Cultural Encounters on Byzantium's Northern Frontier,
c. AD 500–700

In the sixth century Byzantine emperors secured the provinces of the Balkans by engineering a frontier system of unprecedented complexity. Drawing on literary, archaeological, anthropological, and numismatic sources Andrei Gandila argues that cultural attraction was a crucial component of the political frontier of exclusion in the northern Balkans. If left unattended, the entire edifice could easily collapse under its own weight. Through a detailed analysis of the archaeological evidence the author demonstrates that communities living beyond the frontier competed for access to Byzantine goods and reshaped their identity as a result of continual negotiation, reinvention, and hybridization. In the hands of "barbarians" Byzantine objects, such as coins, jewelry, and terracotta lamps, possessed more than functional or economic value, bringing social prestige, conveying religious symbolism embedded in the iconography, and offering a general sense of sharing in the Early Byzantine provincial lifestyle.

ANDREI GANDILA is Assistant Professor of History and Director of Ancient and Medieval Studies at the University of Alabama in Huntsville. His numerous publications include articles in *Byzantinische Zeitschrift, Dumbarton Oaks Papers, Numismatic Chronicle, Revue Numismatique, American Journal of Numismatics*, and *Archaeologia Bulgarica*.

Cultural Encounters on Byzantium's Northern Frontier, c. AD 500–700

Coins, Artifacts and History

ANDREI GANDILA
University of Alabama, Huntsville

CAMBRIDGE
UNIVERSITY PRESS

University Printing House, Cambridge CB2 8BS, United Kingdom

One Liberty Plaza, 20th Floor, New York, NY 10006, USA

477 Williamstown Road, Port Melbourne, VIC 3207, Australia

314–321, 3rd Floor, Plot 3, Splendor Forum, Jasola District Centre, New Delhi – 110025, India

79 Anson Road, #06–04/06, Singapore 079906

Cambridge University Press is part of the University of Cambridge.

It furthers the University's mission by disseminating knowledge in the pursuit of education, learning, and research at the highest international levels of excellence.

www.cambridge.org
Information on this title: www.cambridge.org/9781108470421
DOI: 10.1017/9781108470421

© Andrei Gandila 2018

This publication is in copyright. Subject to statutory exception and to the provisions of relevant collective licensing agreements, no reproduction of any part may take place without the written permission of Cambridge University Press.

First published 2018

Printed in the United Kingdom by TJ International Ltd. Padstow Cornwall

A catalogue record for this publication is available from the British Library.

Library of Congress Cataloging-in-Publication Data
Names: Gândilă, Andrei, author.
Title: Cultural encounters on Byzantium's Northern Frontier, c. AD 500-700 : coins, artifacts and history / Andrei Gandila.
Description: Cambridge, United Kingdom ; New York, NY : Cambridge University Press, 2018. | Includes bibliographical references and index.
Identifiers: LCCN 2018016125 | ISBN 9781108470421 (hardback : alk. paper)
Subjects: LCSH: Lower Danube River Valley–Antiquities, Byzantine. | Lower Danube River Valley–Commerce–History–To 1500. | Coins, Byzantine–Lower Danube River Valley. | Byzantine Empire–History–527-1081. | Byzantine Empire–History–To 527.
Classification: LCC DR49.24 G36 2018 | DDC 949.6/02–dc23
LC record available at https://lccn.loc.gov/2018016125

ISBN 978-1-108-47042-1 Hardback

Cambridge University Press has no responsibility for the persistence or accuracy of URLs for external or third-party internet websites referred to in this publication and does not guarantee that any content on such websites is, or will remain, accurate or appropriate.

*To my mother, Virginia
and my wife, Crina*

Contents

Acknowledgments [*page* viii]
Abbreviations [xi]
Figures [xv]
Illustration Credits [xvii]

Introduction [1]

1 The Roman Frontier in Late Antiquity [10]

2 Cultural Diversity in the Danube Region and Beyond: An Archaeological Perspective [33]

3 Christianity North of the Danube [101]

4 Contact and Separation on the Danube Frontier [131]

5 The Flow of Byzantine Coins Beyond the Frontier [154]

6 Putting the Danube into Perspective: Money, Bullion, and Prestige in Avaria and Transcaucasia [191]

7 Money and Barbarians: Same Coins, Different Functions [243]

Conclusions [280]

Bibliography [289]
Index [363]

Acknowledgments

An essay on frontiers could hardly pass over one's own limitations. While researching this book I have incurred many debts, which I am happy to acknowledge. This project would not have been completed successfully without help, advice, and cooperation from a large number of people. I am particularly grateful to my mentor, Florin Curta, for his constant guidance and intellectual rigor. I would like to thank the readers of my dissertation out of which this book developed, Bonnie Effros, David Geggus, Susan Gillespie, and Andrea Sterk, for their advice and encouragement. The research for this study, conducted in Europe and the United States, was made possible with generous support from a number of institutions including the Dumbarton Oaks Research Library and Collection, the Medieval Academy of America, the American Numismatic Society, the International Association of Byzantine Studies, the International Numismatic Commission, the Center for the Humanities and the Public Sphere, University of Florida, and the Humanities Center of the University of Alabama in Huntsville.

A book is a journey not a destination, if I may adapt a famous quote about life often attributed to Ralph Waldo Emerson. Indeed, this book is the outcome of a long and exciting intellectual adventure started almost a decade ago. My dissertation defended in 2013 marked the first phase of this project which then meandered through several more years of extensive revision. I wrote the first chapter at Dumbarton Oaks during a short-term predoctoral residency in 2011, building on two early papers presented at the Medieval Congress in Kalamazoo. The text took its final shape in the summer of 2015 in the Art Deco building of the John Miller Burnam Classical Library (Cincinnati) where I was able to travel on a research grant provided by University of Alabama in Huntsville's Humanities Center. Research for the second, third, and fourth chapters began in Florida in 2011 and continued in Romania in 2012 with generous support from the Medieval Academy of America. In the following years Florin Curta's comprehensive archaeological database has provided a goldmine of information, without which the research period devoted to these chapters would have become agonizingly long. Archaeological research conducted at

Capidava since 2001, as part of a larger team led by Ioan C. Opriș from the University of Bucharest, has provided indispensable hands-on experience with archaeological material from the frontier region.

The fifth and sixth chapters, dealing with the numismatic evidence, are the result of several visits at the American Numismatic Society in New York from 2009 to 2015, where I have taken advantage of its unparalleled numismatic library. I have conducted additional research in Romania with generous funding from University of Florida's Center for the Humanities and the Public Sphere and the Humanities Center of the University of Alabama in Huntsville. Preliminary work for the seventh chapter required two stages. The beginnings of the project date back to my time as an Assistant Curator at the National History Museum of Romania in Bucharest, where I have benefited from the guidance and advice of Ernest Oberländer-Târnoveanu who initiated me into the fascinating world of numismatics. My narrative took shape in New York during the 2009 Summer Seminar generously sponsored by the American Numismatic Society, where I had the privilege to study one of the largest collections of Early Byzantine coins in the world. I enjoyed much help and hospitality from the ANS curators and I still treasure the frequent numismatic conversations with Robert Hoge, Peter van Alfen, Elena Stolyarik, and the late Richard Witschonke. My growing interest in the numismatic aspect of the frontier question was fueled by animated discussions at an international conference in Cracow in 2007 where I discovered the intellectual potential of the subject as well as the significant misconceptions attached to it. The original structure of the numismatic chapters developed in the genial atmosphere of Dumbarton Oaks during my one-year Junior Fellowship (2012–2013), where I availed myself of its wonderful library with great gusto. Indeed, its unrivaled collection of books and journals invited a much more ambitious undertaking than initially planned.

As the project expanded I have benefited from close collaboration with scholars from Bulgaria, Hungary, Macedonia, Georgia, Turkey, and Israel who generously gave me access to unpublished data and offered precious advice and comparanda material. I would like to thank Georges Abou Diwan, Gabriela Bijovsky, Zeliha Demirel-Gökalp, Maja Hadji-Maneva, Stoyan Mihaylov, Péter Somogyi, and Alena Tenchova for sharing the results of their research. As a member of the project "Framing the Late Antique and Early Medieval Economy" (FLAME) directed by Princeton University I gained a deeper appreciation of the large-scale implications of monetary production and circulation in the Mediterranean world.

Numerous discussions with Alan Stahl and my enthusiastic colleagues have helped me contextualize my own research in the frontier region.

At Dumbarton Oaks, Princeton, and elsewhere I have benefited from numerous thought-provoking conversations about history, archaeology, and numismatics with Cécile Morrisson, Alan Stahl, Julian Baker, Bruno Callegher, Rebecca Darley, Kuba Kabala, and Axel Nielsen. I have presented early versions of most chapters at scholarly meetings in Europe and the United States. Conference audiences in Kalamazoo, Princeton, Glasgow, Cracow, Sofia, Varna, and Taormina have made many useful and thoughtful comments for which I am grateful. The numismatic chapters, which have been in many ways the most challenging and time-consuming, required the collection of significant material from elusive local journals as well as unpublished finds, now available in the companion Catalogue published on Cambridge University Press' webpage (www.cambridge.org/ 9781108470421). I would like to thank Deborah Stewart, Librarian for Byzantine Studies at Dumbarton Oaks, David Hill, Francis D. Campbell Librarian of the American Numismatic Society, and Charlotte Olson, Librarian at University of Alabama in Huntsville and chief liaison with the wonderful world of Interlibrary Loan. Special thanks are due to my friend and colleague Alexandru Tudorie whose ability to locate obscure and seemingly unreachable publications continues to puzzle me.

Michael Sharp and Dave Morris at Cambridge University Press have been encouraging collaborators throughout the book's editorial process. I appreciate their patient support as well as the helpful insights of the two anonymous reviewers, whose judicious comments and constructive criticism saved me from errors and pointed me in new directions. Family members always come last in the acknowledgment section of academic books and that is not really fair because their contribution is truly indispensable. I would like to thank my wife, Crina, and my mother, Virginia, for their love, unwavering confidence, and unconditional support. A pious memory to my father, Mircea, who taught me to love history and writing. Sit tibi terra levis.

Abbreviations

AA	*American Anthropologist* (Washington, 1888–).
AAASH	*Acta Archaeologica Academiae Scientiarum Hungaricae* (Budapest, 1951–).
AAC	*Acta Archaeologica Carpathica* (Cracow, 1958–).
AAnth	*American Anthropologist* (Washington, DC, 1888–).
Acta Orientalia	*Acta Orientalia Academiae Scientiarum Hungaricae* (Budapest, 1950–).
AJA	*American Journal of Archaeology* (New York, NY, 1885–).
AJN	*American Journal of Numismatics* (New York, NY, 1989–).
Akten XII	Dassmann, E., K. Thraede, and J. Engemann, eds. *Akten des XII. Internationalen Kongresses für Christliche Archäologie*. Münster: Aschendorffsche Verlagsbuchhandlung, 1995.
AM	*Arheologia Moldovei* (Bucharest, 1961–).
AMN	*Acta Musei Napocensis* (Cluj-Napoca, 1964–).
Anzeiger	*Anzeiger der Österreichischen Akademie der Wissenschaften. Philosophisch-historische Klasse* (Vienna, 1947–).
ARA	*Annual Review of Anthropology* (Palo Alto, CA, 1972–).
ArchBulg	*Archaeologia Bulgarica* (Sofia, 1997–).
ArchDelt	*Archaiologikon Deltion* (Athens, 1915–).
ArchÉrt	*Archaeologiai Értesítő* (Budapest, 1881–).
ASGE	*Arkheologicheskii Sbornik Gosudarstvennogo Ermitazha* (Leningrad, 1959–).
Atlante	Carandini, A., ed. *Atlante délle forme ceramice, I. Ceramica fine romana nel Bacino Mediterraneo (medio e tardo Imperio)*. Rome: Istituto della Enciclopedia Italiana, 1981.
BAR	*British Archaeological Reports* (Oxford, 1974–).
BASOR	*Bulletin of the American Schools of Oriental Research* (Ann Arbor, MI, 1919–).
BCH	*Bulletin de correspondance hellénique* (Athens/Paris, 1877–).
BMGS	*Byzantine and Modern Greek Studies* (Oxford, 1975–).
BOR	*Biserica Ortodoxă Română* (Bucharest, 1874–).

Broneer	Broneer, O. *Terracotta Lamps. Corinth, IV, Part II.* Cambridge, MA: Harvard University Press, 1930.
BS	*Balkan Studies* (Thessaloniki, 1960–).
BSNR	*Buletinul Societăţii Numismatice Române* (Bucharest, 1904–).
BV	*Bayerische Vorgeschichtsblätter* (Munich, 1921–).
Byzantine Coins	Wołoszyn, M., ed. *Byzantine Coins in Central Europe Between the 5th and 10th Century.* Cracow: Polish Academy of Sciences, 2009.
BZ	*Byzantinische Zeitschrift* (Munich, 1892–).
CAB	*Cercetări arheologice în Bucureşti* (Bucharest, 1963–).
CAH	*Communicationes Archaeologicae Hungariae* (Budapest 1981–).
CN	*Cercetări Numismatice* (Bucharest, 1978–).
DOC	Bellinger, A. R. and P. Grierson. *Catalogue of the Byzantine Coins in the Dumbarton Oaks Collection and in the Whittemore Collection.* Vols. I–II. Washington, DC: Dumbarton Oaks Center for Byzantine Studies, 1966–1968.
Donaulimes	Schwarcz, A., P. Soustal, and A. Cholakova, eds. *Der Donaulimes in der Spätantike und im Frühmittelalter.* Miscellanea Bulgarica 22. Vienna: LIT, 2016.
DOP	*Dumbarton Oaks Papers* (Washington, DC, 1941–).
EB	*Études Balkaniques* (Sofia, 1964–).
EBPB	*Études Byzantines et Post-Byzantines* (Bucharest, 1979–).
EN	*Ephemeris Napocensis* (Cluj-Napoca, 1991–).
FHG	*Fragmenta Historicorum Graecorum.*
GRBS	*Greek, Roman and Byzantine Studies* (Cambridge, MA, 1959–).
Hayes	Hayes, J. W. *Excavations at Saraçhane in Istanbul. Vol. II. The Pottery.* Princeton, NJ: Princeton University Press, 1992.
IAI	*Izvestiia na Arkheologicheskiia Institut* (Sofia, 1950–).
Iconomu	Iconomu, C. *Opaiţe greco-romane.* Constanţa: Muzeul regional de arheologie, 1967.
IMIB	*Izvestiia na Muzeite ot Iugoiztochna Bulgariia* (Plovdiv, 1976–).
INMV	*Izvestiia na Narodniia Muzei Varna* (Varna, 1965–).
Istoria românilor 1	Petrescu-Dîmboviţa, M. and A. Vulpe, eds. *Istoria românilor. Vol. 1: Moştenirea timpurilor îndepărtate.* Bucharest: Editura Enciclopedică, 2001.
Istoria românilor 2	Protase, D. and A. Suceveanu, eds. *Istoria românilor. Vol. 2: Daco-romani, romanici, alogeni.* Bucharest: Editura Enciclopedică, 2001.

Istoria românilor 3	Pascu, Ş. and R. Teodorescu, eds. *Istoria românilor. Vol. 3: Genezele româneşti*. Bucharest: Editura Enciclopedică, 2001.
JRA	*Journal of Roman Archaeology* (Ann Arbor, MI, 1988–).
JRS	*Journal of Roman Studies* (London, 1911–).
KSIA	*Kratkie Soobshcheniia Instituta Arkheologii* (Moscow, 1952).
Kuzmanov	Kuzmanov, G. *Antichni lampi. Kolektsiia na Natsionalniia Arkheologicheski Muzei*. Sofia: Izdatelstvo na Bulgarskata Akademiia na Naukite, 1992.
Lychnological Acts 2	Roman, C. A. and N. Gudea, eds. *Lychnological Acts 2. Trade and Local Production of Lamps from the Prehistory until the Middle Age. Acts of the 2nd International Congress on Ancient and Middle Age Lightning Devices (Zalău – Cluj-Napoca, 13th–18th May 2006)*. Zalău/Cluj-Napoca: Mega, 2008.
MAIET	*Materialy po arkheologii, istorii i etnografii Tavrii* (Simferopol, 1990–).
MCA	*Materiale şi cercetări de arheologie* (Bucharest, 1955–).
MFMÉ	*A Móra Ferenc Múzeum Évkönyve. Studia Archaeologica* (Szeged, 1995–).
MGH: AA	*Monumenta Germaniae Historica: Auctores Antiquissimi*.
MGH: SRM	*Monumenta Germaniae Historica: Scriptores Rerum Merovingicarum*.
MGH: SS	*Monumenta Germaniae Historica: Scriptores Rerum Germanicarum in Usum Scholarum Separatim Editi*.
MIB	Hahn, W. *Moneta Imperii Byzantini*. 3 vols. Vienna: Verlag der Österreichischen Akademie der Wissenschaften, 1973–1981.
MIBE	Hahn, W. and M. Metlich, *Money of the Incipient Byzantine Empire*. Vienna: Österreichische Forschungsgesellschaft für Numismatik am Institut für Numismatik und Geldgeschichte, 2000, rev. 2013.
MIBEC	Hahn, W. and M. Metlich, *Money of the Incipient Byzantine Empire Continued (Justin II – Revolt of the Heraclii 565–610)*. Vienna: Österreichische Forschungsgesellschaft für Numismatik, 2009.
Perlzweig	Miltner, F. *Das Cömeterium der Sieben Schläfer. Forschungen in Ephesos IV*. Baden: Rudolf M. Rohrer, 1937.
Money and Modernity	Akin, D. and J. Robbins, eds. *Money and Modernity: State and Local Currencies in Melanesia*. Pittsburgh, PA: University of Pittsburgh Press, 1999.

Money and Morality	Parry, J. and M. Bloch, eds. *Money and the Morality of Exchange.* Cambridge: Cambridge University Press, 1989.
Money in Africa	Eagleton, C., H. Fuller, and J. Perkins, eds. *Money in Africa.* London: British Museum, 2009.
NC	*Numismatic Chronicle* (London, 1838–).
Neglected Barbarians	Curta, F., ed. *Neglected Barbarians.* Turnhout: Brepols, 2008.
Perlzweig	Perlzweig, J. *The Athenian Agora. Lamps of the Roman Period VII.* Princeton, NJ: Princeton University Press, 1961.
Pontic-Danubian Realm	Ivanišević, V. and M. Kazanski, eds. *The Pontic-Danubian Realm in the Period of the Great Migration.* Paris/Belgrade: Association des amis du Centre d'histoire et civilisation de Byzance/Arheološki Institut, 2012.
Relations	Constantinescu, M., Ş. Pascu, and P. Diaconu, eds. *Relations Between the Autochthonous Population and the Migratory Populations on the Territory of Romania.* Bucharest: Editura Academiei RSR, 1975.
RESEE	*Revue des études sud-est européennes* (Bucharest, 1963–).
RESS	*Revue européenne des sciences sociales (Cahiers Vilfredo Pareto)* (Geneva, 1963–).
RIC	*Roman Imperial Coinage.* 10 vols. London: Spink, 1923–1994.
RIN	*Rivista Italiana di Numismatica e Scienze Affini* (Milan, 1888–).
RN	*Revue Numismatique* (Paris, 1836–).
SA	*Sovetskaia Arkheologiia* (Moscow, 1933–).
SCIV(A)	*Studii şi Cercetări de Istorie Veche (şi Arheologie)* (Bucharest, 1950–).
SCN	*Studii şi cercetări de numismatică* (Bucharest, 1957–).
SF	*Südost-Forschungen* (Leipzig, 1936–).
Shifting Frontiers	Mathisen, R. W., and H. S. Sivan, eds. *Shifting Frontiers in Late Antiquity.* Bodmin, Cornwall: Variorum, 1996.
Transition	Poulter, A. G., ed. *The Transition to Late Antiquity on the Danube and Beyond.* Proceedings of the British Academy 141. Oxford: Oxford University Press, 2007.
Trésors	Morrisson, C., V. Popović, and V. Ivanišević, eds. *Les trésors monétaires byzantins des Balkans et d'Asie Mineure (491–713).* Paris: Lethielleux, 2006.
VV	*Vizantiiskii Vremennik* (Moscow, 1947–).
ZfA	*Zeitschrift für Archäologie* (Berlin, 1967–).
ZPE	*Zeitschrift für Papyrologie und Epigraphik* (Bonn, 1967–).

Figures

1. Early Byzantine frontier provinces and regions in *barbaricum* referred to in the text   [*page* 35]
2. "Non-Roman" handmade pottery finds in the frontier provinces   [39]
3. Amphora finds in *barbaricum*   [47]
4. Finds of Danubian lamps   [54]
5. Finds of Anatolian lamps and local imitations   [60]
6. Finds of North African lamps and imitations   [62]
7. Finds of Palestinian lamps and imitations   [66]
8. Finds of handmade lamps   [68]
9. Distribution of metallurgical activity   [70]
10. Distribution of metallurgical implements from *barbaricum*   [72]
11. Finds of fibulae with bent stem   [78]
12. Cast fibulae with bent stem found in *barbaricum* and their typological analogues in the frontier provinces   [83]
13. Sixth-to-seventh-century "Slavic" bow fibulae in the frontier region and their parallels in *barbaricum*   [89]
14. Main types of Byzantine buckles found in the frontier region   [95]
15. Distribution of bronze liturgical lamps, clay lamps with cross-shaped handle or cross/Chi-Rho on discus/nozzle, and Menas flasks   [121]
16. Distribution of crosses and molds for the production of crosses   [123]
17. Main categories of Byzantine artifacts found in *barbaricum*: amphorae, clay lamps, fibulae, buckles, Christian objects   [143]
18. Sixth-to-seventh-century fibulae and buckles: fibulae with bent stem, Sucidava buckle, cast fibulae with bent stem, and bow fibulae   [145]
19. Sixth-to-seventh-century molds from *barbaricum*   [146]
20. Early Byzantine lamps and imitations: Danubian lamps, Anatolian lamps, North African lamp, imitation after North African lamp, Palestinian lamp, and handmade lamps   [149]
21. Sixth-to-seventh-century Byzantine coin finds in *barbaricum*   [158]
22. Coin finds by mint   [158]
23. Coin finds by denomination   [158]
24. Byzantine gold, silver, and bronze hoards in *barbaricum*   [158]
25. Sixth-to-seventh-century Byzantine gold coins in *barbaricum*   [158]
26. Early Byzantine coin finds north of the Lower Danube   [164]
27. Early Byzantine coin finds north of the Black Sea   [165]

28. The chronology of Early Byzantine coin finds from the Danube frontier and *barbaricum*   [166]
29. Mints and denominations in *barbaricum* (Lower Danube and Black Sea)   [166]
30. Mints and denominations in the Byzantine bridge-head forts (Sucidava, Drobeta, and Dierna)   [166]
31. Early Byzantine coin finds in Transcaucasia   [195]
32. Chronology of Early Byzantine coin finds from eastern Anatolia and Transcaucasia   [197]
33. Mints and denominations in Transcaucasia   [197]
34. Mints and denominations in eastern Anatolia   [197]
35. Early Byzantine coin finds in the Carpathian Basin   [218]
36. Early Byzantine coin finds north of the Middle and Upper Danube   [219]
37. Early Byzantine coin finds in the Carpathian Basin (491–680)   [220]
38. First-to-third-century mummy portraits with coin-necklaces and coin-pendants   [257]
39. Coins as jewelry: coin-necklace from Dzhiginka, Russia; coin-set from Malo Pereshchepyne, Ukraine; and early modern coin-necklace from Madagascar   [275]
40. Early Byzantine gold, silver, and bronze coins modified to be displayed as jewelry   [276]

Illustration Credits

Figure 18, nos. 1, 2, 3, 4, and 9: F. Topoleanu, *Ceramica romană și romano-bizantină de la Halmyris* (Tulcea: Institutul de Cercetări Eco-Muzeale, 2000), 350-357, pl. LVIII/470, pl. LIX/474-475, pl. LX/485, and pl. LXV/525. [*page* 145]

Figure 18, nos. 5, 8, and 10: A. Diaconescu, "Lămpi târzii și paleobizantine din fosta provincie Dacia," *EN* 5 (1995): 265-279, pl. III/1a, pl. V/5a, and pl. VII/1a. [145]

Figure 18, no. 6: M. Glumac, "Glinene svetiljke iz kasnoantichke zbirke Narodnog Muzeja u Beogradu," *Zbornik Narodnog Muzeja* 17, no. 1 (2001): 218, fig. 8. [145]

Figure 18, no. 7: K. Kalchev, "Antichni i kusnoantichni lampi ot Stara Zagora," *IMIB* 5 (1982): 15, pl. IV/4. [145]

Figure 18, no. 11: Z. Hajnal, "Késő antik jellegű kerámia a Kölked-Feketekapui avar kori telepről 2005," *CAH* (2005): 180, fig. 2/1. [145]

Figure 18, no. 12: S. Dolinescu-Ferche and M. Constantinescu, "Un établissement du VIe siècle à Bucarest (Découvertes de la rue Soldat Ghivan)," *Dacia* 25 (1981): 319, fig. 16/7a. [145]

Figure 19, nos. 1-2: A. Măgureanu and B. Ciupercă, "The 6th-8th centuries metallurgical activity from Budureasca Valley. The molds," *AMN* 41-42, no. 1 (2004-2005): 313, fig. 5/2 and 5/9. [146]

Figure 19, no. 3: D. G. Teodor, "Ateliers byzantins des VIe-VIIIe siècles au nord du Bas-Danube," *EBPB* 5 (2006): 196, fig. 4. [146]

Figure 19, no. 4: D. G. Teodor, *Civilizația romanică la est de Carpați în secolele V-VII (așezarea de la Botoșana-Suceava)* (Bucharest: Editura Academiei RSR, 1984), 99, fig. 20/1. [146]

Figure 19, nos. 5-6: I. S. Vinokur, *Slov'ians'kyi iuveliry Podnistrov'ia. Za materialamy doslidzhen' Bernashivs'kogo kompleksu seredyny I tys. n. e.* (Kam'ianets' Podil's'kyy: Oium, 1997), 54, fig. 16; 81, fig. 34. [146]

Figure 20, no. 1: A. V. Bodianskii, "Arkheologicheskie nakhodki v Dneprovskom nadporozh'e," *SA* (1960), no. 1: 273, fig. 1/7. [149]

Figure 20, no. 2: L. M. Rutkovskaia, "Arkheologicheskie pamiatniki IV-VI vv. v raione Kremenchugskogo moria (Ukraina)," *Slovenská Archeológia* 27 (1979): 341, fig. 22/9. [149]

Figure 20, no. 3: D. G. Teodor, "Fibules byzantines des Ve-VIIe siècles dans l'espace carpato-danubien-pontique," *EBPB* 3 (1997): 73, fig. 3/9. [149]

Figure 20, no. 4: L. V. Vakulenko and O. M. Prykhodniuk, *Slavianskie poseleniia I tys. n.e. u s. Sokol na Srednem Dnestre* (Kiev: Naukova Dumka, 1984), 57, fig. 32/9. [149]

Figure 20, no. 5: R. Popovici, "Două piese vestimentare din secolele VI-VII descoperite la Borniș-Neamț," *AM* 12 (1988): 250, fig. 1/2. [149]

Figure 20, no. 6: D. G. Teodor, *The East-Carpathian Area of Romania in the V-XI Centuries A.D.* BAR International Series 81 (Oxford: BAR, 1980), fig. 11/3. [149]

Figure 20, no. 7: A. Petre, *La romanité en Scythie Mineure (IIe-VIIe siècles de notre ère). Recherches archéologiques* (Bucharest: AIESEE, 1987), pl. 145/239d. [149]

Figure 20, no. 8: A. Kharalambieva, "Dva tipa kusnoantichni fibuli vuv Varnenskiia muzei," *INMV* 25 (1989): pl. VI/7. [149]

Figure 20, no. 9: G. I. Petre and A. Stoican, "O fibulă digitată din nordul Olteniei," *SCIVA* 27, no. 1 (1976): 115, fig. 1a. [149]

Figure 20, no. 10: D. G. Teodor and C. Chiriac, "Noi fibule digitate din Dobrogea," *Peuce* 3-4 (2005-2006): 249, fig. 2. [149]

Figure 20, no. 11: J. Herrmann, "Die fruhmittelalterlichen Siedlungen auf dem Gelände des Kastells Iatrus," in *Iatrus Krivina. Spätantike Befestigung und frühmittelalterliche Siedlung an der unteren Donau. Band I: Ergebnisse der Ausgrabungen 1966-1973*, eds. G. von Bülow et al. (Berlin: Akademie-Verlag, 1979), 114, fig. 46a. [149]

Figure 20, no. 12: A. Kharalambieva, "Bügelfibeln aus dem 7. Jh. südlich der unteren Donau," in *Actes du XIIe Congrès international des sciences préhistoriques et protohistoriques, Bratislava, 1-7 septembre 1991*, ed. J. Pavuj (Bratislava: Institut Archéologique de l'Académie Slovaque des Sciences, 1993), 26, fig. 1/1. [149]

Figure 38, nos. 1-2 and 4: K. Parlasca, *Repertorio d'arte dell'Egitto Greco-Romano*, ed. A. Adriani, Series B/ Volume I (Palermo: Fondazione "Ignazio Mormino" del Banco di Sicilia, 1969), pl. 19/78, pl. 34/142, and pl. 56/226. [257]

Figure 38, no. 3: K. Parlasca, *Repertorio d'arte dell'Egitto Greco-Romano*, ed. A. Adriani, Series B/ Volume II (Palermo: Fondazione "Ignazio Mormino" del Banco di Sicilia, 1977), pl. 98/397. [257]

Figure 39, nos. 1-2: V. V. Kropotkin, *Klady vizantiiskikh monet na territorii SSSR* (Moscow: Izd-vo Akademii nauk SSSR, 1962), pl. 14/1 and pl. 16/13-20. [275]

Illustration Credits   xix

Figure 39, no. 3:   J. Chauvicourt and S. Chauvicourt, *Numismatique malgache. Fasc. 3. Les premières monnaies introduites à Madagascar* (Antananarivo: Trano Printy Loterana, 1968), 9, fig. 3.   [275]

Figure 40, no. 1:   S. V. Gusev, *Severo-Vostochnyi Kavkaz v epokhu srednevekov'ia: monety rasskazyvaiut* (Moscow: Institut etnologii i antropologii RAN, 1995), 46, fig. 1/1.   [276]

Figure 40, nos. 2-3 and 5-6:   P. Somogyi, *Byzantinische Fundmünzen der Awarenzeit in ihrem europäischen Umfeld* (Budapest: Institut für Archäologische Wissenschaften, 2014), 101, fig. 12; 196, fig. 38; 198, fig. 42; 201, fig. 47.   [276]

Figure 40, nos. 4 and 8:   P. Somogyi, *Byzantinische Fundmünzen der Awarenzeit* (Innsbruck: Universitätsverlag Wagner, 1997), 34, no. 17; 67, no. 52.   [276]

Figure 40, no. 7:   G. Poenaru Bordea, R. Ocheşeanu, and A. Popeea. *Monnaies byzantines du Musée de Constanţa (Roumanie)* (Wetteren: Moneta, 2004), fig. 753.   [276]

Figure 40, no. 9:   V. Radić and V. Ivanišević, *Byzantine Coins from the National Museum in Belgrade* (Belgrade: Narodni Muzej, 2006), pl. 20/318.   [276]

Figure 40, no. 10:   T. Abramishvili, *Sakartvelos sakhelmts'ipo muzeumis bizant'iuri monet'ebi* (Tbilisi: Mecniereba, 1965), pl. V/74.   [276]

Introduction

André Piganiol closed his *Empire Chrétien* with two sentences destined to become famous in the following decades: "La civilisation romaine n'est pas morte de sa belle morte. Elle a été assassinée" (The Roman civilization did not die a natural death. It was assassinated).[1] Half a century ago the frontier question was not really a question at all. The "decline and fall" of the Roman Empire was the dominant paradigm and had been firmly in place since the enlightened days of Edward Gibbon. Frontier drama loomed large in this fatalistic scenario which saw wave after wave of savage barbarians crashing through the Roman defenses and eventually plunging Western civilization into a dark cultural abyss. And yet there were important signs announcing a major historiographical shift. The articulation of Late Antiquity as an independent field and an unprecedented turn toward the study of social and economic phenomena forever changed our understanding of ancient frontiers. The Anglo-American school of Late Antique studies, the French "Annales School," and indeed, the creation and expansion of the European Union have brought a renewed interest in frontiers as well as new and exciting vistas for the study of interaction between different cultures and civilizations.

Because of the uneven development of the field, only certain areas of the Late Roman frontier stretching on three continents have been thoroughly researched. The Western provinces enjoy the most privileged position as several generations of scholars painstakingly reassessed the dissolution of Roman structures and the transition to the Middle Ages. Important work has been done in other regions as well. The Early Byzantine frontier in North Africa has long been a central focus for historians interested in the transition from the Vandal to the Byzantine, and later Arab, domination. In the Near East our understanding of the role and function of the desert frontier is still very much influenced by the seminal thesis of Benjamin Isaac and the subsequent works built on his concept of an open frontier. On the other hand, there is still much to be learned about the evolution of

---

[1] A. Piganiol, *L'empire chrétien (325–395)* (Paris, 1947), 422.

the Danube frontier in Late Antiquity and its many functions, as it separated and at the same time brought together the Early Byzantine Empire and the northern *barbaricum.*

The argument in the following chapters operates on three different planes. The first is the broad debate surrounding frontier culture, the role of liminal spaces, and the creation of identities. Scholars have long been fascinated by Justinian's work of fortification in the Balkans and have used archaeological and literary sources to emphasize the emperor's efforts to create separation rather than foster communication between the frontier provinces and the world of "barbarians." Drawing on anthropological models I will argue that natural frontiers like the Danube are in fact multidimensional. Their political, geographic, demographic, and cultural aspects are complementary rather than conflicting but their study requires different research questions and methodological tools. The Early Byzantine frontier on the Danube can be perceived as a political and military border of exclusion due to its strategic advantages, but also as a cultural frontier zone open to negotiation and facilitating the circulation of ideas, objects, and people. The cultural dimension, however, remained subservient to the political one. The chain of fortifications fastened on the southern bank of the river ensured that Byzantine emperors would continue to hold the key unlocking cross-cultural interaction. In the sixth century when the empire was no longer able to launch major campaigns north of the Danube, cultural integration became a complementary strategy of protecting the Balkans used in tandem with physical defenses.

The second theme is the archaeology of cultural contact on the periphery with special emphasis on the role of Byzantine money outside the frontier. I argue that cultural interaction was essentially non-economic and relied on barbarians recruited in the Roman army to act as cultural brokers transmitting goods and fashions from the northern Balkans to *barbaricum.* I am using the latest developments in world-systems analysis to describe the Danube region as a semiperiphery where a unique type of culture was created in relation to the Byzantine core and the "barbarian" periphery. This fertile ground of cultural negotiation and hybridization sustained the development of identities and social values in *barbaricum* in relation to the Byzantine world. Communities from the lands north of the Danube competed for access to Byzantine goods and one of the main observations is that several other cultural frontiers can be identified beyond the classical antithesis, "Empire vs. Barbarians." Competition in *barbaricum* as well as the relative proximity to the frontier dictated what type of fashions would be adopted. Inclusion and exclusion are complementary rather than antithetical notions as they both generated an increasing demand for Byzantine goods. Although channeled by different tastes and preferences, the circulation of ideas and styles across the Danube was closely related to the militarized nature of the frontier and depended on a fragile balance of power.

The analysis of coin finds reveals a chiefly non-economic function of Byzantine money outside the Empire. The social value of Byzantine coins resided in their direct association with the Roman way of life and the emulation of Roman practices. Against current economistic interpretations of the numismatic evidence, I argue that low-value bronze coins had little or no monetary function. They did not sustain an exchange system fueled by coinage, nor did they support the development of a market economy. Communities in *barbaricum* treated coins like any other Byzantine object and invested them with social meaning. In addition, precious-metal coinage crossed the frontier through political channels. Early Byzantine emperors employing a well-honed *Realpolitik* used diplomatic gifts to create alliances or tilt the balance of power in their favor and lavished barbarian leaders with large quantities of *solidi* and ceremonial silver. Byzantine gold and silver coins were subsequently woven into the social fabric of communities from the frontier region, being melted down to produce jewelry and other objects which became an index of social distinction. Some were included in graves to highlight the social status of the deceased, while others were hoarded as symbols of wealth.

Finally, the third theme is an important historiographical question – and, indeed, a highly politicized issue – regarding the creation of Early Medieval ethnicities, languages, and states in Eastern Europe. The debate is one of "continuity vs. discontinuity" or "autochthony vs. immigrationism," best illustrated by the opposing views of the Romanian and Hungarian schools, although historians, archaeologists, and linguists across the Balkans had to grapple with this question in their struggle to understand an important formative period in their nation's past. For it is political ideology that really stood behind this fierce polemic, from eighteenth-century enlightenment to nineteenth-century nationalism and twentieth-century communism. On the basis of linguistic and archaeological evidence, Romanian scholars have emphasized the continuity of Roman culture in the territory of present-day Romania, striving to demonstrate that the ancestors of modern Romanians successfully preserved their Latin language, Christian religion, and Roman identity against centuries of pressure from incoming barbarian groups. Under the aggressive nationalism promoted by the communist regime in the 1970s and 1980s the discourse became radicalized into one proclaiming the cultural superiority of the autochthonous population and the inevitable assimilation of the newcomers. Unaware of the ongoing debate over the political and cultural function of Roman frontiers – a popular topic in western scholarship at that time – Romanian researchers underscored the permeability of the Danube frontier for purely ideological reasons, because it served their chief purpose of proving the uninterrupted contact between "proto-Romanian" communities and the Byzantine Empire.

Such views continued to be opposed by Hungarian scholarship, and occasionally Bulgarian – to be sure, with equal bias. Nineteenth-century Austro-Hungarian imperialism had described Transylvania as a *terra deserta* at the arrival of the Magyars, so no Romanic continuity could be accepted as it could undermine the Hungarian claims over this province. Still, medieval Romanians had to be accounted for somehow so an immigrationist solution was offered. The polemic was reignited during the communist decades when the Hungarian school felt compelled to provide an inflammatory response to the nationalistic distortions tirelessly cultivated by Romanian historians. Unsurprisingly, Hungarian scholars revived the "immigrationist" thesis stating that Romanian ethnicity (and the Romanian language, by extension) was a creation of the lands south of the Danube, exported north of the river much later in the 12th to 13th centuries.

Those who look for partisanship in this book will be disappointed. Furthermore, the present analysis will not attempt to establish a "golden mean" – for the theories are mutually exclusive – but to propose a different paradigm of interaction that cuts across ethnicities and sees the process of cultural interaction in light of the Empire's pragmatic political agenda. This has less to do with ideology, propaganda, or the imperial rhetoric often invoked by historians. Byzantine emperors divided the world of *barbaricum* into friends and foes regardless of ethnic background – a fluid concept always susceptible to unexpected and radical change as dictated by political expediency. Throughout the sixth and seventh centuries the Empire fought and made up with the Gepids, the Avars, the Lombards, and the Antes, to name only the most conspicuous cases mentioned in contemporary accounts. Previous conflict never precluded future collaboration against common enemies and it often appears that aggression against the Empire was the necessary test for being taken seriously by the imperial administration (i.e. the extraction of tribute or subsidies). The Latin-speaking and Christian communities north of the Danube – the main obsession of Romanian scholarship – were hardly the only target for the

Empire's cultural tactic expressed in the surge of Byzantine goods across the frontier. While the descendants of the Roman colonists never disappeared from Transylvania and the Danube plain, Byzantine emperors did not pay special attention to their welfare. Elucidating the ethnic profile of communities living in the empire's shadow is beyond the scope of this book – the author wonders if it can be achieved at all – but it seems clear that Romanization, in the wide sense of the concept, was available to anyone willing to help defend imperial interests on the Lower Danube. This is not a question of massive population movement (immigrationist thesis) or stubborn cultural survival against all adversity (continuity thesis); it is a political game whose cultural consequences transcend modern perceptions of frontiers, clear-cut ethnicity, and nationalism.

The source material which forms the basis for discussion in the following chapters combines evidence drawn from the written record, archaeological and anthropological data, as well as my own research in numismatic collections from various museums and the field work undertaken since 2001 at Capidava, an important Late Roman fortress on the Lower Danube frontier. The main methodological goal is to highlight the numismatic evidence as the primary source of a monograph which attempts to weave numismatics, archaeology, history, and ethnographic research into a homogeneous interdisciplinary narrative. In many ways this book is an invitation to dialogue. A common thread of all chapters is the realization that only by pulling together various strands of information, often the province of diverse disciplines and specializations, can we build a nuanced and multifaceted narrative of frontier history. The reader will not find a brand new theoretical framework for analyzing frontiers and cross-cultural interaction but a long overdue fusion between concepts and definitions which often seemed mutually exclusive. Indeed, the frontier in its complexity and chameleonic nature defies total encapsulation by a single universal model.

The book has seven chapters organized thematically. The first chapter is a reinterpretation of the Roman frontier in Late Antiquity. In the last decades historians have described frontier rivers as primarily facilitating communication and cultural contact and less as borders of exclusion; contrariwise, archaeologists still concentrate their efforts on the military dimension. Under the spell of the postmodernist turn the former have approached frontiers through a polysemic kaleidoscope of cultural, intellectual, and symbolic lenses, while the latter remained entrenched in the traditional focus on fortifications and lines of defense. In many ways this dichotomy was engendered by insufficient conversation between historians and archaeologists and has delayed the development of a conceptual model which could help bridge such disciplinary divides. The chapter is an attempt to offer such a model, drawn from the anthropological study of frontiers. By doing so it is necessary to intrude upon several of the major and still outstanding questions of Byzantine history. What was the Byzantine worldview on frontiers? Is there any change from the early Roman centuries? Was there a Grand Strategy in Late Antiquity? A careful comparative study reveals enduring literary *topoi* but also an ongoing concern to use reinforced natural obstacles as political frontiers able to act as convenient barriers against "barbarians." This chapter reemphasizes the strategic role of the Danube in Late Antiquity and its political function of separation. This reality must be acknowledged before anything else if we hope to understand the cultural dimension of the Danube frontier in all its complexity.

Drawing on post-colonial theory and new directions in world-systems analysis, the second, third, and fourth chapters offer an archaeological interpretation of the Danube region as a cultural interface between Early Byzantium and northern *barbaricum* based on a variety of Byzantine goods found outside the Empire. The study of archaeological evidence confirms the fact that economic, cultural, and political borders are not coterminous; the Empire's influence can be traced far beyond its administrative limits. The surge of Byzantine artifacts across the frontier, such as amphorae, lamps, brooches, and buckles, points to different channels of distribution and particular preferences associated with the creation of elite identity and social prestige in relation to Byzantium. This cultural dynamic reshaped the nearby *barbaricum* into a "negotiated periphery" due to the active agency of "barbarians" in taking control of their cultural identity, while interaction itself brought benefits to both sides. However, it also developed into a "bipolar periphery," since cultural contact was equally the result of cooperation and conflict, of "barbarians" drawn into the empire's service and "barbarians" drawn by the empire's wealth and bent on plunder. In the end both helped spread Byzantine goods, fashions, and religious ideas in the northern world. More importantly, it becomes clear that the Danube's political function of separation could not function unless there was sufficient cultural interaction between the two sides of the river to avoid a permanent state of conflict. Byzantine emperors could not muster the material and human resources needed to support a 1,000 km-long frontier from Belgrade to the Danube Delta, if continuous pressure from *barbaricum* was not prevented through diplomatic action and the implementation of long-term cultural strategies.

The fifth and sixth chapters reevaluate the flow of Early Byzantine coins beyond the political border by analyzing their distribution on a wide geographical area from Central Europe to the Caucasus, with special emphasis on the Lower Danube. When properly placed in their historical and archaeological context coins can illuminate some of the outstanding issues regarding the nature of cultural contact in the frontier region often obscured by the limitations of the written evidence. The coin is not only the most widely and frequently circulated Byzantine object in *barbaricum*, but also the most reliable and chronologically sensitive. If conclusions drawn on the basis of other artifacts often command no confidence because of their erratic nature, the standardized and bureaucratic aspect of Byzantine coins, often dated with the regnal year of the ruler, provides a unique type of evidence. Notwithstanding its own limitations, numismatic material affords the rare opportunity to analyze vast frontier regions in comparison through the lens of a single historical source. Gold is most abundant in the Carpathian Basin where the Avars – just like the Huns in the previous century – received millions of gold *solidi* in the form of annual tribute; this immediately developed into the most potent symbol of the khagan's power and the main instrument for maintaining the loyalty of the peoples under his suzerainty. In the Lower Danube region copper coins dominate the numismatic corpus, as a testament of the significant pressure exerted by the frontier system whose influence projected over wide regions south and east of the Carpathians. Finally, silver predominates in Transcaucasia where ceremonial *miliarensia* were used to buy the loyalty of Caucasian tribes, while the hexagram became the main unit of payment for the troops fighting against Persia in the seventh century, particularly in Armenia and Iberia where the Sasanian silver drachm had been for a long time the dominant coinage.

The last chapter explores the problem of economic vs. non-economic functions performed by coins. While precious-metal coins have been connected with political payments, current interpretations of Byzantine copper coins found outside the frontier are chiefly economic. Given the fiduciary nature of Byzantine bronze coinage, the question therefore ineluctably arises as to how they could act as monetary media of exchange outside the confines of the issuing authority. Previous arguments have been couched in preconceived notions regarding the Early Byzantine monetary economy and the untested assumption that parts of *barbaricum* followed the same conditions prevailing in the imperial provinces. Ethnographic research assessing the impact of money on traditional societies in the colonial period can shed some light on the Byzantine case. Although set in a different time and space, the situations discussed in this chapter are brought together by a common denominator, which is cultural contact between monetized empires ("world systems") and small rural communities ("mini-systems"). Drawing on such anthropological parallels for the use of monetary instruments by traditional communities, I argue that coins served mainly non-economic purposes. From an economic, but non-monetary, perspective coins were more attractive for their intrinsic value as raw material for the production of jewelry. As one moves farther from the border, the social appropriation of coins as amulets, souvenirs, and objects of prestige increases.

A note on terminology is required. Historical periodization can be notoriously confusing and Late Antiquity makes no exception. The book covers its final phase from the late fifth to the late seventh century, or the *spätere Spätantike* as Peter Brown defined it. The weight rests on the "long sixth century," from the accession of Anastasius (491–518) to the reign of Heraclius (610–641), which roughly corresponds to the renewal of the Byzantine frontier on the Danube and its ultimate demise, respectively. Depending on region, language, and intellectual tradition Late Roman, Early Byzantine or Byzantine may be used as labels for the period covering the sixth and seventh centuries. Archaeological terminology such as Roman-Byzantine in the Balkans, Late Byzantine in Near East, and Early Medieval or Late Migration for cultures from the Central European *barbaricum* only add to the general confusion to which the non-specialist may easily succumb. In the following chapters only Roman and Early Byzantine will be used, the former for general statements (e.g. Roman way of life, Roman tradition, "Romans and barbarians") and the latter for chronologically sensitive contexts and in relation to the fact that sixth-to-seventh-century coinage is universally described as Early Byzantine. I am using Latin terminology for names or the English equivalent long established in scholarship (e.g. Anastasius, Justinian) and Latin or Greek terms for coinage, reflecting the evolution of this technical vocabulary during Late Antiquity (e.g. *solidus*; *hexagrammon*). "Copper" designates the low-value Byzantine coinage, although the metal itself is a copper alloy, sometimes described as "bronze" in the numismatic literature, where the terms are used interchangeably.

Since this is a work about frontiers, the reader may be puzzled by the variety of seemingly synonymous words used to describe them. I am using "frontier" as a general term which has been unofficially applied to this academic subfield (frontier studies), while "border" specifically designates a linear political demarcation (i.e. the Danube river). "Danubian borderlands" signifies a region corresponding to the cultural semiperiphery described in the second chapter, while *barbaricum* is a northern periphery outside the empire's direct political control. No clear cultural delimitation exists between these two regions as they were constantly negotiated and subject to change. For the sake of brevity, *barbaricum* will therefore be used to designate lands outside the Byzantine provincial administration, although no uniformity must be expected. Throughout the book regions beyond the frontier are sometimes labeled *Gepidia*, *Avaria*, or *Sklavinia*, but their political and cultural boundaries are hard to define in the ever-changing world of *barbaricum*. On the other hand, the term "barbarian" will be used sparingly and only in generic contexts, lest the reader should be left with the impression that various groups may be lumped together under the same cultural umbrella. Finally, I am using Romanization to describe the adoption or imitation of Roman practices; this venerable concept no longer fashionable in many academic circles should be understood here in light of more recent developments in post-colonial theory and archaeological research.

1 | The Roman Frontier in Late Antiquity

1.1 The Frontier Question

For more than a century historians and archaeologists have struggled to define Roman frontiers. Frontiers and borders have always been unwieldy notions as they belong to two different worlds and yet they are their own cultural universe.[1] Since separation is one of the most enduring themes in human history, one of the major challenges has been the negotiation of modern realities which constantly distort our understanding of what frontiers meant to the ancient Romans. Running the risk of falling into the trap of presentism, a number of scholars based their argumentation on implicit or explicit comparisons with modern frontiers. Nineteenth-century efforts to redraw the map of Europe based on nationalistic views of political, cultural, and linguistic identity have prompted historians to rethink the function of Roman frontiers by projecting modern concepts onto ancient contexts. The ensuing debate has shaped two schools of thought. Scholars had to grapple with several frustrating questions: was the Roman frontier a linear barrier separating two worlds or was it an area of economic, cultural, and religious contact? What was the role of geography in sustaining imperial policy in frontier regions? Did frontier rivers unite or divide? Although the static frontier thesis has fallen out of favor with historians of the Roman Empire, the main goal of this chapter is to show that political conditions in Late Antiquity favored frontiers of exclusion and the Danube river will be used as a compelling example of a natural linear border which Roman emperors desperately tried to

---

[1] The quest for a proper terminology has not yet yielded a universally accepted vocabulary. For the problem, see H. Elton, *Frontiers of the Roman Empire* (Bloomington, IN, 1996), 3–9. For an interdisciplinary approach, see L. Rodseth and B. J. Parker, "Introduction: theoretical considerations in the study of frontiers," in *Untaming the Frontier in Anthropology, Archaeology and History*, eds. B. J. Parker and L. Rodseth (Tucson, AZ, 2005), 9–11. See also B. A. Feuer, *Boundaries, Borders and Frontiers in Archaeology: A Study of Spatial Relationships* (Jefferson, NC, 2016), esp. ch. 1. For post-colonial theory on the polysemic nature of borderlands, see H. Bhabha, "Culture's in-between," in *Questions of Cultural Identity*, eds. S. Hall and P. du Gay (London, 1996), 52–60.

maintain. They were not always successful, but for the present discussion the desideratum is more important than the outcome.

The notion of frontier as a line of demarcation between different civilizations had already been put forward by Edward Gibbon in the eighteenth century and later informed the pioneering thesis developed by Frederick Turner. Even to this day, in almost any study dealing with the conceptualization of Roman frontiers, it is *de rigueur* to introduce the topic by citing Turner's seminal work. The American historian argued that the westward expansion was the driving force behind American development, while the frontier itself represented the confluence between savagery and civilization.[2] Entwined with attitudes derived from the modern experience of colonialism, on the old continent such ideas dominated the intellectual discourse in the first half of the twentieth century.[3] Andreas Alföldi's description of the Danube and the Rhine as "moral barriers" separating Roman civilization from the barbarian threat remains notable to this day.[4] This was clearly reminiscent of Turner's meeting point between the forces of civilization and the savage wilderness, later echoed by Owen Lattimore's classic study of the Great Wall, whose ideological purpose was to protect Chinese civilization from the barbarian "outer darkness."[5] Such developments revealed the potential value of comparative analyses but also foreshadowed what would remain for decades the dominant approach in Roman frontier studies, defined by a strong focus on military installations.[6]

---

[2] F. J. Turner, *The Frontier in American History* (New York, NY, 1893). The Turnerian frontier has a long history of criticism and revision in American historiography. For a review and new directions, see K. L. Klein, "Reclaiming the "F" word, or being and becoming postwestern," *Pacific Historical Review* 65, no. 2 (1996): 179–215. For the current legacy of the Turnerian thesis, see L. F. Kutchen, "The neo-Turnerian frontier," *Early American Literature* 40, no. 1 (2005): 163–171.

[3] For the influence of Turner in Roman studies, see W. Pohl, "Conclusion: the transformation of frontiers," in *The Transformation of Frontiers. From Late Antiquity to the Carolingians*, eds. W. Pohl, I. Wood, and H. Reimitz (Leiden, 2001), 248.

[4] A. Alföldi, "The moral barrier on Rhine and Danube," in *The Congress of Roman Frontier Studies, 1949*, ed. E. Birley (Durham, 1952), 1–16.

[5] O. Lattimore, *Inner Asian Frontiers of China* (Boston, MA, 1962), 238, although for Lattimore the Great Wall was far from being a static frontier of exclusion. This type of rhetoric is still being explored, a recent example being the southern border of Egypt separating the "civilized" Nile Valley from the "chaotic" desert, for which see A. L. Boozer, "Frontiers and borderlands in imperial perspectives: exploring Rome's Egyptian frontier," *AJA* 117, no. 2 (2013): 275–292.

[6] For the methodology of the comparative approach, see S. L. Dyson, "The role of comparative frontier studies in understanding the Roman frontier," in *Actes du IXe Congrès international d'études sur les frontières romaines, Mamaia 6–13 sept. 1972*, ed. D. M. Pippidi (Bucharest, 1974), 277–283; J. W. Eadie, "Peripheral vision in Roman history: strengths and weaknesses of the comparative approach," in *Ancient and Modern: Essays in Honor of Gerald F. Else*, eds. J. H. D'Arms and J. W. Eadie (Ann Arbor, MI, 1977), 215–234; I. Kopytoff, "The Roman frontier and

Alföldi's essay opened the first edition (1949) of a series of conferences dedicated to the study of Roman frontiers (*Limeskongresse*), held periodically to this day, in which historians and archaeologists present their work on different sections of the Roman and Early Byzantine *limes*.[7] The results of this prestigious conference perpetuate the concept of a linear fortified border, as the program has only recently begun to include studies on aspects unrelated to military strategy, such as the role of economy, religion, and group identity.[8]

Surprisingly, the most influential, yet controversial, thesis has come from Edward Luttwak, a modern military strategist of the Cold War era. His "Grand Strategy" of the Roman Empire, and more recently, his "Grand Strategy" of the Byzantine Empire, have championed the view of a rational, pragmatic, and well-informed frontier policy, which adapted to external threats.[9] According to Luttwak, the frontier strategy of the Late Roman Empire was characterized by an in-depth defense system, based on a network of fortifications able to absorb the shock of barbarian invasions. Perhaps the greatest achievement of his episodic incursions into Roman history has been the incisive body of scholarship produced to refute his arguments.[10] In doing so, scholars engaged in the frontier debate have

---

the uses of comparison," in *Frontières d'empire. Nature et signification des frontières romaines*, eds. P. Brun, S. van der Leeuw, and C. R. Whittaker (Nemours, 1993), 144. Comparisons between the Chinese Wall and the Roman frontier system are still in fashion, e.g. T. Wilmott, "Towers and spies on Chinese and Roman frontiers," in *The Army and Frontiers of Rome. Papers Offered to David J. Breeze on the Occasion of his Sixty-fifth Birthday and his Retirement from Historic Scotland*, ed. W. S. Hanson (Portsmouth, RI, 2009), 127–133.

[7] The common usage of *limes* with the meaning of "frontier" (usually fortified) is a modern adaptation of the Roman term which had a different connotation, for which see B. Isaac, "The meaning of the term *limes* and *limitanei*," *JRS* 78 (1988): 125–147. See also G. Forni, "Limes. Nozioni e nomenclature," in *Il confine nel mondo clasico*, ed. M. Sordi (Milan, 1987), 272–294.

[8] For a review of the problem, see D. H. Miller, "Frontier societies and the transition between Late Antiquity and the Early Middle Ages," in *Shifting Frontiers*, 161. See, however, Mortimer Wheeler's early attempt to address exchange patterns beyond the frontier, M. Wheeler, *Rome beyond the Imperial Frontier* (London, 1954). See also J. H. Eggers, *Der römische Import im freien Germanien* (Hamburg, 1951).

[9] E. N. Luttwak, *The Grand Strategy of the Roman Empire. From the First Century AD to the Third* (Baltimore, MD, 1976); E. N. Luttwak, *The Grand Strategy of the Byzantine Empire* (Cambridge, MA, 2009).

[10] The merits of an in-depth defense strategy have been questioned by archaeological research conducted in the Near East, for which see B. Isaac, *The Limits of Empire. The Roman Army in the East* (Oxford, 1990). For North Africa, see D. Pringle, *The Defence of Byzantine Africa from Justinian to the Arab Conquest. An account of the Military History and Archaeology of the African Provinces in the Sixth and Seventh Centuries* (Oxford, 1981), 94–109; D. Cherry, *Frontier and Society in Roman North Africa* (Oxford, 1998), 24–74. For the Balkans, see A. G. Poulter, "Cataclysm on the Lower Danube: the destruction of a complex Roman landscape," in *Landscape of Change: Rural Evolutions in Late Antiquity and the Early Middle Ages*, ed. N.

reshaped and refined the frontier paradigm. In the light of growing interest in social, economic, and religious issues, military strategy has been forced into the background.[11] The role and function of "frontier societies" looms large in recent studies, as part of a broader intellectual shift stressing the transformation of the Roman world, a process in which *romanitas* and *barbaritas* blend together in a formative symbiosis.[12]

The pendulum swing in the recent historiography has a main thrust and a number of subsidiary channels. Although the frontier question is far from being solved, it is now widely accepted that Late Roman frontiers were neither static lines of defense, nor barriers holding back barbarian tides.[13] More importantly, C. R. Whittaker has shown that frontiers need to be understood as homogeneous contact zones incorporating regions on both sides of the military installations, a theory which gained widespread recognition.[14] According to this interpretation, borders and boundaries are two distinct notions, which need to be treated by using distinct methodological tools.[15] While borders refer to political and military edges of society,

---

Christie (Aldershot, 2004), 223–253. For a recent attempt to resurrect the "Grand Strategy" model, see K. Kagan, "Redefining Roman Grand Strategy," *Journal of Military History* 70, no. 2 (2006): 333–362.

[11] In the last two decades collective volumes on the topic of late antique and medieval frontiers have started to include separate sections on intellectual and religious frontiers; see for example A. Rousselle, ed., *Frontières terrestres, frontières célestes dans l'antiquité* (Paris: Diffusion De Boccard, 1995); *Shifting Frontiers*; O. Merisalo, ed., *Frontiers in the Middle Ages: Proceedings of the Third European Congress of Medieval Studies (Jyväskylä, 10–14 June 2003)* (Louvain-la-Neuve, 2006); J. H. F. Dijkstra and G. Fisher, eds., *Inside and Out: Interactions between Rome and the Peoples on the Arabian and Egyptian Frontiers in Late Antiquity* (Leuven, 2014).

[12] "The Transformation of the Roman World," a massive project sponsored by the European Science Foundation, had a major role in shaping this new approach in the 1990s. That it soon became the leading paradigm is evident in recent volumes on the same topic; see for instance R. W. Mathisen and D. Shanzer, eds., *Romans, Barbarians, and the Transformation of the Roman World. Cultural Interaction and the Creation of Identity in Late Antiquity* (Farnham, 2011).

[13] *Shifting Frontiers*; Pohl et al., *The Transformation of Frontiers*; F. Curta, ed., *Borders, Barriers, and Ethnogenesis. Frontiers in Late Antiquity and the Middle Ages* (Turnhout, 2005); Isaac, *Limits of Empire*; C. R. Whittaker, *Frontiers of the Roman Empire. A Social and Economic Study* (Baltimore, MD, 1994). This interpretation is not unanimously accepted; cf. D. Williams, *The Reach of Rome. A History of the Roman Imperial Frontier 1st–5th Centuries AD* (New York, NY, 1996), 299; P. Parker, *The Empire Stops Here. A Journey along the Frontiers of the Roman World* (London, 2009); M. W. Graham, *News and Frontier Consciousness in the Late Roman Empire* (Ann Arbor, MI, 2006), 50.

[14] Whittaker, *Frontiers*; C. R. Whittaker, "Frontiers," in *The Cambridge Ancient History*, eds. A. K. Bowman, P. Garnsey, and D. Rathbone, vol. XI (Cambridge, 2000), 293–319; C. R. Whittaker, *Rome and Its Frontiers: The Dynamics of Empire* (New York, NY, 2004).

[15] Whittaker, *Rome and Its Frontiers*, 4–6. For the Danube frontier, see E. Zanini, "Confine e frontiera: il limes danubiano nel VI secolo," in *MILION. Studi e ricerche d'arte bizantina*, eds. C. Barsanti, A. G. Guidobaldi, and A. Iacobini (Rome, 1988), 257–271.

boundary studies address the mechanics of cultural interaction and the social transformation brought by long-term contact, leading to the creation of the frontier as a unique area with a different outlook than the core regions of the Empire.

Although convincingly arguing against the monolithic definition of static frontiers, historians have yet to develop an inclusive model of interaction and for the most part the community remains trapped in a dichotomous discourse of linear vs. non-linear borders.[16] More weight needs to be placed on the changing nature of frontiers from the early Roman period to the Early Byzantine. While the early imperial centuries have traditionally been the focus of frontier studies, both historical and archaeological, the treatment of Late Antique developments – fifth-to-seventh century in particular – is a more recent concern.[17] The transition to the Early Middle Ages in the West shifted the research focus to a new set of questions, deflecting attention away from the Eastern European frontier of Byzantium which survived the western collapse by some 150 years.[18] This explains the tendency to generalize based on research concentrating on the old northern frontier of the Western Empire and to some extent the Near East and North Africa. Particularly lacking are book-length studies dealing with the Early Byzantine frontier in the northern Balkans and the Transcaucasus. The separate identity of various Roman frontiers

---

[16] This polemical approach is more typical of English-language scholarship, although see Elton, *Frontiers*, 1–9. The French *Annales* tradition has long emphasized the polysemic nature of frontiers in a complementary rather than dissonant fashion, although the various facets were often stated but not fully explored. See L. Febvre, "La Frontière: le mot et la notion," *Revue de Synthèse Historique* 45 (1928): 31–44 and especially F. Braudel, *La Méditerranée et le monde méditerranéen à l'époque de Philippe II*, 2nd edn. (Paris, 1966), 155: "C'est de cent frontières qu'il faut parler à la fois: celles-ci à la mesure de la politique, ces autres de l'économie ou de la civilisation" ("We should speak in terms of a hundred frontiers, some political, some economic, and some cultural"). Annalist influence on Dick Whittaker's seminal thesis focusing on the social aspect of Roman frontiers is most apparent in the early French version of his work, *Les frontières de l'Empire romain* (Paris, 1989).

[17] Archaeological surveys of the Danube region often do not go beyond the fifth century when the Lower Danube became a purely Balkan frontier, disconnected from western affairs; see in particular J. J. Wilkes, "The Roman Danube: an archaeological survey," *JRS* 95 (2005): 124–225. Balkan scholars as well as western scholars directly involved in archaeological research in the Lower Danube region are a lot more sensitive to later developments, for which see more recently V. Dinchev, "The fortresses of Thrace and Dacia in the Early Byzantine period," in *Transition*, 479–546; A. G. Poulter, "The Lower Danubian frontier in Late Antiquity: evolution and dramatic change in the frontier zone, c. 296–600," in *Zwischen Region und Reich: das Gebiet der oberen Donau im Imperium Romanum*, eds. P. Herz, P. Schmid, and O. Stoll (Berlin, 2010), 11–42.

[18] The most glaring example illustrating this tendency is the 14-volume "Transformation of the Roman World" project which deals mostly with conditions in Central and Western Europe.

(as opposed to a uniform Grand Strategy) emphasized in most recent works has taught us that frontiers can only be understood in a comparative fashion. In my view this can only be achieved if we approach Roman frontiers comprehensively in both geographic and chronological terms.

This chapter brings into focus the Lower Danube frontier and its political role of separation as illuminated by ancient texts, while the next chapters will home in on the archaeological evidence to show that cultural contact, while allowing for, and even being driven by individual agency, remained subservient to the political agenda promoted by sixth- and seventh-century emperors. Although historians have long struggled with the multifaceted nature of frontiers, the field commonly labeled "Frontier Studies" is multidisciplinary and has already offered a number of theoretical frameworks coming from an anthropological perspective.[19] The model proposed by Bradley Parker is particularly suitable as a starting point for the study of Late Antique borderlands.[20] Parker developed a frontier spectrum ("The Continuum of Frontier Dynamics"), ranging from static to fluid, which can be defined in terms of five categories: geographic, political, demographic, cultural, and economic.[21] Each of these "boundary sets" has a number of subcategories but only some of those are germane to our case study. The geographic category refers to the physical character of frontier regions, the presence or absence of physical features which may create separation, such as rivers or mountains. The presence of the Danube in the northern Balkans, as well as the Caucasus, east of the Black Sea, make the geographic dimension of the northern Byzantine frontier particularly salient. The political category, which also includes administrative

---

[19] Feuer, *Boundaries*, esp. ch. 2; M. Naum, "Re-emerging frontiers: post-colonial theory and historical archaeology of the borderlands," *Journal of Archaeological Method and Theory* 17, no. 2 (2011): 101–131; T. Wendl and M. Rösler, "Frontiers and borderlands. The rise and relevance of an anthropological research genre," in *Frontiers and Borderlands: Anthropological Perspectives*, eds. T. Wendl and M. Rösler (Frankfurt am Main, 1999), 1–27; E. M. Shortman and P. A. Urban, "Culture contact structure and process," in *Studies in Culture Contact: Interaction, Culture Change, and Archaeology*, ed. C. Cusick (Carbondale, IL, 1998), 102–25; K. G. Lightfoot and A. Martinez, "Frontiers and boundaries in archaeological perspective," *ARA* 24 (1995): 471–492; C. Chase-Dunn and T. D. Hall, "Conceptualizing Core/Periphery hierarchies for comparative study," in *Core/Periphery Relations in Precapitalist Worlds*, eds. C. Chase-Dunn and T. D. Hall (Boulder, CO, 1991), 5–44; S. W. Green and S. M. Perlman, "Frontiers, boundaries, and open social systems," in *The Archaeology of Frontiers and Boundaries*, eds. S. W. Green and S. M. Perlman (New York, NY, 1985), 3–13.

[20] B. J. Parker, "Understanding of borderland processes," *AAnt* 71, no. 1 (2006): 77–100. This is a particularly convenient model for the comparative study of river frontiers in antiquity since it grew out of Parker's own research on the Assyrian frontier established on the Upper Tigris.

[21] Ibid., 82, fig. 2.

and military boundaries, became preeminent during the long sixth century and is well documented in contemporary accounts. The demographic, cultural, and economic categories are harder to separate although the researcher may still be able to focus on an individual aspect while maintaining a broader perspective. Finally, demographic boundaries are particularly meaningful in the Early Byzantine case because population movement across the frontier had a major role in cultural diffusion, the creation of cultural identity, as well as stimulating trade.

Although interconnected, it must be recognized that the study of different types of frontiers often require different research tools and will sometimes yield seemingly opposed results. It should not be surprising then that this book will on the one hand argue that the Danube in Late Antiquity was meant to be a fortified static border of political and military exclusion, while on the other emphasize the significance of demographic movement, social and religious interaction, and economic exchange.[22] The Danube frontier was clearly multidimensional.[23] Indeed, boundary sets reinforce each other rather than operating in separate or antagonistic spheres. Parker's model includes a "Borderland Matrix" where the five types of boundaries interact and are placed on equal footing.[24] In the sixth century, however, when state dirigisme in the Balkans reached its apex, the political aspect became overarching. Therefore, Parker's generic model needs some adjustment. Although all boundary sets remain interconnected, they gravitate around the more dominant political manifestation. To be sure, its power should not be exaggerated. We should resist the temptation of being overly drawn into the scenario depicting an overcontrolling government

---

[22] Fortunately, there is some hope of developing a standard set of borderland characteristics applicable to pre-modern imperial realms across time and space. Parker's methodology has been adopted in Andean archaeology, for which see U. Matthies Green and K. E. Costion, "Modeling ranges of cross-cultural interaction in ancient borderlands," in *Frontiers of Colonialism*, ed. C. D. Beaule (Gainesville, FL, 2017), 480–539. A similar conceptual framework emphasizing multidimensionality has been applied in the case of the Inka imperial frontier, for which see A. Alconini, "The dynamics of military and cultural frontiers on the southeastern edge of the Inka Empire," in *Untaming the Frontier*, 115–46; as well as to the Aztec frontier, for which see F. F. Berdan, "Borders in the Eastern Aztec Empire," in *The Postclassic Mesoamerican World*, eds. M. E. Smith and F. F. Berdan (Salt Lake City, UT, 2003), 73–77.

[23] S. Brezeanu, "The Lower Danube frontier during the 4th–7th centuries. A notion's ambiguity," *Annuario Istituto Romeno di Cultura e Ricerca Umanistica* 5 (2003): 19–46. More generally on the multidimensional nature of the Byzantine frontier, see H. Ahrweiler, "La frontière et les frontières de Byzance en Orient," in *Actes du XIVe congrès international des études byzantines: Bucarest, 6–12 septembre 1971*, eds. M. Berza and E. Stănescu, vol. I (Bucharest, 1974), 209–230; D. Obolensky, "Byzantine frontier zones and cultural exchanges," in *Actes*, eds. Berza and Stănescu, 303–313.

[24] Parker, "Understanding of borderland," 90, fig. 3.

orchestrated by historians and panegyrists absorbed by political and diplomatic concerns. On the other hand, the physical remains of sixth-century military installations built throughout the Balkans should not be ignored as they lend additional credibility to the active involvement of the government in the frontier region.[25]

The interaction that takes place within and between boundary sets through time is the essence of Parker's boundary dynamics. Indeed, change over time adds another important dimension to the ongoing political concerns voiced by sixth-century observers. Conditions during Late Antiquity altered the traditional view of Roman frontiers and prompted the development of a new type of official rhetoric. Although Roman ideology may have remained unchanged in terms of an *imperium sine fine* under the new Christian identity, the reality on the ground changed dramatically.[26] The endemic civil wars of the third century and the collapse of the tetrarchic system in the fourth century transferred the military initiative to various barbarian tribes and the sprawling Empire was often forced to fight on several fronts. Conquering new territories or subduing new peoples was no longer as high a priority as preserving the Empire and keeping the barbarians at bay. Consequently, unlike early historians, writers of the Late Empire developed a real obsession with frontiers and constantly deplored the loss of territory. The often-cited account of the fourth-century anonymous author of *De rebus bellicis* is a case in point, notwithstanding the rhetorical tone:

> Above all it must be recognized that wild nations are pressing upon the Roman Empire and howling about it everywhere, and treacherous barbarians, with the cover of natural places, are assailing every frontier [...] Among the measures taken by the State for its own advantage there is also the effective care of the frontier-works which surround all the borders of the Empire. Their safety will be better provided for by a continuous line of forts constructed at intervals of one mile with firm walls and very powerful towers.[27]

---

[25] For sixth-century imperial initiatives in the Balkans, see recently A. Sarantis, *Justinian's Balkan Wars: Campaigning, Diplomacy and Development in Illyricum, Thrace and the Northern World AD 527–65* (Francis Cairns: Prenton, 2016), 113–226.

[26] For the Byzantine ideology on frontiers, see G. Dagron, "Byzance et la frontière. Idéologie et réalité," in *Frontiers in the Middle Ages*, ed. Merisalo, 303–318. On the contrast between reality and ideology, see P. Trousset, "La frontière romaine et ses contradictions," in *La frontière: séminaire de recherche*, ed. Y. Roman (Paris, 1993), 25–33.

[27] *De Rebus Bellicis*, 6.1 and 20 (trans. Thompson): *in primis sciendum est quod imperium Romanum circumlatrantium ubique nationum perstringat insania et omne latus limitum tecta naturalibus locis appeat dolosa barbaries* [...] *Est praeterea inter commode Reipublicae utilis*

Although "frontier drama" developed into a recurring theme which abounded in repetitive and formulaic phrases, there is every reason to believe that it was an issue of major concern for both the authors and their readership from the fourth to the seventh century. Indeed, as the Empire grew weaker, frontier consciousness grew stronger.[28] Such concerns apply not only to the Danube frontier but suggest an empire-wide effort. Based on this new ideology, Late Roman emperors often received praise for strengthening the frontier. The practice began in earnest with the transformations brought by the Tetrarchy and remained an important literary device until the empire's final collapse. In an early panegyric, Maximianus was held in high regard because he protected the Rhine frontier, while another text belonging to the same genre mentioned the camps of cavalry units and infantry restored by the Tetrarchy on the Rhine, Danube, and Euphrates.[29] More than two centuries later, little seems to have changed; Procopius spoke of the defenses with which Justinian "surrounded the farthest limits of the territory of the Romans," and of "all the fortifications whereby this Emperor preserved the Empire, walling it about and frustrating the attacks of the barbarians on the Romans."[30] Later in that century, Agathias was still fully aware of ongoing concerns with the loss of territory when he reminded his readers of the shameful defeat of Julian in Persia, "confining thereafter the extent of his Empire within new frontiers, whittling away its far-flung corners."[31] This was a lesson to be heeded on more than one frontier in the second half of the sixth century, when Agathias was forced to acknowledge the shaky legacy of Justinian's imperial effort.[32]

---

limitum cura ambientium ubique latus imperii, quorum tutelage assidua melius castella prospicient, ita ut millenis interiecta passibus stabili muro et firmissimis turribus erigantur. For the frontier question in *De rebus bellicis*, see J. Arce, "Frontiers of the Late Roman Empire: perceptions and realities," in *The Transformation of Frontiers*, eds. Pohl et al., 5–13.

[28] For a recent discussion of this complex phenomenon, see Graham, *News and Frontier*, part I.

[29] *Panegyrici Latini* 8.13.3 and 9.18.4: *toto Rheni et Histri et Eufrate limite restituta.*

[30] Procopius, *De Aedificiis*, 2.1.2–3 (trans. Dewing): τὸ δὲ λοιπὸν ἐπὶ τὰ ἐρύματα ἡμῖν ἰτέον, [καὶ] οἷσπερ τὰς ἐσχατιὰς περιέβαλε Ῥωμαίων τῆς γῆς [...] ἀλλὰ τὰ ὀχυρώματα σύμπαντα, οἷς ὁ βασιλεὺς οὗτος τὴν βασιλείαν ἐσώσατο, τειχισάμενός τε αὐτὴν καὶ ἀμήχανον τοῖς βαρβάροις καταστησάμενος τὴν ἐς Ῥωμαίους ἐπιβουλήν. The propagandistic tone does not reduce the historical value of Procopius' account and perhaps the best piece of evidence in his defense is the well-known inscription found at Byllis in Albania honoring Viktorinos, Justinian's architect in the Balkans, who was responsible for building the forts of Thracia and Illyricum; see D. Feissel, "L'architecte Viktôrinos et les fortifications de Justinien dans les provinces balkaniques," *Bulletin de la Société Nationale des Antiquaires de France* (1988): 136–146.

[31] Agathias, *Historiae*, 4.25.7 (trans Frendo): περιστέλλων ἐς τὰ ὀπίσω καινοῖς ὁρίοις καὶ ὑποτεμνόμενος τῆς οἰκείας ἀρχῆς τὸ περαιτέρω ἐκβαῖνον.

[32] The best analysis of Agathias remains A. Cameron, *Agathias* (Oxford, 1970).

Before exploring the empire's frontier on the Danube, we should remember that the main political priority remained the border with Persia, the archrival and ideological antithesis of Rome. No emperor could afford to ignore it as the consequences could prove catastrophic. Indeed, Procopius showed that the need for establishing a firm frontier had a long tradition in Late Antiquity: "it was forbidden in the treaty which the Emperor Theodosius once concluded with the Persian nation, that either party should construct any new fortress on his own land where it bordered on the boundaries of the other nation."[33] Unlike the Danube region which rarely produced a monolithic challenge to Rome, the frontier with Persia is as close as we can get to the familiar notion of militarized borders between rival states. During the sixth century, frontier forts such as Dara in Mesopotamia became central in the military and diplomatic relations between Byzantium and Sasanian Persia. The capture of the fortress by the Persians literally drove Emperor Justin II insane.[34] The only similar episode in the Balkans, the loss of Sirmium, seems to have provoked a less dramatic effect on the imperial house.[35] Although events such as the loss of Dara may seem only remotely significant for conditions in the northern Balkans, the shock waves rippled across the empire. Resources were spread dangerously thin and failure on the principal theater(s) could take supplies and manpower away from regions placed lower on the empire's strategic plan. The transfer of troops from the Balkans to other theaters, frequently referred to in contemporary sources, should teach us that politics and diplomacy on the Danube frontier can only be understood in a much

---

[33] Procopius, *De Aedificiis*, 2.1.5 (trans Dewing): ἅσπερ ποτὲ βασιλεὺς Θεοδόσιος ἔθετο πρὸς τὸ Περσῶν γένος, μηδετέρους ἐν χωρίῳ οἰκείῳ ἐν γειτόνων που τοῖς τῶν ἑτέρων ὁρίοις κειμένῳ ὀχύρωμα νεώτερόν τι ἐπιτεχνᾶσθαι. Moreover, the regulation of trade at the Persian border in a rescript from 408/9 suggested that boundaries should be strictly enforced and traffic closely monitored, since no trade was permitted beyond Nisibis, Callinicum, and Artaxata; see *Corpus Iuris Civilis*, 4.63.4 (408/9).

[34] John of Ephesus, *Historia Ecclesiastica*, 3.4. For the strategic significance of Dara, see B. Croke and J. Crow, "Procopius and Dara," *JRS* 73 (1983): 143–159; M. Whitby, "Procopius' description of Dara ("Buildings" II 1–3)," in *The Defence of the Roman and Byzantine East. Proceedings of a Colloquium Held at the University of Sheffield in April 1986*, eds. P. Freeman and D. L. Kennedy (Oxford, 1986), 737–783.

[35] In the sixth century Sirmium passed from the Goths (504), to the Gepids (536), the Romans (567), and finally to the Avars (582). For the events, see Sarantis, *Justinian's Balkan Wars*, 60; M. Whitby, *The Emperor Maurice and His Historian: Theophylact Simocatta on Persian and Balkan Warfare* (Oxford, 1988), 88–89.

broader context. The Balkan provinces may have pinned their hopes on the local Danubian system but their fate was crafted elsewhere.[36]

1.2 Rome's Frontier on the Danube: *Topos* and Reality

> [...] for this we have resolved after countless considerations, that it be more beneficial to us and to the entire Europe that the Danube be reinforced with fortresses. For this is the water of resistance [*aqua contradictionis*], where Heraclius battled with Chosroes to defend the Roman Empire, and where in spite of surprise or fierce attacks we fought the Mongols for ten months, our kingdom almost deprived of fortresses and defenders.[37]

This is how the Hungarian king Béla IV appealed to Pope Innocent IV in a letter dated on the Ides of November 1254 when rumors of another massive Mongol invasion spread panic in the Hungarian kingdom. Although the geography of the conflict with Persia became confused in the thirteenth-century text, it was nothing short of an ideological return to the Roman frontier guarded by the Danube, described as *aqua contradictionis*, with deliberate Biblical connotations (Num. 20:13), and seen as a bulwark against barbarian invaders. A discussion of the Early Byzantine frontier on the Danube, which will be the focus of the following pages, raises again the issue of rivers as frontiers of exclusion. If Alföldi's "moral frontier" is no longer tenable, emphasizing the role of rivers as "bureaucratic choices" primarily facilitating transport, communication, and supply or as "ritual boundaries to be crossed" is equally problematic.[38]

---

[36] The mutiny of 602 which ended with the deposition of Maurice and renewed hostilities with Persia could be invoked as evidence that events in the Balkans shaped the Empire's destiny. However, it must be remembered that the military maneuvers of the late 590s in the Danube region were nothing but a desperate attempt to compensate for two decades of inaction and poor diplomatic choices in the northern Balkans. For the events, see Whitby, *The Emperor Maurice*, 156–169. For the imminent conflict with Persia, irrespective of the 602 episode, see J. H. W. G. Liebeschuetz, "The Lower Danube under pressure: from Valens to Heraclius," in *Transition*, 129.

[37] *Codex Diplomaticus Hungariae Ecclesiasticus ac Civilis*, ed. G. Fejér, vol. IV/1 (Buda, 1829), 222.

[38] This view is generally upheld by scholars who choose to view the frontier in non-linear terms. It gained ground especially after Luttwak published his controversial thesis; see Isaac, *The Limits of Empire*, 410–413, and more forcefully at Whittaker, *Frontiers of the Roman Empire*, 171: "the Danube was rarely if ever the political or military frontier." For earlier views, see C. M. Wells, *The German Policy of Augustus* (Oxford, 1972), 24; C. J. Mann, "The frontiers of the Principate," in *Aufstieg und Niedergang der römischen Welt. II. Principat. 1. Politische Geschichte (Allgemeines)*, ed. H. Temporini (Berlin, 1974), 513. Historians often cite Lord

Fortunately, there are reasons to believe that the frontier-river is not a defunct concept.[39]

The Danube frontier is an excellent case for testing such assumptions against the available literary and archaeological evidence. The Lower Danube may not have been the inevitable Roman frontier in Eastern Europe but it certainly developed into one when the empire was forced into a defensive position in Late Antiquity. Arguing against a coherent frontier strategy, some scholars have pointed out that an ambitious emperor like Trajan could afford to bypass the Danube and establish a new province (Dacia) which eventually took many legions to defend.[40] In hindsight this was a poor strategic move but for contemporaries who could admire the emperor's new forum dominating the skyline, it was well worth the effort. Furthermore, the new Carpathian frontier was not necessarily a failure considering that it lasted for ca. 165 years. But it did not prove to be the wisest choice either. When disaster struck in the third century the transdanubian provinces were abandoned without remorse and the entire length of the Lower Danube became once again Rome's border in the Balkans. This lends further weight to the argument that the Danube was in the end the most sustainable option and its longevity certainly proves it. The Romans continued to regard the river as the legal border of the Empire until the administration of the northern Balkans finally collapsed and the Byzantine state – followed by the Ottoman – maintained this *de iure* claim for much longer.[41]

Curzon's 1907 lecture on frontiers as a historiographical foundation for their claim that rivers connect rather than separate; see Lord Curzon, *Frontiers. The Romanes Lecture* (Oxford, 1908), 21. On that same page, however, Lord Curzon also stated that rivers provided "a convenient line of division, easily capable of defense" and specifically referred to the cases of the Rhine and the Danube under the Romans.

[39] For the symbolic and practical role of separation, see M. J. Nicasie, *Twilight of Empire. The Roman Army from the Reign of Diocletian until the Battle of Adrianople* (Amsterdam, 1998), 123–125; Graham, *News and Frontier*, 56–72; Parker, *The Empire Stops*, 4. For the role of rivers and water defenses, see B. Rankov, "Do rivers make good frontiers?" in *Limes XIX. Proceedings of the XIXth International Congress of Roman Frontier Studies Held in Pécs, Hungary, September 2003*, ed. Z. Visy (Pécs, 2005), 175–181; B. Campbell, *Rivers and the Power of Ancient Rome* (Chapel Hill, NC, 2012), 186–197; N. Christie, "From the Danube to the Po: the defence of Pannonia and Italy in the fourth and fifth centuries AD," in *Transition*, 570–573; C. S. Sommer, "Why there? The positioning of forts along the riverine frontiers of the Roman Empire," in *The Army and Frontiers*, ed. Hanson, 103–114; N. Hodgson, "Relationships between Roman river frontiers and artificial frontiers," in *Roman Frontier Studies 1995. Proceedings of the XVIth International Congress of Roman Frontier Studies*, ed. W. Groenman-Van Waateringe (Oxford, 1997), 61–66.

[40] Whittaker, *Rome and Its Frontiers*, 34–35, with a discussion of previous theories.

[41] E. Chrysos, "Die Nordgrenze des byzantinischen Reiches im 6. bis 8. Jahrhundert," in *Die Völker Südosteuropas im 6. bis 8. Jarhrhundert*, ed. B. Hänsel (Munich, 1987), 27–40. Imperial rhetoric continued to claim the Danube as the official border even after the creation of the

The Danube had played a political function as a natural obstacle long before the Romans, although it was far from being impregnable.[42] Ancient Greek writers did not fail to notice that the greatest weakness of the river was its tendency to freeze during winter, which allowed an easy crossing just like "a plain over which men ride."[43] Rome would have to face the same problem. Since the establishment of the province of Moesia, the Romans regarded the Danube as a line separating them from the peoples living north of the river, especially the Dacians, whose inroads south of the Danube are described by Annaeus Florus: "whenever the Danube froze and bridged itself [*gelu Danuvius iunxerat ripas*], under the command of their king Cotiso, they used to make descents and ravage the neighboring districts."[44] A similar reference to the frozen river is made on Trajan's column, in the depiction of the heavily armed Dacian and Sarmatian cavalry crossing the frozen Danube for a surprise counteroffensive in the winter of 101.[45] The same recurring problem troubled Late Roman writers. In the fourth century Libanius mentioned the raids of the "Scythians" which he "could not bear to look upon," praying that "the ice on the Danube should not be frozen solid, to be sufficient for their crossing,"[46] while in the sixth century Agathias wrote in the same vein about the terrifying invasion of the Cutrigurs in 559:

> As usual, with the approach of winter, the river froze to a considerable depth and the ice was already hard enough to be crossed on horseback. Whereupon Zabergan, the leader of the Cutrigurs galloped across the

---

Bulgar kingdom; see recently O. Damian, *Bizanțul la Dunărea de Jos (secolele VII–X)* (Brăila, 2015), 205–214; T. Stepanov, "Danube and Caucasus – the Bulgar(ian)s' real and imagined frontiers," in *Donaulimes*, 299–309.

[42] The earliest reference is Herodotus' account of the campaign led by Darius the Great in 514 BC, which entailed a complicated crossing of the Danube; see Herodotus, *Historiae*, 4.89.

[43] Aristotle, *De Mirabilibus Auscultationibus*, 168 (182): καὶ θέρους μὲν ναυσίπορον ἔχουσι τὸ ῥεῖθρον, τοῦ δὲ χειμῶνος παγέντες ὑπὸ κρύους ἐν πεδίου σχήματι καθιππεύονται.

[44] Annaeus Florus, *Epitome*, 2.28 (trans. Forster). For a discussion of the frozen Danube as an ancient literary *topos* in Greek and Roman literature, see F. Hornstein, "ΙΣΤΡΟΣ ΑΜΑΞΕΥΟΜΕΝΟΣ. Zur Geschichte eines literarischen Topos," *Gymnasium* 64 (1957): 154–161, and more recently S. Patoura, "Emporio kai synallages ste dounabike methorio: he Autokratoria kai hoi 'barbaroi'," in *He methorios tou Dounabe kai o kosmos tes sten epoche tes metanasteuses ton laon (4os–7os ai.)*, ed. S. Patoura-Spanou (Athens, 2008), 195–221. Several other examples from the early Roman period are discussed in Rankov, "Do rivers make," 178–179.

[45] L. Rossi, *Trajan's Column and the Dacian Wars* (Ithaca, NY, 1971), 146–148. For the Danube as symbolic frontier on the Column, see M. Galinier, "La Colonne trajane: images et imaginaire de la frontière," in *Frontières terrestres*, ed. Rouselle, 274–276.

[46] Libanius, *Oratio 59*, 90 (trans. Dodgeon, rev. Vermes and Lieu): αὕτη δὲ ἦν μὴ παγῆναι βέβαιον ἐν Ἴστρῳ κρύσταλλον, ὥστε καὶ ἐπελθεῖν ὑπάρχειν.

frozen waters with a huge force of cavalry and crossed over without difficulty into the territory of the Romans.⁴⁷

References to invasions facilitated by the frozen Danube continued to be made during the Middle Byzantine period, a chilly reminder that nature itself was the Empire's worst enemy in the northern Balkans.⁴⁸ Indirectly, such descriptions suggest that the unfrozen river was considered to be an efficient barrier.⁴⁹ The general impression is that as long as the river flowed and the fleet could operate in coordination with static defenses on the right bank, the Balkan provinces were not in serious danger.

To be sure, the role of the river as a communication artery should not be overlooked, especially after Dacia became a Roman province, but it would be a mistake to understate the strategic value of the river in regulating access from and to the left bank.⁵⁰ This remained a central preoccupation throughout the Roman presence in the region, starting with the early phase of conquest. Trajan built the celebrated stone bridge across the Danube for his second campaign in Dacia, but his successor Hadrian wanted to remove it fearing attacks from barbarians who would use it to sweep into Moesia.⁵¹ An easy crossing of the Danube was clearly a double-edged sword. After the abandoning of Dacia, the Danube became the first line of defense and its function of separation was not lost on Late Roman historians writing about frontiers. A few examples will throw light on this enduring concern. In the geographical introduction to his *Historiarum adversum paganos*, Orosius described the territory which the "Danube cuts off from barbarian

---

[47] Agathias, *Historiae*, 5.11.6 (trans. Frendo): τότε δὴ οὖν τοῦ χειμῶνος ἐπιλαβομένου, τὰ μὲν ῥεῖθρα τοῦδε τοῦ ποταμοῦ κατὰ τὸ εἰωθὸς ὑπὸ τοῦ κρύους ἐπήγνυτο ἐς βάθος καὶ ἦσαν ἤδη σκληρὰ καὶ βάσιμα καὶ ἱππήλατα. Ζάβεργάν δὲ ὁ τῶν Κοτριγούρων Οὔννων ἡγεμὼν σὺν πλείστοις ὅσοις ἱππόταις ἐπιδραμὼν καθάπερ χέρσον τὰς δίνας ἐς τὴν Ῥωμαίων ἐπικράτειαν εὐκολώτατα διαβαίνει.

[48] Mauropos, 182 (St. George speech, April 23, 1049); Psellos, *Chronographia*, 67 (Isaac Komnenos); Kedrenos, *Synopsis*, 514; Staurakios, *Logos eis ta thaumasia tou Agiou Dimitriou*, 1.5.

[49] Isaac, *The Limits of Empire*, 413, turns the argument on its head by suggesting that such accounts prove that the Danube was not an efficient natural barrier.

[50] I. Barnea, "Le Danube, voie de communication byzantine," in *He epikoinonia sto Byzantio. Praktika tou B' diethnous symposiou, 4–6 oktobriou 1990*, ed. N. Moschonas (Athens, 1993), 577–595; A. Barnea, "Voies de communication au Bas-Danube aux IVe–VIe s. ap. J. C.," *EBPB* 3 (1997): 29–43. For a nuanced view of the *ripa* and its function in the frontier context, see P. Trousset, "La notion de 'ripa' et les frontières de l'empire," in *Le fleuve et ses métamorphoses. Actes du Colloque international tenu à l'Université Lyon 3 – Jean Moulin les 13, 14 et 15 mai 1992*, ed. F. Piquet (Paris, 1993), 141–152.

[51] Cassius Dio, *History*, 68.13.6.

lands down as far as Our Sea."[52] Zosimus noted that according to the peace terms imposed on the Goths by Valens, "the barbarians were forbidden to cross the river or ever again to set foot inside the Roman borders."[53] Such arrangements never lasted and Jerome could only lament the state of the Danube frontier shattered by barbarian invasions (*fracta Danubii limite*), after which "Rome had to fight within her own borders not for glory but for bare life."[54] During the dark days of the Hunnic domination at the Danube, Attila managed to extend his control south of the river and according to Priscus of Panium he moved the frontier to Naissus, "which he had laid waste and established as the border point between the Scythian and the Roman territory."[55] Later, he reacknowledged the Danube as the official frontier as he vowed to keep the peace on the same terms and to withdraw from the Roman territory bordering on the river.[56] The status quo remained quite unchanged in the sixth century when Procopius was writing that the Danube "clearly forms the boundary between the barbarians, who hold its left bank, and the territory of the Romans, which is on the right."[57] Although such accounts were often written with more attention to rhetoric than truth, they all seem to converge on the notion that the Danube was meant to separate, rather than unite.

The practical function of rivers was often reinforced by ideological principles. Rivers had a symbolic meaning for the Romans as boundaries that should not be crossed or as natural frontiers between two peoples, acting as neutral territory.[58] Naturally, rivers could also bind as long as the

---

[52] Orosius, *Historiarum adversum Paganos Libri VII*, 1.2.54 (trans. Fear): *nunc quidquid Danuuius a barbarico ad mare Nostrum secludit expediam*. Interestingly, the river's role of separation echoed Seneca's own understanding – more than three centuries earlier – of the fact that the Danube separated what was Roman from what was "Sarmatian" as he ridiculed the "boundaries of mortals," for which see Seneca, *Naturales Quaestiones*, 1.9 (praefatio), 4: *Danuuius Sarmatica ac Romana disterminet*.

[53] Zosimus, *Historia Nova*, 4.11 (trans. Buchanan and Davis): βαρβάροις τε ἀπέγνωστο μὴ περαιοῦσθαι μηδὲ ὅλως ποτὲ τοῖς Ῥωμαίων ἐπιβαίνειν ὁρίοις.

[54] Jerome, *Epistula* 123.17 (trans. Fremantle): *Romam in gremio suo, non pro gloria, sed pro salute pugnare*.

[55] Priscus, *History*, fr. 11.1 (trans. Blockley): Ναϊσσῷ, ἣν ὅριον ὡς ὑπ' αὐτοῦ δῃωθεῖσαν τῆς Σκυθῶν καὶ Ῥωμαίων ἐτίθετο γῆς.

[56] Priscus, *History*, 4.15.4 (Blockley).

[57] Procopius, *De Aedificiis*, 4.5.10: Δακίας δὲ ὡς ἀγχοτάτω γενόμενος, ἐνταῦθα διορίξων φαίνεται πρῶτον τούς τε βαρβάρους, οἳ δὴ αὐτοῦ τὰ ἐπ' ἀριστερᾷ ἔχουσι, τήν τε Ῥωμαίων γῆν ἐν δεξιᾷ οὖσαν.

[58] For the symbolic meaning of crossing or bridging rivers, see D. Braund, "River frontiers in the environmental psychology of the Roman world," in *The Roman Army in the East*, ed. D. Kennedy (Ann Arbor, MI, 1996), 43–47.

Romans were the ones regulating traffic. In this respect, rivers were sometimes used for propagandistic purposes on visual media where one can find several of its functions intertwined. One such example is the medallion from Lyon struck during the Tetrarchy showing *Germani* crossing the Rhine bridge at Mainz leaving behind their homeland to embrace Roman civilization.[59] The propagandistic scene alludes to the *receptio* of foreign groups, a practice whose frequency would only increase in the next century. The symbolic image of the river as a dividing line would not be lost on contemporary eyes and its impact on the Late Roman construction of otherness should not be underestimated. Similar symbolism can be attached to the bridge built by Constantine across the Rhine at Cologne "more to add glory to your command and an ornament to the frontier than to give yourself an opportunity, as often as you wish, of crossing into enemy territory," in the words of a panegyric typically fraught with rhetorical devices.[60] The Danube made no exception. The stone bridge opened in 328 connecting Oescus with Sucidava on *ripa Gothica* was meant to place Constantine on equal footing with Trajan, although he never came close to reclaiming Carpathian Dacia for the Empire.[61] Nevertheless, here as well medallions were struck to commemorate the event.[62] Clearly, bridges across frontier rivers were not built only for campaigns into enemy territory and ceremonies of *receptio*. They were strong statements of Roman power and such ideological bravado was most needed in times of insecurity.

From a diplomatic perspective the neutral symbolism of rivers is made apparent by the fact that peace negotiations were sometimes held symbolically close to an important river. Romans had met the Persians on the

---

[59] For an illustration of the medallion, see T. S. Burns, *Barbarians within the Gates of Rome: A Study of Roman Military Policy and the Barbarians, ca. 375–425 AD.* (Bloomington, IN, 1994), 14, ill. 1.

[60] *Panegyrici Latini*, 6.13.1 (trans. Nixon and Rodgers): *cum tamen hoc tu magis ad gloriam imperii tui et ornatum limitis facias quam ad facultatem, quotiens uelis, in hosticum transeundi.*

[61] Only briefly mentioned by Aurelius Victor, *De Caesaribus*, 41.18: *pons per Danubium ductus*. For the significance of the bridge, see A. Madgearu, "Military operations commanded by Constantine the Great north of the Danube," in *Cruce și misiune. Sfinții Împărați Constantin și Elena - promotori ai libertății religioase și apărători ai Bisericii*, eds. E. Popescu and V. Ioniță, vol. II (Bucharest, 2013), 588–590; D. Tudor, *Les ponts romains du Bas-Danube* (Bucharest, 1974), 135–166; I. Barnea and O. Iliescu, *Constantin cel Mare* (Bucharest, 1982), 107–111.

[62] *RIC* VII, 298, showing a bridge with three arches and the legend "Danubius." See more recently E. Paunov, "Konstantinoviiat most na Dunava pri Escus – Sukidava izobrazen na bronzov medal'on," *Reverse* 1, no. 1 (2016): 28–33. The stone bridge is sometimes confused with the temporary pontoon bridge linking Transmarisca and Dafne, e.g. Whittaker, *Rome and Its Frontiers*, 38.

Euphrates for negotiations in the first century, in the fourth century Valentinian negotiated with the Alamans on a ship in the middle of the Rhine, while Valens met Athanaric on the Danube.[63] After the dissolution of the Hunnic empire, the sons of Attila came to Emperor Leo I to ask that Romans and Huns should meet at the Danube for a peace treaty, "in the old manner" (τὸ παλαιὸν ἔθος), and establish a market.[64] No doubt Priscus had in mind the fourth-century precedent with the Goths playing the role of the barbarian. In the sixth century, the Avars having reached "the banks of the Scythian Hister" and threatening to invade the Roman province sent envoys to Constantinople requesting stipends from Justin II.[65] These examples show that barbarians themselves acknowledged the political and military dimension of the river. Although such practices are most typical for the Roman era, their longevity is truly impressive. The Danube retained its diplomatic function into the Middle Byzantine period, when Sviatoslav sailed along the river in a "Scythian" boat to meet Emperor Tzimiskes for peace negotiations.[66] Half a millennium later, a treaty from 1444 between the Ottomans and the Hungarians was establishing the Danube as a frontier which they pledged not to violate.[67] As usual, such promises were rarely kept.

The border between symbolical and practical was easy to cross and the Danube often became a convenient separation line. In the early seventh century Georgios Pisides contemplated the role of the Danube against the threat of the Avars in the same vein as Late Roman historians had, the river being described metaphorically as a "boundary to savagery" and "a fence and a new wall:"[68]

> Until now the river provided by unwritten (natural) law a border (to the Empire), (nonetheless) how much damage has the state suffered from the wicked barbarians! On the one hand, they always tried to break through the established frontier, on the other hand, the power of the Romans prevented them from invading our land.[69]

---

[63] Ammianus Marcellinus, *Res Gestae*, 30.3.4–5; 31.4.13; Tacitus, *Annales*, 2.58.
[64] Priscus, *History*, 6.46 (Blockley).
[65] Corippus, *In laudem Iustini Augusti minoris*, 3.300–302: *nunc ripas Scythici victor rex contigit Istri, densaque per latos figens tentoria campos ad tua nos, princeps, haec splendida moenia misit.*
[66] Leo the Deacon, *Historiae*, 9.11.   [67] Chalcocondyl, *Historiarum*, 6.
[68] Note how the symbolic function of the river had changed since the Principate when god Danubius on Trajan's column was helping Roman troops cross into Dacia (Scene III) and the same aggressive imagery was being used on coins issued shorty after the first war, with Danubius pressing his knee on the female personification of Dacia (*RIC* II, 556).
[69] Georgios Pisides, *Bellum Avaricum*, 30–40: ὁ Ποντογείτων Ἴστρος ἴσχυσεν μόλις ὡς ῥευστὸν ἀντίφραγμα καὶ τεῖχος νέον· τεῖχος γὰρ αὐτοῖς ἀντέβη τὰ κύματα καὶ φραγμὸς ἑστὼς εἰς ἀείδρομον φύσιν. τέως μὲν οὖν τὸ ῥεῖθρον ἀγράφῳ κρίσει τούτους μεσάζον τοὺς ὅρους ἐπήξατο, ὅσην δὲ

Pisides wrote during the tumultuous days of Heraclius' reign, but the passage clearly reflects a deep-seated mentality, whose echo still resonated in twelfth-century Byzantium.[70] Especially when the Empire was not strong enough to assert its influence north of the river, the Danube was specifically indicated as the northern border of Byzantium. Such was the case in the treaty sealed by Emperor Maurice with Baian, the khagan of the Avars, according to which "the Ister was agreed as intermedium between Romans and Avars, but there was provision for crossing the river against Slavs."[71] It would seem that the Romans were sometimes in the strategic position of initiating offensive campaigns north of the Danube, to be sure, an ambition of little relevance in Pisides' time. The fact that the Empire was able to embark on such expeditions only twice during the long sixth century shows that the Danube was not necessarily the desired frontier, but certainly the more convenient and affordable one at that time. Trajan's and Constantine's achievements in bridging the two sides of the river could not be replicated in the sixth century, despite Procopius' efforts to present Justinian as the quintessential *restitutor orbis romani*. It was not the inability to produce such technological feats – the Sangarius Bridge comes to mind – but the futility of such actions that prompted sixth-century emperors to adopt a more pragmatic strategy of entrenchment behind the Danube.[72]

Furthermore, an argument can be made that the few expeditions north of the Danube did not bring anything good in the long term, but rather caused additional trouble for the frontier provinces. On the rare occasions when the Empire was on the offensive beyond the Danube, the main purpose was not the annexation of transdanubian regions but the

---

λοιπὸν ἡ πολιτεία βλάβην ἐκ τῶν ἀθέσμων βαρβάρων ὑφίστατο, τῶν μὲν θελόντων τοὺς πεπηγμένους ὅρους ἀεὶ σαλεύειν, τοῦ δὲ Ῥωμαίων κράτους εἴργοντος αὐτοῖς τὰς καθ' ἡμῶν εἰσόδους. For a discussion of this particular work of Pisides, see P. Speck, *Zufälliges zum Bellum Avaricum des Georgios Pisides* (Munich, 1980). However, these particular lines (30–40) concerning the Danube frontier have received little historical attention. For a brief mention, see Patoura, "Emporio kai synallages," 399, n. 7; Brezeanu, "The Lower Danube," 27.

[70] A similar metaphor can be found in the speech to Manuel Comnenus written by Constantine Manasses in 1173: ἡ γὰρ φύσις ἀνέκαθεν τὰς ἀρχὰς ἄμφω ταῖς Ἴστρου ῥοαῖς ἀπετείχισε καὶ πύργον ὑγρὸν καὶ κινούμενον αὐταῖς ἐσχεδίασε, in E Kurtz, "Eshchte dva neizdann'ikh proizvedeniia Konstantina Manassi," VV 12 (1906): 92 (lines 134–135).

[71] Theophylact Simocatta, *Historia*, 7.15.14 (trans. Whitby): διομολογεῖται δὲ Ῥωμαίοις καὶ Ἀβάροις ὁ Ἴστρος μεσίτης, κατὰ δὲ Σκλαυηνῶν ἐξουσία τὸν ποταμὸν διανήξασθαι. For the Danube as the political border of Byzantium in the sixth century, see also Chrysos, "Die Nordgrenze," 27–40.

[72] M. Whitby, "Justinian's bridge over the Sangarius and the date of Procopius' de Aedificiis," *Journal of Hellenic Studies* 105 (1985): 129–148.

pacification of barbarian groups who were often crossing into the Empire for plunder. Inevitably, this generated a climate of increasing hostility toward the Empire. After a few years of successful incursions north of the river led by Chilbudius, during which "not only did no one succeed in crossing the Danube against the Romans, but the Romans actually crossed over to the opposite side many times," in 533 the general was killed in battle and as a result "the river became free for the barbarians to cross at all times as they wished, and the possessions of the Romans were rendered easily accessible."[73] Although this is typical of Procopius' dramatic tone when it came to the defense of the Balkans, it is no less true that it took some six decades for the Romans to venture again north of the Danube.[74] When that happened an even more terrible disaster struck; after a series of successful expeditions in the late 590s, in 602 Petrus was ordered to spend the winter in enemy territory, an unpopular decision which led to a general mutiny and eventually to the deposition of Maurice.[75] Clearly, during the long sixth century the Danube emerged as the natural frontier behind which the Empire was hoping to maintain its hold over the Balkans. The transdanubian legacy of Trajan and Constantine loomed large in panegyrical works, but the objective reality was unforgiving: creating a buffer region in *barbaricum* with the force of arms was no longer a viable option.

It is no less true that contemporary discourses often favored extreme interpretations. Most accounts either refer to tragic episodes when the Danube was crossed by barbarians or constitute opportunities to praise some emperor for securing the border, which indirectly suggests that it had been breached in the past. However, this is not an attempt to demonstrate that the Danube was potentially impenetrable – what frontier is? – but to make the case that the river created a serious problem for groups trying to cross into the Empire. The river itself was of course insufficient for keeping the frontier under control. A chain of fortifications built on the right bank

---

[73] Procopius, *Bella*, 7.14.3 and 7.14.6 (trans. Dewing, rev. Kaldellis): οὐχ ὅσον διαβῆναι τὸν Ἴστρον ἐπὶ τοὺς Ῥωμαίους οὐδεὶς ἴσχυσεν, ἀλλὰ καὶ Ῥωμαῖοι ἐς ἤπειρον τὴν ἀντιπέρας […] καὶ τὸ λοιπὸν ὅ τε ποταμὸς ἐσβατὸς ἀεὶ τοῖς βαρβάροις κατ' ἐξουσίαν καὶ τὰ Ῥωμαίων πράγματα εὐέφοδα γέγονε.

[74] For the chronology of the Byzantine campaigns north of the Danube in the 590s, see Whitby, *The Emperor Maurice*, 156–169.

[75] Theophylact Simocatta, *Historia*, 8.6. The idea that the Danube *limes* collapsed in 602 has been long refuted, for which see A. Barnea, "Einige Bemerkungen zur Chronologie des Limes an der unteren Donau in spätrömischer Zeit," *Dacia* 34 (1990): 283–290. However, the old dating of the collapse has not yet disappeared from scholarship; see recently L. Ellis, "Elusive places: a chorological approach to identity and territory in Scythia Minor," in *Romans*, eds. Mathisen and Shanzer, 251.

was meant to supplement the strategic value of the natural barrier and compensate for its inherent vulnerabilities, while a functional fleet became indispensable for monitoring the river.[76] The program of reconstruction in the Balkans was initiated most probably before Justinian, who was responsible for taking it to an unprecedented scale.[77] At least one of its purposes was very clear to contemporaries, as they looked back on the state of the frontier before the onslaught of the Huns:

> The Roman emperors of former times, by way of preventing the crossing of the Danube by the barbarians who live on the other side, occupied the entire bank of this river with strongholds, and not the right bank of the stream alone, for in some parts of it they built towns and fortresses on the other bank.[78]

No doubt Procopius had in mind Justinian's recent *renovatio imperii* and the complete overhaul of the Danube frontier in the first half of the sixth century, including the control over a few strategic bridge-head forts on the left bank, such as Litterata (Lederata) and Recidiva, mentioned in Novella

---

[76] The fact that the river and its system of fortifications constituted a viable frontier line is confirmed by the Byzantine return to the Danube in the tenth century; some of the old fortresses were reused and the river was once again guarded by the imperial fleet; see especially P. Stephenson, *Byzantium's Balkan Frontier: A Political Study of the Northern Balkans, 900–1204*, rev. ed. (Cambridge, 2006); see also A. Madgearu, "Dunărea în epoca bizantină (secolele X–XII): o frontieră permeabilă," *Revista Istorică* 10, no. 1–2 (1999): 41–55; E. Condurachi, I. Barnea, and P. Diaconu, "Nouvelles recherches sur le Limes byzantin du Bas-Danube aux Xe-XIe siècles," in *Proceedings of the XIIIth International Congress of Byzantine Studies. Oxford, 5–10 September 1966*, eds. J. M. Hussey, D. Obolensky, and S. Runciman (London, 1967), 179–193. For the Danubian fleet, see O. Bounegru and M. Zahariade, *Les forces navales du Bas Danube et de la Mer Noire aux Ier-VIe siècles* (Oxford, 1996), 108–109; F. Himmler, *Untersuchungen zur schiffsgestützten Grenzsicherung auf der spätantiken Donau (3.-6. Jh. n. Chr.)* (Oxford, 2011).

[77] For studies of early Byzantine fortifications on the frontier region of the Balkans, see in particular M. Biernacka-Lubańska, *The Roman and Early Byzantine Fortifications of Lower Moesia and Northern Thrace* (Wrocław, 1982); Zanini, "Confini e frontiera," 257–271; R. Ivanov, ed., *Roman and Early Byzantine Settlements in Bulgaria*, vol. II (Sofia, 2002); S. Torbatov, *Ukrepitelnata sistema na provintsiia Skitiia (kraia na III–VII v.)* (Veliko Turnovo, 2002); M. Vasić, "Le limes protobyzantin dans la province de Mésie Première," *Starinar* 45–46 (1994–1995): 41–53; M. Vasić and V. Kondić, "Le limes romain et paléobyzantin des Portes de Fer," in *Studien zu den Militärgrenzen Roms III. 13. internationaler Limeskongreß Aalen 1983. Vorträge* (Stuttgart, 1986), 542–560; Dinchev, "The fortresses of Thrace," 479–546.

[78] Procopius, *De Aedificiis*, 4.5.2 (trans. Dewing): οἱ Ῥωμαίων τὸ παλαιὸν αὐτοκράτορες τοῖς ἐπέκεινα ᾠκημένοις βαρβάροις τὴν τοῦ Δανουβίου διάβασιν ἀναστέλλοντες ὀχυρώμασί τέ κατέλαβον τούτου δὴ τοῦ ποταμοῦ τὴν ἀκτὴν ξύμπασαν, οὐ δὴ ἐν δεξιᾷ τοῦ ποταμοῦ μόνον, ἀλλὰ καὶ αὐτοῦ ἐνιαχῇ ἐπὶ θάτερα πολίσματά τε καὶ φρούρια τῇδε δειμάμενοι. For the view and terminology of Procopius on frontiers, see J. P. Arrignon and J. F. Duneau, "La frontière chez deux auteurs byzantins: Procope de Césarée et Constantin VII Porphyrogénète," *Geographica Byzantina* (1981): 17–30.

XI of 535, Sucidava (Sykibida), Dafne, and possibly other fortifications "built from the ground" briefly mentioned by Procopius.[79] A massive crossing of the Danube was virtually impossible as long as the frontier was properly guarded.[80] The importance of the river and the adjacent fortifications is well illustrated by Menander's description of the Avar campaign against the Sclavenes ordered by Tiberius II Constantine in the summer of 578. The Avar horsemen were ferried into the Empire and escorted along the right bank of the Danube only to cross the river again to attack the Slavic tribes living in eastern Wallachia.[81] The right bank was more suitable to stage various military maneuvers as long as the fortresses remained functional. Indeed, the last quarter of the sixth century brought an increased awareness of the danger entailed in leaving frontier fortifications poorly defended. Emperor Maurice's priority in the northern Balkans is revealed by Theophylact with a disarmingly blunt statement: "the barbarians would not remain quiet unless the Romans kept a very strict guard on the Ister."[82]

This fortified landscape came in sharp contrast with the world north of the river, completely rural, dominated by small open settlements, and never included in the Empire's expansionist agenda. It becomes clear that the Byzantine administration did not see this region as entirely homogeneous. A firm demarcation line was drawn between the Danubian provinces and the lands stretching north of the river. According to Procopius, Justinian reorganized the Danube frontier "wishing, as he did, to make the Ister River the strongest possible line of first defense before them and

---

[79] *Corpus Iuris Civilis*, Novella 11.2 (535 AD): *Recidiva et Litterata, quae trans Danubii sunt*. Procopius, *De Aedificiis*, 4.6.5: ἐν δὲ τῇ ἀντιπέρας ἠπείρῳ ἄλλα τε πολλὰ φρούρια ἐκ θεμελίων [καὶ ταῦτα] τῶν ἐσχάτων ἐδείματο. Archaeological research on the northern bank of the Danube has uncovered sixth-century settlements at Drobeta and Dierna (perhaps Procopius' Zernes, mistakenly placed on the southern bank), which may have been included in Justinian's program; on this question, see A. Madgearu, "The 6th century Lower Danubian bridgeheads: location and mission," *EN* 13 (2003): 295–314.

[80] This is clearly implied by the Cutrigurs' inability to cross into the Balkan provinces without the assistance of the Gepids who held Sirmium, Procopius, *Bella*, 8.18.17: ἐπεὶ δὲ Ῥωμαῖοι τὴν διάβασιν ποταμοῦ Ἴστρου ἐς τὸ ἀκριβὲς ἔν τε Ἰλλυριοῖς καὶ τοῖς ἐπὶ Θρᾴκης χωρίοις ἐφρούρουν, αὐτοὶ τούτους δὴ τοὺς Οὔννους ἐν χώρᾳ τῇ κατ' αὐτοὺς διαπορθμεύσαντες ποταμὸν Ἴστρον ἐς τὰ Ῥωμαίων ἤθη ἀφίεσαν.

[81] Menander, *Historia*, fr. 21 (Blockley). For the strategic road along the Danube, see G. Kardaras, Ho 'dromos tou Dounabe' kata ten Hystere Archaioteta (4os–7os ai.), in *He methorios tou Dounabe kai o kosmos ten sten epoche tes metanasteuses ton laon (4os-7os ai.)*, ed. S. Patoura-Spanou (Athens, 2008), 267–284.

[82] Theophylact Simocatta, 6.6.2 (trans. Whitby): ἔφασκε γὰρ ὁ αὐτοκράτωρ τῷ Πρίσκῳ, οὐκ ἂν ἠρεμοίη τὸ βαρβάρον, εἰ μὴ τὸν Ἴστρον ἐς τὰ μάλιστα τὸ Ῥωμαϊκὸν περιφρουρήσοιτο.

before the whole of Europe."[83] In addition, he covered the Balkans with a network of fortifications claiming that "each farm either has been converted into a stronghold or lies adjacent to one which is fortified."[84] Leaving aside the rhetorical nature of these statements, the fortifications themselves must have created a vivid sense of physical and psychological separation. For the Danubian provincials Justinian's system was designed to instill a feeling of security and protection, while for the barbarians on the other bank, fear, intimidation, and discouragement.[85] There were few doubts regarding the place that transdanubian lands occupied in the Byzantine universe: Edict 13 from 538 stipulated that officers unwilling to assist in the collection of taxes in Egypt would be punished by being sent north of the Danube to defend the border. This was undoubtedly meant to be a severe punishment as the Romans typically sent deportees to areas on the fringes of the civilized world.[86] From a legal, strategic, and mental standpoint, the two sides of the river belonged to two different worlds which often met but never fused.

All evidence suggests that in the sixth century static frontiers mattered more than ever. Separation, rather than inclusion, seems to have been the order of the day. Having to manage provinces scattered on three continents, Roman emperors were compelled to make the most of the regions where nature afforded a convenient line of defense. The strategic role of the

---

[83] Procopius, *De Aedificiis*, 4.1.33 (trans. Dewing): πρόβολον δὲ ἰσχυρότατον αὐτῶν τε καὶ πάσης Εὐρώπης Ἴστρον ποταμὸν ποιεῖσθαι ἐθέλων.

[84] Procopius, *De Aedificiis*, 4.1.35 (trans. Dewing): οὕτω συνεχῆ τὰ ἐρύματα ἐν τοῖς χωρίοις ἀπεργασάμενος ὥστε ἀγρὸς ἕκαστος ἢ φρούριον ἀποτετόρνευται, ἢ τῷ τετειχισμένῳ πρόσοικός ἐστιν. On this question, see F. Curta, "Horsemen in forts or peasants in villages? Remarks on the archaeology of warfare in the 6th to 7th c. Balkans," in *War and Warfare in Late Antiquity*, eds. A. Sarantis and N. Christie (Leiden, 2013), 809–852.

[85] Procopius, *De Aedificiis*, 4.4.1 can be easily dismissed as rhetorical flourish: καὶ εἰ μὲν παρ' ἄλλοις ἀνθρώπων τισὶ μακρά τε ᾠκημένοις καὶ πολιτείαν ἑτέραν ἔχουσι τὸν κατάλογον ἐποιούμεθα τῶν τῇδε φρουρίων, ἅπερ Ἰουστινιανῷ βασιλεῖ εἴργασται, ἵνα δὴ ἔμελλεν ὁ λόγος ἀμάρτυρος εἶναι, εὖ οἶδ' ὅτι μυθολόγος τε ἂν τῶν ἔργων τῷ ἀριθμῷ ἔδοξεν εἶναι καὶ ἄπιστος ὅλως. On the other hand, the complete absence of any such fortified strongholds north of the Danube adds some realism to his statement.

[86] *Corpus Iuris Civilis*, Edict 13 (538): *universa cohors e regione mota in loca quae ultra Istrum sive Danubium sunt transferatur, ut illis limitibus custodiae causa adhaereat*. The banishment of criminals or even higher ranked officials fallen into disgrace to peripheral regions seems to have been common practice, as evidenced by the case of Petra in Palaestina Tertia in the sixth century, or the desert oases of Egypt, for which see Z. T. Fiema, "Late-antique Petra and its hinterland: recent research and new interpretations," in *The Roman and Byzantine Near East. Volume 3: Late-antique Petra, Nile Festival Buildings at Sepphoris, Deir Qual'a Monastery, Khirbet Qana Village and Pilgrim Site, 'Ain-'Arrub Hiding Complex, and Other Studies*, ed. J. H. Humphrey (Portsmouth, RI, 2002), 193 and n. 20; Boozer, "Frontiers and borderlands," 281–283.

Danube increased tremendously as Justinian and his successors found themselves entangled in long episodes of conflict with Persia, while stubbornly clinging to their western ambitions. Although the northern Balkans was rarely granted highest priority status, systemic failure on the Danube could prove catastrophic and Byzantine emperors could not afford to neglect a frontier unlocking access to Constantinople.[87] Indeed, the collapse of the Danube frontier in the early decades of the seventh century would become a major watershed in the history of the Balkans and trigger fundamental political and cultural changes. Perhaps more than elsewhere, on the Danube sixth-century emperors tried to create a frontier of exclusion and were ready to unleash the full might of Roman political and diplomatic genius to achieve that goal. However, was the Danube an impermeable frontier or could cultural contact actually play a central role in frontier policy?

---

[87] See Procopius, *De Aedificiis*, 4.1.4: γεγένηται γὰρ ἐπαξίως τῷ τε γειτονήματι ποταμοῦ Ἴστρου καὶ τῇ ἐνθένδε διὰ τοὺς ἐγκειμένους τῇ χώρᾳ βαρβάρους ἀνάγκῃ.

2 | Cultural Diversity in the Danube Region and Beyond: An Archaeological Perspective

2.1 The Cultural Background

One of the most important questions emerging from the previous discussion concerns the culture of the "barbarian" lands located in the proximity of the Danube, whose development and manipulation became part and parcel of the empire's frontier strategy. What is the cultural background of the Late Roman Danubian borderlands? After abandoning the transdanubian provinces Roman emperors reinforced their natural frontier in the northern Balkans. The entire length of the Lower Danube became once again a convenient line of separation and protection against external threats. The longevity of the river frontier is impressive. Despite several crises, the Empire held its position for more than three centuries after Emperor Aurelian ordered the tactical retreat south of the river in the mid-270s. However, the Danube would never develop into a watertight cultural frontier of exclusion. The political connection with the lands north of the river was broken, but the cultural one endured for centuries. A major communication artery in the second and the third century after the Empire conquered Dacia, the Danube continued to facilitate contact between its two banks. This is attested by the rich archaeological record discussed in the following pages, as well as by peace negotiations between the Romans and various barbarians who insisted on maintaining access to Roman goods through trade points along the Lower Danube.[1] Furthermore, the river acted as an interface between Byzantium and *barbaricum* not only for customary items required by the tribal aristocracy, but also for items prohibited from export like precious metals, weapons, and goods like oil and wine, whose flow north of the Danube could not be prevented.[2]

---

[1] F. Curta, "Frontier ethnogenesis in Late Antiquity: the Danube, the Tervingi, and the Slavs," in *Borders, Barriers, and Ethnogenesis. Frontiers in Late Antiquity and the Middle Ages*, ed. F. Curta (Turnhout, 2005), 173–204.

[2] S. Patoura, "Ho Dounabes stis istoriographikes peges kata ten periodo tes metanasteuseos ton laon; mythoi kai pragmaikoteta," *Historikogeōgraphika* 9 (2002): 410 and n. 55. For such interdictions in relation to the frontier, see J.-M. Carrié, "1993: ouverture des frontières

Cultural interaction on the Danube frontier was more than a reflection of the human desire to exchange goods. It was a carefully engineered imperial policy toward populations in *barbaricum* especially after Roman military incursions north of the river stopped in the early 530s. Since the creation of a buffer zone could not be achieved by force, as Constantine the Great had done in the fourth century, it was time for "plan B." The demand for Roman goods was often exploited for political gain as sixth-century emperors were hoping to achieve a greater degree of cultural integration in the frontier region. Despite the absence of written records attesting the regularization of trade in the sixth century similar to the ones available for the fourth and fifth centuries, it is hard to believe that the issue escaped Justinian's thorough administrative overhaul of the Danubian provinces. Much of the exchange was probably conducted through the Byzantine bridge-head forts on the northern bank of the river which could have acted as trade ports. Official channels, however, were only the driving force behind cultural interaction which gained a life of its own through merchants looking to make a profit and mercenaries and prisoners who brought the two sides of the river in closer contact. Realistically speaking the Early Byzantine government would have been unable to monitor such small-scale traffic, let alone prevent private initiative, and there is little indication that such a separation was ever intended in the first place. As much as possible, sixth-century emperors tried to attract and control rather than antagonize the populations living in the lands north of the river.

Although interaction took place, the regions north and south of the Danube were by no means developing similar cultures during the long sixth century (Figure 1). The dissolution of the Chernyakhov culture and the subsequent chaos brought by the Hunnic onslaught in the fifth century led to increased fragmentation in *barbaricum*. To be sure, the imperial machine regained momentum toward the end of the fifth century and repaired some of the damage produced by the Huns in the Danubian provinces.[3] North of the river, however, the situation was quite different and the remnants of the Hunnic confederation could not achieve the homogeneity and impressive geographic reach of the Chernyakhov cultural

---

romaines?," in *Frontières terrestres, frontières célestes dans l'antiquité*, ed. A. Rousselle (Paris, 1995), 50–51.

[3] J. H. W. G. Liebeschuetz, "The Lower Danube under pressure: from Valens to Heraclius," in *Transition*, 101–134. For Anastasian efforts in the region, see A. Sarantis, *Justinian's Balkan Wars: Campaigning, Diplomacy and Development in Illyricum, Thrace and the Northern World AD 527–65* (Prenton, 2016), 124–129.

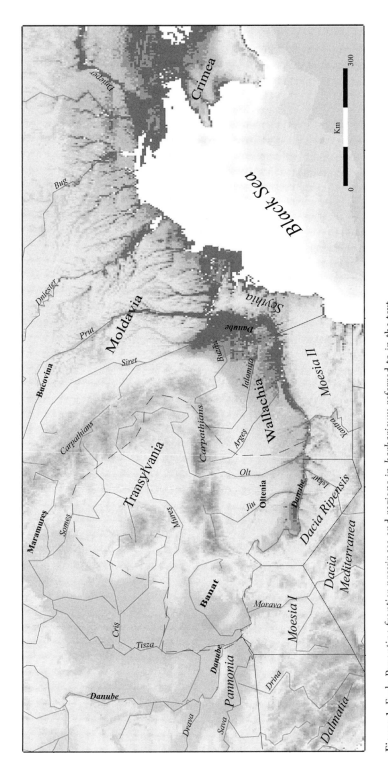

Figure 1 Early Byzantine frontier provinces and regions in *barbaricum* referred to in the text. The dotted line marks the former province of Dacia.

horizon. In this climate of political and cultural confusion a number of traditions came to be recycled, though they had never been totally abandoned, relying on a mix of Roman provincial, Carpic, Sarmatian, and Chernyakhovian influences.[4]

Because of the nature of the evidence archaeologists are forced to rely heavily on ceramic evidence and, incidentally, this is where we see some of the most important cultural distinctions. Indeed, in the case of pottery there is not much borrowing from contemporary wheelmade pots produced in the Danubian provinces. A study based on the ceramic assemblage from Iatrus on the Lower Danube has shown that the ceramic types typical for the frontier fortresses on both sides of the Danube did not influence the ceramics produced in *barbaricum*.[5] Even the regions closest to the river display distinct patterns of ceramic production. In most cases, the shapes follow the different cultural traditions practiced by the mosaic of populations that dominated the lands north of the Danube at one time or another since the early Roman period. For example, at Botoșana, in Moldavia, there is a clear dichotomy between the handmade pottery of so-called Slavic tradition and the wheelmade pottery of Roman inspiration, while in other settlements from Bucovina the study of ceramic assemblages has led to the conclusion that the region was already dominated by Slavic culture in the sixth century.[6] Moreover, several additional influences harked back to the Chernyakhov tradition and the Carpathian barrow culture in settlements from Bucovina such as Rashkiv and Kodyn.[7]

Closer to the Danube frontier, the coexistence of handmade and wheelmade pottery is best exemplified by the finds from Dulceanca in Wallachia. Both types were produced together, as evidenced by a kiln found in the settlement Dulceanca I, where a large wheelmade bowl was associated with 11 handmade pots.[8] To be sure, almost half of the ceramic assemblage from Dulceanca was produced using the fast wheel, while in the close vicinity, at Sfințești, wheelmade pottery is predominant, including some

---

[4] R. Harhoiu, *Die frühe Völkerwanderungszeit in Rumänien* (Bucharest, 1997); I. Mitrea, "Observații privind sfârșitul culturii Sântana de Mureș și începuturile culturii Costișa-Botoșana-Hansca, în stadiul actual al cercetărilor arheologice," *Carpica* 34 (2005): 131–142; V. Teodorescu et al., "Așezarea daco-romană din secolele IV–V de la Cireșanu, jud. Prahova," *MCA* 17 (1993), vol. II, 389–416.

[5] E. S. Teodor, "Ceramica de uz comun din Muntenia de la sfârșitul veacului al V-lea până la mijlocul veacului al VII-lea," PhD Dissertation, A. I. Cuza University, Iași, 2001, 69–70.

[6] D. G. Teodor, "Slavii la nordul Dunării de Jos în secolele VI–VII d. H.," *AM* 17 (1994): 223–251.

[7] Teodor, "Ceramica de uz comun," 95–97.

[8] S. Dolinescu-Ferche, *Așezările din secolele III și VI în sud-vestul Munteniei. Cercetările de la Dulceanca* (Bucharest, 1974), 90.

Gray Gritty Ware pots typical for the Byzantine frontier fortresses.[9] The pottery becomes more "Roman" moving westward into the territory of the former province of Dacia. For instance, the storage capacity of the ceramic containers from Gropșani seems to follow the Roman system.[10] Moreover, Ipotești, in western Wallachia represents a cultural horizon dominated by wheelmade pottery whose initial phase has been traced back to the end of the fifth century and the beginning of the sixth.[11] Clearly the regions west of the Olt river, once part of Trajanic Dacia, were more sensitive to developments in the Empire.

Further east, pottery shows very little standardization. The ceramic assemblages from the area of modern Bucharest show a perplexing diversity of types and influences given their close proximity. The pottery from Ciurel sometimes considered to be early Slavic has been attributed recently to a Chernyakhovian tradition, while the tall pots from Cățelu Nou resemble the shapes characteristic to the culture of the Carpi who dominated Moldavia in the second and third centuries. At Străulești-Lunca we encounter one of the rare occasions when the Byzantine influence can be traced on the local production of wheelmade pottery.[12] Finally, the "Slavic" cemetery from Sărata-Monteoru, by far the largest in central and southeastern Europe, boasts a series of ceramic urns, whose shape has been recently ascribed to a local tradition despite the funerary ritual, which is believed to be early Slavic.[13]

In what concerns the dating of the complexes, two coins of Justinian found at Bucharest–Străulești–Măicănești suggest a dating of this and other contemporary settlements toward the middle of the sixth century, although the archaeological context of the coins invites caution.[14] A common characteristic is the higher concentration of wheelmade pottery in the first half of the sixth century, but this often appears to be a circular argument as

---

[9] Ibid., figs. 174–175.
[10] Teodor, "Ceramica," 242–243; O. Toropu, V. Ciucă, and C. Voicu, "Noi descoperiri arheologice în Oltenia," *Drobeta* 2 (1976): 98–102.
[11] P. Roman and S. Dolinescu-Ferche, "Cercetările de la Ipotești (jud. Olt) (observații asupra culturii materiale autohtone din sec. al VI-lea în Muntenia)," *SCIVA* 29, no. 1 (1978): 89–90.
[12] Ciurel: S. Dolinescu-Ferche, "Ciurel, habitat des VIe–VIIe siècles des notre ère," *Dacia* 23 (1979): 179–230. For the interpretation of Ciurel as Slavic, see more recently P. Diaconu, "Cui aparține cultura Ciurel?" *Istros* 10 (2000): 491–493. For a new interpretation of finds from Cățelu Nou and Străulești-Lunca, see Teodor, "Ceramica," 117–118 and 122.
[13] Teodor, "Ceramica," 133–134.
[14] Both coins were found outside the sunken-featured buildings, in the so-called "cultural layer"; see M. Constantiniu, "Șantierul arheologic Băneasa-Străulești," *CAB* 2 (1965): 182 and 189, fig. 93.

dating often relies on the proportion between handmade and wheelmade pots. The assumption is that ceramics simplified in the course of the sixth century as the Slavic influence became more pronounced and handmade pottery came to dominate the ceramic assemblages. This tendency, however, was not exclusive to the Lower Danube region. A similar process seems to have been at work in Cyprus, for example, where good quality ceramics coexisted with an increasing number of handmade cooking vessels. This was seen as an adaptive response to the changing social and economic realities of the time.[15]

If the Empire's influence is rarely seen on the sixth-century ceramics produced in *barbaricum*, many Early Byzantine fortresses have yielded a variety of handmade pots, typical for the regions north of the Danube (Figure 2). The ceramic types are not restricted to the well-known Penkovka and Korchak groups usually associated with the Antes and the early Slavs, respectively.[16] The inventory of handmade pottery includes shapes deriving from the pre-Roman tradition or influenced by the Sarmatic or Germanic groups settled in the frontier region. Based on such influences, fortresses located in the same province show major differences in the handmade pottery assemblages found on the site. In Scythia the majority of shapes from Dinogetia, Beroe, and Halmyris belong to the Penkovka type, while at Capidava the Sarmatic tradition is much more powerful.[17] Further west, in northern Illyricum fortresses on the Danube have yielded

---

[15] M. Rautman, "Handmade pottery and social change: the view from Late Roman Cyprus," *Journal of Mediterranean Archaeology* 11, no. 1 (1998): 95.

[16] For the Prague type, see F. Curta, "The Prague type: a critical approach to pottery classification," *ArchBulg* 5 (2001): 73–106. For the Penkovka culture, see recently B. S. Szmoniewski, "The Antes: eastern 'brothers' of the Sclavenes?" in *Neglected Barbarians*, 53–82.

[17] E. S. Teodor, "Handmade pottery from the Late Roman fortress at Capidava," in *Between the Steppe and the Empire. Archaeological Studies in Honour of Radu Harhoiu at 65th Anniversary*, eds. A Măgureanu and E. Gáll (Bucharest, 2010), 211–223; F. Topoleanu and E. S. Teodor, "Handmade pottery from Halmyris and its cultural context," *Peuce* 7 (2009): 347–360; D. Vîlceanu and A. Barnea, "Ceramica lucrată cu mîna din așezarea romano-bizantină de la Piatra Frecăței (sec. VI e.n.)," *SCIVA* 26, no. 2 (1975): 209–218; M. Comșa, "Contribution à la question de la pénétration des Slaves au sud du Danube durant les VIe–VIIe siècles d'après quelques données archéologiques de Dobroudja," in *I Międzynarodowy Kongres Archeologii Słowiańskiej, Warszawa 14–18 IX-1965*, vol. III (Wrocław, 1970), 322–330; A. Petre, "Contribuția culturii romano-bizantine din secolele VI-VII la geneza culturii feudale timpurii din spațiul balcano-ponto-danubian," in *2050 de ani de la făurirea de către Burebista a primului stat independent și centralizat al geto-dacilor* (Bucharest, 1980), 193–214; M. Comșa, "La Province de la Scythie Mineure (Dobroudja) et les Slaves pendant les VI–VII ss.," in *Istoriia i kul'tura drevnik i srednevekovykh slavian*, ed. V. V. Sedov (Moscow, 1999), 301–313.

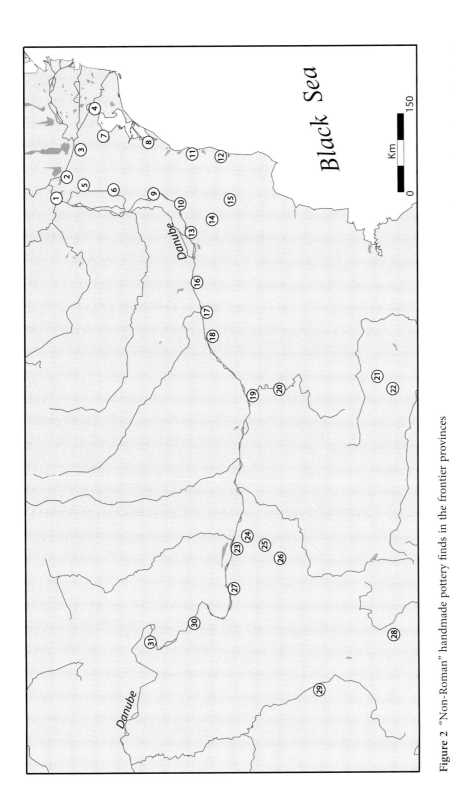

Figure 2 "Non-Roman" handmade pottery finds in the frontier provinces

1. Dinogetia; 2. Niculiţel; 3. Tulcea; 4. Halmyris; 5. Troesmis; 6. Beroe (Piatra Frecăţei); 7. Halmyris; 8. Histria; 9. Capidava; 10. Axiopolis; 11. Tomis; 12. Callatis; 13. Dervent; 14. Tropaeum Traiani; 15. Golesh; 16. Durostorum; 17. Nigriniana; 18. Nova Cherna; 19. Iatrus; 20. Sturmen; 21. Beroe (Stara Zagora); 22. Karasura; 23. Kosloduy; 24. Augusta; 25. Vulchedrum; 26. Jakimovo; 27. Kabyle; 28. Pautalia; 29. Caričin Grad; 30. Dorticum; 31. Velesnica.

ceramic evidence pointing to a significant Germanic presence.[18] The wide distribution of handmade pots in the northern Balkans suggests that military manpower was recruited from a multiethnic environment.[19] This is the first clear sign that the political strategy of sixth-century emperors was to exploit the human resources of *barbaricum* for the defense of the border. In other words, cultural interaction and negotiation was not only possible but actually required for Justinian's frontier system of exclusion to function.

The kaleidoscope of influences behind the production of handmade pottery illustrated by the examples presented above might suggest that the "barbarians" themselves, recruited to defend the Empire's frontier, subscribed to different cultural traditions. To be sure, there is a risk in ascribing the handmade pottery to outside groups alone. The example from Cyprus warns us that the decline of the ceramic industry and the shift toward a more localized production of handmade pottery can be symptoms of more profound social and economic transformations.[20] The archaeological context in which the handmade pots have been found at Capidava in Scythia, for instance, presents us with a perplexing association of such "inferior" types with a large quantity of regular Roman amphorae and cooking wares. The complex, which was destroyed probably in the late 570s, reflects such cultural changes whereby the new recruits from *barbaricum* may have compounded the general economic decline of the Empire.[21] Likewise, the simplification of residential building techniques observed in the study of houses in the northern Balkans may reflect the "barbarization" of frontier culture, although here as well it is not always easy to distinguish between changing ethnic structures and general cultural decline.[22]

---

[18] P. Špehar, "The Danubian *limes* between Lederata and Aquae during the Migration Period," in *Pontic-Danubian Realm*, 48–51; V. Ivanišević, M. Kazanski, and A. Mastykova, *Les nécropoles de Viminacium à l'époque des grandes migrations* (Paris, 2006), 119–124.

[19] Z. Kurnatowska, "Słowianie Południowi," in *Wedrowka i etnogeneza w starozytnosci i sredniowieczu*, eds. M. Salamon and J. Strzelczyk (Cracow, 2004), 205; S. Angelova and R. Koleva, "Archäologische Zeugnisse frühslawischer Besiedlung in Bulgarien," in *Post-Roman Towns, Trade and Settlement in Europe and Byzantium. Vol. 2: Byzantium, Pliska, and the Balkans*, ed. J. Henning (Berlin, 2007), 281–307. G. Kardaras, "The Byzantine–Antic treaty (545/46 AD) and the defense of the Scythia Minor," *Byzantinoslavica* 58 (2010): 77–80. For an early version of this theory, see Comșa, "Contribution à la question," 327–328.

[20] A similar interpretation has been long suggested as a possible explanation for the appearance of handmade pots at Beroe, for which see Vîlceanu and Barnea, "Ceramica lucrată," 216–217.

[21] A. Gandila, "Early Byzantine Capidava: the numismatic evidence," *CN* 12–13 (2006–2007): 103.

[22] V. Dinchev, "Household substructure of the Early Byzantine settlements on the present Bulgarian territory," *ArchBulg* 1 (1997): 47–63.

The apparent lack of dialogue between the regions south and north of the Danube can be ascribed to the more conservative nature of ceramic production and the greater resistance in replacing ancestral shapes. Indeed, there was little motivation to do so. A variety of objects could fill the need to follow fashions from the frontier provinces. In order to look more "Roman," populations in *barbaricum* chose to imitate different categories of items like lamps, buckles, and brooches, or to import them directly from the Empire. To what extent can this circulation be tied to larger political considerations in the Danube region? A closer investigation of the main categories of imports and imitations will shed more light on the nature of cultural contact on the frontier, and the factors favoring or limiting its extent. Cultural interaction could mean commerce in some cases, although trade remains an elusive activity on the sixth-century Danube frontier. The exact goods offered by "barbarians" in return for Roman products are very hard to identify in the archaeological record perhaps because of their perishable nature. Without denying the role of economic exchange, a far more promising avenue by which to explain the circulation of Byzantine artifacts is to attempt a closer examination of the movement of people in the context of political, diplomatic, and military developments in the frontier region, documented both by archaeological and literary sources.

2.2 Byzantine Imports and Imitations in *Barbaricum*

For lack of a better term imports will be defined here as any object produced in the Empire and brought to the territories beyond the Danube *limes* through economic or non-economic channels, either as basic goods or prestige items. Besides coins, discussed in the second part of the book, ceramics (amphorae, lamps), metal items (brooches, buckles, jewelry), and a number of Christian objects that cut across these categories constitute the main types of goods found north of the Danube. By necessity, the analysis of archaeological material often results in dense prose but it remains an indispensable component of any interpretive framework. Indeed, any attempt to gauge the Empire's cultural influence in *barbaricum* needs to be founded on a solid understanding of the archaeological evidence in its proper chronological and spatial context. This chapter will concentrate on the diffusion of the main types of Byzantine imports, while the next will explore the role of Christianity in light of the available sources. Finally, the historical significance of cultural contact in the frontier region seen through the lens of material evidence will be discussed in Chapter 4.

The Roman legacy in southeastern Europe remains a sensitive topic, always susceptible to manipulation in the service of various ideological agendas. More specifically, the presence of Byzantine objects in *barbaricum* has been used to demonstrate the development of a homogeneous culture which had embraced and preserved the Roman heritage, not only in Trajanic Dacia but also in the regions south and east of the Carpathians.[23] Any "non-Roman" influences were downplayed, denied, or presented as a barbaric interference with the cultural progress of the autochthonous population. Such interpretations were developed to support nationalistic discourses rather than being a critical and dispassionate assessment of the evidence.[24] Although to some extent the manipulation of archaeological material was true of most Eastern European schools between 1945 and 1989,[25] the Romanian case became the most conspicuous in its attempt to distort the past in order to serve the communist regime's quest for legitimacy in the 1970s and 1980s.[26] Along with the pressures of an increasingly abusive dictatorship, Romanian scholars had to struggle against the

---

[23] M. Constantiniu, "Elemente romano-bizantine în cultura materială a populaţiei autohtone din partea centrală a Munteniei, în secolele VI-VII e.n.," *SCIVA* 17, no. 4 (1966): 665–678; D. G. Teodor, "Elemente şi influenţe bizantine în Moldova, în sec. VI-XI," *SCIVA* 21, no. 1 (1970): 97–128; L. Bârzu, *La continuité de la création matérielle et spirituelle du peuple roumain sur le territoire de l'ancienne Dacie* (Bucharest, 1980), 77–83; I. Barnea, "Sur les rapports avec Byzance du territoire situé au Nord du Bas-Danube durant la période Anastase Ier-Justinien Ier (491–565)," *EBPB* 2 (1991): 47–57; D. G. Teodor, "Éléments et influences byzantins dans la civilisation des VIe–VIIe siècles après J. Chr. au nord du Bas-Danube," *EBPB* 2 (1991): 59–72.

[24] F. Curta, "The changing image of the early Slavs in the Rumanian historiography and archaeological literature. A critical survey," *SF* 53 (1994): 235–276.

[25] For the connection between politics and archaeology, see T. Kaiser, "Archaeology and ideology in Southeast Europe," in *Nationalism, Politics, and the Practice of Archaeology*, eds. P. L. Kohl and C. Fawcett (Cambridge, 1995), 99–119; P. Novaković, "The present makes the past: the use of archaeology and changing national identities in Former Yugoslavia," in *Auf der Suche nach Identitäten: Volk, Stamm, Kultur, Ethnos*, eds. S. Rieckhoff and U. Sommer (Oxford, 2007), 181–192; J. Lászlovszky and Cs. Siklódi, "Archaeological theory in Hungary since 1960: theories without theoretical archaeology," in *Archaeological Theory in Europe: The Last Three Decades*, ed. I. Hodder (New York, NY, 1991), 272–298; J. Rassamakin, "Die Archäologie der Ukraine: vom 'entwickelten' Sozialismus zur 'Selbstständigkeit'," in *Archäologien Europas. Geschichte, Methoden und Theorien*, eds. P. F. Biehl, A. Gramsch, and A. Marciniak (Münster, 2002), 271–282; S. Babić, "Still innocent after all these years? Sketches for a social history of archaeology in Serbia," in *Archäologien Europas*, eds. Biehl et al., 309–321.

[26] For a good overview, see M. Anghelinu, "Failed revolution: Marxism and the Romanian prehistoric archaeology between 1945 and 1989," *ArchBulg* 11, no. 1 (2007): 1–36. The nationalistic agenda was not new; it simply resurrected a venerable intellectual concern dating back to the late eighteenth-century "Transylvanian School," for which see I. Lungu, *Şcoala Ardeleană. Mişcare culturală naţională iluministă* (Bucharest, 1995), 127–206. There have been only modest attempts to rebuke the exaggerations inherent to this type of discourse and attempt a more dispassionate approach, e.g. C. Opreanu, "The North-Danube regions from the Roman province of Dacia to the emergence of the Romanian language (2nd–8th Centuries)," in *History*

2.2 Byzantine Imports and Imitations in Barbaricum

residual legacy of Austro-Hungarian claims, on one hand, and Slavic nationalism, on the other, forcing them to develop a defensive obsession with the nation's role as a "Latin island" in Eastern Europe. From an ideological standpoint, the most profitable avenue was to mystify the "continuity thesis," an important historiographical question regarding the linguistic and ethnic development of Balkan populations during Late Antiquity and the Early Middle Ages. Proponents of this theory strove to defend the uninterrupted occupation of the lands north of the Danube by a Christian Romanized population, whose culture slowly but inexorably spread from Roman Dacia to other regions of modern-day Romania and maintained its identity untainted against centuries of adversity. Despite genuine merits grounded in the historical, archaeological, and linguistic evidence, its credibility was compromised in the hands of overzealous cultural mandarins.[27]

What is more disturbing, however, is the lingering effect of such a discourse casting its long shadow into the third millennium. Indeed, a recent multivolume work designed to become the definitive treatise of Romanian history introduced the topic by tracing a clear boundary between the durable and culturally entrenched local population and the invading foreigners, bent on destruction.[28] Moreover, this *topos* became central to the interpretation of historical conditions in Late Antiquity when the Romans were no longer in direct control of the regions north of the Danube. Working within this paradigm, historians and archaeologists – most of them trained during the *ancien régime* – chose to ascribe to the autochthonous (i.e. Daco-Roman) population any traces of contact with the Early Byzantine Empire, as well as any evidence of local "sophistication" (technologies, exchange systems, etc.). Population groups coming from elsewhere were seen as savage nomads who could not possibly appreciate civilization, although somehow they were always destined to be taught and assimilated into the dominant Romanic culture.[29] Finally, the enduring link with the Empire was deemed so strong that the entire *barbaricum* was described as a Byzantine "cultural province."[30]

---

    of Romania: Compendium, eds. I. A. Pop, I. Bolovan, and S. Andrea (Cluj-Napoca, 2006), 59–132, at 104–108.

[27] For a critique, see G. A. Niculescu, "Archaeology, nationalism, and the 'History of the Romanians'," *Dacia* 48–49 (2004–2005): 99–124.

[28] V. Tufescu, "Teritoriul și populația României," in *Istoria românilor 1*, 3–6.

[29] D. Protase, "Populația autohtonă în Dacia postromană (anul 275–secolul al VI-lea)," in *Istoria românilor 2*, 602–603.

[30] G. Popilian, "Stăpânirea romano-bizantină la Dunărea de Jos," in *Istoria românilor 2*, 616. The phrase was borrowed verbatim from L. Bârzu, "Retragerea aureliană și romanitatea nord-dunăreană," in L. Bârzu and S. Brezeanu, *Originea și continuitatea românilor. Arheologie și*

To be sure, neighboring schools were no less inclined to mystify and distort in the name of nationalism. In Bulgarian scholarship ideological influences pushed the discourse in the opposite direction, with Scythia and Moesia II (modern Dobrudja) becoming the main battleground, and significant efforts were made to overemphasize cultural discontinuity and demonstrate the settlement of the Slavs in the Balkan provinces at an early date. According to such views, the creation of the first Bulgar state took place in a region heavily "barbarized" during the troubled centuries of Late Antiquity when the Roman culture and identity slowly faded into insignificance.[31] Likewise, certain circles of Hungarian scholarship have remained deeply attached to the nineteenth-century "immigrationist thesis" developed in the context of Austro-Hungarian imperialism and continued to downplay the level of Romanization in Dacia, while maintaining that the Romanian ethnolinguistic genesis took place in the Balkans during the Early Middle Ages. Conveniently, the Magyars were already in control of Transylvania when a Romanian-speaking population supposedly migrated to this region in the thirteenth century, somehow returning to the exact same province abandoned by their ancestors when they left Dacia in the third century.[32]

tradiție istorică (Bucharest, 1991), 207. Another book published that same year described this region as an "extension of Byzantine civilization": A. Madgearu, Rolul creștinismului in formarea poporului român (Bucharest, 2001), 78.

[31] For medieval archaeology in Bulgaria in the last decades of the twentieth century, see V. Nikolov, "Die bulgarische Archäologie im letzten Jahrzehnt des 20. Jahrhunderts," in *Archäologien Europas*, eds. Biehl et al., 303–7. For the interpretation of early Slavic settlement, see D. Angelov, "La formation de la nationalité bulgare," *EB* 4 (1969): 14–37; S. Angelova, "Po vuprosa za rannoslavianskata kultura na iug i na sever ot Dunav prez VI–VII v.," *Arkheologiia* 12 (1980), no. 4: 1–12; V. Vulov, "Ranni zaselvaniia na slaviani v pridunavskite oblasti na Balkanskiia poluostrov," in *Bulgariia 1300. Institutsii i durzhavna traditsiia. Dokladi na tretiia kongres na Bulgarskoto Istorichesko Druzhestvo, 3–5 oktombri 1981*, ed. E. Buzhashki, vol. II (Sofia, 1982), 169–177; V. Velkov, "L'état ethnique de Dobrudža au cours du IVe–VIe s.," in *Dobrudža. Études ethno-culturelles: recueil d'articles*, eds. D. S. Angelov and D. Ovcharov (Sofia, 1987), 13–21. See more recently N. Khrisimov, "Ranneslavianskie pamiatniki v severo-vostochnoi chasti Balkanskogo poluostrova," *Stratum plus* (2015), no. 5: 309–344; A. Dancheva-Vasileva, "Serdika i slavianskite nashestviia vuv Vizantiiskata imperiia VI–VII v.," in *Eurika. In honorem Ludmilae Donchevae-Petkovae*, eds. V. Grigorov, M. Daskalov, and E. Komatarova-Balinova (Sofia, 2009), 79–92; Angelova and Koleva, "Archäologische Zeugnisse," 481–508.

[32] E. Pamlényi, ed., *A History of Hungary* (London, 1975), 22–25; E. Illyés, *Ethnic Continuity in the Carpatho-Danubian Area* (Boulder, CO, 1992); E. Tóth, "The Roman province of Dacia," in *History of Transylvania*, ed. B. Köpeczi (Budapest, 1994), 28–61; L. Makkai, "The emergence of the Estates (1172–1526)," in *History of Transylvania*, ed. Köpeczi, 178–243, at 178–198. See more recently A. Zsoldos, "Hongria als segles XII i XIII," in *Princeses de terres llunyanes. Catalunya i Hongria a l'edat mitjana*, eds. F. Makk et al. (Barcelona, 2009), 145–163. Romanian revisionist histories denouncing the nationalistic bias have been promptly published in English

This historiographical legacy deeply fraught with ideological prejudice forces us to commence with a reassessment of the evidence by surveying the main categories of Byzantine artifacts and their diffusion in *barbaricum*. The main purpose is not to attach new ethnic labels to archaeological finds or to perpetuate a time-honored debate – which in my view needs to be shelved – but to understand the nature of cultural contact in its real complexity.[33] This can only be achieved by going back to the sources. Rather than attempting a comprehensive treatment of all categories of imports, the discussion in this chapter addresses a selected number of diagnostic items that lend themselves to multifaceted analysis through their wide distribution, variety of types, and ability to shed new light on the social, economic, and religious realities of the frontier. Various other small finds of Byzantine origin, usually pieces of jewelry, circulated in *barbaricum* and have been diligently gathered and published. The fact that most of them are unique finds precludes any analysis of distribution, while the lack of archaeological context reduces their usefulness for answering the type of historical questions that interest us most. To be sure, the main categories of imports discussed below are themselves not free of such problems, but there are sufficient finds in secure contexts to permit a series of historical and archaeological observations.

While primarily focusing on genuine imports from the Danubian provinces or more distant corners of the Empire, we should not ignore the local production of a wide variety of goods of Byzantine inspiration, most of them made of copper alloy and modeled after Byzantine prototypes. The large number of metallurgical implements, especially molds, discussed below in a separate section, implies the mass production of certain items, in the limited sense of the term. Although these are not Byzantine objects per se, they can still be treated as evidence of contact with the Empire as well as being an original attempt to create culture in relation to Byzantium based on local preferences. Finally, they are valuable indicators of local

---

by the press of Central European University in Budapest; e.g. L. Boia, *History and Myth in Romanian Consciousness* (Budapest, 2001); S. Mitu, *National Identity of Romanians in Transylvania* (Budapest, 2001).

[33] The absurdity of the debate was best encapsulated by J. Nouzille, *La Transylvanie: terre de contacts et de conflits* (Strasbourg, 1994), 50: "Deux thèses opposent donc les historiens, l'une faisant appel à la logique contre les sources historiques, l'autre réfutant la logique pour s'appuyer sur les textes, même s'ils sont contradictoires" ("Two opposed theories divide the scholarly community, one using logic against the historical sources and the other using conflicting sources against logic").

demand and perhaps betraying the inability to procure genuine Byzantine goods in sufficient quantity.

2.2.1 Amphorae

The Early Byzantine amphora is one of the most common artifacts found in hilltop fortresses from the northern Balkans, being primarily related to the state-controlled *annona* system designed to supply the frontier garrisons.[34] Unfortunately, very few sites have so far benefited from quantitative studies of well-stratified ceramic assemblages. Based on the available archaeological monographs, the amphora occasionally accounts for almost half of the ceramic remains from a site. In most cases either LR1 or LR2 is the most frequent type.[35] This is hardly the case north of the river. With the exception of the major bridge-head fort of Sucidava, the rural settlements in *barbaricum* have produced only a small quantity of amphora fragments (Figure 3). Their concentration in the close proximity of the Danube is unsurprising, but the similar density of amphora finds a few hundred kilometers to the north, in Moldavia, appears unusual if we are

---

[34] O. Karagiorgou, "LR2: a container for the military *annona* on the Danubian border?" in *Economy and Exchange in the East Mediterranean during Late Antiquity. Proceedings of a Conference at Somerville College, Oxford, 29th May, 1999*, eds. S. Kingsley and M. Decker (Oxford, 2001), 129–166.

[35] I. C. Opriş, *Ceramica romană târzie şi paleobizantină de la Capidava în contextul descoperirilor de la Dunărea de Jos (sec. IV–VI p. Chr.)* (Bucharest, 2003), 50; F. Topoleanu, "Ceramica," in A. Suceveanu et al., *Halmyris I. Monografie arheologică* (Cluj-Napoca, 2003), 226–227; M. Mackensen, "Amphoren und Spatheia von Golemanovo Kale," in S. Uenze et al., *Die Spätantiken Befestigungen von Sadovec (Bulgarien)* (Munich, 1992), 239–254; L. Bjelajac, "La céramique et les lampes," in *Caričin Grad II: Le quartier sud-ouest de la ville haute*, eds. B. Bavant, V. Kondić, and J. M. Spieser (Rome, 1990), 174–176 and pl. XXI; Đ. Janković, *Podunavski deo oblasti Akvisa u VI i pochetkom VII veka* (Belgrade, 1981), 147–153; G. Kuzmanov, "Ceramica del primo periodo bizantino a Ratiaria," *Ratiarensia* 3–4 (1987): 115–116; G. Kuzmanov, "Ranovizantiiska bitova keramika ot Gradishteto (severozapaden sector)," in V. Dinchev, *Bulgaro-britanski razkopki na gradishteto pri s. Dichin, Velikoturnovska oblast, 1996–2003: rezultati ot prouchvaniiata na bulgarskiia ekip* (Sofia, 2009), 174–178; R. K. Falkner, "The pottery," in A. G. Poulter, *Nicopolis ad Istrum: A Roman to Early Byzantine City. The Pottery and Glass* (London, 1999), 117, fig. 8.4; C. Scorpan, "Ceramica romano-bizantină de la Sacidava," *Pontica* 8 (1975): 263–313; B. Böttger, "Die Gefäßkeramik aus dem Kastell Iatrus," in B. Döhle et al., *Iatrus-Krivina. Spätantike Befestigung und frühmittelalterliche Siedlung an der unteren Donau. Band II: Ergebnisse der Ausgrabungen 1966–1973* (Berlin, 1982), 33–148. At Viminacium LR2 and LR1 types represent an overwhelming majority of 96.6 percent, for which see M. Popović, "Svetinja, novi podaci o ranovizantijskom Viminacijumu," *Starinar* 38 (1987): 36. On the other hand, at Saraçhane, Istanbul, LR1 and LR2 account for ca. 25 percent of the sixth- and seventh-century deposits, for which see *Hayes*, 62–71.

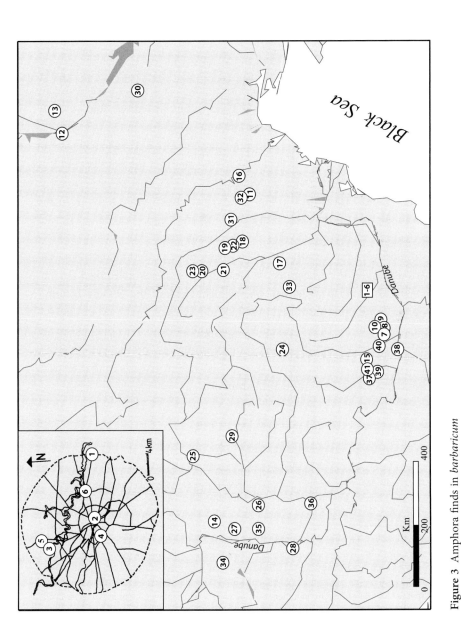

Figure 3 Amphora finds in *barbaricum*

1. Bucharest–Cățelu Nou; 2. Bucharest–Foișorul Mavrocordaților; 3. Bucharest–Străulești–Măicănești; 4. Bucharest–Mihai Vodă; 5. Bucharest–Băneasa; 6. Bucharest–Soldat Ghivan; 7. Vedea; 8. Dulceanca; 9. Olteni; 10. Sfințești; 11. Hansca; 12. Kiev; 13. Svetil'ne; 14. Dány; 15. Gropșani; 16. Speia; 17. Gutinaș; 18. Bâcu; 19. Bârlești; 20. Botoșani; 21. Conțești; 22. Păușești; 23. Vlădeni; 24. Bratei; 25. Tiszavasvári; 26. Gátér; 27. Kunbábony; 28. Kölked-Feketekapu; 29. Biharea; 30. Pastyrs'ke; 31. Seliște; 32. Dănceni; 33. Târgul Secuiesc; 34. Csákberény; 35. Kiskőrös-Pohibuj; 36. Óbecse/Bečej; 37. Craiova–Fântâna Obedeanu; 38. Orlea; 39. Făcăi; 40. Fărcașul de Sus; 41. Ișalnița.

looking for a strictly economic explanation. It is more likely that Byzantine amphorae and their content acquired different social values depending on various factors such as the distance from the Danube frontier and the main channels responsible for bringing such goods in *barbaricum*.

The main question, therefore, is whether such amphorae with a wide circulation in the Danubian provinces performed a similar function in *barbaricum*. Since containers were related to *annona militaris*, their scarcity or complete absence in parts of *barbaricum* can be ascribed to the limited reach of the Roman military beyond the bridge-heads established on the northern bank of the Danube. If this is the case, then the few known LR1 and LR2 north of the river in Wallachia probably arrived through trade – perhaps in exchange for grain – which may have been part of an official strategy of supplying the frontier fortresses. Unlike dress accessories, discussed later in this chapter, amphorae were too large to count as "souvenirs" and could not be displayed (i.e. worn) as objects of prestige. On the other hand, access to oil or wine from the Empire could, of course, enhance one's social standing.

An economic function can also be ascribed to amphora finds from the western edge of the Balkans, in Slovenia, where a good number of sites of the frontier region produced a conspicuously large quantity of *spatheia* customarily produced in the Western Mediterranean.[36] Similar channels of distribution might be responsible for finds of *spatheia* at Kölked-Feketekapu, an Early Avar settlement on the right bank of the Middle Danube. Amphorae and other imported material from Kölked-Feketekapu suggest a route coming from the western Balkans and even Italy, rather than the usual provenance from the Lower Danube provinces and the western Black Sea coast.[37] Kölked-Feketekapu seems to be at a crossroads in that respect, since it also yielded LR1 and LR2 amphorae.

---

[36] For Spain and North Africa in particular, see D. P. S. Peacock and D. F. Williams, *Amphorae and the Roman Economy. An Introductory Guide* (New York, NY, 1986), 202–203. See also P. M. Pröttel, *Mediterrane Feinkeramikimporte des 2. bis 7. Jahrhunderts n. Chr. im oberen Adriaraum und in Slowenien* (Espelkamp, 1996). For finds in Slovenia (Adjovski gradec, Crnomelj, Križna gora, Vranje, Kranj, and Koper), see M. Bausovac, "Late Roman amphorae from Rifnik near Celje (Slovenia)," in *LRCW3. Late Roman Coarse Wares, Cooking Wares and Amphorae in the Mediterranean. Archaeology and Archaeometry. Comparison Between Western and Eastern Mediterranean*, ed. S. Menchelli (Oxford, 2010), 695–701; Z. Modrijan, "Keramika," in *Poznoantična utrjena naselbina Tonovcov grad pri Kobaridu. Najdbe*, eds. Z. Modrijan and T. Milavec (Ljubljana, 2011), 121–219; 514–556.

[37] A eulogy flask with no analogies in the eastern Balkans adds weight to this proposition, for which see Z. Hajnal, "Késő antik jellegű kerámia a Kölked-Feketekapui avar kori telepről 2005," *CAH* (2005): 477–480.

These types of amphorae are also found in burial assemblages of the Middle Avar period from the region between the rivers Tisza and the Danube, such as Tiszavasvári and Kunbábony.[38] These and other finds of amphorae in *Avaria* originated from the western Black Sea area, and were acquired most likely after the collapse of the Danubian frontier system, since most of the finds are associated with material securely dated to the Middle Avar period (ca. 630 to ca. 670).[39] Recent studies have shown that such amphorae represent a symbol of prestige for the Avar nobility who received such items in their burial assemblages, but they also reflect the changing nature of political contacts between the Empire and the Avar Khaganate after the failed siege of Constantinople (626).[40]

A similar interpretation was recently suggested for the fragments of amphorae found in settlements belonging to the so-called Ipoteşti-Cândeşti and Botoşana cultures, south and east of the Carpathians, respectively. Andrei Măgureanu argued that the presence of amphorae must be connected with the local elite that chose to display its economic power through such artifacts imported from the Empire.[41] Indeed, some amphora fragments have been retrieved from houses that stand out as being larger and richer, as it is clearly the case of the building B10 at Bucharest–Soldat Ghivan Street, where fragments of several imported amphorae were associated with a local imitation of an Early Byzantine amphora, a ladle used to pour metal, and a mold designed to produce jewelry. Although the outstanding house at Soldat Ghivan displays the largest number of amphorae to be found in a single building north of the Danube, there are other sunken-featured buildings in the same settlement which produced artifacts

---

[38] T. Vida, *Die Awarenzeitliche Keramik I. (6.–7. Jh.)* (Budapest, 1999), pl. 38/3 and pl. 39/3.

[39] For other amphora finds, see Vida, *Die Awarenzeitliche Keramik*, 242–243; É. Garam, *Funde byzantinischer Herkunft in der Awarenzeit vom Ende des 6. bis zum Ende des 7. Jahrhunderts* (Budapest, 2001), 166–168, pl. 123–124. For the circulation of amphorae in Avaria, see recently F. Curta, "Amphorae and seals: the 'Sub-Byzantine' Avars and the quaestura exercitus," in *Festschrift for Csanád Bálint*, ed. Á. Bollók (Budapest, 2016), 1–28.

[40] G. Csiky and P. Magyar-Hárshegyi, "Wine for the Avar elite? Amphorae from Avar period burials in the Carpathian Basin," in *The Danubian Lands between the Black, Aegean and Adriatic Seas (7th Century BC–10th Century AD)*, eds. G. R. Tsetskhladze et al. (Oxford, 2015), 175–182. The practice of including amphorae in burials is not restricted to the Avar Khaganate; an Early Byzantine amphora was found in an inhumation grave (M 21) from Kushnarenkovo (Bashkortostan, Russia) together with amber beads, bronze and silver fibulae, and a buckle, for which see V. F. Gening, "Pamiatniki u s. Kushnarenkovo na r. Beloi (VI–VII vv. n.e.)," in *Issledovaniia po arkheologii Iuzhnogo Urala*, eds. R. G. Kuzeev, N. A. Mazhitov, and A. Kh. Pshenichniuk (Ufa, 1976), 102, fig. 9/1.

[41] A. Măgureanu, "About power in the sixth–seventh century in the Extra-Carpathian area," in *Potestas et Communitas. Interdiciplinary Studies of the Constitution and Demonstration of Power Relations in the Middle Ages East of the Elbe*, eds. A. Paroń et al. (Warsaw, 2010), 80–81.

that could very well have played the role of prestige items, such as fibulae or even the handmade lamp found in the building B5.[42]

Since any goods imported from the Empire could in principle become an index of social distinction, what is at stake here is the relative value of amphorae among other imported items. On that note, it should be said that Soldat Ghivan is just one of the sixth-century settlements in Bucharest to provide such finds. Indeed, no less than five other locations in Bucharest have yielded amphora fragments, of which only the sunken-featured building L15 from Străuleşti-Măicăneşti can be compared with the one at Soldat Ghivan, being larger than the other houses.[43] The inventory, however, is less spectacular, although it boasts three storage jars of 100 liters each.[44] The presence of metallurgical implements along with amphorae at Soldat Ghivan (house B10) is not unique and has been attested south and east of the Carpathians, at Dulceanca (house B2) and Gutinaş (house L4), respectively. In both cases amphora fragments are associated with scrap pieces of bronze and in the case of Dulceanca, the sunken-featured building B2 also produced a stone mold for jewelry.[45] Moreover, the association of amphora fragments with military brooches or buckles in houses from Dulceanca, Olteni, and Hansca seems to suggest a higher social status for their owners.[46] They were perhaps soldiers who fought in the Roman army and accumulated enough wealth to aspire to elite status in their community. However, in many instances amphora fragments are either found in inconspicuous buildings or the archaeological context was not documented, making it hard to determine whether the amphora,

---

[42] S. Dolinescu-Ferche and M. Constantiniu, "Un établissment du VIe siècle á Bucarest (Découvertes de la rue Soldat Ghivan)," *Dacia* 25 (1981): 320, with fig. 17/16 and 323, fig. 19/1.

[43] Căţelu Nou: V. Leahu, "Raport asupra săpăturilor arheologice efectuate în 1960 la Căţelu Nou," *CAB* 1 (1963): 39, with fig. 26/1. Bucureşti–Foişorul Mavrocordaţilor: M. Turcu and C. Marinescu, "Consideraţii privind 'Foişorul Mavrocordaţilor'," *Bucureşti. Materiale de istorie şi muzeografie* 6 (1968), 125 fig. 6/8. Bucharest–Mihai Vodă: G. Cantea, "Cercetările arheologice pe dealul Mihai Vodă şi împrejurimi," in *Bucureştii de odinioară în lumina săpăturilor arheologice*, ed. I. Ionaşcu (Bucharest, 1959), 33–34; 93–96, pl. LXXIII/1–3; Bucharest–Băneasa: Constantiniu, "Şantierul arheologic Băneasa-Străuleşti," 79; 91–94.

[44] M. Constantiniu, "Săpăturile de la Străuleşti-Măicăneşti. Aşezarea feudală II," *CAB* 2 (1965): 185, with fig. 83/5.

[45] Dulceanca: Dolinescu-Ferche, *Aşezările*, 96, fig. 106/6, 8. Gutinaş: I. Mitrea, C. Eminovici, and V. Momanu, "Aşezarea din secolele V–VII de la Ştefan cel Mare, jud. Bacău," *Carpica* 18–19 (1986–1987): 247, fig. 14/4.

[46] Dulceanca: Dolinescu-Ferche, *Aşezările*, figs. 85/6–8 and 92. Olteni: S. Dolinescu-Ferche, "Aşezarea din sec. VI e.n. de la Olteni-judeţul Teleorman, 1966," *MCA* 10 (1973): 205. Hansca: I. A. Rafalovich, *Slaviane VI–IX vekov v Moldavii* (Kishinew, 1972), 32, fig. 3/1 and 38, fig. 8/8.

2.2 Byzantine Imports and Imitations in Barbaricum

and more precisely its content (wine/oil), held a higher symbolic value in relation to other imports.[47]

Amphora finds are not restricted to the region north of the Danube. A LR1 amphora was found at Klimovka on the upper Volga, the easternmost find of Early Byzantine amphorae. In addition, a number of Pontic amphorae belonging to the type Kuzmanov XVI/ Scorpan IX are known from the region of Kiev.[48] A type-based distribution of amphorae in *barbaricum* has already been attempted and it clearly shows that most finds north of the Black Sea, especially on the Dnieper, belong to a series of amphorae produced in the Pontic area, which could suggest trading connections with the Empire, possibly through the Crimea.[49] By contrast, the region north of the Lower Danube produced mostly finds of LR1 and LR2. Such amphorae became dominant in the northern Balkans after the creation of *quaestura exercitus* in 536, which brought under the same administrative umbrella some of the production centers of these amphora types.[50] The scarcity of imported amphorae from the first half of the sixth

---

[47] For the possible content of LR1 and LR2 amphorae, see Karagiorgou, "LR2: a container," 146–149. For other amphora finds north of the Danube, see S. Dolinescu-Ferche, "Cercetările arheologice din com. Vedea (jud. Teleorman)," *MCA* 16 (1986): 205, fig. 2; V. Teodorescu, "O nouă cultură arheologică recent precizată în țara noastră, cultura Ipotești-Cîndești (sec. V–VII)," in *Sesiunea de comunicări științifice a muzeelor de istorie, dec. 1964*, vol. II (Bucharest, 1971), 130, fig. 6/4; G. Popilian and M. Nica, *Gropșani. Monografie arheologică* (Bucharest, 1998), 23–25; S. Dolinescu-Ferche, "Un complex din secolul al VI-lea la Sfințești," *SCIV* 18, no. 1 (1967): 130, fig. 3/5; G. Popilian and M. Nica, "Așezarea prefeudală de la Craiova (Fântâna Obedeanu)," *Drobeta* 15 (2005), pl. VII/8 (LR2); O. Toropu, *Romanitatea tîrzie și străromânii în Dacia traiană sud-carpatică (secolele III–XI)* (Craiova, 1976), 205–217, nos. 52, 53, 76, and 92, with pl. V (LR1 and fragments); D. G. Teodor, *Descoperiri arheologice și numismatice la est de Carpați* (Bucharest, 1997), nos. 49, 59, 106, 195, 343, 512, and 756; I. Tentiuc, "Siturile din secolele V–VII de la Molești-Ialoveni (Republica Moldova)," *AM* 21 (1998): 209; N. Gudea and I. Ghiurco, *Din istoria creștinismului la români. Mărturii arheologice* (Oradea, 1988), 197; B. Ciupercă and A. Măgureanu, "Locuințe din a doua jumătate a mileniului I p. Chr. descoperite la Târgșoru Vechi," in *Arheologia mileniului I p. Chr. Cercetări actuale privind istoria și arheologia migrațiilor*, ed. L. M. Voicu (Bucharest, 2010), 156–157.

[48] Kiev: A. M. Shovkoplias, "Ranneslavianskaia keramika s gory Kiselevki v Kieve," in *Slaviane nakanune obrazovaniia Kievskoi Rusi*, ed. B. A. Rybakov (Moscow, 1963), 140, fig. 2/1; O. M. Prikhodniuk, *Arkheologychny pam'iatki seredn'ogo Pridniprov'ia VI–IX st. n.e.* (Kiev, 1980), 130; 63, fig. 44/9. Svetil'ne: Shovkoplias, "Ranneslavianskaia keramika," 140. Klimovka: V. V. Priimak, "Kulturnye transformatsii i vzaimovliianiia v Dneprovskom regione na iskhode rimskogo vremei i v rannem Srednevekov'e," in *Doklady nauchnoi konferentsii, posviashchennoi 60-letiiu so dnia rozhdeniia E. A. Goriunova (Sankt Petersburg, 14–17 noiabria 2000 g.)* (St. Petersburg, 2004), fig. 3B.

[49] Curta, *The Making of the Slavs*, 244, fig. 37.

[50] For *quaestura exercitus*, see A. Gkoutzioukostas and X. M. Moniaros, *He peripheriake dioiketike anadiorganose tes byzantines autokratorias apo ton Ioustiniano A' (527–565): he periptose tes quaestura Iustiniana exercitus* (Thessaloniki, 2009). See also S. Torbatov, "Quaestura exercitus: Moesia Secunda and Scythia under Justinian," *ArchBulg* 1 (1997): 78–87.

century in the Crimea and the northern Balkans points to major difficulties in supplying the Danube frontier and was probably one of the main reasons for the creation of this atypical administrative unit.[51]

Finally, among the amphorae found north of the Danube three appear to be local imitations. One of them was already mentioned, the fragment from the B10 building at Bucharest–Soldat Ghivan found in association with a Byzantine amphora; the second was found at Bratei in Transylvania, in the sunken-featured building B5, also associated with a genuine amphora; and finally an amphora handle comes from the sixth–seventh century settlement at Târgșoru Vechi in Wallachia (building B41).[52] Such imitations strengthen the hypothesis that imported amphorae represented one way that communities in *barbaricum* imitated the Roman lifestyle, while their owners increased their prestige through their ability to procure oil or wine from the Empire. There is, however, very little to suggest that the ability to acquire such goods was the exclusive privilege of a particular ethnic group. Rather, it appears to be a more general phenomenon in the northern world as a symbol of participation in the militaristic culture of the Byzantine frontier.

2.2.2 Lamps

2.2.2.1 Danubian Lamps

Byzantine lamps constitute one of the most important, yet insufficiently explored, categories of imports in *barbaricum*. They have been traditionally associated with the Roman way of life and often connected to Christian practice.[53] Clay lamps provide the greatest diversity and potential for a study of geographical distribution and they will be the main focus of the next pages.[54] Bronze lamps, on the other hand, are interesting due to their higher value

---

[51] V. G. Swan, "Dichin (Bulgaria): interpreting the ceramic evidence in its wider context," in *Transition*, 263.

[52] Soldat-Ghivan: Dolinescu-Ferche and Constantiniu, "Un établissment," 318–319, fig. 16/1, possibly imitating an Early Byzantine LR2; Bratei: E. Zaharia, "La station n. 2 de Bratei, dép. de Sibiu (VIe–VIIIe siècles), *Dacia* 38–39 (1995), 305. Târgșoru Vechi: B. Ciupercă and A. Măgureanu, "Locuințe din a doua jumătate a mileniului I p. Chr. descoperite la Târgșoru Vechi," in *Arheologia mileniului I p. Chr. Cercetări actuale privind istoria și arheologia migrațiilor*, ed. L. M. Voicu (Bucharest, 2010), 155; 167, fig. 6.

[53] A. Diaconescu, "Lămpi romane târzii și paleobizantine din fosta provincie Dacia," *EN* 5 (1995): 255–299, remains the only synthetic treatment of this category of artifacts, valuable for its contribution to the typology of lamps found in *barbaricum*.

[54] For a recent comprehensive analysis of lamps in the sixth–seventh century Balkans, see recently F. Curta, "Shedding light on a murky matter: remarks on 6th to early 7th century clay lamps in the Balkans," *AB* 20, no. 3 (2016): 51–116.

and well-documented parallels in the Byzantine world. The Christian bronze lamp from Luciu on the left bank of the Danube, the only such find outside the former province of Dacia, has to be mentioned for its perfect resemblance to lamps found at Archar and Athens, in Illyricum, while the Christian lamp from Tápiógyörgye in *Avaria* has good analogies in Dardania at Kalaja and Bujanovac, in Asia Minor at Ephesus, and in Crete.[55] Other fifth-to-sixth-century bronze lamps have been found in Dacia, most of which have a Coptic origin.[56] However, most bronze lamps from *barbaricum* have good analogies in the Balkans, so there is no reason to assume a direct connection between Dacia and Egypt. Adriatic or Aegean sources are more likely alternatives given the concentration of finds in Illyricum.

If most bronze lamps are long-distance imports, the largest percentage of clay lamps was produced in the Balkans. They are usually referred to in the literature as "Danubian lamps" because they are mostly found in settlements from the Lower Danube provinces (Figure 4).[57] Although they are a typical creation of frontier culture, it seems that some lamp designs

---

[55] Luciu: I. Barnea, *Christian Art in Romania. Vol. 1: 3rd–6th Centuries* (Bucharest, 1979), pl. 112. Archar: *Kuzmanov*, no. 443. Athens: *Perlzweig*, no. 2984. A similar lamp found in Greece is now in the Vatican Museum, for which see M. C. De'Spagnolis and E. De Carolis, *Le lucerne di bronzo* (Vatican, 1986), 68, no. 29; another close analogy at Sadovets, for which see Uenze, *Die Spätantiken Befestigungen*, pl. 143/3. A lamp very similar to the one from Luciu was part of a spectacular hoard of coins, jewelry, and liturgical objects recently found in Gaza and buried at the beginning of the seventh century, for which see K. Golan, "Why hide? Hoarding in Late Antiquity in view of the Early Byzantine hoard from the Gaza area," presentation at the 22nd International Congress of Byzantine Studies, Sofia, 2011. Tápiógyörgye: Garam, *Funde*, pl. 133 and XL/4. Ephesus: *Miltner*, n. 356. Kalaja: E. Shukriu, "Frühchristliche Lampen aus der antiken Provinz Dardania," *Mitteilungen zur Christlichen Archäologie* 9 (2003): fig. 1. Bujanovac: O. Ilić, "Early Christian imports and local imitations of imported goods in the territory of the Central Balkans," in *The Roman Empire and Beyond*, eds. E. C. De Sena and H. Dobrzanska (Oxford, 2011), 50, fig. 12/6. Crete (Chania Museum): www.cretekreta.com/files/u2/ ByzantineCollectionBronzeLamp.jpg (visit of January 16, 2017).

[56] Dej, Lipova, Moigrad (Porolissum), and Reşca (Romula): Gudea and Ghiurco, *Din istoria creştinismului*, 143–147. Many similar lamps found their way into western museums, such as the Römisch-Germanischen Zentralmuseum zu Mainz or the British Museum. For a comprehensive list of analogies, see M. Xanthopoulou, *Les lampes en bronze a l'époque paléochrétienne* (Turnhout, 2010).

[57] For the typology, see especially *Iconomu; Kuzmanov; Hayes*. In the classification created for the lamps found on the Yassı Ada shipwreck, Danubian lamps are found under the label "Balkan;" see K. D. Vitelli, "The lamps," in G. E. Bass and F. H. van Doorninck, Jr., *Yassı Ada. Volume I. A Seventh-Century Byzantine Shipwreck* (College Station, 1982), 196–199. The name was also adopted by scholars from the Balkans, for which see K. Kostova and D. Dobreva, "Roman, Late Roman and Early Byzantine lamps from National Archaeological Reserve 'Deultum-Debelt'," in *Lychnological Acts 2*, 164. Their frequency is particularly high in the northern Balkans; at Capidava local lamps account for 66 percent of the total number of finds; see Opriş, *Ceramica romană*, 167, fig. 10. A high proportion (over 50 percent) was also noted for the late occupation levels at Halmyris, for which see Topoleanu, "Ceramica," 244, table 8.

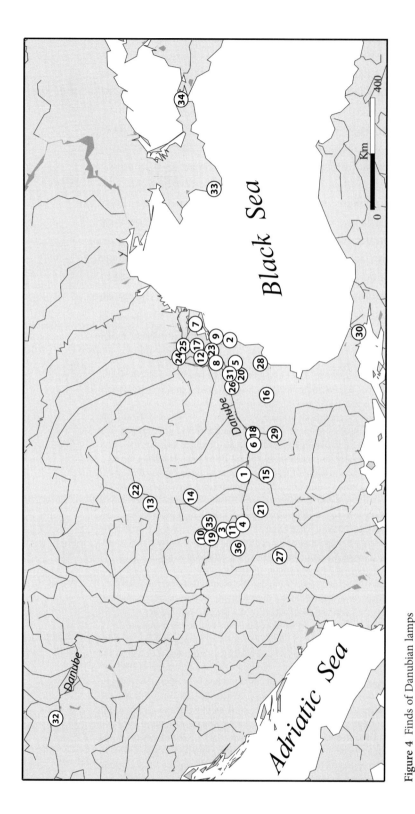

Figure 4 Finds of Danubian lamps

1. Sucidava; 2. Tomis; 3. Aquis; 4. Kovilovo Grad; 5. Tropaeum Traiani; 6. Novae; 7. Halmyris; 8. Capidava; 9. Histria; 10. Dierna; 11. Mokranjske Stene; 12. Beroe; 13. Apulum; 14. Bumbeşti; 15. Sadovec; 16. Shumen; 17. Izvoarele; 18. Iatrus; 19. Hajdučka Vodenica; 20. Golesh; 21. Mihailovgrad; 22. Războieni; 23. Ulmetum; 24. Dinogetia; 25. Noviodunum; 26. Durostorum; 27. Caričin Grad; 28. Odurtsi; 29. Veliko Turnovo; 30. Saraçhane; 31. Oltina; 32. Vienna; 33. Chersonesus; 34. Kertch; 35. Drobeta; 36. Romuliana.

were either produced or had prototypes developed in Constantinople as evidenced by numerous finds from the excavations at Saraçhane.[58] However, in *barbaricum* "Danubian" lamps are not showing up in the quantity we would expect given their immense popularity in almost every Danube fort. The spatial distribution of finds can provide a tentative explanation. The lamp from Bumbești in Oltenia has a perfect analogy at Constanța (Tomis).[59] Here, and also to the south along the Black Sea coast, at Kranevo, as well as on the Danube, at Sacidava, molds for this type have been unearthed proving the local production of these lamps in the eastern Balkans.[60] They were not made only for the local market as such lamps circulated as far as Anemurium in Cilicia.[61] Most of the finds, however, concentrate in the northeastern Balkans. Very similar lamps have been found in Scythia and Moesia II,[62] while a late seventh-century lamp with a cross at the base of the nozzle has been found during excavations at Saraçhane, showing the longevity of that design.[63]

Another Danubian lamp was found at Alba Iulia in the former Roman city (Apulum), its distinctive feature being the handle in the form of a human head.[64] Lamps with human-shaped handles have been found in multiple locations in Scythia, Moesia Secunda, and Dacia Ripensis.[65]

---

[58] *Hayes*, types 11–12.

[59] Diaconescu, "Lămpi romane," 271, pl. V/1 and the analogy from Tomis at pl. V/2.

[60] Constanța: C. Iconomu, "Descoperiri de tipare de opaițe la Tomis," *Pontica* 9 (1976): 135–145. Kranevo: G. Toncheva, "Keramichna rabotilnica krai s. Kranevo," *Izvestiia Bulgarskoto Arkheologichesko Druzhestvo* 9 (1952): 81–104. Sacidava: C. Scorpan, "Descoperiri arheologice diverse la Sacidava," *Pontica* 11 (1978): pl. VI.

[61] H. Williams and P. Taylor, "A Byzantine lamp hoard from Anamur (Cilicia)," *Anatolian Studies* 25 (1975): 80, fig. 4.

[62] Noviodunum: I. Barnea and A. Barnea, "Săpăturile de salvare de la Noviodunum," *Peuce* 9 (1984): pl. X/6. Durostorum: C. Mușețeanu, "Ceramica romană de la Durostorum," PhD Dissertation, University of Bucharest, 1992, 177–178. Murighiol: Topoleanu, "Ceramica," pl. XLVII/ 27; I. Barnea, "Perioada Dominatului (sec. IV–VII)," in R. Vulpe and I. Barnea, *Din istoria Dobrogei*, vol. II (Bucharest, 1968), fig. 51/3. Veliko Turnovo: *Kuzmanov*, no. 305.

[63] *Hayes*, type 16, no. 134. Lamps with cross on the nozzle have been labeled "North African" by Kuzmanov, but similar types are found among the Attic lamps from the Athenian agora. It is well known that Greek lamps of the Early Byzantine period were inspired by African types, so that similar lamps produced in the Balkans could have followed the same practice, see *Kuzmanov*, type XXXVI; *Perlzweig*, no. 2933.

[64] Diaconescu, "Lămpi romane," 273, pl. VI/ 1a–d.

[65] Adamclisi: I. Bogdan Cătăniciu and A. Barnea, "Ceramica și descoperiri mărunte," in *Tropaeum Traiani. I. Cetatea*, ed. I. Barnea (Bucharest, 1979), figs. 173/ 9.5 and 9.6. Capidava: Z. Covacef and E. Corbu, "Considerații asupra unei categorii de opaițe descoperite în sectorul V al cetății Capidava," *Pontica* 24 (1991): figs. 2/1–3, 10. Oltina: M. Irimia, "Cuptoarele romano-bizantine de ars ceramica de la Oltina," *Pontice* 1 (1968): 400, fig. 18/3. Dunăreni: *Iconomu*, 149, no. 778. Beroe: Vîlceanu and Barnea, "Ceramica lucrată," pl. 1/5. Halmyris: Topoleanu, "Ceramica," pl. LIX/10 and LVI/9; for an illustration of this lamp, see below Chapter 4, Figure 18/1. Tomis: I.

The circulation of this type was not restricted to the Lower Danube region since similar examples appear further to the east, in the Crimea and to the west in Pannonia.[66] However, the specimen from Alba Iulia departs from the common design of the lamps mentioned above, most of which display the usual short strokes on the rim. Instead, we find a zigzag pattern with small globules reminiscent of the popular lamps produced in Asia Minor during the fifth and sixth centuries and sometimes imitated in the northern Balkans.[67] Anatolian influences on the specimen from Apulum should not be surprising, since lamps with human-shaped handles have been found in Constantinople, as well as at Sardis in Lydia.[68] More significantly, the lamp from Apulum remains a singular find despite what appears to have been a significant level of production and circulation of lamps with human-shaped handles in the frontier region.

Other types of lamps did not even circulate farther than the Byzantine bridge-heads on the northern side of the river. They are still worth mentioning. The lamp discovered at Orşova (Dierna) boasts a handle in the shape of a ram's head, with strong analogies in Scythia.[69] A similar

---

Barnea, O. Iliescu, and C. Nicolescu, *Cultura bizantină în România* (Bucharest, 1971), 171, no. 344. Novae: A. Dimitrova, "Arkheologicheskie raskopki v vostochnom sektore Nove v 1963 godu," *IAI* 28 (1965): 60, fig. 31. Iatrus: G. von Bülow, B. Böttger, and S. Conrad, eds., *Iatrus-Krivina. Spätantike Befestigung und frühmittelalterliche Siedlung an der unteren Donau. Band VI: Ergebnisse der Ausgrabungen 1992-2000* (Mainz am Rhein, 2007), pl. 40/2284. Mokranjske Stene and Aquis: Janković, *Podunavski*, pl. XI/3 and XI/5. Romuliana: S. Petković, "Late Roman Romuliana and Mediaeval Gamzigrad from the end of 4th to 11th centuries AD," in *Keszthely-Fenékpuszta im Kontext spätantiker Kontinuitätsforschung zwischen Noricum und Moesia*, ed. O. Heinrich-Tamáska (Leipzig, 2011), 274, fig. 8a.

[66] Chersonesus: L. Chrzanovski and D. Zhuravlev, *Lamps from Chersonesus in the State Historical Museum – Moscow* (Rome, 1998), 172–174, nos. 109–110. Kerch: T. I. Makarova, "Bospor-Korchev po arkheologicheskim dannym," in *Vizantiiskaia Tavrika. Sbornik nauchnykh trudov (v XVIII kongressu vizantinistov)*, ed. P. P. Tolochko (Kiev, 1991), 135, fig. 15/2. Vienna: D. Ivanyi, *Die Pannonischen Lampen: eine typologisch-chronologische Übersicht* (Budapest, 1935), n. 1224, pl. LXVII/8 (very similar to the lamp found at Mokranjske Stene, for which see Janković, *Podunavski*, pl. XI/5).

[67] A mold for such imitations was found at Halmyris, for which see F. Topoleanu, *Ceramica romană şi romano-bizantină de la Halmyris* (Tulcea, 2000), 211–214.

[68] *Hayes*, type 11, pl. 21/64–65; J. Stephens Crawford, *The Byzantine Shops at Sardis* (Cambridge MA, 1990), fig. 93 (shop W8).

[69] Tomis: C. L. Băluţă, "Lămpile antice din colecţia Severeanu," *Apulum* 31 (1994): pl. VII/7. Capidava: Covacef and Corbu, "Consideraţii," fig. 2/9. Histria (associated with a sixth-century coin): D. M. Pippidi, G. Bordenache, and V. Eftimie, "Şantierul arheologic Histria," *MCA* 7 (1961): fig. 15/2. Halmyris (described as an "oriental" type): Topoleanu, "Ceramica," pl. LV/23; for an illustration of this lamp, see below Chapter 4, Figure 18/2. Occasionally, the ram's head is replaced with a bull's head, for which see: Adamclisi: I. Bogdan Cătăniciu and A. Barnea, "Ceramica şi descoperiri," fig. 173. Ulmetum: V. Pârvan, "Cetatea Ulmetum III," *Academia Română Memoriile Secţiei Istorice* 37 (1914–1915): pl. VI/3.

lamp was found at Sucidava, the most important Byzantine settlement on the northern bank of the Danube, but no such finds are known deeper in *barbaricum*.[70] Additional lamps of the Balkan type have been found at Sucidava, among which a few lamps with cross-shaped handle. One of them was found in the Early Byzantine church together with coins dated 587/8 and 596/7, which securely pushes the *terminus post quem* of this model to the end of the sixth century and the beginning of the seventh.[71] Similar lamps with different cross shapes and designs on the handle are known throughout the northern Balkans and on the northern bank of the Danube, at Drobeta.[72] The type was also popular in Constantinople, which might indicate a possible center of production, especially since lamps with cross-shaped handle also appear on Anatolian sites, such as Amorium.[73] Interestingly, there is no trace of such lamps with Christian symbolism north of the Danube border, in *barbaricum*, although they were clearly available everywhere along the Lower Danube.

Yet another common group of lamps features a palmette or leaf-shaped handle, and sometimes a stylized "Tree of Life." Models displaying superior craftsmanship have been found in Asia Minor, suggesting a possible source of inspiration.[74] One specimen with a handle in the shape of an upright sprig from Sucidava has good analogies at Tomis and Halmyris, in Scythia,

---

[70] D. Tudor, "Sucidava IV. Campania a șaptea (1946) și a opta (1947) de săpături și cercetări arheologice în cetățuia dela Celei, reg. Craiova, raionul Corabia," *Materiale arheologice privind istoria veche a RPR*, vol. I (Bucharest, 1953): fig. 12/f.

[71] Ibid., fig. 11/d.

[72] Halmyris: Topoleanu, "Ceramica," pl. LXVII/10; for an illustration of this lamp, see below Chapter 4, Figure 18/3. Tomis: Barnea et al., *Cultura bizantină*, 170, no. 338. Capidava: Opriș, *Ceramica romană*, pl. LXI/416; Covacef and Corbu, "Considerații," fig. 1/11–12. Novae (two specimens are associated with a sixth-century coin): D. P. Dimitrov et al., "Arkheologicheskie raskopki v vostochnom sektore Nove v 1962 godu," *IAI* 27 (1964): fig. 18; D. P. Dimitrov et al., "Arkheologicheskie raskopki v vostochnom sektore Nove v 1963 godu," *IAI* 28 (1965): fig. 30; L. Press et al., "Novae – sektor zachodni, 1971. Sprawozdanie tymczasowe z wykopalisk ekspedycji archeologicznej Uniwersytetu Warszawskiego," *Archeologia* 24 (1973): figs. 55 and 65. Kovilovo Grad and Aquis: Janković, *Podunavski*, pl. XI/1–2. Drobeta: Barnea, *Christian Art*, pl. 114/1.

[73] Constantinople: Hayes, type 11, pl. 22 and 24. Amorium: M. A. V. Gill and N. T. Şen, "Roman and Early Byzantine terracotta lamps. With a discussion and two appendices by C. S. Lightfoot," in *Amorium Reports II. Research Papers and Technical Reports*, ed. C. S. Lightfoot (Oxford, 2003), pl. III/5 and III/31.

[74] *Miltner*, type IX. Such lamps are often found on Samos; for their typology see N. Poulou-Papadimitriou, "Lampes paléochrétiennes de Samos," *BCH* 110, no. 1 (1986): fig. 53. Amorium: Gill and Şen, "Roman," figs. III/8, nos. 39–41 and figs. III/25 and III/26. For various hypotheses regarding the origin of this type, see P. Dyczek, "Lamps of the 3rd–6th century AD from the civil architecture in Sector IV at Novae," in *Lychnological Acts 2*, 76.

and Saraçhane in Constantinople,[75] while a second lamp of this kind resembles finds from several locations in the northern Balkans, some of them associated with sixth-century coins.[76] Once again, lamps did not travel further north. Finally, one last "Danubian" lamp found in *barbaricum,* at Feldioara-Războieni in Transylvania, has a perfect analogy at Tomis in Scythia and belongs to the type with grapevine motifs,[77] whose prototype might have been an earlier lamp from Asia Minor,[78] sometimes found in Scythia and also imitated in Greece during the sixth century.[79] A similar design on a lamp found at Caričin Grad in Dacia Mediterranea, a sixth-century foundation, and on lamps from the seventh-century Yassı Ada shipwreck proves that it remained popular for a long time.[80]

All this shows that a great variety of lamp designs were widely available on the Lower Danube frontier and many were produced locally. Clay lamps were fragile, perhaps expensive, and required vegetable oil to function. Since they were not worn like brooches or belt buckles or carried in pockets, like coins, for instance, their non-economic circulation north of the Danube was more limited. Finally, lamps had a more indirect connection with the militarized culture of the northern Balkans to which many communities in *barbaricum* aspired. Their neutral symbolism made them less appealing as markers of social distinction. This undoubtedly explains why such common items of daily use in the frontier provinces do not show up very often in the lands north of the river.

---

[75] Sucidava: Barnea et al., *Cultura bizantină*, 171, no. 348. Tomis: *Iconomu*, fig. 183. Halmyris: Topoleanu, "Ceramica," pl. XLVII/11; for an illustration of this lamp, see below Chapter 4, Figure 18/4. Saraçhane: *Hayes*, type 11, pl. 22/82.

[76] Sucidava: Barnea et al., *Cultura bizantină*, 172, no. 350; Histria: Popescu et al., "Şantierul arheologic Histria," fig. 15/3; Sadovets: S. Uenze, ed., *Die spätantiken Befestigungen*, pl. 46/22. Shumen: V. Antonova, "Arkheologicheski prouchvaniia na Shumenskata krepost (Prevaritelno suobshtenie za trakiiskoto, rimskoto i rannovizantiiskoto selishte)," *Izvestiia na Narodniia Muzei Shumen* 6 (1973): fig. 1; Novae: Dyczek, "Lamps," pl. 29/11.

[77] Diaconescu, "Lămpi romane," 271, pl. V/5a–c; for the Tomis analogy, see pl. V/6; for an illustration of the lamp found at Feldioara-Războieni, see below Chapter 4, Figure 18/5.

[78] *Miltner*, type X. See also the lamps from a large hoard found at Anemurium; Williams and Taylor, "A Byzantine lamp," 81, form II, type 15.

[79] Adamclisi: Bogdan Cătăniciu and Barnea, "Ceramica," fig. 173/9.1. Sacidava: Scorpan, "Descoperiri arheologice," pl. XV/10. Halmyris: Topoleanu, "Ceramica," pl. XLIII/19. A similar lamp was found at Stobi, in Macedonia; see M. Glumac, "Glinene svetiljke iz kasnoantičke zbirke Narodnog Muzeja u Beogradu," *Zbornik Narodnog Muzeja* 17, no. 1 (2001): 218, no. 8 for an illustration of this lamp, see below Chapter 4, Figure 18/6.

[80] Caričin Grad: L. Bjelajac, "La céramique," 189, type V, pl. XXII/5. Yassı Ada: Vitelli, "Lamps," 190, L1, and fig. 9/2.

2.2.2.2 Lamps from Asia Minor, North Africa, and Palestine

The second major category of lamps described here were either imported from Asia Minor or borrowed motifs from the most popular models produced in the Byzantine heartland and circulated in the Balkans during the Early Byzantine period (Figure 5). Only one such lamp has been found north of the Danube, at Sucidava, on the left bank of the river, while in *barbaricum* proper no sixth-century lamps from Asia Minor have been reported to date. The lamp found at Sucidava belongs to the most common type, characterized by the presence of small globules on the rim.[81] An attempt was made to divide this type into two chronological groups: lamps with a round shape and no channel toward the nozzle, dated to the late fifth and early sixth century, and examples with a more elongated shape and a small channel from the discus to the nozzle, dated to the later sixth century.[82] Such a division finds a possible confirmation in the finds from the early seventh-century shipwreck from Yassı Ada where only the later type has been found.[83] As it is, the specimen from Sucidava belongs to *Hayes* type 2, dated to the later sixth century. As a matter of fact, most lamps with globules on the rim imported from Asia Minor or imitating this popular design found in the Danubian provinces belong to Hayes type 2.[84] Molds found at Halmyris in Scythia prove that the type was imitated and

---

[81] D. Tudor, "Sucidava III. Quatrième (1942), cinquième (1943) et sixième (1945) campagnes de fouilles et de recherches archéologiques dans la forteresse de Celei, département de Romanați," *Dacia* 11–12 (1945–1947), fig. 20/4.

[82] *Hayes*, 82; for an illustration of this model, see below Chapter 4, Figure 18/7.

[83] Vitelli, "Lamps," 193, L12, and fig. 9–3.

[84] Sadovets: Uenze, ed., *Die spätantiken Befestigungen*, pl. 44/8. Pernik: V. Liubenova, "Selishteto ot rimskata i rannovizantiiskata epokha," in *Pernik I. Poselishten zhivot na khulma Krakra ot V khil. pr. n.e. do VI v. na n.e.*, ed. T. Ivanov (Sofia, 1981), fig. 68/1–3. Beroe (associated with sixth-century coins): Vîlceanu and Barnea, "Ceramica lucrată," fig. 1/3–4. Aquis: Janković, *Podunavski*, pl. X/4; Histria: D. M. Pippidi et al., "Șantierul arheologic," 240, fig. 15. Callatis: N. Harțuche and O. Bounegru, "Opaițe grecești și romane din colecțiile Muzeului Brăila," *Pontica* 15 (1982): pl. VII/1. Karasura: V. Stoikov, "Kusnoantichni lampi ot Karasura (Predvaritelno suobshtenie)," in *Paleobalkanistika i starobulgaristika. Vtori esenni mezhdunarodni cheteniia Profesor "Ivan Gulubov," Veliko Turnovo, 14–17 noemvri 1996*, ed. I. Kharalambiev et al. (Veliko Turnovo, 2001), pl. 1/4–5. Sacidava: Scorpan, "Descoperiri arheologice," pl. IV/17. Capidava: Opriș, *Ceramica romană*, pl. XLIII/427–428; C. Matei, "Cercetări arheologice în zona instalației portuare antice de la Capidava (II), *Cultură și Civilizație la Dunărea de Jos* 5–7 (1988–1989), fig. 9/7. Iatrus: M. Wendel et al., *Iatrus-Krivina. Spätantike Befestigung und frühmittelalterliche Siedlung an der unteren Donau. Band III: Die mittelalterlichen Siedlungen* (Berlin, 1986), pl. 59/494.

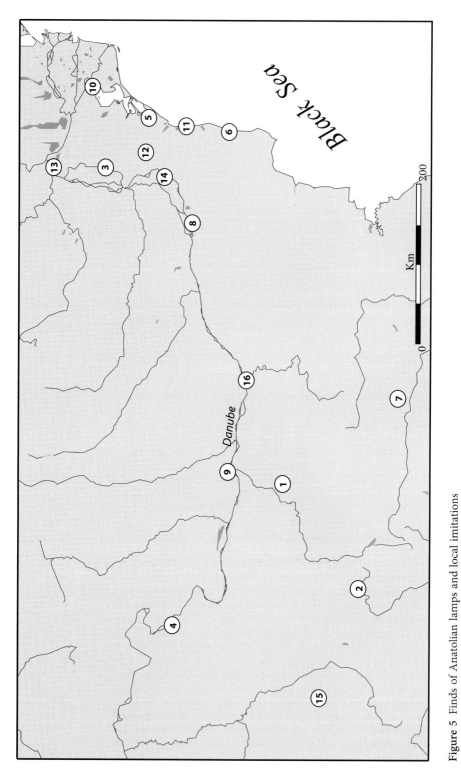

Figure 5 Finds of Anatolian lamps and local imitations

1. Sadovec; 2. Pernik; 3. Beroe; 4. Aquis; 5. Histria; 6. Callatis; 7. Karasura; 8. Sacidava; 9. Sucidava; 10. Halmyris; 11. Tomis; 12. Ulmetum; 13. Dinogetia; 14. Axiopolis; 15. Caričin Grad; 16. Iatrus.

produced locally.[85] It is, therefore, highly probable that the specimen from Sucidava did not come from Asia Minor but from a closer production center in the northern Balkans. The next group of lamps brings together original pieces imported from North Africa and imitations produced in Greece or in the Danube region (Figure 6).[86] The distribution map reveals the fact that North African models found in *barbaricum* were almost as popular as the common "Danubian" types found in great numbers in the Byzantine provinces of the northern Balkans. North African lamps type Hayes 2B/ Atlante X, most typical for the sixth century, have been found at Turda (Potaissa), Alba Iulia (Apulum), and Reşca (Romula), three former urban centers of Dacia where the Roman provincial lifestyle was still cherished.[87] North African lamps are more common in Illyricum,[88] although several finds are known in the Thracian diocese, some of them being local imitations.[89] However, no direct parallels can be established between the type of lamps found in *barbaricum* and the lamps from

---

[85] Topoleanu, *Ceramica*, 211–214. Similar lamps from Caričin Grad, a sixth-century Justinianic foundation, have been described as local imitations, for which see Bjelajac, "La céramique et les lampes," 188.

[86] Many such lamps are Attic products, for which see *Perlzweig*, pl. 38 sq., or Corinthian, for which see *Broneer*, types XXVIII–XXXIII. Several such imitations were found in a villa urbana from Nea Anchialos in a context dated with coins from Justinian I, for which see P. Lazaridis, "Nea Ankhialos," *ArchDelt* 20 (1965), pl. 393β. Another lamp combining African and Anatolian motifs was produced in the region of Stobi, in Macedonia, see Glumac, "Glinene svetiljke," 216, n. 6. A number of locally produced African imitations have been found at Novae, on the Lower Danube, for which see recently Dyczek, "Lamps," 74. A mold for African lamps was found at Dinogetia, for which see I. Barnea, *Les monuments paléochrétiennes de Roumanie* (Vatican, 1977), 241.

[87] Turda and Alba Iulia: Diaconescu, "Lămpi romane," 265, pl. III/1a–d and 3a–c; for an illustration of this lamp, see below Chapter 4, Figure 18/8. Reşca: N. Gudea and I. Ghiurco, "Un opaiţ de bronz bizantin de la Porolissum," *Acta Musei Porolissensis* 10 (1986), fig. 3b.

[88] For finds of African lamps in the Adriatic region, see P. M. Pröttel, *Mediterrane Feinkeramikimporte des 2. bis 7. Jahrhunderts n. Chr. im oberen Adriaraum und in Slowenien* (Espelkamp, 1996), 69–81; B. Vikić-Belančić, *Antičke svjetilijke u Arheološkom Muzeju u Zagrebu* (Zagreb, 1976). For the distribution of African lamps type *Atlante* VIII and X in the Danube region, see recently V. Părău, "La diffusione delle lucerne nordafricane dei sec. IV–VI DC nelle ex-provincie central e sud danubiane. La lucerna del tipo Atlante VIII–X con chrismon," in *Lychnological Acts 2*, 197–206, and pl. 135.

[89] Tomis: G. Papuc, "Opaiţe de import la Tomis," *Pontica* 9 (1976): 201–205; C. L. Băluţă, "Lămpile antice," pl. VIII/1–3, 5. Adamclisi: Barnea, ed., *Tropaeum Traiani*, pl. 173/ 9.2. A. Diaconescu argued that the lamp from Adamclisi has monetary impressions of Theodosius II and must be dated after 430; see Diaconescu, "Lămpi romane," 257, no. 4. Halmyris: Topoleanu, "Ceramica," pl. LVII/13; for an illustration of this lamp, see below Chapter 4, Figure 18/9. Capidava: Opriş, *Ceramica romană*, pl. XLIII/433. Dinogetia: Barnea, *Christian Art*, pl. 107. Novae: Dyczek, "Lamps," pl. 28/4. More lamps from Dobrudja at F. Topoleanu, *Lămpile antice din colecţiile Muzeului Judeţean de Istorie şi Arheologie Prahova – Ploieşti* (Ploieşti, 2012), 187–192.

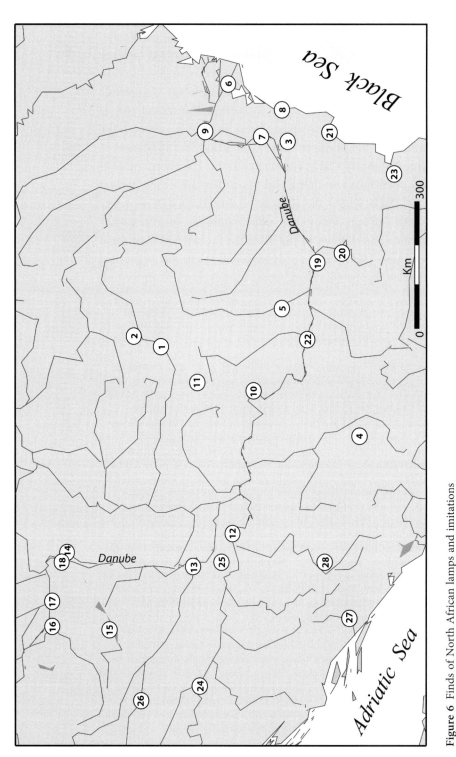

Figure 6 Finds of North African lamps and imitations

1. Apulum; 2. Potaissa; 3. Tropaeum Traiani; 4. Caričin Grad; 5. Romula; 6. Halmyris; 7. Capidava; 8. Tomis; 9. Dinogetia; 10. Drobeta; 11. Sarmizegetusa; 12. Sirmium; 13. Osijek; 14. Budapest; 15. Kekkut; 16. Győr; 17. Oszöny; 18. Obuda; 19. Novae; 20. Nicopolis ad Istrum; 21. Dionysopolis; 22. Kozloduy; 23. Deultum; 24. Siscia; 25. Vinkovci; 26. Poetovio; 27. Mogorjelo; 28. Židova Stena.

Scythia, which might indicate that the western Black Sea region was not the main supplier of such items, but probably the Aegean or the Dalmatian coast.[90] Indeed, we find closer parallels in the central and western Balkans, the most obvious being the African lamp type Atlante X found at Caričin Grad in Dacia Mediterranea, which has an excellent analogue at Koper (Capris, on the Adriatic coast).[91] A lamp type Atlante VIII A1a found at Tomis has a good analogy at Siscia (Sisak) in Croatia, which testifies once again to the importance of sea routes in the diffusion of North African goods.[92] Original lamps imported in towns close to the sea coast were imitated in the Danube region or in the heart of the Balkans where genuine pieces were more difficult to procure. A perfect example is offered by two similar lamps, type Atlante X C2 with palm on the discus, one being a genuine import found at Dionysopolis on the Black Sea coast and the other a local imitation from Kozloduy, in Dacia Ripensis.[93]

It has been argued that North African lamps should be associated with Christian liturgy and the significance of light in Christian symbolism.[94] However, not just North African lamps had a Christian design but also some of those produced in the Balkans, as we have already seen. Since a number of cheaper alternatives were available for liturgical purposes closer to home, imported lamps in *barbaricum* must have possessed a significant social value beyond their practical use or religious symbolism. The African lamps brought to transdanubian Dacia might be related to the long-distance circulation of Christian artifacts, which also included Coptic bronze lamps. A route from Italy or through the Adriatic is very probable, given the high density of finds in the western Balkans, as well as on the

---

[90] African lamps were being imitated on a large scale in Greece throughout the sixth century. Many of the types commonly found in the Danube region have analogies at Delphi, where a late sixth-century cemetery has produced a large quantity of well-preserved imitations of African lamps, for which see P. Petridis, *La céramique protobyzantine de Delphes: une production et son contexte* (Athens, 2010), 85–92.

[91] Caričin Grad: Bjelajac, "La céramique," pl. XX/1. Koper: P. Bitenc and T. Knific, eds., *Od Rimljanov do Slovanov Predmeti* (Ljubljana, 2001), fig. 92.

[92] Tomis: Barnea, *Christian Art*, pl. 105/1. Siscia: Vikić-Belančić, *Antičke svjetiljke*, 42, n. 304 and pl. XVII/7. Both lamps seem to be local imitations. The type originated most probably in Tunisia, for which see A. Ennabli, *Lampes chrétiennes de Tunisie (Musées du Bardo et de Carthage)* (Paris, 1976), pl. XLVII/865 and pl. LI/923. Imports of African Chi-Rho lamps were also reported in Crimea together with imitations, probably following the same route in the Aegean and the Black Sea, for which see Chrzanovski and Zhuravlev, *Lamps from Chersonesus*, 158, n. 96.

[93] For both lamps, see *Kuzmanov*, 42, no. 302 and 303, pl. IV/6.

[94] Diaconescu, "Lămpi romane," 289.

Middle Danube.[95] The lamps could have traveled by sea with larger cargoes bringing *spatheia* from North Africa, and then redistributed on land routes and rivers to regions beyond the frontier. Justinian's reconquest of Dalmatia may have facilitated such access and this seems to be confirmed by the numismatic evidence discussed in Chapter 6.

The western connection was probably interrupted more rapidly than the eastern one, since after ca. 550 African Red Slip Ware became rare even on parts of the Dalmatian coast, a traditional destination for African goods during Late Antiquity.[96] This must have affected the general circulation of imports from the Western Mediterranean, which typically reached the lands north of the Danube through the mediation of intermediary trading ports in the western Balkans.[97] The lamps found in Scythia, on the other hand, were more easily brought via the Black Sea and the Aegean together with Greek imitations, such as the specimen found at Tomis.[98] Lamps imitating North African models are also present north of the Danube, at Drobeta, and further to the north at Sarmizegetusa.[99] To be sure, a route

---

[95] For possible routes of distribution, see Părău, "La diffusione," pl. 136–140. For the role of the Adriatic in the diffusion of western imports, see V. Vidrih Perko, "Seaborne trade routes in the North-East Adriatic and their connections to the hinterland in the Late Antiquity," in *L'Adriatico dalla tarda antichità all'età carolingia*, eds. G. Broglio and P. Delogu (Rome, 2005), 49–77.

[96] J.-P. Sodini, "The transformation of cities in Late Antiquity within the provinces of Macedonia and Epirus," in *Transition*, 330. A possible decline in production in North Africa is testified by the increased presence of eastern imports, such as LR1, for which see J. A. Riley, "The coarse pottery," in *Excavations at Sidi Khrebish, Benghazi (Berenice)*, ed. J. A. Lloyd, vol. II (Tripoli, 1979), 121, fig. 2. In central and southern Greece there seems to be a persistence of African imports as late as the seventh century, for which see recently Petridis, *La céramique*, 126–127. For the decline of African Red Slip Ware in the Adriatic region, see M. Buora, "La ceramica di importazione (sigillata africana e anfore) come indicatore archeologico per il periodo bizantino nell'alto Adriatico," *Quaderni friulani di archeologia* 15 (2005): 163–167.

[97] Gudea and Ghiurco, *Din istoria creștinismului*, 128. Cf. D. Protase, *Autohtonii în Dacia II: Dacia postromană până la slavi* (Cluj-Napoca, 2000), 80, who argues that the territory north of the Danube was isolated from the western world due to the presence of Gepids and later Avars.

[98] Barnea et al., *Cultura bizantină*, 169, no. 331. The image on the discus has been described as a rabbit but in fact is a stag, a common depiction on African lamps type *Atlante* X C2. For a close parallel, see Ennabli, *Lampes chrétiennes*, pl. XX/391. Imitations of this type have been found at Chersonesus, for which see Chrzanovski and Zhuravlev, *Lamps from Chersonesus*, 162–164, nos. 102–103.

[99] Drobeta: Barnea et al., *Cultura bizantină*, 172, no. 353, very similar to a lamp from Athens, for which see *Perlzweig*, no. 2591. An imitation from the Danube region was probably used as a model for the "North African" lamp from Sarmizegetusa: Diaconescu, "Lămpi romane," 268, pl. IV/2a–b. A third Greek lamp was found at Apulum, being a typical product of Athens and Corinth, for which see Diaconescu, "Lămpi romane," 273, pl. VI/4a–c. Greek imitations after African lamps are also common in Bulgaria; see Kostova and Dobreva, "Roman," pl. 121; and in Serbia; see J. C. Rubright, "Lamps from Sirmium in the museum of Sremska Mitrovica," in

from the western Black Sea was not the only means by which such objects could find their way north of the Danube, since they could have been procured directly from the Danubian provinces.

Finally, Palestinian lamps are among the most exotic finds in the Lower Danube region, and highly sought after because of their connection to the Holy Land (Figure 7). Few such lamps have been reported in the Balkans, but it may well be that some are either misattributed or misdated. Alexandru Diaconescu has redated the specimens found in *barbaricum* based on the typology established for lamps found in Syria-Palestine. Thus, two lamps found at Gherla and Ploiești, the latter found in an inhumation grave, belong to the so-called "candlestick" type produced in the Holy Land from the sixth century onward.[100] They must have followed the same communication routes responsible for the import of North African lamps, Egyptian bronze lamps, and Menas flasks. A third lamp, found at Răcari, in the former Roman *castrum*, has a more problematic attribution.[101] Although it has been assigned to the early "Jerash" category, the typological parallels from Palestine are less convincing.[102] A certain degree of skepticism is also warranted by closer parallels with lamps from the Balkans, similar "barge-shaped" lamps having been found in the heartland of the Thracian diocese, but also in Dobrudja and southern Russia.[103] Their dating to the sixth century is not certain as they may well belong to an earlier period.[104] Indeed, some of them might constitute local imitations of Syro-Palestinian Late

---

Sirmium III. Archaeological Investigations in Syrmian Pannonia, eds. V. Popović and E. L. Ochsenschlager (Belgrade, 1973), pl. V/56.

[100] Diaconescu, "Lămpi romane," 279, pl. VII/1a–c and VII/6; for an illustration of this lamp, see below Chapter 4, Figure 18/10.

[101] Ibid., pl. VIII/1a–c.

[102] T. Scholl, "The chronology of Jerash lamps: Umayyad period," *Archeologia* 42 (1991): 65–84. Diaconescu associated the Răcari lamp with Scholl's type IV, subgroup 2 (fig. 7), but the analogy is dubious since the type boasts a handle ending with a zoomorphic head, impossible to verify in the case of the Răcari lamp whose handle is now missing. The pattern on the rim is also different. Finally, the dating of this type to the second half of the seventh century is yet another reason to look for parallels elsewhere, since it is highly unlikely that Umayyad lamps were exported north of the Danube. The lamp from Răcari is in fact much closer to *Kuzmanov* type XXXII; indeed, Kuzmanov recognized the influence of fourth-century Syro-Palestinian models. The concentration of these lamps in central and southeastern Bulgaria suggests a possible center of production in that region.

[103] Karasura: Stoikov, "Kusnoantichni lampi," pl. I/1–2; *Kuzmanov*, n. 291. Iambol: N. Tantcheva-Vassilieva, "Antichni glineni lampi ot Muzeia v Iambol," *IMIB* 5 (1982), pl. III/18. Deultum: Kostova and Dobreva, "Roman," 166, with the bibliography and further analogies in Dobrudja and southern Russia, and pl. 119–20; Stara Zagora: K. Kalchev, "Antichni i kusnoantichni lampi ot Stara Zagora," *IMIB* 5 (1982): 7–22.

[104] For a recent typology, see Kostova and Dobreva, "Roman," 164–166, with a dating spanning the entire Late Antique period.

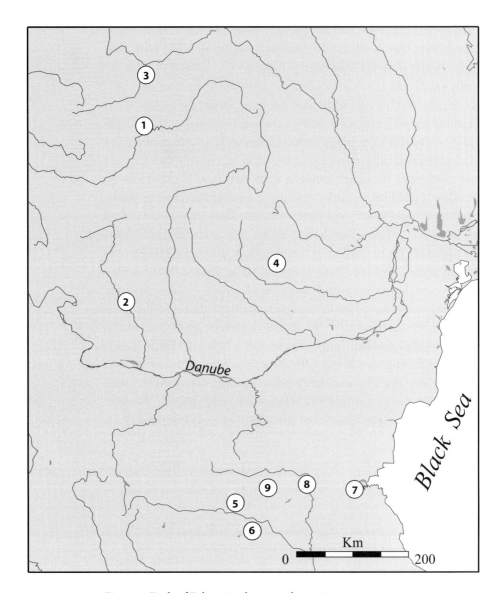

Figure 7 Finds of Palestinian lamps and imitations
1. Potaissa; 2. Răcari; 3. Gherla; 4. Ploieşti; 5. Karasura; 6. Haskovo; 7. Deultum; 8. Iambol; 9. Beroe.

Antique models in the shape of a boat with a tall and curved handle, with some Anatolian influences traceable in the style of the decoration.

2.2.2.3 Handmade Lamps

Not all lamps from *barbaricum* are Byzantine imports. Handmade lamps have been largely neglected although they are an excellent indicator of the decline of Roman life in urban centers of the Early Byzantine provinces and an example of *imitatio* in the case of lamps produced in *barbaricum* (Figure 8). Indeed, handmade lamps have been found on the last phase of occupation at Caričin Grad, where a modified Roman brick was transformed into a makeshift lamp, and at Sacidava on the Danube where a handmade cup was used for that purpose.[105] A third lamp, in the form of a "Getic" cup, was found in a cremation grave from Nalbant in the northern part of Scythia.[106] The decline of urban production toward the end of the sixth century is probably responsible for the appearance of such improvised lamps in the frontier provinces of the Balkans. As for the handmade lamps produced in *barbaricum,* most of them are found in Wallachia east of the river Olt. An important contrast becomes apparent: imported lamps manufactured in various centers of the Empire concentrate in the former province of Dacia, while handmade lamps are most often found in Wallachia. All handmade lamps have been found in sunken-featured buildings in sixth-to-seventh-century contexts, most of which not suggesting a particularly high social status.[107] The lamps from Bratei, Bucharest–Soldat Ghivan, and Cândești have a similar shape and constitute attempts to imitate Early Byzantine lamps. Interestingly, good analogies for these lamps can be found at Dunaújváros (Intercisa) and Kölked-Feketekapu, in *Avaria*, while no such lamps can be found in between, from Bratei to the Middle Danube, the demand for lamps being satisfied through imports from the Empire.[108] Given the rather unprepossessing nature of the buildings in which handmade lamps have been found, their production was justified

---

[105] Caričin Grad: Bjelajac, "La céramique," pl. XXII/8. For the "ruralization" of Caričin Grad in its last occupation phase, see also V. Popović, "La descente des Koutrigours, des Slaves et des Avars vers la Mer Égée: le témoignage de l'archéologie," *Comptes rendus de l'Académie des Inscriptions et Belles-Lettres* 6 (1978): 634. Sacidava: C. Scorpan, "Imitații getice după opaițe greco-romane," *Pontice* 2 (1969): figs. 15–17.

[106] G. Simion, "Necropola feudal-timpurie de la Nalbant (jud. Tulcea)," *Peuce* 2 (1971), pl. V/3.

[107] Cândești: E.-M. Constantinescu, *Memoria pământului dintre Carpați și Dunăre* (Buzău, 1999), fig. 12/4. Bratei: Zaharia, "La station n. 2 de Bratei," fig. 13/12 (building H7). Malu Roșu: B. Filipescu, "Cercetări în stațiunea arheologică Malu Roșu, com. Fierbinți-tîrg, jud. Ialomița," *Cercetări arheologice* 7 (1984): pl. II/2 (building L C79). Bucharest–Soldat Ghivan: Dolinescu-Ferche and Constantiniu, "Un établissement," fig. 16/7a–b (building B5); for an illustration this lamp, see below Chapter 4, Figure 18/12.

[108] Dunaújváros: G. Kálmán, "A kishegyesi régibb középkori temető," *ArchÉrt* 31 (1907): fig. 75c. Kölked-Feketekapu: Z. Hajnal, "Mécsesek a Kölked-Feketekapui avar telepről," *Archaeologiai Értesítő* 128 (2003): 180, fig. 2/1, 6/4, and 9 (buildings 120 and 135); for an illustration of this lamp, see below Chapter 4, Figure 18/11.

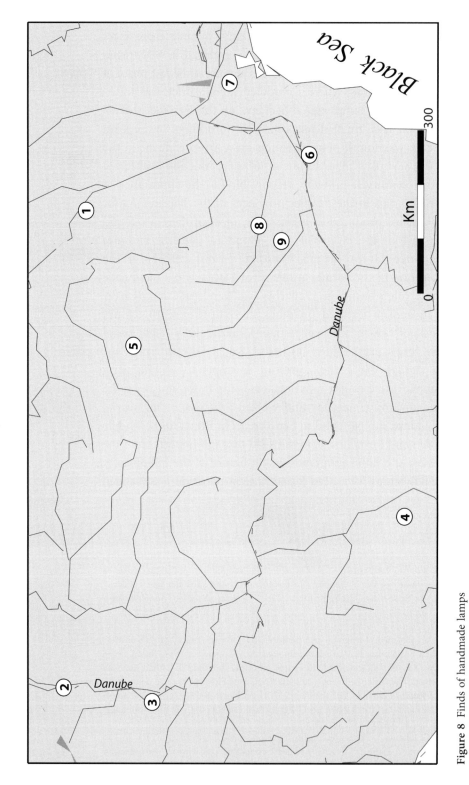

Figure 8 Finds of handmade lamps
1. Cândeşti; 2. Dunaújváros; 3. Kölked-Feketekapu; 4. Caričin Grad; 5. Bratei; 6. Sacidava; 7. Nalbant; 8. Malu Roşu; 9. Bucharest–Soldat Ghivan.

by the need to find a convenient alternative to Early Byzantine lamps. Unfortunately, none of the genuine Byzantine lamps from *barbaricum* has been found in a good stratigraphic context. Their social value is therefore impossible to determine with any certainty, although the practice of imitation and the high availability of lamps on the Lower Danube suggest a lack of motivation rather than the inability to obtain such items.

2.2.3 Molds and Metallurgical Production

If the circulation of amphorae points to a combination of trade and *annona*-related movements, other categories of objects are even more firmly connected to the military environment of the northern Balkans. Metallurgical activity north of the Danube has long captured the attention of scholars trying to assess the cultural influence of the Empire in *barbaricum*.[109] Molds in particular have been considered one of the most fascinating, yet unwieldy types of imports.[110] Indeed, the very notion of import attached to molds is counterintuitive as many of them could have been produced outside the Empire, and the same is true for other metallurgical implements which are often found together in archaeological contexts (Figure 9). It is *imitatio* rather than genuine import, some of the items

---

[109] G. Postică, *Civilizația medievală timpurie din spațiul pruto-nistrean (secolele V–XIII)* (Bucharest, 2007), 155–173; D. G. Teodor, "Ateliers byzantins des VIe–VIIIe siècles au nord du Bas-Danube," *EBPB* 5 (2006): 198–201; Ș. Olteanu, *Societatea carpato-danubiano-pontică în secolele IV–XI. Structuri demo-economice și social-politice* (Bucharest, 1997); D. G. Teodor, *Meșteșugurile la nordul Dunării de Jos în secolele IV–XI* (Iași, 1996); V. Teodorescu, "Centre meșteșugărești din sec. V/VI–VII în București," *București* 9 (1972): 73–99.

[110] B. Ciupercă and A. Măgureanu, "Unele observații asupra problemei tiparelor din secolele V–VII descoperite în spațiul extra-carpatic," *Buletinul Muzeului Județean Teleorman* 1 (2009): 149–157; A. Măgureanu and B. Ciupercă, "The 6th–8th centuries metallurgical activity from Budureasca Valley. The molds," *AMN* 41–42, no. 1 (2004–2005): 291–318; D. G. Teodor, "Tipare din secolele V–XI d. Hr. în regiunile carpato-nistrene," *AM* 28 (2005): 159–174; B. S. Szmoniewski, "Production of Early Medieval ornaments made of non-ferrous metals: dies from archaeological finds in North-East Romania," *AAC* 37 (2002): 111–135; E. Iu. Tavlinceva, "K voprosu o metallicheskom bisere v riazno-okskikh mogil'nikakh (po materialam Shokshinskogo mogil'nika)," in *Nauchnoe nasledie A. P. Smirnova i sovremennye problemy arkheologii Volgo-Kam'ia. Materialy nauchnoi konferencii*, ed. I. V. Belocerkovskaia (Moscow, 2000), 109–115; H. Kóčka-Krenz, "The beginning of metal casting in Polish territories in the Early Middle Ages (the 6th–13th centuries)," in *Trudy V Mezhdunarodnogo Kongressa arkheologov-slavistov, Kiev 18–25 sentiabria 1985 g.*, ed. P. P. Tolochko (Kiev, 1988), 83–89; N. Dănilă, "Tipare de turnat cruci din secolele IV–VI, descoperite pe teritoriul României," *BOR* 101 (1983): 557–561.

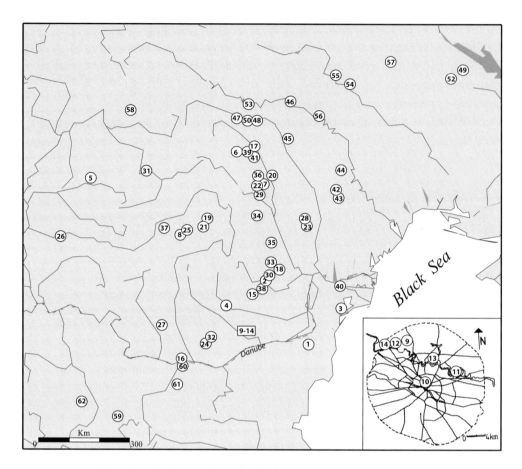

Figure 9 Distribution of metallurgical activity
1. Tropaeum Traiani (Adamclisi); 2. Aldeni; 3. Argamum; 4. Băleni-Români; 5. Biharea; 6. Botoşana; 7. Borşeni; 8. Bratei; 9. Bucharest–Băneasa; 10. Bucharest–Casa Armatei; 11. Bucharest–Soldat Ghivan; 12. Bucharest–Străuleşti; 13. Bucharest–Tei; 14. Bucharest–Dămăroaia; 15. Budureasca; 16. Sucidava; 17. Cucorani; 18. Coroteni; 19. Corund; 20. Costeşti; 21. Cristuru Secuiesc; 22. Davideni; 23. Dodeşti; 24. Dulceanca; 25. Dumbrăveni; 26. Felnac; 27. Gropşani; 28. Gura Idrici; 29. Izvoare; 30. Izvoru Dulce; 31. Lozna; 32. Olteni; 33. Poieniţa; 34. Prăjeşti; 35. Răcoasa; 36. Rădeni; 37. Sânmiclăuş; 38. Sărata Monteoru; 39. Suceava; 40. Tulcea; 41. Udeşti; 42. Dănceni; 43. Hansca; 44. Selişte; 45. Şapte-Bani; 46. Bernashivka; 47. Gorecha; 48. Kodin; 49. Mikhailyvka; 50. Novoselitsia; 51. Parievka; 52. Pastyrs'ke; 53. Rashkiv; 54. Samchincy; 55. Semenki; 56. Skibincy; 57. Teterevka; 58. Volos'ke; 59. Gorna Sekirna; 60. Oescus; 61. Sadovec; 62. Caričin Grad.

produced with those molds being of Byzantine inspiration, mostly small pieces of jewelry and ornaments. The technique itself, pseudo-granulation and lost-wax casting, might have been borrowed from the Empire. Moreover, as we shall soon find out, many of the items were in fact produced for further "exporting" somewhere else in *barbaricum*. The task of the researcher is to go beyond the mere description and attempt to trace the objects produced with the molds in the archaeological record. More often than not, pieces of jewelry resembling the ones carved on a mold are completely unknown in the region where the mold was found, which has important implications for understanding the production and circulation of such items.

The question of production is particularly problematic, although many scholars have argued that Byzantine itinerant craftsmen had a crucial role in metallurgical activity in *barbaricum*. Much has been made of the account of Procopius who suggested that many merchants and craftsmen were fleeing the country because of the abuses which reduced them to poverty. Leaving aside the fact that the *Secret History* – a vitriolic *Kaiserkritik* – should rarely be taken at face value, Procopius does not even refer specifically to the Danube region, but to the East:

> In the cities I mentioned, virtually the entire populace suddenly found themselves beggars. Craftsmen and manual workers, as you can imagine, had to struggle against hunger, and because of this many of them fled, expatriated themselves, and took up with the Persians.[111]

The account was conveniently truncated in an early seminal study in order to emphasize the strong connection between the Byzantine Empire and the Romanized communities in the lands north of the Danube, and later adopted uncritically to suggest that such craftsmen may be the ones responsible for the presence of molds north of the Danube.[112] Such specialists may very well have operated in *barbaricum*, attracted by a larger demand for jewelry of Byzantine inspiration or commissioned to produce certain types of items. The ethnicity of such craftsmen is, however, impossible to determine in the absence of any solid evidence regarding their activity. Furthermore, there are reasons to believe that local production was perhaps more important than the activity of itinerant specialists. The buildings whose material remains included metallurgical implements look no different than the ordinary sunken-featured residences so common in *barbaricum*. The association of molds with crucibles, ladles, scrap metal,

---

[111] Procopius, *Historia Arcana*, 25.25 (trans. Kaldellis): βάναυσοι γὰρ ἄνθρωποι καὶ χειρώνακτες λιμῷ παλαίειν, ὡς τὸ εἰκός, ἠναγκάζοντο, πολλοί τε ἀπ' αὐτοῦ τὴν πολιτείαν μεταβαλλόμενοι φεύγοντες ᾤχοντο ἐς τὰ Περσῶν ἤθη.
[112] Teodorescu, "Centre meșteșugărești," 92, n. 50; Teodor, "Ateliers byzantins," 190; Ciupercă and Măgureanu, "Unele observații," 152.

Settlement	Molds	Crucibles	Ladles	Scrap metal	Tools	Settlement	Molds	Crucibles	Ladles	Scrap metal	Tools
Adamclisi (RO)	x					Davideni (RO)	x	x	x	x	
Aldeni (RO)	x					Dodești (RO)	x			x	
Argamum (RO)	x					Dulceanca (RO)	x	x	x	x	
Băleni-Români (RO)	x	x				Dumbrăveni (RO)	x				
Biharea (RO)		x				Felnac (RO)	x				
Botoșana (RO)	x	x	x			Gropșani (RO)		x	x	x	
Borșeni (RO)		x				Gura Idrici (RO)	x				
Bratei (RO)		x	x			Izvoare (RO)			x		
Bucharest-Băneasa (RO)		x				Izvorul Dulce (RO)	x				
Bucharest- Casa Armatei (RO)		x				Lozna (RO)	x				
Bucharest-Soldat Ghivan (RO)	x		x		x	Olteni (RO)	x				
Bucharest-Străulești (RO)	x					Poienița (RO)	x				
Bucharest-Tei (RO)	x		x			Prăjești (RO)	x				
Bucharest-Dămăroaia (RO)	x		x			Răcoasa (RO)	x				
Budureasca (RO)	x	x	x	x	x	Rădeni (RO)	x				
Celei-Sucidava (RO)	x					Sânmiclăuș (RO)	x				
Cucorani (RO)		x				Sărata Monteoru (RO)		x			
Coroteni (RO)	x					Suceava (RO)		x			
Corund (RO)	x					Tulcea (RO)					
Costești (RO)	x					Udești (RO)			x		
Cristuru Secuiesc (RO)	x					Kuzhendeevsky (RU)	x				
Dănceni (MD)	x					Bancerovsko (RU)		x	x		
Hansa (MD)		x	x			Osechen (RU)	x				
Seliște (MD)	x		x			Podol (RU)			x		
Șapte-Bani (MD)		x	x			Rozhdestveno (RU)	x				
Bernashivka (UKR)	x		x			Shokshino (RU)	x		x		
Gorecha (UKR)		x				Somovsko (RU)	x		x		
Khyttsi (UKR)		x				Stan (RU)	x	x	x		
Kodyn (UKR)		x				Ufa (RU)			x		
Mikhailyvka (UKR)			x			Usogorsk (RU)		x	x		
Novoselitsia (UKR)	x					Uzmen' (RU)		x	x		
Parievka (UKR)	x	x				Gorna Sekirna (BG)	x				
Pastyrs'ke (UKR)	x					Ghigen (BG)	x				
Rashkiv (UKR)		x	x			Sadovec (BG)	x			x	
Samchyntsi (UKR)	x					Caričin Grad (SR)	x				
Semenki (UKR)	x		x			Hacki (PL)	x				
Skybyntsi (UKR)	x	x				Nowa Huta (PL)	x				
Teterevka (UKR)	x					Szeligi (PL)	x				
Volos'ke (UKR)			x			Żukovice (PL)	x				
Zimne (UKR)	x		x	x		Kuzebaevo (RU)	x	x	x	x	x

Figure 10 Distribution of metallurgical implements from *barbaricum*

and specific tools such as tweezers and carvers point to the existence of ad hoc local activity (Figure 10). Indeed, there is less evidence of centralized production of jewelry in specialized workshops. Rather, it seems to be a household activity or at least not restricted to a single workshop in the community, judging by the fact that in many settlements metallurgical implements and molds have been found in several residences.[113]

The production and use of molds is unlikely to have been the exclusive province of a Romanized population considering the diffusion of such artifacts on a vast geographic area from the Volga river to Central Europe. To be sure, there is a larger concentration of molds in the territories adjacent to the frontier, especially those used to produce Christian crosses, but this does not seem to follow practices from the Danubian provinces, or at least not as closely as has been suggested. A considerably smaller number of molds have been found in the Balkans, which begs the question whether metallurgical production using molds was essentially a "barbarian" practice. Many types of Byzantine jewelry and ornaments followed this technique, while production itself is well attested in the Balkans in towns like Sadovets, Caričin Grad, and Adamclisi.[114] Given the superior concentration of molds in *barbaricum*, it is possible that non-Romans were in fact coordinating this activity in the Balkan provinces and producing jewelry and dress accessories fashionable in the military environment of the frontier.

The few molds found in the Balkans throw some light on the connection between metallurgical activity on the frontier and what was transmitted beyond, in *barbaricum*. Fashions seem to have developed somewhat independently, as only a few of the items carved on molds from the Empire can be found on molds from *barbaricum*. The triangle-shaped pendant from the mold found in the late sixth-century occupation level at Adamclisi in Scythia has good parallels at Budureasca, Bernashivka, and as far north as

---

[113] Botoşana: D. G. Teodor, *Civilizația romanică la est de Carpați în secolele V–VII (așezarea de la Botoșana-Suceava)* (Bucharest, 1984), 98, fig. 19/6; 99, fig. 20/3 and fig. 20/1; 100, fig. 21/1 a–c. Davideni: I. Mitrea, *Comunități sătești la est de Carpați în epoca migrațiilor. Așezarea de la Davideni din secolele V–VII* (Piatra Neamț, 2001), 325, figs. 65/1 and 65/5. Seliște: I. A. Rafalovich, "Issledovaniia ranneslavianskikh poselenii v Moldavii," in *Arkheologicheskie issledovaniia v Moldavii v 1970–1971 gg.*, ed. G. F. Chebotarenko (Kishinew, 1973), 140, figs. 3/1 and 3/2; I. A. Rafalovich and V. L. Lapushnian, "Raboty Reutskoi arkheologicheskoi ekspeditsii," in *Arkheologicheskie issledovaniia v Moldavii v 1972 g.* (Kishinew, 1973), 133, fig. 10/4. Budureasca: Măgureanu and Ciupercă, "The 6th–8th centuries," 291–318. Zimne: V. V. Aulikh, *Zimnyvs'ke gorodishche – slov'ians'ka pam'iatka VI–VII n.e. v zakhydnyi Voliny* (Kiev, 1972), pl. XIV/1–3, XIV/5, and fig. XV/1–7.

[114] Sadovets: Uenze, *Die spätantiken Befestigungen*, fig. 9/6. Caričin Grad: B. Bavant, "Les petits objects," in *Caričin Grad,* eds. Bavant et al., 220–224. Adamclisi: Barnea, ed., *Tropaeum Traiani*, 218, fig. 169/10/14. See also B. Dumanov, "The Late Antique workshops of jewelry south of the Lower Danube. Direct and indirect evidence of local production," in *The Lower Danube Roman Limes (1st–6th c. AD)*, eds. L. Vagalinski, N. Sharankov, and S. Torbatov (Sofia, 2012), 405–428.

Loosi in Estonia.[115] The belt buckles and belt ornaments on the molds from Caričin Grad resemble to some degree artifacts found in burial assemblages from Kerch and Luchistoe (Crimea), although this fashion also gained some popularity in the core regions of the Avar Khaganate.[116] The pyramidal earring pendants from a mold found near Oescus have good analogies in Early Avar assemblages (earrings of the Deszk type), but also in the steppe lands north of the Black Sea.[117] Similar connections with *Avaria* can be traced on the mold found accidentally at Gorna Sekirna in Illyricum, which boasts a class of earrings imitating the shape of twisted wires, having good analogies at Kölked-Feketekapu.[118] Moving to the Thracian diocese, the granulated column pendants on a mold from Argamum represents a very common style of ornamentation visible on molds across *barbaricum*. Pseudo-granulation, a typically Byzantine technique, can be found on very similar molds from Budureasca, Cristuru Secuiesc, Bucharest–Străulești, Bernashivka, and in simplified forms on molds from Russia, dated from the sixth to the eleventh century.[119] Finally, the mold for Maltese crosses from Sadovets constitutes a special case as both molds and actual crosses are found north of the Danube.[120] With two exceptions,

---

[115] Budureasca: Măgureanu and Ciupercă, "The 6th–8th centuries," 315, fig. 7. Bernashivka: I. S. Vynokur, *Slov'ians'kyi iuveliry Podnistrov'ia. Za materialamy doslidzhen' Bernashivs'kogo kompleksu seredyny I tys. n. e.* (Kam'ianets' Podil's'kyy, 1997), fig. 23. Loosi: M. Schmiedehelm and S. Laul, "Asustusest ja etnilisest oludest Kagu-Eestis I aastatuhande," in *Studia archaeologica in memoriam Harri Moora*, eds. M. Schmiedehelm, L. Jaanits, and J. Selirand (Tallinn, 1970), 160 and fig. 4; pl. IV.

[116] Bavant, "Les petits objects," 220–224; B. Bavant, "Un moule d'orfèvre protobyzantin au British Museum," in *Mélanges Jean-Pierre Sodini* (Paris, 2005), 643, fig. 6.

[117] M. Daskalov and D. I. Dimitrov, "Za prozvodostvoto na nakiti prez VI–VII v. v bulgarskite zemi," *Arkheologiia* 42 (2001): 69, fig. 1; C. Bàllint, "Probleme der archäologischen Forschung zur awarischen Landnahme," in *Ausgewählte Probleme europäischer Landnahmen des Früh- und Hochmittelalters*, eds. M. Müller-Wille and R. Scheider (Sigmaringen, 1993), 237–238; Garam, *Funde*, pl. 10.

[118] M. Daskalov, "Kalapi za metalni nakiti i kolanni ukrasi (VI-VII v.) ot Iuzhna Bulgariia," *Arkheologiia* 45 (2004): 91, fig. 1; A. Kiss, *Das awarenzeitlich-gepidische Gräberfeld von Kölked-Feketekapu A.* (Innsbruck, 1996), 268, fig. 45/187.

[119] Budureasca: Măgureanu and Ciupercă, "The 6th–8th centuries," 318, fig. 10/9–10. Cristuru: Z. Székely, "Aşezări din secolele VII–VIII în bazinul superior al Tîrnavei Mari," *SCIVA* 39, no. 2 (1988): 182 and 186; fig. 19/6. Bucharest–Străulești: Teodorescu, "Centre meșteșugărești," 83 fig. 5/4. Bernashivka: Vynokur, *Slov'ians'kyi iuveliry*, figs. 22, 27, 36, 37, 38, 40. Russia: Tavlinceva, "K voprosu o metallicheskom," 112, fig. 3. For an illustration of molds showcasing this technique, see below Chapter 4, Figure 19/1–2; 6.

[120] Olteni: C. Preda, "Tipar pentru bijuterii din secolul al VI-lea e.n., descoperit la Olteni (r. Videle, reg. București), *SCIV* 18, no. 3 (1967): 513–515; Sucidava and Sânmicláuș: Dănilă, "Tipare de turnat," 559, no. 2 and 560, no. 6. Izvoru Dulce: I. Miclea and R. Florescu, *Daco-romanii*, vol. II (Bucharest, 1980), 209 and pl. 760. Davideni: D. G. Teodor, *Creștinismul la est de Carpați de la origini și pînă în secolul al XVI-lea* (Iași, 1991), 162, fig. 8/3. Botoșana: Teodor,

2.2 Byzantine Imports and Imitations in Barbaricum

all molds from this category are found outside the limits of Trajanic Dacia. This pattern stands in sharp contrast with the distribution of Byzantine lamps with Christian motifs, very common in Dacia but rare south and east of the Carpathians. Religious identity was clearly expressed in several different ways in the lands north of the Danube.

The molds, the pieces of jewelry, as well as the most typical metallurgical implements are not restricted to the frontier region but seem to have a lot in common with similar artifacts having an impressive geographic reach. The mold from Bucharest–Străulești designed to produce small granulations has clear analogies not only at Budureasca and Davideni, but also at Bernashivka in Ukraine and at Supruty and Kuzhendeevsky in Russia, where they have been found in graves applied on clothing and not on pieces of jewelry.[121] The dating of such items is not always helpful; they are also found in later medieval contexts indicating the longevity of such ornaments, which should not be surprising given their basic shape. For instance, the interesting file carved on a mold from Budureasca 5 has very good parallels both in *Avaria* at Vác-Kavicsbánya and at Zimne in Ukraine, while tweezers similar to the one from Bucharest–Soldat Ghivan have been found at Bancerovoe (Belarus) and Usugorsk (Russia).[122] Equally, crucibles and ladles with very similar shapes can be found in most Early Medieval metallurgical complexes in Central and Eastern Europe, from the Czech Republic to the Baltic and the Upper Volga region (Figure 10).

Perhaps the most interesting conclusion resulting from the geographical distribution of metallurgical implements is the fact that many of the items produced with molds have clear analogies in the Avar world. Several molds from Budureasca as well as the mold from Vadu Săpat were used to produce punched appliqués, pendants, belt ornaments, and earring

---

Civilizația romanică, 99–100, figs. 20/1 and 21/1 a–c; for an illustration of this mold, see below Chapter 4, Figure 19/4. Bucharest–Străulești: Teodorescu, "Centre meșteșugărești," 81, fig. 3/6. Hansca: I. Hâncu, "Semnificația unor vestigii de cult la Hansca-Ialoveni, *Analele Științifice ale Universității de Stat din Moldova-seria științe socio-umane* (1998): 29–31, fig. 1.

[121] For Bucharest–Străulești, Budureasca, and Davideni, see above n. 119–120. Supruty and Kuzhendeevky: Tavlinceva, "K voprosu," 112, fig. 3/1–3.

[122] Budureasca: Măgureanu and Ciupercă, "The 6th–8th centuries," 316, fig. 8. Vác-Kavicsbánya: S. Tettamanti, *Das awarenzeitliche Gräberfeld in Vác-Kavicsbánya* (Budapest, 2000). Zimne: Aulikh, *Zimnyvs'ke gorodishche*, 74 and pl. XV/1. Bucharest–Soldat Ghivan: Dolinescu-Ferche and Constantiniu, "Un établissement," 321 and fig. 18/13. Bancerovsko: A. G. Mitrofanov, "Bancerovskoe gorodishche," *Belorusskie drevnosti* (1967): 255. Usugorsk: A. M. Murygyn, "Poselenie Usugorsk III na srednei Mezeni," *Materialy po arkheologii Evropeiskogo Severo-Vostoka* 8 (1980): 81.

components, identifiable in the archaeological repertoire of the Early and Middle Avar milieu.[123] In addition, some of the molds found east of the Carpathians have recently been redated based on analogies with artifacts belonging to the Middle Avar period.[124] What is then the explanation for the use of molds designed to produce objects of Avar inspiration but Byzantine technique? The concentration of molds in *barbaricum* and the frontier region coincides with the presence of troops and the development of a highly militarized society. The growing connection with the Avar Khaganate reflected in the production of jewelry is a good indicator of the declining influence of Byzantine culture and its use in the service of the Avar aristocracy, especially in the seventh century when the Danube frontier was abandoned. The northern *barbaricum* developed into a contested periphery in the second half of the sixth century with the Avars gradually pulling the region away from the Byzantine orbit. Local communities responded in various ways, often betraying a state of cultural confusion: deliberately avoiding Avar fashions, emulating the social values of the Avar aristocracy, or simply producing such objects for the Avar warrior class whose influence was increasingly felt throughout the region.

2.2.4 Brooches

2.2.4.1 Fibulae with Bent Stem

Among the various imports of Byzantine origin brought to the lands north of the Danube during the long sixth century, fibulae (brooches) are by far the most diverse group from a typological perspective. The fibula with bent stem and its derivation, the cast fibula with bent stem, have a long reputation of resisting any attempt to create a coherent and universally accepted classification based on style, size, and chronology. Although the sixth-century fibula follows the model of a fourth-century type produced by the Sântana de Mureș-Chernyakhov culture, it is larger and has a U-shaped stem, which along with other stylistic details safely dates it to the sixth century.[125] In addition, unlike its fourth-century precedent, the sixth-century fibula with bent stem is no longer a creation of the lands north of the Danube, but a typical product of the frontier fortresses acquired in

---

[123] Măgureanu and Ciupercă, "The 6th–8th Centuries," 297–299.
[124] Szmoniewski, "Production," 122–127 (molds from Costești, Cucuteni, Răcoasa, and Rădeni).
[125] Uenze, *Die Spätantiken Befestigungen*, 146–154; I. O. Gavritukhin, "Fibula iz Luki-Kavechinskoi v kontekste slaviano-vizantiiskih sviazei," in *Słowianie i ich sąsiedzi we wczesnym średniowieczu*, ed. M. Dulinicz (Lublin, 2003), 201.

barbaricum as a Roman import. Consequently, the overwhelming difference in the number of finds from the Balkans compared to the regions outside the Empire's borders comes as no surprise (Figure 11).

The chronology of the fibula with bent stem is particularly important for understanding the historical circumstances which made these brooches fashionable in *barbaricum*. Fortunately, there are sufficient datable finds to permit a tentative chronological attribution of the main categories of fibulae with bent stem.[126] Syna Uenze has advanced a date in the first half of the sixth century for the fibula with bent stem, which was replaced in the second half of the century by its cast version.[127] However, evidence from various regions of the Balkans, the Crimea, and also from *barbaricum* clearly suggests a continuous use of fibulae with bent stem throughout the sixth century and perhaps even more intensely in the second half of that century. There is only one coin-dated fibula known so far, at Terechovo in Russia, at a great distance from the Danubian frontier where a quarter-*follis* of Justinian was associated with a cast fibula in a warrior burial.[128] In two other two cases, Nea Anchialos (Macedonia) and Histria (Scythia), fibulae have been found in proximity of coins struck for Justin II (565–578).[129] In a third case, a fibula with bent stem was found near a house in the Sadovets-Golemannovo kale fort, an area which also produced coin finds, the latest of which are issues of Justin II.[130] Unfortunately, no stratigraphical correlation can be established between the fibulae and the

---

[126] F. Curta and A. Gandila, "Sixth-century fibulae with bent stem," *Peuce* 11 (2013): 173, fig. 29.

[127] Uenze, *Die Spätantiken Befestigungen*, 149–151. Several other finds confirm this dating. A fibula found in grave 155 in Suuk Su (Crimea) was associated with two bow fibulae of Zaseckaia's class IV62 firmly dated to the first half of the sixth century, for which see N. I. Repnikov, "Nekotorye mogil'niki oblasti Krymskikh gotov," *Zapiski Odesskogo obshchestva istorii i drevnostei* 27 (1907): 117–118; I. P. Zaseckaia, "Datirovka i proiskhoidenie palchatikh fibul bosporskogo nekropolia rannesrednevekovogo perioda," *MAIET* 6 (1997): 450. In the Balkans, a fibula from grave 100 in Stari Kostolac was associated with a shield-on-tongue buckle, which also suggests a dating within the first half of the sixth century, for which see Ivanišević et al., *Les nécropoles*, 160. For the dating of shield-on-tongue buckles, see J. Cseh et al., *Gepidische Gräberfelder im Theissgebiet II* (Budapest, 2005), 154.

[128] I. Akhmedov, "Rannevizantiiskie nakhodki na R. Oke v central'noi Rossii (predvaritel'nye soobshchenie)," in *Od Bachórza do Światowida ze Zbrucza. Tworzenie się słowiańskiej Europy w ujęciu źródłoznawczym. Księga jubileuszowa Profesora Michała Parczewskiego*, eds. B. Chudzińska, M. Wojenka, and M. Wołoszyn (Cracow, 2016), 172.

[129] Nea Anchialos: Lazaridis, "Nea Anchialos," 326–334; pl. 394β. For a discussion of the coin finds, see Curta and Gandila, "Sixth-century fibulae," 113, n. 48. Histria: E. Condurachi et al., "Șantierul arheologic," *MCA* 4 (1957): 16–21. For the coins, see C. Preda and H. Nubar, *Histria III. Descoperirile monetare de la Histria 1914–1970* (Bucharest, 1973), 209–216.

[130] A hoard of gold coins was also found in that house, with the later coins struck for Emperor Maurice; see Uenze, *Die Spätantiken Befestigungen*, 116, 118–119, 302, 332–333, 403, and 477–478.

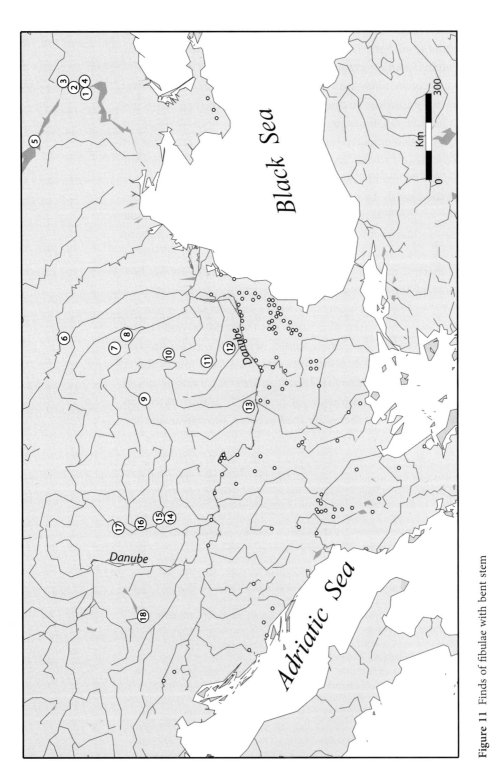

Figure 11 Finds of fibulae with bent stem
1. Voloske; 2. Zvonets'ke; 3. Igren'; 4. Kizlevo; 5. Hradyz'ke; 6. Kavetchina; 7. Davideni; 8. Moldoveni; 9. Moreşti; 10. Poian; 11. Târgşor; 12. Bucharest; 13. Sucidava; 14. Berekhát; 15. Kiszombor; 16. Szolnok; 17. Keszthely.

coins to secure the dating. In other contexts, the later dating is indicated by the association of fibulae with artifacts for which we have better chronological information. Such an example is the assemblage from grave 112 in Stari Kostolac which includes the remains of a wooden bucket with iron handle and hoops, a practice unknown before the settlement of the Avars in Pannonia (ca. 570).[131] Finally, at Bucharest–Militari a fibula with bent stem was found inside a sunken-featured building in association with fragments of handmade pottery typical for the second half of the sixth or the early seventh century.[132]

Only ca. 10 percent of the total number of finds are from outside the Empire, despite the otherwise impressive geographic distribution of fibulae with bent stem from Lake Balaton (Hungary) to the Oka River (Russia). Furthermore, out of 12 classes identified in a recent classification, only four are present in *barbaricum*.[133] Whether or not the preference for certain classes reflects fashions outside the Empire is a matter of speculation, but a comparative analysis between finds from *barbaricum* and the Balkans can shed some light on possible routes of distribution and areas of contact between the two worlds. The largest category of finds belongs to the group of fibulae with the bow wider than the stem and zigzag ornament which is one of the most common types in the Balkans as well. The closest parallels can be found in the provinces of Moesia II and Scythia, in the northeastern Balkans.[134] In addition, the more distant finds from the Dnieper region have clear analogies in the same frontier provinces.[135] As we move closer

---

[131] Ivanišević et al., *Les nécropoles*, 162.

[132] V. Zirra and G. Cazimir, "Unele rezultate ale săpăturilor arheologice de pe Cîmpul lui Boja din cartierul Militari," *CAB* 1 (1963): 60 and 63; M. Sgîbea, "Fibule din sec. III și VI e.n. descoperite în săpăturile arheologice de la Militari," *CAB* 1 (1963): 373 and 378–380; 379 pl. II/1; Teodorescu, "Centre meșteșugărești," 93 and 78, fig. 2/3.

[133] For a recent typology, see Curta and Gandila, "Sixth-century fibulae," 101–176.

[134] The fibula from Davideni has a close correspondent at Pet Mogilii in Moesia II; see Mitrea, *Comunități sătești*, 138–139; 329, fig. 68/1; A. Kharalambieva and G. Atanasov, "Novopostupili fibuli ot III–VII v. v Shumenskiia muzei," *INMV* 28 (1992): 100, pl. III/5.

[135] The specimen from Zvonets'ke (below, Chapter 4, Figure 20/1) has a close parallel at Zdravkovec in Moesia II, for which see A. V. Bodianskii, "Arkheologicheskie nakhodki v Dneprovskom nadporozh'e," *SA* (1960), no. 1: 273–275, with fig. 1/7. K. Koicheva and A. Kharalambieva, "Fibuli ot Istoricheskiia muzei v Gabrovo (III–VII vek)," *Godishnik na muzeite ot Severna Bulgariia* 19 (1993): 70; pl. VII/9. The fibula from Igren', has a common decoration found on several specimens from Scythia and Moesia II, but also from Bucharest; Igren': O. M. Prykhodniuk, *Pen'kovskaia kul'tura. Kul'turno-khronologicheskii aspekt issledovaniia* (Voronezh, 1998), 140, fig. 71/2. Adamclisi: Barnea, ed., *Tropaeum Traiani*, 223, fig. 174/10.3. General Kantardzhievo: A. Kharalambieva, "Dva tipa kusnoantichni fibuli vuv Varnenskiia muzei," *INMV* 25 (1989), 34 and 37; pl. III/2. Golesh: G. Atanasov, "Martyrium et ἁγιασμον dans le castel bas-byzantin près du village de Golech, région de Silistra (communication

to the Danube border, the parallels extend west to Dacia Ripensis and Dacia Mediterranea. Bucharest seems to have been at a crossroads in this respect, as a fibula found in a neighboring settlement has good analogies at Stari Kostolac, Aquis, and Korbovo in the Iron Gates region, and also at Sucidava, on the left bank of the Danube.[136] A number of specimens of this class have been found at Pernik in western Bulgaria, which suggests that this particular version was mainly produced in the diocese of Dacia.[137]

The second largest group of finds from *barbaricum* is represented by fibulae with bows and stems of similar width, some of which have no analogies in the Empire.[138] Two fibulae found in Moldavia have loose parallels in the Balkans, the specimen from Davideni being a basic one with no decoration, very common in Moesia II, while the fibula from Moldoveni finds its closest analogue at Pernik.[139] The fibula from Davideni was found in a sunken-featured building together with amphora fragments and a metallurgical ladle, suggesting that the owner had close ties to the Byzantine world. The third class boasts a trapeze-shaped stem as its most distinctive feature and is typically found in the Dnieper region.[140] A fibula

---

préliminaire)," in *Von der Scythia zur Dobrudža*, eds. Kh. Kholiolchev, R. Pillinger, and R. Hahrreiter (Vienna, 1997), 127–129; 138, fig. 5/4. Bucharest: Sgîbea, "Fibule din sec. III," 378–380, with pl. II.

[136] Bucharest–Militari: Zirra and Cazimir, "Unele rezultate," 56–63; 69, fig. 17/3. Stari Kostolac: Ivanišević et al., *Les nécropoles*, 160–161, with pl. 10/T100.2. Aquis: Korbovo: Janković, *Podunavski*, 215; 126, fig. 70. Sucidava: D. Tudor, "Sucidava III," 196–197, with fig. 41/14.

[137] Liubenova, "Selishteto ot rimskata," 168–171, with fig. 110/7. Interestingly, the specimen found in a female grave at Szolnok on the Middle Danube finds no parallels in the Iron Gates region, being somewhat similar to a specimen from Venchan in Moesia II, for which see I. Bóna and M. Nagy, *Gepidische Gräberfelder am Theissgebiet I* (Budapest, 2002), 220; 376, pl. 102.8; Kharalambieva, "Dva tipa," 33–39, with pl. III/6.

[138] The most interesting are the specimens from Hradyz'ke (below, Chapter 4, Figure 20/2) on the Middle Dnieper and Keszthely in Hungary, for which see L. M. Rutkivs'ka, "Arkheologicheskie pamiatniki IV–VI vv. v raione Kremenchugskogo moria (Ukraina)," *Slovenská Archeológia* 27 (1979), no. 2: 358; 341, fig. 22/9; R. Müller, "Sági Károly temetőfeltárása a Keszthely-fenékpusztai erőd déli fala előtt," *Zalai Múzeum* 9 (1999): 158 and 173, fig. 4/23.1. Kramolin: Koicheva and Kharalambieva, "Fibuli ot istoricheskiia," 70; pl. VI/4. Suuk Su: Repnikov, "Nekotorye mogil'niki," 116–117; 146, fig. 111.

[139] Davideni: Mitrea, *Comunități sătești*, 121–122; 326, fig. 66/6. Moldoveni: I. Mitrea, "Cîteva fibule romano-bizantine descoperite în Moldova," *SCIV* 24, no. 4 (1973): 663–665, with fig. 1/1. Pernik: Liubenova, "Selishteto ot rimskata," 168–171, with fig. 110/5.

[140] Volos'ke: Prykhodniuk, *Pen'kovskaia kul'tura*, 156; 142, fig. 74/4. Hradyz'ke: Rutkivs'ka, "Arkheologicheskie pamiatniki," 358; 341, fig. 22/9. Parallels in NE Bulgaria, for which see A. Kharalambieva, "Fibulite ot I–VII v. v muzeia na Dulgopol," *INMV* 32–33 (1996–1997): 113; 128 pl. XII/107. General Kantardzhievo: Kharalambieva, "Dva tipa kusnoantichni," 34; 37, pl. II/4. Poian: Z. Székely, "Așezări din secolele VI–XI p. Ch. în bazinul Oltului superior," *SCIVA* 43, no. 2 (1992): 263; 269, fig. 17; for an illustration of this fibula, see below Chapter 4, Figure 20/3.

of this type was found at Poian in Transylvania, somewhat resembling the shape of a specimen from the L'viv region in Ukraine as well as one from Gabrovo, south of the Danube.[141] The fibula from Poian is also important for establishing the chronology of this variant, as it was found in a house together with handmade pottery and fragments of clay pans dated to the second half of the sixth century.[142] Finally, the last category of fibulae displays a triangular bow section. Only one such find has been recorded so far, at Kavetchina on the Dniester and despite its larger size it resembles the style noticed on several other pieces known from Illyricum.[143]

The prolonged production and circulation of such brooches beyond the first half of the sixth century have important implications for their presence in *barbaricum* at a time when the northern Balkans became a major theater of military operations. Justinian's massive program of reconstruction in the northern Balkans as well as his active diplomatic activity intensified the production and circulation of military brooches. Although the fibulae with bent stem may have been fashionable in the Balkans as early as the first decades of the sixth century, the growing militarization of the frontier provinces in the later sixth century and the connection between fibulae with bent stem and frontier fortresses offers the necessary explanation for their popularity. Well-dated finds from the lands north of the Danube suggest that fibulae with bent stem continued to be brought to *barbaricum* in the second half of the century by "barbarians" of different ethnic extraction who served in the Roman army and chose to display this hybrid identity after returning to their homeland. Indeed, their social value was sufficiently significant to justify the local production of imitations as a cheaper alternative to genuine Byzantine brooches.

2.2.4.2 Cast Fibulae with Bent Stem

The cast fibula with bent stem is known in the literature as "Roman-Byzantine," "Danubian–Byzantine," or "cast fibula with fake spiral" (*gegossene Fibel mit Scheinumwicklung*), being a typical product of the military forts on the Danube. Establishing a firm typology and identifying production centers have been the main objectives of archaeologists working with

---

[141] Koicheva and Kharalambieva, "Fibuli," 69, fig. II/4.
[142] Curta, *The Making of the Slavs*, 296.
[143] L. V. Vakulenko and O. M. Prykhodniuk, *Slavianskie poseleniia I tys. n.e. u s. Sokol na Srednem Dnestre* (Kiev, 1984), 82 and 57, fig. 32/9; for an illustration of this fibula, see below Chapter 4, Figure 20/4; Curta and Gandila, "Sixth-century fibulae," 126.

this class of brooches. Syna Uenze was the first to notice the heavy concentration of finds in the area of the Iron Gates of the Danube.[144] The existence of an important production center in this area was confirmed by the publication of the casts found in the "Theodora Tower" of the Late Roman fort in Drobeta, which Adrian Bejan identified as an additional workshop on the left bank of the Danube.[145] The functioning of a workshop north of the river might explain the popularity gained by this type of fibula in *barbaricum*.[146] However, a growing body of finds from the last decades seems to contradict the earlier hypothesis that the cast fibula with bent stem originated only in the borderlands between Moesia I and Dacia Ripensis. Two specimens with unfiled edges from the region of Shumen (Moesia II) led Anna Kharalambieva to the justified conclusion that such fibulae were in fact produced in several different centers in the Balkans.[147] Additional finds from central Bulgaria as well as a mold found at Caričin Grad give additional weight to Kharalambieva's argument.[148] Due to the lack of standardization in the production of this type of fibula there is no consensus regarding the precise criteria for establishing a reliable typology, and in fact none is completely satisfactory.[149] As far chronology is concerned, most datable assemblages indicate a date within the second half of the sixth century, which seems to have been the golden age of such fibulae (Figure 12).

---

[144] S. Uenze, "Gegossene Fibeln mit Scheinumwicklung des Bügels in den östlichen Balkanprovinzen," in *Studien zur vor- und frühgeschichtlichen Archäologie: Festschrift für Joachim Werner zum 65. Geburtstag*, eds. G. Kossack and G. Ulbert (Munich, 1974), 483–494.

[145] A. Bejan, "Un atelier metalurgic de la Drobeta-Turnu Severin," *AMN* 13 (1976): 257–268.

[146] Roman captives taken from the Balkans could also contribute to spreading this fashion, for which see Đ. Janković, "Pozdneantičnie fibuli VI–VII vekov i slaviane," in *Rapports du IIIe Congres International d'archéologie slave, Bratislava 7–14 Septembre 1975*, vol. I (Bratislava, 1980), 171.

[147] A. Kharalambieva, "Production of dress ornaments in the fortresses and small settlements in North Bulgaria during the period from the 5th till the 7th century AD," in *The Roman and Late Roman City. The International Conference (Veliko Turnovo 26–30 July 2000)*, eds. L. Ruseva-Slokoska, R. T. Ivanov, and V. Dinchev (Sofia, 2002), 393–397.

[148] A. Măgureanu, "Fibulele turnate romano-bizantine," *MCA* 4 (2008): 141.

[149] For an ample critique, see recently, F. Curta and A. Gandila, "Too much typology, too little history: a critical approach to the classification and interpretation of cast fibulae with bent stem," *ArchBulg* 15, no. 3 (2011): 51–81. Classifications have been based on several criteria. For a typology based on the section of the bow or the length of the fibula, see Janković, "Pozdneantičnie fibuli," 173; Kharalambieva, "Dva tipa," 29–40; I. O. Gavritukhin, "Fibuly vizantiiskogo kruga v Vostochnoi Evrope (litye dunaisko-illiriiskie)," *MAIET* 9 (2002): 232–233; D. G. Teodor, "Considerații privind fibulele romano-bizantine din secolele V–VII in spațiul carpato-danubiano-pontic," *AM* 12 (1988): 197–223. A more recent typology favored a classification based entirely on decoration, for which see Măgureanu, "Fibulele turnate," 100–111.

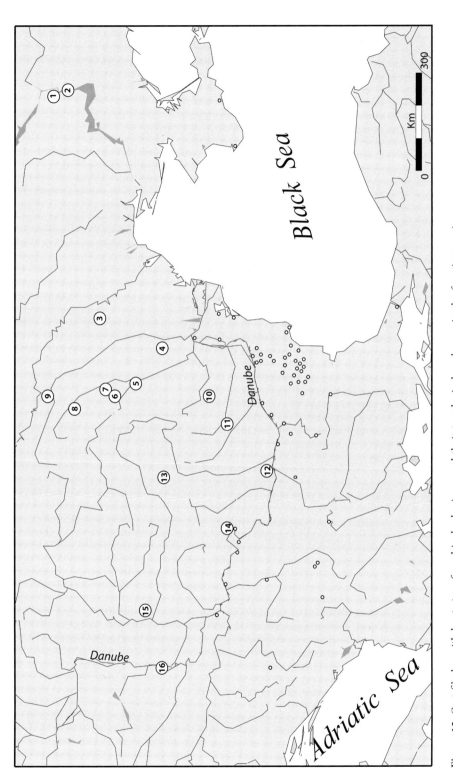

Figure 12 Cast fibulae with bent stem found in *barbaricum* and their typological analogues in the frontier provinces
1. Volos'ke; 2. Zvonets'ke; 3. Hansca; 4. Bârlălești; 5. Bacău; 6. Borșeni; 7. Davideni; 8. Suceava; 9. Chornivka; 10. Sărata Monteoru; 11. Târgșor; 12. Sucidava; 13. Bratei; 14. Drobeta; 15. Hódmező-vásárhely; 16. Kölked-Feketekapu.

Not all types of cast fibulae with bent stem known from the Balkans circulated in *barbaricum*. One of the most interesting pieces is the fibula from Davideni, which belongs to the group with human faces on the bow. The find has been interpreted as a badge of Christian identity under the assumption that the human faces are portraits of saints.[150] The prototype may indeed have been designed to portray religious images but the symbolism was lost on many such fibulae which display a very schematic decoration.[151] The fibula from Davideni might have actually been produced in the Balkans, as the closest analogies come from Pernik, where no less than four specimens have been found.[152] That the fibula from Davideni had religious meaning cannot be completely ruled out, but the archaeological context of house 51 where it was found in association with fragments of wheelmade and handmade pottery, is not explicitly Christian. In addition, a popular category of cast fibulae with bent stem with cross-shaped foot produced in the Balkans are so far unknown in *barbaricum*, which seems to suggest that fibulae embedding explicit or implicit Christian symbolism were not particularly fashionable.[153]

A second important class, fibulae with a rectangular section of the bow, is very common in the northern Balkans especially in the provinces of Scythia and Moesia II but is rarely found in *barbaricum*. One of the two known examples was found in house 25 from Borniş, in Moldavia, together with a belt buckle of the Sucidava class, typical of military assemblages from the frontier region, and illustrative of the higher status of the owner.[154] It is likely that the owner of the fibula from Borniş was a mercenary attracted by warfare in the Danube region in the second half of the sixth century. The shape of the bow resembles specimens such as the ones found in the Danubian provinces at Ibida and Venchan, but it is clearly an imitation with important modifications such as the absence of

---

[150] Mitrea, *Comunități sătești*, 92–3; 326, fig. 66/3.
[151] Chornivka (Ukraine): Gavritukhin, "Fibuly vizantiiskogo," 239–240; 250, fig. 6/1.
[152] Liubenova, "Selishteto ot rimskata," 172, fig. 112/4–7 and 173, fig. 113/1–4.
[153] Curta and Gandila, "Too much typology," 52. Some brooches may have been found on the northern bank of the Danube in the Iron Gates area, for which see D. Tănase and M. Mare, "Piese de port și de podoabă din secolele III–VII în colecția Pongrácz. Catalog," *Analele Banatului* 9 (2001): 202, pl. IV/2.
[154] R. Popovici, "Două piese vestimentare din secolele VI–VII descoperite la Borniș-Neamț," *AM* 12 (1988): 249–250, fig. 1/1; for an illustration of this fibula, see below Chapter 4, Figure 20/5. The other brooch was found very far from the frontier, at Bukhlichskii Khutor, near Petrikov, Mozyr region (Belarus), for which see V. S. Viargei, "Poseleniia prazhskoi kul'tury Belorusskogo Poles'ia," in *Problemy slavianskoi arkheologii*, ed. V. V. Sedov (Moscow, 1997), 35–36, with fig. 2/3.

the fake spiral and the rectangular shape of the bent stem. Imitation seems to have been ordinary practice in *barbaricum* to the point where locally produced fibulae followed other imitations rather than original prototypes. The fibula from Bârlălești is a perfect example, the shape of its foot closely resembling an earlier imitation from *barbaricum,* the iron fibula with bent stem (not cast) from Davideni.[155] Such practices remain important indicators of local tastes and social stratification in the lands north of the Danube. The connection to the Byzantine world was not stable enough to allow unrestricted access to the latest fashions developing in the frontier region and older designs came to be recycled, innovated upon, and perhaps valued as original contributions.

Finally, fibulae with a semicircular section of the bow belong to the type of design most commonly found in the frontier region, with a correspondingly significant presence in *barbaricum*, from the Middle Danube to the Middle Dnieper. Two fibulae have been found at Kölked in Avar-age burial assemblages. One of them is a child burial, the fibula being associated with bronze and iron chains as well as two silver earrings and glass beads with eye-shaped inlays. The second, a female burial, has a rich inventory including a silver fibula of the Cividale class, typical for the early seventh century, earrings, belt mounts, and strap ends, all made of silver.[156] A good parallel for this practice can be found in the province of Scythia, where a child burial from Piatra Frecăței produced a pair of cast fibulae with bent stem in association with two silver earrings with star-shaped pendants and a large number of glass and lead beads.[157] East of the Carpathians, three fibulae with a semicircular section have been found at Hansca, Borșeni, and

---

[155] D. G. Teodor, *The East-Carpathian Area of Romania in the V–XI Centuries AD* (Oxford, 1980), 12; fig. 11/3; for an illustration of this fibula, see below Chapter 4, Figure 20/6. The fibula from Bârlălești has a further analogy at Zvonets'ke, for which see Prikhodniuk, *Pen'kovskaia kul'tura,* 157; 142, fig. 74/10. For Davideni, see Mitrea, *Comunități sătești,* 329, fig. 68/1.

[156] A. Kiss, *Das awarenzeitlich-gepidische,* 132; 503, pl. 89/492.3; A. Kiss, *Das awarenzeitliche Gräberfeld in Kölked-Feketekapu B* (Budapest, 2001), 35; pl. 30/40. An iron fibula of this type was found in Budapest, also in a burial assemblage, for which see M. Nagy, *Awarenzeitliche Gräberfelder im Stadtgebiet von Budapest* (Budapest, 1998), 29; pl. 33/21. A cast fibula with zigzag ornament on the bow has been found at Hódmezővásárhely, associated with a belt buckle with rectangular plate with embossed decoration, for which see Bóna and Nagy, *Gepidische Gräberfelder,* 45 and 346, pl. 72/2.

[157] A. Petre, *La romanité en Scythie Mineure (IIe–VIIe siècles de notre ère). Recherches archéologiques* (Bucharest, 1987), 79; pl. 145/239d (grave E143); for an illustration of this fibula, see below Chapter 4, Figure 20/7. The association of glass beads with cast fibulae with bent stem is also documented in the large cemetery at Sărata-Monteoru (grave 763). Two other graves produced such fibulae, in one case, a cremation burial, the cast fibula with bent stem being found together with unidentifiable fragments of other fibulae, for which see U. Fiedler,

Bacău, the latter being associated with handmade pottery and clay pans from the late sixth century.[158] No perfect analogies are known south of the Danube, although the shapes are somewhat similar to many of the cast fibulae found in the frontier provinces at Novae, Kapitan Dimitrovo, and Accres (Cape Kaliakra).[159]

Surprisingly, most cast fibulae with bent stem from *barbaricum* do not find their closest parallels in the Iron Gates area, which was initially considered to be the main area of production, but in the provinces of Moesia II and Scythia. Significant production in the northeastern Balkans explains the larger number of finds in Moldavia, a region with an easier access to goods from the two Danubian provinces. It is no accident that frontier forts defending these provinces also produced the largest quantity of "non-Roman" handmade ceramics, often attributed to outside populations, Slavs and Antes in particular, and dated to the second half of the sixth century and the beginning of the seventh. Since the golden age of the production and distribution of cast fibulae with bent stem seems to have been the second half of the sixth century, this dovetails nicely with other categories of finds. It suggests that the movement of soldiers recruited from *barbaricum* to man the walls of the Danubian fortresses may have been responsible for the circulation of cast fibulae with bent stem in the region east of the Carpathians. Written accounts present the Slavs as perpetual enemies of the Empire, but the political decentralization of the Slavic world allowed for a much more complex relationship reflected in such archaeological finds.[160] Furthermore, such fashions forged in the multicultural

---

Studien zu Gräberfeldern des 6. bis 9. Jahrhunderts an der unteren Donau (Bonn, 1992), 80–83, figs. 11/8, 11/11, and 11/16.

[158] Hansca: I. A. Rafalovich, "Issledovaniia ranneslavianskikh," 152–153, fig. 10/2. Borşeni: I. Mitrea, "Romanitate şi creştinism în secolele V–VI în lumea satelor din spaţiul carpato-nistrean," *Zargidava* 1 (2002): 24; 39, fig. 9/7. Bacău: I. Mitrea and A. Artimon, "Descoperiri prefeudale la Curtea Domnească Bacău," *Carpica* 4 (1971): 236; 242, fig. 13/1. A variation of the fibula with semicircular bow, having two vertical incisions has been recorded in the same region, at Suceava, for which see D. G. Teodor, "La pénétration des Slaves dans les régions du sud-est de l'Europe d'après les données archéologiques des régions orientales de la Roumanie," *Balcanoslavica* 1 (1972): fig. 4/3.

[159] Kapitan Dimitrovo: A. Kharalambieva, "Fibuli ot I–VII v. v Dobrichkiia muzei," *Dobrudzha* 9 (1992): 137–138; 134 pl. III/7. Accres: Kharalambieva, "Dva tipa kusnoantichni," 39; pl. VI.7; for an illustration of this fibula, see below Chapter 4, Figure 20/8. Novae: S. Stefanov, "Kusnorimski fibuli ot Nove," in *Izsledvaniia v pamet na Karel Shkorpil*, eds. K. Miiatev and V. Mikov (Sofia, 1961), 345, fig. 4/24–26.

[160] The author of the *Strategikon* makes a similar point when he describes the factionalism dominating Slavic society, advising that alliances should be forged with individual Slavic warlords close to the frontier in order to attract them to the Roman cause; see *Strategikon* 11.4.128–131.

crucible of the frontier came to be adopted by communities in present-day Ukraine, hundreds of kilometers away from the Lower Danube.[161] Far from being the ethnic badge of Daco-Roman communities north of the Danube, Byzantine fibulae became markers of social distinction in relation to Byzantium which cut across ethnic boundaries in *barbaricum*.[162]

2.2.4.3 Bow Fibulae

The stylistic variety of the Byzantine fibulae with bent stem which created so many problems to archaeologists trying to establish a firm typology turns into nightmare in the case of the so-called "Slavic" bow fibulae, whose diversity defies any attempt to create a universally accepted classification. Given that additional finds have done nothing but increase that confusion, it is not surprising that the most influential classification is also the oldest. Joachim Werner's typology is based on the shape of the terminal lobe, either a human face or an animal head, and the firm conviction that the bow fibulae should be considered an ethnic badge of the early Slavs.[163] For all its methodological shortcomings, Werner's typology is still employed by historians and archaeologists as a common foundation for further analyses, most of which depart from Werner's system of classification to create some new typological arrangement. Despite the great efforts of Balkan historians to bring order to a very large and exasperatingly diverse body of finds, general consensus is yet to be reached.[164]

---

[161] Even further east, a cast fibula with bent stem was found in the Shilovo region, Ryazan district, Russia, a cultural horizon attributed to the Ryazan Finns, for which see I. Akhmedov, "Rannevizantiiskie nakhodki," 172.

[162] Cf. Teodor, "Ateliers byzantins," 191.

[163] J. Werner, "Slawische Bügelfibeln des 7. Jahrhunderts," in *Reinecke Festschrift zum 75. Geburtstag von Paul Reinecke am 25. September 1947*, eds. G. Behrens and E. Schneider (Mainz, 1950), 150–172. For early reactions to his methodology, see H. Kühn, "Das Problem der masurgermanischen Fibeln in Ostpreussen," in *Documenta Archaeologica Wolfgang La Baume dedicata 8.II.1955*, ed. O. Kleeman (Bonn, 1956), 79–108; I. Nestor, "L'établissement des Slaves en Roumanie à la lumière de quelques découvertes archéologiques récentes," *Dacia* 5 (1961): 429–449; A. Petre, "Contribuția atelierelor romano-bizantine la geneza unor tipuri de fibule 'digitate' din veacurile VI–VII e.n.," *SCIV* 17, no. 2 (1966): 255–275.

[164] L. Vagalinski, "Zur Frage der ethnischen Herkunft der späten Strahlenfibeln (Finger- oder Bügelfibeln) aus dem Donau-Karpaten-Becken (M. 6.–7. Jh.)," *ZfA* 28 (1994): 261–305; C. Katsougiannopoulou, "Studien zu ost- und südosteuropäischen Bügelfibeln," PhD Dissertation, University of Bonn, 1999; D. G. Teodor, "Fibule digitate din secolele VI–VII în spațiul carpato-dunăreano-pontic," *AM* 15 (1992): 119–152; F. Curta, "'Slavic' bow fibulae: twenty years of research," *Bericht der Römisch-Germanischen Kommission* 93 (2012): 235–242.

Two major historical issues are at stake, aside from the taxonomical inclinations of archaeologists: the chronology and the ethnic attribution of the sixth-to-seventh-century bow fibulae. First of all, unlike the fibulae with bent stem discussed in the previous pages, bow fibulae are far more common in *barbaricum* than they are in the Balkan provinces (Figure 13).[165] Second, the "Slavic" bow fibula is not an original creation of the sixth century. It is generally accepted that the shape derives from the East Germanic fibula of the late fifth century, with semicircular head and terminal lobes, itself drawing on previous shapes combining Gothic (Chernyakhov) and Roman provincial elements. Its "Slavic" counterpart is no less a mix of "barbaric" and Early Byzantine features. Based on the production of the earlier "Germanic" type in the frontier region it was suggested that the main production centers must have been located south of the Danube. Another argument brought in favor of this hypothesis was the Byzantine decoration on some "Slavic" fibulae, the naturalistic human faces in particular.[166] Indeed, bow fibulae of superior craftsmanship, often gilded, have been found in the Balkans at Lezhë, Liuliakovo, and Istanbul, all belonging to Werner's class I B. Such specimens are also recorded in *barbaricum*, the most spectacular being the large fibula from Coşovenii de Jos, close to the Danube.[167] In the absence of molds or workshops, stylistic features and patterns of diffusion remain the only criteria for attributing them to Early Byzantine production centers in the Danube region. By contrast, the production of bow fibulae in *barbaricum* was effectively proven by the find of prototypes at Felnac, Bucharest–Tei, and in Banat and especially by the spectacular hoard of 64 molds found in a building from Bernashivka (Ukraine), which included a mold designed to produce a type of bow fibula so far unknown.[168]

Chronology is perhaps the only chance of bringing some order to the large corpus of bow fibulae, given that their stylistic variation prevents any

---

[165] For the distribution of "Slavic" bow fibulae in East-Central, Southeastern, and Eastern Europe, see Curta, "'Slavic' bow fibulae," 260, fig. 21.

[166] Petre, "Contribuţia atelierelor," 267–275; Teodor, "Fibule digitate," 123. Alternatively, some have placed the original production centers in the Crimea, for which see B. A. Rybakov, "Drevnie rusi. K voprosu ob obrazovanii iadra drevnerusskoi narodnosti v svete trudov I. V. Stalina," *SA* 17 (1953): 23–104.

[167] I. Nestor and C. S. Nicolaescu-Plopşor, "Der völkerwanderungszeitliche Schatz Negrescu," *Germania* 22, no. 1 (1938): 33–35, with pl. 7.

[168] E. A. Shablavina and B. S. Szmoniewski, "The forming model of the Kertch type finger-shaped fibula," *Sprawozdania Archeologiczne* 58 (2006): fig. 5; Vynokur, *Slov'ians'kyi iuveliry*, 57, fig. 18; for an illustration of this mold, see below Chapter 4, Figure 19/5.

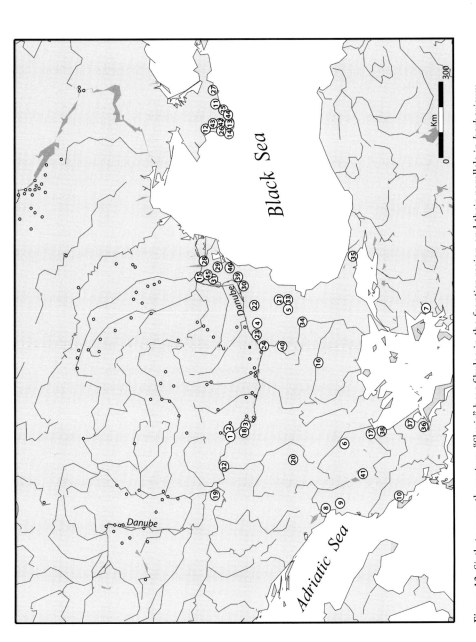

Figure 13 Sixth-to-seventh-century "Slavic" bow fibulae in the frontier region and their parallels in *barbaricum*

1. Velesnica; 2. Korbovo; 3. Aquis; 4. Kamenovo; 5. Rish Pass; 6. Viničani; 7. Pergamon; 8. Lezhë; 9. Krujë; 10. Butrint; 11. Luchistoe; 12. Skalistoe; 13. Fărcașu de Sus; 14. Chersonesus; 15. Garvăn; 16. Plovdiv; 17. Edesa; 18. Negotin; 19. Novi Banovci; 20. Caričin Grad; 21. Shumen; 22. Sturmen; 23. Iatrus; 24. Vardim; 25. Alushta; 26. Eski Kermen; 27. Suuk Su; 28. Somova; 29. Ibida; 30. Dervent; 31. Beroe; 32. Dubovac; 33. Liuliakovo; 34. Iambol; 35. Istanbul; 36. Nea Anchialos; 37. Demetrias; 38. Dion; 39. Tropaeum Traiani; 40. Carevec; 41. Sv. Erazmo; 42. Chufut Kale; 43. Bakla; 44. Artek; 45. Căprioara; 46. Târgușor.

classification based on shape.[169] Unfortunately, a great number of bow fibulae found in Eastern Europe lack archaeological context, this issue being compounded by their significant longevity. Being one of the few artifacts to have survived the great cultural upheaval of the early seventh century, the Byzantine retreat from the Lower Danube cannot be invoked as a chronological boundary. Indeed, many of the "Slavic" bow fibulae found in stratigraphic context south of the Danube were almost certainly lost or deposited after the abandonment of the *limes* in the Balkans (ca. 615). Such is the case of the fibula type I B found in grave 36 and the fibula type I C from the grave 32 at Lezhë in Albania, a cemetery dated to the middle and especially the second half of the seventh century.[170] The pair of fibulae class I C from grave 28 at Kruje, also from Albania, has a similar dating suggested by its association with a buckle of the Corinth class.[171] A close analogy is the fibula found accidentally at Căprioara in northern Dobrudja, which might be contemporary with the pair of fibulae from Kruje.[172] The gilt fibula from Liuliakovo in Bulgaria resembles the one probably found in Istanbul and by extension with the impressive fibula from Coșovenii de Jos, found together with silver earrings with star-shaped pendants, typical for the seventh century.[173] An even later dating should be accepted for the two class I C fibulae from the hoard found at Kamenovo in northern Bulgaria, which also included a pair of fibulae class I F, the only ones of this type

---

[169] In his 1950 contribution Werner dated all "Slavic" bow fibulae to the seventh century, but later he allowed for an earlier dating going back to the second half of the sixth century, for which see J. Werner, "Neues zur Frage der slawischen Bügelfibeln aus süd-osteuropäischen Länders," *Germania* 38 (1960): 114–120. A more radical chronology was suggested by Uwe Fiedler based on similarities between the late fifth-century "Germanic" bow fibulae and "Slavic" bow fibulae, which Fiedler dated to the sixth century; see Fiedler, *Studien zu Gräberfeldern*, 101. For the latest chronology, see Curta, "Slavic bow fibulae," 35–36, table 1.

[170] F. Prendi, "Një varrëze e kulturës arbërore në Lezhë," *Iliria* 9–10 (1979–1980): 129; 166–167, pl. 20/3 and 21/2. A strikingly similar specimen was found at Dubovac in Serbia, unfortunately a stray find, which might also date from this period, for which see D. Dimitrijević, "O etničkim problemima Vojvodine u vreme doseljenja Slovena," in *Simpozijum "Predslavenski etnički elementi na Balkanu u etnogenezi južnih Slovena," održan 24–26. oktobra 1968 u Mostaru*, ed. A. Benac (Sarajevo, 1969), 88 and fig. 1.

[171] S. Anamali and H. Spahiu, "Varrëza arbërore e Krujes," *Iliria* 9–10 (1979–1980): 61–62, with pl. 7/11 and 11/1.

[172] D. G. Teodor and C. Chiriac, "Noi fibule digitate din Dobrogea," *Peuce* 3–4 (2005–2006): 241; 249, fig. 2; for an illustration of this fibula, see below Chapter 4, Figure 20/10.

[173] S. Mikhailov, "Die Bügelfibeln in Bulgarien und ihre historische Interpretation," in *Archäologie als Geschichtswissenschaft. Studien und Untersuchungen*, ed. J. Herrmann (Berlin, 1977), 317–318; pl. 7; Werner, "Neues zur Frage," 119; pl. 2.

found in the Danube region, as well as a strap end with scrollwork decoration, most typical for the Late Avar period (after 700).[174]

On the other hand, an equally large number of brooches can be dated with some certainty before the fall of the Danube frontier.[175] No doubt the safest dating is that of the fibula type I H found during excavations in the Danubian fortress of Iatrus, in the building 66/23N, together with a sixth-century coin, whose exact dating is unfortunately unspecified in the publication.[176] The excavators have dated the complex to the last phase of the fortress which also covers the first two decades of the seventh century. In addition, the pair of similar I H fibulae found in the inhumation burial B42 at Piatra Frecăței on the Danube has been recently dated to the sixth century based on the association with copper-alloy bracelets typical for this period.[177] Another coin-dated fibula was found at Dervent, close to the Danube, having a *terminus post quem* 570/1, but the stratigraphical connection between the two artifacts is not secure. The fibula belongs to Werner's class II A, as do a few other finds from the same region, the three stray finds from Somova and the specimen found during archaeological excavations at Slava Rusă. All of them display a scrollwork motif whose quality of execution suggests an early date in the sixth century.[178]

---

[174] R. Rashev, *Prabulgarite prez V–VII vek* (Veliko Turnovo, 2000), 189, pl. 83/12–15. A fibula class I F was also found in an unknown location in Bulgaria; see S. Mikhailov, "Rannosrednovekovni fibuli v Bulgariia," *IAI* 24 (1961): 41–43, with fig. 3/1.

[175] This list can also include a pair of fibulae class I D found in an inhumation burial at Edessa in Greece and a fibula of the same class found at Dinogetia, with good parallels in the Crimea, for which see P. Petsas, "Archaiotetes kai mnemeia Kentrikes Makedonias," *ArchDelt* 24 (1969): 307, and fig. 320/ε; I. Nestor, "L'établissement des Slaves," 440; 444, fig. 3/1a–b; I. S. Pioro, *Krymskaia Gotiia (Ocherki etnicheskoi istorii naseleniia Kryma v pozdnerimskii period i rannee srednevekov'e)* (Kiev, 1990), 135; 111, fig. 31. For eagle-headed buckles found in the Crimea, see E. A. Shablavina, "O rannesrednekovoi produkcii Bosporskikh iuvelirov (na primere orlinogolovykh priazhek," *Arkheologicheskie vesti* 13 (2006): 230–251.

[176] J. Herrmann, "Die archäologischen Forschungen des Zentralinstituts für Alte Geschichte und Archäologie 1973 und im ersten Halbjahr 1974," *Ausgrabungen und Funde* 19, no. 6 (1974): 303; pl. 44/b.

[177] A. Petre, "Predvaritel'nye svedeniia v sviazi s khronologiei mogil'nika v Piatra Frecăței," *Dacia* 6 (1962): 226, fig. 12/1-b/1; F. Curta, "Werner's Class I C: *erratum corrigendum cum commentariis*," *EN* 21 (2011): 67–68. A similar chronology can be advanced for the fibula found in an inhumation burial at Tulcea in northern Scythia, which was found together with a ceramic pitcher and nine amber beads, for which see G. Simion, "Un nouveau groupe de fibule digitales découvertes dans la région du Dobroudja," *Studia antiqua et medievalia. Miscellanea in honorem annos LXXV peragentis Professoris Dan Gh. Teodor oblata*, ed. D. Aparaschivei (Bucharest, 2009), 412, fig. 1.

[178] Dervent: P. Diaconu, "Fibula digitată descoperită la Dervent (reg. Dobrogea)," *SCIV* 13, no. 2 (1962): 447–448 and fig. 1. Somova: Simion, "Un nouveau groupe," 414–416; figs. 2–3. Slava Rusă: A. Opaiț, "O săpătură de salvare în orașul antic Ibida," *SCIVA* 41, no. 4 (1990): 37–38; 48, fig. 19/37.

Finally, an equally secure dating before the collapse of the frontier is provided by two settlement finds of class II C fibulae from Tsarevets and Caričin Grad, both found together with six-century fibulae with bent stem.[179]

In conclusion, although not much can be said about the bulk of the finds of "Slavic" bow fibulae from the Balkans, it is clear that their presence spans a long period of time, from before and certainly continuing after the demise of the military frontier on the Lower Danube. Recent distribution maps as well as inventories of finds show that most of the "Slavic" bow fibulae from Eastern Europe have been found in *barbaricum* making it the typical female dress ornament of a privileged social class beyond the frontier. Whether or not such fibulae were an exclusive social and ethnic marker of "foreigners" from *barbaricum*, they were clearly not as popular in frontier forts as they were north of the Danube, judging by the number of finds in both regions, and they certainly did not surpass the popularity of the fibulae with bent stem. Since it was rarely used by Roman women, the bow fibula became a marker of distinction expressed through gender whereby warriors of various background in *barbaricum* displayed their hybrid identity. Unlike the Byzantine fibula with bent stem which reflected the willingness to conform to Roman practices, the "Slavic" bow fibula may have become a symbol of opposition in the competitive world of *barbaricum*, where successful warfare against the Empire was celebrated through such identity markers.

Identifying the bow fibula as the ethnic badge of a certain group, as Werner and others have suggested by attributing them to the Slavs, has become increasingly unconvincing since the corpus of finds has come to include a variety of cultural contexts. The distribution map reveals a greater concentration of finds in the northeastern Balkans, in the provinces of Moesia II and Scythia, where a correspondingly larger quantity of Penkovka and Korchak ceramics has been found, usually associated with the Antes and the Slavs, respectively. Is this an additional piece of evidence to suggest that the Slavs were in the end the main ethnic group using bow fibulae? The answer must be negative, since many of the contexts are not

---

[179] A. Kharalambieva, "Bügelfibeln aus dem 7. Jh. südlich der unteren Donau," in *Actes du XIIe Congrès international des sciences préhistoriques et protohistoriques, Bratislava, 1–7 septembre 1991*, ed. J. Pavuj (Bratislava, 1993), 25 and 26, fig. 1/1; for an illustration of this fibula, see below Chapter 4, Figure 20/12; V. Popović, "Byzantins, Slaves et autochtones dans les provinces de Prévalitane et Nouvelle Epire," in *Villes et peuplement dans l'Illyricum protobyzantin. Actes du colloque organisé par l'École Française de Rome, Rome 12–14 mai 1982* (Rome, 1984), 175; 176, fig. 188.

otherwise indicative of what may be viewed as early Slavic material culture. Bow fibulae have been found not only in the Danubian provinces, but also at Caričin Grad in Dacia Mediterranea and even further west at Butrint in Epirus. An interesting concentration of finds was identified in the Iron Gates region, on both sides of the river, an area under constant Avar pressure, especially after the fall of Sirmium (582). An even larger number of specimens have been found in inhumation burials from the provinces of Scythia and Macedonia, as well as in a number of cemeteries from the Crimea.[180]

One might argue that perhaps Slavs recruited to defend the frontier provinces adopted local customs including the practice of inhumation, but such finds are also reported north of the Danube. To be sure, "Slavic" bow fibulae are sometimes found with cremations such as those of the large cemetery at Sărata-Monteoru, but also in inhumation graves, such as those from Bratei, Selişte, Dănceni, and Pruneni.[181] Found in a variety of contexts, singly or in pairs, associated with the Slavs, Avars, Gepids, and the Early Byzantine fortresses and cemeteries in the Balkans, the sixth-to-seventh-century bow fibula is more convincing as an international badge of "barbarian" elevated social status rather than a strictly ethnic one. The fact that it became a particularly fashionable dress accessory on both sides of the river around the time when the Byzantines lost control of the frontier is no coincidence. As the Empire was losing ground in this space of cultural negotiation, the prestige of non-Roman objects increased. Being Roman was falling out of fashion.

---

[180] Adamclisi: G. Papuc, "O fibulă digitată de la Tropaeum Traiani şi cîteva consideraţii asupra fibulelor de acest tip," *Pontica* 20 (1987): 207–210; fig. 1/a-b. Viničani: M. Čorović-Ljubinković, "Les Slaves du centre balkanique du VIe au XIe siècle," *Balcanoslavica* 1 (1972): 47; fig. 1/3. Sv. Erazmo: V. Malenko, "Ranosrednovekovnata materijalna kultura vo Okhrid i Okhridsko," in *Okhrid i Okhridsko niz istorijata*, ed. M. Apostolski (Skopje, 1985), 289; pl. VI/4. A large number of "Slavic" bow fibulae have been found in cemeteries from the Crimea at Luchistoe, Skalistoe, Chufut Kale, Eski Kermen and Suuk Su, for which see especially A. I. Aibabin, "Khronologiia mogil'nikov Kryma pozdnerimskogo i rannesrednevekovogo vremeni," *MAIET* 1 (1990): 5–68; G. F. Korzukhina, "Klady i sluchainye nakhodki veshchei kruga "drevnostei antov" v srednem Podneprov'e. Katalog pamiatnikov," *MAIET* 5 (1996): 352–435 and 586–705.

[181] Sărata Monteoru: Fiedler, *Studien zu Gräberfeldern*, 83, fig. 11. Bratei: L. Bârzu, *Ein gepidisches Denkmal aus Siebenbürgen. Das Gräberfeld 3 von Bratei* (Cluj-Napoca, 2010), 208; 301, pl. 23/G130/2 (with several other specimens). Selişte: Rafalovich and Lapushnian, "Raboty Reutskoi," 139; 131, fig. 9/2. Dănceni: I. A. Rafalovich, *Dancheni. Mogil'nik cherniakhovskoi kul'tury* (Kishinew, 1986), 25–26 and pl. 14/1. Pruneni: M. Comşa, "Die Slawen im karpatischen-donauländischen Raum im 6.-7. Jahrhundert," *ZfA* 7 (1973): 210.

2.2.5 Buckles

The great variety of types and variants noted in the case of fibulae is also shared by sixth-to-seventh-century Byzantine buckles found in the frontier region and beyond (Figure 14). This category of artifacts is, however, less homogeneous and only a few types have been studied and classified. While a large number of buckles of basic shape and no decoration found in *barbaricum* are often named "Byzantine," their dating largely depends on the archaeological context. Many of them may well be local products, possibly imitations, but their connection with contemporary buckles from the Danube region remains uncertain. There are, however, at least four well-established types in the literature, dated to the sixth and seventh centuries, which will constitute the main basis for assessing the function of Byzantine buckles in the regions north of the Lower Danube.

The Sucidava class is by far the most common along with its derivation known as Beroe in the literature, after the sixth-century cemetery excavated at Piatra Frecăței in Scythia.[182] The type was defined by Joachim Werner in 1955 based on finds from Sucidava and securely dated to the second half of the sixth century.[183] The corpus has increased significantly since the 1950s and several new classifications and chronologies have been developed.[184] We can now rely on a large inventory of ca. 150 buckles from the Middle and Lower Danube region.[185] Although Sucidava buckles are another typical product of frontier culture, their geographical footprint is not restricted to the

---

[182] A. Madgearu, "The Sucidava type of buckles and the relations between the Late Roman Empire and the barbarians in the 6th century," *AM* 21 (1998): 217–222. For buckles found at Piatra-Frecăței, see Petre, *La romanité*, 67, with pl. 122 and fig. 187 a–f.

[183] J. Werner, "Byzantinische Gürtelschnallen des 6. und 7. Jahrhunderts aus der Sammlung Diergardt," *Kölner Jahrbuch für Vor- und Frühgeschichte* 1 (1955): 39–40.

[184] Uenze, *Die Spätantiken Befestigungen*, 184–187; D. G. Teodor, "Piese vestimentare bizantine din secolele VI-VIII în spațiul carpato-dunăreano-pontic," *AM* 14 (1991): 118–125; V. Varsik, "Byzantinische Gurtelschnallen im mittleren und unteren Donauraum im 6. und 7. Jahrhundert," *Slovenská Archeológia* 40, no. 1 (1992): 78–80; Fiedler, *Studien Gräberfeldern*, 71–73; A. Madgearu, *Continuitate și discontinuitate culturală la Dunărea de Jos în secolele VII–VIII* (Bucharest, 1997), 39.

[185] Many were found in sixth-century settlements; see Madgearu, "The Sucidava type," 218; M. Daskalov and K. Trendafilova, "Kolanut v iuzhnodunavskite vizantiiski provintsii prez VI–VII v.," in *The Bulgarian Lands in the Middle Ages 7th–18th Centuries. International Conference, a Tribute to the 70th Anniversary of Prof. Alexander Kuzev, Varna, Septempre 12th–14th, 2002*, ed. V. Iotov (Varna, 2005), 7–18; M. Daskalov, *Kolani i kolanni ukrasi ot VI–VII vek (ot dneshna Bulgariia i susednite zemi)* (Sofia, 2012), 38–41 and 64–66.

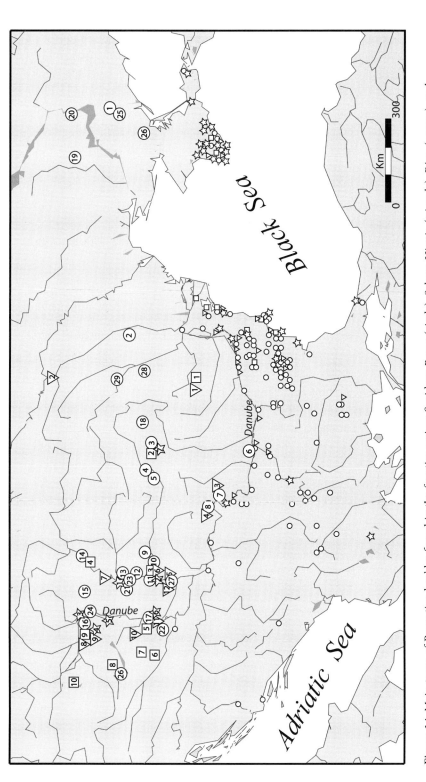

Figure 14 Main types of Byzantine buckles found in the frontier region: Sucidava-Beroe (circle), Salona–Histria (triangle), Pápa (square), and Syracuse (star)

*a) Sucidava-Beroe:*1. Veliki Tokmak; 2. Dăneşti; 3. Brateî; 4. Noşlac; 5. Apulum; 6. Sucidava; 7. Drobeta; 8. Dierna; 9. Pecica; 10. Klárafalva; 11. Szöreg; 12. Hodmezővásárhely-Kishomok; 13. Szentes-Nagyhegy; 14. Tiszafüred; 15. Jánoshida; 16. Tatabanya; 17. Kölked-Feketekapu; 18. Cristuru Secuiesc; 19. Sukhanova; 20. Volos'ke; 21. Kecskemét; 22. Pécs; 23. Szegvár; 24. Törökbálint; 25. Sivashivka; 26. Keszthely; 27. Mokrin; 28. Ştefan cel Mare; 29. Borniş. *b) Salona-Histria:* 1. Sărata Monteoru; 2. Brateî; 3. Drobeta; 4. Dierna; 5. Aradac; 6. Deszk; 7. Tiszadersz; 8. Környe; 9. Csákberény; 10. Szekszárd; 11. Kölked-Feketekapu; 12. Szeghegy. *c) Pápa:* 1. Sărata Monteoru; 2. Brateî; 3. Deszk; 4. Kunszentmárton; 5. Kölked-Feketekapu; 6. Gyód; 7. Pécs-Köztemető; 8. Keszthely; 9. Környe; 10. Pápa. *d) Syracuse:* 1. Szelevény; 2. Szeged-Fehértó; 3. Százhalombatta; 4. Csákberény; 5. Dunapentele; 6. Kölked-Feketekapu; 7. Brateî.

Danubian borderlands.[186] The large concentration of finds in the northern Balkans betrays a significant local production, but their presence in Constantinople, in Asia Minor, and as far as Palmyra in Syria has led some scholars to suggest that the activity of multiple workshops must be responsible for this diversity.[187] Still, it is more likely that Sucidava buckles were brought to these regions by troops transferred from the Balkans to the Near East in the second half of the sixth century.[188]

The production of Sucidava buckles probably took off sometime in the first decades of the sixth century, as suggested by specimens found in association with coins. At Mokranjske Stene in eastern Serbia a Sucidava buckle was found together with a coin of Anastasius, while at Izvor, close to Pernik in western Bulgaria, a similar buckle was associated with a *follis* minted for Justin I.[189] Further south, at Nea Anchialos, a buckle of the Sucidava-Beroe II sub-type was found together with a coin of Justinian.[190] In all three cases the association is not direct, in that the buckles and the coins were not found within the same assemblage; instead, the coins simply date the "layer" in which the buckles were found. Indeed, in all cases the buckles might date from a later period since the coins remained in circulation during the entire sixth century. At any rate, Sucidava buckles are mostly associated with Early Byzantine hilltop sites from the frontier region along the Danube, from Belgrade through Aquis, Oescus, Novae, Durostorum to Dinogetia in northern Scythia and the larger towns of the western Black Sea coast, Histria, Tomis, and Odessos.[191] It is widely accepted that the production of Sucidava buckles stopped after the Byzantine Empire lost control of the Danube at the beginning of the seventh

---

[186] Sucidava buckles have been found in Western Europe, as far as Normandy, for which see M. Schulze-Dörrlamm, *Byzantinische Gürtelschnallen und Gürtelbeschläge im Römisch-Germanischen Zentralmuseum. Teil I: Die Schnallen ohne Beschläg, mit Laschenbeschläg und mit festem Beschläg des 5. bis 7. Jahrhunderts* (Mainz, 2002), 150, fig. 54. The Beroe buckles, deriving from the Sucidava type, have a wider circulation in the east as far as Petropavlovo in Udmurtia, Russia and Brody, close to the Ural mountains, for which see V. A. Semenov, "Petropavlovskii mogil'nik VI–VII vv. V iuzhnoi Udmurtii," *Voprosy arkheologii Urala* 7 (1967): 170, pl. II/22; R. D. Goldina and N. V. Vodolago, *Mogil'niki nevolinskoi kul'tury v Priural'e* (Irkutsk, 1990), 124, pl. XXVII/43. Such finds are also attested in the Caucasus, for instance in the cemetery of Tsibilium in Abkhazia, for which see Y. Voronov, *Tsibilium: la nécropole apsile de Tsibilium (VIIe av. J.-C.–VIIIe ap. J.-C). (Abkhazie, Caucase)* (Oxford, 2007), 72; 258, fig. 146 (grave 313).

[187] Madgearu, "The Sucidava Type," 218.

[188] For the presence of Balkan units in the Near East, see recently A. Madgearu, "Militari 'sciți' și 'daci' în Egipt, Italia și Palestina în secolele VI–VII," *SCIVA* 65, no. 1–2 (2014): 49–58.

[189] Varsik, "Byzantinische Gürtelschnallen," 78; Daskalov and Trendafilova, "Kolanut," 9.

[190] Lazaridis, "Nea Ankhialos," pl. 394.   [191] Daskalov and Trendafilova, "Kolanut," 10, fig. 1.

century, which indirectly links this fashion with the presence of garrisons defending the Byzantine frontier in the Balkans.

Sucidava buckles were also fashionable outside the Empire, but at least in Wallachia and Moldavia they are less popular than expected. Excepting the Byzantine bridge-heads from the left bank of the Danube – Dierna, Drobeta, and Sucidava – none of the settlements where amphorae and fibulae are commonly found also yielded Byzantine buckles of the Sucidava class, or any other type for that matter. In Moldavia only three finds have been recorded so far, including a settlement find from Borniş, which seems to be a local imitation rather than a genuine import, a specimen from an inhumation grave at Dăneşti, and another from a sixth-century settlement from Ştefan cel Mare.[192] Given the great concentration of finds in the provinces of Scythia and Moesia II, the scarcity of Byzantine buckles in the corresponding regions across the Danube appears even more perplexing. The same people who were so eager to obtain Byzantine artifacts such as fibulae, crosses, and various types of jewelry appear to have been relatively uninterested in Byzantine buckles.

The same is true for the other three important classes of Byzantine buckles which can be dated before the fall of the Danube frontier: Salona-Histria, Pápa, and Syracuse.[193] The first two classes have the same function, that of attaching a small purse to the belt, the difference between the two being the presence of a pair of stylized animal heads on the Pápa type. The production of Pápa buckles postdates the Salona-Histria type, from which it derives, although both may have been in use around year 600. Their presence in Early Avar assemblages in Környe and

---

[192] Borniş: R. Popovici, "Două piese vestimentare din secolele VI–VII descoperite la Borniş-Neamţ," *AM* 12 (1988): 249–251, 250, fig. 1. For an illustration of this buckle, see below Chapter 4, Figure 20/5. Dăneşti: D. G. Teodor, *Spaţiul carpato-dunăreano-pontic în mileniul marilor migraţii* (Buzău, 2003), 250, fig. 2/7. Ştefan cel Mare: I. Mitrea and C. Eminovici, "Ştefan cel Mare, jud. Bacău," in *Cronica Cercetărilor Arheologice în România 1983–1992. A XXXI-a sesiune naţională de rapoarte arheologice* (Bucharest, 1997), 105–106, n. 70 (house 17).

[193] For Pápa buckles, see S. Uenze, "Die Schnallen mit Riemenschlaufe aus dem 6. und 7. Jahrh.," *Bayerische Vorgeschichtsblätter* 31, nos. 1–2 (1966): 142–181. For Salona-Histria and Syracuse, see Varsik, "Byzantinische Gürtelschnallen," 80–82; Daskalov and Trendafilova, "Kolanut," 11, fig. 2. See also R. Oanţă-Marghitu, "Argamum între Imperiul Roman Târziu şi 'barbari'. Obiectele mărunte ca ipostaze ale comunicării," in *Orgamé/Argamum. Supplementa I. À la recherche d'une colonie. Actes du Colloque International à l'occasion du 40ème anniversaire des fouilles à Orgamé/Argamum, Bucarest-Tulcea-Jurilovca, 3–5 octobre 2005*, ed. M. Mănucu-Adameşteanu (Bucharest, 2006), 348–352 and pl. V. For the distribution of Syracuse and Pápa buckles outside the Balkans, see Schulze-Dörrlamm, *Byzantinische Gürtelschnallen*, 176, fig. 62 and 226, fig. 82.

Kölked-Feketekapu substantiates this hypothesis.[194] In addition, both types of buckles have been found in the large "Slavic" cemetery from Sărata-Monteoru.[195] In the Early Byzantine provinces of the Balkans Salona-Histria and Pápa buckles display the same pattern of distribution as the Sucidava type, although Pápa buckles are so far missing from the provinces of Dacia Ripensis and Moesia I. Unlike Sucidava buckles, whose popularity brought them to Western Europe, the circulation of Pápa and Salona-Histria buckles was restricted mostly to the Middle and Lower Danube regions and the Crimea, where they are common finds in all the major sixth-to-seventh-century cemeteries. We are facing the same paradox, with finds concentrating in *Avaria*, the northeastern Balkans, and the Crimea, while they are almost completely absent north of the Danube in Wallachia and Moldavia. This is even more surprising since a workshop for the production of Salona-Histria buckles has been found at Drobeta on the left bank of the Danube and could have easily facilitated the distribution of such items further north in *barbaricum*.[196] The concentration of Pápa buckles in the regions under Avar control has led to the conclusion that they were locally produced outside the empire, perhaps by Byzantine craftsmen working for the Avars.[197] Therefore, it is possible that the workshop at Drobeta served the needs of the Avar warriors at a time when the Byzantine frontier in northern Illyricum had been shattered.

The production of the last type of buckle under discussion, known as Syracuse in the literature, took off close to the time when the Empire was losing control of the Danube frontier. The popularity of Syracuse buckles in the Balkans is more limited and only a few are known from the provinces of Moesia II and Scythia, where the Empire retained some influence in the first decades of the seventh century due to the presence of the fleet in the Black Sea.[198] The largest density of finds can be found in

---

[194] Környe (graves M 66, M 106, and M 109): A. Salamon and I. Erdély, *Das völkerwanderungszeitliche Gräberfeld von Környe* (Budapest, 1971), 24, pl. 19 (Salona-Histria) and 20, pl. 9/6 (Pápa); Kölked-Feketekapu (graves M 223, M 259, M 385, M 425, and M 647): Kiss, *Das awarenzeitlich-gepidische*, 75–76, pl. 57 (Salona-Histria) and 165–166, pl. 102 (Pápa). In both cases the Salona-Histria buckles were associated with reused Late Roman coins (Valentinian I-Gratian).

[195] Uenze, "Die Schnallen," fig. 1/6 and 5/35 (graves 564 and 1/1943).

[196] Bejan, "Un atelier metalurgic," pl. VI. For finds in the Balkans, see also Daskalov, *Kolani i kolanni*, 47–48 and 68.

[197] A. Madgearu, "Despre cataramele de tip Pápa și unele probleme ale secolului al VII-lea," *SCIVA* 44, no. 2 (1993): 171–183.

[198] Histria: H. Nubar, "Contribuții la topografia cetății Histria în epoca romano-bizantină. Considerații generale asupra necropolei din sectorul bazilicii extra muros," *SCIV* 22, no. 1 (1971): 208–209, fig. 7/1; Sacidava: C. Scorpan, "Descoperiri arheologice diverse de la

the Crimea, where almost every cemetery yielded buckles of the Syracuse class, followed in popularity by the Middle Danube region. Given such discrepancies, it is likely that Syracuse buckles might not have originated from the Lower Danube region but from the Crimea, where the cultural and political influence of the Avars is clearly visible in the archaeological record.

The impressive density of finds of Byzantine buckles in the regions controlled by the Avars has been explained in the context of the political and diplomatic contacts between the Empire and the Early Avar Khaganate.[199] Since most buckles were associated with weapons in Avar and Gepid graves, they were probably pieces of military equipment, although occasionally they are found in female graves.[200] Some scholars have described Byzantine buckles as the ethnic badge of a Romanic population in *barbaricum*, but in reality none of the types and variants can be firmly attached to an ethnic group, since they have been found in a variety of contexts – inhumation and cremation, male and female graves, hilltop settlements from the frontier region, towns on the Black Sea coast, as well as away from the frontier region, in Asia Minor.[201] Such contexts have been associated with the Romans, the Slavs, the Avars, the Gepids, and the Crimean Goths, making these buckles elements of military fashion on a wide area.

It was the changing political climate that made them popular in some parts of *barbaricum*. The Avar influence is undeniable in Transylvania where the Gepids and the Romanic communities were closer to the Avar center of power than populations in Wallachia and Moldavia. Indeed, Byzantine buckles are unusually rare in the lands south and east of the Carpathians. What explains this paradox? During a time when the Avar pressure north of the Danube was intensifying, population groups which had been in closer contact with Byzantium struggled to protect their cultural identity by refusing to adopt Avar fashions, a conscious rejection

---

Sacidava," *Pontica* 11 (1978): 160–175; pl. XI/54 and XIX/54. Balta Verde: D. Berciu and E. Comşa, "Săpăturile arheologice de la Balta Verde şi Gogoşu," *MCA* 2 (1956): 403–404; fig. 132/1. Karnobat: D. Momchilov, "Kolanni ukrasi V-VII v. ot arkheologicheskiia fond na Karnobatski muzei," *Preslav. Sbornik* 7 (2013): 406, 410; 415, fig. 1/1. Sv. Kirik: Daskalov, *Kolani i kolanni*, 43.

[199] A. Madgearu, "A buckle of Pápa type found in the Early Byzantine fortress Halmyris (Murighiol, Tulcea County)," *Peuce* 15 (2003), 171–172; Varsik, "Byzantinische Gürtelschnallen," 89.

[200] Kölked-Feketekapu: Kiss, *Das awarenzeitlich-gepidische Gräberfeld*, 75–76, pl. 57 (M 425); Kiss, *Das awarenzeitliche Gräberfeld*, 144, fig. 43 (M 457).

[201] Teodor, "Éléments et influences," 64–65.

of some of the items that distinguished Avar warriors toward year 600. These were probably the same communities which had provided soldiers for the frontier garrisons and who chose to develop a system of social value in relation to the Byzantine world, or Slavic communities who resented the growing power of the khaganate after the successful Avar campaign in Wallachia (579). Such cultural resistance was not a uniform tactic, however. As we have seen, the same communities produced jewelry of Avar inspiration using stone molds even if it did not become part of local fashions. The cultural confusion experienced north of the Danube clearly reflects the shifting balance of power in *barbaricum* at the turn of the seventh century. Byzantium was rapidly losing ground in favor of a new hegemonic power.

3 | Christianity North of the Danube

3.1 Religious Life in *Barbaricum* After the Roman Retreat (ca. 275)

Christianity is one of the major cultural interfaces connecting the frontier provinces with the regions north of the Danube. Its significance for the creation of cultural identities in the Late Antique and Early Medieval Balkans cannot be overstated. A series of monographs written in the past decades have established an almost unchallenged narrative concerning the process of Christianization in *barbaricum*.[1] Indeed, the nationalistic discourse dominating the last communist decades in Eastern Europe distorted not only the interpretation of the archaeological evidence discussed in the previous chapter, but also views on the development of Christianity. Most studies shared a common agenda: to demonstrate the cultural continuity of the Daco-Roman population across centuries of vicissitude when the descendants of the Roman colonists had to deal with numerous barbarian invasions, while struggling to maintain their connection to the Roman world and assimilate the newcomers into their superior culture. The standard narrative describes Christianization as going hand in hand with the process of Romanization. The abandoning of Dacia in 275 did nothing to stop the process. On the contrary, it spread and intensified, gaining a life of its own away from direct Roman oversight. It has been argued not only that the Romanized population was very attached to its identity, but also that by the sixth century a cultural uniformity was achieved in the provinces of modern-day Romania through the circulation of people and

---

[1] A. Madgearu, *Rolul creștinismului în formarea poporului român* (Bucharest, 2001); N. Zugravu, *Geneza creștinismului popular al românilor* (Bucharest, 1997); M. Păcurariu, *Geschichte der Rumänischen Orthodoxen Kirche* (Erlangen, 1994); E. Popescu, *Christianitas daco-romana. Florilegium studiorum* (Bucharest, 1994); D. G. Teodor, *Creștinismul la est de Carpați. De la origini și pînă în secolul al XIV-lea* (Iași, 1991); L. Bârzu, *La continuité de la création matérielle et spirituelle du peuple roumain sur le territoire de l'ancienne Dacie* (Bucharest, 1980); I. Barnea, *Les monuments paléochrétiens de Roumanie* (Vatican, 1977).

Christian ideas from Trajanic Dacia to the "barbarian" regions south and east of the Carpathians.[2]

The goal was to show that by the beginning of the Dark Age following the Byzantine retreat from the Danube Christianization north of the river had become a firmly entrenched and irreversible process. The lack of official missions and systematic institutional guidance was not seen as a major problem, because the Daco-Roman population living in *barbaricum* never severed its ties to the Christian community from the Balkans. Archaeological evidence was adduced in support of this theory, as historians and archeologists alike strove to gather and publish all early Christian material found north of the Danube.[3] The absence of churches and the rarity of Christian burials were attributed to the independent development of Christianity in these lands.[4] Faced with an inconclusive literary and archaeological record, historians have advanced an alternative interpretation relying on the concept of Folk Christianity, a popular form of religion developing in an irregular fashion away from any institutional hierarchies or canonical constraint.[5] The end result of the entwined processes of

---

[2] A. Madgearu, "The significance of the Early Christian artefacts in post-Roman Dacia," in *Christianisierung Europas. Entstehung, Entwicklung und Konsolidierung im archäologischen Befund. Internationale Tagung im Dezember 2010 in Bergisch-Gladbach*, eds. O. Heinrich-Tamáska, N. Krohn, and S. Ristow (Regensburg, 2012), 299–317; D. G. Teodor, "Populația autohtonă din regiunile extracarpatice în secolele V–VII," in *Istoria românilor 2*, 654; Ș. Olteanu, M. Rusu, and R. Popa, "Modul de viață a comunităților umane: așezări, locuințe, necropole, credințe," in *Istoria românilor 3*, 91–92; M. Rusu, "Paleocreștinismul nord-dunărean și etnogeneza romînilor," *Anuarul Institutului de Istorie și Arheologie Cluj-Napoca* 26 (1983–1984): 57; I. Barnea, "Le christianisme sur le territoire de la Republique Socialiste de Roumanie aux IIIe–XIe siècles," *EB* 1 (1985): 97; Bârzu, *La continuité*, 77.

[3] I. Mitrea, "Considerații privind etnicitatea și spiritualitatea la est de Carpați în secolul al VI-lea pe baza surselor arheologice," in *Adevărul omenește posibil pentru rânduirea binelui*, eds. L. Cornea, M. D. Drecin, and B. B. Ștefănescu (Oradea, 2001), 299–306; M. Rusu, "Paleocreștinismul din Dacia romană," *EN* 1 (1991): 81–112; N. Gudea and I. Ghiurco, *Din istoria creștinismului la români. Mărturii arheologice* (Oradea, 1988); N. Dănilă, "Viața creștină în secolele IV–VI în lumina documentelor romano-bizantine," *Mitropolia Olteniei* 36, nos. 5–6 (1984): 325–341; N. Dănilă, "Izvoare literare, epigrafice, arheologice și numismatice privind prezența bizantină în Banat în secolele IV–VI," *Mitropolia Banatului* 34, nos. 3–4 (1984): 150–161; I. Catrinoiu, "Rolul Bizanțului în viața religioasă din Muntenia în secolele IV–VI în lumina izvoarelor literare și arheologice," *BOR* 110, no. 7 (1983): 589–599. N. Dănilă, "Considerații asupra noilor materiale arheologice paleocreștine din Transilvania," *BOR* 100, nos. 7–8 (1982): 731–742; D. Protase, *Problema continuității în Dacia în lumina arheologiei și numismaticii* (Bucharest, 1966), 141–153.

[4] Madgearu, *Rolul creștinismului*, 105–106; Zugravu, *Geneza creștinismului*, 326–330.

[5] D. Protase, "Populația autohtonă în Dacia postromană (anul 275 – secolul al VI-lea)," in *Istoria românilor 2*, 599–600; D. G. Teodor, "Creștinism și păgânism la est de Carpați în a doua jumătate a mileniului I d. Hr.," *Pontica* 28–29 (1994–1995): 221–222; Zugravu, *Geneza creștinismului*, 19–59. A. Madgearu, "Romanizare și creștinare la nordul Dunării în

Romanization and Christianization was the Romanian ethnogenesis, the formation of a Christian and Neo-Latin-speaking nation which managed to preserve its Roman identity against all odds. Despite some criticism, such theories developed in the 1970s and 1980s in the context of national-communism remain firmly entrenched in historiography to this day.[6] They downplay the multiethnic nature of *barbaricum* in Late Antiquity, streamline the process of Christianization, and give it a "manifest destiny" aura. To be sure, much of the argument is nothing but a partisan reading of evidence whose existence should not be denied but simply reinterpreted. The whole problem needs to be reassessed in light of the archaeological material and the scanty information available from written sources.

Sixth-century Christianity north of the Danube can be understood only in the context of long-term imperial efforts to establish strategic buffer zones in *barbaricum*. Such actions were driven by political and diplomatic motivations, rather than religious, as Late Roman emperors were hoping to pacify barbarian tribes and attract them into the Empire's cultural orbit. However, the chronological boundaries of this process, the reigns of Constantine (306–337) and Justinian (527–565), are separated by two centuries of sporadic and uneven imperial initiatives in the lands north of the Danube. For many decades, the local population would be left to its own devices and it is unclear whether religious developments in *barbaricum* were always in favor of the Empire's official religion. Indeed, sixth-century Christianity raises questions of continuity, on the one hand, and conformity to Christian canons, on the other.

Many historians have argued that the process of Christianization started before Dacia was abandoned by Emperor Aurelian. According to such theories, "unofficial missionaries," which included Roman colonists, traders, soldiers, and prisoners, came to Dacia from regions where Christianity had established an early foothold.[7] These efforts remained marginal

---

secolele IV–VII," *Anuarul Institutului de Istorie "A. D. Xenopol"* 31 (1994): 482; Gudea and Ghiurco, *Din istoria creştinismului*, 110.

[6] The most balanced discussion remains A. Timotin, "Paleocreştinismul carpato-danubian," *Archaeus* 2, no. 2 (1998): 43–172. For a thorough critique of the nationalist thesis, see G. A. Niculescu, "Archaeology, nationalism, and the 'History of the Romanians'," *Dacia* 48–49 (2004–2005): 99–124. For the role of Christianity in national identity, see S. Mitu, *National Identity of Romanians in Transylvania* (Budapest, 2001), 249–250.

[7] This idea pervades the entire literature on the subject, but see more recently M. Bărbulescu, "Paleocreştinismul în România. Probleme metodologice şi aspecte istoriografice româneşti şi străine," in *Slujitor al bisericii şi al neamului. Părintele Prof. Univ. Dr. Mircea Păcurariu, membru corespondent al Academiei Române, la împlinirea vârstei de 70 de ani* (Cluj-Napoca, 2002), 171–178; S. D. Cârstea, "Creştinismul românesc din primele secole. Puncte de vedere,"

because of the general climate of distrust and persecution, but we are told that the development of Christianity gained momentum after 275 when any official limitation on its growth disappeared from the lands north of the Danube along with the Roman army and administration.[8] The theory is problematic because the last decades of the third century brought the so-called "Little Peace of the Church" and there is no reason to believe that the Christian community would have faced serious adversity had Dacia remained in the provincial system.[9] Moreover, it was simply assumed that the effects of the Roman retreat, which by necessity led to a weakening of the cultural and economic ties to the Roman world, would not have negatively impacted the growth of Christianity. If anything, the abandoning of Dacia delayed the process of Christianization and made it less fluid and systematic in the next century.

To be sure, even without Roman institutional support, the presence of Christianity in *barbaricum* increased significantly after Constantine's political and religious reforms. Historians and archaeologists often refer to the substantial body of archaeological material as evidence that Christianity received additional impetus in the fourth century after it was embraced by the imperial house. The defining features of this process promptly revealed themselves. First, imperial initiatives were political, rather than religious, and second, the growth of Christianity, or at least its pace, seemed to depend closely on Roman intervention. Through an uncritical reading of panegyrical and ecclesiastical sources, it has been repeatedly argued that Constantine reached out to protect and expand the Christian community in *barbaricum*, being deeply concerned with its spiritual well-being.[10] In reality, Constantine's agenda was purely political and his religious initiatives were subservient to his larger goals.

What exactly were the effects of his actions on the Lower Danube and the northern world? Only half a century after the official abandoning of Dacia, Constantine could still hope to rely on the remaining Roman

---

Revista Teologică 2 (2008): 129. The archaeological evidence is inconclusive, but see Madgearu, *Rolul creștinismului*, 18–32.

[8] Protase, "Populația autohtonă," 589; I. Ionescu, *Începuturile creștinismului românesc daco-roman (sec. II–VI, VII)* (Bucharest, 1998), 21–22; N. Stoicescu, *The Continuity of the Romanian People* (Bucharest, 1983), 181.

[9] H. A. Drake, *Constantine and the Bishops: The Politics of Intolerance* (Baltimore, MD, 2002), 114–115; See also W. H. C. Frend, "Persecutions: genesis and legacy," in *The Cambridge History of Christianity. Volume 1: Origins to Constantine*, eds. M. M. Mitchell and F. M. Young (Cambridge, 2006), 517–518.

[10] Catrinoiu, "Rolul Bizanțului," 594; E. Popescu, "Le christianisme en Roumanie jusqu'au VIIe siècle à la lumière des nouvelles recherches," in *Christianitas daco-romana*, 84.

structures in order to reestablish some degree of control north of the Danube. For his campaigns against the Goths, the emperor built or restored several important fortresses on the Gothic bank of the Danube. The most significant was Dafne, whose strategic value was still remembered by Procopius in the sixth century.[11] In addition, Constantine ordered the building of a stone bridge across the Danube connecting Oescus with Sucidava, inaugurated in 328 in the emperor's presence.[12] This impressive technological feat fueled the propaganda machine as Constantine wanted to present himself as the restorer of the most glorious age of Roman expansionism, associated with emperor Trajan.[13] The bridge also served practical purposes and the left side of the river must have been sufficiently pacified to ensure that it would remain functional and easily guarded. Indeed, this level of security was achieved after Constantine established more than 20 bridge-heads on the left bank.[14] The complete reconquest of Trajanic Dacia was never accomplished and perhaps never seriously contemplated by Constantine, although he took the title *Dacicus Maximus*.[15] The emperor's main goal was the creation of a sizeable buffer region between *Romania* and *Gothia*, a spearhead into *barbaricum* allowing a more direct involvement in local politics and ensuring a better protection of the Danube frontier. Imperial intervention may have also included the Christianization of local communities in Dacia as well as in *Gothia*. The terms of the peace treaty of 332 may have stipulated the freedom of

---

[11] Procopius, *De Aedificiis*, 4.7.7.

[12] The most detailed description remains D. Tudor, *Les ponts romains du Bas-Danube* (Bucharest, 1974), 135–166. For recent research, see P. Gherghe and L. Amon, "Noi date în legătură cu podul lui Constantin cel Mare de la Sucidava," *Pontica* 40 (2007): 359–369. The bridge seems to have remained usable for at least four decades. Valens chose to cross the river on a pontoon bridge at Dafne for his campaign against the Goths in 367, but perhaps the decision was taken out of strategic considerations, Constantine's bridge being located some 250 km upstream. For the event, see Ammianus, *Res Gestae*, 27.5.2.

[13] Medallions were issued to commemorate the event, for which see recently E. Paunov, "Konstantinoviiat most na Dunava pri Escus – Sukidava izobrazen na bronzov medal'on," *Reverse* 1, no. 1 (2016): 28–33; For the numismatic evidence identifying Trajan as Constantine's imperial model, see M. R. Alföldi, "Das trajanische Bild Constantins," in *Die constantinische Goldprägung: Untersuchungen zu ihrer Bedeutung für Kaiserpolitik und Hofkunst* (Mainz, 1963), 57–69. See also the medallions with the legend *Gothia* and Constantine hailed as *Debellator Gentium Barbarorum* (*RIC* VII, 531).

[14] V. Mărculeț, "Un problème de géopolitique de la politique danubienne du Constantin le Grand (324–337): la reconquête et la domination de la Dacie méridionale," *Pontica* 41 (2008): 302.

[15] Cf. G. Popilian, "Stăpânirea romano-bizantină la Dunărea de Jos," in *Istoria românilor 2*, 611, where Constantine's intention to reconquer Dacia is considered an undisputed fact. For a more skeptical interpretation, see N. Lenski, *Failure of Empire: Valens and the Roman State in the Fourth Century AD* (Los Angeles, CA, 2002), 122–124. For Constantine's imperial titles, see T. D. Barnes, "The Victories of Constantine," *ZPE* 20 (1976): 149–155.

religion, although Eusebius and Socrates offer only generic remarks on this subject.[16] In any case, the plan worked because the emperor's actions brought several decades of peace on the Lower Danube.

Relative stability on the frontier allowed Constantius II to support in the 340s a semi-official mission north of the Danube led by Ulfilas. According to his pupil Auxentius, the bishop served the local Christian community by preaching not only in the language of the Goths, but also in Greek and Latin, a clear sign that his activity targeted multiethnic communities.[17] The ethnic diversity of communities in *barbaricum*, whose Christianity must have been strong enough to justify the presence of a bishop, could have been enhanced by the large number of Christian prisoners brought by the Goths after their massive raids in Asia Minor in the second half of the third century.[18] In addition, the transdanubian Christian community of the mid-fourth century may have included some of the Romans who sought refuge among barbarians during the Great Persecution, a practice lamented by Eusebius.[19] Equally, it must be remembered that the persecution launched in the late 340s forced Ulfilas to leave *Gothia* taking with him a significant number of Christians and this would have weakened the community in *barbaricum*.[20] Unfortunately, any attempt to estimate the size of the Christian population beyond the frontier is frustrated by the constant movement of people north and south of the river from the fourth to the seventh century.

---

[16] Eusebius, *Vita Constantini*, 4.14.1; Socrates, *Historia ecclesiastica*, 1.18. For an interpretation of these passages in favor of Constantine's ecumenical ambitions, see E. Chrysos, "Gothia Romana. Zur Rechtslage des Föderatenlandes der Westgoten im 4. Jh.," *Dacoromania* 1 (1973): 62–64; E. Popescu, "La hiérarchie ecclésiastique sur le territoire de la Roumanie. Sa structure et son évolution jusqu'au VIIe siècle," in *Christianitas daco-romana*, 206–207. For a more skeptical reading, see M. Kulikowski, *Rome's Gothic Wars: From the Third Century to Alaric* (Cambridge, 2007), 107.

[17] Auxentius, *Epistula*, 53: *grecam et latinam et goticam linguam sine intermissione in una et sola eclesia Cristi predicauit*. This supports Sozomen's statement that not only the Goths embraced Christianity but also the neighboring communities close to the Danube, for which see Sozomen, *Historia Ecclesiastica*, II, 6.1: καὶ Γόθοι, καὶ ὅσοι τούτοις ὅμοροι τὸ πρὶν ἦσαν ἀμφὶ τὰς ὄχθας Ἴστρου ποταμοῦ.

[18] Philostorgius, *Historia Ecclesiastica*, 2.5.

[19] Eusebius, *Vita Constantini*, 2.53. Eusebius' statements refer generically to "barbarians" welcoming Christian refugees from the Empire, without any specific mention of the Danube region: αὐχοῦσι νῦν ἐπ' ἐκείνοις οἱ βάρβαροι οἱ τοὺς κατ' ἐκεῖνο καιροῦ ἐξ ἡμῶν φεύγοντας ὑποδεδεγμένοι καὶ φιλανθρώπῳ τηρήσαντες αἰχμαλωσίᾳ, ὅτι οὐ μόνον τὴν σωτηρίαν ἀλλὰ καὶ τὰ τῆς σεμνότητος αὐτοῖς κατέστησαν ἐν ἀσφαλείᾳ ἔχειν.

[20] Auxentius, *Epistula*, 58–59: *sanctissimus uir beatus Ulfila cum grandi populo confessorum de uarbarico pulsus in solo Romaniae*.

Although it has been argued that the active policy initiated by Constantine and continued by Constantius II north of the Danube resulted in a "second Romanization" in Dacia the effects were less spectacular as the Gothic problem returned with a vengeance during Valens' reign.[21] Once again, political expediency took precedence and religion became a tool and a means to an end rather than a standalone imperial goal. Rome's allies in *barbaricum* received additional impetus to convert when Valens' military intervention (367–369) was followed by a more insidious *divide et impera* strategy of supporting the Christian community in *Gothia*. Indeed, Valens interfered in the civil war tearing apart Gothic society north of the Danube by showing favor to Fritigern, the Gothic leader who converted to Christianity along with his supporters.[22] We can be sure that Christianity already had deep roots throughout the region and across the social spectrum since Athanaric used violent persecution (369–372) as a way of strengthening his grip on his lands and openly opposing Rome and the pro-Roman Gothic factions. On the other hand, the exact strength of the Christian community at this point is hard to gauge. Athanaric's agenda was political and had less to do with the number of Christians in *Gothia* and more with an ideological show of strength in the aftermath of his recent military setback. In any case, another wave of Christians fled persecution by seeking shelter in the Balkan provinces.[23]

The archaeological evidence points to a larger concentration of Christian artifacts on the territory of the former province of Dacia. Although the finds' provenance and context are often insufficiently documented, the number of artifacts alone can be used as a tentative indicator of considerable demand for goods associated with the practice of Christianity. Aside from their religious significance, such imports reflect close contacts between transdanubian Dacia and the Illyrian and Pannonian regions, at least until the arrival of the Huns. Most finds come from Roman towns such as Apulum, Porolissum, Sarmizegetusa, and Potaissa where urban life – or rather "life in the city" – continued for some time despite a natural

---

[21] A. Madgearu, "Military operations commanded by Constantine the Great north of the Danube," in *Cruce și misiune. Sfinții Împărați Constantin și Elena - promotori ai libertății religioase și apărători ai Bisericii*, eds. E. Popescu and V. Ioniță, vol. II (Bucharest, 2013), 592. Cf. H. Wolfram, *The Roman Empire and Its Germanic Peoples* (Los Angeles, CA, 1997), 75–76.

[22] Socrates, *Historia Ecclesiastica*, 4.33.4. For the religious circumstances and Fritigern's position, see Kulikowski, *Rome's Gothic Wars*, 116–122. For the political context, see P. Heather and J. Matthews, *The Goths in the Fourth Century* (Liverpool, 1991), 17–26. For the date of Fritigern's conversion, see N. Lenski, "The Gothic civil war and the date of the Gothic conversion," *GRBS* 36 (1995): 51–87.

[23] Epiphanius, *Audians*, 15.4.248.

process of ruralization after the province was abandoned. Locally produced Christian items, such as terracotta lamps, are the most convincing finds. Unlike imported luxury goods, which could be connected with the creation of social distinction rather than reflecting religious belief, the Christian significance of local products cannot be questioned.[24] On the other hand, the association of certain artifacts with churches and the Christian liturgy is more conjectural. Although items such as the bronze lamps found in several locations in Dacia, the Eucharistic bowl from Porolissum, and the fragmentary chandelier from Biertan originally served liturgical purposes, we cannot automatically assume an identical function once they were brought to Dacia. Few of these artifacts have been found in well-documented contexts, although this problem was often ignored. Indeed, no room was left for alternative interpretations, despite the unknown circumstances of most finds which left ample room for ambiguity.

The famous fourth-century *donarium* found accidentally at Biertan in the eighteenth century perfectly reflects the uncritical interpretation of finds as well as its ideological prejudice. Based on the original description, the assemblage appears to be a hoard of copper objects including a pitcher, a bowl, a medallion decorated with a Chi-Rho, and a votive *tabula ansata* with the openwork inscription *Ego Zenovivs Votvm Posvi*.[25] According to the original report, the pitcher ("Kanne") and the bowl ("Schüssel") were found in poor condition and abandoned. Although they are lost and no details are known, these objects were later labeled as "liturgical vessel" (*herniboxeston*).[26] Zenobius himself became a munificent Romanic leader contributing to the local church, a priest, or even a "bishop of the Daco-Roman population in Transylvania."[27] The existence of a church was assumed although no archaeological evidence was found and no

---

[24] Madgearu, *Rolul creștinismului*, 114–117, nos. 1, 7, and 12–13; Barnea, *Christian Art*, 32–33.

[25] K. Horedt, "Eine lateinische Inschrift des 4. Jahrhunderts aus Siebenbürgen," *Anuarul Institutului de Studii Clasice* 4 (1941–1943): 10–16.

[26] Barnea, *Christian Art*, 32; Zugravu, *Geneza creștinismului*, 290; Madgearu, *Rolul creștinismului*, 115, nos. 4–6; Gudea and Ghiurco, *Din istoria creștinismului*, 138. A. Diaconescu and C. Opreanu, "Cîteva puncte de vedere în legătură cu evoluția societății autohtone în epoca daco-romană tîrzie și în perioada migrațiilor," *Anuarul Institutului de Istorie și Arheologie din Cluj* 29 (1989): 593. For the original description of the objects (1779), see Horedt, "Eine lateinische Inschrift," 10: "Es waren noch kleine Überbleibsel einer Kanne und einer Schüssel von gleichem Erze dabei, aber so verdorben, dass sie (nicht) verdieneten, aufbehalten zu werden" ("There were also small remains of a pitcher and a bowl of the same metal, but they were so damaged that they were not worth retrieving").

[27] E. Popescu, *Inscripțiile grecești și latine din secolele IV–XIII descoperite în România* (Bucharest, 1976), 389; Madgearu, *Rolul creștinismului*, 41.

fourth-century settlements are known in the immediate vicinity.[28] The *donarium* has been unanimously described as one of the most important documents confirming the Christianity and continuity of the Daco-Roman population in Transylvania.[29] Any revisionist interpretation was swiftly dismissed.[30] In fact, the find from Biertan may have a more prosaic explanation; it shows many similarities with the late sixth-century hoard of coins and copper objects found at Horgești in Moldavia, in the sense that both appear to be accumulations of copper items whose intrinsic value determined the owner to bury them for safekeeping.[31] The monetary function of the coins from Horgești, discussed in Chapter 7, should be questioned just as much as the Christian significance of the objects from Biertan. While the religious interpretation remains in the realm of possibility, it should be allowed that the find from Biertan could be the result of plunder in Illyricum or Pannonia anytime between the fourth and the sixth century.[32] This applies equally to all undocumented finds of imported luxury items from Dacia. Furthermore, the ethnic background and religious belief of the owners are impossible to determine, given the multicultural nature of Transylvania in Late Antiquity and the changing balance of power in the region.[33]

Along with archaeological material, linguistic evidence has long been used to confirm the existence of a well-established Christian community north of the Danube in Late Antiquity.[34] Christian terminology in

---

[28] For the archaeological survey, see K. Horedt, "Kleine Beiträge," *Dacia* 23 (1979): 343.

[29] Barnea, *Christian Art*, 126; Diaconescu and Opreanu, "Cîteva puncte," 579.

[30] The *donarium* from Biertan has been attributed to Gothic raids, for which see U. Fiedler, "Biertan. Ein Zeugnis heidnischer Opferstätten im nachrömischen Siebenbürgen," *Dacia* 40–42 (1996–1998): 389–397; For a rebuttal, see A. Madgearu, "The spreading of the Christianity in the rural areas of post-Roman Dacia (4th–7th centuries)," *Archaeus* 8 (2004): 46–52.

[31] S. Musteață, "Unele concretizări privind vasul de metal din tezaurul monetar de la Horgești, jud. Bacău, Romania," in *Arheologia între știință, politică și economia de piață*, eds. S. Musteață, A. Popa, and J.-P. Abraham (Chișinău, 2010), 99–127.

[32] Madgearu dismisses the possibility based on the unfounded assumption that barbarians would only seek objects made of silver and gold; see Madgearu, *Rolul creștinismului*, 41–42, n. 31. On the other hand, Fiedler suggested that the assemblage was an offering made by a Germanic warrior to the spirit of the spring flowing nearby, without considering the possibility that the place may have been deliberately chosen as a convenient point of reference for later retrieval; see Fiedler, "Biertan," 390–391.

[33] For the cultural background, see R. Harhoiu, "Allgemeine Betrachtungen zum Bestattungssittenbild Siebenbürgens im 4. und bis zur Mitte des 9. Jahrhunderts," *Dacia* 48–49 (2004–2005): 283–334.

[34] Protase, "Populația autohtonă," 597–599; Madgearu, *Rolul creștinismului*, 53–57; Zugravu, *Geneza creștinismului*, 187–194; Barnea, "Le christianisme," 93–94; Ionescu, *Începuturile creștinismului*, 41–66. For a comprehensive treatment of the linguistic heritage, see I. Popinceanu, *Religion, Glaube und Aberglaube in der rumänischen Sprache* (Nürnberg, 1964).

Romanian has ancient Latin roots, which was taken to mean that the faith had been firmly established long before the cultural transformations brought by the Byzantine retreat from the northern Balkans. Such terms include *christianus* (creştin = Christian), *crux* (cruce = cross), *domine deo* (Dumnezeu = God), *angelus* (înger = angel), *sanctus* (sânt = saint), *basilica* (biserica = church) and many others relating to the Christian calendar, liturgy, and practices. This Latin vocabulary developed in the fourth century in the Danube region and was transferred to the Latin-speaking population in transdanubian Dacia in the context of the empire's expansionist policy.[35] The issue is, however, less straightforward than it may appear when following the broad political and cultural developments.[36] Despite reams of scholarly speculation, a consensus is far from being reached regarding the territory where the Romanian language developed, the historical time frame of the process, and the circumstances in which the so-called "Balkan Romance" split into several dialects.

A time-honored debate between linguists, historians, and archaeologists, whose roots reach back to late eighteenth-century enlightenment and nineteenth-century nationalism, offers two opposing interpretations. On the one hand, it has been argued that the Romanian language is the direct result of Romanization in the province of Dacia and constant cultural contact with the Roman world south of the Danube. According to this view, the Christian vocabulary developed between the fourth and the seventh century and was firmly in place when Slavonic became the dominant language of the medieval church in the Balkans. In other words, this interpretation served the "continuity thesis," postulating an uninterrupted cultural development of the Daco-Roman population on the territory of present-day Romania, with or without the political presence of Rome.[37]

---

[35] Cf. J. Kramer, "Bemerkungen zu den christlichen Erbwörtern des Rumänischen und zur Frage der Urheimat der Balkanromanen," *Zeitschrift für Balkanologie* 34 (1998): 15–22, where the historical and archaeological context is completely ignored and the lands north of the Danube are described as being completely cut off from the Roman world.

[36] For a concise overview of the linguistic debate, see E. Banfi, "Cristianizzazione nei Balcani e formazione della lega linguistica balcanica," in *Christianity Among the Slavs: The Heritage of Saints Cyril and Methodius. Acts of the International Congress Held on the Eleventh Centenary of the Death of St. Methodius, Rome, October 8–11, 1985*, eds. G. Farrugia, R. F. Taft, and G. K. Piovesana (Rome, 1988), 145–163. For the historical coordinates of the problem, see E. Popescu, "Continuité daco-romaine. Ethnogénèse du people roumain et sa langue. Rôle du christianisme," in *Christianitas daco-romana*, 30–57. For a well-organized conspectus of the older literature, see Stoicescu, *The Continuity*, 9–101.

[37] Works from the last few decades include N. Saramandu, *Originea dialectelor româneşti* (Bucharest, 2005); S. Dumistrăcel and D. Hreapcă, "Histoire des dialects dans la Romania: Romania du Sud-Est," in *Romanische Sprachgeschichte/ Histoire linguistique de la Romania*,

On the other hand, opponents of this theory have claimed that Romanization left insignificant cultural and linguistic traces north of the Danube. Romanian language developed as a result of a presumed immigration of Romance-speaking groups in the Middle Ages, on which written sources are completely silent.[38] More recent research has exposed both theories as excessively rigid, a defining feature of all scholarly assumptions serving nationalistic or imperialistic ideologies.[39] Indeed, the concept of "mobile continuity" is more in tune with the historical evidence suggesting a constant circulation of population groups north and south of the Danube in Late Antiquity and the Early Middle Ages, from the so-called Jireček Line in the Central Balkans to the Carpathians. The transdanubian linguistic tradition from Transylvania (*Romania antiqua*) coexisted with and became reinforced by cultural and linguistic influences on both sides of the Danube (*Romania nova*), which may have proven decisive for the development of Latin-language Christianity. This process probably continued after the collapse of the Danube frontier in the seventh century, especially since the river could be crossed freely without any authority regulating traffic.

If archaeological, literary, and linguistic evidence points to the existence of a growing Christian community in the fourth-century *barbaricum*, sometimes receiving institutional support from the Lower Danube provinces, the fifth century was a time of confusion and crisis. Both written and

---

eds. G. Ernst et al. (Berlin, 2008), 2459–2476; M. Sala, *De la latină la română* (Bucharest, 1998), 11–34; E. Scărlătoiu, *Istroromânii și istroromâna: relații lingvistice cu slavii de sud: cuvinte de origine veche slavă* (Bucharest, 1998), 52–84; Păcurariu, *Geschichte*, 22–30.

[38] The theory goes back to the nineteenth century but continues to find supporters despite the absence of any documented tradition recording a massive migration from the Balkans to the lands north of the Danube; see more recently H. Lüdtke, *Der Ursprung der romanischen Sprachen. Eine Geschichte der sprachlichen Kommunikation* (Kiel, 2005), 415–440; J. Kramer, "Sprachwissenschaft und Politik. Die Theorie der Kontinuität des Rumänischen und der balkanische Ethno-Nationalismus im 20. Jh.," *Balkan-Archiv* 24–25 (1999–2000): 105–163; A. du Nay, *The Origin of the Rumanians: The Early History of the Rumanian Language* (Toronto, 1996); G. Schramm, *Ein Damm bricht. Die römische Donaugrenze und die Invasionen des 5.–7. Jahrhunderts im Lichte von Namen und Wörtern* (Munich, 1997). For a critical review, see N. Saramandu, "À propos de l'origine du roumain," *RESEE* 47 (2009): 315–321.

[39] For the linguistic explanation, see A. Niculescu, "Le daco-roumain – *Romania antiqua, Romania nova* et la continuité mobile. Une synthèse," in *Actes du XVIIIe Congrès international de linguistique et philologie romanes: Université de Trèves (Trier) 1986*, ed. D. Kremer (Tübingen, 1992), 86–104. For a historical discussion of this phenomenon in light of linguistic and archaeological research, see C. Opreanu, "The North-Danube regions from the Roman province of Dacia to the emergence of the Romanian language (2nd–8th centuries)," in *History of Romania: Compendium*, eds. I. A. Pop, I. Bolovan, and S. Andrea (Cluj-Napoca, 2006), 129–132.

material sources are conspicuously silent and the fifth-century Lower Danube appears to have experienced its lowest cultural ebb.[40] Already after the massive crossing of the Goths into the Balkan provinces the empire lost the ability to remain directly involved in the lands north of the Danube. Moreover, the Hunnic storm made such intervention impossible, as the emperor in Constantinople had a difficult time maintaining some semblance of control at the Lower Danube.[41] The Christian community in *barbaricum* was weakened by the massive migration south of the river in the late 370s and perhaps continuing after the arrival of the Huns, despite information about the activity of Gothic bishops such as Goddas and the martyrdom of queen Gaatha.[42] With the frontier shattered in the middle decades of the fifth century we can assume an easier crossing of the unguarded Danube, but it is doubtful that Christians from the Balkans would have found the lands north of the river particularly auspicious.[43] The former province of Dacia, including the territories reconquered by Constantine, which had enjoyed relative stability and uninhibited access to the Roman world, was the region most affected by the Hunnic invasion since Attila's center of power was established on the Middle Danube. The provinces of Pannonia and northern Illyricum were ravaged and Dacia's connection to the Roman world was only reestablished in the sixth century, perhaps as late as the reign of Justinian.

Although a contraction of the Christian community in *barbaricum* was not inevitable, after the fourth century religion evolved without any close institutional guidance and by the sixth century it came to encompass a variety of practices and achieved an ethnic diversity which many historians struggle to acknowledge. What was the state of Christianity in *barbaricum* when the Empire officially reconnected with the lands north of the Danube? Although the circulation of people and fashions was never interrupted, imperial intervention was the main catalyst for the dissemination of religious ideas and Roman culture in general. It accelerated processes

---

[40] For a survey of the archaeological evidence, see R. Harhoiu, *Die frühe Völkerwanderungszeit in Rumänien* (Bucharest, 1997).

[41] Even the province of Scythia, one of the more sheltered regions during the height of the Hunnic power, shows signs of decline and isolation, for which see L. Oța, "Hunii in Dobrogea," *Istros* 10 (2000): 363–387.

[42] Heather and Matthews, *The Goths*, 127–131. See also Z. Rubin, "The conversion of the Visigoths to Christianity," *Museum Helveticum* 38 (1981): 39–45.

[43] For political developments in the Danube region, see recently H. J. Kim, *The Huns* (New York, NY, 2016), 77–95.

already in motion and redirected them from the more meandered path carved by the ever-changing ethnic balance and relations of power in *barbaricum*. If Constantine's active policy north of the Danube came only a few decades after the abandoning of Dacia, Justinian had to acknowledge the fact that a century and a half had passed since the last vigorous imperial initiative in the lands north of the Danube. Nevertheless, Justinian's ambition was to walk in the footsteps of his illustrious predecessors, Trajan and Constantine, and he was destined to surpass their achievements if we believe sixth-century panegyrists. The reality, however, was less gratifying. Not only that Justinian did not regain control of former Dacia, as Lydus seems to suggest, but the extent of Roman influence was a lot more modest than the buffer zone established in *barbaricum* through Constantine the Great's efforts.[44]

If the fourth-century emperor managed to secure at least 20 outposts on the left bank of the Danube, build a spectacular stone bridge, and advance deep into former Dacia, Justinian only restored several bridge-head forts, Litterata, Recidiva, Zernes (Dierna), and Sykibida (Sucidava) – the latter perhaps already functional – as well as Constantine's foundation Dafne. Procopius is vague about Justinian's other achievements on the northern bank of the river, where he mentions that the emperor built from the ground (ἐκ θεμελίων) many other fortresses.[45] None are named and archaeology has not been able to locate their remains yet. However, Procopius does mention one old fortification, Theodora, placed on the northern bank of the river close to the ruins of Trajan's bridge.[46] Unlike Trajan and Constantine, Justinian had no intention of building a bridge across the

---

[44] Lydus, *De magistratibus*, 2.28: συνεῖδεν, αὐτὸς κατὰ μηδὲν Τραϊανῷ παραχωρῶν, περισῶσαι Ῥωμαίοις ἥδε ποτὲ ἀφηνιάζουσαν τὴν βορείαν. D. Protase took the account at face value and claimed that Justinian had plans to reconquer Dacia, for which see Protase, "Populația autohtonă," 586. For a similar interpretation, see Barnea, *Christian Art*, 34.

[45] Procopius, *De Aedificiis*, 4.6.5. On the reliablility of Procopius' *Buildings* and the reconstruction of the Danube frontier, see S. A. Ivanov, "Oborona Vizantii i geografiia 'varvarskikh' vtorzhenii cherez Dunai v pervoi polovine VI v.," *VV* 44 (1983): 27–47.

[46] The name has often been associated with Justinian's wife Theodora, for which see I. Barnea, "Sur les rapports avec Byzance du territoire situé au Nord du Bas Danube durant la période Anastase Ier-Justinien Ier (491–565)," *EBPB* 2 (1991): 54; and more recently, Popilian, "Stăpânirea romano-bizantină," 614. However, Procopius clearly states that Justinian paid no attention to this fortress, which would have been unlikely if he had just renamed it himself. In fact, Justinian gave his wife's name to fortresses built in Moesia, Theodoropolis and Pulchra Theodora, for which see Procopius, *De Aedificiis*, 4.7.5 and 4.11.20. It is more probable that the name of the transdanubian fortification referred to Theodora, wife of Constantius Chlorus, for which see A. Madgearu, "The 6th century Lower Danubian bridgeheads: location and mission," *EN* 13 (2003): 297.

Danube and he also felt that Theodora was too exposed to barbarian attacks to be worth restoring.[47]

Military initiatives north of the Danube were equally unimpressive. Unlike fourth-century emperors who successfully campaigned in *barbaricum*, Justinian's efforts simply aimed to punish the Slavs who were making frequent inroads in the frontier provinces and to instill terror and fear, a traditional Roman weapon in dealing with the transdanubian *barbaricum*.[48] Although Roman armies crossed the river into enemy territory multiple times, Slavic resistance prevented the emperor from devising a more ambitious agenda. After several years of successful attacks, in 533 the Roman commander Chilbudius was killed and the imperial armies did not return north of the Danube until the last decade of the century. Justinian's defensive policy after this date, which included the heavy fortification of the river, implies that his plan to create a deeper buffer region in *barbaricum* was dropped or at least postponed until the successful conclusion of hostilities on the western front.

Did this mean that the cultural connection with the Christian community north of the Danube would also be abandoned? The evidence suggests a negative answer, as the empire's short-term aggressive plan was replaced by a long-term cultural tactic of inclusion. Novella XI (535) concerning the archbishopric of Justiniana Prima remains the most important official document regarding the sixth-century religious policy in the Danube region.[49] The creation of an archbishopric in the Dacian diocese was part of Justinian's program of administrative reform meant to reshape the ecclesiastical hierarchies and administrative apparatus. It also had the purpose of reestablishing Roman structures in Illyricum, the emperor's birthplace and the area most affected by Hunnic destruction. Even in the sixth century, the region remained the Achilles' Heel in the defense of the Balkans after the Gepids established themselves at Sirmium and gained control of the core areas of Attila's former empire. On the other hand, it is not clear whether the presence of Gepids and Herules in northern Illyricum affected the development of Christianity as both

---

[47] Procopius, *De Aedificiis*, 4.6.18.

[48] In his oration *On the Peace of Valens* delivered in 370, Themistius argued emphatically that it was not a river or a wall keeping the Goths at bay, but fear and a sense of inferiority to Rome; see Themistius, *Oratio X*, 138d. In the sixth century, Procopius was using the same *topos* when arguing that even the weakly defended towers on the Danube were enough to scare the barbarians and dissuade them from crossing the river; see *De Aedificiis*, 4.5.4–5.

[49] *Corpus Iuris Civilis*, Novella 11.3.94.

groups had either adopted Christianity or were undergoing this process in the sixth century.[50]

According to Novella XI, the jurisdiction of the new archbishopric extended north of the Danube to include the Byzantine bridge-heads of Litterata and Recidiva.[51] Scholars have often used this legal source to suggest that the Christian population living north of the Danube was placed under the jurisdiction of the bishop of Aquis, an important town in the Iron Gates region. That the measure was taken shortly after Chilbudius' death is not a coincidence. Justinian's militaristic policy in *barbaricum* had failed and in less than a decade the geo-strategic map would suffer dramatic changes. The Italian front needed the emperor's full attention after Belisarius' initial *blitzkrieg* came to a halt (537), a potentially disastrous revolt in North Africa required immediate intervention (536), the Persians invaded Syria (540), and a great plague was crippling the Byzantine cities (542). In these new circumstances, which also included the loss of Sirmium to the Gepids (536), a more active cultural tactic north of the Danube became the emperor's solution for destabilizing the local political structures and encouraging Romanization. Although no official missions have been recorded in the written sources, more modest initiatives could have been organized from the existing bishoprics on the Lower Danube. In addition, many of the soldiers recruited from *barbaricum* would have embraced Christianity becoming themselves agents of Christianization in their homeland. The same role could have been played by the Christian Latin-speaking communities which had survived the great cultural transformations of the past century.[52]

---

[50] For Byzantine diplomacy targeting the Gepids and the Herules, see recently A. Sarantis, *Justinian's Balkan Wars: Campaigning, Diplomacy and Development in Illyricum, Thrace and the Northern World AD 527–65* (Prenton, 2016), 40–65. Archaeological evidence shows that Christianity was already influent among the Gepids in the fifth century, for which see C. Opreanu, "Creștinismul și neamurile germanice în secolele IV–V în Transilvania," *EN* 5 (1995): 237–249.

[51] The location of Recidiva is still controversial with some scholars identifying it as Arcidava or even Sucidava, while more recently it has been located at Stari Dubovac; see D. Tudor, *Oltenia romană* (Bucharest, 1978), 466; Barnea, "Sur les rapports," 56; Madgearu, "The 6th century," 297. For the location of Litterata (Lederata), see A. Jovanović, "The problem of the location of Lederata," in *Roman Limes on the Middle and Lower Danube*, ed. P. Petrović (Belgrade, 1996), 69–72. Viminacium, also mentioned by Justinian's novella, is on the southern bank near Kostolac, Serbia; for the Early Byzantine settlement, see M. Popović, "Svetinja, novi podanci o ranovizantijskom Viminacijumu," *Starinar* 38 (1987), 1–37.

[52] Nelu Zugravu goes as far as calling the Latin-speaking Christians north of the Danube "true anonymous apostles"; see Zugravu, *Geneza creștinismului*, 411.

This is the context in which we must situate the archaeological evidence pertaining to the circulation of Christian objects in *barbaricum*. This movement targeted the existing Christian communities of Latin heritage but mixed ethnic composition whose connection to the Roman world was renewed and strengthened, but also pagan groups willing to adopt a more positive attitude toward Roman culture. Some scholars have interpreted the wide diffusion of Christian objects north of the Danube in the sixth century as a sign of the thorough Romanization of the region, the culmination of a centuries-long process.[53] In reality, the diffusion of Christian values in the sixth-century *barbaricum* has more to do with the absence of a central power beyond the frontier to oppose Roman influence in the manner of fourth-century Thervingian leaders. Slavic society was a lot more decentralized, adaptable, and generally tolerant if we accept the statements made in the *Strategikon*.[54] In any case, much like its fourth-century precedent, sixth-century Christianization remained a by-product of imperial political ambition.

3.2 Sixth-Century Christianity: The Material Evidence

The common wisdom regarding the process of Christianization in *barbaricum* was recently challenged by a different interpretation of the archaeological evidence. The main contention has been that the presence of Christian artifacts in the lands beyond the frontier should not be seen as evidence for the existence of a Christian population. Items such as flasks, lamps, and crosses were not brought north of the river out of religious consideration, but as items required by local elites, part of the cultural process described as *imitatio imperii*.[55] Although such views are refreshing, a strictly dichotomous discourse is not likely to further our understanding of the religious process. There is certainly enough evidence to support the claim that power groups in *barbaricum* needed access to Roman goods in order to maintain their social standing. The elite north of the Danube frontier could achieve that either by opposing or by joining imperial efforts in the region. Those who resisted would want to limit the "cultural contamination" and preserve their ethnic identity, while acquiring certain

---

[53] Madgearu, *Rolul creștinismului*, 78. See also Barnea, "Le christianisme," 92.
[54] *Strategikon*, 11.4.8–16 and 11.4.128–140.
[55] F. Curta, "Limes and cross: the religious dimension of the sixth-century Danube frontier of the Early Byzantine Empire," *Starinar* 51 (2001): 64–65.

Roman goods as symbols of their strength in relation to other competing forces in *barbaricum*. On the other hand, some elements of the barbarian elite and even ambitious commoners sought access to Roman goods by serving in the Roman army or by providing the empire with an ally north of the Danube frontier. Establishing closer relations may have included the adoption of Christianity as a way of gaining mutual trust.[56] Back home, however, there was no pressure to conform to specific Christian practices and none could be imposed by the Byzantine church.

From an archaeological perspective, Christianization appears sporadic and unsystematic. Indeed, the number of liturgical items, such as the bronze lamps found in the former province of Dacia, is insufficient to document the existence of a strong Christian community, since most of them are chance finds with no archaeological context to give them more meaning. Moreover, the absence of churches dated to the sixth century adds to this uncertainty.[57] It has been repeatedly suggested that sixth-century churches north of the Danube could have been made of wooden structures or other perishable materials, impossible to trace in the archaeological record.[58] While this hypothesis cannot be completely ruled out, the absence of churches remains problematic, especially since such examples exist in *barbaricum,* the most spectacular being the basilica and extramural cemetery at Fenékpuszta, on the western shore of Lake Balaton.[59] The basilica with three apses from Fenékpuszta has good analogies

---

[56] Colonial examples can provide some guide for the motivations behind the adoption of Christianity. See for instance: J. Blackburn, *The White Men: The First Response of Aboriginal Peoples to the White Men* (London, 1979), 50: "The people are often eager to please this high being. They give up their rituals, customs and beliefs [...] and wait for the moment when their period of initiation is over and they are now rewarded with as much power and as many possessions as the white men now have."

[57] Curches functioned in Byzantine bridge-head forts from the northern bank, the best studied being the church from Sucidava where an inscription written on a Byzantine amphora mentions a "Lukonochos, son to Lykatios, presbyter," for which see Barnea, *Christian Art*, 122 and pl. 43.

[58] Teodor, *Creștinismul la est*, 82; Barnea, *Les monuments*, 27; Madgearu, *Rolul creștinismului*, 82; Zugravu, *Geneza creștinismului*, 337; D. Protase, *Autohtonii în Dacia II: Dacia postromană până la slavi* (Cluj-Napoca, 2000), 77.

[59] O. Heinrich-Tamáska, "Megjegyzések a fenékpusztai II. számú kora keresztény bazilika keltezésehez," *MFMÉ* 12 (2011): 225–234. For the cemetery next to the basilica, see R. Müller, *Die Gräberfelder vor der Südmauer der Befestigung von Keszthely-Fenékpuszta* (Budapest, 2010). On the archaeological evidence for the presence of Christianity in Pannonia, see E. B. Thomas, "Die Romanität Pannoniens im 5. und 6. Jahrhundert," in *Germanen, Hunnen und Awaren: Schätze der Völkerwanderungszeit: Germanisches Nationalmuseum, Nürnberg, 12. Dezember 1987 bis 21. Februar 1988: Museum für Vor- und Frühgeschichte der Stadt Frankfurt am Main, 13. März bis 15. Mai 1988*, eds. W. Menghin, T. Springer, and E. Wamers (Nuremberg, 1987), 284–294.

in the Lower Danube frontier region, which raises the question of why such religious buildings are so far missing from the lands north of the Danube. The complete ruralization of *barbaricum* could support the hypothesis that private houses could serve as gathering place and *domus ecclesiae*, but it also favored the preservation of pagan practices or even a lapse in faith given the fragility of the Christian community in the fifth century.

The rarity of Christian inhumation burials is also striking. With the exception of the burial assemblages from Moldoveni, Săbăoani, Secuieni, and Dănești (all in Moldavia), which have been interpreted as Christian because of their west–east orientation and the presence of Byzantine grave goods, other inhumation graves south and east of the Carpathians cannot be described as Christian with any certainty.[60] In addition, the absence of any notable inhumation cemeteries to contrast large cremation cemeteries such as the one excavated at Sărata-Monteoru adds to the uncertainty regarding the dominant religion north of the Danube. Sixth-century burials from *barbaricum* reflect a wide variety of practices, incineration and inhumation (non-Christian) being attributed both to the local population and the Slavic groups. This problem has proven insurmountable even for the partisans of the "Christian continuity" thesis, who have always been reluctant to allow that the Slavs could exert such cultural pressure on the Daco-Roman population as to provoke a massive return to the practice of incineration. Faced with a perplexing funerary record, historians and archaeologists remained true to their original theories and argued that burial practices were among the most conservative cultural features and in fact incineration did not contradict the Christian doctrine of salvation.[61]

What cannot be denied, however, is the absolute increase in the number and diversity of objects bearing Christian symbols found in the sixth-century *barbaricum*, many of which are direct imports from the Empire.[62] Whereas most Christian objects dated to the fourth and fifth centuries concentrated in the former province of Dacia, the long sixth century witnessed a dramatic increase in such finds in Wallachia and Moldavia. An official policy of Christianization would provide the easiest explanation

---

[60] Teodor, *Creștinismul*, nos. 17, 26, 31, and 32. The religious symbolism of the fibula with cross-shaped motifs from the grave at Moldoveni and of the Sucidava buckle from Dănești is debated. A similar grave, found at Dănceni in Moldova, contained two "Slavic" bow fibulae, glass beads, and a handmade pot, for which see I. A. Rafalovich, *Dancheni. Mogil'nik cherniakhovskoi kul'tury* (Kishinew, 1986), 25–27.

[61] This dominant interpretation is well reflected in Madgearu, *Rolul creștinismului*, 87–91 and 97–103; 91, for the inferior Slavic culture.

[62] Madgearu, *Rolul creștinismului*, pl. II and V.

but the sources are completely silent on this matter.[63] Since the Empire used mission as a political device during the Justinianic age in various peripheral areas such as the Transcaucasus, Yemen, and Nubia, we can only conclude that little could be gained politically from such initiatives north of the Danube.[64] The Christianization of the Slavs was not taken into consideration by sixth-century emperors, which comes in sharp contrast with fourth-century interests in the area when Ulfilas was preaching the Gospel in *Gothia*.[65] The decentralized nature of transdanubian society was perhaps the main impediment to the usual top-down strategy of Christianization which Justinian applied elsewhere on the northern frontier. The investiture and baptism of various barbarian leaders at Constantinople, such as the Hun king Grod, the Herul king Grepes, or the Lazi king Tzath, are set-piece stories in contemporary accounts and although they do not tell us much about systematic efforts to convert populations in *barbaricum*, they remain indicative of the emperor's diplomatic and cultural agenda.[66]

Novella XI of 535 regarding the jurisdiction of the new archbishopric established at Justiniana Prima was often described as having "exceptional significance," although in reality it tells us nothing about the Christian community north of the river.[67] Scholars have often used this source to suggest that the Christian population was placed under the jurisdiction of the archbishop of Justiniana Prima, based on the fact that two bridge-head fortifications from the northern bank are mentioned in the document. While Justinian's cultural strategy of integration seems clear, no bishoprics were established here and it is doubtful that such isolated Danubian

---

[63] Cf. Păcurarîu, *Geschichte*, 69, who posits the existence of bishoprics in the Byzantine bridgehead forts from the northern bank.

[64] I. Engelhardt, *Mission und Politik in Byzanz: ein Beitrag zur Strukturanalyse byzantinischer Mission zur Zeit Justins und Justinians* (Munich, 1974); G. Fowden, *Empire to Commonwealth: Consequences of Monotheism in Late Antiquity* (Princeton, NJ, 1993), 100–137; W. Seibt, "Westgeorgien (Egrisi, Lazica) in frühchristlicher Zeit," in *Die Schwarzmeerküste in der Spätantike und im frühen Mittelalter*, eds. R. Pillinger, A. Pülz, and H. Vetters (Vienna, 1992), 137–144; P. Wood, "Christianity and the Arabs in the sixth century," in *Inside and Out: Interactions between Rome and the Peoples on the Arabian and Egyptian Frontiers in Late Antiquity*, eds. J. H. F. Dijkstra and G. Fisher (Leuven, 2014), 355–370.

[65] F. Curta, "Before Cyril and Methodius: Christianity and barbarians beyond the sixth- and seventh-century Danube frontier," in *East Central and Eastern Europe in the Early Middle Ages*, ed. F. Curta (Ann Arbor, MI, 2005), 186–189.

[66] Malalas, *Chronographia*, 17.9 (Tzath); 18.6 (Grepes); 18.14 (Grod).

[67] G. Ștefan, "Justiniana Prima și stăpînirea bizantină la Dunărea de Jos în secolul al VI-lea e.n.," *Drobeta* 1 (1974): 65–70; Barnea, "Sur les rapports," 56. Nelu Zugravu considered that the creation of the archbishopric at Justiniana Prima led to a stricter adherence to Christian canons and hierarchies in *barbaricum*, for which see Zugravu, *Geneza creștinismului*, 420–421. For a more skeptical interpretation, see Madgearu, *Rolul creștinismului*, 80–81.

fortresses could project much political and religious influence deep into the hinterland. A similar role was envisaged for the well-established bishoprics of Scythia, whose authority would have extended beyond the Danube. Such views present the regions of Wallachia and southern Moldavia as being caught into a cultural pincer movement with Christian influences converging from Dobrudja and Dacia.[68] Even if such initiatives were real, they were short-lived and soon curtailed by the growing insecurity toward the middle of the sixth century when the Danube frontier became highly unstable. The lack of any evidence of attempts to institutionalize Christianity north of the river corroborated by the absence of any documented churches warrants a high degree of skepticism as to the precise influence of Byzantine bishoprics in the lands beyond the frontier.

Nevertheless, the diffusion of an unprecedented number of Christian objects deserves a more satisfactory explanation. While their presence cannot be ascribed to a coherent policy of Christianization, they reflect the Empire's desire to encourage *imitatio* in *barbaricum,* and more precisely to Justinian's ecumenical ambitions, which might have taken different forms. How successful were these initiatives? A recent gazetteer of Christian objects boasts a kaleidoscope of items showing up north of the river, which prima facie seems to paint the picture of a vibrant Christian community.[69] However, a closer examination of their context and spatial distribution casts some doubt on this optimistic assessment. Lamps, flasks, pectoral crosses, and molds for the production of crosses are the most interesting Christian objects imported or produced in *barbaricum*. The map reveals different patterns of distribution (Figure 15). We have already noted the large concentration of Early Byzantine lamps in Trajanic Dacia, many of which bear Christian symbols. The bronze liturgical lamps are particularly interesting, as are some of the Danubian and African clay lamps, most of them found in former Roman towns. All Christian lamps have been connected with the existence of churches in Dacia, although the finds lack any context to even allow a direct association with the religious beliefs of their owners.[70] On the other hand, very few lamps have been found south and east of the Carpathians. The often-cited lamp from Luciu, accidentally found close to the left bank of the Danube, was most likely not

---

[68] Barnea, *Les monuments*, 26; Păcurariu, *Geschichte*, 61–65; D. G. Teodor, *Creștinismul*, 60–61; N. Zugravu, "Cu privire la jurisdicția asupra creștinilor nord-dunăreni în secolele II–VIII," *Pontica* 28–29 (1995–1996): 176–179; Protase, *Autohtonii în Dacia*, 87; for a more skeptical interpretation, see Gudea and Ghiurco, *Din istoria creștinismului*, 128.
[69] Madgearu, *Rolul creștinismului*, 120–127.
[70] Madgearu, *Rolul creștinismului*, 82; Protase, "Populația autohtonă," 591.

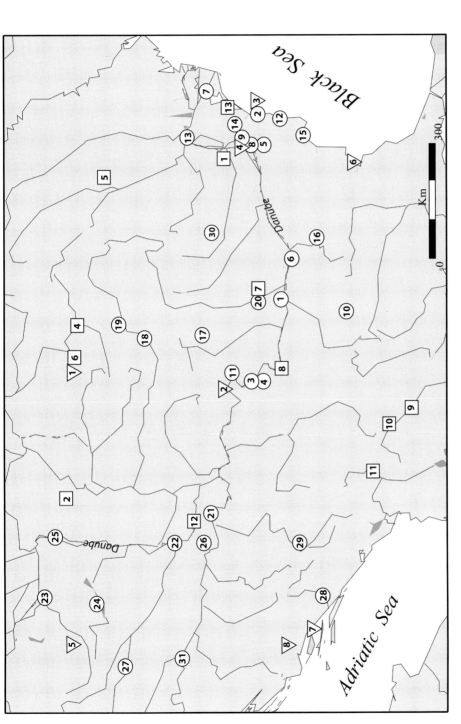

Figure 15 Distribution of bronze liturgical lamps (square), clay lamps with cross-shaped handle or cross/Chi-Rho on discus/nozzle (circle), and Menas flasks (triangle) *a) Bronze lamps*: 1. Luciu; 2. Tápiógyörgye; 3. Ratiaria; 4. Dej; 5. Lipova; 6. Porolissum; 7. Romula; 8. German; 9. Stobi; 10. Scupi; 11. Kalaja; 12. Nova Palanka; 13. Histria. *b) Clay lamps*: 1. Sucidava; 2. Tomis; 3. Aquis; 4. Kovilovo Grad; 5. Tropaeum Traiani; 6. Novae; 7. Halmyris; 8. Capidava; 9. Axiopolis; 10. Pirdop; 11. Drobeta; 12. Callatis; 13. Dinogetia; 14. Ulmetum; 15. Dionysopolis; 16. Gorni Trumbesh; 17. Bumbeşti; 18. Apulum; 19. Potaissa; 20. Romula; 21. Sirmium; 22. Osijek; 23. Gyor; 24. Kekkut; 25. Budapest; 26. Vinkovci; 27. Poetovio; 28. Mogorjelo; 29. Zidova Stena; 30. Ploieşti; 31. Siscia. *c) Menas flasks*: 1. Porolissum; 2. Dierna; 3. Tomis; 4. Capidava; 5. Szombathely; 6. Anchialos; 7. Makarska; 8. Č.tluk.

obtained by means of trade.[71] More probably, the bronze lamp was part of the booty taken from one of the Roman fortresses in Scythia. Along with lamps, flasks from the Holy Land and Egypt, especially Menas flasks, have been described as liturgical implements. They seem to have been relatively popular north of the Danube if one considers the finds from Moigrad (Porolissum), Orșova (Dierna), and Szombathely.[72] Menas flasks are very common in Italy and the Dalmatian coast, but also north of the Alps in the Rhine region, although the local provenance of some of the finds is not always certain.[73] Therefore, the flasks found in *barbaricum* may reflect contacts with the Dalmatian coast, rather than an eastern connection to Constantinople.[74]

Some conspicuous differences in the pattern of distribution remain important for understanding the variety of preferences and fashions in *barbaricum*. If Christian lamps rarely circulated outside the former province of Dacia, pectoral crosses are often found in Wallachia and Moldavia (Figure 16). Most of them are Maltese crosses usually made of copper or lead, such as the ones found at Davideni, Rashkiv, Ruginoasa, Valea Voievozilor and in *Avaria*, at Balatonfüzfő-Szalmássy and

---

[71] For the commercial explanation, see Zugravu, *Geneza creștinismului*, 415; Madgearu, *Rolul creștinismului*, 79; Protase, "Populația autohtonă," 594; C. Chiriac, *Civilizația bizantină și societatea din regiunile extracarpatice ale României în secolele VI–VIII* (Brăila, 2013), 76; D. G. Teodor, "Christian Roman Byzantine imports north of the Lower Danube," *Interacademica* 2–3 (2001): 118–120.

[72] I. Barnea, "Menasampullen auf dem Gebiet Rumäniens," in *Akten XII*, 509–514 and pl. 61; Z. Kadar, "*Die Menasampulle von Szombathely*," in *Akten XII*, 886–888. An additional Menas flask is kept at the Brukenthal Museum in Sibiu and was probably found in the former province of Dacia; see V. Moga, "Observații asupra unor piese paleocreștine inedite," *Apulum* 37, no. 1 (2000): 430, fig. 1.

[73] P. Linscheid, "Untersuchungen zur Verbreitung von Menasampullen nördlich der Alpen," in *Akten XII*, 982–986; Demeglio, "Ampolle devozionali," fig. 6. For the caveat, see S. Bangert, "Menas ampullae: a case study of long-distance contacts," in *Incipient Globalization? Long-distance Contacts in the Sixth Century*, ed. A. Harris (Oxford, 2007), 29; 29–33, for the long-distance circulation of Menas flasks. For pilgrim routes to Europe based on *ampullae*, see C. Lambert and P. P. Demeglio, "Ampolle devozionali ed itinerari di pellegrinaggio tra IV e VII secolo," *Antiquité Tardive* 2 (1994): 205–231.

[74] Curta, "Limes and cross," 59, n. 136; Lambert and Demeglio, "Ampolle devozionali," 219; cf. Madgearu, *Rolul creștinismului*, 52–53, who argued that the region north of the Danube had little or no connection with the West. Four Menas flasks are known from the northeastern Balkans, but Scythia seems a less probable supplier of such items to Trajanic Dacia; cf. Barnea, "Menasampullen," 514. Some flasks were produced locally and probably have no religious symbolism, for which see recently F. Topoleanu, "Vase de tip ploscă descoperite recent în Dobrogea (sec. VI p. Chr.)," in *Moesica et Christiana. Studies in Honour of Professor Alexandru Barnea*, eds. A. Panaite, R. Cîrjan, and C. Căpiță (Brăila, 2016), 455–461.

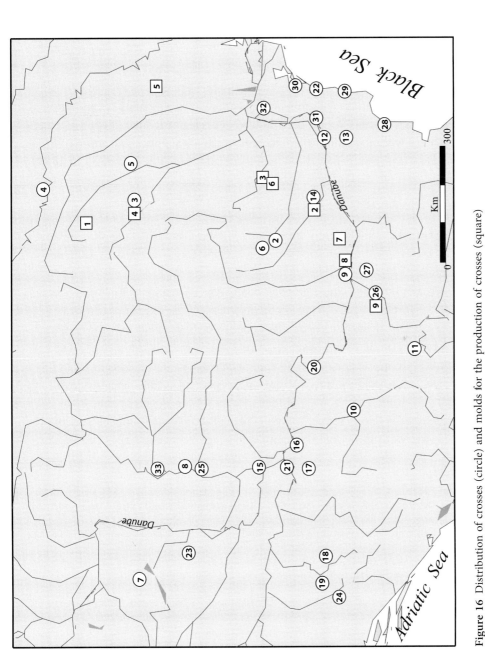

Figure 16 Distribution of crosses (circle) and molds for the production of crosses (square)
a) Crosses: 1. Porolissum; 2. Băleni-Români; 3. Davideni; 4. Rashkov; 5. Ruginoasa; 6. Valea Voievozilor; 7. Balatonfűzfő; 8. Székkutas; 9. Sucidava; 10. Naissus; 11. Pernik; 12. Sucidava (Izvoarele); 13. Golesh; 14. Bucharest; 15. Novi Banovci; 16. Ram; 17. Batočina; 18. Mihaljevići; 19. Čipuljići; 20. Aquis; 21. Višnjica; 22. Tomis; 23. Závod; 24. Gornje Turbe; 25. Deszk; 26. Sadovec; 27. Bezhanovo; 28. Odessos; 29. Callatis; 30. Histria; 31. Axiopolis; 32. Beroe; 33. Kiszombor. *b) Molds:* 1. Botoşana; 2. Bucharest-Străuleşti; 3. Cândeşti; 4. Davideni; 5. Hansca; 6. Izvoru Dulce; 7. Olteni; 8. Sucidava; 9. Sadovec.

Székkutas.⁷⁵ It seems that the parallel between the Middle Danube region, on one hand, and Moldavia and Wallachia, on the other, illustrated by the study of handmade lamps, is also valid for pectoral crosses, with Dacia following a different pattern. Unlike lamps, many crosses have been found in a clear archaeological context, in association with other sixth-century artifacts and sometimes with molds used to produce such crosses. Molds for Maltese crosses have been found at Botoșana, Davideni, Bucharest–Străulești-Lunca, Sânmiclăuș, and Olteni and clearly point to the local production of such items.⁷⁶ On the basis of molds, it has been suggested that crosses were mass produced for a growing Christian community.⁷⁷ That such a Christian community existed is beyond doubt; it is, however, unclear to what extent we are dealing with a significant production, since an almost equal number of crosses and molds have been found. In addition, some of those molds had multiple designs and were used to produce a variety of ornaments and pieces of jewelry, aside from pectoral crosses.

As we have seen, pectoral crosses are also found in the heart of the Avar Khaganate, although no molds are known from this region. Unlike brooches and buckles, crosses were not specifically associated with the military. This may explain why populations in Wallachia and Moldavia were not bothered by the growing popularity of such items in *Avaria*. The fact that most crosses found north of the Danube frontier are Maltese may have been a deliberate attempt to develop a distinct identity on the eastern periphery of the Avar Khaganate. At the same time, Maltese crosses were a typical dress accessory of women on fortified sites in the Danubian provinces.⁷⁸ Christianity was a strong component of Roman identity in the sixth century and we are told that frontier officers were expected to be a model of religious virtue.⁷⁹ Given this cultural climate, any "barbarians" serving the Empire would be tempted to adopt some religious practices and

---

[75] A. Madgearu, "Semnificația purtării crucilor pectorale descoperite la nord de Dunăre în secolele VI–VII," *AM* 30 (2007): 129–136; F. Curta, "Limes and cross," 58–62. Similar crosses are often found south of the Danube, for which see Curta, "Before Cyril," 185 and fig. 8.5. There are many Avar-period crosses from Hungary usually found in female graves, of which the lead crosses are the closest analogies for the ones found in Romania; see E. Garam, *Funde byzantinischer Herkunft in der Awarenzeit vom Ende des 6. bis zum Ende des 7. Jahrhunderts* (Budapest, 2001), 64, fig. 6 and pl. 40.

[76] Dănilă, "Tipare de turnat," 559–560.   [77] Madgearu, *Rolul creștinismului*, 81.

[78] F. Curta, "New remarks on Christianity beyond the sixth- and early seventh-century frontier of the Empire," in *Keszthely-Fenékpuszta im Kontext spätantiker Kontinuitätsforschung zwischen Noricum und Moesia*, ed. O. Heinrich-Tamáska (Leipzig, 2011), 307.

[79] *On Strategy*, 9: γνώριμον μὲν ἐπ' εὐσεβείᾳ τυγχάνειν μετὰ καὶ τῶν ἄλλων ὅσα πρέπει ἄρχουσι.

perhaps either marry local Christian women or simply export to their homeland the fashion of wearing crosses.[80] Not only soldiers returning home, but also Christian prisoners taken after successful raids into the Balkans helped spread this fashion in *barbaricum*. Indeed, Procopius tells us of the multitude of women taken captive by the Slavs, even if his numbers are most likely exaggerated.[81]

Still, we remain in the realm of uncertainty and unable draw a clear distinction between social value and religious meaning. More specifically, how can we distinguish between *imitatio* and genuine adherence to the Christian creed? Unlike the genuine Byzantine imports found in *Avaria*, north of the Lower Danube the unaffordable Byzantine crosses were often replaced by cheaper local imitations. Although these may have been mass produced for the local Christian community, the full spectrum of Byzantine imports discussed in the previous chapter does not indicate a special preference for Christian objects. On the contrary, some of the common dress accessories from the Balkans which bear Christian symbols – without being themselves religious items – are rare or non-existent in the lands north of the Danube. The most important are the Sucidava buckles with cross-shaped openwork decoration, fibulae with bent stem with Christian inscriptions (Minna, Amin, Maria, etc.), and cast fibulae with bent stem with cross-shaped foot.[82] Finally, none of the Christian terracotta lamps manufactured in the Danube region or imported from North Africa found their way in *barbaricum*, south and east of the Carpathians, although they were very common across the Danubian provinces and therefore easy to procure.[83] Their size and fragile nature cannot fully account for their absence.

---

[80] Although marriage between provincials and barbarians was banned by fourth-century legislation, carried over into the fifth-century Theodosian Code, by the sixth century the reality had changed significantly. For evidence of mixed marriages in the Danube region in Late Antiquity, see V. Velkov, *Cities in Thrace and Dacia in Late Antiquity* (Amsterdam, 1977), 277–279. On the legal aspects of intermarriage, see especially R. Mathisen, "*Provinciales, gentiles*, and marriages between Romans and barbarians in the Late Roman Empire," *JRS* 99 (2009): 140–155; R. C. Blockley, "Roman–barbarian marriages in the Late Empire," *Florilegium* 4 (1982): 63–79.

[81] Procopius, *Bella*, 7.38.18.

[82] The only known example is the cast fibula with bent stem and human faces on the bow found in house 52 from Davideni, for which see I. Mitrea, *Comunități sătești la est de Carpați în epoca migrațiilor. Așezarea de la Davideni din secolele V–VIII* (Piatra Neamț, 2001), 92–93; 326, fig. 66/3. This and several other Christian artifacts from Davideni, including a cross, a mold for the production of crosses, and a comb made of bone with a cross handle, compelled Mitrea to describe the settlement as a "true apostolic center" in Moldavia, for which see Mitrea, "Considerații privind," 303–304.

[83] Barnea, *Les monuments*, 240–245. For lamps, see above Chapter 2.2.2.

Christian symbols on local handmade pottery have also been connected with the religion of local communities in *barbaricum,* especially in Moldavia and Wallachia.[84] Recent attempts to classify the incisions made on local pots have led to inconclusive results and complete uncertainty regarding their religious significance.[85] To be sure, crosses appear not only on traditional pots whose shape can be traced back to the pre-Roman period, but also on Slavic wares of the so-called Korchak type found in the sixth-to-seventh-century settlements from Cucorăni and Suceava-Șipot in Moldavia.[86] Moreover, swastikas and other symbols appear on handmade pottery from Bucharest and Dulceanca in Wallachia and might have carried a different cultural symbolism than the iconography associated with Christianity.[87] What is particularly important about this practice, which seems to be so common in *barbaricum,* is the fact that it occurs only on handmade pottery. Despite a recent reassessment, its cultural symbolism related to identity formation is far from being fully understood.[88]

In the absence of documented churches, the presence of devotional objects such as the lead *ampulla* from Iași (Moldavia), the bronze bowl for holy water found at Periam (Banat), or the bird-headed distaff from Craiova (Oltenia) suggests that Christianity may have been adopted at an individual level, but not in an institutionalized form, if we even accept that such items retained their religious meaning in *barbaricum.*[89] Indeed, the function of some of these objects is still controversial. Bird-headed distaffs and dress-pins are common in the northern Balkans and some scholars have associated their symbolism with Christian belief and funerary

---

[84] For a recent inventory, see Madgearu, *Rolul creștinismului,* 127–137.

[85] E. S. Teodor and I. Stanciu, "About crosses on wet clay as cultural markers," *EN* 19 (2009): 129–155; Madgearu, *Rolul creștinismului,* 83–84. Previous publications offered a more optimistic interpretation, for which see especially Teodor, *Creștinismul,* 82–84.

[86] Teodor, *Creștinismul,* fig. 14/4 and 15/1, 4.

[87] S. Dolinescu-Ferche, *Așezările din secolele III și VI în sud-vestul Munteniei. Cercetările de la Dulceanca* (Bucharest, 1974), fig. 70/1; S. Dolinescu-Ferche and M. Constantiniu, "Un établissement du VIe siècle à Bucarest (Découvertes de la rue Soldat Ghivan)," *Dacia* 25 (1981): fig. 9/6.

[88] Teodor and Stanciu, "About crosses," 141.

[89] Iași: V. Macarie, "Un vas bizantin de cult descoperit la Iași," *SCIVA* 32, no. 2 (1981): 299–302. Craiova: Popilian and Nica, "Așezarea prefeudală," 154. Periam: D. Țeicu, "Căldarea de lut paleocreștină de la Periam," *Thraco-Dacica* 11 (1990): 153–156. The function of the liturgical bowl from Periam is problematic. Like many other accidental finds from the lands dominated by the Avars, it could have been taken during one of the frequent inroads made in Illyricum. For a religious interpretation, see Madgearu, "The spreading of Christianity," 46; Rusu, "Paleocreștinismul nord-dunărean," 61, n. 83.

practices.[90] An attempt to connect them to the heresy of Bonosus on account of their concentration in the Iron Gates region of the Danube has been met with skepticism.[91] To be sure, a silver dress-pin bearing the inscription BONOSA was found at Keszthely-Fenékpuszta horreum, and although the upper part is missing there might be a connection with the known bird-headed distaffs.[92] Regardless of its precise function, which still remains a matter for conjecture, the piece found at Craiova in *barbaricum* is more likely to reflect practices from the Danubian provinces where such items remained in fashion with slight modifications from the fourth to the sixth century.

What is the evidence telling us so far? Conversion to Christianity or adherence to at least some Christian traditions firmly in place since the fourth century was most likely not synonymous with a full adoption of Christian norms and precepts, since inhumation seems to have been practiced on a limited scale north of the Danube. Very few of the key artifacts invoked for the Christianization of *barbaricum* have a good stratigraphical context; some were acquired from private collectors and their original provenance is seldom known. Crosses and molds for the production of crosses are often found north of the Danube, most of the time in archaeological context, but no clear distinction can be drawn between cultural *imitatio* and religious belief. Members of the privileged class north of the Danube, which had fewer means than the Avar aristocracy, may have very well expressed their connection to the Byzantine world through common items such as bronze or lead crosses as a public display of their religious belief.[93] Finally, some of the items produced in provinces far from the Danube, such as North African lamps or Egyptian *ampullae*, could also reflect long distance social and economic connections. These

---

[90] For a list of finds and a distribution map, see recently A. Madgearu, "A stick with dove head found at Halmyris," *Cultură și civilizație la Dunărea de Jos* 24 (2008): 221–230. We should add the finds from Novi Banovci and Iatrus, absent from Madgearu's list, for which see Z. Vinski, "Arheološki spomenici velike seobe naroda u Srijemu," *Situla* 2 (1957): 70, n. 56; G. Gomolka-Fuchs, "Die Kleinfunde vom 4. bis 6. Jh. aus Iatrus," in *Iatrus-Krivina II. Ergebnisse der Ausgrabungen 1966–1973* (Berlin, 1982), pl. 64/286.

[91] The heresy dates back to the fourth century and is known for denying the perpetual virginity of Mary. See N. Zugravu, *Erezii și schisme la Dunărea de Mijloc și de Jos în mileniul I* (Iași, 1999), 81; Đ. Janković, *Podunavski deo oblasti Akvisa u VI i pochetkom VII veka* (Belgrade, 1981), 176–177.

[92] Garam, *Funde*, pl. 41/3 (grave 5).

[93] Cf. Madgearu, "Semnificația purtării," 132. Settlement patterns north of the Danube have very little to offer in terms of spectacular residences, while gold and silver objects, with or without religious symbolism, are extremely rare finds; see A. Măgureanu and B. S. Szmoniewski, "Domestic dwellings in Moldavia and Wallachia in the initial phase of the Early Middle Ages," *AAC* 38 (2003): 111–136.

could include regions like Dalmatia and even the Holy Land, through pilgrimage, in the case of Menas flasks. Communities from the former province of Dacia had been exposed to Christianity since the fourth century and important foundations were already in place, but it is significant to note that the Hunnic invasion in the fifth century did not completely sever Dacia's connection to the Mediterranean world.

Encouraged by the cultural porosity of the Danube frontier, some individuals or communities of different ethnic background living in the shadow of the Empire decided to adopt the religion of Byzantium as a result of constant interaction. Byzantine emperors would certainly approve of such cultural integration. However, the decision was taken at a personal level and actual practices departed from the official canons, as they sometimes did south of the Danube. Once again, a connection with the circulation of people to and from the militarized Danube frontier seems inescapable. Objects with religious designation arrived north of the Danube, either as prestige objects for local elites or as Christian artifacts for believers whose ethnic identity is not always clear.[94] Some of these may have been Christian prisoners from the Empire allowed to practice their religion while in captivity, but their exact contribution to further conversions in *barbaricum* is hard to assess.[95] Justinian's frontier policy in the Balkans included not only the program of fortification, but also alliances with the Herules, the Lombards, the Antes, and the Utigurs. Most of the new converts were barbarian soldiers having federate status who helped spread Christian ideas and artifacts in *barbaricum*, similar to the Germanic auxiliaries of the early imperial period who brought statues of Jupiter, Mars, and Mercury back to their homeland.[96] Both the literary and

---

[94] Historians have drawn attention to a later account of Theophanes Confessor who mentions the help offered by a Christian Gepid during a Roman campaign north of the Danube in 593. Since no Gepids were supposedly living in northeastern Wallachia, it has been suggested that the Christian scout used by the Roman army belonged to a local Romanized community. While this is a plausible assumption, this anecdote is of little use for a broader understanding of Christianity north of the Danube. For the episode, see Theophanes, *Cronographia*, 271, AM 6085 [592/3]. For the ethnic attribution, see Teodor, *Creștinismul*, 61.

[95] On the topic of prisoners in the Danube region, see N. Lenski, "Captivity among the barbarians and its impact on the fate of the Roman Empire," in *The Cambridge Companion to the Age of Attila*, ed. M. Maas (Cambridge, 2014), 230–246. On the role of prisoners for explaining the presence of Christian artifacts in *barbaricum*, close to the Danube, see M. Comşa, "Die Slawen im karpatisch-donauländischen Raum im 6.–7. Jh," *ZfA* 7 (1973): 217.

[96] R. Stupperich, "Bemerkungen zum römischen Import im sogenannten Freien Germanien," in *Aspekte römisch-germanischer Beziehungen in der frühen Kaiserzeit: Vortragsreihe zur Sonderausstellung "Kalkriese-Römer im Osnabrücker Land," 1993 in Osnabrück*, ed. G. Franzius (Espelkamp, 1995), 65–67, with fig. 11a–c.

archaeological evidence places them on the Lower Danube frontier, although the empire's recruiting strategy may have also resorted to unofficial channels as pressure increased in the second half of the sixth century and constant fighting on several fronts created a shortage of manpower.[97] Indeed, the whole purpose of Justinian's cultural integration tactic was the exploitation of the human reservoir in the lands beyond the frontier. Apparently, this approach was not carried on successfully by his successors. So much can be deduced from the late sixth-century *Strategikon* where caution was advised when dealing with a category of Romanized individuals (perhaps also Christian), who "have given in to the times, forget their own people, and prefer to gain the good will of the enemy."[98]

Despite general optimism on the spread of Christianity north of the frontier, we still have too many loose ends because the evidence is inconclusive and often outright contradictory. Showcasing their trademark pragmatism honed over many centuries of dealing with "barbarians" (for better or worse), sixth-century emperors included religion in their repertoire of political solutions. However, this otherwise formidable arsenal lacked a strong military dimension and Byzantine rulers were unable to project much political power beyond the frontier. Christians from old settlements which had been in contact with the Empire for centuries were left to their own devices as direct imperial intervention seldom reached beyond the Danube line.[99] Without a coherent institutional framework to guide and regulate practices, religion evolved in an unsystematic fashion, allowing for a unique mixture of Christian and pagan practices.[100] It is simply unrealistic to expect standardized Christian behavior in a decentralized rural society beyond Byzantium's frontier. Ample evidence from the

---

[97] This was the legacy of Justinian's political ambition, for which see A. Kaldellis, "Classicism, barbarism, and warfare: Prokopios and the conservative reaction to Later Roman military policy," *American Journal of Ancient History* 3–4 (2004–2005): 204–218.

[98] *Strategikon*, 11.4.133–135. The source calls them refugees (ρεφούγοι), a technical Latin term which has sparked controversy; see A. Madgearu, "About Maurikios, Strategikon, XI.4.31," *RESEE* 35, nos. 1–2 (1997): 119–121.

[99] It has been argued that the Christian community north of the Danube may have been administered by *clerici illiterati* through analogy with the well-known episode from the Carolingian age when the conquest of the Avar heartland revealed the existence of a local Christian community served by illiterate priests. For the parallel, see Diaconescu and Opreanu, "Cîteva puncte," 594–595.

[100] This image is reinforced by linguistic evidence, for which see Niculescu, "Le daco-roumain," 101: "les territoires nord-danubiennes [...] apparaissent, à la lumière de ces analyses, comme une zone romanisé et abandonnée à son sort, rurale, discontinue, fragile même" ("in light of this analysis, the lands north of the Danube appear as a region Romanized but left to its own devices, rural, fragmented, and fragile").

western Middle Ages where a society dominated by the institution of the church still left room for popular religious practices that deviated from Catholic doctrine should provide a cautionary tale of just how resilient a pre-Christian folkloric past can be. Historians of the medieval Orthodox church should regard Late Antiquity as an indispensable formative period which provided the foundation on which to build a solid religious structure, but teleological assumptions must be avoided. As far as the sixth century is concerned, we can only conclude that Christianity was hardly an unequivocal phenomenon in the lands north of the Danube and it will take more solid archaeological evidence to change this conviction.

4 | Contact and Separation on the Danube Frontier

It is perhaps the right time to pull together the chief observations made so far and advance some historical propositions based on the baffling amount of archaeological evidence explored in the previous chapters. The study of written and material sources concerning the Danube frontier presents an ostensible paradox. Often used as a rhetorical device by sixth-century writers, the Danube was described as a linear frontier which capable emperors were able to hold against barbarian tides. The river was truly "the first line of defense," to use the words of Procopius, not metaphorically, however, but through the fleet monitoring the river.[1] The Empire's stance was mostly defensive. No attempts were made to conquer regions north of the Danube, except for efforts to reestablish a number of bridgehead forts which had the strategic mission of acting as a spearhead in *barbaricum*. On the Roman side of the river, archaeologists have revealed a long chain of fortifications rebuilt in the first half of the sixth century and this conveniently dovetails with the concerns raised by contemporary observers. All sources seem to be in agreement and converging toward an inescapable conclusion: the Empire's priority in the northern Balkans was to prevent, or at least contain, a massive crossing of the Danube that could endanger Constantinople and to discourage small bands of raiders set on plundering the frontier provinces. And yet, this is in many ways a misleading scenario. Despite such strategic precautions, a wide variety of Byzantine goods found their way north of the Danube throughout the sixth century and into the seventh, a paradox which needs further explanation. How could the same frontier be a daunting system of watertight barriers and yet culturally permeable?

To be sure, Early Byzantine emperors were following time-honored practices. In the previous centuries Rome had developed a model of interaction on the northern frontier which supposed the existence of several interrelated structures. This type of interaction was articulated by historians and archaeologists based on world-systems theory: a Roman

---

[1] Procopius, *De Aedificiis*, 4.1.33. For the activity of the fleet, see F. Himmler, *Untersuchungen zur schiffsgestützten Grenzsicherung auf der spätantiken Donau (3.–6. Jh. n. Chr.)* (Oxford, 2011).

system (the peripheral provinces), a buffer area between Rome and the Germanic world (client kingdoms), and the independent Germanic system.[2] The buffer zone maintained strong connections with the Empire, which can be seen in the large quantity of Roman goods and coins.[3] A version of this strategy was still practiced in the sixth century on a different frontier. The Ghassanids in Arabia and the "kingdoms" of Transcaucasia represented such buffer lands between Early Byzantium and Sasanian Persia, although the material evidence for these regions has not yet been fully explored.[4] In order to avoid misleading generalizations we should test for the existence of such concerns north of the Danube against the abundant archaeological evidence presented in the previous chapters. This is particularly important because north of the Danube the empire had neither a diplomatic partner, nor a rival of the magnitude of Persia. Furthermore, the region lacks any of the missionary activity which otherwise characterizes imperial efforts on most other frontiers. All this

---

[2] L. Hedeager, "A quantitative analysis of Roman imports in Europe north of the limes (0–400 AD), and the question of Roman–Germanic exchange," in *New Directions in Scandinavian Archaeology*, eds. K. Kristiansen and C. Paludan-Müller (Copenhagen, 1979), 191–216. For further discussion, see in particular M. G. Fulford, "Roman and barbarian: the economy of Roman frontier systems," in *Barbarians and Romans in North-West Europe: From the Later Republic to Late Antiquity*, eds. J. C. Barrett, A. P. Fitzpatrick, and L. Macinnes (Oxford, 1989), 81–95; P. S. Wells, "Production within and beyond imperial boundaries: goods, exchange, and power in Roman Europe," in *World-Systems Theory in Practice: Leadership, Production, and Exchange*, ed. P. N. Kardulias (Boulder, CO, 1999), 85–101.

[3] M. C. Galestin, "Roman artefacts beyond the northern Frontier: interpreting the evidence from the Netherlands," *European Journal of Archaeology* 13, no. 1 (2010): 64–88; A. Gardner, "Fluid frontiers: cultural interaction on the edge of empire," *Stanford Journal of Archaeology* 5 (2007): 43–60; M. Erdrich, *Rom und die Barbaren. Das Verhältnis zwischen dem Imperium Romanum und den germanischen Stämmen vor seiner Nordwestgrenze von der späten römischen Republik bis zum Gallischen Sonderreich* (Mainz, 2001); G. Franzius, ed., *Aspekte römisch-germanischer Beziehungen in der frühen Kaiserzeit: Vortragsreihe zur Sonderausstellung "Kalkriese-Römer im Osnabrücker Land," 1993 in Osnabrück* (Espelkamp, 1995); U. L. Hansen, *Römischer Import im Norden: Warenaustausch zwischen dem Römischen Reich und dem freien Germanien während der Kaiserzeit unter besonderer Berücksichtigung Nordeuropas* (Copenhagen, 1987). For the numismatic evidence, see A. Bursche, *Later Roman–Barbarian Contacts in Central Europe: Numismatic Evidence* (Berlin, 1996).

[4] The comparison between different frontier regions of the Late Roman world has gained more ground in the recent decades; see, for example, J. Crow, "Amida and Tropaeum Traiani: a comparison of Late Antique fortress cities on the Lower Danube and Mesopotamia," in *Transition*, 435–455; Z. Visy, "Similarities and differences in the Late Roman defense system on the European and Eastern frontiers," in *Limes XVIII: Proceedings of the XVIIIth International Congress of Roman Frontier Studies, Amman, Jordan (September 2000)*, eds. P. Freeman et al. (Oxford, 2002), 71–75; P. Mayerson, "The Saracens and the *limes*," *BASOR* 262 (1986): 39. For an anthropological perspective, see T. D. Hall, "Puzzles in the comparative study of frontiers: problems, some solutions, and methodological implications," *Journal of World-Systems Research* 15, no. 1 (2009): 25–47.

suggests that the northern *barbaricum* should display several unique features. Did sixth-century emperors attempt to establish a buffer zone north of the Danube or was it a no man's land, a backwater with no real place in the large scheme of things? What type of theoretical framework best explains cultural interaction on the Danube frontier?

Approaches informed by Wallerstein's world-systems theory have gradually lost momentum in the last two decades. Indeed, the overwhelming focus on core–periphery connections and the unilinear nature of the discussion has provided only a limited model for the study of ancient *barbaricum*, where many communities corresponded to what Wallerstein has defined as "mini-systems."[5] The original theory portrayed the periphery as passive and peoples on the fringes of world systems as powerless, exploited, and uncapable of any decision-making process in their cultural dealings with more "advanced" civilizations. World-systems analysis, however, remains valuable for understanding frontier culture by adapting the original paradigm to pre-capitalist realities and by designating an eclectic approach to frontier studies.[6] Unlike early modern contexts, interaction on the Early Byzantine frontier relied heavily on the circulation of prestige goods, something that has long been identified as a defining characteristic of ancient systems.[7] Indeed, most categories of artifacts discussed below, while items of daily use in the Roman world, became an index of social distinction in *barbaricum*. A particularly illuminating contribution is the post-colonial concept of "negotiated peripherality," which allows individuals living in the shadow of a world system to negotiate and decide which

---

[5] I. Wallerstein, "A world-system perspective on the social sciences," *The British Journal of Sociology* 27, no. 3 (1976): 345–346.

[6] For such efforts, see C. Chase-Dunn and T. D. Hall, "Conceptualizing Core/Periphery hierarchies for comparative study," in *Core/Periphery Relations in Precapitalist Worlds*, eds. C. Chase-Dunn and T. D. Hall (Boulder, CO, 1991), 5–44; P. M. Rice, "Context of contact and change: peripheries, frontiers, and boundaries," in *Studies in Culture Contact: Interaction, Culture Change, and Archaeology*, ed. C. Cusick (Carbondale, IL, 1998), 44–66; P. N. Kardulias, "Preface," in *World-Systems Theory in Practice: Leadership, Production, and Exchange*, ed. P. N. Kardulias (Lanham, MD, 1999), xvii–xxi; T. D. Hall, "Frontiers, ethnogenesis, and world-systems: rethinking the theories," in *A World-Systems Reader: New Perspectives on Gender, Urbanism, Cultures, Indigenous Peoples, and Ecology*, ed. T. D. Hall (Lanham, MD, 2000), 237–270. For a review of recent contributions in this direction, see M. L. Galaty, "World-systems analysis and anthropology: a new détente?," *Reviews in Anthropology* 40 (2011): 3–26, esp. 14–16 on frontiers; T. D. Hall, P. N. Kardulias, and C. Chase-Dunn, "World-systems analysis and archaeology: continuing the dialogue," *Journal of Archaeological Research* 19 (2011): 233–279; M. Naum, "Re-emerging frontiers: postcolonial theory and historical archaeology of the borderlands," *Journal of Archaeological Method and Theory* 17, no. 2 (2011): 101–108.

[7] J. Schneider, "Was there a precapitalist world-system?" *Peasant Studies* 6, no. 1 (1977): 20–29.

cultural traits to adopt.[8] The archaeological evidence from the Danube frontier discussed in this chapter provides important confirmation of such practices. The circulation of Byzantine goods was more the result of human agency than of systematic action coordinated from the imperial core, although the Danube border's cultural porosity was a politically deliberate attempt to stimulate integration at a time when military intervention and conquest were no longer realistic options.[9]

Despite all criticism, Wallerstein's original core–semiperiphery–periphery model in its barebone condition may yet be of use if we consider the Danube frontier a semiperiphery with a strong cultural identity and the location of significant innovation and change, while the nearby *barbaricum* constituted a periphery acting as a reservoir of manpower and strategic resources, as both literary and archaeological sources seem to suggest.[10] But this system was far from being unilinear. During the course of the long sixth century the northern *barbaricum* gradually developed into a "contested periphery," as the Avars challenged the Byzantine control of the region and eventually destroyed the frontier system altogether marking an important milestone in the history of the Balkans.[11] The core did not manipulate the periphery, in this case; moreover, marginal regions proved to be decisive agents of cultural change.

Perhaps not unlike other imperial frontiers of the pre-modern world, the circulation of cultural influences and the forging of identities on the northern frontier of Byzantium resulted from a combination of cooperation and conflict. This is neither ironic nor accidental. Justinian's building program in the Balkans, undertaken at an unprecedented scale, served more than one function. Its practical purpose of creating obstacles for invaders and securing the Danubian provinces was doubled by the psychological desire to intimidate which Roman imperialism had perfected over the centuries. The Balkan system devised by Justinian was meant to instill feelings like awe, fear, and admiration in the hearts and minds of "barbarians" living north of the river, who should find the whole enterprise

---

[8] For the concept, see P. N. Kardulias, "Negotiation and incorporation on the margins of world-systems: examples from Cyprus and North America," *Journal of World-Systems Research* 13, no. 1 (2007): 56–57.

[9] For some theoretical underpinnings, see G. J. Stein, "From passive periphery to active agents: emerging perspectives in the archaeology of interregional interaction," *AAnth* 104, no. 3 (2002): 903–909.

[10] For a theoretical model, see C. Chase-Dunn and T. D. Hall, *Rise and Demise: Comparing World-Systems* (Boulder, CO, 1997), ch. 5.

[11] For the concept, see M. Allen, "Contested Peripheries: Philistia in the Neo-Assyrian World-System," PhD Dissertation, University of California, Los Angeles, CA, 1996.

"fabulous and altogether incredible."[12] As a "new Trajan," Justinian had the duty to pacify the transdanubian *barbaricum*, if not reclaiming this region for the empire.[13] Consequently, this greatly polarized barbarian attitudes toward Byzantium. Submissiveness and the desire to emulate the Byzantine way of life was one type of response, while the other was the ambition to prove oneself against the most prestigious adversary, a timeless benchmark of barbarian success.[14] Byzantine fashions could be brought to *barbaricum* by men who served the empire as soldiers, but also by thousands of Byzantine prisoners taken north of the Danube during episodes of conflict. Likewise, Byzantine goods could reflect the activity of merchants, for which only tantalizing evidence exists in contemporary accounts, but also the much better-documented raids of plunder in the Balkan provinces. Because of this duality, the northern frontier of Byzantium appears to be a "bipolar periphery," caught in a Janus-like dynamic where culture flowed through channels which may seem mutually exclusive, but in the end complemented each other in the process of forging new cultural behaviors and practices.

Acknowledging the fact that cultural interaction in frontier regions is the result of a complicated process of negotiation instead of unilateral domination brings us back to the sphere of post-colonial theory and its application in archaeology. Richard White's definition of the frontier as a "middle ground" located between empires and rural societies seems like a perfect description of communities living in the shadow of the Early Byzantine Empire.[15] And yet White's middle ground assumes that accommodation results from the fact that none of the actors is able to impose their will. The diffusion of Byzantine goods north of the Danube, as well as the local imitation of such items, shows that communities in *barbaricum* depended on continuous access to the Byzantine world. They took the Empire as a cultural frame of reference and competed for gaining access to this world,

---

[12] Procopius, *De Aedificiis*, 4.4.1, using the traditional Roman *topos* of the "overawed" barbarian.
[13] Lydus, *De Magistratibus*, 2.28; Procopius, *De Aedificiis*, 4.6.11–18; Justinian's political involvement in the northern world is well documented, although here both authors are using a very distinctive panegyrical tone.
[14] For Justinian's policy in the northern Balkans, see recently, A. Sarantis, *Justinian's Balkan Wars: Campaigning, Diplomacy and Development in Illyricum, Thrace and the Northern World AD 527–65* (Prenton, 2016). For the connection between raids of plunder and the creation of social prestige in *barbaricum*, see D. Syrbe, "Reiternomaden des Schwarzmeerraums (Kutriguren und Utiguren) und byzantinische Diplomatie im 6. Jahrhundert," *Acta Orientalia* 65, no. 3 (2012): 291–316.
[15] R. White, *The Middle Ground: Indians, Empires and Republics in the Great Lakes Region, 1650–1815* (Cambridge, 1991), esp. ch. 2.

either peacefully or violently. Equally, Byzantium needed to exploit the human and material resources of *barbaricum*. Consequently, the region comes closer to the notion of an "interdependent borderland," according to the typology established by Oscar Martínez, at least until the abandoning of the military border on the Danube when cultural contact gained new coordinates.[16]

Cultural encounters were mutually beneficial although they mirrored the political strength of the partners. Interaction gradually led to cultural change and the reshaping of certain social values in relation to Byzantium. One would be inclined to place this process within the "acculturation" framework, an explanatory model once prominent but no longer held in high esteem.[17] It can be more accurately described as the result of an "interstitial agency" in a space of negotiation where power is unequal and yet insufficiently so as to allow for uncompromising domination.[18] Brad Bartel's matrix of imperialism applied to the study of conditions on the Danube frontier in Upper Moesia provides a suitable parallel, although the cultural response in the sixth-century *barbaricum* seems to fall between his "Acculturation" and "Equilibrium" outcomes, the latter being characterized by a pronounced maintenance of the indigenous culture.[19] Indeed, the archaeological evidence points to a peculiar form of acculturation shaped by the insufficient political force of the imperialist power and allowing for a more selective form of cultural borrowing. This type of interaction does not lead to the loss of cultural distinctiveness through assimilation into the dominant culture. It corresponds to Homi Bhabha's "Third Space" as a cultural area of continual negotiation, reinvention, and hybridization.[20] It is

---

[16] O. J. Martínez, *Border People. Life and Society in the US–Mexico Borderlands* (Tucson, AZ, 1994), 8–9. His typology of borderland interaction includes four categories defined in terms of intensity: alienated, coexistent, interdependent, and integrated.

[17] Unless of course we may return to the original program which defined acculturation as "those phenomena which result when groups of individuals having different cultures come into continuous first-hand contact, with subsequent changes in the original patterns of either or both groups," for which see R. Redfield et al., "Memorandum for the study of acculturation," *AA* 38 (1936): 149. For the history of the concept and criticism, see J. C. Cusick, "Historiography of acculturation: an evaluation of concepts and their application in archaeology," in *Studies in Culture Contact*, ed. Cusick, 126–145. For an interesting comeback of acculturation in frontier contexts, see B. A. Feuer, *Boundaries, Borders and Frontiers in Archaeology: A Study of Spatial Relationships* (Jefferson, NC, 2016), 72–78.

[18] For "interstitial" agency, see H. Bhabha, "Culture's in-between," in *Questions of Cultural Identity*, eds. S. Hall and P. du Gay (London, 1996), 58.

[19] B. Bartel, "Colonialism and cultural responses: problems related to Roman provincial analysis," *World Archaeology* 12, no. 1 (1980): 11–26.

[20] H. Bhabha, *The Location of Culture* (London, 1994), 37–39.

a place decidedly more elusive than Wallerstein's economist system, but not necessarily incompatible in light of the new directions in world-systems analysis.[21]

What makes the Danube a particularly interesting frontier is the fact that the lands north of the river do not fall under the standard definition of *barbaricum,* because much of the region had been a Roman province for more than 150 years (Trajan's Dacia). With all the controversy regarding the level of Romanization and the demographic impact of the Roman retreat south of the Danube in the last quarter of the third century, we cannot question the fact that the region had been deeply permeated by Roman culture.[22] Generations later, communities in Dacia still maintained the Roman way of life, albeit in a residual manner, and struggled to remain in contact with the Empire. However, this post-provincial society was not the only one seeking Roman goods and it would be a mistake to place ethnic labels when it comes to motivations behind cultural interaction. The fourth-century Chernyakhov culture, whose degree of homogeneity was impressive given its presumed multiethnic background, developed in the shadow of the Empire and the high priority given to commercial relations in treaties between Late Roman emperors and the Goths is revealing. Things remained unchanged in the next century when Attila's sons decided that their chief priority was to persuade Emperor Leo I to resume trading relations with the Huns; access to Roman goods remained crucial for securing and maintaining power in *barbaricum.*[23]

Did any of this change in the sixth century? The Empire was slow to recover from the dark days of the fifth century but with the reign of Anastasius we witness the first major attempt to reestablish a firm imperial control on the Lower Danube. Facing a much more divided political landscape north of the river, the empire lacked a redoubtable partner for

---

[21] Cultural anthropologists will find here similarities with the model of interaction proposed by Edward Shortman and Patricia Urban, although the distinction between their "coevolving interaction systems" and "hierarchical interaction systems" is not always clear-cut in the sixth-century Danube region where the duality of dominant/dominated often appears to be ambiguous; see E. M. Shortman and P. A. Urban, "Culture contact structure and process," in *Studies in Culture Contact*, ed. Cusick, 111–117.

[22] For a recent discussion, see I. Oltean, *Dacia: Landscape, Colonisation, and Romanisation* (London, 2007). Romanization itself has become a controversial concept under the influence of post-colonial theory; the literature is abundant, but for the main coordinates of the debate see J. Webster, "Creolizing the Roman provinces," *AJA* 105, no. 2 (2001): 209–225. For new archaeological directions, see recently M. J. Versluys, "Understanding objects in motion. An archaeological dialogue on Romanization," *Archaeological Dialogues* 21, no. 1 (2014): 1–20, as well as the accompanying essays in the volume.

[23] Priscus, *History*, 6.46 (Blockley).

negotiations and this may explain the silence of the sources on the question of trade on the Danube frontier. In the post-Hunnic world, most diplomatic activity was concentrated in the northwestern Balkans, targeting the Herules, the Gepids, and the Lombards, or in the nomadic steppes north of the Black Sea, a region disputed by Cutrigur and Utigur tribes. Out of this historical background, whose undertones projected back to the abandonment of Dacia by Emperor Aurelian, emerged the mixed ethnic communities which would be the main recipients of Byzantine goods in the sixth century.[24] Some of them lived in Dacia, now mostly under the control of the Gepids, whose political relations with Constantinople remained unstable, while others were located south and east of the Carpathians, caught between the Empire to the south, Gepids to the west, and Cutrigurs to the east.

Conspicuously absent from accounts recording imperial diplomatic initiatives, this region became an important reservoir of military manpower for the garrisons defending the Danube frontier. It is revealing that the only forays north of the river led by Chilbudius in the early 530s aimed to take prisoners, presumably not with the intention of collecting ransoms but to weaken the warlike Slavic communities while gaining additional recruits for use in the Balkans and elsewhere.[25] In the following decades, plague, endemic warfare, and frequent resettlement of population would only increase the shortage of manpower and with it the strategic significance of human resources from *barbaricum*.[26] That Justinian's policy was a

---

[24] For cultural contacts between Roman Dacia and the neighboring regions, see C. Opreanu, *Dacia romană și Barbaricum* (Timișoara, 1998). Historians who endorse the "continuity of Roman life" thesis in post-Roman Dacia (Transylvania) often overlook the major cultural transformations that the region had undergone since the abandoning of the province in the third century. See more recently, A.-M. Velter, *Transilvania în secolele V–XII. Interpretări istorico-politice și economice pe baza descoperirilor monetare din bazinul Carpatic, secolele V–XII* (Bucharest, 2002), 40–41.

[25] Procopius, *Bella*, 5.27.2, 6.26.18–20, and 7.14.6, for Danubian Slavs used on other theaters. Almost a century has passed since Ernst Stein first drew attention to the demographic potential of tribes north of the Danube, for which see E. Stein, *Studien zur Geschichte des byzantinischen Reiches, vornehmlich unter den Kaisern Justinus II u. Tiberius Constantinus* (Stuttgart, 1919), 119–120.

[26] On population movement in the Balkans, see W. Liebeschuetz, "The refugees and evacuees in the age of migrations," in *The Construction of Communities in the Early Middle Ages*, eds. R. Corradini, M. Diesenberger, and H. Reimitz (Leiden, 2003), 71–74. On the settlement of the Slavs in the Balkans under Justinian, see F. Montinaro, "Byzantium and the Slavs in the reign of Justinian: comparing the two recensions of Procopius' Buildings," in *Pontic-Danubian Realm*, 89–114. For the socioeconomic implications of the sixth-century plague, see P. Sarris, "Bubonic plague in Byzantium: the evidence of non-literary sources," in *Plague and the End of Antiquity: The Pandemic of 541–750*, ed. L. K. Little (Cambridge, 2008), 119–132.

temporary success is testified by the relative pacification of the Slavs whose raids are no longer mentioned until the late 570s.[27]

In addition to human resources, Byzantine emperors wanted to secure access to local agriculture. The advice given by the author of the *Strategikon* repeatedly refers to grain and food supplies as one of the major resources to be taken from the lands north of the Danube.[28] This is only indirect evidence for potential trade contacts involving the procurement of foodstuffs from the lands north of the Danube, although we can extrapolate from better-documented cases dating to the early Roman period to assume that the insufficient resources available in the Balkans would have motivated economic contacts with *barbaricum*.[29] And, indeed, the region was suffering from an endemic shortage of food. Demand must have been substantial given the desolating picture offered by the archaeology of rural spaces in the Balkans, where large-scale agriculture all but disappeared in the aftermath of the Hunnic storm and never recovered.[30] Archaeological research has revealed an abundance of amphora types associated with the state-directed *annona* distributed across the Balkans, while sixth-century legislation frequently mentions the difficulty of collecting taxes from the impoverished provinces of the Thracian diocese.[31]

Justinian's massive building program in the Balkans required enormous quantities of food, a voracious demand which the new *quaestura exercitus* could not satisfy.[32] There can be no doubt that the garrisons stationed on the Lower Danube frontier would have actively sought to supplement the *annona* with supplies procured from *barbaricum*. Settlement patterns north of the Danube confirm the fact that agriculture and husbandry were

---

[27] F. Curta, *The Making of the Slavs: History and Archaeology of the Lower Danube Region, c. 500–700* (Cambridge, 2001), 89.

[28] *Strategikon*, 11.4.136–140.

[29] C. R. Whittaker, *Rome and Its Frontiers: The Dynamics of Empire* (New York, NY, 2004), 107–108.

[30] A. G. Poulter, "Cataclysm on the Lower Danube: the destruction of a complex Roman landscape," in *Landscape of Change: Rural Evolutions in Late Antiquity and the Early Middle Ages*, ed. N. Christie (Aldershot, 2004), 223–253; F. Curta, "Peasants as 'makeshift soldiers for the occasion:' sixth-century settlement patterns in the Balkans," in *Urban Centers and Rural Contexts in Late Antiquity*, eds. T. S. Burns and J. W. Eadie (Lansing, MI, 2001), 199–217.

[31] E.g. *Corpus Iuris Civilis*, CJ, 10.27.2, 10 (3). For a discussion of the problem, see E. Popescu, "Le village en Scythie Mineure (Dobroudja) à l'époque protobyzantine," in *Les villages dans l'Empire byzantin (IVe–XVe siècle)*, eds. J. Lefort, C. Morrisson, and J.-P. Sodini (Paris, 2005), 363–380. For amphora finds, see above, Chapter 2.2.1.

[32] S. Torbatov, "*Quaestura exercitus*: Moesia Secunda and Scythia under Justinian," *ArchBulg* 1 (1997): 78–87.

the main economic activities.[33] Several settlements had storage pits where remains of grains have been found, most frequently wheat, rye, millet, and barley.[34] At Dulceanca in the Danube plain, archaeologists have found large quantities of bones – mostly cattle, sheep, goats, pigs, and horses – and this seems to be typical for the region.[35] It is unclear, however, to what extent these activities could be developed beyond the subsistence level in order to become a reliable source of food for the Danubian forts and even less certain whether frontier garrisons came to depend on it. At Iatrus, some 75 km south of Dulceanca local need for animal protein had to be supplemented with hunting, so the existence of demand in the northern Balkans seems obvious.[36] Moreover, at Histria in Scythia a strain of wheat (*Triticum compactum*) not cultivated in the Greco-Roman Balkans was probably imported from across the Danube.[37] Although substantial evidence is still lacking, some type of interdependence must have been established since more than a dozen settlements north of the Danube were abandoned after the collapse of the frontier system early in the seventh century.[38]

Economic gain was only a secondary concern deriving from the Empire's main political priorities in the region which aimed to attract local communities into its cultural orbit. The river was by no means an "Iron Curtain" as the Empire had neither the strength nor the energy to ensure a clear separation. In the end, what did it mean to be Roman in the sixth-century Balkans? Influenced by the discourse of contemporary writers, modern historians have often viewed the northern frontier region in terms of a long struggle between "Romans" and "Barbarians" with different names but similar agendas. In reality, the Danubian provinces had been a multi-ethnic environment long before the Slavs and Avars in the sixth century.[39]

---

[33] Ș. Olteanu, *Societatea carpato-danubiano-pontică în secolele IV–XI. Structuri demo-economice și social-politice* (Bucharest, 1997), 58–101; S. Stanc, *Relațiile omului cu lumea animală. Arheozoologia secolelor IV-X pentru zonele extracarpatice de est și de sud ale României* (Iași, 2006).

[34] Olteanu, *Societatea*, 87.

[35] S. Dolinescu-Ferche, *Așezările din secolele III și VI în sud-vestul Munteniei. Cercetările de la Dulceanca* (Bucharest, 1974), 108.

[36] L. Bartosiewicz and A. M. Choyke, "Animal remains from the 1970–1972 excavations of Iatrus (Krivina), Bulgaria," *AAASH* 43 (1991): 181–209.

[37] M. Cîrciumaru and E. Ionescu, "Semințe de cereale și leguminoase din așezarea de la Histria (secolul al VI-lea e.n.)," *SCIVA* 36, no. 4 (1977): 267–270.

[38] O. Toropu, *Romanitatea tîrzie și străromânii în Dacia traiană sud-carpatică (secolele III–XI)* (Craiova, 1976), 124.

[39] For a useful overview of fourth-century developments, see M. Kulikowski, *Rome's Gothic Wars: From the Third Century to Alaric* (Cambridge, 2007). For long-term developments, see

Especially after the 530s when the Empire found itself engaged in wars on multiple fronts, while having to cope with an unprecedented series of natural disasters, the defense of the Balkans faced a potential systemic failure. Justinian tried to prevent that by forging alliances with various groups, such as the Antes, the Herules, and the Utigurs, or by manipulating conflicts within *barbaricum* through the customary *divide et impera*.[40] As a consequence, peripheral Roman identity became even more diluted.[41]

In the frontier region there was a much more active mobility and congregation of people from different cultural backgrounds than historians have been willing to admit in their quest for clear-cut ethnicity and group identity. Furthermore, the general tendency has been to lump together regions from *barbaricum* conveying a false sense of homogeneity in their dealings with Byzantium.[42] In reality, their access to various categories of goods from the Empire depended on a series of conditions, of which the most important were availability, relations of power, and the social fabric of communities in *barbaricum* which might have placed different value on artifacts of Roman origin. The periphery was not just a passive recipient of cultural influences anxious to be acculturated. A vertical negotiation with the Byzantine world was probably doubled by a horizontal one between power circles in *barbaricum*. The fluidity of these exchanges means that such cultural distinctions do not always overlap with the political sphere of groups that dominated the region during the sixth and seventh century. Pre-modern cultural and political frontiers are rarely coterminous.

The circulation of Roman goods in *barbaricum* is the direct result of social interaction and social conflict between the sixth-century Roman government (core), the ethnically mixed Roman militarized culture of the Lower Danube (semiperiphery), and outside "barbarians" who could

---

A. G. Poulter, "The Lower Danubian frontier in Late Antiquity: evolution and dramatic change in the frontier zone, c. 296–600," in eds. P. Herz, P. Schmid, and O. Stoll (Berlin, 2010), 11–42. For the multiethnic structure of Balkan populations in Late Antiquity, see V. Velkov, *Cities in Thrace and Dacia in Late Antiquity* (Amsterdam, 1977), 261–281.

[40] For the military requirements of the Danube frontier, see Curta, *The Making of the Slavs*, 183, table 7; for the shortage of defenders and the use of barbarians, see M. Pillon, "Armée et defense de l'Illyricum byzantin de Justinien à Héraclius (527–641). De la reorganization justinienne à l'émergence des 'armées de cité'," *Erytheia* 26 (2005): 46–55.

[41] On sixth-century Roman identity, more generally, see G. Greatrex, "Roman identity in the sixth century," in *Ethnicity and Culture in Late Antiquity*, eds. S. Mitchell and G. Greatrex (London, 2000), 267–292.

[42] See more recently L. M. Stratulat, "Continuitate și discontinuitate la nordul Dunării de Jos (secolele IV–VIII d.Hr.)," *Carpica* 31 (2002): 59–78; D. G. Teodor, "Considerații privind continuitatea autohtonă în spațiul carpato-dunărean în mileniul I d. Hr," *Carpica* 34 (2005): 143–150.

either join this world or oppose it as a means of creating and maintaining social prestige (periphery). The easiest way to become "Roman" was to serve in the garrisons stationed on the frontier. Here much of Roman identity revolved around wearing a military dress adorned with Byzantine brooches and belt buckles and living in a fortress where life depended on the arrival of the state-controlled *annona*, wine and oil received in standardized containers, mostly amphorae known as LR1 and LR2. These are precisely the artifacts most often found in the lands north of the Danube: fragments of amphorae, oil lamps, and dress accessories associated with the traditional military culture of the Balkans which had elevated more than a dozen officers to the imperial purple from the third to the sixth century (Figure 17). Being Roman on the sixth-century Danube frontier was a fluid concept, a negotiated identity defined by several practices: adopting the provincial life style, living under Roman law, speaking Latin, adhering to Christianity, and possibly acquiring Roman wives.[43]

In light of such preconditions, it comes as no surprise that amphorae are commonly found in the close proximity of the Danube, north of Sucidava, the main Byzantine possession on the left bank of the river. However, no Byzantine brooches or buckles have been found in this region, although they were readily available from Sucidava or from any one of the Byzantine forts in the Iron Gates area. The only possible conclusion is that communities in Oltenia had no interest in expressing their identity in such a manner or adopting fashions connected to the military hilltop sites on the Danube. They may have chosen to distance themselves culturally from the Avar world where such fashions were becoming increasingly popular or it may simply be the closer contact with the Byzantine world – historically going back to Trajanic Dacia – that rendered these common items less powerful as an index of social standing. By contrast, amphorae are often found in Moldavia, some 150 miles away from Dinogetia, the closest Byzantine fortress, which implies that communities east of the Carpathians placed a premium on gaining access to wine and oil, the main products transported in amphorae. The same communities sought to procure Byzantine dress accessories such as fibulae with bent stem and cast

---

[43] For intermarriage we might extrapolate from the northeastern frontier where this was common practice, according to Procopius, *De Aedificiis*, 3.3.10–12. For the language spoken in the northern Balkans, see the famous *torna, torna* anecdote in Theophylact Simocatta, *Historia*, 2.15.7–9, later retold, perhaps from a different source, with a bit more detail about the popular Latin spoken by the common soldiers in the Balkans, by Theophanes, *Chronographia*, 258, AM 6079 [586/7]: ἑνὸς γὰρ ζώου τὸν φόρτον διαστρέψαντος, ἕτερος τὸν δεσπότην τοῦ ζώου προσφωνεῖ τὸν φόρτον ἀνορθῶσαι τῇ πατρῴᾳ φωνῇ· "τόρνα, τόρνα, φράτερ."

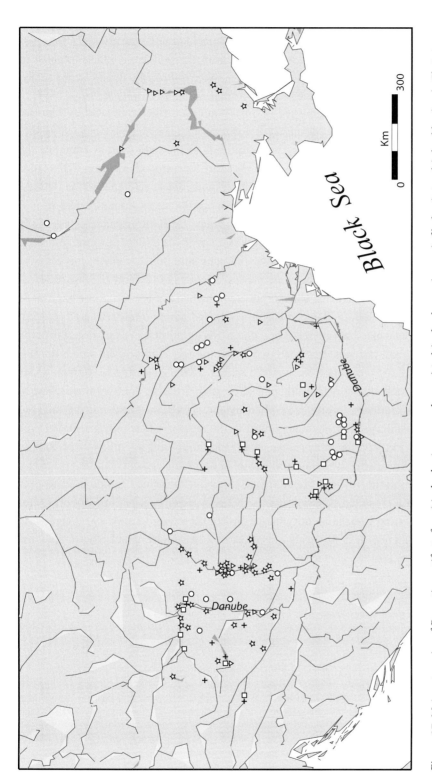

Figure 17 Main categories of Byzantine artifacts found in *barbaricum*: amphorae (circle), clay lamps (square), fibulae (triangle), buckles (star), Christian objects (cross)

fibulae with bent stem, as well as Byzantine buckles of the Sucidava class (Figure 18). This may be a reflection of the political contacts established with the Antes, who became federates and brought their culture to the Lower Danube while spreading Roman influences in *barbaricum*.[44]

The alliance established by Justinian and further cultivated by Maurice may have offered additional opportunities.[45] The area of Moldavia permeated by Slavic culture in the second half of the sixth century emulated the Early Byzantine frontier way of life more than any other region in the lands north of the Danube. The *Strategikon* makes clear reference to the political fragmentation of the Slavic world which the savvy Roman leader should exploit by attracting certain Slavic groups to the Roman cause, especially those close to the frontier.[46] This strategy had a double purpose: to drive a wedge between various Slavic factions and to strengthen the Danube frontier. Many of the mercenaries recruited to defend the fortresses of Moesia and Scythia, whose cultural influence can be seen in the handmade pottery found there, may have hailed from Moldavia and eastern Wallachia. Such mercenaries who acted as cultural brokers brought home Roman fashions mostly related to the military environment which dominated the Lower Danube region and increased the demand for Roman goods as well as the social value placed on such artifacts. Some of them came to be produced locally as testified by the significant number of molds and metallurgical implements found in the region.[47] This shows a special type of initiative in the process of appropriation and assimilation of Roman culture whereby communities in *barbaricum* created culture instead of simply borrowing. Metallurgical implements include molds used to produce crosses, a possible sign that Christian practices became important for creating a social identity based on Roman values (Figure 19). There is no evidence of a full-scale adoption of Christianity which shows that the

---

[44] For the strategic mission of the Antes, see G. Kardaras, "The Byzantine–Antic treaty (545/46 AD) and the defense of the Scythia Minor," *Byzantinoslavica* 58 (2010): 74–85. For the archaeological evidence, see B. S. Szmoniewski, "The Antes: eastern 'brothers' of the Sclavenes?" in *Neglected Barbarians*, 53–82. See also C. Bonev, "Les Antes et Byzance," *EB* 19 (1983), 3: 109–120.

[45] Procopius, *Bella*, 7.14.32–33; Michael the Syrian, *Chronicon*, 10.21 (ed. Chabot, 362).

[46] *Strategikon*, 11.4.128–131: Πολλῶν δὲ ὄντων ῥηγῶν καὶ ἀσυμφώνως ἐχόντων πρὸς ἀλλήλους, οὐκ ἄτοπόν τινας αὐτῶν μεταχειρίζεσθαι ἢ λόγῳ ἢ δώροις καὶ μάλιστα τοὺς ἐγγυτέρω τῶν μεθορίων καὶ τοῖς ἄλλοις ἐπέρχεσθαι, ἵνα μὴ ἡ πρὸς πάντας ἔχθρα ἕνωσιν ἢ μοναρχίαν ποιεῖ, expressing a deep-seated view, beautifully reminiscent of Tacitus, *Germania*, 33: *maneat, quaeso, duretque gentibus, si non amor nostri, at certe odium sui, quando urgentibus imperii fatis nihil iam praestare fortuna maius potest quam hostium discordiam*.

[47] See above, Chapter 2, Figure 9–10.

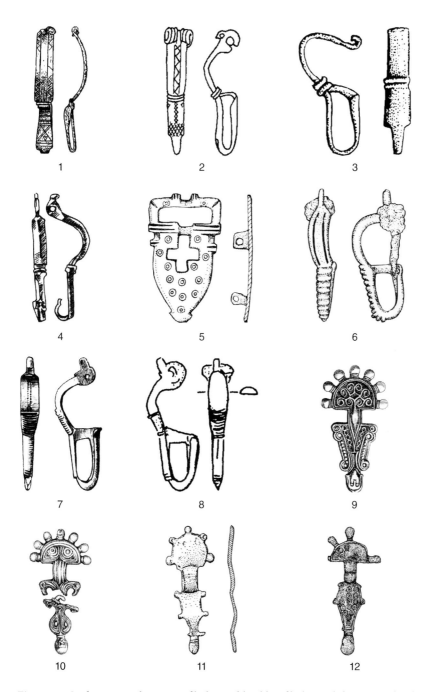

Figure 18 Sixth-to-seventh-century fibulae and buckles: fibulae with bent stem (1–4), Sucidava buckle (5), cast fibulae with bent stem (6–8), and bow fibulae (9–12)

146   *Contact and Separation on the Danube Frontier*

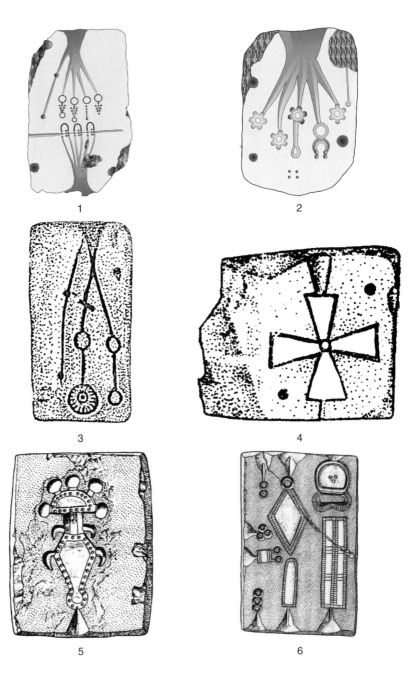

Figure 19 Sixth-to-seventh-century molds from *barbaricum*

empire did not exert significant cultural pressure, while communities in *barbaricum* were not willing to forego their non-Roman identity.

Between Oltenia, the land closest to the Lower Danube, and Moldavia lies a region of mixed cultural influences best seen in the local ceramics discussed in Chapter 2. Interestingly, there are surprisingly few settlements closer than 20 km from the Danube. The existence of a "no man's land" in the Danube valley could be ascribed to the Empire's policy of preventing frequent crossings of the river or the creation of power centers too close to the military frontier. The cultural profile of the area is dominated by the controversy regarding the role of the Slavs, the great cemetery from Sărata-Monteoru, and the mosaic of settlements around Bucharest which produced diverse ceramic shapes and settlement patterns, but also an important number of Byzantine imports betraying close ties to the Byzantine world.[48] Almost all categories of Byzantine artifacts can be found in those settlements illustrating an easy access to goods, which can be explained by their relative proximity to the Danube (ca. 75 km). The metallurgical activity of the region is also impressive with no less than six settlements in Bucharest yielding a variety of tools. Further north, several settlements on the Buzău valley and the Subcarpathian hills, Budureasca in particular, were also notable for their metallurgical workshops.[49]

Yet another region with strong local particularities, as we have already seen, is the territory of the former province of Dacia, especially Transylvania. Here, the Roman tradition going back to the Trajanic province was coupled with another defining trait, a stronger domination of the Hunnic confederation in the fifth century and of the Gepids and Avars in the sixth. Romanian historians, in particular, have insisted on the great upheaval produced by the Huns whose domination of the Middle Danube brought an end to cultural contacts with the western Roman world and prompted a reorientation toward Constantinople.[50] In reality, the break with the West was not an event but a long cultural process in which the Huns were but one episode. With chunks of the western Balkans under the direct control of Attila a reorientation toward Constantinople is hard to conceive and in fact there is very little evidence that such a reorientation ever occurred. There is also no evidence to suggest that the western

---

[48] For the main coordinates of the debate, see Curta, *The Making of the Slavs*, esp. ch. 6.

[49] A. Măgureanu and B. Ciupercă, "The 6th–8th centuries metallurgical activity from Budureasca Valley. The molds," *AMN* 41–42, no. 1 (2004–2005): 291–318.

[50] Velter, *Transilvania*, 28–29; D. Protase, *Autohtonii în Dacia II: Dacia postromană până la slavi* (Cluj-Napoca, 2000), 80; I. Barnea, "Le christianisme sur le territoire de la Republique Socialiste de Roumanie aux IIIe–XIe siècles," *EB* 1 (1985): 96.

connection was completely broken before the seventh century. In any case, Dacia's strongest link with the Roman world was neither the west nor the east, but the nearby frontier region of northern Illyricum where diplomatic action resulted in the cooption of the Herules as federates and the manipulation of the Gepid–Lombard feud. Such initiatives brought Dacia in closer contact with the provinces of the Balkans.

In any case, once the Hunnic storm passed, Dacia resumed its cultural contacts with the West, favored by the reconquest of Dalmatia and Italy by Justinian. Some of the imported items virtually unknown in other parts of *barbaricum*, such as bronze lamps, Menas flasks, and genuine North African lamps, may have arrived in Trajanic Dacia through the mediation of Adriatic ports (Figure 20). Crosses or molds for the production of crosses, so often found south and east of the Carpathians are absent in Dacia. Common Byzantine dress accessories appear in Gepid and Early Avar contexts and generally follow cultural trends from the Middle Danube and Tisza valleys. In this region, pieces of military equipment of Byzantine origin are found in association with artifacts typical for the Carpathian Basin milieu or following fashions from the eastern corners of the Avar Khaganate, whose influence extended to the lands north of the Black Sea. Sometimes cemeteries excavated in this region offer a glimpse into the wealth of the Early Avar power center in Pannonia. Grave inventories combine Byzantine and Eastern elements, an exquisite taste which the Avar aristocracy was able to afford after the Empire sent an estimated total 27 tons of gold in the form of tribute.[51] The rise of the Avars as the hegemonic power in the Carpathian Basin forced the populations in *barbaricum* to make certain cultural decisions or shift their political allegiance. The archaeological evidence reflects such tensions as some communities were clearly oscillating between Byzantine and Avar influence.

The movement of people and perhaps the activity of Byzantine and "barbarian" merchants north of the river ensured a steady flow of Byzantine goods to *barbaricum*. Most of them were unique creations of Danubian frontier culture which constituted what world-systems theorists describe as a semiperiphery where a great deal of innovation takes place.[52] Such items had an important social value in the lands north of the Danube,

---

[51] W. Pohl, *Die Awaren: Ein Steppenvolk in Mitteleuropa, 567–822 n. Chr.* (Munich, 1988), 398. For the evidence of graves, see especially R. Harhoiu, "Quellenlage und Forschungsstand der Frühgeschichte Siebenbürgens im 6.–7. Jahrhundert," *Dacia* 43–45 (2001): 97–158.

[52] Chase-Dunn and Hall, "Conceptualizing Core/Periphery," 30.

Contact and Separation on the Danube Frontier 149

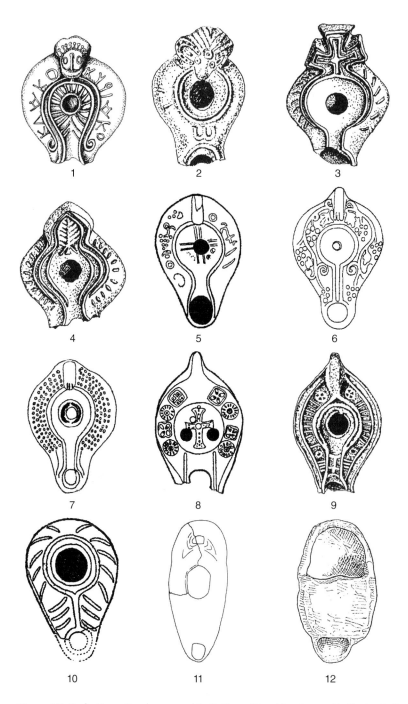

Figure 20 Early Byzantine lamps and imitations: Danubian lamps (1–5), Anatolian lamps (6–7), North African lamp (8), imitation after North African lamp (9), Palestinian lamp (10), and handmade lamps (11–12)

but it is important to note that not all categories of goods typical for the frontier settlements were equally popular. Roman glass, an accessory of the military elite otherwise abundantly documented on sites in the northern Balkans was perhaps too fragile to be transported north of the river.[53] Moreover, various types of jewelry and dress accessories are missing in *barbaricum*, which seems to suggest that communities beyond the frontier received only a number of basic items, lead and copper crosses instead of silver, buckles and brooches made of iron or copper alloy, and the most common ceramic containers in which soldiers received their rations. Oil lamps were not sought after, although they are found in abundance in frontier fortresses and clearly easy to come by. Sometimes communities from *barbaricum*, except those from Trajanic Dacia, chose to manufacture crude handmade imitations. There is not any real wealth in this region beyond the frontier that archaeologists can speak of. Silver and gold objects are extremely rare and the ones recorded do not have a clear archaeological context and might reflect expeditions of plunder in the Balkans. To be sure, single finds of precious-metal objects are also scarce in the Danubian provinces. Here Justinian had to invent a special administrative unit, *quaestura exercitus*, in a desperate attempt to feed the northern Balkans which housed many garrisons but possessed few resources.

Many of the Byzantine imports found in *barbaricum* are therefore nothing but a fragmentary reflection of the *annona militaris*, which took on a different meaning after crossing the frontier, becoming reconstituted and "translated," and perhaps fulfilling certain traditional values of gift-giving and gift exchange.[54] The existence of commercial activity on the frontier and beyond cannot be ruled out, but the Danube as a contact zone presupposed a more important set of relations, of a non-economic nature.[55] The movement of objects documented by archaeological means

---

[53] For recent publications, see G. Jeremić, "Glass artefacts from Roman and Late Roman fortification at Saldum on the Middle Danube. Social and economic background," in *Annales du 18e Congrès de l'Association internationale pour l'histoire du verre. Thessaloniki, 2009*, eds. D. Ignatiadou and A. Antonaras (Thessaloniki, 2012), 284–291; V. Ivanišević and S. Stamenković, "'Glass' workshop from Caričin Grad (Iustiniana Prima)," in *Glass Along the Silk Road from 200 BC to AD 1000. International Conference Within the Scope of the "Sino-German Project on Cultural Heritage Preservation" of the RGZM and the Shaanxi Provincial Institute of Archaeology, December 11th–12th 2008*, ed. B. Zorn (Mainz, 2010), 39–52; M. Križanac, "Glass from Early Byzantine Gradina on Mount Jelica (Serbia)," in *Late Antique/Early Byzantine Glass in the Eastern Mediterranean*, ed. E. Laflı (Izmir, 2009), 265–284.

[54] For the post-colonial concept of "translation," see C. Gosden, *Archaeology and Colonialism: Cultural Contact from 5000 BC to the Present* (Cambridge, 2004), 82–86.

[55] For a strictly economic interpretation, see D. G. Teodor, "Éléments et influences byzantins dans la civilisation des VIe–VIIe siècles après J. Chr. au nord du Bas-Danube," *EBPB* 2 (1991): 59–72.

dovetails nicely with sixth-century accounts documenting the movement of people, including large numbers of prisoners taken from the provinces of the Balkans into captivity north of the Danube.[56] This two-way street of Romans forcibly taken to *barbaricum* and "barbarians" serving in frontier garrisons produced a largely non-economic kind of cultural contact, whose material remains are the Roman objects found in *barbaricum*, the non-Roman objects found in frontier provinces, as well as the multicultural influences traceable on several categories of artifacts discussed in the previous chapters.

Despite such interaction, the culture of the Danubian borderlands and the nearby *barbaricum* did not grow into a homogeneous, distinctive culture. A "middle ground" environment developed, but not necessarily in the sense defined by Richard White, mainly because a state of cultural equilibrium could not be established.[57] Although interaction was not a one-way street, the cultural pull of Byzantium was evidently stronger. What made this possible was not just the empire's prestige, wealth, and the sophistication of its culture, but also the political fragmentation in the lands beyond the frontier which favored emulation and competition. On the other hand, although basic Byzantine items of mundane value in the frontier fortresses acquired prestige attributes once they crossed into *barbaricum*, emulation had practical limits. Settlement patterns are in sharp contrast, the fortified hilltop sites of the Balkans being replaced by defenseless open settlements in the lands north of the river. The ceramic production in *barbaricum* did not follow contemporary shapes from the Empire and the import of fine wares is almost non-existent. Instead, it relied on traditional pots, some of them going back to the Roman provincial shapes of the first centuries AD. Finally, Christianity, a crucial component of sixth-century Roman identity, was present north of the Danube but in modified forms which departed from the accepted norms regarding burial rites and the practice in churches so far missing in *barbaricum*.

Interwoven, these remarks throw light on a group of societies living in the shadow of the Empire but adopting only certain cultural practices, a decision shaped by the balance of power in the region and the degree to which the Danube could function both as a military frontier and as a cultural interface between the Empire and the northern world. This leaves a lot more room for cultural choice than was allowed by the traditional

---

[56] C. Chiriac, "Unele observații asupra informațiilor literar-istorice bizantine privitoare la regiunea Dunării de Jos în secolele V–X," *AM* 20 (1997): 118–120.
[57] White, *The Middle Ground*, ix.

Roman view which saw barbarians "becoming different without knowing it."[58] Similar to the observations made by S. T. Parker on *Limes Arabicus* or D. Cherry in North Africa we can argue that on the Danube there was cultural diversity and rejection as much as there was cultural symbiosis, or "peculiar types of culture-sympathy and culture-clash" as Homi Bhabha described this duality.[59] The Danube remained a daunting natural and political barrier regardless of the facet we wish to emphasize, be it demographic, economic or religious. Continuous cultural interaction was not meant to engender some kind of "open frontier" but to reinforce and secure the existing one. Byzantine goods filtered through the deliberate – and, indeed, inevitable – permeability of the Danube frontier and embarked on a journey which took them through several levels of value and meaning, from functional, close to the frontier, to symbolical in more distant regions in *barbaricum*.[60]

To conclude, the partially successful attempt to create political buffer zones in Arabia and Transcaucasia, where the stakes were high because of rival Persia, was not replicated in the more obscure political climate of the transdanubian world. Although we see several emperors engaged on the diplomatic front in the northern Balkans and the Black Sea steppe, the lack of direct intervention makes the northern *barbaricum* appear dominated by a *laissez-faire* type of approach. This is a sign of pragmatism, not of passivity. Early Byzantine emperors lacked the political and military muscle and were forced to adopt a cultural strategy. The dilemma faced by sixth-century rulers, who by choice or necessity had to spend elsewhere the dwindling resources of the Empire, explain the particular culture developed north of the Danube in relation to Byzantium. Deeply concerned with the fate of the Balkan provinces, Anastasius and his successors strengthened the Danube border but welcomed any outside help they could get to defend it. This *Realpolitik* favored the creation of a unique frontier culture, which I have described as a "bipolar periphery," reverberating deep into *barbaricum* through the channels of cooperation and conflict. Indeed,

---

[58] Cassius Dio, *History*, 56.18.3, speaking about Germani on the first-century Rhine frontier.

[59] Bhabha, "Culture's in-between," 54; S. T. Parker, "The defense of Palestine and Transjordan from Diocletian to Heraclius," in *The Archaeology of Jordan and Beyond: Essays in Honor of James A. Sauer*, eds. L. E. Stager, J. A. Greene, and M. D. Coogan (Winona Lake, IN, 2000), 367–388; D. Cherry, *Frontier and Society in Roman North Africa* (Oxford, 1998).

[60] The same pattern is clearly visible in the early Roman period, for which see P. Wells, "Tradition, identity, and change beyond the Roman frontier," in *Resources, Power and Interregional Interaction*, eds. E. M. Shortman and P. A. Urban (New York, NY, 1992), 185.

the static defensive line on the Danube could not function without constant cultural contact of a more fluid nature.

Despite the great assortment of Byzantine artifacts circulating north of the Danube, none is sufficiently versatile and chronologically sensitive as to capture the rhythm of cultural exchange in the frontier region. The numismatic evidence can strengthen the propositions advanced in the previous pages and throw more light on three fundamental questions. How did Byzantine goods travel across the frontier? Who were the owners? Was there a continuous flow of Byzantine goods toward *barbaricum* or was traffic purely situational? Coins are the only type of Byzantine artifact which can offer a precise dating, being inscribed with the regnal year of the ruling emperor, and are sufficiently standardized to prevent any taxonomical pitfalls. Coins are also the most common artifacts of Byzantine origin found in *barbaricum* and often the best published. Due to the wealth of information they provide and the variety of functions they perform coins lend themselves to multiscalar analysis and can answer questions regarding their role in facilitating cultural contact between Byzantium and the northern world. They can illuminate important issues such as the non-economic function of money, as Byzantine coins combined the natural appeal of intrinsic value (i.e. gold, silver, and copper) with the imperial iconography and Christian symbolism directly related to the question of *aemulatio* discussed in the previous chapters. They can further illustrate the social effect of political payments which Byzantine emperors made in silver and gold coin. Finally, they reveal the traffic of people coming from the military border where "barbarian" soldiers received monetary payments for their services to the empire. In many ways coins are the most complex and intriguing Byzantine objects and it is particularly to this type of source that we need now turn.

5 | The Flow of Byzantine Coins Beyond the Frontier

5.1 General Remarks

Among other virtues, to the modern scholar ancient coinage presents two unique qualities: standardization and high frequency. Unlike the bewildering variety of artifacts ordered by archaeologists according to somewhat artificially defined criteria, coinage needs no such arrangements. Byzantine money has already been classified by the issuing authority into different denominations, mints, and dates and the same coins circulating in the Empire can be found outside the frontier. To be sure, the function performed by Byzantine coins differed from place to place and from one context to another, but the distribution of coin finds on a map affords the same kind of preliminary observations whether those coins have been found inside or outside the political borders of the Early Byzantine Empire. Such comparisons are most welcome, as communication routes and directions of circulation can be fleshed out by examining the mints responsible for striking the coins found in a certain area. Much of the argument in the following two chapters derives from multivariate analyses in time and space which may highlight clusters of small change in one region, the predominance of gold coins in another, the frequency of distant mints, or comparisons between the age-structure of single finds and hoards. The discussion is organized chronologically, taking advantage of the precise dating of Byzantine coinage, another important feature distinguishing coins from other artifacts.

In geographic terms, the nature of the numismatic evidence invites a much broader discussion, not least because coins, by their very nature, were meant to circulate and exchange hands even when they served nonmonetary purposes. This chapter will analyze the flow of Byzantine coins beyond the Danube frontier in the context of the literary and archaeological evidence discussed earlier in the book. Although the Lower Danube remains the main geographic unit of analysis, the functions performed by Byzantine coins beyond this frontier cannot be properly understood without venturing into the regions flanking it to the west (the Carpathian Basin) and to the east (the Black Sea region including Transcaucasia).

This comparison will be developed in Chapter 6. Unfortunately, an undertaking of such geographic magnitude cannot be expanded to include the entire archaeological record due to the fragmentary nature of the evidence, the level of publication, and indeed the sheer quantity of material and the cultural variety of the contexts in which Byzantine artifacts are found. Coins, however, have been published with regularity partly because numismatics developed early as an independent discipline with its own tools, literature, and areas of specialization, while other types of artifacts have received less systematic attention. Furthermore, cultural comparisons between the Danube region, the Pontic steppe, and the Caucasus are particularly familiar to scholars who study the diffusion of cultural influences, the history and archaeology of the Avar period, or the westward migration of the Bulgars and the creation of their first kingdom in the Balkans.[1] The methodological dilemma raised by the cultural diversity inevitably encountered in such a large geographic area is somewhat vindicated by the homogeneous distribution of similar samples of coin finds, which facilitates comparison. The proximity to Byzantine provinces and to important war theaters is another feature shared by the three areas under discussion, the Lower Danube, Transcaucasia, and the Carpathian Basin. Indeed, Byzantine attempts to manipulate the balance of power in the lands beyond the frontier shaped the flow of coins to all these regions. Soldiers' salaries, diplomatic payments, occasional imperial gifts for VIPs, ransom for POWs, and plunder in the Byzantine provinces are the most important documented means through which coins traveled across frontiers. Finally, based on this discussion, Chapter 7 will offer a historical and anthropological interpretation of the functions performed by coins in communities from *barbaricum*.

---

[1] The literature is abundant, but see especially T. Stepanov, "Danube and Caucasus – the Bulgar(ian)s' real and imagined frontiers," in *Donaulimes*, 299–310; I. Ivanov, "Bolgi, Bersili, Esegeli - osnovni prabulgarski rodove na Kavkaz, Volga, Dunav i v Makedoniia," in *Bulgariia v svetovnoto kulturno nasledstvo. Materialy ot tretata natsionalna konferentsiia po istoriia, arkheologiia i kulturen turizum. Putuvane kum Bulgariia – Shumen, 17–19.05.2012 g.*, ed. I. Iordanov (Shumen, 2014), 179–193; D. Glad, "The Empire's influence on the barbarian elites from the Pontic region to the Rhine (5th–7th centuries)," in *Pontic-Danubian Realm*, 349–362; P. Somogyi, "New remarks on the flow of Byzantine coins in Avaria and Wallachia during the second half of the seventh century," in *The Other Europe in the Middle Ages: Avars, Bulgars, Khazars and Cumans*, ed. F. Curta (Boston, MA, 2008), 83–149; I. Bóna, "'Barbarische' Nachahmungen von byzantinischen Goldmünzen im Awarenreich," *RIN* 95 (1993): 529–538; C. Bálint, "Kontakte zwischen Iran, Byzanz und der Steppe. Das Grab von Üç Tepe (Sowj. Azerbajdžan) und der beschlagverzierte Gürtel im 6. und 7. Jahrhundert," in *Awarenforschungen*, ed. F. Daim, vol. I (Vienna, 1992), 309–496.

The contexts in which Byzantine coins have been found, singly or in hoards, and their usefulness for the integration of numismatic evidence into the broader historical narrative require some clarification. The inventory of Byzantine coin finds from *barbaricum* includes some 1,200 single finds and several more thousands in hoards (Appendix A), but only some have been found during archaeological excavations (Appendix B, Table 15).[2] Most single finds from the Danubian provinces resulted from systematic excavations in coastal towns and frontier fortresses, but the nature of the settlements in *barbaricum* – much smaller and unfortified – made them vulnerable to destruction during agricultural works. Even though few coins have been found in stratigraphic context, the fact that finds usually cluster along major river valleys or in the proximity of known settlements affords a general analysis of circulation patterns.[3] To add to the problem, many unprovenanced coins from museum collections may not have been found locally but brought by collectors from Byzantine provinces. The controversy surrounding the presence of Byzantine coins in England is the most notorious example, but similar concerns regarding the collection of the National Museum in Budapest, much closer to the Empire, illustrates some limitations of the numismatic evidence.[4] Whenever possible, such coins must be judged against context-embedded finds or indirect confirmation should be sought in a wide frequency of stray finds from the same area.

Information about hoards is equally incomplete. More than half of the total number of hoards have been dispersed, either divided between finders or otherwise lost in unknown circumstances (Appendix B, Table 16). This poses serious methodological problems for the researcher looking to

---

[2] The appendix can be accessed freely at www.cambridge.org/9781108470421.

[3] It is tempting to connect this geographic pattern with the statement made by the author of the *Strategikon* who claimed that the settlements of the Slavs and Antes lie in a row along the rivers, very close to one another, *Strategikon*, 11.4.

[4] For England, see R. Abdy and G. Williams, "A catalogue of hoards and single finds from the British Iles c. 410–675," in *Coinage and History in the North Sea World, c. AD 500–1250. Essays in Honour of Marion Archibald*, eds. B. Cook and G. Williams (Leiden, 2006), 11–73. For a recent discussion, see C. Morrisson, "Byzantine coins in Early Medieval Britain: a Byzantinist's assessment," in *Early Medieval Monetary History: Studies in Memory of Mark Blackburn*, eds. M. Allen, R. Naismith, and E. Screen (New York, NY, 2016), 207–242. For Budapest, see A. Kiss, "Die "barbarischen" Könige des 4.–7. Jahrhunderts im Karpatenbecken, als Verbündete des römischen bzw. byzantinischen Reiches," *Communicationes Archaeologicae Hungaricae* (1991): 122–123; P. Somogyi, *Byzantinische Fundmünzen der Awarenzeit* (Innsbruck, 1997), 111–117; P. Somogyi, "New remarks on the flow of Byzantine coins in Avaria and Wallachia during the second half of the seventh Century," in *The Other Europe in the Middle Ages: Avars, Bulgars, Khazars and Cumans*, ed. F. Curta (Leiden, 2008), 90–103 with the previous literature.

attribute their deposition to a specific historical context, as the date of concealment is always inferred on the basis of the latest coin in the assemblage. Unless there is a large concentration of hoards in a small region, such as the case of the string of incomplete hoards from Bohemia ending in the reign of Justinian I, such fragmentary finds offer very few certainties. Furthermore, few hoards have been found during archaeological excavations. Hoards such as those found in Magraneti, Pityus, and Archaeopolis in Georgia or Hrozová in the Czech Republic are important exceptions. Finally, for the majority of hoards it is uncertain whether the process of accumulation took place in the same region where they were hidden for safekeeping or the sum of money was brought as a purse from a Byzantine province and buried in conditions of emergency before it could be dispersed locally.

A number of general observations can be drawn from the statistical analysis of Early Byzantine coins in *barbaricum* (Figure 21 to Figure 25). The largest number of coins are issues of Justinian I, but his reign is also the longest. By taking into account the length of each reign, the highest percentage goes to Justin II, followed closely by Justin I (Figure 21) (Appendix B, Tables 1 and 13). All types of Byzantine coins can be found in *barbaricum* – gold, silver, and copper – but in varying proportions depending on emperor and region. The fewest gold coins are those struck for Justin I and Justin II, respectively, while the largest concentration of gold is found in the seventh century (Appendix B, Tables 2 and 3). The largest number of gold coins have been found in the Carpathian Basin and the neighboring regions, chiefly on the territory of the Avar Khaganate where many cemeteries have yielded Byzantine *solidi*. Before the Avar age, the largest concentration of finds are *solidi* of Anastasius found in coastal areas of the Baltic and the Adriatic and *solidi* and *tremisses* of Justinian from Central Europe.

Almost 80 percent of the silver coins are seventh-century hexagrams. The reign of Heraclius witnessed the most intense production, although its levels are uneven. Indeed, almost 50 percent of all seventh-century hexagrams are issues dated 625–629. The largest number of hexagrams can be found in Transcaucasia and the heaviest concentration dates from the time of Heraclius' massive counteroffensive against Persia in the 620s. In fact, Transcaucasia boasts the highest overall proportion of silver coins, 17 percent. This may seem rather unimpressive, but it should be remembered that sixth-century silver coinage was mostly ceremonial (imperial largesse), which makes it rare in *barbaricum*; to be sure, it is equally exotic in the Byzantine provinces. Most of the sixth-century silver coins from

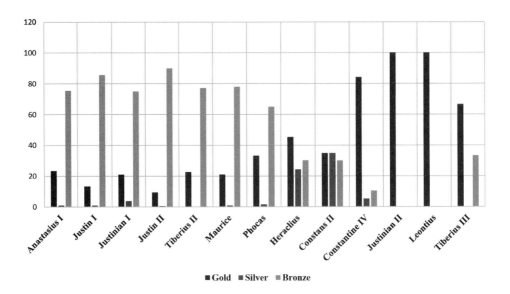

Figure 21 Sixth-to-seventh-century Byzantine coin finds in *barbaricum*

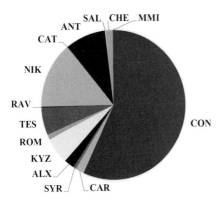

Figure 22 Coin finds by mint
Abbreviations in Appendix B, Table 4

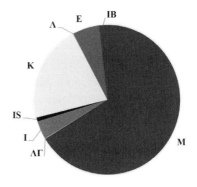

Figure 23 Coin finds by denomination
Abbreviations in Appendix B, Table 6

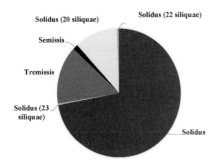

Figure 24 Byzantine gold, silver, and bronze hoards in *barbaricum*

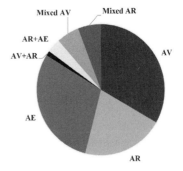

Figure 25 Sixth-to-seventh-century Byzantine gold coins in *barbaricum*

Transcaucasia – *siliquae* and *miliarensia* – date from the reign of Justinian, as do the few pieces found in the Carpathian Basin.

The vast majority of numismatic finds in *barbaricum* are copper issues and this is no different from the general pattern of coin circulation documented in the Byzantine provinces. Over 65 percent of the coins are copper and the proportion could be higher were it not for the predominance of gold in the Carpathian Basin (Appendix B, Table 2). The largest concentration of copper coins can be found in the Lower Danube region (ca. 85 percent), the closest to a heavily militarized frontier. Within individual reigns, the largest percentage of copper coins goes to Justin II (over 90 percent) and the frequency remains high throughout the long sixth century until the accession of Heraclius, when the proportion gradually drops to less than a third. Explanations should be sought not only in *barbaricum* and in circumstances related to the collapse of the frontier system in the Balkans, but also in Byzantine monetary policies and in fluctuations of mint output. The great advantage of copper coins, aside from their sheer number, is their accurate dating by *lustrum* and even by regnal year after 538 (Appendix B, Table 4).[5] The chronological sequence of finds in *barbaricum* reveals a significant concentration of coins issued between 512 and 538, when the Byzantine monetary system was remarkably stable. The best represented, however, is the coinage of 538–542 featuring the impressively large *folles* of Justinian, apparently very popular outside the Empire. A general decline can be noticed in the last quarter of the sixth century, while coins struck after 620 are rare even in the Balkans, south of the Danube.[6]

Mints and denominations can provide additional comparative insight. In both geographic and quantitative terms, the distribution of coins by mint depends on proximity and output as well as on local preference. As expected, the central mint in Constantinople accounts for over 55 percent of the finds, followed by Nicomedia and Antioch (Figure 22) (Appendix B, Table 5). The Syrian mint is particularly influential in Transcaucasia, although it is far from being exotic in the Lower Danube region. The importance of provincial mints increased in the second half of the sixth century and in many contexts Thessalonica, Nicomedia, and Antioch

---

[5] For dating patterns based on the *lustrum* cycle, see W. Hahn, "Emission und Lustrum in der byzantinischen Münzprägung des 6. Jahrhunderts," *Anzeiger* 108 (1971): 215–221.

[6] A. Gandila, "A few rare Byzantine coins found in Dobrudja and the extent of Byzantine control in the seventh-century Balkans," *CN* 17 (2016): 53–64; S. Mihaylov, "Seventh-to-eighth century Byzantine bronze coins from Northeastern Bulgaria," *Cultură și Civilizație la Dunărea de Jos* 26 (2008): 77–85.

surpass Constantinople. Coins from the Western mints opened after Justinian's *reconquista* are more frequent in Central Europe, where connections with the western Mediterranean were stronger. Finally, the statistical breakdown by denomination reveals an overwhelming dominance of the *follis* (over 65 percent), while the small change typically used for everyday transactions in Byzantine urban markets, *decanummia* (quarter-*follis*) and *pentanummia* (eighth-*follis*), covers only ca. 10 percent of the finds from *barbaricum* (Figure 23) (Appendix B, Table 6).

It does not take much effort to notice that the flow of Byzantine coins during the sixth and seventh centuries was anything but linear. What are, then, the explanations for the chronological and spatial distribution of Byzantine coins in *barbaricum*? What are the local and broader historical circumstances that influenced the availability of Byzantine coins in lands beyond the frontier? How did Byzantine emperors use coinage to manipulate the balance of power in peripheral regions? These are some of the main questions addressed in this chapter and the next along with some attempts to clarify methodological issues regarding the use of numismatic evidence.

5.2 The Lower Danube: The Land of Bronze

5.2.1 Reconstruction and the Age of Justinian (ca. 490–565)

From a strictly numismatic point of view the Byzantine coin series begins with the reform of Anastasius in 498. However, such a periodization seems artificial if we consider certain historical processes long in motion when Anastasius implemented his monetary policy. At least three major stages of development can be identified. They provide historical perspective on sixth-century realities although the mechanisms of circulation were too unstable to speak about any coherent *longue durée* phenomena. The first phase was shaped by the abandoning of Dacia ordered by Aurelian in the early 270s. As a result, in the following centuries the cultural distinction between the territory of the former Roman province and the regions east and south of the Carpathians became blurred.[7] Coin finds of the early fourth century still concentrate in the area of the former Roman towns in Transylvania and Oltenia, but by the sixth century the direction of the coin

---

[7] For the Roman influence in the regions neighboring transdanubian Dacia, see more recently C. Opreanu, "The barbarians and Roman Dacia. War, trade and cultural interaction," in *The Roman Empire and Beyond*, eds. E. C. De Sena and H. Dobrzanska (Oxford, 2011), 125–136.

influx would shift toward Moldavia and Wallachia. The second stage was marked by the development of the so-called Sântana de Mureș-Chernyakhov culture, a mixture of Roman, Germanic, Sarmatian and other local, sometimes pre-Roman influences overlapping under Gothic hegemony. The period of its greatest extent and flourishing coincides with renewed Roman ambitions on the Lower Danube and beyond. The shifting balance of power in the region is reflected in the fourth-century peace negotiations with the Goths. The provisions regarding the regulation of trade have been used by historians and numismatists to explain the presence of Late Roman coins north of the Danube.[8] Finally, the third stage witnessed the cultural and political transformation of the region under the brutal domination of the Huns. The terms most frequently associated with the Hunnic storm in the Balkans and the Carpathian Basin are devastation, collapse, social, economic, and demographic decline. Indeed, there is a sharp decline in the flow of Roman coins to *barbaricum* in the first half of the fifth century, but this also coincides with a more general decline of the Late Roman monetary system, reflecting a deeper internal weakness of the Empire at the turn of the fifth century.[9]

From a historical perspective a numismatic understanding of sixth-century interaction in the frontier region must begin with the transitional decades following the dissolution of Attila's confederation. The second half of the fifth century was marked by an almost complete breakdown of the low-value currency system as a direct consequence of the political catastrophe which took the western provinces away from Roman control. From an archaeological point of view the effects of the Hunnic onslaught north of the Danube are still hard to gauge. Fatalistic scenarios aside, both elements of continuity and major cultural change must be considered.

---

[8] P. Heather and J. Matthews, *The Goths in the Fourth Century* (Liverpool, 1991), 51–102; G. Gomolka-Fuchs, ed., *Die Sîntana de Mureș-Cernjachov-Kultur: Akten des internationalen Kolloquiums in Caputh vom 20. bis 24. Oktober 1995* (Bonn, 1999); F. Petrescu, *Repertoriul monumentelor arheologice de tip Sântana de Mureș-Cerneahov de pe teritoriul României* (Bucharest, 2002); M. Kulikowski, *Rome's Gothic Wars: From the Third Century to Alaric* (Cambridge, 2007), 86–99.

[9] For Late Roman coins north of the Danube, see D. Moisil, "The Danube *limes* and the *barbaricum* (294–498 AD): a study in coin circulation," *Histoire et Mesure* 17, nos. 3–4 (2002): 79–120; C. Preda, "Circulația monedelor postaureliene în Dacia," *SCIVA* 26, no. 4 (1975): 441–486; V. M. Butnariu, "Monedele romane postaureliene în teritoriile carpato-dunăreano-pontice (anii 275–491): III. Perioada 383–491," *AM* 14 (1991): 67–107; V. M. Butnariu, "Monedele romane postaureliene în teritoriile carpato-dunăreano-pontice (anii 275–491): II. Perioada 323–383," *AM* 12 (1988): 131–196; V. M. Butnariu, "Monedele romane postaureliene în teritoriile carpato-dunăreano-pontice (anii 275–491): I. Perioada 275–324," *AM* 11 (1987): 113–140.

The Gepids replaced the Huns as the hegemonic power in the Tisza basin and by extension in Transylvania and Banat, but no coherent political unit existed in the northern Danubian plain. This may explain the lack of information about any economic and religious initiatives undertaken by sixth-century emperors in the region. Until the rise of the Avar Khaganate in the last quarter of the sixth century, Byzantine emperors focused their diplomatic activity in the northwestern Balkans where the Gepids could not match the political ambition of previous Gothic and Hunnic confederations.[10]

Historians often emphasize cultural continuity north of the Danube, the use of Early Byzantine coins being described as the exclusive privilege of Daco-Roman communities in *barbaricum* on account of their long history of monetary contact with the Roman world.[11] Such processes must be analyzed with caution as they often rely on brush strokes hiding important particularities and developments measured in decades rather than centuries. As a result of the major transformations taking place from the late third to the late fifth century many of the cultural coordinates in place before the third-century crisis were no longer traceable when Anastasius acceded to the throne. This includes the culture of the Danubian provinces, not just the ethnic profile of the lands north of the river. The Empire was struggling to reestablish the frontier system after almost five decades when Byzantine emperors had to deal not only with the Huns but also with the aggression of the Ostrogoths. Successful reconstruction in the sixth century – despite spectacular achievements – produced an artificial edifice. The Balkan provinces came to be dominated by a dense network of fortifications which lacked sufficient support from the countryside and had to rely on official *annona* sent from elsewhere under the administrative auspices of peculiar arrangements such as *quaestura exercitus*.[12] Urban life can be found almost exclusively on the coast of the Black Sea and the Aegean and in strategic locations of the interior; the direct implication is that much of the monetary economy in the northern Balkans reflects

---

[10] For the role of the Gepids in the region, see recently A. Sarantis, *Justinian's Balkan Wars: Campaigning, Diplomacy and Development in Illyricum, Thrace and the Northern World AD 527–65* (Prenton, 2016), 266–277.

[11] The literature is vast, but see more recently D. G. Teodor, "Considerații privind unele aspecte ale etnogenezei românești," *AM* 34 (2011): 177–185. This question is discussed in more detail in Chapter 7.

[12] A. G. Poulter, "Cataclysm on the Lower Danube: the destruction of a complex Roman landscape," in *Landscape of Change: Rural Evolutions in Late Antiquity and the Early Middle Ages*, ed. N. Christie (Aldershot, 2004), 223–253.

soldiers' salaries and their expenditure rather than a real market. Yet historians and numismatists continue to speak about intensive trade and coin use in *barbaricum* based on the assumption that the mere presence of coins must reflect a resuming of such activities in the sixth century – if they ever existed in the first place.[13]

A survey of sixth-to-seventh-century coin finds is a necessary starting point for understanding fluctuations in coin supply and ultimately the function of Early Byzantine coins outside the Empire (Figure 26–Figure 30). Many Early Byzantine bronze coins are dated with the regnal year of the ruler, which induces a false sense of precision. While accurate dating facilitates a detailed analysis of coin flow over time, it also conceals a number of methodological pitfalls to which many historians and numismatists have succumbed. One of the most common mistakes is to assume that coins arrived in a region immediately after they were minted, ignoring the fact that coins issued in a certain year continued to circulate as long as they remained legal tender. Hoards with the latest coins struck in the seventh century often include early sixth-century issues and, notwithstanding the normal attrition rate, coins of sixth-century emperors remained in use for many decades. To be sure, the age-structure of hoards suggests a steady release of fresh coin disbursed in the form of payment to soldiers defending the fortresses of the Balkans, but their free circulation prohibits any firm statement regarding the time when they were lost in *barbaricum* other than establishing a *terminus post quem*. The degree of wear which constitutes an important indication of prolonged circulation cannot be verified in most cases, unfortunately, because bronze coins are seldom illustrated in publications. This realization takes away some of the power of numismatic evidence, but the reward is a much more responsible use of coins as a primary source for dating archaeological complexes and for assessing social and economic phenomena.

The early post-reform coinage of Anastasius (498–512) is perhaps an exception as its weight standard was doubled in 512 making it anomalous and susceptible to official withdrawal from circulation after this date. The fact that some late sixth-century hoards from the Balkans still include such early issues is an invitation to caution in generalizing the nature of its

---

[13] C. Chiriac, *Civilizația bizantină și societatea din regiunile extracarpatice ale României în secolele VI–VIII* (Brăila, 2013), 82; A.-M. Velter, *Transilvania în secolele V–XII. Interpretări istorico-politice și economice pe baza descoperirilor monetare din bazinul Carpatic, secolele V–XII* (Bucharest, 2002), 33–35; L. M. Stratulat, "Continuitate și discontinuitate la nordul Dunării de Jos (secolele IV–VIII d. Hr.)," *Carpica* 31 (2002): 70–71; A. Madgearu, *Continuitate și discontinuitate culturală la Dunărea de Jos în secolele VII–VIII* (Bucharest, 1997), 68.

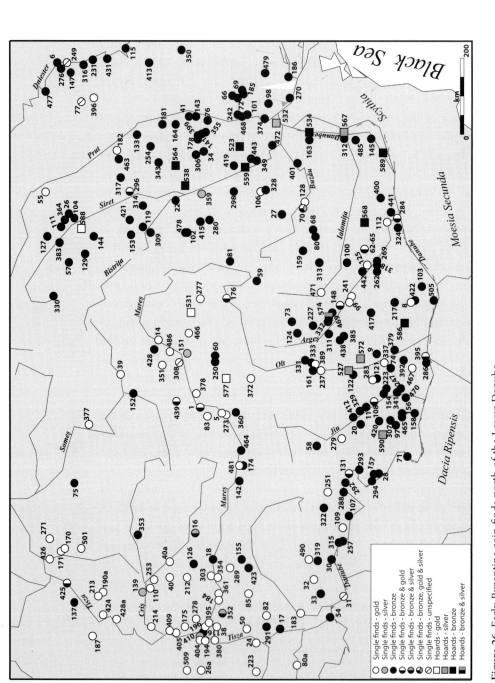

Figure 26 Early Byzantine coin finds north of the Lower Danube. Numbers on the map refer to numbers in Appendix A.2.

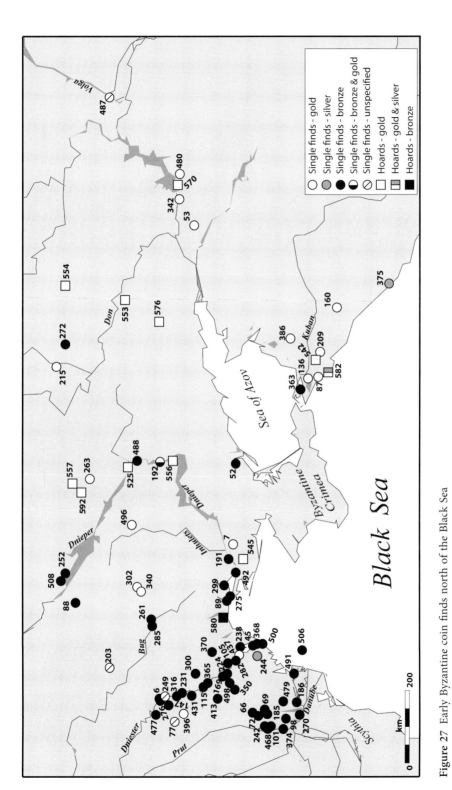

Figure 27 Early Byzantine coin finds north of the Black Sea. Numbers on the map refer to numbers in Appendix A.2.

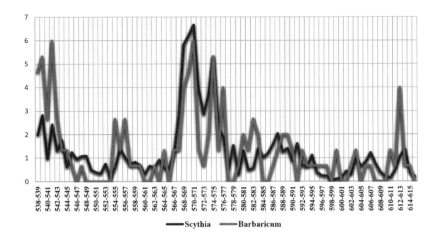

Figure 28 The chronology of Early Byzantine coin finds from the Danube frontier and *barbaricum*

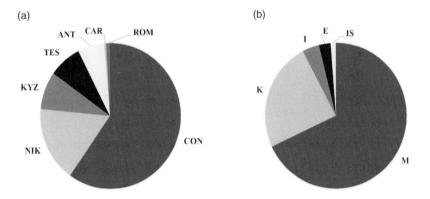

Figure 29a–b Mints and denominations in *barbaricum* (Lower Danube and Black Sea) Abbreviations in Appendix B, Tables 4 and 6

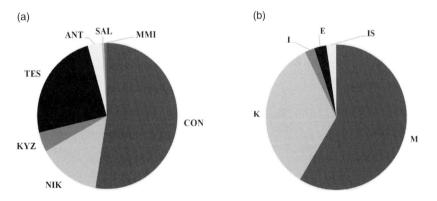

Figure 30a–b Mints and denominations in the Byzantine bridge-head forts (Sucidava, Drobeta, and Dierna)

successful withdrawal soon after 512.[14] In any case, only two early issues are so far known in *barbaricum*, both found east of the Carpathians, a *follis* from Slobozia Mare (Moldova), not far from the Danube, and another one from the area of Bârlad (Romania).[15] As both finds are relatively close to the Byzantine province of Scythia, one is tempted to ascribe their presence to the emperor's reconstruction efforts on the Danube frontier, well documented by archaeological sources.[16] The other two early reform issues of Anastasius have been found at Drobeta, an important Byzantine bridgehead fortress in the Iron Gates region.[17] A well-known inscription from Ratiaria, if indeed dating from the reign of Anastasius, confirms the emperor's strategic interest in northern Illyricum.[18] Based on the numismatic evidence, it has been suggested that reconstruction efforts in the Danube region had been initiated as early as the reign of Marcian (450–457).[19] However, the process of restoration was long and uneven, being hindered by renewed conflict with the Ostrogoths in the 480s and the revolt of Vitalianus in the 510s.

Mint output during the experimental stage which preceded the final reform of 512 was low compared to the following decades even if we assume a rapid withdrawal of this coinage.[20] The rarity of finds in *barbaricum* mirrors the situation south of the Danube, the northeastern Balkans remaining the best documented region.[21] On the other hand, from a

---

[14] A. Gandila, "Early Byzantine coin circulation in the eastern provinces: a statistical approach," *AJN* 21 (2009): 166 and n. 67.

[15] A. A. Nudel'man, *Topografiia kladov i nakhodok edinichnykh monet* (Kishinew, 1976), 87, no. 46; E. Oberländer-Târnoveanu and E. Popușoi, "Monede bizantine din colecția muzeului 'Vasile Pârvan' din Bîrlad," *Carpica* 13, no. 2 (1992): 228, no. 1.

[16] I. Barnea, "Contributions to Dobrudja history under Anastasius I," *Dacia* 4 (1960): 363–374; A. Suceveanu and A. Barnea, *La Dobroudja romaine* (Bucharest, 1991), 170–172.

[17] E. Oberländer-Târnoveanu, "Tranziția de la antichitate la evul mediu timpuriu la marginea imperiului (II). De la prima dispariție a circulației monetare la renașterea ei în zona Porților de Fier ale Dunării (circa 375–565)," *Muzeul Național* 16 (2004): 55, n. 50.

[18] V. Velkov, "Napis na car Anastasiie (491–518) ot Ratiariia," *Arkheologiia* (1984), nos. 1–2: 92–94. Vladislav Popović has interpreted the inscription *Anastasiana Ratiaria semper floreat* as referring to the rebirth of the town (ἀνάστασις) rather than to the emperor's name as a builder; see V. Popović, "Trois inscriptions protobyzantines de Bregovina," *Starinar* 40–41 (1989–1990): 283.

[19] Oberländer-Târnoveanu, "Tranziția de la antichitate," 53; Sarantis, *Justinian's Balkan*, 129–134.

[20] The most comprehensive statistical study of Anastasius' early reform coinage remains D. M. Metcalf, *The Origins of the Anastasian Currency Reform* (Chicago, IL, 1969).

[21] S. Mihaylov, "Etapi v parichata tsirkulatsiia prez rannovizantiiskata epocha (498–681) v provintsiia Vtora Miziia," *Numizmatika, sfragistika i epigrafika* 6 (2010): 111, fig. 1; A. Gandila, "Some aspects of monetary circulation in the Byzantine province of Scythia during the 6th and 7th century," in *Numismatic, Sphragistic and Epigraphic Contributions to the History of the Black Sea Coast*, ed. I. Lazarenko, vol. I (Varna, 2008), 306, table 2. The rarity of finds cannot be

statistical perspective the post-512 coinage of Anastasius is more abundant in *barbaricum* than it is in the Danubian provinces. Although most finds concentrate in the region close to the Danube, two half-folles have been found in Transylvania, at Gherla (Romania) and Dorobanți (Romania), the latter retrieved from an inhumation grave. The coin was found in a pot said to be Gepidic.[22] A similar connection might be supposed for the barbarous imitation of a *follis* bearing the name of Anastasius found at Drobeta. Such imitations are known in Serbia and Bulgaria deep into the hinterland and almost all use pre-538 coin types as models, which suggests that they were produced in the first decades of the sixth century.[23] This period coincides with the Gepid domination of the western Balkans but also with the presence of the Herules whose cultural footprint in the region has received increasing attention in the past few years.[24] Since many such imitations have been found in the provinces of Thracia and Haemimontus, a connection with the movement of Herul federates is more probable although the coins may have been issued by the Gepids.[25] Gold coins were also imitated; a *tremissis* of Anastasius was found at Viminacium on the right bank of the Danube, perhaps issued at Sirmium where the Gepids opened a mint.[26]

---

connected with the attacks of "Bulgars" in 493, 499 and 502; cf. Oberländer-Târnoveanu, "Tranziția de la antichitate," 54.

[22] Velter, *Transilvania*, 291, no. 53; V. M. Butnariu, "Răspîndirea monedelor bizantine din secolele VI–VII în teritoriile carpato-dunărene," *BSNR* 131–133 (1983–1985): 219, no. 44.

[23] I. Iurukova, "Imitations barbares de monnaies de bronze byzantines du VIe siècle," *Byzantinoslavica* 30 (1969): 83–87; D. Gaj-Popović, "The appearance of the barbarized folises (folles) in the 6th century in the Balkan Peninsula," *Balcanoslavica* 2 (1973): 95–100; V. Ivanišević, "La monnaie paléobyzantine dans l'Illyricum du nord," in *Mélanges Cécile Morrisson* (Paris, 2010), 446–448.

[24] A. Kiss, "Heruler in Nordserbien," in *Interaktionen der mitteleuropäischen Slawen und anderer Ethnika im 6.–10. Jahrhundert. Symposium Nové Vozokany 3.–7. Oktober 1983*, ed. P. Šalkovský (Nitra, 1984), 133–137; H. Gračanin, "Gepidi, Heruli, Langobardi i južna Panonija," *Scrinia slavonica* 7 (2007): 7–64; A. Sarantis, "The Justinianic Herules: from allied barbarians to Roman provincials," in *Neglected Barbarians*, 361–402; R. Steinacher, "The Herules: fragments of a history," in *Neglected Barbarians*, 319–360; V. Ivanišević and M. Kazanski, "Geruly Iustiniana v Severnom Illirikume i ikh arheologicheskie sledy," *Stratum plus* (2010), 5: 141–157; I. Bugarski and V. Ivanišević, "Pogranich'e rimskoi imperii i varvarov: sistema oborony imperii ot Kutsiia do Lederaty," in *Lesnaja i lesostepnaia zony vostochnoi Evropy v epohi rimskikh vliianii i velikogo pereseleniia narodov* (Tula, 2012), 482–511.

[25] A. Tenchova, "Beobachtung der Münzzirkulation am Mittellauf des Maritzaflusses im 6.–7. Jahrhundert," presentation at "22nd International Congress of Byzantine Studies, Sofia, 22–27 August 2011."

[26] V. Ivanišević, "Vizantijski novac (491–1092) iz zbirke Narodnog Muzeja u Požarevacu," *Numizmatičar* 11 (1988): 90.

The post-reform coinage of Anastasius found in *barbaricum* along the Lower Danube, in the Carpathian Basin, and north of the Black Sea as far as Kiselivka Hill in Kiev might constitute an immediate echo of the emperor's successful overhaul of the monetary system. However, it is equally possible that some of the coins were brought to these regions and lost under his successors, sometime before 538 when Justinian undertook another major monetary reform, or even later (Appendix B, Table 13). We can be even less certain about the chronology of gold coins of Anastasius found in *barbaricum,* as Byzantine gold was far more stable than the petty currency and Roman legislation itself encouraged the use of *solidi* issued by former emperors.[27] Consequently, the *solidi* found at Bucharest–Măgurele and Craiova, less than 75 km away from the Danube, may well reflect later sixth-century subsidies or plunder expeditions in the provinces of the Balkans.[28]

The period from 512 to 538 – covering the final regnal years of Anastasius, the reign of Justin I, and the first decade of Justinian's reign – is characterized by unprecedented monetary stability. In the western section of the frontier issues of Justin I are well represented in the Byzantine bridge-head forts at Sucidava and Drobeta, their coverage extending to the Roman *castrum* at Pojejena as well as to Dierna-Zernes, one of the fortresses reclaimed by the Empire on the left bank of the Danube.[29] Furthermore, three coins of Justin I have been found at Răcari, a former Roman *castrum*, including a *pentanummium*, a rare denomination in *barbaricum,* which suggests a direct connection with the Byzantine provinces of the Balkans where such coins were more common.[30] Belonging to the same category of small change, a *decanummium* of Justin I was found in the old *castrum* at Pojejena, a fortification attached to the defense system of Moesia Prima.[31]

---

[27] M. F. Hendy, *Studies in the Byzantine Monetary Economy c. 300–1450* (Cambridge, 1985), 366.

[28] B. Mitrea, "Découvertes monétaires en Roumanie: 1981, 1982 et 1983," *Dacia* 28 (1984): 188, no. 131; Butnariu, "Răspîndirea monedelor," 218, no. 39.

[29] Sucidava: Butnariu, "Răspîndirea monedelor," 226, nos. 2–6; A. Vîlcu and E. Nicolae, "Monede bizantine descoperite la Sucidava," in *Arheologia Mileniului I p. Chr. Cercetări actuale privind istoria și arheologia migrațiilor,* eds. L. M. Voicu and B. Ciupercă (Bucharest, 2010), 300, nos. 1–3. Drobeta: Oberländer-Târnoveanu, "Tranziția de la antichitate," 60–61, n. 63. Pojejena: Butnariu, "Răspîndirea monedelor," 221, no. 117. Dierna: Oberländer-Târnoveanu, "Tranziția de la antichitate," 62, n. 65. In the case of Dierna we have to rely on private collections of coins acquired from the area of the ancient settlement; see E. Oberländer-Târnoveanu, "La răscruce de vremuri: tranziția de la antichitate la evul mediu timpuriu în zona Porților de Fier ale Dunării – un punct de vedere numismatic," *CN* 8 (2002): 126.

[30] Butnariu, "Răspîndirea monedelor," 222, nos. 123–125.   [31] Ibid., 221, no. 117.

Further east, *pentanummia* of Anastasius have been found at Vadul lui Isac (Moldova) and Kherson (Ukraine) and might indicate similar connections with Byzantine Scythia and the Crimea, respectively.[32] Another *pentanummium* issued after the reform of 512 was found at Domnești (Romania) and was probably lost by someone traveling on the communication route along the Argeș river, a major artery linking the Lower Danube with the Carpathians.[33] The Argeș river valley and its main tributaries is a region rich in finds from the first decades of the sixth century (Figure 26). Several sixth-century settlements have been excavated in the area of modern-day Bucharest, some of them yielding coin finds of Justinian.[34] More coins of Justin I and Justinian dated between 522 and 538 have been found at Ulmeni close to the mouth of Argeș river. The unusually large number of finds from Ulmeni as well the heavy concentration of late sixth-century issues in the general area are reasons to suspect that the coins were originally part of a hoard subsequently dispersed.[35]

If coins of Anastasius did not travel very far from the Danube, coins of Justin I and early issues of Justinian are found in greater number in northern Moldavia, in the Siret-Prut interfluve and in the highland region of the eastern Carpathians. This area also features a high concentration of Late Roman amphorae and an intense metallurgical activity, whose beginnings might date from this period.[36] Two *folles* of Justinian from 527–537 have been found during archaeological excavations in the large settlement of Botoșana, in two sunken-featured buildings, in association with metallurgical implements.[37] In most other cases there is no stratigraphic context, but the occasional association of coins with sixth-century pottery and dress

---

[32] E. S. Stolyarik, *Essays on Monetary Circulation in the North-Western Black Sea Region in the Late Roman and Early Byzantine Periods: Late 3rd Century–Early 13th Century AD* (Odessa, 1993), 132, no. 2 and 133, no. 9.

[33] G. Poenaru Bordea and P. I. Dicu, "Monede romane tîrzii și bizantine (secolele IV–XI) descoperite pe teritoriul județului Argeș," *SCN* 9 (1989): 78, no. 85.

[34] E. Oberländer-Târnoveanu, "Barbaricum apropiat – populațiile din Muntenia și Imperiul Bizantin (secolele VI–X) – mărturia numismaticii," *Ialomița* 4 (2004): 333, n. 12; Butnariu, "Răspîndirea monedelor," 217, nos. 19, 21–22; M. Constantiniu, "Săpăturile de la Străulești-Măicănești. Așezarea feudală II," *CAB* 2 (1965): 174–189 and fig. 93/1–3. It has been long suggested that the region of Bucharest was the center of the Slavic tribal union ruled by Ardagast, for which see M. Comșa, "Les formations politiques (cnezats de vallée) du VIe siècle sur le territoire de la Roumanie," *Prace i materiały. Muzeum Archeologicznego i Etnograficznego w Łodzi. Seria Archeologiczne* 25 (1978): 109–117.

[35] Butnariu, "Răspîndirea monedelor," 223, nos. 159–162; Oberländer-Târnoveanu, "Barbaricum apropiat," 332.

[36] For distribution maps, see above Chapter 2, Figure 3 and Figure 9.

[37] D. G. Teodor, *Civilizația romanică la est de Carpați în secolele V–VII (așezarea de la Botoșana-Suceava)* (Bucharest, 1984), 61, figs. 30/1–2 and 31/6–8.

accessories suggests the existence of settlements.[38] In the same region, but closer to the Danube, at Cudalbi laborers found a small hoard of copper coins hidden in a ceramic container, ending with issues of Justin I. Its interpretation as reflecting the first Slavic attacks on the Danube frontier should be taken with caution as it is not supported by any archaeological evidence.[39]

Gold coins of Justin I are so far unknown in the region between the Eastern Carpathians and the Dnieper, while the two gold coins of Justinian I found at Borolea and Iași have been published with insufficient details and cannot be dated more precisely within Justinian's long reign.[40] We find gold issues of Justin I – two *solidi* and a *tremissis* – closer to the Danube in Oltenia, the area where the influence of Byzantine forts from the northern bank is most obvious.[41] In eastern Wallachia, at Găești, not far from the impressive Slavic cemetery at Sărata-Monteoru, a *solidus* dated between 527 and 538 might signal the early development of a power center in the region, if indeed the coin was lost in the first half of the sixth century.[42] Along with the coins – some of them modified to be worn as pendants – imitations of Late Roman amphorae and handmade lamps following Byzantine prototypes, as well as the production of Byzantine-style jewelry, suggest that access to Byzantine culture played an important role as an index of social distinction.[43]

A number of patterns emerge from the distribution of coin finds dating from the first decades of the sixth century. In Oltenia coin circulated along the valleys of rivers Olt and Jiu through the mediation of the Byzantine fortresses on the northern bank of the Danube. In Wallachia, Moldavia, and the northwestern Black Sea steppe the coin flow was dictated by

---

[38] At Sărățeni (Vaslui, Romania) and Cârja (Vaslui, Romania) coins of Justin I were found in association with remains of handmade pots, for which see D. G. Teodor, *Descoperiri arheologice și numismatice la est de Carpați (contribuții la continuitatea daco-romană și veche românească)* (Bucharest, 1997), 64, no. 156 and 144, no. 619.

[39] *Trésors*, no. 351; E. Oberländer-Târnoveanu, "Societate, economie și politică – populațiile de pe teritoriul Moldovei și lumea sud-est europeană în secolele IV–XIV în lumina descoperirilor monetare," *Suceava* 26–28 (1999–2001): 317.

[40] Oberländer-Târnoveanu, "Tranziția de la antichitate," 61, n. 63; Butnariu, "Răspîndirea monedelor," 217, no. 15 and 220, no. 76.

[41] Vădastrița: Butnariu, "Răspîndirea monedelor," 224, no. 171; Olari: Oberländer-Târnoveanu, "Tranziția de la antichitate," 61, n. 63.

[42] Butnariu, "Răspîndirea monedelor," 219, no. 51.

[43] A *solidus* from 527–537 found at Almăjel (Mehedinți, Romania) was pierced and a loop was attached later; for an illustration of the coin, see A. Vîlcu, T. Isvoranu, and E. Nicolae, *Les monnaies d'or de l'Institut d'Archéologie de Bucarest* (Wetteren, 2006), 150, no. 441 and pl. 15/441.

developments in the provinces of Moesia Secunda, Scythia, and the Byzantine possessions in the Crimea at a time when the empire was reestablishing its domination in the northern Balkans through diplomatic action or reconstruction and entrenchment on the Danube. Most of the Byzantine coins crossing the river were copper issues from the central mint in Constantinople, which is also typical for the Balkans at a time when the Early Byzantine monetary system was still in its infancy. Three coins of Justinian from Antioch were found not far from the Danube border and reflect communication routes in the Black Sea or perhaps the movement of soldiers from one theater to another. The few gold coins from the Danubian plain are accidental finds and may fulfill different scenarios – the payment of soldiers and mercenaries, plunder in the Balkan provinces, or diplomatic gifts sent to petty chieftains. It is tempting to link these finds to the state of the frontier as described by Procopius who lamented the death of the capable general Chilbudius in 533, after which "the river became free for the barbarians to cross at all times as they wished, and the possessions of the Romans were rendered easily accessible."[44] Although Procopius often exaggerated for dramatic effect, it may not be coincidental that most gold coins from the lands north of the Danube are Justinianic *solidi* struck before 550, the majority being issues from 527–538.[45] This might constitute a strong indication that they were lost sometime in the second quarter of the sixth century when Justinian's massive building program created a large manpower demand fulfilled by transdanubians.[46]

Finds of dated coinage of Justinian (538–565) display a remarkable series of contrasts. The most striking is the unusual concentration of coins dated between 538 and 545, especially issues struck on the heavy standard employed after the reform (Figure 29; Appendix B, Table 4).[47] The heavy coins of Justinian, whose role in the Byzantine economy was discussed elsewhere, were extremely popular in *barbaricum* on account of their

---

[44] Procopius, *Bella*, 7.14.6 (trans. Dewing; rev. Kaldellis): καὶ τὸ λοιπὸν ὅ τε ποταμὸς ἐσβατὸς ἀεὶ τοῖς βαρβάροις κατ' ἐξουσίαν καὶ τὰ Ῥωμαίων πράγματα εὐέφοδα γέγονε.

[45] Appendix A, nos. 11a, 55, 128, 148, 182, 279, 337, 389, and 471. In the Black Sea steppe later hoards reflect Justinian's diplomatic intervention in the region dominated by Cutrigur and Utigur tribes, for example the hoard from Beloyariv'ka, for which see V. V. Kropotkin, *Klady vizantiiskikh monet na territorii SSSR* (Moscow, 1962), 36, no. 253.

[46] For the chronology of fortification work in the Balkans, see recently Sarantis, *Justinian's Balkan*, 172–176.

[47] Oberländer-Târnoveanu, "Barbaricum apropiat," 338. His argument that coins from 527–538 are more abundant in Wallachia than later issues of Justinian is not valid since it does not take into account the fact that the period covers 11 years while coins after 538 are dated with the regnal year and statistical calculations are made on a one-year basis.

size.[48] Indeed, almost 18 percent of all Early Byzantine copper coins found between the Iron Gates of the Danube and the Dnieper are Justinianic issues minted between 538 and 542 (Figure 28).[49] The 30 find spots are not evenly distributed on the map; they cluster in Moldavia and in the Pontic steppe where Justinian engineered an alliance with the Antes.[50] Some of the coins were found close to the Danube, while others were lost very far from the river, at Băiceni in Moldavia and Zolotonosha on the Middle Dnieper.[51] In both cases, however, the Danubian provinces supplied the coins.

This unprecedented increase in the number of finds from *barbaricum* came to an abrupt end ca. 545 and there is a conspicuous hiatus in finds from 548 to 554. The coin flow picked up again from 555–560 followed by several gaps between 560 and 565 (Appendix B, Table 4). Current interpretations serve preconceived scenarios in which the numismatic evidence had to play its designated role. The explanation most often invoked by historians and numismatists rests on the methodological traps mentioned above: the assumption that coins must have arrived in *barbaricum* close to the time when they were issued and the tendency to explain fluctuations in coin supply by reference to military events or the arrival of new ethnic groups. Recent analyses of the coin flow to *barbaricum* during the age of Justinian have linked the sharp decline in the second half of his reign to successive incursions of Slavs, Bulgars, and Cutrigurs in the provinces of Illyricum and Thracia and the permanent settlement of the Slavs east and south of the Carpathians, closer to the Danube frontier.[52] Scholars diligently mined the written sources for events taking place in those years for which coin finds are missing. While this method can provide some

---

[48] A. Gandila, "Heavy money, weightier problems: the Justinianic reform of 538 and its economic consequences," *RN* 168 (2012): 363–402.

[49] The only hoard closed in this period is the small accumulation from Stary Biliary (Odesa, Ukraine), with the closing coin dated 542/3, for which see E. S. Stolyarik, "Klad vizantiiskikh bronzovykh VI v. iz Starye Beliary, Odesskoi oblasti," in *Severnoe Prichernomor'e: materialy po arkheologii: sbornik nauchnykh trudov*, ed. G. A. Dzis-Raiko (Kiev, 1984), 136–138 and pl. 1–2.

[50] G. Kardaras, "The Byzantine–Antic treaty (545/46 AD) and the defense of the Scythia Minor," *Byzantinoslavica* 58 (2010): 74–80; S. Patoura, "Une nouvelle considération sur la politique de Justinien envers les peuples du Danube," *Byzantinoslavica* 58 (1997): 81–82.

[51] D. G. Teodor, *Teritoriul est-carpatic în veacurile V–XI e.n.: contribuții arheologice și istorice la problema formării poporului român* (Iași, 1978), 23 and fig. 16/2; V. V. Kropotkin, *Klady vizantiiskikh*, 37, no. 275.

[52] Oberländer-Târnoveanu, "Barbaricum apropiat," 339–341; E. S. Teodor, "O frontieră incertă a lumii romane – Cîmpia Dunării de Jos în epoca lui Justinian," *Cercetări arheologice* 12 (2003): 334; Madgearu, *Continuitate și discontinuitate*, 68–89.

working hypotheses, it is rarely sufficient for drawing definitive conclusions. To be sure, archaeological evidence was adduced in support of such theories, but the use of coins to date complexes often made the argument appear circular.[53] The alternative interpretation, a presumed "economic closure" of the frontier as a result of Justinian's fortification program, is also untenable as evidence from the frontier provinces has revealed the same pattern of circulation marked by sudden drops.[54]

In reality, the explanation is quite different and has little to do with events in *barbaricum*. The chronological gaps correspond to low points in mint output traceable in finds from the Balkans and from other regions of the Early Byzantine Empire.[55] Coin finds in *barbaricum* mirror fluctuations in output at the imperial mints and in the supply of fresh coin to the frontier fortresses. Whether or not new Slavic groups settled in the Danubian plain around 550 continues to be debated by historians and archaeologists of the Early Middle Ages, but coins have little to offer toward a successful resolution of this historiographical question. The only meaningful observation is that whatever changes occurred in the ethnic background of the region, the monetary connection to the Empire was not broken until the Danube itself ceased to be under direct Byzantine rule. The decentralized nature of Slavic politics led to the cooption of certain Slavic groups into the frontier system, which made ethnic changes in *barbaricum* less dramatic.[56] In any case, there is no strong indication that the general flow of Byzantine goods was seriously disrupted; the opposite seems to be true, as we shall soon find out.

The heavy coins of Justinian from 538–542, and by extension to 550, were popular not only in *barbaricum* but also in the Byzantine outposts from the left bank of the Danube, as testified by numerous finds resulted from archaeological excavations at Sucidava.[57] Some of the soldiers defending the Byzantine forts in *barbaricum* were recruited from the region north of the river and they helped distribute Justinian's coins on

---

[53] M. Comșa, "Unele date cu privire la Banatul de sud în sec. IV–VII," in *In Memoriam Constantini Daicoviciu*, ed. H. Daicoviciu (Cluj, 1974), 96.

[54] F. Curta, "Frontier ethnogenesis in Late Antiquity: the Danube, the Tervingi, and the Slavs," in *Borders, Barriers, and Ethnogenesis. Frontiers in Late Antiquity and the Middle Ages*, ed. F. Curta (Turnhout, 2005), 186. Wolf Liebeschuetz's contention that coin finds from 558 to 582 are virtually absent is obviously contradicted by the evidence; see J. H. W. G. Liebeschuetz, "The Lower Danube under pressure: from Valens to Heraclius," in *Transition*, 114. For the same "closure" hypothesis, see Sarantis, *Justinian's Balkan*, 280. For coin circulation in the northern Balkans, see Gandila, "Some aspects," 307; Mihaylov, "Etapi v parichata," 115.

[55] Gandila, "Early Byzantine," 208, fig. 3.   [56] *Strategikon*, 11.4.

[57] Butnariu, "Răspîndirea monedelor," 226–227, nos. 11–17.

the much wider geographic area from which they hailed. Chilbudius himself, the general celebrated by Procopius for his victories north of the Danube, had a non-Roman origin and it is safe to assume that many of the soldiers under his command were not Roman-born. Excavations at Sucidava also produced a significant number of *decanummia*, a small denomination typical for low-value market transactions. Such coins are rare in *barbaricum* and always worth highlighting. The three *decanummia* from Calafat, Cioroiu Nou, and Ulmeni were found close to the Danube, but this is not a general rule if we consider the finds from Bacău and Tecuci in Moldavia.[58] The imperial mints issued high quantities of *decanummia* in the last decade of Justinian's reign in order to meet the needs of a market flooded with higher denominations in the previous decades.[59] A lower output of *folles* explains the gaps noticed in the corpus of finds from *barbaricum*, given the local preference for heavier coins. Once again, fluctuations reflect monetary policies in the Empire and not military events on the Danube frontier.

Two *decanummia* (Bacău and Calafat) were minted in Rome, an important development pointing to the growing complexity of the monetary system during the reign of Justinian and renewed – probably military – connections to Italy.[60] Mints other than Constantinople account for more than 45 percent of the finds of Justinianic issues north of the Danube and northwest of the Black Sea (Appendix B, Table 7). One *pentanummium* from Parutyne (Ukraine) was issued by the Crimean mint in Cherson, while a half-*follis* from Salona was found at Drobeta in the Iron Gates region of the Danube, possibly signaling the movement of federate troops from the Balkans during the Gothic wars in Italy.[61] Procopius informs us of Justinian's effort to increase the strength of his army by recruiting from *barbaricum* for his campaigns in the west and the presence of western

---

[58] Calafat and Cioroiu Nou: Oberländer-Târnoveanu, "Tranziția de la antichitate," 68, n. 70. Ulmeni: Butnariu, "Răspîndirea monedelor," 223, no. 163. Bacău: Oberländer-Târnoveanu, "Societate," 317, n. 31. Tecuci: D. G. Teodor, "Elemente și influențe bizantine în Moldova în secolele VI–XI," *SCIV* 21, no. 1 (1970): 121, fig. 9/4.

[59] S. Mihaylov, "Vidovete nominali v monetnoto obrashtenie na bizantiiskite provintsii Scitiia i Vtora Miziia (498–681 g.)," in *Numismatic, Sphragistic and Epigraphic Contributions to the History of the Black Sea Coast*, edited by I. Lazarenko, vol. I (Varna, 2008), 280–281, tables 3–4.

[60] A. Gandila, "Going east: western money in the Early Byzantine Balkans, Asia Minor and the Circumpontic region (6th–7th c.)," *RIN* 117 (2016): 147–150.

[61] Stolyarik, *Essays*, 137, no. 42; Oberländer-Târnoveanu, "Tranziția de la antichitate," 68, n. 70. For cultural connections between the Balkan frontier and the Crimea facilitated by the movement of troops, see A. Furasiev, "Byzance et la Crimée du sud-ouest au VIe siècle: relations culturelles et particularités du costume feminin," in *Pontic-Danubian Realm*, 372–377.

mints north of the Danube lends credibility to his account.[62] Finally, some of the gold coins of Justinian dated before 550 as well as the rare silver *miliarensia* from Oltenia and Banat may constitute stipends and gifts sent by Justinian to buy the loyalty of certain groups from the area dominated by Herules and Gepids.[63]

5.2.2 Money, Warfare, and Collapse (ca. 565–680)

With the accession of Justin II we witness a heavy influx of Byzantine coins north of the Danube prompted by a drastic change in the imperial attitude toward barbarian groups. The new emperor decided to discontinue diplomatic payments and rely instead on internal resources for securing the Danube frontier, an attitude best encapsulated in Agathias' *Cycle*: "let no barbarian, freeing himself from the yoke-strap that passes under his neck, dare to fix his gaze on our King, the mighty warrior."[64] Although Agathias himself is inconsistent in his assessment of Justin's new strategy,[65] the Danube frontier was probably strengthened and the direct consequence is an absolute increase in the number of coin finds from frontier fortresses in the Balkans.[66] The policy was coordinated with the imperial mints, Thessalonica being commissioned to strike huge quantities of half-*folles* to pay the troops. Against this background, the increase of the monetary stock in the northern Balkans was also felt in *barbaricum*.

The balance of power in the northern world was about to shift with the arrival of the Avars in Pannonia ca. 568 followed by their swift subjugation of the Gepids and the Slavs. Potential changes in the ethnic structure of the

---

[62] J. L. Teall, "The barbarians in Justinian's armies," *Speculum* 40, no. 2 (1965): 294–322; H. Ditten, "Slawen im byzantinischen Heer von Justinian I. bis Justinian II," in *Studien zum 7. Jahrhundert in Byzanz. Probleme der Herausbildung des Feudalismus*, eds. H. Köpstein and F. Winkelmann (Berlin, 1976), 59–72; M. Whitby, "Recruitment in Roman armies," in *The Byzantine and Early Islamic Near East III: State, Resources and Armies*, ed. A. Cameron (Princeton, NJ, 1995), 61–125, esp. 103–110.

[63] C. Preda, "O monedă bizantină de argint inedită," *BSNR* 86–87 (1992–1993): 123–124; Oberländer-Târnoveanu, "Tranziția de la antichitate," 69–70, n. 72; Vîlcu et al., *Les monnaies d'or*, 153, no. 460; A. Kharalambieva, "Gepids in the Balkans: a survey of the archaeological evidence," in *Neglected Barbarians*, 245–262; Sarantis, "The Justinianic Herules," 361–402. For the lands next to the Danube frontier, which were under the control of the Herules and the Gepids, see P. Špehar, "The Danubian *limes* between Lederata and Aquae during the Migration Period," in *Pontic-Danubian Realm*, 35–56; Bugarski and Ivanišević, "Pogranich'e rimskoi," 482–511.

[64] Agathias, *Cycle* 4.3.47–48 (trans. Paton): μή τις ὑπαυχενίοιο λιπὼν ζωστῆρα λεπάδνου βάρβαρος ἐς βασιλῆα βιημάχον ὄμμα τανύσσῃ.

[65] A. Cameron, *Agathias* (Oxford, 1970), 124–130.   [66] Gandila, "Early Byzantine," 179.

5.2 The Lower Danube: The Land of Bronze

communities living north of the Danube cannot be traced in the numismatic evidence as coins seem to have followed the same paths as they had in the first half of the sixth century. The large production of half-*folles* by Thessalonica is reflected in the finds from Sucidava and Drobeta on the Danube's left bank and by extension in Banat and Oltenia, but also as far as northern Moldavia at Cucorăni where a coin was found in a sixth-century settlement (Figure 30a).[67] The year-by-year flow reveals two major spikes corresponding to years 570 and 575, a reflection of the quinquennial *donativum*, a payment discontinued by Justinian but reinstated by Justin II; these irregular grants were distributed to the garrisons defending the frontier and promptly exchanged into copper coin for daily expenditure (Figure 28).[68] The fact that both the military frontier and the northern *barbaricum* display the same fluctuations strengthens the observation that coins and other Byzantine goods circulated through the mediation of people of different ethnic background involved in the defense of the northern Balkans.

Because of such military channels of distribution, the chronology of finds from *barbaricum*, the Danubian provinces, and the Byzantine bridgehead forts on the northern bank of the river remains highly correlated. The only departure from the common pattern is the superior frequency of coins issued by the Nicomedian mint in *barbaricum* – mostly *folles* – compared to those from Thessalonica, dominant in frontier fortresses of the Balkans (Figure 29a). Once more, the explanation lies in the preference for higher denominations in *barbaricum, folles* of Nicomedia and Constantinople being favored against half-*folles* of Thessalonica on account of their size (Figure 29b). This type of discrimination based on size and weight stems from the non-monetary function of coins beyond the frontier discussed in the last chapter. The military nature of coin circulation in the Byzantine outposts north of the Danube is also testified by the presence at Drobeta of coins issued by mobile mints, the so-called *Moneta Militaris Imitativa* and of issues of Antioch at Sucidava pointing to the transfer of troops to the Balkans.[69] The constant presence of the Syrian mint among finds throughout the sixth century (over 6 percent; Figure 30 and Appendix B, Table 7) could also be related to finds of Palestinian lamps, flasks, and other

---

[67] Teodor, *Teritoriul est-carpatic*, 23 and fig. 16/5.
[68] This is best seen in the chronological structure of finds from the Danubian province of Scythia, for which see Gandila, "Some aspects," 308.
[69] Oberländer-Târnoveanu, "La răscruce de vremuri," 124, n. 17; Butnariu, "Răspîndirea monedelor," 227, no. 32; Vîlcu and Nicolae, "Monede bizantine," 303, no. 22.

devotional objects from the Holy Land in *barbaricum,* although a military explanation seems more plausible at this point.[70]

Recent attempts to draw a distinction between Oltenia, Wallachia, and Moldavia based on the chronology of finds from Justin II are not convincing.[71] The assumption that certain gaps in finds from Wallachia testify that the Slavs were hindering cultural contact between local communities and the Empire cannot be supported by reference to the current coin sample, substantial enough to make general remarks about a large geographical area from northern Serbia to southern Ukraine, but too thin to trace annual developments in more circumscribed areas.[72] A common characteristic of the three regions is the scarcity of gold coins of Justin II. Only one find is known, a *solidus* from Mănăstioara; another *solidus* is a Gepid imitation found at Romula, while three more gold coins were found in Banat and might be connected to the growing Avar center of power in the Middle Danube region.[73] The rarity of *solidi* might have something to do with Justin II's policy of checking the flow of gold outside the frontier. Still, the virtual absence of *solidi* from the 570s remains a mystery since the end of this decade was marked by important incursions of the Slavs who took plunder and prisoners to their homeland north of the river.[74] A potential decrease in mint output during Justin II's reign or a complete impoverishment of the Balkans are improbable hypotheses given the high frequency of his gold coins in hoards from this region.[75]

---

[70] For the circulation of devotional items from the Holy Land, see above, Chapter 2, Figure 7 and Chapter 3, Figure 15.

[71] Oberländer-Târnoveanu, "Barbaricum apropiat," 348–349.

[72] For the role of the Slavs, see M. Comşa, "Socio-economic organization of the Daco-Romanic and Slav population on the Lower Danube during the 6th–8th centuries," in *Relations*, 171–200; S. Dolinescu-Ferche, "La culture Ipoteşti–Ciurel–Cîndeşti (Ve–VIIe siècles). La situation en Valachie," *Dacia NS* 28 (1984): 117–147.

[73] Mănăstioara: Butnariu, "Răspîndirea monedelor," 220, no. 81. Reşca: Oberländer-Târnoveanu, "La răscruce," 143, n. 147. Banat (unknown locations): P. Somogyi, "Byzantinische Fundmünzen der Awarenzeit. Eine Bestandsaufnahme, 1998-2007," *AAC* 42–43 (2007–2008): 292–294, nos. 23–25.

[74] Menander, *Historia*, fr. 21 (Blockley); John of Ephesus, *Historia Ecclesiastica*, 6.25. Gold coins account for only ca. nine percent of all finds from Justin II in the entire region from the Baltic Sea to the Caspian Sea (Appendix B, Table 1).

[75] Almost all gold coin hoards hidden in the Balkans in the last quarter of the sixth century contain issues of Justin II. In one hoard from Thessalonica 85 out of 115 coins were issues of Justin II, while the proportion is lower, around one-third, in most other cases, but still high enough to exclude the possibility of a low mint output during his reign. For the hoards, see *Trésors*, nos. 19, 65, 82, 103, 117, 151, and 244–246. Furthermore, the collection of the Romanian Academy in Bucharest includes many gold coins of Justin II, for which see A. Vîlcu, *Les monnaies d'or de la Bibliothèque de l'Académie roumaine. II. Monnaies Byzantines* (Wetteren, 2009), 49–54, nos. 87–117.

Political developments, however, left their mark in the form of copper coin hoards whose number increases on both sides of the Danube. The only hoard from *barbaricum* echoing these events was found at Gropeni (Romania) and was concealed sometime after 577. Contemporary hoards were hidden along the Danube from west to east at Veliko Orašje (578/9), Veliko Gradište (580/1), Boljetin (577/8), Tekija (578/9), Slatinska Reka (575/6), Axiopolis (578/82), and Capidava (579/82).[76] These hoards as well as several others from the hinterland dating from the last years of Justin II's reign and from the reign of Tiberius II into the early 580s can be attributed to increased warfare in the region, marked by Slavic incursions in the Balkans and retaliation of the Byzantines allied with the Avars. The account of Menander shows that the growing insecurity of the Danube frontier was alarming; instead of pacifying the region, the Avaro-Byzantine expedition of 579 which led to the destruction of the Slavic center of power in eastern Wallachia strengthened the Avar influence north of the Danube.[77] Justinian's diplomatic genius was apparently lost on his immediate successors. The hoard from Gropeni, hidden on the left bank of the river is perhaps a reflection of these events, but cannot tell us much about the flow of Byzantine coins to *barbaricum*. Given the proximity to the military border, the hoard from Gropeni constitutes a sum of money brought from the province of Scythia, buried for safekeeping in the context of the conflict between Byzantines, Avars, and Slavs, and never retrieved.[78]

The years between 577 and 582 are marked by several gaps in the chronology of finds from *barbaricum*, but this reflects the state of the Danube provinces affected by insecurity and warfare (Figure 28). Most of the coins of Tiberius II have been found in Byzantine fortresses at Sucidava, Drobeta, and Ostrovu Banului, or very close to the Danube, at Giurgița.[79] Many are issues of Thessalonica, the mint responsible with

---

[76] *Trésors*, nos. 65, 248, 249, 259, 264, and 265; A. Gandila, "Un tezaur de monede bizantine timpurii descoperit la Capidava," *CN* 15 (2009): 87–105.

[77] Menander, *Historia*, fr. 21 (Blockley); Madgearu, *Continuitate și discontinuitate*, 18–19; C. Chiriac, "Expediția avară din 578–579 și evidența numismatică," *AM* 16 (1993): 191–203.

[78] A recent attempt to argue that only the coins of Justin II were brought from the Empire in the 570s, the earlier ones being drawn from the local stock, is unconvincing; see Oberländer-Târnoveanu, "Barbaricum apropiat," 346. Another hoard, found in Bucharest before World War II in unknown circumstances, ends with coins from 580/1, but the original composition of the hoard remains uncertain; see *Trésors*, no. 350.

[79] Sucidava: Butnariu, "Răspîndirea monedelor," 227; Vîlcu and Nicolae, "Monede bizantine," 304–305, nos. 30–34; Oberländer-Târnoveanu, "La răscruce de vremuri," 129, n. 57. Drobeta: Oberländer-Târnoveanu, "La răscruce de vremuri," 129, n. 56. Giurgița and Ostrovu Banului: Butnariu, "Răspîndirea monedelor," 219, no. 67 and 221, no. 102.

sustaining the war effort in Illyricum. The *pentanummium* from Drobeta proves that low-value exchanges were still taking place on the Lower Danube despite the political and economic crisis and the inflationary tendencies of Justin II's monetary policy. Only two finds can be placed with certainty outside the sphere of the Byzantine bridge-heads on the left bank of the river, two *folles* from Buzău and Bacău, respectively.[80] The *solidus* from Coada Izvorului (Romania) found in mint state probably belongs to a dispersed hoard and could have been brought north of the Danube after one of the frequent plunder expeditions lamented by contemporary writers.[81]

Archaeological evidence shows that warfare in the Danube region, which led to the loss of Sirmium to the Avars in 582, did not stop the flow of Byzantine goods north of the river. As we have seen, growing militarization in the northern Balkans in the last quarter of the sixth century brought a large quantity of Byzantine cast fibulae with bent stem and buckles in *barbaricum,* which are typical for the military hilltop fortresses of the Lower Danube. Frontier culture was also responsible for the development and spread of the so-called "Slavic" bow fibulae, a fashion that can be traced on both sides of the Danube but especially in *barbaricum*.[82] In addition, a steady influx of fresh coin can be noticed until after 600 with brief interruptions in 584–586 and 600–602. Coins from the last years of Maurice's reign are rare even in the Danubian provinces, the case of Scythia being the best documented.[83] It is most likely a problem of mint output during these years, rather than a result of successful Byzantine campaigning north of the Danube.[84] A financial crisis caused by an acute shortage of metal is made apparent by an intensification of the emergency practice of restriking old coinage at the Propontic mints.[85] Antioch seems to have become the most stable mint, but this could hardly affect the Balkans where the Syrian mint was never dominant.

---

[80] E. Oberländer-Târnoveanu and E.-M. Constantinescu, "Monede romane târzii și bizantine din colecția Muzeului Județean Buzău," *Mousaios* 4 (1994): 319, n. 28.

[81] Butnariu, "Răspîndirea monedelor," 219, no. 51.

[82] For the diffusion of fibulae and buckles in *barbaricum*, see above, Chapter 2, Figure 12– Figure 14.

[83] Gandila, "Some aspects," 320, table 1.

[84] It has been argued that the impact of the Byzantine campaigns against the Slavs in Wallachia led to the interruption of relations with Byzantium, but the presence of coins of Phocas and Heraclius in the same region makes this hypothesis improbable; see Oberländer-Târnoveanu, "Barbaricum apropiat," 354.

[85] Gandila, "Heavy money," 370–371. On pay cuts, see Theophylact Simocatta, *Historia*, 3.1.2 and 7.1.2.

With the reign of Maurice, the Danube frontier entered its final phase. Coin finds have been recorded on the left bank of the Danube from the Iron Gates to the mouths of the river. Many of the finds may be related to the Avar offensive in the 580s and the Byzantine counteroffensive which included a number of incursions north of the river led by general Priscus and by the emperor's brother Petrus between 594 and 602.[86] Both Drobeta and Sucidava remained important military outposts throughout Maurice's reign. Coin finds are recorded until 599, when Sucidava probably fell under the attacks of the Avars. The finds include gold issues, a *tremissis* at Sucidava and a light weight *solidus* of 20 *siliquae* at Drobeta, reflecting the movements of the Avars or perhaps the last military payments sent to the local garrison.[87] An unusual concentration of light weight *solidi* of Maurice – typically associated with the regular payments sent to the Avars – can be noticed in the province of Scythia at a time when the khagan was in Anchialus negotiating an increase of the tribute to 100,000 *solidi*, but actually preparing to plunder the rich towns along the Black Sea coast.[88]

Three coins from Antioch found north of the Danube may signal the movement of troops after the conflict with Persia was brought to an end and Maurice redeployed his troops in the northern Balkans.[89] One issue of Antioch and another of Thessalonica have been found at Buzău, while two *solidi* are recorded in the region of Wallachia where several Slavic political centers are mentioned by Theophylact Simocatta.[90] Coins of Maurice were also found far away from the Danube frontier, at Vășcăuți (Moldova) and

---

[86] F. Curta, *The Making of the Slavs: History and Archaeology of the Lower Danube Region, c. 500–700* (Cambridge, 2001), 100; A. Madgearu, "The province of Scythia and the Avaro-Slavic invasions (576–626)," *BS* 37, no. 1 (1996): 42–51; M. Whitby, *The Emperor Maurice and His Historian: Theophylact Simocatta on Persian and Balkan Warfare* (Oxford, 1988), 140–165. Coins of Maurice have been found at Ostrovu Mare, Gogoșu, Goicea, Orlea, Zimnicea, Prundu, Fetești, Novosils'ke, and Vasylivka, for which see Appendix A, nos. 145, 157, 158, 270, 286, 294, 324, 479, and 505.

[87] Oberländer-Târnoveanu, "La răscruce de vremuri," 132, n. 70; Vîlcu, *Les monnaies d'or*, 60, no. 148.

[88] For the context, see Whitby, *The Emperor Maurice*, 142–143. For the coins, see Vîlcu, *Les monnaies d'or*, 10.

[89] Theophanes, *Chronographia*, 267, AM 6082 [589/90], is very clear on the transfer of troops from Anatolia to Thracia: διὰ τοῦτο ὁ αὐτοκράτωρ Μαυρίκιος τὰς δυνάμεις ἀπὸ ἀνατολῆς ἐπὶ τὴν Θρᾴκην μετήγαγεν.

[90] Theophylact Simocatta, *Historia*, 6.6–10; Oberländer-Târnoveanu and Constantinescu, "Monede romane," 317–319, nos. 29 and 31; Oberländer-Târnoveanu, "Barbaricum apropiat," 353, n. 40; B. Mitrea, "Découvertes récentes et plus anciennes de monnaies antiques et byzantines sur le territoire de la République Populaire Roumaine," *Dacia* 7 (1963): 597, no. 52.

Pavlivka (Ukraine).[91] The Early Byzantine monetary economy was slowly breaking down in the Balkans, a process whose effects were inevitably felt in *barbaricum* where only one denomination below the half-*follis* is so far known, a *decanummium* found at Bârlad in Moldavia.[92]

More than two decades of warfare in the northern Balkans left a trail of hoards found on both sides of the Danube in different contexts but hidden and lost under the same circumstances. Although numismatists often exaggerate the connection between hoarding and warfare, the massive concentration of hoards during the last decades of the sixth century cannot be accidental. The Avar offensive from the mid-580s led to the concealment of several copper and gold hoards in the Danubian provinces.[93] The geographical distribution of finds shows that the diocese of Thracia was most affected by these attacks coordinated by the new Avar khagan in alliance with the Slavs led by Ardagast.[94] No echo of this hoarding frenzy can be traced north of the Danube, unless the hoard from Troianul in Wallachia was closed early in Maurice's reign.[95] The hoard is a medley of Late Roman coins and Early Byzantine small denominations of Justinian, Justin II, and Maurice. The coin of Maurice cannot be dated with precision but the entire accumulation fits the pattern of small change used on a daily basis in market transactions in one of the large towns of the Black Sea coast or the Aegean.

The next group of hoards dating to the last decade of the sixth century is connected with the Byzantine campaigns north of the Danube aimed at destroying the Slavic centers of power in Wallachia and southern Moldavia and at reestablishing the balance of power in the Middle Danube region by checking the expansion of the Avars. Although most of the late hoards on the Danube frontier are from Illyricum, the hoards from *barbaricum* were found across the Danube in the lands bordering the province of Scythia.[96] The hoard from Unirea hidden after 594/5 was found on the river's left bank and appears to be connected with the Byzantine counteroffensive led by Priscus and Petrus in Wallachia.[97] The second hoard was found quite far from the Danube, at Horgești in Moldavia and was concealed

---

[91] Nudel'man, *Topografiia kladov*, 83, no. 14; Stolyarik, *Essays*, 140, no. 59.
[92] Oberländer-Târnoveanu and Popușoi, "Monede bizantine," 229, no. 5.
[93] The hoards from Koprivets, Provadiia, Adamclisi, Zulud, Zaldapa, Slava Rusă, and Sadovets, for which see *Trésors*, nos. 47, 52, 61, 63, 79, 82 and 240–245.
[94] Whitby, *The Emperor Maurice*, 140–145; Liebeschuetz, "The Lower Danube," 117–120.
[95] *Trésors*, no. 364.
[96] The hoards from Bosman, Reselets, and Rakita, for which see *Trésors*, nos. 238, 239, and 260.
[97] *Trésors*, no. 366. For the context, see Whitby, *The Emperor Maurice*, 156–161.

after 597/8 in circumstances related to the same military events in *barbaricum*. The hoard itself is a collection of metal objects – a copper-alloy pitcher, a bronze chain, and scrap pieces of bronze – and may be the result of plunder during this decade of insecurity.[98] It is tempting to make a connection with statements made by the author of the *Strategikon* who claimed that the Slavs used to bury their most valuable possessions in secret places.[99] Clearly, some of them were never retrieved.

Although a treaty in 598 was establishing the Danube as the official frontier agreed between the Avars and the Byzantines, war resumed shortly after. The rebellion of 602 erupted at a moment when the Byzantine army was camped north of the Danube.[100] Archaeological research in the past decades has confirmed the survival of certain sections of the frontier well after this turning point in the history of the northern Balkans. The Danubian provinces were still worth defending. In 604 Phocas sealed a new treaty with the Avars, agreeing to increase the annual tribute to 140,000 *solidi*.[101] Although the emperor transferred the troops to the East to engage the Persians, the Balkans enjoyed several years of peace. The Avars themselves needed time to recover; the Byzantine *tour de force* in the 590s had seriously shaken the Avar position on the Danube and bruised the khagan's prestige in the northern world. The river remained the frontier between Avars and Romans until ca. 615 when the Balkan provinces could no longer absorb a new wave of attacks. The final eclipse of the Roman frontier on the Danube came swiftly. The Persian conquest of Jerusalem in 614, the loss of Egypt in 619, and the devastation of the Byzantine heartland in Asia Minor taxed the remaining resources of an already impoverished Empire fighting for survival. The abandonment of the Lower Danube region was an inevitable consequence.[102]

Byzantine coins continued to cross the Danube without any major interruption until 615, confirming the survival of some Byzantine fortresses on the Lower Danube. No coins after 599 have so far been recorded

---

[98] *Trésors*, no. 355. See C. Chiriac, *Civilizația bizantină*, 74; 87, for the presence of scrap metal as an indication that the hoard belonged to an itinerant artisan.

[99] *Strategikon*, 11.4.25–27: τὰ ἀναγκαῖα τῶν πραγμάτων αὐτῶν ἐν ἀποκρύφῳ χωννύουσιν, οὐδὲν περιττὸν ἐν φανερῷ κεκτημένα.

[100] Whitby, *The Emperor Maurice*, 161–165.

[101] Theophanes, *Chronographia*, 292, AM 6096 [603/4].

[102] For events in the East, see G. Greatrex and S. N. C. Lieu, eds., *The Roman Eastern Frontier and the Persian Wars. Part II, AD 363–630. A Narrative Sourcebook* (New York, NY, 2002), 187–197; J. Howard-Johnston, *Witnesses to a World Crisis: Historians and Histories of the Middle East in the Seventh Century* (Oxford, 2010). For the Danube frontier, see Madgearu, *Continuitate și discontinuitate*, 24.

at Sucidava and it is possible that its role as a military outpost ended after the Avar attacks in the last decade of the sixth century. Drobeta continued to receive Byzantine bronze coins well into the seventh century, after a long gap between 599 and 612, as did a number of fortresses on the right bank, such as Novae, Durostorum, Capidava, and Noviodunum, although their defensive capabilities at this point seem greatly reduced.[103] Most strategic points in the western sector of the frontier had already been lost and apparently never recovered judging by the interruption of coin circulation in important fortresses such as Aquis, Viminacium, Ratiaria, and Singidunum.[104] The coins of Phocas found in *barbaricum* are primarily half-*folles*, a situation encountered in Scythia as well, but since very few were stamped with the regnal year (because of changes in iconography) we can no longer follow the annual influx of coins north of the Danube.[105] Given the steady annual supply between 610 and 615 it can be supposed that the same was true for the reign of Phocas (602–610). Very few finds are known in Oltenia and Banat, the destruction of the Byzantine *limes* in Moesia Prima and Dacia Ripensis and the proximity to the Avar center of power being the main reasons for reduced cultural contact with communities living north of the Danube. Coins of Phocas are more abundant in Wallachia and Moldavia, with finds clustering close to the Danube and further to the north, in the lands between the rivers Prut and Dniester.[106]

Renewed efforts to reestablish the Byzantine control on the Danube at the beginning of Heraclius' reign brought payments to the small garrisons stationed at Drobeta and Dierna.[107] This policy was also felt in *barbaricum*,

---

[103] Novae: K. Dimitrov, "Poznorzymskie i wczesnobizantyjskie monety z odcinka iv w Novae z lat 294–612," *Novensia* 11 (1998): 110–111. Durostorum: E. Oberländer-Târnoveanu, "Monnaies byzantines des VIIe–Xe siècles découvertes à Silistra dans la collection de l'Académicien Péricle Papahagi conservées au Cabinet des Medailles du Musée National d'Histoire de Roumanie" *CN* 7 (1996): 117–120; Capidava: A. Gandila, "Early Byzantine Capidava: the numismatic evidence," *CN* 12–13 (2006–2007): 118. Noviodunum: G. Poenaru Bordea, E. Nicolae, and A. Popescu, Contributions numismatiques à l'histoire de Noviodunum aux VIe–VIIe siècles, *SCN* 11 (1995): 157–161.

[104] Aquis: Đ. Janković, *Podunavski deo oblasti Akvisa u VI i pochetkom VII veka* (Belgrade, 1981), 72, table 6. Viminacium: V. Ivanišević, "Vizantijski novac (491–1092) iz zairke Narodnog Myzeja y Pojarevci," *Numizmatičar* 11 (1988): 87–99. Ratiaria: B. Boshkova, "Coins from the excavations of the antique town Ratiaria," *Ratiarensia* 2 (1984): 105–116. Belgrade: V. Ivanišević, "Vizantijski novac sa Beogradske tvrđave," *Numizmatičar* 10 (1987): 88–107. For a synopsis of finds from northern Illyricum, see more recently Ivanišević, "La monnaie paléobyzantine," 441–454.

[105] Gandila, "Some aspects," 318, table 5.

[106] The finds from Oltenița, Gropeni, Salcia, and Iuzhnoe, for which see Oberländer-Târnoveanu, "Societate," 320; Oberländer-Târnoveanu, "Barbaricum apropiat," 356.

[107] Oberländer-Târnoveanu, "La răscruce," 138, n. 111 and n. 121.

a significant number of finds being recorded in Oltenia in the proximity of the Byzantine bridge-heads. All coins are copper issues dated between 610 and 616 when the frontier was still relatively functional. Since the Avar pressure had significantly decreased since 602, Heraclius reverted to Justinian's policy of looking for allies in *barbaricum* while concentrating his resources on the Eastern front. Two *solidi* have an unknown finding place in Oltenia but we are better informed about gold coins from regions of *barbaricum* across the diocese of Thracia and north of the Black Sea. The power centers of the Slavs in southern Moldavia and northern Wallachia were the main recipients of gold coins as testified by several interesting finds.[108] These include the *solidus* found at Buzău and more significantly the small hoard of *solidi* from Udești in northern Moldavia (616–625).[109] The money belonged to a local "big man," judging by the rich archaeological context in which the coins have been found; he may have achieved his status during this time of conflict on the northern frontier of Byzantium.[110] Meanwhile, the smaller communities in Moldavia continued to receive Byzantine copper coins. Two *folles* of which one is an issue of 619–620, a late date even for the provinces of the Balkans, were found together with Early Medieval pottery at Comănești.[111] A hoard found at Movileni on the bank of Siret river was hidden shortly after 614 and has the typical structure of a purse withdrawn from circulation from one of the frontier provinces, since it included *decanummia* commonly used in the urban marketplace, as well as several coins from Antioch.[112] The most probable origin is one of the larger frontier towns of Scythia. The available numismatic evidence testifies that several

---

[108] Oberländer-Târnoveanu and Constantinescu, "Monede romane," 311, no. 32; A *solidus* from a collection in Cotești (Vrancea, Romania) was mistakenly described as a local find when in fact the coin was found at Axiopolis on the Danube frontier; see Oberländer-Târnoveanu, "Societate," 320, n. 46. For the correction, see Vîlcu, *Les monnaies d'or*, 12.

[109] M. Gogu, "Monedele bizantine aflate în colecția numismatică a Muzeului Național al Bucovinei din Suceava," *Suceava* 26–28 (1999–2001): 296–297 and 310, fig. 7/26–28.

[110] A. Rădulescu, "Casa cnezială de la Udești," *Magazin Istoric* 11 (1977): 49.

[111] Teodor, *Teritoriul est-carpatic*, 23, fig. 16/6–7.

[112] *Trésors*, no. 358. The latest coin in the hoard is a follis from Cyzicus dated 613/4. A mistake in the original publication of the hoard where the last coin was dated to 600 continues to be used in more recent interpretations of this hoard despite the correction made more than three decades ago, e.g. E. S. Teodor, "Epoca romană târzie și cronologia atacurilor transdanubiene. Analiza componentelor etnice și geografice (partea a doua, de la 565 la 626)," *Muzeul Național* 15 (2003): 29. For the revised dating, see G. Poenaru Bordea and R. Ocheșeanu, "Probleme istorice dobrogene (secolele VI–VII) în lumina monedelor bizantine din colecția Muzeului de Istorie Națională și Arheologie din Constanța," *SCIVA* 31, no. 3 (1980): 395, n. 49.

fortresses were functional and still guarding the lower sector of the Danubian *limes* in the second decade of the seventh century.[113]

Further east, three *solidi* found in burial assemblages in the region of Kirovohrad in central Ukraine are later issues from the third decade of the seventh century and signal major political transformations following the Byzantine retreat from the northern Balkans.[114] At a time when Heraclius was desperately looking for allies against the Avars and Persians who assaulted the walls of Constantinople, the strategic role of the Pontic steppe increased tremendously. The rising influence of the Bulgars brought a large quantity of Byzantine coined gold and silver as well as jewelry and plate found in a number of spectacular seventh-century burials and hoards. Nikephoros and John of Nikiu describe the successful diplomatic contacts between Byzantium and "Great Bulgaria" in the 630s, concluded when Heraclius honored Kubrat with the title of *patricius*.[115] Heraclius and his successor motivated Kubrat not only with symbolic titles but also with more tangible treasures whose remains can be traced in the archaeological record. By far the most spectacular find is the rich burial from Malo Pereshchepyne (Ukraine), which many historians attribute to Kubrat himself.[116] The treasure included some 70 Byzantine gold coins, the majority being lightweight *solidi* of 20 *siliquae* struck for Heraclius and Constans II. The latest issues can be dated no later than 646. Most of the coins were either pierced or mounted into sets. The gold hoards from Kelegeia, Maistrov, and Zachepylivka, in Ukraine, belong to the same cultural horizon of wealth accumulated through political payments sent to the Black Sea steppe by emperors of the Heraclian house.[117]

---

[113] Gandila, "Some aspects," 311–312.

[114] Pechenaya: Kropotkin, *Klady vizantiiskikh*, 33, no. 196. Rivne: Stolyarik, *Essays*, 141, no. 70 and fig. 14/3. Yosypivka: O. S. Beliaev and I. O. Molodchikova, "Pokhovannia kochyvnikov na r. Orel," *Arkheolohiia* 28 (1978): 86, fig. 2/4.

[115] Nikephoros, *Breviarum*, 22; John of Nikiu, *Chronicle* 120.47; For Byzantine–Bulgar relations, see O. V. Komar, "'Kubrat' i 'Velyka Bulgariia': problemy dzhereloznavchogo analizu," *Skhodoznavstvo* (2001), nos. 13–14: 133–155; E. G. Galkina, "K voprosu o roli Velikoi Bulgarii v etnopoliticheskoi istorii Vostochnoi Evropy," *Studia Slavica et Balcanica Petropolitana* 9 (2011), no. 1: 5–32; V. Vachkova, "Danube Bulgaria and Khazaria as parts of the Byzantine *oikoumene*," in *The Other Europe*, ed. Curta, 343–345.

[116] J. Werner, *Der Grabfund von Malaja Pereščepina und Kuvrat, Kagan der Bulgaren* (Munich, 1984); I. V. Sokolova, "Monety Pereshchepinskogo klada," in *Sokrovishcha Khana Kubrata*, ed. O. Fedoseenko (St. Petersburg, 1997), 17–41. However, there is no consensus regarding the ethnic attribution of the find, for which see especially O. V. Komar and V. M. Khardaev, "Zachepilovskii ("Novosanzharskii") kompleks rubezha VII–VIII vv," in *Stepi Evropy v epokhu srednevekov'ia. Khazarskoe vremia. Sbornik nauchnykh trudov*, ed. A. V. Evgelevskii (Donetsk, 2012), 243–296, esp. 278–281 for the discussion of coin finds.

[117] Kelegeia: A. Semenov, "Vizantiiskie monety Kelegeiskogo kompleksa," *ASGE* 31 (1991): 121–130. Maistrov: Kropotkin, *Klady vizantiiskikh*, 31–32, no. 159. Zachepylivka: O. V. Komar

Although the Empire was forced to abandon the Danube frontier, cultural contact with the territories north of the river was not completely interrupted. The declining prestige of the Avar Khaganate after the failed siege of Constantinople and the Byzantine retrenchment after the initial shock of the Arab storm in the East permitted a more active policy in the Balkans. Instead of being filtered through the Danube frontier, which had performed the role of cultural semiperiphery until ca. 615, the circulation of Byzantine goods and coins became the subject of direct connections between the Byzantine core and the peripheral *barbaricum*. In the seventh century political payments controlled from the center replaced the semi-independent practice of day-to-day interaction sustained by the frontier system in the previous century. The numismatic reflection of this dramatic change is a tremendous increase in the flow of precious-metal coins especially silver hexagrams. In the second half of the seventh century a trail of hoards dating from the reign of Constantine IV can be followed from southern Russia to Slovakia, with the largest concentration being recorded in the Danubian plain (Romania). With the exception of the dispersed hoard from Drăgășani, the other hoards of Byzantine silver have a closing date in the 670s and seem to belong to the same historical context.[118] Since the date dovetails nicely with the migration of the Onogur Bulgars, most historians have interpreted the finds as an illustration of the shifting balance of power in the Lower Danube region. Constantine IV was desperately trying to find allies against the rising influence of the Bulgars at a time when the Byzantines had just survived the first Arab siege of Constantinople by the skin of their teeth (678).[119] On the other hand,

---

and V. M. Khardaev, "Kolekciia Zachepylivs'kogo ("Novosanzhars'kogo") kompleksu 1928 r.: vtrachene i zberezhene," in *Starozhytnosti livoberezhnogo Podniprov'ia 2011. Zbirnyk naukovykh prats'*, eds. G. Iu. Ivakin, I. F. Koval'ova, and I. Kulatova (Kiev, 2011), 101–115. For a recent discussion of finds from the second half of the seventh century in the Black Sea region, see Somogyi, "New remarks," 108–125. See also J. Smedley, "Seventh-century Byzantine coins in Southern Russia and the problem of light weight solidi," in *Studies in Byzantine Gold Coinage*, eds. W. Hahn and W. E. Metcalf (New York, NY, 1988), 120–122.

[118] Drăgășani: Somogyi, *Byzantinische Fundmünzen*, 131, no. 34. Piua Petrii: M. Pauker, "Monete antice și grecești, romane și bizantine găsite la Piua Pietrei," *Cronica numismatică și arheologică* 135–136 (1945): 53. Priseaca: B. Mitrea, "Date noi cu privire la secolul VII. Tezaurul de hexagrame bizantine de la Priseaca (jud. Olt)," *SCN* 6 (1975): 113–125; E. Oberländer-Târnoveanu, "From the Late Antiquity to the Early Middle Ages – the Byzantine coins in the territories of the Iron Gates of the Danube from the second half of the 6th century to the first half of the 8th century," *EBPB* 4 (2001): 63. Galați: Somogyi, *Byzantinische Fundmünzen*, 128, no. 21.

[119] F. Curta, "Invasion or inflation? Sixth-to-seventh century Byzantine coin hoards in Eastern and Southeastern Europe," *Annali dell'Istituto Italiano di Numismatica* 43 (1996): 114–116; Somogyi, "New remarks," 115–135.

the invigorated prestige of Byzantium left room for fresh diplomatic maneuvers promptly exploited by the emperor.

The large quantity of hexagrams from *barbaricum* reflect either gifts to appease the Bulgars or stipends sent to Slavic centers. The two interpretations are not mutually exclusive as the geographical location of the hoards indicates two different areas of concentration. The hoards from Galați and Piua Petrii were found on the left bank of the Danube across the former province of Scythia. From the northeastern Balkans we know about a potential hoard from Valea Teilor and three other single finds of hexagrams dating from the reign of Constantine IV.[120] All these finds must be related to the presence of the Bulgars led by Asparuch in the area of the Danube Delta. On the other hand, the second area of concentration lies some 300 km to the west, in Oltenia, the finds from Vârtop, Priseaca, and Drăgășani being located in the same general area demarcated by the Danube to the west and the Olt river to the east. They may indeed constitute military payments and gifts sent to power centers of mixed ethnic composition, whose leaders emerged as potential allies against the Bulgars. The same region produced a rich burial with a spectacular inventory (Coșoveni), which belongs to the same cultural horizon.[121] The Byzantines seem to have played two cards at the same time, hoping to achieve some stability in the northern Balkans.

Byzantine coppers from the second half of the seventh century are not completely absent in *barbaricum*; they are worth mentioning because low-value coins reflect cultural contact of a different nature. The few bronze coins of Constans II were found not very far from the Danube, at Reșca in Oltenia, Novaci in Wallachia, and Bârlad in Moldavia.[122] The coins were probably lost in the 650s–660s. The half-follis found at Novaci is an issue of Carthage, which should not be surprising. Several seventh-century coins issued by mints from Italy and North Africa have been found in the northeastern Balkans.[123] The hoard from Obârșeni in Moldavia was

---

[120] F. Curta, "Byzantium in Dark-Age Greece (the numismatic evidence in its Balkan context)," *BMGS* 29, no. 2 (2005): 130, nos. 72, 74, 78 and 79.

[121] I. Nestor and C. S. Nicolaescu-Plopșor, "Der völkerwanderungszeitliche Schatz Negrescu," *Germania* 22, no. 1 (1938): 33–41.

[122] Reșca: Oberländer-Târnoveanu, "La răscruce," 143, n. 150. Novaci: Butnariu, "Răspîndirea monedelor," 220, no. 86. Bârlad: Oberländer-Târnoveanu and Popușoi, "Monede bizantine," 230, nos. 7–8. A *solidus* find was reported at Curcani (Călărași, Romania), for which see Oberländer-Târnoveanu, "Barbaricum apropiat," 357, n. 48. It was recently argued that the *solidus* in question was in fact bought by a collector from Curcani, without necessarily being a local find, for which see Vîlcu, *Les monnaies d'or*, 13.

[123] Coins of Heraclius and Constans II issued in Alexandria, Carthage, Ravenna, and Syracuse found in Moesia Secunda and Scythia, for which see Gandila, "A few rare," 53–64; Curta, "Byzantium in Dark-Age," 124–135; Oberländer-Târnoveanu, "Monnaies byzantines," 119–120.

concealed in the late 650s and included issues of Alexandria, Carthage, and Syracuse, which account for more than one-third of the total number of coins in the hoard.[124] This suggests that Constans II was already making efforts to reestablish a foothold in the northern Balkans by transferring troops and resources from the west. Theophanes informs us that the emperor staged a major campaign against the Slavs in the Balkans in 658 and his political ambitions, never to materialize, might have included a much wider area up to the Danube, the traditional frontier of the Empire.[125]

The western Black Sea region remained in Byzantine hands at least until 680 judging by the coin finds covering some 450 km along the coast from Constanța (Romania) to Akhtopol (Bulgaria).[126] A hoard from Tomis on the Black Sea coast included coins from Alexandria, Carthage, and Rome confirming the concentration of resources on this strategic front.[127] These finds can be connected with the major campaign mounted by Constantine IV against the Bulgars in 680 and more generally with efforts to defend the Byzantine positions in Dobrudja, often with the help of the fleet.[128] Furthermore, the presence of coins and seals indicates that late seventh-century emperors did not abandon all ambition in the Danube region and beyond.[129] In *barbaricum* a *follis* of Tiberius III (698–705) minted at Ravenna was found at Berezeni (Vaslui, Romania) and indeed most finds from this late period are located in southern Moldavia where the Empire was probably trying to find allies or recruits in order to reestablish its strategic position at the mouths of the Danube.[130]

---

[124] *Trésors*, no. 359. A *follis* of Constans II from Syracuse was found further north at Pinsk in Belarus, for which see Kropotkin, *Klady vizantiiskikh*, 38, no. 299.

[125] Theophanes, *Chronographia*, 347, AM 6149 [656/7].

[126] Curta, "Byzantium in Dark-Age," 124–135. For an updated catalogue of bronze coins, see Mihaylov, "Seventh-to-eighth," 77–85.

[127] *Trésors*, no. 67.

[128] For the significance of ports, see F. Karagianni, "Networks of Medieval city-ports on the Black Sea (7th–15th century). The archaeological evidence," in *Harbours and Maritime Networks as Complex Adaptive Systems*, eds. J. Preiser-Kapeller and F. Daim (Mainz, 2015), 83–104. For the role of the Byzantine fleet, see S. Cosentino, "Constans II and the Byzantine navy," *BZ* 100, no. 2 (2007): 577–603. For seventh-century western coins in Dobrudja, see Gandila, "A few rare," 53–64.

[129] For seventh-century coin finds in the region of Durostorum, see Oberländer-Târnoveanu, "Monnaies byzantines," 97–127; the often-invoked hoard of silver coins from Constantine IV in fact dates to the sixth century; see Curta, "Invasion or inflation," 169; Somogyi, "New remarks," 113. For the redating, see *Trésors*, no. 56.

[130] The same general area produced a hexagram of Constantine IV from the beginning of his reign found at Scurta, for which see Butnariu, "Răspîndirea monedelor," 222, no. 137. Further south, an early seventh-century *follis* of Justinian II was found during excavations in Bucharest, for

The creation of the Bulgar state after 680 marks the beginning of a new era in the history of the northern Balkans. The cultural semiperiphery on the Lower Danube pulverized along with the military frontier and new peripheries were created deep into the Balkan Peninsula and dangerously close to the Byzantine capital. For more than two centuries from the dissolution of Attila's confederation to the rise of the Bulgars, the Byzantine Empire maintained cultural ties with peoples and centers of power located beyond its military border on the Danube. More importantly, the constant and almost uninterrupted coin flow to the transdanubian *barbaricum* suggests a continuous traffic of goods, such as those discussed at length in the previous chapters. Regardless of the ethnic background of communities in *barbaricum,* some preserving elements of Roman provincial culture, others being mixed cultural groups forged under the domination of the Huns, the Gepids, or the Avars, having access to the Byzantine world remained crucial for the creation and preservation of social status. From the Empire's point of view, whether dealing with Antes, Herules, Slavs or Cutrigurs, priorities were dictated by political expediency and the need to secure the frontier in the northern Balkans. A successful policy would not only protect Constantinople but also allow the deployment of men and resources on the main theaters of operations in Italy, Anatolia, and Transcaucasia. As the numismatic evidence testifies, this was attempted – and sometimes achieved – through recruitment, retrenchment, diplomatic initiative, and the ability to create tension in *barbaricum* through the customary *divide et impera.*

which see E. Oberländer-Târnoveanu and G. Mănucu-Adameşteanu, "O monedă de la începutul secolului al VIII-lea descoperită în Bucureşti, pe amplasamentul 'Teatrul Naţional'," in *Teatrul Naţional din Bucureşti (1846–1947): cercetări arheologice,* ed. G. Mănucu-Adameşteanu (Bucharest, 2005), 357–375.

6 | Putting the Danube into Perspective: Money, Bullion, and Prestige in Avaria and Transcaucasia

6.1 Transcaucasia: The Land of Silver

6.1.1 The Price of Diplomacy in Lazica and Iberia (ca. 522–562)

Bordered by the Greater Caucasus range to the north, Transcaucasia was part of the northern frontier as much as it was part of the long Eastern frontier which ran from Trapezus to Aila. The Romans had a vested interest in controlling the eastern Black Sea coast where they established a number of military outposts as early as the first century. A political periphery under the Principate, Transcaucasia and its small kingdoms became one of the highest priorities of Byzantine diplomacy in Late Antiquity. The strategic value of the region was deemed so important that Procopius even feared the Persians might launch a naval expedition against the Byzantine capital should Lazica fall in their hands.[1] Even if Procopius' anxiety was somewhat unrealistic, the fact that Justinian's Persian treaty of 562 is dominated by Caucasian politics demonstrates the strategic significance of the region for both powers.[2] Perhaps more than elsewhere, in Transcaucasia diplomacy was a tool as powerful as military action.[3] The rivalry with Persia over Armenian lands dictated the main coordinates of this political dynamic, whose roots can be traced back to the old Pompeian system of client states established in the last century of the Republic.[4] But diplomacy between great powers can sometimes act in unexpected ways, leaving room for fruitful cooperation when common interest demands it.

---

[1] Procopius, *Bella*, 2.28.23.
[2] Menander, *Historia*, fr. 6 (Blockley). For Caucasian politics, see G. Greatrex and S. N. C. Lieu, eds., *The Roman Eastern Frontier and the Persian Wars. Part II, AD 363–630. A Narrative Sourcebook* (New York, NY, 2002). For the strategic geography of the east, see M. Whittow, *The Making of Orthodox Byzantium, 600–1025* (Los Angeles, CA, 1996), 25–36.
[3] One can still confidently refer to C. Toumanoff, "Caucasia and Byzantium," *Traditio* 27 (1971): 111–158. See also A. Carile, "Il Caucaso e l'Imperio bizantino (secoli VI–XI)," in *Il Caucaso: cerniera fra culture dal Mediterraneo alla Persia (secoli IV–XI)*, vol. I (Spoleto, 1996), 9–80.
[4] For the Pompeian legacy, see E. Frezouls, "Les fluctuations de la frontière de l'Empire Romain," in *La géographie administrative et politique d'Alexandre à Mahomet: actes du Colloque de Strasbourg, 14–16 juin 1979* (Leiden, 1981), 183; E. W. Gray, "The Roman Eastern limes from Constantine to Justinian," *Proceedings of the African Classical Association* 12 (1973): 34–35.

The defense of the Caucasus passes is a case in point. It became a major issue in negotiations under the Flavians when the Alans invaded Media Atropatene through the Caucasian Gates and resurfaced several times in Late Antiquity, eventually leading to open conflict during the reign of Anastasius.[5] The matter remained unsettled in the sixth century and fueled a bitter competition whose monetary consequences will be discussed in the following pages.

For most of the sixth century Lazica and its vassals – the Suani, Apsili, Abasgi, and other small tribes living on the southern foothills of the Caucasus – remained in the Byzantine orbit as a buffer region, a client confederation which retained its formal independence. From a strategic point of view, the region acted as a Roman frontier reinforced with fortresses planted deep into Lazi territory, at Sarapana and Scanda, to protect it from potential threats from Iberia, the eastern kingdom controlled by the Sasanian king.[6] Direct access from Iberia was extremely difficult although Pompey had managed to cross into Colchis by taking this route. In the sixth century, Procopius did not hesitate to praise the Persians for managing to cut up a strategic road linking the two regions.[7] The Byzantine writer did not identify any other natural frontier acting as a dividing line besides the difficult terrain surrounding Lazica, although he discussed the strategic role of the Phasis river.[8] The difficult terrain was perhaps less insurmountable than the chronic factionalism of

---

[5] Suetonius, *Domitianus*, 2.2. For instances of cooperation and shared interest in Late Antiquity, see B. Dignas and E. Winter, *Rome and Persia in Late Antiquity: Neighbours and Rivals* (Cambridge, 2007), ch. 6. For Alan incursions in the sixth century, see A. Alemany, "Sixth-century Alania: between Byzantium, Sasanian Iran and the Turkic world," in *Ērān ud Anērān. Studies Presented to Boris Il'ich Marshak on the Occasion of His 70th Birthday*, eds. M. Compareti, P. Raffetta, and G. Scarcia (Venice, 2006), 43–50.

[6] D. Braund, *Georgia in Antiquity: A History of Colchis and Transcaucasian Iberia, 550 BC-AD 562* (Oxford, 1994), 290–291; C. Zuckerman, "The Early Byzantine strongholds in Eastern Pontus," *Travaux et Mémoires* 11 (1991): 527–540; M. Van Esbroeck, "Lazique, Mingrélie, Svanéthie et Aphkhazie du IVe au IXe siècle," in *Il Caucaso*, vol. I, 209–214; G. M. Berndt, "Shifting frontiers in the Caucasus Mountains: the Suani," in *Shifting Cultural Frontiers in Late Antiquity*, eds. D. Brakke, D. Deliyannis, and E. Watts (Burlington, VT, 2012), 255–270; Iu. N. Voronov, "The Eastern Pontus within the sphere of Byzantine political and cultural activities, the sixth–eighth centuries," in *XVIIIth International Congress of Byzantine Studies. Selected Papers: Main and Communications, Moscow 1991. Volume II: History, Archaeology, Religion, Theology*, eds. I. Shevchenko and G. G. Litavrin (Shepherdstown, WV, 1996), 167–172.

[7] Procopius, *Bella*, 8.13.5.

[8] Procopius, *Bella*, 2.29.23–26. For the physical geography of Lazica and its strategic implications, see D. Braund, "Coping with the Caucasus: Roman responses to local conditions in Colchis," in *The Eastern Frontier of the Roman Empire. Proceedings of a Colloquium Held at Ankara in September 1988*, eds. D. French and C. Lightfoot (Oxford, 1989), 31–43.

Transcaucasian states which often welcomed external intervention. Such invitations were usually too tempting to pass on. The Caucasian frontier district was established through diplomatic means but continuously negotiated through the force of arms as the small kingdoms of Transcaucasia ceaselessly wavered between Roman and Persian overlordship.

Political instability in the region was compounded by the absence of a convenient natural border. Unlike the frontier on the Euphrates, Transcaucasia offered no apparent line of demarcation and the spheres of influence were subject to constant change and adjustment depending on the strength of the two empires. This made the northeastern frontier of Byzantium far more volatile than the frontier zone delineated by the Danube. From a different perspective, however, the Lower Danube and the Transcaucasus seem to share some key features. Both were deemed strategically important by the Byzantine Empire and for good reason. The Lower Danube guarded the access to the provinces of the Balkans and to Constantinople itself, which could be reached both by land and by sea. It also controlled access to important trade routes leading north to the Baltic. As a consequence, sixth-century emperors saw fit to rebuild some of the old Roman fortifications on the northern bank of the Danube in order to use them as outposts in *barbaricum*. Quite similarly, Transcaucasia guarded the Caucasian Gates through which nomad raiders from the north could launch plunder expeditions into Asia Minor and target the eastern Black Sea coast. The same passes were linking eastern and western trade routes connecting with the Silk Road.[9] As a reflection of similar agendas, fortresses such as Sucidava and Drobeta on the Lower Danube found their strategic equivalents at Pityus and Sebastopolis on the northeastern Black Sea coast.

The political fragmentation of the region into a mosaic of tribes inhabiting the southern foothills of the Caucasus and subjected to the Lazian king might not have been very different from the confederacy of clients established by the Avars in the Danube region. Written sources, however, are far more generous when it comes to Transcaucasian affairs. For it is the nature of the evidence that shapes our understanding and sets these two frontier regions apart. In the sixth century stakes were much higher in Transcaucasia as the whole region became the main theater of operations in the

---

[9] M. Kazanski and V. A. Mastykova, "Centry vlasti i togoviye puti Zapadnoi Alanii V–VI vv.," in *Severnyi Kavkaz: istoriko-arkheologicheskie ocherki i zametki*, eds. M. P. Abramova and V. I. Markovin (Moscow, 2001), 138–161.

conflict opposing Byzantium and Persia.[10] The political and diplomatic priorities of Byzantium are reflected unequivocally in the amount of space and energy that contemporary writers were willing to devote to the description of foreign peoples. If the Empire launched only two major campaigns north of the Danube during the sixth century, Lazica, Iberia, Albania, and Armenia saw continuous decades of warfare which feature prominently in the works of Procopius, Menander, and Agathias. The ideological conflict between two archenemies in a region fraught with centuries-long political and cultural competition was more fascinating than obscure events taking place in the post-Hunnic *barbaricum* north of the Danube. Given the nature of frontier politics on the Lower Danube and in Transcaucasia, the presence of Byzantine and Sasanian coins in Georgia and Armenia has slightly different historical coordinates. To be sure, in both regions preserving imperial interests remained the main priority and money was used as a powerful tool. The scale of the enterprise is what really makes the difference, for while the Danube frontier was flooded with copper coins used by soldiers recruited from *barbaricum*, in Transcaucasia the Byzantine emperor was forced not only to outmaneuver but also outbid the Persian ruler, which could only be achieved through heavy spending of silver and gold.

For completely different reasons which have to do with modern scholarship, another significant difference between the two regions is the pattern of recording and preserving the numismatic evidence. Although Transcaucasia – Georgia in particular – produced a number of copper coin finds comparable to that yielded by the lands north of the Danube, only in a few cases has the information about the finding place been properly recorded (Appendix B, Table 2).[11] Based on the heavy concentration of finds in the western half of modern Georgia, we can responsibly speculate that most of the unprovenanced Byzantine coins now in the Janashia Museum of Georgia were found on the territory of the Lazian kingdom (Figure 31).[12] The chronological structure of the finds largely corresponds to what we know about coin circulation in a number of Byzantine centers in eastern and northeastern Anatolia, although the level of publication is far from matching the corpus available for the Danube

---

[10] For a recent overview, see Dignas and Winter, *Rome and Persia*.
[11] The appendix can be accessed freely at www.cambridge.org/9781108470421.
[12] The main source of information about hoards and single finds of Byzantine coins in Georgia remains the work of Tamara Abramishvili, for which see especially T. Abramishvili, *Sakartvelos sakhelmts'ipo muzeumis bizant'iuri monet'ebi* (Tbilisi, 1965); T. Abramishvili, *Sakartvelos sakhelmts'ipo muzeumis bizant'iuri monet'ebi (1966–1984)* (Tbilisi, 1989).

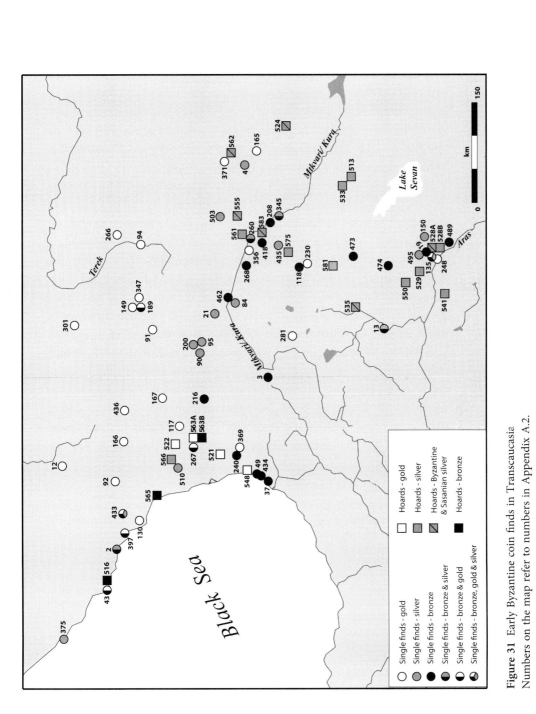

Figure 31 Early Byzantine coin finds in Transcaucasia
Numbers on the map refer to numbers in Appendix A.2.

frontier (Figure 32–Figure 34).[13] Even if we are not always able to contextualize the Georgian finds, a chronological – sometimes year-by-year – analysis is still possible. Unlike the Balkan situation, the annual flow of coins to Transcaucasia is paralleled by an almost equally precise sequence of events and developments recorded in contemporary accounts. This can guide our interpretation when the archaeological context is inconclusive, although a close correlation with historical events can often downplay the non-political channels of coin circulation. On the other hand, the presence of rare sixth-century ceremonial silver *miliarensia* and the massive quantity of seventh-century hexagrams found in Transcaucasia truly identify this region as a "land of silver," while the abundance of gold further confirms the political ambitions of Byzantine rulers.

The chronology of bronze coinage can help us understand the changing priorities of Byzantium (Figure 32). In Transcaucasia, the percentage of finds dated between 498 and 538 – before Justinian's monetary reform – is double compared to the Lower Danube. These are decades of consolidation in Lazica under the renewed suzerainty of Byzantium. Traditionally, the Roman Empire claimed control of the eastern Black Sea coast from Trapezus to Pityus and extended its political influence in the immediate hinterland. The eastern half of today's Georgia, the ancient kingdom of Iberia, as well as Albania, to the southeast, were under Persian control. This balance of power, however, was upset in the second half of the fourth century when failure in the East and in the Balkans led to the humiliating death of two emperors, Julian and Valens, respectively. The Roman garrisons on the Black Sea coast fell under Persian sway, although Pityus (Bich'vinta) and Sebastopolis (Sukhumi) were probably restored under Theodosius I.[14] As regards Pityus, we at least know that it was the

---

[13] Unfortunately very few publications exist from eastern Turkey, the provinces of Armenia Prima and Armenia Secunda being closest to Transcaucasia. There is indication of a substantial collection in the museum from Erzurum but just a short synopsis is currently available, for which see H. Özyurt Özcan, "Erzurum Arkeoloji Müzesi'ndeki bizans sikkeleri," in *Araştırma Sonuçları Toplantısı* 24, no. 1 (2007): 1–16. The most substantial remain the catalogues of finds from Amasya and Malatya, although the samples from Sinop and Amasra can be useful for the larger implications of circulation in the Black Sea; see Z. Demirel Gökalp, *Malatya Arkeoloji Müzesi bizans sikkeleri kataloğu* (Istanbul, 2014); S. Ireland, *Greek, Roman and Byzantine Coins in the Museum at Amasya* (London, 2000); S. Ireland and S. Ateşoğulları, "The ancient coins in Amasra Museum," in *Studies in Ancient Coinage from Turkey*, ed. R. Ashton (London, 1996), 115–137; J. Casey, *A Catalogue of the Greek, Roman and Byzantine Coins in Sinop Museum (Turkey) and Related Historical and Numismatic Studies* (London, 2010).

[14] C. Zuckerman, "The Early Byzantine strongholds in Eastern Pontus," *Travaux et Mémoires* 11 (1991): 527–540.

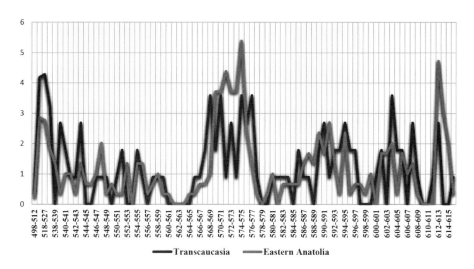

Figure 32 The chronology of Early Byzantine coin finds from eastern Anatolia and Transcaucasia

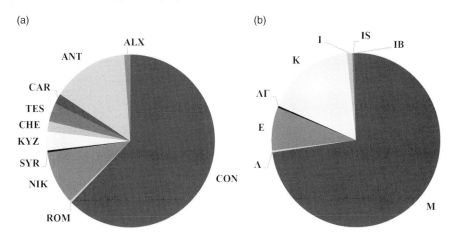

Figure 33a–b Mints and denominations in Transcaucasia
Abbreviations in Appendix B, Tables 4 and 6

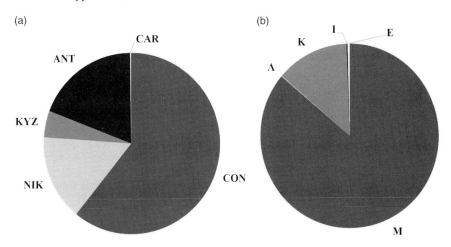

Figure 34a–b Mints and denominations in eastern Anatolia
Abbreviations in Appendix B, Tables 4 and 6

designated place of exile for John Chrisostomos in 407.[15] Even if Theodosius II regained a foothold in Lazica, the Roman position was still weak and relied mostly on religious ties with peoples of Transcaucasia who had started the process of Christianization in the first half of the fourth century.[16]

The kingdom of Lazica had strong ties to Sasanian Persia, something that sixth-century writers in Byzantium tried to conceal as the political climate of the region became more auspicious. It is revealing, however, that Lazian rulers were appointed by the Persian king, a practice which remained in place in the second half of the fifth century and until 522 when Lazica reentered the Byzantine orbit. In a move typical for Transcaucasian politics in Late Antiquity the Lazian king Tzath decided to renounce his allegiance to Persia and throw in his lot with Byzantium. The Byzantine response was equally traditional: Tzath was baptized by Justin I, received a Byzantine wife, and returned to Lazica as a client king.[17] The same decade saw the pacification of the Tzani, a troublesome tribe in the mountains of Pontus. Early in his reign, Justinian built fortresses and churches in Tzanica, taking control of this strategic region securing access to both Lazica and Armenia.[18] In addition, the Iberian king rebelled against the Persian encroachment in local religious affairs and reached for help from the Byzantine emperor. The Byzantine position in Transcaucasia had improved dramatically.[19]

We learn more about Justinian's intentions from Novella XXVIII (535) where the emperor boasted his submission of the Tzani and his suzerainty over the "Lazian Empire," a heterogeneous confederation which included the northern tribes of the Suani, the Abasgi, the Apsili, the Scymni, and the Misimiani. The cities mentioned in this official document include Archaeopolis (Nokalakevi) – the Lazian capital – Rhodopolis (Vartsikhe), Petra (Tzikhisdziri), as well as two settlements which the document classifies as fortresses (rather than towns) – Pityus and Sebastopolis – attached to the province of Pontus Polemoniacus.[20] These developments find an

---

[15] W. Seibt, "Westgeorgien (Egrisi, Lazica) in frühchristlicher Zeit," in *Die Schwarzmeerküste in der Spätantike und im frühen Mittelalter*, eds. R. Pillinger, A. Pülz, and H. Vetters (Vienna, 1992), 139.

[16] C. Haas, "Mountain Constantines: the Christianization of Aksum and Iberia," *Journal of Late Antiquity* 1, no. 1 (2008): 101–126; R. W. Thomson, "Mission, conversion, and Christianization: the Armenian example," *Harvard Ukrainian Studies* 12–13 (1988/1989): 28–45. See also G. Fowden, *Empire to Commonwealth: Consequences of Monotheism in Late Antiquity* (Princeton, NJ, 1994), 104–109

[17] Malalas, *Chronographia*, 17.9.   [18] Procopius, *De Aedificiis*, 3.6.1–14.

[19] Braund, *Georgia in Antiquity*, 282–284.   [20] *Corpus Iuris Civilis*, Novella 28 (535 AD).

excellent reflection in coin finds from this period. Although still adhering to the caveat that some coins might have arrived at a much later date after their striking, it is still safe to assume that many of the coins issued during these decades (498–538) reached Transcaucasia before Justinian's monetary reform of 538. Although Procopius credits Justinian with expanding and consolidating the Byzantine influence in Lazica, the large number of coin finds from his predecessors might reflect earlier efforts, at least since Tzath sided with the Byzantine Empire in 522. Both Pityus and Sebastopolis produced a significant number of finds from Anastasius, while a halffollis from Archaeopolis is actually an early reform issue from 507–512.[21] Two coins of Anastasius found at Petra, Justinian's brand new foundation, were probably lost later although older settlements are known in the area of Tzikishdziri. One more coin was found at Batumi, possibly the location of ancient Portus Altus. All these finds point to a stronger Byzantine control along the Black Sea coast.[22] Furthermore, the defection of Iberia to Justin I in 525 was followed by an extension of Byzantine ambitions to the south, in Armenia, where Dorotheus and Sittas had led successful campaigns in the years preceding the "eternal peace" of 532.[23] The large number of coin finds from Ani (Kars, Turkey) is probably a good indicator of the Byzantine military presence in Armenia.[24]

The reign of Justin I which saw this major shift in political allegiance in Transcaucasia brought an even larger quantity of coin to Lazica, especially to the main Byzantine strongholds on the coast. Excavations at Pityus produced no less than 18 coins of Justin I of which seven are *pentanummia*, pointing to the fact that the fortress was firmly connected to the Byzantine monetary system and perhaps to the trade network in the

---

[21] Pityus: I. Tsukhishvili, "Bich'vint'is bizant'iuri monet'ebi," in *Didi Pit'iunt'i. Arkeologiuri gatkhrebi Bich'vint'ashi*, vol. II, ed. A. M. Apakidze (Tbilisi, 1977), 314–315, nos. 11–16 and 605, figs. 11–15. Sebastopolis: S. M. Shamba, *Monetnoe obrashchenie na territorii Abkhazii: (V v. do n.e.–XIII v. n.e.)* (Tbilisi, 1987), 77–78, nos. 111–112. Archaeopolis: T. Abramishvili, "Nokalakevisa da nojikhevis monet'ebi," in *Nokalakevi-Arkeopolisi. Arkeologiuri gatkhrebi 1978–1982*, ed. P. Zakaraia (Tbilisi, 1987), 277, no. 12.

[22] Abramishvili, *Sakartvelos sakhelmts'ipo (1966–1984)*, 11, no. 29. For the location of Portus Altus, see G. R. Tsetskhladze, *Pichvnari and Its Environs, 6th c BC–4th c AD* (Paris, 1999), 85. The Byzantine presence on the northeastern Black Sea coast was also confirmed by a spectacular silver plate probably found in a fortress or cemetery in Abkhazia, for which see Y. Pyiatnisky, "New evidence for Byzantine activity in the Caucasus during the reign of the Emperor Anastasius I," *AJN* 18 (2006): 113–122.

[23] Greatrex and Lieu, eds, *The Roman Eastern*, 94 96.

[24] Kh. Mousheghian, A. Mousheghian, and C. Bresc, *History and Coin Finds in Armenia. Coins from Ani, Capital of Armenia (4th c. BC–19th c. AD)* (Wetteren, 2000), 72, nos. 19–23.

Black Sea.[25] Moreover, a hoard of 55 *pentanummia*, all issues of Justin I, was found near the north wall during archaeological excavations in 1961.[26] The hoard is unique in the Black Sea and the wider Eastern Mediterranean region and the coins were clearly intended for use at the marketplace. Copper coins of Justin I have been found not only close to the coast, at Sebastopolis and Archaeopolis, but also in the hinterland, at Kutaisi and Urbnisi.[27] The specimen from Sebastopolis is an issue of Antioch, a rare find in the Black Sea region, which points to the transfer of troops on the large theater of operations from the Caucasus to the Euphrates. The ceremonial silver heavy *miliarense* found at Zugdidi, close to the Lazian capital of Archaeopolis, is a clear reflection of diplomatic gifts necessary to cement the new alliance between Byzantium and Lazica.[28] Four *solidi*, of which one has a known finding place at Gveso (Georgia), may reflect similar political payments dating from the early stage of the Byzantine presence in Lazica.[29]

Such practices were continued and even intensified in the first decade of Justinian's reign. His plans in Transcaucasia were far more ambitious. Although Lazica was never included in the provincial system, Justinian's tendency to encroach upon the administrative and political structures of Armenia and Lazica made him extremely unpopular with the local princes. The Lazi confederation of clients was particularly fragile and relied on the loyalty of the northern tribes, which was hardly unwavering. The Abasgi, the Apsili, the Misimiani, and the Suani, whose main strategic purpose was to guard the two major passes of Klukhor and Marukha in the western Caucasus, were lavished with occasional gifts to ensure their pro-Byzantine position. Later events would prove that their willingness to cooperate should not be taken for granted.

---

[25] Tsukhishvili, "Bich'vint'is bizant'iuri," 315–318, nos. 17–27 and 606–607, figs. 19–24, 26–28.

[26] Tsukhishvili and Depeyrot, *History and Coin*, 72–73, no. 4.

[27] Sebastopolis: Shamba, *Monetnoe obrashchenie*, 78, no. 113. Archaeopolis: Abramishvili, "Nokalakevisa da nojikhevis monet'ebi," 277–278, nos. 13–15. Kutaisi: Tsukhishvili and Depeyrot, *History and Coin*, 24, no. 2. Urbnisi: Abramishvili, *Sakartvelos sakhelmts'ipo*, 123, no. 33a.

[28] Abramishvili, *Sakartvelos sakhelmts'ipo*, 40–41, no. 56. Ceremonial silver coins are a far more reliable chronological marker, since they were distributed by the emperor. They probably had no monetary function and therefore it is likely that they arrived to their final destination immediately after they were issued; cf. Tsukhishvili and Depeyrot, *History and Coin*, 25, who state that silver coins were intended for the foreign market.

[29] M. Tsotselia, *Coin Finds in Georgia: (6th Century BC–15th Century AD)* (Wetteren, 2010), 130, no. 692; Abramishvili, *Sakartvelos sakhelmts'ipo*, 40, nos. 53–55.

In the 530s the Abasgi were converted to Christianity and their dual monarchy abolished.[30] This decision did not come for free. Two ceremonial silver *miliarensia* dated between 527 and 538 were found in *Apsilia* and *Abasgia*, at Akhali Atoni and Tsibilium, respectively, while a *solidus* found in the fortress of Ch'khalt'a (Abkhazia) might date from the same period.[31] A light *miliarense* from Sochi in Krasnodar has a wider dating (537–565) but may belong to the same historical context.[32] New churches were being built and the material cultural betrays Justinian's ambitions of acculturation in this region. In addition, the Byzantine fortresses of the northeastern coast became more integrated into the Mediterranean world judging by the quantity of amphorae found in settlements of the coast and the finds of coins from Antioch, Alexandria, and Carthage at Pityus and Akhali Atoni in Abkhazia.[33] Indeed, Agathias described the Lazi as wealthy because they had access to the Black Sea and carried on a thriving commerce.[34] The coins from North Africa may well reflect trade but also the movement of people such as the Tzani who fought in Justinian's army in Italy. Finally, one of the *folles* found at Pityus is a Balkan imitation and

---

[30] G. Greatrex, "Byzantium and the east in the sixth century," in *The Cambridge Companion to the Age of Justinian*, ed. M. Maas (Cambridge, 2005), 497.

[31] Akhali Atoni and Tsebelda: Shamba, *Monetnoe obrashchenie*, 78–79, no. 114 and 116. Ch'khalt'a: Kropotkin, *Klady vizantiiskikh,* 46, no. 477. Two *miliarensia* and a *solidus* of Justinian were part of a belt found in a grave from Tsibilium; for the archaeological context, see Iu. N. Voronov and V. A. Iushin, "Pogrebenie VII v. n. e. v s. Tsebel'da v Abkhazii," *KSIA* 128 (1971): 100–105. For the dating of the assemblage, see C. Bálint, "Der Gürtel im frühmittelalterlichen Transkaukasus und das Grab von Üč Tepe," in *Awarenforschungen*, ed. F. Daim (Vienna, 1992), 378–380; N. Khrisimov, "Der frühmittelalterliche Gürtel von Üç Tepe (Azerbajdžan) und die dazugehörige Ausrüstung. Ein Rekonstruktionsversuch," *ArchBulg* 8, no. 1 (2004): 79–96.

[32] Kropotkin, *Klady vizantiiskikh*, 22, no. 22.

[33] D. Braund, "Procopius on the economy of Lazica," *The Classical Quarterly* 41, no. 1 (1991), 223 with the older literature; Iu. N. Voronov and O. Kh. Bgazhba, *Materialy po arkheologii Tsebel'dy (itogi issledovanii Tsibiliuma v 1978–1982 gg.)* (Tbilisi, 1985); N. Inaishvili and N. Vashakidze, "Typology and chronology of Greek, Roman and Early Byzantine amphorae from Petra-Tsikhisdziri," in *PATABS I: Production and Trade of Amphorae in the Black Sea: actes de la table ronde internationale de Batoumi et Trabzon, 27–29 avril 2006*, eds. D. Kassab Tezgör and N. Inaishvili (Paris, 2010), 151–152; M. Zamtaradze, "Nokalakevshi aghmochenili amforebi," in *Nokalakevi-Arkeopolisi: III. Arkeologiuri gatchrebi 1983–1989*, ed. P. Zakaraia (Tbilisi, 1993), 158–175. Coin finds at Pityus: Tsukhishvili, "Bich'vnt'is bizant'iuri," 321, nos. 42–43. Akhali Atoni: Shamba, *Monetnoe obrashchenie*, 81, no. 123. Three additional unprovenanced coins of Cherson in Abramishvili, *Sakartvelos sakhelmts'ipo*, 49–51, nos. 100–102. Interestingly, no coins from African mints have been found at Sinop and Amasra, on the southern Black Sea coast, for which see Casey, *A Catalogue*, 79–86; Ireland and Ateşoğulları, "The ancient coins," 132–135.

[34] Agathias, *Historiae*, 3.5.3.

may have been brought by the "Bulgar" prisoners taken by Mundus and sent to Lazica and Armenia to defend the frontier.[35]

Justinian was also aiming further east in Iberia where a growing Byzantine presence can be felt in these decades. Copper coins of Anastasius, Justin I, and Justinian have been found at K'rts'anisi, Nost'e, Rustavi, Dmanisi, and Mtskheta.[36] A silver *miliarense* pierced to be worn as a pendant was found in a grave from the Iberian capital of Mtskheta, possibly pointing to diplomatic gifts sent to Iberian rulers.[37] Gold coins of Anastasius also reached the region controlled by the Alans who guarded the Dariel Pass (Alan Gates). Justinian went a step further by securing the allegiance of queen Boa of the Sabir Huns won over "with gifts of imperial raiment and a variety of silver vessels and not a little money."[38] The money was well spent as the powerful queen defeated other Hunnic groups allied with the Persians.[39]

Byzantine diplomatic activity is also evident northwards on the Black Sea coast, toward the Taman peninsula and Bosporus. By 520 Bosporus was under the rule of Grod, the pro-Byzantine leader of the Huns who dominated the region in cooperation with the Tetraxite Goths. The study of burial assemblages from the region points to strong cultural ties between Bosporus and the northern Caucasus.[40] Further internal turmoil in Bosporus was swiftly resolved by Justinian who sent an army across the Black Sea to retake the city in 534–535. Two *solidi* of Justin I found at Dzhiginka and Goryachi Klyuch in Krasnodar may be related to this political context. The specimen from Dzhiginka is in fact a rare joint reign issue of Justin I and Justinian I struck in April–August 527. The ceremonial nature of the coinage was doubtlessly recognized by the owner who attached the coin to

---

[35] Abramishvili, *Sakartvelos sakhelmts'ipo (1966–1984)*, 16, no. 49. For the events, see Theophanes, *Chronographia*, 219, AM 6032 [539/40]. The episode actually took place around 530 after the cooption of Mundus in the Balkans, the defection of Iberia, and the subjugation of the Tzani in Transcaucasia.

[36] K'rts'anisi, Nost'e, Rustavi: Abramishvili, *Sakartvelos sakhelmts'ipo*, 39, no. 49; 123, nos. 23 and 33. Dmanisi: Abramishvili, *Sakartvelos sakhelmts'ipo*, 42, no. 63; Abramishvili, *Sakartvelos sakhelmts'ipo (1966–1984)*, 13, no. 36; Mtskheta: Kropotkin, *Klady vizantiiskikh*, 44, no. 424.

[37] Abramishvili, *Sakartvelos sakhelmts'ipo*, 44, no. 74.

[38] Malalas, *Chronographia* 18.13 (trans. Jeffreys, Jeffreys, and Scott): καὶ προτραπεῖσα ὑπὸ τοῦ βασιλέως Ἰουστινιανοῦ ξενίοις πολλοῖς βασιλικῆς φορεσίας καὶ σκευῶν διαφόρων ἐν ἀργύρῳ καὶ χρημάτων οὐκ ὀλίγων.

[39] Greatrex and Lieu, eds., *The Roman Eastern*, 82.

[40] I. O. Gavritukhin and M. Kazanski, "Bosporus, the Tetraxite Goths, and the Northern Caucasus region during the second half of the fifth and the sixth centuries," in *Neglected Barbarians*, 83–136.

a gold necklace with precious stone pendants.[41] Access to such Byzantine coins was becoming an important index of social distinction.

Justinian's golden decade ended abruptly and unexpectedly. The successful Persian invasion of Byzantine Syria in 540 was not without consequences in Transcaucasia. Alienated by Justinian's policy and his corrupt officials who forced the Lazi to accept import duties and to support the Byzantine troops by ensuring the provision of supplies at low prices, king Gubazes II turned to Chosroes for help. The Persians promptly invaded Lazica and took Petra, while the Byzantine garrisons from *Abasgia* withdrew from Pityus and Sebastopolis after razing the fortresses to the ground. Coins of Justinian found in a burned layer at Pityus confirm Procopius' account.[42] Sebastopolis was later rebuilt according to the same author who no longer mentions Pityus in his list, although coin finds from the second half of the sixth century prove that the fortress remained in use.[43]

The Persian king tried to impose Zoroastrianism by force in his intention to burn the most important cultural bridge uniting Byzantium and Lazica and to curb Justinian's ecumenical ambitions in the Caucasus.[44] In addition, Lazica found itself isolated from the Black Sea network, which affected its economy. Soon enough Gubazes II realized that Chosroes was even less accommodating than Justinian and decided to make amends and reach back to the Byzantine emperor. War resumed in Lazica in 547. In his usual manner, Justinian invited the Alans and the Sabir Huns to attack Persian Iberia and was ready to spend three *centenaria* of gold (21,600 *solidi*) to enlist their support.[45] Three years of warfare did not settle the matter, as the Persians still held Petra despite a number of victories won by the Byzantine-Lazian armies.

Another episode of sudden reversal – unmistakable trademark of Caucasian diplomacy – unfolded on the political scene of the mid-sixth

---

[41] Dzhiginka and Goryachi Klyuch: Kropotkin, *Klady vizantiiskikh*, 21, no. 7 and no. 9 and fig. 14. On finds of joint reign *solidi* of Justin I and Justinian I, see W. E. Metcalf, "The joint reign gold of Justin I and Justinian I," in *Studies in Byzantine Gold Coinage*, eds. W. Hahn and W. E. Metcalf (New York, NY, 1988), 19–27.

[42] Tsukhishvili and Depeyrot, *History and Coin*, 21. For the events, see Greatrex and Lieu, eds., *The Roman Eastern*, 115.

[43] Tsukhishvili and Depeyrot, *History and Coin*, 21; 25, associate the scarcity of finds from the second half of the sixth century at Pityus with a general decline in mint output throughout the empire; finds from any Byzantine province from the Danube to Arabia disprove this claim.

[44] Justinian's actions in the first half of his reign targeted not just the Transcaucasus but also the Huns living in the steppes north of the Caucasus, for which see Pseudo-Zachariah, *Chronicle*, 12.216–217.

[45] Procopius, *Bella*, 2.29.27–32. For the Byzantine *kentenarion*, see G. Dagron and C. Morrisson, "Le Kentènarion dans les sources byzantines," *RN* 17 (1975): 145–162.

century. Byzantine taxation and political intervention in *Abasgia* became so unpopular that the Abasgi asked Chosroes for help. The Persians advanced from Iberia to *Apsilia* and restored the Abasgian monarchy under Persian suzerainty. In addition, a Lazi defector offered the Apsilian fortress of Tsibilium to the Persians.[46] Although Justinian finally recaptured and destroyed Petra in 551 and punished the rebellious Abasgi, the Persian army led by Mermeroes remained in control of eastern Lazica and Suania. A Persian assault on western Lazica was successfully repelled after Justinian transferred more troops to the Transcaucasus.[47] The murder of king Gubazes II in 555 followed by a well-timed Tzani revolt in 558 made the Byzantine position in Lazica even more tenuous as the Lazi withdrew their military support.[48] There are only three coin finds dated between 558 and 565 known in Lazica. The explanation should be sought not only in these episodes of regional insecurity but also in a serious reduction of mint output during these last years of Justinian's reign, whose effects we have already analyzed for the Danubian case.

Coin finds in Transcaucasia mirror the bitter conflict between 541 and 562, which roughly corresponds with the dated coinage of Justinian (538–565), and highlight the precarious position of Byzantium.[49] The heavy series of 538–542 which is so well represented in the Lower Danube region, as we have seen, was not equally popular in Transcaucasia (Figure 32). Nevertheless, the period 538–545 produced almost the same number of finds as the last two decades of Justinian's reign (545–565). Copper coins from the early years after the 538 reform have been found in Armenia, at Ani and Vanadzor and in Abkhazia, at Pityus and Sebastopolis.[50] The two important fortresses had been destroyed and abandoned in 541 but Procopius might have exaggerated this episode. At Sebastopolis five post-reform issues of Justinian have been retrieved, of which three specimens date from the 540s. To be sure, some of them might have been lost later, together with coins of Justin II.

The numismatic reflection of diplomatic initiatives during these decades of conflict left a few important traces in western Georgia. After

---

[46] Braund, *Georgia in Antiquity*, 300.
[47] Greatrex and Lieu, eds., *The Roman Eastern*, 118–121.
[48] Ibid., 122; Braund, *Georgia in Antiquity*, 308.
[49] Hoards of Sasanian drachms from Iberia (Tolenji, Dusheti, and Urbnisi) concealed during these decades must be associated with the same events; see M. Tsotselia, *History and Coin Finds in Georgia: Sasanian Coin Finds and Hoards* (Wetteren, 2003), 49–57.
[50] Ani and Vanadzor: Mousheghian et al., *History (Ani)*, 73–74, nos. 32–33 and 180, no. 2. Pityus: Tsukhishvili, "Bich'vint'is bizant'iuri," 321–322, nos. 44 and 49. Sebastopolis: Shamba, *Monetnoe obrashchenie*, 80–81, nos. 122, 124, and 125.

the ill-timed murder of Gubazes II, Justinian saw fit to entrust general Soterichus with distributing four *centenaria* of gold (28,800 *solidi*) to barbarian tribes from the Lazian confederation. The stakes were raised when the Misimiani killed Soterichus and helped themselves to the money. A Roman army under generals Martin and John Dacnas punished the rebels and retrieved the gold.[51] Indeed, gold was not in short supply in Transcaucasia. John Dacnas was entrusted with 400 pounds of gold to be distributed to worthy soldiers fighting in *Misimia*. Justinian had shown similar generosity a few years earlier when he sent his pursebearer Rusticus to Lazica with gifts (δῶρα) for the soldiers, as they were struggling to check Mermeroes' advance into Lazica.[52] The dispersed hoards of *solidi* of Justinian from Chkhorotsqu and Kobuleti may belong to this context.[53]

Further north, two ceremonial silver *miliarensia* and one *solidus* found at Tsebelda may reflect Justinian's efforts to strengthen the loyalty of the Apsili at a time when their Misimiani neighbors had rebelled, the Abasgi had been barely pacified after their defection to Persia, and the Suani were yet to be punished for a similar defection in 552.[54] In fact, Justinian's diplomatic efforts at the beginning of this decade targeted the entire northern Black Sea front as he was striving to convince the Utigurs and the Tetraxite Goths to attack the Cutrigurs. The hoard from Ilych in Krasnodar made of 140 third-to-fourth-century gold issues of Bosporan kings and *solidi* of Justinian hidden in an amphora may reflect such initiatives.[55] Finally, the arrival of the Avars sometime in the 550s intensified diplomatic contacts in the Caucasus and the eastern Black Sea region. Justinian sent gifts of gold and silk to the Avars hoping to attract them to the imperial cause in the Caucasus, although it is not clear whether the Avars received regular subsidies and

---

[51] Agathias, *Historiae* 4.12–20, for the episode, and 4.20.9, for the sum of money involved.
[52] Agathias, *Historiae* 3.2.3–4 and 4.17.3.
[53] Abramishvili, *Sakartvelos sakhelmts'ipo*, 124, no. 42; Kropotkin, *Klady vizantiiskikh*, 45, no. 444.
[54] Voronov and Iushin, "Pogrebenie," 103, fig. 43; Shamba, *Monetnoe obrashchenie*, 79, no. 115. For the Suani, see recently G. M. Berndt, "Shifting frontiers," 255–270. The Byzantine army used the fortresses of *Apsilia* as bases to attack Misimia, for which see Braund, *Georgia in Antiquity*, 310. For archaeological evidence from the region, see M. Kazanski, "Contribution à l'histoire de la défense de la frontière pontique au Bas-Empire," *Travaux et Mémoires* 11 (1991): 488–493.
[55] N. A. Frolova and E. Ia. Nikolaeva, "Il'ichevskii klad monet 1975 g.," *VV* 39 (1978): 173–179. For the historical and archaeological evidence, see M. Kazanski and A. Mastykova, *Les peuples du Caucase du Nord. Le début de l'histoire (Ier-VIIe siècle apr. J.-C.)* (Paris, 2003), 141. For the gifts sent by Justinian to the Utigurs, see John of Antioch, *Historia Chronike*, 217.

federate status at this point.[56] The aging Justinian could hardly foresee the tremendous impact of the newcomers on the fate of his European provinces.

6.1.2 Wavering between Byzantium, Persia, and the Caliphate (ca. 562–670)

Peace followed in 562, after Dagistheus (*magister militum per Armeniam*) won a major victory at Phasis (Poti) near the Black Sea coast in Lazica. The theater of operations moved southwards into Armenia during the reign of Justin II. In 571 the Armenians revolted against the Persian *marzban* who tried to impose Zoroastrianism in the Armenian capital of Dvin and limit the religious freedom of Armenians long granted by Shapur III (383–388). Vardan, the leader of the Armenian rebellion received help from Justin II and managed to take control of Dvin. Drawn into this game of shifting loyalties, Iberia joined the revolt against Persia and between 572 and 574 Roman armies advanced deep into Albania toward the Caspian Sea. The turn of events was so surprising that John of Biclar writing from distant Spain was convinced that "the emperor Justin made Armenia and Iberia Roman provinces."[57] The Byzantine success was, however, less enduring and by 580 Persia regained the initiative in the Transcaucasus. Desperate to restore his foothold in the region, Tiberius II decided to recruit 15,000 "Germans" from the northern Balkans and send them to the East.[58] The transfer of troops from the Balkans is suggested by the significant number of half-*folles* of Thessalonica found in Georgia, given that the Macedonian mint was supplying the army defending the Danube frontier (Appendix B, Table 9).[59]

Coin finds of Justin II are abundant in Transcaucasia, especially copper issues. His coins were found during excavations at Ani and Dvin and the majority were struck by the mint of Nicomedia, which was probably commissioned to support the war effort in Armenia.[60] Coins from

---

[56] W. Pohl, *Die Awaren: Ein Steppenvolk in Mitteleuropa, 567–822 n. Chr.* (Munich, 1988), 206.

[57] John of Biclar, *Chronica*, 20–21, "Iustinus imperator Armeniam et Hiberiam repulsis Persis Romanas provincias facit." For the events, see Greatrex and Lieu, eds., *The Roman Eastern*, 138–149.

[58] Greatrex and Lieu, eds., *The Roman Eastern*, 151.

[59] Thessalonica is less well represented or completely missing among finds from Sinop, Amasya, and Malatya, for which see Casey, *A Catalogue of the Greek*, 79–86; Ireland and Ateşoğulları, "The ancient coins," 132–135; Demirel Gökalp, "Malatya arkeoloji," 37–43.

[60] Mousheghian et al., *History (Ani)*, 74–75, nos. 42–51; Kh. Mousheghian et al., *History and Coin Finds in Armenia: Coins from Duin, Capital of Armenia (4–13th c.); Inventory of Byzantine and*

Antioch have been found at Vardenut and Vosketap, in Armenia, and also at Melitene, a major Roman base during this decade of conflict.[61] On the other hand, things were quiet in Lazica and we can envisage a period of reconstruction and consolidation as testified by coin finds from Pityus, Archaeopolis, and Kutaisi.[62] A hoard of copper coins from Archaeopolis spanning the reigns of Anastasius to Justin II might have been concealed during renewed insecurity in Lazica in 574–575.[63] A half-*follis* from a mobile military mint striking coins imitating the mint of Rome was found at Akhaltsikhe close to the Mtkvari river and confirms the movement of troops from the west.[64] Pityus was perhaps the main base for such movements as another half-*follis* of Tiberius II or Maurice from the military mint labeled "Rome" was found during archaeological excavations in the fortress.[65] The transfer of troops might be connected with the war effort in Albania and the revolt of Iberia supported by Justin II. A *follis* from 570/1 found in Iberia at Dmanisi is perhaps related to the same events.[66]

As we have already seen, Justin II was not very keen on sending gold to barbarians. However, the balance of power in the steppe north of the Caucasus was rapidly changing. By the end of his reign the Turks would become the masters of this wide region after subjugating the Sabir Huns, the Alans, and the Utigurs.[67] *Solidi* of Justin II and his predecessors as well as a copper coin of Justin II have been found in the Alan cemetery of Kamunta (North Ossetia-Alania), a gold-plated imitation comes from the Mokraya Balka cemetery, and a *solidus* of Justin II with a suspension loop was part of the inventory of a grave from Pechanka

---

Sasanian Coins in Armenia (6–7th c.) (Wetteren, 2000), 62, nos. 19–24. Cf. Tsukhishvili and Depeyrot, *History and Coin*, 19, who believe that the mint of Nicomedia had lost its importance during the reign of Justinian I; evidence from the Balkans, Asia Minor, and the Near East clearly refutes this claim.

[61] Demirel Gökalp, "Malatya arkeoloji," 42–43, nos. 184–193. Melitene was sacked by the Persians in 576, for which see R. W. Thomson, "Eastern neighbours: Armenia (400–600)," in *The Cambridge History of the Byzantine Empire c. 500–1492*, ed. J. Shepard (Cambridge, 2008), 168.

[62] Pityus: Tsukhishvili, "Bich'vint'is bizant'iuri," 323–324, nos. 50–53 and 609–610, figs. 50–53. Archaeopolis: Abramishvili, "Nokalakevisa da nojikhevis," 278, nos. 17–18. Kutaisi: Tsukhishvili and Depeyrot, *History and Coin*, 24, no. 4. Unprovenanced coins from Georgia: Abramishvili, *Sakartvelos sakhelmts'ipo*, 50–52, nos. 105–107 and 109–120.

[63] Greatrex and Lieu, eds., *The Roman Eastern*, 153.

[64] Abramishvili, *Sakartvelos sakhelmts'ipo (1966–1984)*, 21, no. 73, with n. 114; Gandila, "Going east," 149.

[65] Abramishvili, *Sakartvelos sakhelmts'ipo (1966–1984)*, 19, no 63.

[66] Ibid., 20, no. 71 and pl. IV/71. A hoard of Sasanian drachms from Mtskheta may be related to the same events; see Tsotselia, *History and Coin*, 61–64.

[67] Kazanski and Mastykova, *Les peuples du Caucase*, 150.

(Kabardino-Balkaria).[68] An exceptionally rare find from Mokraya Balka, a light weight *solidus* of 22 *siliquae* from the joint reign of Justin II and Tiberius II (26 September 578–4 October 578), pierced twice, reminds of the find from Dzhiginka and probably has the same significance.[69] All these finds, as well as others from the Kislovodsk basin, may be part of the political and diplomatic context of the 570s when Justin II managed to finally punish the Suani who had switched sides in favor of Persia two decades earlier.[70] As a symbol of their definitive victory, the Romans captured the Suani king and brought him as a captive to Constantinople together with his royal treasure.[71] No doubt, the protection of the Dariel Pass remained a major strategic priority for both Byzantium and Persia. This much can be deduced from the assortment of Byzantine and Sasanian coins and artifacts found in such cemeteries.[72] Although long-term efforts in the region are well documented, it must be noted that many gold coins date from the seventh century and it is therefore impossible to ascertain that Justin II's issues arrived in the region during his reign.

By the beginning of Maurice's reign the Persians had restored their control over Iberia and Albania. For almost a decade war would continue with fierce battles in the southern sector of the frontier, quite far from the Caucasus. Nevertheless, the region remained strategically important in the larger scheme. In 589 Maurice paid the Iberians to invade Albania, trying to take advantage of the Persian weakness in the region after they were forced to transfer troops to the east to face an invasion of the Turks. The Georgian Chronicles tell us that Maurice supplied the Iberian *curopalates* Guaram with ample coin to recruit an army from the tribes of the northern Caucasus.[73] A *solidus* of Maurice from Saskhari (Georgia) may belong to this political context.[74] Returning general Bahram retaliated by launching a campaign against the Suani but his efforts were thwarted by a major defeat to the south, close to Araxes river. The subsequent rebellion of Bahram against Hormizd and the rightful heir Chosroes proved to be a decisive

---

[68] Kamunta and Pechanka: Kropotkin, *Klady vizantiiskikh*, 30, nos. 138/3, 11. and 30, no. 132. Mokraya Balka: E. V. Rtveladze and A. P. Runich, "Novye nakhodki vizantiiskikh monet i indikacii v okrestnostiakh Kislovodska," *VV* 37 (1976): 153.

[69] Rtveladze and Runich, "Novye nakhodki," 151 and fig. 1/1–2.

[70] Y. A. Prokopenko, "Byzantine coins of the 5th–9th century and their imitations in the Central and Eastern Ciscaucasus," in *Byzantine Coins*, 545–550 and fig. 1.

[71] G. M. Berndt, "Shifting frontiers," 269, discussing the account of John of Biclar.

[72] Kazanski and Mastykova, *Les peuples du Caucase*, 565.

[73] Greatrex and Lieu, eds., *The Roman Eastern*, 171; R. W. Thomson, trans., *Rewriting Caucasian History. The Medieval Armenian Adaptation of the Georgian Chronicles* (Oxford, 1996), 230.

[74] Abramishvili, *Sakartvelos sakhelmts'ipo*, 55, no. 131.

moment for the balance of power in Transcaucasia. Maurice's successful campaign against Bahram and the restoration of Chosroes under the terms imposed by the emperor meant that Byzantium would gain unprecedented influence in the east. In exchange for "a great sum of money," the Persian king agreed to give up control of Persarmenia as far as Dvin and Lake Van and of Iberia as far as Tbilisi.[75] Relations with Persia remained good until the death of Maurice, especially since the emperor was determined to deal with the Avars in the Balkans while Chosroes II had to establish his rule in Persia.[76]

Coins of Maurice are common in Transcaucasia, particularly issues from the 590s after the war with Persia was brought to an end. Coins from Antioch are particularly abundant in Armenia at Ani and in Lazica at Pityus and Kutaisi.[77] Pityus continued to receive coins from Thessalonica in significant numbers signaling an uninterrupted traffic from the Balkans via the Black Sea. Two copper coins from 589/90 and 594/5 have been found in the most important centers of Iberia, at Mtskheta and Tbilisi, respectively, confirming the extension of Byzantium's influence east of Lazica, according to the terms accepted by Chosroes.[78] A small hoard found at Nekresi comprised of two silver Sasanian drachms and one *siliqua* of Maurice is another testament to the mixed Byzantine-Persian influence in Iberia.[79] A silver light *miliarense* and three *solidi* have no recorded finding place, but they can be situated in the same historical context.[80]

Although peace was restored in Transcaucasia and the emperor diverted his attention to the Balkans, the consolidation of the Roman presence in Lazica must have remained an important priority. A hoard of 23 *solidi* found during archaeological excavations at Archaeopolis is extremely important for understanding Maurice's military and diplomatic efforts in Lazica, not always recorded in written sources. Many of the *solidi* are

---

[75] Theophylact Simocatta, *Historia*, 5.2.6: ὁ δὲ τοῦ Ῥωμαϊκοῦ βασιλεὺς μετὰ τῆς συμμαχίας τῶν ὅπλων καὶ τὴν τῶν χρημάτων αὐτῷ μεγίστην ῥοπὴν ἐχαρίζετο.
[76] Whitby, *The Emperor Maurice*, 292–304.
[77] Ani: Mousheghian et al., *History (Ani)*, 75–76, nos. 53–60. Pityus: Tsukhishvili, "Bich'vint'is bizant'iuri," 324–326, nos. 54–57 and 610–611, figs. 54–57; Abramishvili, *Sakartvelos sakhelmts'ipo (1966–1984)*, 23–24, nos. 81 and 83. Kutaisi: Tsukhishvili and Depeyrot, *History and Coin*, 24, no. 6.
[78] Abramishvili, *Sakartvelos sakhelmts'ipo*, 125, no. 58; Abramishvili, *Sakartvelos sakhelmts'ipo (1966–1984)*, 21, no. 74 and 23, no. 79.
[79] Tsotselia, *Coin Finds*, 142, no. 755.
[80] Abramishvili, *Sakartvelos sakhelmts'ipo (1966–1984)*, 21, no. 75 and pl. IV/75; Abramishvili, *Sakartvelos sakhelmts'ipo*, 54–55, nos. 130, 132 and 134.

die-linked which means they were brought fresh from the mint. They were not regular *solidi* but lightweight issues worth 23 *siliquae* which suggests a political payment sent to the Lazian capital in the last decade of his reign.[81] A copper hoard found in Ochamchire (Abkhazia), whose context was unfortunately poorly recorded, contained some 58 bronze coins from Justin I to Maurice, the last issue being dated 601/2.[82] Its concealment during the events following the death of Maurice seems plausible. This is in fact one of the rare copper coin hoards found in Transcaucasia where we do not see the hoarding frenzy that characterizes the last decades of the sixth century in the Balkans. In Lazica and Armenia most hoards are of gold or silver which tells us that soldiers on the Eastern front were detailed to a higher pay grade.[83]

War with Persia resumed during the reign of Phocas and would continue for more than two decades. The murder of Maurice and his family was the perfect excuse for Chosroes II, whose gratitude toward Constantinople was already growing thin in the decade after his restoration to the Persian throne. The main objective was to reconquer Armenia but as Persian forces advanced with unusual ease the road was open for a much more ambitious expedition into the Byzantine heartland.[84] Phocas had already sealed a new deal with the Avars in 604 and was probably trying to gain the loyalty of Caucasian tribes judging by the finds of gold and silver coins from the area. A ceremonial *siliqua* was found at Ch'iatura (Georgia), and a *solidus* at Dranda in Abkhazia.[85] Grave finds from cemeteries such as Chmi and Kamunta in North Ossetia-Alania included *solidi* of Phocas, sometimes pierced to be worn as jewelry.[86] Two light *siliquae* of Maurice and Phocas, respectively, were found in a grave from Mokraya Balka, indicating that such payments were also sent north of the Caucasus.[87] The Byzantine emperor was probably trying to compensate for

---

[81] Tsukhishvili and Depeyrot, *History and Coin*, 74, no. 5 and pl. 1; T. Abramishvili, "Nokalakevskii klad," *VV* 23 (1963): 158–165.

[82] T. Abramishvili, "Ochamchireshi aghmochenili sp'ilendzis bizant'iuri monet'ebi," *Akad. S. Janashias sachelobis sakartvelos sachelmts'ipo muzeumis moambe* 24-B (1963): 57–59 and pl. I/1–6.

[83] Mobile troops were clearly paid better than frontier garrisons. If any real gold was spent in the Balkans this happened precisely at times when emperors transferred professional troops to the region, as Maurice did in the 590s when the hoarding of gold clearly spikes in the northern Balkans, e.g. *Trésors*, nos. 79, 82, 243, 244, and 247.

[84] Greatrex and Lieu, eds., *The Roman Eastern*, 186–187.

[85] Abramishvili, *Sakartvelos sakhelmts'ipo (1966–1984)*, 24, no. 86 and pl. VI/86; Kropotkin, *Klady vizantiiskikh*, 43, no. 408.

[86] Kropotkin, *Klady vizantiiskikh*, 31, no. 142/2–3; Ibid., 30, no. 138/6.

[87] Rtveladze and Runich, "Novye nakhodki," 151–153 and fig. 1/3–5.

the weak defense of the region, most of his troops no doubt having been moved to the main theater of operations in the south. It is important to note that no bronze coins of Phocas are so far recorded on the eastern Black Sea coast, although there are indeed quite a few unprovenanced coins of Phocas in Georgian museums.[88] Copper coin finds are always worth highlighting. Unlike precious-metal coinage, low-value coins can tell us a lot more about Roman garrisons in the Transcaucasus and the activity of enlisted soldiers, some of them recruited locally, who received regular pay for daily needs rather than ceremonial gifts of silver and gold.

The conflict escalated to new heights at the beginning of Heraclius' reign opening a dark period in Byzantine history. Within a decade, the Persians conquered Egypt and brought a trail of destruction in Syria-Palestine and Asia Minor, while the Avars and the Slavs ravaged the Balkans. Heraclius contemplated moving the capital to Carthage but ended up by melting down church property to produce a brand new coinage – the hexagram – which he intended to use for paying the army and the administration at half the old rate.[89] The Byzantine recovery started in Transcaucasia and was made possible not only through the emperor's energetic reforms, but also by the fateful alliance with the Turks who proved decisive in shifting the balance in Heraclius' favor. After arranging a new treaty with the Avars in 620, Heraclius concentrated all his resources on the Persian front. A first major achievement was the sacking of Dvin in 624 but then the war moved to the north. Movses Dashkurantsi tells us about the emperor's diplomatic initiatives as he sought to gain the loyalty of Caucasian tribes while struggling to outmaneuver three superior Persian armies.[90] The deal with the Turks bore immediate fruit as the nomads poured through the Caspian Gates and invaded Albania in 626. Having joined his Turkish allies at Tbilisi in the spring of 627 Heraclius proceeded to the south through Armenia to achieve a final and complete victory against Persia.[91]

The coins of Heraclius found in Transcaucasia date mostly from this period of warfare. A drastic reduction in the number of copper coins bespeaks the heavy reliance on allies and mercenaries.[92] Pityus continued to receive copper issues at least until 630 but no other coins with a known finding place can be mentioned, although at least a dozen coins are

---

[88] Abramishvili, *Sakartvelos sakhelmts'ipo*, 61–62, nos. 170, 172–173, 176–180.
[89] Greatrex and Lieu, eds., *The Roman Eastern*, 187–197.   [90] Ibid., 202–205.
[91] J. Howard-Johnston, "Heraclius' Persian campaigns and the revival of the Eastern Roman Empire, 622–630," *War in History* 6, no. 1 (1999): 1–44.
[92] Cf. Tsukhishvili and Depeyrot, *History and Coin*, 24, claiming that copper coins of the seventh century "vanished in West Georgia."

preserved in Georgian museums.[93] There is only one significant find from the beginning of Heraclius' reign, the dispersed hoard of Chibati (Georgia) which contained some 2,000 gold coins of which only 124 have been preserved.[94] Much like the hoard of Maurice from Archaeopolis, which lies at a close distance to the northeast, most of the coins from Chibati are die-linked. The coins of Phocas cover almost 85 percent of the accumulation, a strong indication that the hoard was concealed at the beginning of Heraclius' reign rather than later. The hoard of Chibati suggests that both emperors were interested in cultivating the loyalty of the Lazi. Moreover, their actions can be felt on a much larger front along the northern Black Sea coast, judging by the finds from Sennaya and Starodzhereliyevskaya in Krasnodar.[95] Local imitations of Byzantine silver and gold coins of Phocas and Heraclius from the Kislovodsk basin reveal the continuity of Byzantine diplomatic initiatives in the northern Caucasus, as well as the creation of social identities and status in relation to Byzantium.[96]

Most hoards of the period were concealed in Georgia where Heraclius conducted an aggressive diplomatic activity aimed at gaining the support of the local tribes. Movses Dashkurantsi informs us that the emperor sent a letter to convince Caucasian princes to join his cause, but a lot more than clever words was needed to build an alliance. It was also here that Heraclius bought the loyalty of the Turks after pledging to "satisfy the thirst of the savage, gold-loving people of long hair," in the words of the same chronicler.[97] There are no gold coins in the region which can be dated to the 620s, aside from the *solidus* from Didi Chqoni in Lazica.[98] There are, however, many hexagrams found in Georgia, both single finds and hoards

---

[93] Abramishvili, *Sakartvelos sakhelmts'ipo*, 64–68, nos. 188–194, 196–197, 199–204, 206–211 and 213–214; Abramishvili, *Sakartvelos sakhelmts'ipo (1966–1984)*, 33, no. 127.

[94] T. Abramishvili, "Bizant'iuri okros monet'ebi (Chibatis gandzi)," in *Akad. S. Janashias sachelobis sakartvelos sachelmts'ipo muzeumis moambe* 25-B (1968): 159–176; Tsukhishvili and Depeyrot, *History and Coin*, 75–79 and pl. 2–6. We might add a contemporary hoard of Sasanian drachms from Urbnisi (Shida Kartli, Georgia) concealed after 617, for which see Tsotselia, *History and Coin*, 77.

[95] Kropotkin, *Klady vizantiiskikh*, 22, nos. 19a and 25.

[96] Rtveladze and Runich, "Novye nakhodki," 153; E. V. Rtveladze and A. P. Runich, "Nakhodki indikacii vizantiiskikh monet vblizi Kislovodska," *VV* 32 (1971): 220 and fig. 1/3; Y. A. Prokopenko, "K voprosu o Severo-Kavkazskikh podrazhaniiakh bizantiiskim monetn'im obraztsam," *Vestnik stavropol'skogo gosudarstvennogo pedagogichescogo universiteta* 1 (1995): 63–67.

[97] For the attitude of Moses of Dashkura toward nomadic peoples of the steppes, see J. Howard-Johnston, "Armenian historians of Heraclius: an examination of the aims, sources and working-methods of Sebeos and Movses Daskhurantsi," in *The Reign of Heraclius (610–641): Crisis and Confrontation*, eds. G.J. Reinink and B. H. Stolte (Leuven, 2002): 41–62.

[98] Abramishvili, *Sakartvelos sakhelmts'ipo*, 64, no. 186.

most of which concentrate in Persian Iberia rather than in Lazica. In Iberia, Heraclius had to deal with Stephen I who remained in communion with the church in Constantinople but chose a political alliance with Chosroes II.[99] Single hexagrams have been found in Iberia at Ak'ura, Ch'andrebi, Mtskheta, and Ts'ints'karo;[100] two small hoards found at Mtskheta and Sarachilo were probably concealed during the same events.[101] A third hoard of the period found at Odishi is another typical example of a political payment sent to the Lazian center of power around Archaeopolis. The hoard includes two ceremonial *siliquae* of Maurice as well as hexagrams of Heraclius dated 625–629, showing a gradual accumulation of monetary gifts by the local elite.[102] Not all finds should be associated with the war effort against Persia, as several more Byzantine coins from Georgia are clearly dated after 630 when the war was successfully concluded. A *solidus* from Ch'iora and a hexagram found in a grave from Zhebot'a date from 632–635 and 635–637, respectively and a *solidus* from Shilda dates from 641.[103] Two very large mixed silver hoards of Sasanian drachms and Byzantine hexagrams from Dedoplitskaro and Tbilisi, concealed sometime around 641 prove that wealth in Iberia still relied on the dominant presence of Sasanian coins.[104]

These developments extended to the south, in Armenia, where the concentration of silver coinage coincides with the Byzantine

---

[99] Greatrex and Lieu, eds., *The Roman Eastern*, 179 and 209.

[100] Ak'ura: Abramishvili, *Sakartvelos sakhelmts'ipo (1966–1984)*, 27, no. 92. Ch'andrebi, Mtskheta, and Ts'ints'karo: Abramishvili, *Sakartvelos sakhelmts'ipo*, 126, nos. 66–67 and 71.

[101] Kropotkin, *Klady vizantiiskikh*, 44, no. 425; Abramishvili, *Sakartvelos sakhelmts'ipo (1966–1984)*, 30, nos. 111–113 and pl. VII/111–112; Tsukhishvili and Depeyrot, *History and Coin*, 82, no. 9 and pl. 7.

[102] Tsukhishvili and Depeyrot, *History and Coin*, 81, no. 8 and pl. 6 and 29, arguing that the coins represent a homogeneous group; Abramishvili, *Sakartvelos sakhelmts'ipo (1966–1984)*, 22, n. 120; 22–31, nos. 76–77, 88, 94–102, and 119.

[103] Ch'iora and Zhebot'a: Abramishvili, *Sakartvelos sakhelmts'ipo*, 64, no. 187 and 126, no. 74. Shilda: Abramishvili, *Sakartvelos sakhelmts'ipo (1966–1984)*, 25, no. 87 and pl. VI/87. Cf. P. Somogyi, "New remarks on the flow of Byzantine coins in Avaria and Wallachia during the second half of the seventh Century," in *The Other Europe in the Middle Ages: Avars, Bulgars, Khazars and Cumans*, ed. F. Curta (Leiden, 2008), 121, arguing that the flow of Byzantine *solidi* to Lazica was interrupted after 613. Cf. Tsukhishvili and Depeyrot, *History*, 28, arguing that no gold coins of Phocas and Heraclius were found in Iberia.

[104] I. Dzhalagania, *Inozemnaia moneta v denezhnom obrashchenii Gruzii V–XIII vv.* (Tbilisi, 1979), 10–33; I. Dzhalagania, *Monety klady Gruzii: klad sasanidskikh i vizantiiskikh monet iz Tsiteli Tskaro (pervaia chast')* (Tbilisi, 1980); M. Tsotselia, *History and Coin Finds in Georgia: Sasanian and Byzantine Coins from Tsitelitskaro (AD 641)* (Wetteren, 2002), 86–87; Tsotselia, *Coin Finds*, 140, no. 742. Tsukhishvili and Depeyrot, *History and Coin*, 27, associate these hoards with trade relations trade with Byzantium. For the presence of Sasanian coins in Georgia, see Tsotselia, *History and Coin*.

counteroffensive led by Heraclius and his Turkish allies.[105] Hoards of hexagrams have been found at Iğdır, Dvin, and Grtchi.[106] The first hoard from the Persarmenian capital of Dvin ends with issues dated between 638 and 641, but the bulk of the hoard is made up of issues from 625–629, a probable reflection of mint output. The second hoard from Dvin is another example of a mixed Sasanian-Byzantine hoard in which the Persian issues are numerically superior. Heraclius was well aware of the fact that Armenian loyalties were eminently unstable given the political climate of fragmentation which had characterized Armenia since the abolishing of the monarchy in 428.[107] However, the Byzantine emperor had little time to devise a new strategy after the momentous victory against Chosroes because the rising Caliphate would soon capitalize on the weakness of the two empires. Epigraphic evidence shows that the last years of Heraclius' reign witnessed an intense campaign to attract Armenian princes by granting them honorary titles.[108] A *solidus* found at Masis dated to 641 might indicate that loyalties were bought with money, not only with titles, especially since the Arabs got dangerously close after a successful raiding of Dvin in 640.[109]

In fact, the Arab conquest of Transcaucasia was already under way despite Byzantine resistance. Constans II and Constantine IV made great efforts to maintain a foothold in Georgia and Armenia through a combination of diplomacy and warfare when internal turmoil in the Caliphate offered good opportunities for action. Coin hoards from the 650s testify to the energetic activity of Constans II in Armenia especially after Muawiya offered very generous terms in 652 should Armenian nobles decide to switch sides.[110] Only one hoard was found in Georgia, in a burned layer from a destroyed seventh-century residence in Magraneti (Georgia), comprising an almost equal number of Sasanian drachms and Byzantine hexagrams.[111] The other

---

[105] Ani: Mousheghian et al., *History (Ani)*, 77, nos. 66–73. Dvin and Yerevan: Mousheghian et al., *History (Duin)*, 63, nos. 26–51 and 197.

[106] Iğdır: Kropotkin, *Klady vizantiiskikh*, 42, no. 370. Dvin and Grtchi: Mousheghian et al., *History (Duin)*, 107–108 and pl. 9; 131–133 and pl. 9; 194–195.

[107] Thomson, "Eastern neighbours," 160. See also Whittow, *The Making of Byzantium*, 202–203.

[108] T. W. Greenwood, "A corpus of Early Medieval Armenian inscriptions," *DOP* 58 (2004): 27–91.

[109] Mousheghian et al., *History (Duin)*, 168–169; T. W. Greenwood, "Armenian neighbours: 600–1045," in *The Cambridge History*, ed. Shepard, 341; Whittow, *The Making of Byzantium*, 209–210.

[110] Greenwood, "Armenian neighbours," 342.

[111] T. Abramishvili, "Klad monet iz Magraneti," in *Numizmaticheskii sbornik: posviashchaetsia pamiati D. G. Kapanadze*, ed. V. A. Lekvinadze (Tbilisi, 1977), 73–82 and pl. VII.

four hoards were found in Armenia in the Mtkvari-Araxes interfluve, north of Dvin, at Echmiazdin, Gyumri, Kosh, and Stepanavan, and can be connected with Constans II's campaign of 654 and his general efforts to reestablish the Byzantine domination in Armenia.[112] Six single finds of hexagrams of Constans II are known from Transcaucasia, most of which were found in Georgia, rather than in Armenia as we would have expected based on the geographical distribution of hoards. Such coins were found both in Lazica, at Zugdidi (Samegrelo-Zemo Svaneti) and Ch'orvila (Imereti), and in Iberia, at At'ots'i (Shida Kartli) and Rustavi (Kvemo Kartli).[113] Bracteates struck on thin gold foil imitating *solidi* from 654–667 were found in a grave from Dzhaga (Karachayevo-Cherkesiya) evidencing continuing relations with tribes from the northern Caucasus.[114]

The Second Fitna following the death of Muawiya was promptly exploited by Constantine IV who invaded Cilicia, while the new dominant group of the northern steppe, the Khazars, invaded Armenia. Although the new caliph Abd-al Malik offered very good terms, the Byzantine position in Transcaucasia remained precarious. Despite the efforts of Justinian II to buy the loyalty of Armenian and Albanian nobles in the same manner as his predecessors, by the end of the century the Caliphate extended its influence even farther to the north.[115] Contrary to some opinions, Byzantium did not lose control of the eastern Black Sea coast until the early eighth century.[116] In 662 Constans II exiled monothelite heretics in Lazica, ecclesiastical centers were still in place at Phasis and Sebastopolis, while Smbat Bagratuni, the leader of an Armenian revolt against the Arabs, found refuge at Phasis in 705, a settlement which still had some significance.[117] Coin finds further substantiate this state of affairs. No hoards are known in Transcaucasia after 670 when the importance of the hexagram had already declined, but single finds of *solidi* of Constantine IV,

---

[112] Mousheghian et al., *History (Duin)*, 164–165 and pl. 23–24; 170 and pl. 25; 179–180; 182–183 and pl. 25.

[113] Zugdidi: Abramishvili, *Sakartvelos sakhelmts'ipo (1966–1984)*, 35–36, no. 133. Ch'orvila: Tsotselia, *Coin Finds*, 149, no. 790. At'ots'i and Rustavi: Abramishvili, *Sakartvelos sakhelmts'ipo*, 71, nos. 229 and 123, no. 33. Cf. Somogy, "New remarks," 121, who maintains that no hexagrams from the second half of the seventh century have been found in the region.

[114] Rtveladze and Runich, "Nakhodki indikacii," 220–221 and fig. 1/5–6.

[115] Greenwood, "Armenian neighbours," 344–345.

[116] Whittow, *The Making of Byzantium*, 210.

[117] Greenwood, "Armenian neighbours," 346; B. Martin-Hisard, "La domination Byzantine sur le littoral oriental du Pont Euxin (milieu du VIIe–VIIIe siècles)," *Byzantinobulgaria* 7 (1981): 144–146. A *solidus* of Justinian II from his second reign (705–711) was found at Shemokmedi (Guria, Georgia) not far from Phasis, for which see Abramishvili, *Sakartvelos sakhelmts'ipo (1966–1984)*, 37, no. 140 and pl. IX/140.

Justinian II, Leontius, and Tiberius III have been reported in Georgia and in the steppe north of the Caucasus as far as Serpovoe (Tambov, Russia).[118] The finds concentrate in Lazica but are also known in Iberia.[119] An interesting concentration of late seventh-century *solidi* can be found northeast of the Sea of Azov, on the River Don, where several cemeteries have produced single and collective finds of *solidi* of emperors from Constans II to Justinian II's second reign. The most spectacular are the graves from Podgornenskii and Salovo which seem to share a date at the turn of the eighth century, same as the single finds from Bol'shaia Orlovka, Romanovskaya, and Verbovyi Log.[120] A connection of these finds with gifts from Constantinople to the Khazar allies seems inescapable. Byzantium still had some cards to play.

In conclusion, the Transcaucasian example has provided an interesting parallel for the Balkan case, placing the coin finds from the transdanubian *barbaricum* in a wider perspective. While they did not follow a "grand strategy," Byzantine motivations and tactics in peripheral regions can be discerned through the strategic use of money to gain political advantage. The concerns may have been similar but the intensity and degree of involvement differed. In the northern *barbaricum* beyond the Danube border a cultural approach aimed at containing the barbarian threat worked best. Coin finds as well as other categories of artifacts reveal a cultural policy of inclusion as a more sustainable long-term solution for ensuring the security of the Balkans. Conversely, in Transcaucasia direct intervention and high expenditure were required to counterbalance Persian ambitions seeking conquest and cultural domination, rather than

---

[118] Abramishvili, *Sakartvelos sakhelmts'ipo*, 73–74, nos. 240–241 and 244–246; Kropotkin, *Klady vizantiiskikh*, 29, nos. 125–126.

[119] Pityus, Gvank'iti, Sukhumi, Gurjaani, and Ok'ami: Abramishvili, *Sakartvelos sakhelmts'ipo*, 72, no. 239; 73, no. 242; 74, no. 247; 127, nos. 76 and 84. Shemokmedi: Abramishvili, *Sakartvelos sakhelmts'ipo (1966–1984)*, 37, no. 140 and pl. IX/140.

[120] Podgornenskii and Verbovyi Log: S. I. Bezuglov and S. A. Naumenko, "Novye nakhodki vizantiiskikh i iranskikh importov v stepiakh Podon'ia," *Donskaia arkheologiia* 1 (1999): 35–36. Salovo: V. E. Flerova, "Podkurgannye pogrebreniia vostochnoevropeiskikh stepei i puti slozheniia kul'tury Khazarii," in *Stepi Evropy v epokhu srednevekov'ia. Khazarskoe vremia*, ed. A. V. Evgelevskii (Donetsk, 2001), 172–174, with fig. 4. Bol'shaia Orlovka: S. I. Bezuglov, "O monete iz Bol'shoi Orlovki (k ocenke datiruiushchikh vozmozhnostei)," in *Srednevekovye drevnosti Dona*, ed. I. K. Guguev (Moscow, 2007), 114–118. Romanovskaya: A. Semenov, "K vyiavleniiu central'noaziatskikh elementov v kul'ture rannesrednevekovykh kochevnikov Vostochnoi Evropy," *ASGE* 29 (1988), 109. For a general discussion, see E. V. Kruglov, "Obrashchenie vizantiiskikh monet VI–VIII vv. v vostochnoevropeiskikh stepiakh," in *Vizantiia: obshchestvo i cerkov'*, eds. S. N. Malakhov and N. D. Barabanov (Armavir, 2005), 168–177.

plunder or the mere extraction of subsidies. Viewed from the banks of the Lower Danube, the wealth showered on the Caucasian borderlands is breathtaking. Nothing of the sort had crossed the river since Attila's time and only the creation of the Avar Khaganate on the Middle Danube brought massive Byzantine wealth to the northern world. Bronze coins are dominant in *barbaricum* – the daily currency vehiculated in frontier fortresses on the Lower Danube – while Lazica, Iberia, and Armenia were heavily infused with silver and gold. There was a fierce competition between Byzantine and Sasanian money in a world dominated by opportunistic kingdoms willing to sell their allegiance to the highest bidder. No second bidder existed in the northern Balkans and Byzantine emperors were fully aware of this reality as they engineered their attitudes vis-à-vis the northern world. It was the rise of the Avars as a rival power that completely shattered the Byzantine hopes of limiting the stream of gold pouring out of its treasury.

6.2 The Carpathian Basin: The Land of Gold

6.2.1 Gepids, Lombards, Herules and the Quest for Hegemony (ca. 488–568)

The stakes were high not only in Transcaucasia but also in the Carpathian Basin, where Justinian's Italian campaign and the rise of the Avars stimulated a constant transfer of wealth. Although the history of the Carpathian Basin in the sixth century was shaped by cultural and diplomatic contact with Byzantium, the ties with the Empire were much more volatile than those established in Transcaucasia and in the Lower Danube region. Distance is one factor, as concentrations of Byzantine artifacts, especially coins, are sometimes found 750 kilometers away from the nearest Byzantine province and might have exchanged hands many times traversing a wide region populated by a mosaic of Germanic tribes (Figure 35–Figure 36). Most of the time centers of power in Central Europe might not have had direct access to Byzantine wealth. Although this appears similar to the case of the Suani or Abasgi on the foothills of the Caucasus who received stipends through the mediation of Lazi kings, Byzantine ambitions were much more limited north of the Alps. The distribution of finds reveals four geographic areas of concentration: the Tisza basin and the Middle Danube, corresponding with the core areas of the Gepid kingdom and later the Avar Khaganate, the Drava-Sava

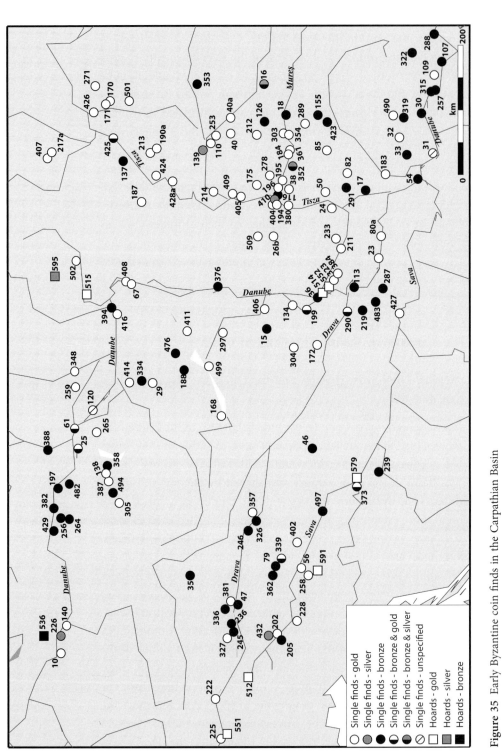

Figure 35 Early Byzantine coin finds in the Carpathian Basin. Numbers on the map refer to numbers in Appendix A.2. For Transylvania, see Figure 26.

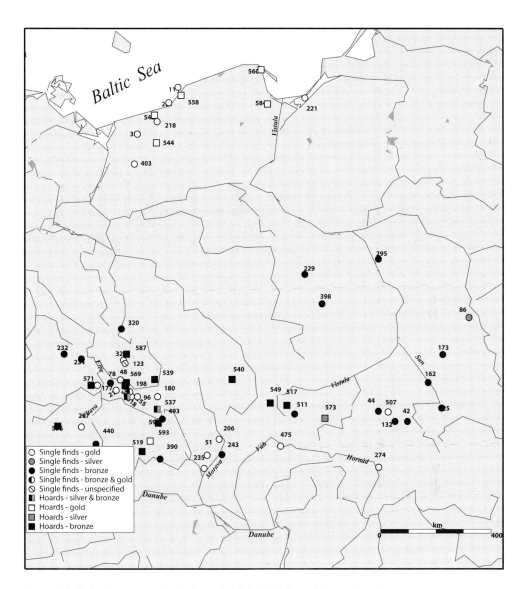

Figure 36 Early Byzantine coin finds north of the Middle and Upper Danube
Numbers on the map refer to numbers in Appendix A.2.

interfluve, an important area of contact between the Empire and *barbaricum*, and the Upper Danube region and Bohemia at the confluence between the late Germanic and early Slavic worlds.

Another distinctive factor is chronology, a somewhat arbitrarily defined unit of analysis but a good indicator of major trends and developments. From a historical perspective the flow of Byzantine coins to the Carpathian Basin can be divided into two major stages, ca. 488–568 and ca. 568–680, respectively. The first stage can be further subdivided into two phases, from

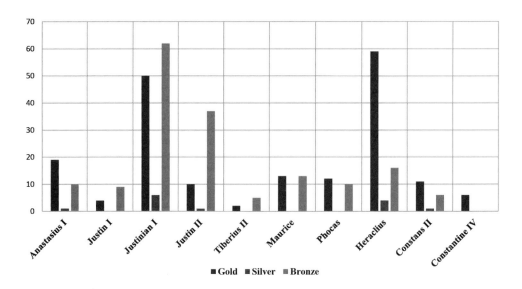

Figure 37 Early Byzantine coin finds in the Carpathian Basin (491–680)

488 when Theodoric the Great took the Ostrogoths to Italy until 535 when Justinian launched his Italian campaign, and from 535 to 568 when the Avars settled in the Middle Danube region and the Lombards migrated to Italy. The second stage is marked by the Avar hegemony in the Carpathian Basin and can be itself subdivided in at least two distinct phases corresponding to the so-called Early and Middle Avar periods, whose transition is marked by the failed siege of Constantinople in 626.

More than anything, political developments in Italy and the western Balkans dictated the nature of contact between Byzantium and the peoples of Central Europe during the sixth and seventh centuries, which often presupposed the typical combination of warfare and diplomatic maneuvers – gifts, stipends, and tribute. This is best reflected in the ratio between gold and copper coins (Figure 37). Four-to-five times more Byzantine gold is to be found in Central Europe than in the Lower Danube region, at the expense of the base metal coinage whose influx always depended on a permanent Byzantine presence (Appendix B, Table 2). The absence of a true hegemonic power in Central and Eastern Europe between the dissolution of Attila's confederation and the rise of the Avar Khaganate made the Carpathian Basin fertile ground for diplomatic initiatives.[121] In the course of the sixth century Herules, Lombards, and Gepids received political

---

[121] A. Sarantis, "War and diplomacy in Pannonia and the Northwest Balkans during the reign of Justinian. The Gepid threat and imperial responses," *DOP* 63 (2009): 15–40.

stipends and served as *foederati* or *symmachoi* in campaigns led by Byzantine emperors on three different continents. In addition, men from smaller or less articulated communities from Central Europe which did not always capture the interest of contemporary chroniclers were attracted by the chance to make one's fortune in successful warfare. The age of Justinian in particular presented many such opportunities, closer to home in northern Italy and Dalmatia or further away in North Africa and in Persia. It comes as no surprise that Procopius complained about the blurring of the traditional distinction between Roman *stratiotai* and barbarian *foederati*.[122]

After the battle of Nedao (454), the Gepids became masters of the regions east of the Middle Danube, into Transylvania and southward to the Lower Danube. At the same time, the Ostrogoths were allowed to settle in Pannonia but their contacts extended further north. A large quantity of *solidi* reached Pomerania, the Baltic islands, and Scandinavia in the second half of the fifth century only to end abruptly after the reign of Anastasius on the Baltic coast of Poland and perhaps a few decades later in Scandinavia.[123] As well as single finds of *solidi*, hoards of *solidi* ending with issues of Anastasius have been found in Poland at Karsibór, Małechowo, and Trąbki Małe.[124] A hoard found at Karlino included *solidi* of Anastasius and also Scandinavian bracteates and jewelry.[125] In addition, a large hoard of 150 gold coins from Mrzezino, included 130 issues of Anastasius – original *solidi* and Ostrogothic imitations – hinting at the fact that most of the gold was channeled to the Baltic through the mediation of the Ostrogoths, the main recipients of Byzantine subsidies.[126] D. M. Metcalf's hypothesis that the gold primarily illustrates commerce in furs on the Baltic is less

---

[122] Procopius, *Bella*, 1.11.3–4. On the barbarization of the army under Justinian, see A. Kaldellis, "Classicism, barbarism, and warfare: Prokopios and the conservative reaction to Later Roman military policy," *American Journal of Ancient History* 3–4 (2004–2005): 189–218.

[123] R. Ciołek, "Der Zufluss von Solidi in die südlichen Ostseegebiete," in *Byzantine Coins*, 217–230; H. Horsnaes, "Late Roman and Byzantine coins found in Denmark," in *Byzantine Coins*, 231–270; I. Hammarberg, B. Malmer, and T. Zachrisson, *Byzantine Coins Found in Sweden* (London, 1989).

[124] Karsibór: R. Ciołek, "Znaleziska monet rzymskich z terenów Pomorza przechowywanie w zbiorach Muzeum Kulturalno-Historycznego w Stralsundzie," *Wiadomości Numizmatyczne* 43 (1999): 176. Małechowo and Trąbki Małe: J. Iluk, "Bałtycki epizod wczesnobizantyskich dziejów. Znaleziska solidów na Pomorzu Nadwiślańskim z V–VI wieku," in *Gdańsk średniowieczny w świetle najnowszych badań archeologicznych i historycznych*, ed. H. Paner (Gdańsk, 1998), 57.

[125] Iluk, "Bałtycki epizod," 57.

[126] R. Ciołek, "Skarb złotych monet z Mrzezina (Gm. Puck) a zespół z Brzezina Gdańskiego," *Wiadomości Numizmatyczne* 42 (1998): 59–60.

convincing, although it may be part of the larger picture.[127] On the other hand, Renata Ciołek was right to assume that Byzantine gold coins in Pomerania reflect contacts within the Germanic world rather than direct connections to Byzantium.[128]

In fact, there is an uninterrupted chain of gold *solidi* and *tremisses* of Anastasius and Justin I running from the Baltic to the Adriatic coast. South of Poland the large concentration of finds in the Czech Republic can be attributed to the Lombard influence in Bohemia and perhaps also to the Thuringians on the Elbe.[129] Few coins have been found in archaeological context, but at least the *solidus* from Lužice comes from a cemetery dating from the migration period. To be sure, the cemetery remained in use for some time as testified by a *tremissis* of Justinian with a suspension loop found in a princely burial.[130] A *tremissis* with suspension loop of Anastasius found at Chotusice in the nineteenth century may have also belonged to a destroyed grave.[131] Four other gold coins from Anastasius and Justin I found in the Czech Republic and Slovakia indicate that the region became strategically important for Byzantium, especially after the Lombards defeated the Herules in 508 and positioned themselves as potential adversaries of the Ostrogoths in Italy.[132] The gold trail meanders east and south into the territory ruled by the Gepids and the Ostrogoths, respectively. An early *solidus* of Anastasius from Balotaszállás (492–507), another *solidus* from the same period found in a grave from the Gepid cemetery in Kiszombor, and a ceremonial silver *miliarense* from a Gepid grave in Szőreg (all in Hungary) reflect political payments sent to the Gepid center in the Tisza-Mureş interfluve or perhaps booty taken from

---

[127] D. M. Metcalf, "Viking-Age numismatics 1: Late Roman and Byzantine gold in the northern lands," *NC* 155 (1995): 413–441.

[128] Ciołek, "Der Zufluss von Solidi," 224–26. See also Iluk, "Bałtycki epizod," 51–63; See also F. Curta, *The Making of the Slavs: History and Archaeology of the Lower Danube Region, c. 500–700* (Cambridge, 2001), 195–196.

[129] E. Droberjar, "À propos des contacts entre l'empire d'Orient et les germans de l'Elbe au VIe siècle," in *Pontic-Danubian Realm*, 297–316.

[130] J. Militký, "Finds of the Early Byzantine coins of the 6th and 7th century in the territory of the Czech Republic," in *Byzantine Coins*, 378–379, no. M28/1–2 (grave 55 and 113).

[131] Ibid., 367, no. C2.

[132] The best surveys on the Lombards remain N. Christie, *The Lombards: The Ancient Longobards* (Cambridge, MA, 1995); K. Christou, *Byzanz und die Langobarden: von der Ansiedlung in Pannonien bis zur endgültigen Anerkennung (500–680)* (Athens, 1991). See also recently, G. Ausenda, P. Delogu, and C. Wickham, eds., *The Langobards Before the Frankish Conquest: An Ethnographic Perspective* (Rochester, NY, 2009). For sixth-century Longobards, see W. Pohl, "The Empire and the Lombards: treaties and negotiations in the sixth century," in *Kingdoms of the Empire: The Integration of Barbarians in Late Antiquity*, ed. W. Pohl (Leiden, 1997), 75–134.

Illyricum by the Gepids led by Mundus.[133] Finds extend to the west into Bosnia, Croatia, and especially into Slovenia, closer to Italy, where four single finds of *solidi* and *tremisses* of Anastasius are known, possibly related to the Ostrogoths and the migration of various groups of Herules after their defeat in 508.[134]

The influx of gold was followed by a more modest penetration of copper coinage. A half-*follis* found together with Gepid pottery in a grave from Dorobanți and another one found in unknown circumstances at Gherla in Transylvania might signal connections with Byzantine fortresses on the Danube where such small change was handled more frequently.[135] Bronze coins of Anastasius and Justin I are not absent from Central Europe, with finds recorded at Kolín and Předlánce (Czech Republic), Štúrovo (Slovakia), Staasdorf and Reisberg (Austria), and further west on the Upper Danube, but they tend to concentrate in the western Balkans, south of the Drava or in the sector of the Roman *limes* between Singidunum and the Iron Gates, where such coins were more readily available from Byzantine fortresses.[136]

The age of Justinian brought the opening of an important war front in Italy and renewed political alliances meant to isolate the Ostrogoths and secure the frontier of the Balkans. Already in 526 the Lombards took over

---

[133] Byzantine emperors started to send annual subsidies to the Gepids after the dissolution of the Hunnic confederation, for which see Jordanes, *Getica,* 264, *annua sollemnia*. Coin finds at Balotaszállás: A. Kiss, "Régészeti és numizmatikai adatok a Duna-Tisza-köz 5. század második felének és a 6. század első felének településtörténetéhez," *MFMÉ* 4 (1998): 191. Kiszombor: D. Csallány, *Archäologische Denkmäler der Gepiden im Mitteldonaubecken* (Budapest, 1961), 174; pl. CXV/11. Szőreg: J. Cseh, et al., *Gepidische Gräberfelder im Theissgebiet II* (Budapest, 2005), 123. On Mundus' career, see B. Croke, "Mundo the Gepid: from freebooter to Roman general," *Chiron* 12 (1982): 125–135. For the cultural fabric of the region at the beginning of the sixth century, see J. Terjal, "Cultural or ethnic changes? Continuity and discontinuity on the Middle Danube ca AD 500," in *Pontic-Danubian Realm*, 115–188.

[134] P. Kos, "The monetary circulation in the Southeastern Alpine region ca 300 BC–AD 1000," *Situla* 24 (1984–1985): 226, nos. 1–4 (finds from Ljubljana, Mokronog, Studeno, and Trbinc). For the Herules, see Sarantis, "The Justinianic Herules," 361–402.

[135] Csallány, *Archäologische Denkmäler*, 145, 292, and pl. CCLXXII/2; A.-M. Velter, *Transilvania în secolele V–XII. Interpretări istorico-politice și economice pe baza descoperirilor monetare din bazinul Carpatic, secolele V-XII* (Bucharest, 2002), 291, no. 53.

[136] Kolín and Předlánce: Militký, "Finds," 367, no. C4 and 374–375, no. C19. Štúrovo: A. Fiala, "Byzantské mince na Slovensku (6.-12. storočie)," *Slovenská Numizmatika* 10 (1989): 57, no. 3. Staasdorf and Reisberg: W. Hahn, "Die Fundmünzen des 5.–9. Jahrhunderts in Österreich und den unmittelbar angrenzenden Gebieten," in *Die Geburt Mitteleuropas. Geschichte Österreichs vor seiner Entstehung, 378–907*, ed. H. Wolfram (Vienna, 1987), 455 and 458. For the upper Danube, see J. Drauschke, "Byzantinische Münzen des ausgehenden 5. bis beginnenden 8. Jahrhunderts in den östlichen Regionen des Merowingerreiches," in *Byzantine Coins*, 288, fig. 12.

Pannonia and rapidly strengthened their position taking advantage of Gothic instability after Theodoric's death; it is likely that the move was orchestrated with the tacit approval of Byzantium.[137] Securing the western Balkans as a bridge between Thracia, Illyricum, and Italy became of paramount importance for Justinian as war broke out in Italy in 535. Diplomatic initiatives targeted all the important groups from the Carpathian Basin – the Gepids, the Herules, and the Lombards. It is possible that they all received occasional stipends from Byzantium, especially since Justinian repeatedly exercised his ability to play off one barbarian group against another. A notable example is the emperor's decision in 547 to stop paying off the Gepids and instead to bestow on the Lombards lands in Pannonia and Noricum as well as "a very large amount of money."[138] His alliance with the Herules settled in the area of Singidunum had already been sealed two decades before this event when the Herul king was baptized in Constantinople and left home with many gifts, not before Justinian reiterated his intention to call on the Herules when their military assistance would be required.[139]

From an archaeological perspective the Herules are still hard to trace.[140] The same cannot be said about the Gepids who left a deep cultural imprint in the archaeological record of Transylvania and the Tisza valley, giving weight to Jordanes' identification of the region as *Gepidia*.[141] Justinian's relations with the Gepids fluctuated depending on the balance of power in *barbaricum*, the emperor's agenda in the western Balkans, and the Gepids' own ambitions after they reconquered the important city of Sirmium (536). The nature of the numismatic evidence suggests that subsidies or occasional gifts were sent to the Gepid centers of power in Transylvania and Banat. Two lightweight *solidi* customarily used in political payments

---

[137] Christie, *The Lombards*, 34–35. [138] Procopius, *Bella*, 7.33.10: χρήμασι μεγάλοις.
[139] Sarantis, "The Justinianic Herules," 373–374.
[140] V. Ivanišević and M. Kazanski, "Geruly Iustiniana v Severnom Illirikume i ikh arheologicheskie sledy," *Stratum plus* (2010), no. 5: 141–157.
[141] Jordanes, *Getica*, 74. For "Gepidia" see also Geographus Ravennas, *Cosmographia*, 4.14. On the Gepids, see I. Bóna, "Gepiden in Siebenbürgen, Gepiden an der Theiss," *AAASH* 23, nos. 1–2 (1979): 9–50; W. Pohl, "Die Gepiden und die Gentes an der mittleren Donau nach dem Zerfall des Attilareiches," in *Die Völker an der mittleren und unteren Donau im fünften und sechsten Jahrhundert*, eds. H. Wolfram and F. Daim (Vienna, 1980), 239–305; A. Khraralambieva, "Gepids in the Balkans: a survey of the archaeological evidence," in *Neglected Barbarians*, 245–262. The evidence from western Banat is less convincing, for which see V. Ivanišević and I. Bugarski, "Western Banat during the Great Migration Period," in *The Turbulent Epoch: New Materials from the Late Roman Period and the Migration Period*, eds. B. Niezabitowska-Wiśniewska, P. Łuczkiewicz, and S. Sadowski (Lublin, 2008), 58.

have been found at Gyula and Banatski Karlovac, both dated 538–542.[142] Three rare ceremonial silver pieces have been found at Gheorghe Doja and Lăureni, in the upper Mureș valley, and in an unspecified location in Arad County.[143] The Mureș region was dominated by the important settlement of Morești, perhaps a Gepid center of power in Transylvania.[144] As we have seen in the case of Transcaucasia, such silver coins reflect diplomatic gifts, less valuable than gold but more indicative of the emperor's intentions as they had a pronounced ceremonial function.

Two gold coins from Vădaș and Sângeorgiu de Câmpie, two other from unspecified locations in Mureș County, and a *solidus* which was perhaps part of a large hoard found at Apalina are fragments of the wealth accumulated by the Gepid elite.[145] An additional hoard (ca. one hundred *solidi* and jewelry) attributed to the Gepids was found at Șeica Mică (Sibiu, Romania), but only 36 coins have been preserved with the most recent struck for Justin I.[146] Further west, a *solidus* of Justinian was found in a Gepid grave from Bočar (North Banat, Serbia).[147] Copper coins found occasionally in Transylvania were probably brought by those Gepids who served in the garrisons defending the Danube frontier or on distant theaters as suggested by a twelve-*nummia* issue from Alexandria found at Timișoara.[148] The gold coins found in unknown circumstances in several other locations in Transylvania reflect redistributions in the Gepid

---

[142] D. Tănase, "Piese de aur din epoca migrațiilor în colecția Muzeului Banatului din Timișoara," in *Între stepă și Imperiu. Studii în onoarea lui Radu Harhoiu*, eds. A. Măgureanu and F. Gáll (Bucharest, 2010), 147, fig. 2/5a–b; E. Oberländer-Târnoveanu, "Tranziția de la antichitate la evul mediu timpuriu la marginea imperiului (II). De la prima dispariție a circulației monetare la renașterea ei în zona Porților de Fier ale Dunării (circa 375–565)," *Muzeul Național* 16 (2004): 69–70, n. 72.

[143] Gheorghe Doja: V. Lazăr, *Repertoriul arheologic al județului Mureș* (Târgu Mureș, 1995), 133, no. XXVI.1. Lăureni: A. Lakatos, "Monede bizantine din perioada avară în Transilvania, vestul și nord-vestul României." *EN* 12 (2002): 248, no. 13. Arad County: Oberländer-Târnoveanu, "Tranziția de la antichitate," 69–70, n. 72.

[144] K. Horedt, *Morești. Grabungen in einer vor- und frühgeschichtlichen Siedlung in Siebenbürgen* (Bucharest, 1979).

[145] Vădaș, Sângeorgiu de Câmpie, and Mureș County: Lakatos, "Monede bizantine," 248, no. 15 and no. 20; 250, no. 26. Apalina: I. Winkler, "Despre activitatea numismatică a lui Michael Pap Szatmári (1747–1812)," *SCN* 3 (1960): 440.

[146] P. Somogyi, "Der Fund von Kleinschelken (Siebenbürgen, 1856) im Lichte neuentdeckter Archivdaten," in *Byzantine Coins*, 417–448.

[147] D. Dimitrijević and M. Girić, "Pesak près de Bočar, nécropole gépide," in *Époque préhistorique et protohistorique en Yougoslavie – Recherches et résultats*, ed. G. Novak et al. (Belgrade, 1971), 191.

[148] Lakatos, "Monede bizantine," 252, no. 44B.

kingdom, some perhaps resulting from a new agreement negotiated in 552 on the eve of a new offensive in Italy.[149]

Gepids, Herules, and Lombards served in the Roman armies of Belisarius and Narses in Italy and some crumbs of wealth accumulated in the service of the Empire are reflected in coin finds from their homeland. One method of tracing their movement is by looking at the mints issuing the coins found in the Carpathian Basin. Finds of coins from the Italian mints of Rome and Ravenna are recorded as far north as Poland. A quarter-*siliqua* from Ravenna was found in an unspecified location in Slovenia and a *tremissis* comes from a grave in Rifnik.[150] More silver Byzantine coins from Italy have been reported in Bavaria where the interests of Romans, Franks, and Ostrogoths collided during the age of Justinian.[151] Bronze *decanummia* from Rome have been found at Sisak (Croatia), Lovosice (Czech Republic), and Przemyśl (Poland) and two twelve-*nummia* issues from Alexandria at Osijek (Croatia) and Stillfried (Austria).[152] Regardless of their ethnic background, men from Central European lands were attracted by warfare in Italy. The fact that many of these coins are small denominations, as are other finds from eastern mints such as the *pentanummia* found at Vienna and Osijek and the already mentioned *decanummium* from Przemyśl, suggests direct access to urban markets.[153] This is not to say that the large *folles* of Justinian, so popular north of the Lower Danube, are absent in the Carpathian Basin. On the

---

[149] Beclean and Vețel: Lakatos, "Monede bizantine," 247, no. 3 and 250, no. 27. Cetea: Velter, *Transilvania*, 289, no. 23. Oarda de Jos: V. Suciu, "Noi descoperiri monetare în județul Alba," *Apulum* 38 (2001): 256 and fig. 2. Pecica: Oberländer-Târnoveanu, "Tranziția de la antichitate," 69, n. 72. Șomcuta Mare: E. Chirilă and A. Socolan, *Tezaure și descoperiri monetare din colecția Muzeului județean Maramureș* (Baia Mare, 1971), 67, no. 9 with pl. IX/10 and pl. XI/2.

[150] P. Kos, *Die Fundmünzen der römischen Zeit in Slowenien*, vol. III (Berlin, 1988), 583, no. 2; L. Bolta, *Rifnik pri Šenturju. Poznoantična naselbina in grobišče* (Ljubljana, 1981), 36 and pl. 17/10.

[151] Drauschke, "Byzantinische Fundmünzen," 289, fig 14 and 294, fig. 18.

[152] Sisak: I. Mirnik and A. Šemrov, "Byzantine coins in the Zagreb Archaeological Museum numismatic collection. Anastasius I (AD 497–518) – Anastasius II (AD 713–715)," *Vjesnik Arheološkog muzeja u Zagrebu* 30–31 (1997–1998): 166, no. 329. Lovosice: Militký, "Finds," 371, no. C14. Przemyśl: M. Wołoszyn, "Byzantinische Münzen aus dem 6.–7. Jh. in Polen," in *Byzantine Coins*, 504, no. 14. Osijek: H. Göricke-Lukić, "Justinijanov novac iz Slavonije i Baranje," in *Radovi XIII. Međunarodnog kongresa za starokršćansku arheologija. Split-Poreč (25.9–1.10.1994)*, vol. II, eds. N. Cambi and E. Marin (Split, 1998), 1154, no. 44. Stillfried: H. Winter, "Die byzantinischen und karolingischen Fundmünzen aus dem österreichischen Bereich der Avaria – eine Neubearbeitung," in *Byzantine Coins*, 341, no. 7 and 351, fig. 6/20.

[153] Winter, "Die byzantinischen," 343, no. 12b/1; Göricke-Lukić, "Justinijanov novac," 1151, no. 20.

contrary, such coins are the most common Justinianic issues from Slovenia to Poland.[154]

The purses of soldiers fighting in Italy and perhaps political payments sent from Constantinople or redistributed in bilateral relations between different tribes in *barbaricum* are also reflected in single finds and hoards of gold coins. *Tremisses*, which became the standard gold denomination of Italy and the western kingdoms, unlike the case of Transcaucasia and the Lower Danube where they are rare finds, are well represented and their frequency increases as one moves westward from the Middle Danube to Bavaria.[155] Two hoards from Slovenia and Croatia, found at Vrh Pri Pahi and Sisak, respectively, included Byzantine issues as well as Lombard imitations after coins of Justinian, either betraying the ethnic background of the owner or the source of accumulation.[156]

Silver pieces with no real monetary function in the Byzantine economy support the interpretation offered for the flow of gold to these regions. The two silver *miliarensia* found at Rabka-Zdrój (Poland) have a ceremonial nature and date from the initial stage of the war in Italy, although they may be also connected with developments in *barbaricum* occasioned by the migration of the Lombards southward into Pannonia. Unfortunately, not enough is known about the circumstances of the find but both coins were struck with the same pair of dies. They were likely part of a larger payment received during an

---

[154] Rifnik (Slovenia): Kos, "The monetary circulation," 226, no. 15. Vinkovci (Croatia): Göricke-Lukić, "Justinijanov novac," 1150, no. 11. Bjelovar (Croatia): Mirnik and Šemrov, "Byzantine coins," 211, no. 3. Týn Nad Vltavou and Maratice (Czech Republic): Militký, "Finds," 371, no. C12 and 380, no. M30. Żywiec and Przemyśl (Poland): Wołoszyn, "Byzantinische Fundmünzen," 503, no. 12 and 506–507, no. 20. Mitterndorf, Klosterneuburg, and Carnuntum (Austria): Winter, "Die byzantinischen," 337, no. 1/9 and 340, no. 2, 4; 350, fig. 6/17–18.

[155] Osijek (Croatia): Göricke-Lukić, "Justinijanov novac," 1149, no. 2. Sisak (Croatia): Mirnik and Šemrov, "Byzantine coins," 149, no. 79. Rifnik (Slovenia): Bolta, *Rifnik*, 36 and pl. 17/1. Kranj (Slovenia): V. Stare, *Kranj. Nekropola iz časa preseljevanja ljudstev* (Ljubljana, 1980), 107. Tolisa (Bosnia and Herzegovina): Mirnik and Šemrov, "Byzantine coins," 149, no. 84. Pécs (Hungary): Winter, "Die byzantinischen," 346, no. 18 and 352, fig. 6/25. Pulst and St Paul im Lavanttal (Austria): Hahn, "Die Fundmünzen," 455. Eisenstadt (Austria): Winter, "Die byzantinischen," 344, no. 13 and 351, fig. 6/21. Lužice (Czech Republic): Militký, "Finds," 378–379, no. M28/2. For finds in Bavaria, see Drauschke, "Byzantinische Fundmünzen," 285, fig. 8.

[156] Ž. Demo, *Ostrogothic Coinage from Collections in Croatia, Slovenia and Bosnia & Herzegovina* (Ljubljana, 1994), 227 and 229–231. Additional gold hoards concealed during the reign of Justinian have been found at Kötschach-Laas (Austria) and Zašovice (Czech Republic), for which see Hahn, "Die Fundmünzen," 454; Militký, "Finds," 379–380, no. M. 29.

official visit to the Byzantine capital.[157] Diplomatic payments could be later redistributed as gifts down the social ladder in *barbaricum*.

The density of finds in the Czech Republic, Bohemia in particular, is perhaps the most intriguing development of this period. As well as six single finds of gold and copper coins, the region yielded no less than six hoards concealed during the reign of Justinian.[158] Although most of the hoards were found accidentally and subsequently dispersed, the available material still offers a suggestive picture of the kind of coins handled in the region. Except for the hoard from Žďár nad Sázavou, all other hoards include ancient Roman coins along with Early Byzantine issues.[159] The hoard from Hradec Králové includes a *decanummium* from 540/1 and so does the hoard of 26 bronze coins from Prague, ending with a *decanummium* from Carthage dated to the same year.[160] Interestingly, the earliest coin in the hoard is a first-century issue of Augustus. Only two coins have been retrieved from the hoard found at Žinkovy, but one is a *decanummium* minted in Ravenna in the 540s.[161] Finally, a hoard of 17 coppers from Turnov is comprised of small Late Roman pieces (AE4) including a Vandal imitation, a small-module half-*follis* of Anastasius, and two *decanummia* of Justinian.[162]

A few conclusions emerge from this enumeration. The owners of such small-value accumulations obviously had access to pocket change and perhaps deliberately selected small pieces for hoarding. Some have associated their deposition with ritual practice or with monetary transactions restricted to the elite, but neither seems plausible.[163] They were more likely exotic souvenirs brought by barbarian soldiers returning home eager to display and share their experience accumulated in the urban culture of the Mediterranean world. Indeed, most of these hoards betray a Mediterranean origin due to the presence of coins from Rome, Ravenna, and Carthage.

---

[157] Wołoszyn, "Byzantinische Fundmünzen," 504–505, no. 16 and 508, figs. 6–7. Another silver coin of Justinian was found in Poland at Chełm, but the exact circumstances of the find are uncertain; see 500, no. 4.

[158] An additional hoard found at Červený Hrádek was made of 20 coins of which only seven survive; the latest coin was struck for Justin I, but the hoard may in fact belog to the same horizon of hoards buried during the age of Justinian; see Militký, "Finds," 368–369, no. C7.

[159] Ibid., 380, no. M31.   [160] Ibid., 370–371, no. C11 and 369–370, no. C10.

[161] Ibid., 369, no. C9.

[162] Ibid., 362 and 371–373, no. C15. The hoard was placed in connection with a Prague-type Slavic settlement, for which see N. Profantová, "Die frühslavische Besiedlung Böhmens und archäologische Spuren der Kontakte zum früh- und mittelawarischen sowie merowingischen Kulturkreis," in *Kulturwandel in Mitteleuropa. Langobarden, Awaren, Slawen*, eds. J. Bemmann and M. Schmauder (Bonn, 2008), 628–631.

[163] Profantová, "Die frühslavische Besiedlung," 365.

Contemporary hoards from North Africa and Italy are often large accumulations of small change reflecting the nature of the local monetary economy and it is conceivable that the similar but comparatively smaller hoards from the Czech Republic constitute groups of coins acquired by mercenaries either hired in Justinian's armies or attracted to the Gothic cause.[164] An ethnic attribution of these finds is notoriously difficult and Czech scholars prefer the neutral label "late Germanic phase," although a more direct connection with the Lombards or groups associated with them is quite probable.[165]

6.2.2 The Avar Pursuit of Byzantine Wealth (ca. 568–680)

The rise of the Avar Khaganate overturned the balance of power in the Carpathian Basin. As early as 558 the Avars sent an embassy to Constantinople seeking an alliance and returned home with "cords worked with gold, couches, silken garment and a great many other objects."[166] Such precious gifts turned out to be only the preamble to the tons of gold absorbed by the Khaganate after the Avars migrated to the Middle Danube a decade later. An annual tribute of 80,000 *solidi* was agreed upon in 574. An Avar offensive in the Balkans brought an increase of the tribute to 100,000 *solidi* in 585 and to 120,000 in 598. The treaty of 604 as well as the negotiations later conducted by Heraclius incurred an additional increase of the tribute; the emperor finally ended up agreeing to a staggering 200,000 *solidi* in 623 when he desperately needed peace in the Balkans to stage his counteroffensive in the East.[167]

---

[164] For the hoarding of Early Byzantine small change together with ancient Greek and Roman coins, see recently F. Curta and A. Gandila, "Hoards and hoarding patterns in the Early Byzantine Balkans," *DOP* 65–66 (2012): 59–62.

[165] Christie, *The Lombards*, 65. See also D. Quast, "Die Langobarden in Mähren und im nördlichen Niederösterreich – ein Diskussionsbeitrag," in *Archaeology of Identity – Archäologie der Identität*, eds. W. Pohl and M. Mehofer (Vienna, 2009), 93–110; Z. Loskotová, "Lombard burial grounds and graves of social elites north of the Middle Danube in the light of recent research," in *Macht des Goldes, Gold der Macht. Herrschafts- und Jenseitsrepräsentation zwischen Antike und Frühmittelalter im mittleren Donauraum. Akten des 23. internationalen Symposiums der Grundprobleme der frühgeschichtlichen Entwicklung im mittleren Donauraum, Tengelic, 16.–19.11.2011*, eds. M. Hardt and O. Heinrich-Tamáska (Weinstadt, 2013), 321–338.

[166] Menander, *Historia*, fr. 5.2 (trans. Blockley): παραχρῆμα τά τε δῶρα ἔστελλεν, σειράς τε χρθσῷ διαπεποικιλμένας καὶ κλίνας ἐσθῆτάς τε στηρικάς καὶ ἕτερα πλεῖστα ἐκμαλθακῶσαι οἷά τε ὄντα ἀλαζομενείας ἀνάπλεα φρονήματα.

[167] J. Iluk, "The export of gold from the Roman Empire to barbarian countries from the 4th to the 6th centuries," *Münstersche Beiträge zur antiken Handelsgeschichte* 4, no. 1 (1985): 93; Pohl, *Die Awaren*, 502 for yearly tribute and 398, n. 32, for total estimations, with the previous literature on the subject.

Historians generally agree that some six million *solidi* (ca. 27 tons of gold) were sent to *Avaria* between 568 and 626. Part of this gold was kept in the royal treasury of the khagan and some of the wealth accumulated in this period might have been seized by Charlemagne in 796. Einhard states that "all the money and treasure they had been hoarding for a long time was seized," which might be taken as a reference to the Byzantine *solidi* accumulated in the Early Avar period.[168] Some of the tribute, however, was promptly distributed by the khagan to his warrior elite. Many coins were probably melted down to produce the spectacular jewelry often found in Avar-age cemeteries, while others ended up as "Charon's obol" in graves, or were remodeled into finger rings or pendants.[169] In any case, gold became the quintessential symbol of elevated social status in the Avar world.

Within a decade after their arrival in Pannonia, the Avars emerged as the hegemonic power of the Carpathian Basin. Already in 566 the Lombard king Alboin renewed hostilities with the Gepids and achieved a decisive victory. The diplomatic initiatives related to this conflict would have long-term consequences for the Danube region. Justin II first backed the Gepids on account of Cunimund's promise to cede Sirmium to the Empire, but his failure to deliver after an initial joint success against the Lombards resulted in a neutral stance adopted by the angered emperor in the final stage of the conflict. The defeated Lombards were forced to seek the alliance of the Avars, themselves eager to gain a foothold in the western Balkans.[170] The might of the Avars and possibly other political calculations led Alboin to

---

[168] Einhard, *Vita Karoli Magni*, 13: *omnis pecunia et congesti ex longo tempore thesauri direpti sunt*. The *Annales Regni Francorum* (796) is even more specific: *thesaurum priscorum regum multa seculorum prolixitate collectum domno regi Carolo ad Aquis palatium misit*. For a discussion of the contemporary sources regarding the Avar treasure, see E. Tóth, "Die awarische Schatzkammer und die Franken," in *Thesaurus Avarorum. Régészeti tánulmanyok Garam Éva tiszteletére*, ed. T. Vida (Budapest, 2012), 773–782. See also J. B. Ross, "Two neglected Paladins of Charlemagne: Erich of Friuli and Gerold of Bavaria," *Speculum* 20 (1945): 221–222.

[169] A. Kiss, "Die Goldfunde des Karpatenbeckens vom 5.–10. Jahrhundert (Angaben zu den Vergleichsmöglichkeiten der schriftlichen und archäologischen Quellen)," *AAASH* 38 (1986): 105–145. On coins as *obolus*, see É. Garam, "A közép avarkor sírobolussal keltezhető leletköre," *ArchÉrt* 105 (1978): 206–216; I. Boná, "Studien zum frühawarischen Reitergrab von Szegvár," *AAASH* 32 (1980): 83–86. For the Avar thirst for Byzantine gold and its social implications, see also M. Hardt, "The nomad's greed for gold: from the fall of the Burgundians to the Avar treasure," in *The Construction of Communities in the Early Middle Ages: Texts, Resources and Artefacts*, eds. R. Corradini, M. Diesenberger, and H. Reimitz (Leiden, 2003), 98–107.

[170] Christou, *The Lombards*, 98–106; Pohl, "The Empire and the Lombards," 96–98. On diplomacy, see F. Wozniak, "Byzantine diplomacy and the Lombardic–Gepid wars," *BS* 20

Italy and it is perhaps now that the Lombards gained direct control over the important fortresses in Slovenia. Although Justinian granted them the entire region north of Dalmatia, Byzantine copper coin finds from settlements such as Rifnik, Ptuj, Sempeter, and Celje are more abundant in the period before 568. They are dominated by small change, *decanummia* and half-*folles*, some of them minted at Rome and Salona, indicating a connection with the war effort. The hoard of *solidi* from Arnoldstein in Carinthia, which included imitations after *solidi* of Justinian and a lightweight *solidus* of 22 *siliquae* from Ravenna, was probably concealed during the events leading to the Lombard conquest of northern Italy.[171]

The Gepid kingdom pulverized after Cunimund's death on the battlefield, but Gepid cultural identity survived in a modified form under the rule of the Avars in Transylvania and western Hungary.[172] Few gold coins of Justin II have been found in a clear Avar context, in graves from Șpălnaca, Szentendre, and Kölked-Feketekapu and provide a *terminus post quem* for the dating of those complexes to the Early Avar period.[173] Two times as many copper coins have been found in *Avaria* and Justin II is in fact the only Avar-age emperor whose copper coins are more abundant than his *solidi*.[174] The early years of the Khaganate on the Middle Danube were marked by Justin II's stubborn refusal to continue paying the tribute, a policy also visible in the lands north of the Lower Danube where his gold coins are very rare, as we have seen in the previous chapter.

The Byzantine recovery of Sirmium and the Gepid presence in Pannonia facilitated the distribution of copper coins to the north. Some of these coins are clearly connected with the military, such as the *follis* issued by a mobile

---

(1979): 139–158; G. Kardaras, *To Byzantio kai oi Abaroi, 6.–9. ai. Politikes, diplomatikes kai politismikes scheseis* (Athens, 2010).

[171] Hahn, "Die Fundmünzen," 454.

[172] On Gepid culture under the Avars, see R. Harhoiu, "Quellenlage und Forschungsstand der Frühgeschichte Siebenbürgens im 6.-7. Jahrhundert," *Dacia* 43-45 (2001), 130–131. For the important cemetery from Bratei, see R. Harhoiu, "Where did all the Gepids go? A sixth- to seventh-century cemetery in Bratei (Romania)," in *Neglected Barbarians*, 209–244. On German culture under the Avars, see A. Kiss, "Germanen im awarenzeitlichen Karpatenbecken," in *Awarenforschungen*, ed. F. Daim, vol. I (Vienna, 1992), 35–134; A. P. Kiss, "A gepidák avar kori továbbélésének vizsgálatáról," in *Középkortörténeti tanulmányok 6. A VI. Medievisztikai PhD-konferencia (Szeged, 2009. június 4–5. előadásai)*, eds. P. G. Tóth and P. Szabó (Szeged, 2010), 119–134.

[173] P. Somogyi, *Byzantinische Fundmünzen der Awarenzeit* (Innsbruck, 1997), 56, no. 39; 79, no. 66; and 87–88, no. 77. The cemetery from Szentendre also produced a *solidus* of Phocas, for which see 88–89, no. 78.

[174] P. Somogyi, "Byzantinische Fundmünzen der Awarenzeit. Eine Bestandaufnahme, 1998–2007," *AAC* 42–43 (2007–2008): 234, table 1 and 237–238, table 3.

military mint found at Carnuntum but also the half-*folles* of Thessalonica from Carnuntum and Tiszakeszi used to pay the soldiers defending the frontier in Illyricum.[175] In addition, the prevalence of coins from Nicomedia rather than Constantinople reminds of the similar observation made for other militarized frontier regions such as Transcaucasia and Arabia.[176] Minting patterns in the Early Byzantine world are still poorly understood, but Nicomedia may have been commissioned to support the frontier. Indeed, it is possible that the transfer of troops facilitated a more intense circulation of bronze coins in the Carpathian Basin. Evagrius praised Tiberius II's aggressive recruiting activity in Pannonia and the Alpine regions for his campaign against Persia in the mid-570s and the initiative clearly left some numismatic traces in the region where these soldiers were recruited.[177]

The arrival of the Avars did not completely disrupt connections between Central Europe and the Mediterranean world. A *decanummium* from Carthage was found in Poland at Łódź showing little circulation wear, while *folles* from Nicomedia have been found at Sulejów (Poland) and in an unspecified location in Moravia.[178] In the Czech Republic a small hoard of silver and copper coins from Trajan Decius to Justin II (573/4) found at Bohouňovice continued the tradition of accumulations containing older Roman coins.[179] Interestingly, no other hoards are recorded in Poland, Slovakia, and the Czech Republic until the seventh century. Although the indirect connection to the Byzantine world was not completely severed, a drastic reduction in coin finds can be noticed in the last quarter of the sixth century. Some scholars have attributed this development to the arrival of Slavic groups, but the hegemony exercised by the Avars is an equally plausible explanation, as the khagan had every reason to exploit the resources and the demographic potential of the region to his own benefit.[180] Closer to the Avar center of power, however, the connection with the

---

[175] Winter, "Die byzantinischen," 338, no. 1/23; Somogyi, "Byzantinische Fundmünzen," 285–286, no. 16.

[176] A. Gandila, "Early Byzantine coin circulation in the eastern provinces: a statistical approach," *AJN* 21 (2009): 216, figs. 14–15.

[177] Evagrius, *Historia ecclesiastica*, 5.14.

[178] Wołoszyn, "Byzantinische Fundmünzen," 501–502, no. 9 and 505, no. 17; Militký, "Finds of the Early," 381, no. M33.

[179] Militký, "Finds of the Early," 374, no. C17.

[180] M. Woloszyn, "Byzantine coins from the 6th and 7th c. from Poland and their East-Central European context," in *Roman Coins Outside the Empire: Ways and Phases, Contexts and Functions*, eds. A. Bursche, R. Ciołek, and R. Wolters (Wetteren, 2008), 201; K. Godłowski, "Das Aufhören der germanischen Kulturen an der mittleren Donau und das Problem des

Mediterranean world was maintained as testified by the three twelve-*nummia* of Maurice and Phocas minted in Alexandria found at Maria Saal and Vienna and the two *decanummia* from Ravenna and Carthage, at Carnuntum.[181]

Finds of *solidi* from the core regions of the Avar Khaganate confirm the flow of gold described by written sources.[182] However, the chronological structure of surviving gold coins does not match the evolution of the tribute recorded by Byzantine writers. Based on the available information and allowing for an almost uninterrupted flow of gold according to the treaties, no less than 3.8 million *solidi* had already reached *Avaria* by 610. Even if we accept that payments were temporarily discontinued during years of intense warfare in the Balkans in the 580s, and especially the late 590s when the Byzantine army was successful, it is still reasonable to suggest that 50 percent of the total amount of gold dispatched to the Avars had already been paid before the accession of Heraclius. How, then, should we account for this disproportionate ratio weighing heavily in favor of coins from the reign of Heraclius? The corpus of finds from *Avaria* confirms the fact that only 36 coins can be dated to the interval 565–610, while 49 coins date from the reign of Heraclius (610–641). The coin/year ratio difference would be ca. 0.8 coins/year compared to ca. 1.6 coins/year, so approximately double in favor of Heraclius. Furthermore, no fewer than 29 coins date from 616–625 (3.2 coins/year) which corresponds to the highest level reached by the tribute.[183] In other words, the survival of Heraclian *solidi* is up to four times higher.

Could it be that contemporary accounts exaggerated the Byzantine willingness to pay the tribute in the last quarter of the sixth century? While this is not impossible, the changing political landscape in the opening decades of the seventh century offers a more plausible explanation. Starting from 614, the Avars and the Slavs ravaged the provinces of the Balkans and delivered the *coup de grâce* to the already crumbling defensive system on

---

Vordringens der Slawen," in *Die Völker*, eds. Wolfram and Daim, 229–230. On the heavy tribute paid by the Slavs, see Fredegar, *Chronicae*, 4.48.

[181] Winter, "Die byzantinischen," 342–343, nos. 11b/1 and 12a; Hahn, "Die Fundmünzen," 454.

[182] Territories in today's Hungary, northeastern Austria, southwestern Slovakia, western Romania, and Vojvodina in Serbia were part of the Avar Khaganate proper; see Pohl, *Die Awaren*, map 2.

[183] Somogyi, "Byzantinische Fundmünzen," 234–237, table 1. A few more coins have been added to the list without changing the statistics, for which see P. Somogyi, *Byzantinische Fundmünzen der Awarenzeit in ihrem europäischen Umfeld* (Budapest, 2014), 237–241.

the Lower Danube.[184] The level of the tribute continued to escalate until the failed siege of Constantinople (626), whereupon the flow of gold from Constantinople effectively stopped. This posed serious problems to the Avars; the khagan had to maintain a sizeable treasury, as the loyalty of the peoples under his suzerainty was maintained with gifts and displays of authority. Seventh-century Avar rulers became less inclined to melt down the coins received from Heraclius. The euphoria of the previous decades when the ever-increasing tribute was being promptly converted into objects of status was replaced by a more conservative strategy after Heraclius successfully defended the capital and completely annihilated the Sasanian kingdom. A periodic redistribution of *solidi* would continue to remind the warrior elite of the khagan's ability to bend the Byzantine ruler to his will.

Tribute was not the only means of gaining access to Byzantine gold. Plunder and ransom for prisoners paid in coin were important alternatives, albeit harder to quantify by the modern historian.[185] Plunder in the Balkans cannot fully account for the overwhelmingly superior number of coins minted for Heraclius found in the Carpathian Basin, especially since many finds are lightweight *solidi* of 20 *siliquae* dated between 616 and 625, probably issued for external payments.[186] Péter Somogyi has listed five other lightweight *solidi* of 20 *siliquae* of Phocas and four *solidi* of Maurice worth between 20 and 23 *siliquae*,[187] which indicates that the practice was probably intensified after the peace of 584 when Maurice agreed to increase the tribute to 100,000 *solidi*.[188] Such finds best reflect the redistribution system in the Avar Khaganate, but also in its wider area of influence, as testified by the finds from Bohuslavice and Kšely in the Czech Republic, and Żółków in Poland, as well as by a large hoard of some 300 *solidi* found at Firtușu in Transylvania.[189] Some of the lightweight *solidi*

---

[184] I. Boná, "Die Awarenfeldzüge und der Untergang der byzantinischen Provinzen an der Unteren Donau," in *Kontakte zwischen Iran, Byzanz und der Steppe im 6.-7. Jahrhundert*, ed. C. Bálint (Budapest, 2000), 163–183.

[185] For example, a nephew of Heraclius was ransomed for an unspecified sum of money (χρήματα), which probably brought additional gold to Avaria in the decades following the failed siege of Constantinople. For the episode, see, *Breviarum*, 21.

[186] Somogyi, "Byzantinische Fundmünzen," 235–236.

[187] Ibid., 234; Somogyi, *Byzantinische Fundmünzen der Awarenzeit*, 198, no. 15/2 and 208–209, no. 30.

[188] For the historical context, see Whitby, *The Emperor Maurice*, 142.

[189] Bohuslavice and Kšely: Militký, "Finds," 360 and 376, nos. C23–24; 361 and 381–382, no. M37. Żółków: Wołoszyn, "Byzantinische Fundmünzen," 506, no. 19 and 511, figs. 6/14. Firtușu: Somogyi, *Byzantinische Fundmünzen*, 137–138; P. Somogyi, "Ismeretlen levéltári adatok a

from the core areas of the Khaganate were repurposed as jewelry and later deposited in graves.[190]

In regions west of the Avar center of power, western mints continued to play an important role, Italy being the most probable mediator of contacts with the central and Eastern Mediterranean world. North African copper coins of Phocas and Heraclius minted at Carthage have been found at Sisak, Carnuntum, and Ostrówek (Poland) and twelve-*nummia* of - Alexandria at Carnuntum and Maria Saal in Austria.[191] A countermarked *follis* from Sicily and a *decanummium* from Catania have been found at Ptuj and Carnuntum, respectively.[192] In addition, a rare half-*follis* minted at Alexandretta in Syria during the revolt of the Heraclii (608–610) was found in Slovakia at Štúrovo, but the exact circumstances of the find have not been properly published.[193] Finally, a hoard was found at Kluk (Czech Republic) in a flooded sand quarry but only one coin is known, a half-*follis* minted at Carthage in 606–607.[194] The practice of burying hoards of small change brought from a Mediterranean milieu would continue in Bohemia until the second half of the seventh century. Although Czech archaeologists traditionally distinguish between Germanic and Slavic contexts based on the type of Byzantine coins brought to the region – gold for the former and copper for the latter – the numismatic evidence points to a greater degree of continuity.

At least three major patterns of diffusion can be discerned in the Avar Khaganate. First, no copper coin finds from western mints are so far known from the core areas of *Avaria*, although several have been recorded in the Lower Danube *barbaricum* and further east in Transcaucasia. Only three gold coins issued by western mints have been found *Avaria*, of which only the *solidus* of Constans II minted in Rome was found in archaeological context – a grave from the Avar-age cemetery of

---

Firtos hegyén 1831-ben talált bizánci aranyakról," in *Hadak útján. A népvándorlás kor fiatal kutatóinak konferenciája*, eds. L. Bende, G. Lőrinczy, and C. Szalontai (Szeged, 2000), 197–204.

[190] Sânpetru German and Hajdúdorog-Városkert: Somogyi, *Byzantinische Fundmünzen*, 43–44, no. 27 and 77, no. 65. Tiszavasvári-Kashalom-dűlő, Szendrő, and Kiszombor-Tanyahalom-dűlő: Somogyi, "Byzantinische Fundmünzen," 274–275, no. 7; 283–284, no. 14; and 286–287, no. 17.

[191] Sisak: Mirnik and Šemrov, "Byzantine coins," 194, no. 699. Carnuntum: Winter, "Die byzantinischen," 339, nos. 25–26 and 28–29. Maria Saal: Hahn, "Die Fundmünzen," 454. Ostrówek: Wołoszyn, "Byzantinische Fundmünzen," 502–503, no. 11.

[192] Kos, "The monetary circulation," 227, no. 28; Winter, "Die byzantinischen," 339, no. 31.

[193] J. Hunka, "Finds of Byzantine coins from the 5th–10th century from the northern part of the Carpathian Basin," in *Byzantine Coins*, 397, table 1, no. 8.

[194] Militký, "Finds," 375, no. C22.

Hajdúnánás-Fürjhalom-járás (Hungary).[195] This is somewhat unexpected since the Avars raided as far as Cividale, sacked in 611, where they could have gained easy access to precious coins from western mints.[196] Second, burying coin hoards was not a common practice in the Avar world, which places the Khaganate in sharp contrast with the surrounding areas. To be sure, there is some indication of gold coin hoards found in the nineteenth century at Kupusina and Bački Monoštor, but they have been dispersed and no coins have been retrieved. Moreover, the available information suggests that none of the coins was dated later than 610.[197] Given the large quantity of Byzantine gold pouring into the Avar Khaganate, the absence of hoards in its core areas is quite perplexing. It is no less true that very few Avar settlements have been studied. Most of the archaeological knowledge of the Avar period derives from burial assemblages in which the deposition of large hoards was not customary. Finally, there is very little silver in *Avaria* to match the silver frenzy in Transcaucasia and the more modest flow of hexagrams to the peripheral areas of the Avar world.[198] Wherever they are found in great quantities, silver pieces are connected with major theaters of war or with political payments sent to allies, which the Empire did not consider important enough to require gold subsidies or whose culture held silver in high regard.[199]

The flow of Byzantine gold to *Avaria* dropped abruptly after 626, and despite the attempt of Attila Kiss to suggest that tribute continued to be paid in smaller amounts after the failed siege of Constantinople, the numismatic evidence found in archaeological context indicates that the Avar Khaganate no longer presented a serious challenge. Few coins struck between 625 and 655 have been found in excavations and the gold pieces from burial assemblages dating from the second half of the seventh century

---

[195] Hajdúnánás-Fürjhalom-járás: Somogyi, "Byzantinische Fundmünzen," 272–273, no. 5. We should also mention here an unprovenanced *tremissis* of Maurice from Rome in the collection of the museum in Miskolc and a *solidus* of Heraclius from Ravenna in the National Museum in Budapest, for which see Somogyi, "Byzantinische Fundmünzen," 291–292, no. 22; Somogyi, *Byzantinische Fundmünzen*, 101–102, no. 91.

[196] Pohl, *Die Awaren*, 238–240.   [197] Somogyi, *Byzantinische Fundmünzen*, 136–139.

[198] Hexagrams of Heraclius have been found at Sânnicolaul Mare and Arad in Transylvania: Oberländer-Târnoveanu, "La răscruce de vremuri," 140, n. 142; Linz (Austria): Hahn, "Die Fundmünzen," 459; Szadzko (Poland): Wołoszyn, "Byzantinische Fundmünzen," 505–506, no. 18 and 511, fig. 6/13.

[199] However, there is an impressive quantity of silver plate from Early Avar-age assemblages; see T. Vida, "The Byzantine vessels of the Avars," in *The Gold of the Avars. The Nagyszentmiklós Treasure. Magyar Nemzeti Múzeum, Budapest, 24 March–30 June, 2002*, eds. T. Kovács and É. Garam (Budapest, 2002), 113–119.

indicate a drastically diminished flow of gold from Byzantium.[200] Still, the renewed infusion of Byzantine coins after a few decades of partial interruption requires an explanation. Continuous, albeit reduced, tribute paid by Heraclius' successors or the association with the migration of a Bulgar group into *Avaria* following the death of Kubrat are not satisfactory solutions.[201] The most plausible so far has been Péter Somogyi's suggestion that the shifting balance of power in the wide region between the Middle Danube and the Caucasus around 650 may have led to renewed diplomatic relations between Byzantium and the now weaker Avar Khaganate. Political pragmatism dictates that old foes can become friends in mutually beneficial circumstances. The Avar embassy of 678 and the plausible assumption that Constans II and Constantine IV feared the growing power of the Bulgars provide sufficient grounds for this interpretation.[202] Gold *solidi* continued to be used as *oboli* in graves from Gyenesdiás, Hajdúnánás-Fürjhalom-járás, and Kiskundorozsma in Hungary.[203] The scarcity of coins in the decades after 626 often led to the use of symbolic round-shaped pieces of gold as *oboli* or the reuse of old Roman coins for this purpose as testified by burial assemblages from Hungary and Slovakia dating from this period.[204]

Before the assault on the Byzantine capital or perhaps shortly after, the Slavs rebelled under the leadership of Samo, a colorful figure who took advantage of the long-term repercussions of the Avar defeat under the walls of Constantinople and established a thirty-five-year-long reign over what is often described as "Samo's empire," a loose political entity stretching from the Elbe to the Middle Danube and the Drava.[205] The gold coins

---

[200] A. Kiss, "Die 'barbarischen' Könige des 4.–7. Jahrhunderts im Karpatenbecken, als Verbündeten des römischen bzw. byzantinischen Reiches," *Communicationes Archaeologicae Hungaricae* (1991): 122–123. For a convincing rebuttal, see Somogyi, *Byzantinische Fundmünzen*, 111–117, and more recently, Somogyi, "New remarks," 90–103 with the previous literature.

[201] I. Bóna, "Barbarische' Nachahmungen von byzantinischen Goldmünzen im Awarenreich," *RIN* 95 (1993): 529–538.

[202] Somogyi, "New remarks," 125–135.

[203] Somogyi, *Byzantinische Fundmünzen*, 43, no. 26; Somogyi, "Byzantinische Fundmünzen," 272–273, no. 5 and 273–274, no. 6.

[204] J. Zábojník, "Antike Münzen im Gebiet der Slowakei aus der Zeit des Awarischen Khaganats," in *Byzantine Coins*, 403–405; Garam, "A közép avarkor," 210–211.

[205] Pohl, *Die Awaren*, 256–261; Curta, *The Making of the Slavs*, 109. For Avar influence on the territory of today's Czech Republic, see N. Profantová, "Awarische Funde in der Tschechischen Republik – Forschungsstand und neue Erkenntnisse," *AAC* 45 (2010): 203–270. For Avar archaeological evidence in Slovakia, see J. Zábojník, "Das Awarische Kaganat und die Slawen an seiner nördlichen Peripherie (Probleme der archäologischen Abgrenzung)," *Slovenská Archeológia* 47, no. 1 (1999): 153–173.

and imitations after coins of Heraclius and Constans II found in the Czech Republic and Slovakia have been associated with Samo's ephemeral state.[206] Seventh-century finds from Poland have also been associated with a Slavic population. The *follis* of Heraclius (613/4) from Grodzisko Dolne was found in a Slavic settlement, while the hexagram from Szadzko and the *solidus* from Żółków are accidental finds.[207] The hoard of precious objects from Poštorná in Moravia which included jewelry of Byzantine inspiration, as well as other Byzantine finds from the Czech Republic, Slovakia, and Poland suggest some level of contact with Byzantine culture either directly or through intermediaries.[208] Slavic influence to the south, perhaps as far as Slovenia, explains the uninterrupted access to the Mediterranean.[209]

Two hoards from the Czech Republic, found at Hrozová and Poděbrady were concealed on the eve or soon after Samo's confederation disintegrated.[210] The structure of the hoards betrays a western origin and confirms the continuous access of communities in Bohemia to the culture of the Mediterranean world, insufficiently documented in contemporary accounts.[211] The connection was established in the context of Justinian's western *reconquista* and the barbarization of his armies and maintained as a side effect of subsequent imperial efforts in Italy and North Africa. The small accumulation found during archaeological excavations on the left bank of the Hrozová river includes four bronze coins, all issues of Carthage, including a Carthaginian issue of Zeugitania from the third century BC. The latest coin is a rare *follis* of Constans II from Carthage,

---

[206] Kšely, Kolín, and Bohuslavice: Militký, "Finds," 381–382, no. M37; 376, nos. C23–24; 378, no. C26; Mostová: Somogyi, "New remarks," 94, n. 33. Šaľa: Somogyi, "Byzantinische Fundmünzen," 288, no. 18. For Samo's political center see recently F. Curta, "The Early Slavs in Bohemia and Moravia: a response to my critics." *Archeologické rozhledy* 61 (2009): 725–754.

[207] Wołoszyn, "Byzantinische Fundmünzen," 500–501, no. 6; 511, fig. 6/12; 505–506, no. 18; 511, fig. 6/13; 506, no. 19; and 511, fig. 6/14.

[208] For the Byzantine influence in Poland, see M. Wołoszyn, "Die byzantinischen Fundstücke in Polen. Ausgewählte Probleme," in *Byzantium and East Central Europe*, eds. G. Prinzing and M. Salamon (Cracow, 2001), 49–59; L. Košnar, "Raně středověký depot stříbrných předmětů z Poštorné, okr. Břeclav," *Praehistorica* 21 (1994): 69–103. See also A. Avenarius, *Die byzantinische Kultur und die Slawen: zum Problem der Rezeption und Transformation (6. bis 12. Jahrhundert)* (Vienna, 2000), 20–49.

[209] For the changing cultural fabric of settlements in Slovenia, see T. Milavec, "Late Antique settlements in Slovenia after the year 600," in *Pontic-Danubian Realm*, 71–88.

[210] Militký, "Finds," 376–377, no. C25; 382, no. M38.

[211] Coins of Constans II including issues from western mints have been found in Slovenia, at Celje and Ptuj, and in Austria, at Neulengbach and Wiener Neustadt indicating a possible communication bridge linking the Mediterranean, Bohemia, and Moravia; see Kos, *Die Fundmünzen*, vol. III, 497, no. 916; Kos, "The monetary circulation," 227, nos. 29–30; Winter, "Die byzantinischen," 341, no. 9; 340–341, no. 5 and 351, fig. 6/19.

dated 662–667. Most probably the coins were brought together from Tunisia, via Italy. The hoard from Poděbrady, of which only seven coins have been preserved, includes only Early Byzantine coins, from Justin II to Constans II (latest coin, 651–657), and displays a kaleidoscope of mints but mostly western (Catania, Rome, and Carthage). Some of these coins may have been gathered in North Africa or southern Italy. This renewed traffic came at a time when Constans II attempted to take advantage of the First Fitna (656–661) and check the Arab expansion, just as he did in Transcaucasia. The emperor established himself in Sicily in 663, despoiled Rome of its remaining treasures including the copper roof tiles of the Pantheon (presumably for minting fresh coins) and imposed heavy taxation on southern Italy while at the same time trying to stabilize the political situation in Africa.[212]

Finally, the hoard from Zemiansky Vrbovok (Slovakia), concealed after 669–674, is not only the northernmost collective find of Byzantine silver but also a unique accumulation in many respects.[213] It is the upscale version of the hoard of coins and scrap bronze concealed at Horgești in Moldavia at the beginning of the seventh century and can be compared only to the collections of Late Roman coins and scrap silver from Gudme in Denmark.[214] Because of the association of coins with silver bowls, plate (Sasanian), jewelry, and scrap silver, the hoard from Zemiansky Vrbovok was attributed to a silversmith, perhaps Byzantine, who worked for the Avars and catered to the tastes of the barbarian elite.[215] To be sure, the association of seventh-century Byzantine silver coins with silver jewelry is

---

[212] For Constans II's policy in Africa, see more recently W. E. Kaegi, *Muslim Expansion and Byzantine Collapse in North Africa* (Cambridge, 2010), 166–199. See also D. Pringle, *The Defence of Byzantine Africa from Justinian to the Arab Conquest. An account of the Military History and Archaeology of the African Provinces in the Sixth and Seventh Centuries* (Oxford, 1981), 46–48. For the role of Sicily in the seventh century, see V. Prigent, "Le rôle des provinces d'Occident dans l'approvisionnement de Constantinople (618–771). Témoignages numismatique et sigillographique," *Mélanges de l'École Française de Rome, Moyen Âge* 118, no. 2 (2006): 269–299.

[213] P. Radomerský, "Byzantské mince z pokladu v Zemianském Vrbovku," *Památky Archeologické* 44 (1953): 109–122; A. Fiala, "K objavu miliarense Constansa II. z pokladu zo Zemianskeho Vrbovku," *Numismatický sborník* 17 (1986): 15–20; Avenarius, *Die byzantinische Kultur*, 37 with fig. 8 for the objects.

[214] P. Vang Petersen, "Excavations at sites of treasure trove finds at Gudme," in *The Archaeology of Gudme and Lundeborg. Papers presented at a Conference at Svendborg, October 1991*, eds. P. O. Nielsen, K. Randsborg, and H. Thrane (Copenhagen, 1994), 30–40.

[215] Hunka, "Finds of Byzantine coins," 396–397; Zábojník, "Antike Münzen," 406–408; Avenarius, *Die byzantinische Kultur*, 36–37; V. Turčan, "K historickému pozadiu uloženia depotu v Zemianskom Vrbovku," in *Byzantská kultúra a Slovensko. Zborník štúdií*, ed. V. Turčan (Bratislava, 2007), 41–47.

not unique to Zemianský Vrbovok. A contemporary but much larger hoard of hexagrams found at Priseaca in Oltenia included two star-shaped silver earrings. However, most of the coins from Zemiansky Vrbovok are not hexagrams but *miliarensia*, ceremonial issues of irregular weight, two times lighter than the regular silver coinage. The pieces are die-linked and uncirculated, the typical features of a diplomatic gift of freshly minted coins; it is hardly a random accumulation of scrap silver carried by an artisan.[216]

Ceremonial silver of the type included in the Zemiansky Vrbovok hoard circulated on a much wider area. One early *miliarense* of Constans II was found in Georgia, the most important destination for Byzantine ceremonial silver pieces.[217] The same region produced the two die-linked gold hoards found at Chibati and Nokalakevi, reflecting political payments much like the collection from Zemiansky Vrbovok. Closer to Slovakia, *miliarensia* of Constans II were found in a grave from Stejanovci (Serbia) and in the area of Dunafalva (Hungary).[218] In addition, the Kiskőrös-type silver imitations after *miliarensia* struck for Constans II and Constantine IV prove that they had been widely known in the Avar Khaganate and highly regarded as status symbol.[219] In conclusion, the hoard from Zemiansky Vrbovok reflects the distribution of imperial largesse, which the original recipient subsequently gave away as raw material for the production of jewelry and plate. The gift may have been occasioned by one of the Avar-Byzantine contacts preceding the embassy of 678, while the hexagrams of Constans II and Constantine IV from the hoard were probably later additions to the original group of *miliarensia* sent to *Avaria* during Constans II's lifetime.[220]

So far the analysis of coin finds in the last two chapters has revealed the existence of two main channels of diffusion, both subservient to the Empire's political agenda in the northern frontier region and *barbaricum*. Political and diplomatic payments have left a long trail of gold and silver extending from the Carpathian Basin to the Caucasus. The fact that such

---

[216] *Miliarense* type *MIB* 60.
[217] Abramishvili, *Sakartvelos sakhelmts'ipo muzeumis,* 70, no. 220 and pl. XIII/220.
[218] Somogyi, *Byzantinische Fundmünzen*, 78–79, no. 68; P. Somogyi, "Byzantinische Fundmünzen als Quelle zur Archäologie der Awaren," fig. 6, in press.
[219] Ibid., 127. See also P. Somogyi, "Bemerkungen zu den silbernen Münzimitationen vom Typ Kiskörös," in *A Népvándorláskor fiatal kutatoinak IV. összejövetele. Visegrád, 1993, szeptember 20–22,* ed. I. Borsody (Visegrád, 1995), 79–89.
[220] Somogyi's suggestion that Constantine IV would dispense ceremonial issues of his predecessor as diplomatic gifts is unlikely and might have been ill-received by the Avar envoys; see Somogyi, "New remarks," 132.

Byzantine coins were often imitated confirms their distinctive social function gained within cultures beyond the frontier. Perhaps more than any other Byzantine objects, gold and silver coins reflected the political and military strength of warlords who could muscle their way into the Byzantine orbit and obtain protection money from the emperor. To be sure, any Byzantine object could bring social prestige, but money – especially gold – had been for a long time the traditional Roman solution for containing the barbarian threat. Its ideological force was therefore unmistakable. On the other hand, it is often impossible to distinguish between political payment and plunder since both are very well recorded in contemporary accounts. Sometimes the coins themselves (lightweight *solidi* and ceremonial *miliarensia*) suggest diplomatic gifts, but precious coinage could have arrived in *barbaricum* in less peaceful circumstances. In any case, it is unlikely that plunder – no matter how successful – could have rivaled the systematic flow of tribute which amounted to millions of *solidi*.

The second major distribution channel is connected with the militarized frontier in the northern Balkans (and to some extent in Transcaucasia), which acted as a catalyst for the diffusion of bronze coinage. Although local garrisons were paid in gold – at least nominally – daily purchases required the use of low-value bronze coinage which official money-changers were ready to provide.[221] Frontier fortresses boasted an ethnically mixed culture where a late version of Romanization took place whereby foreign soldiers embraced Early Byzantine fashions and styles clearly visible in the archaeological record discussed in Chapter 2, while themselves leaving their mark on frontier culture. Although the status quo on the sixth-century northern frontier could be volatile and unpredictable, the constant movement of people ensured the diffusion of bronze coins on a wide area. Unfortunately for the modern observer, the casual circulation of people from the frontier to *barbaricum* was of little interest to contemporary writers who were too busy indulging in the traditional "civilization vs. barbarism" discourse. Artifacts and copper coins provide a window into the untold story of cultural interaction of a more mundane but durable nature that transcends the high levels of diplomacy and military campaigning illustrated by gold and silver coinage.

The circulation of Byzantine artifacts beyond the frontier, and especially its varying intensity over time, can only be discerned with the help of coins,

---

[221] For official money-changers, see C. Asdracha, "Inscriptions chrétiennes et protobyzantines de la Thrace orientale et de l'île d'Imbros (IIIe–VIIe siècles): Présentation et commentaire historique," *ArchDelt* 53 (1998): 494–496.

the most precisely dated instrument of the Byzantine government. Barring inflationary spirals, periods of abundance in the numismatic record are likely to signal high points in the diffusion of Byzantine goods of all kinds, primarily those discussed in the early chapters. Analyzing diffusion patterns and retracing their chronological evolution in the political and diplomatic context of the time has been the first necessary step toward elucidating the flow and function of Byzantine goods in *barbaricum*. It is now time to address another important set of questions: what were the functions performed by Byzantine money in communities living in the Empire's shadow? Could they differ depending on the culture in which those coins were integrated? Can we speak of a real monetary economy based on exchange mediated by copper coins? Finally, what can this tell us about the cultural fabric of the communities that gained access to Byzantine goods? The next chapter will provide several possible interpretations.

7 | Money and Barbarians: Same Coins, Different Functions

7.1 Coins Beyond Frontiers: The Use and Abuse of the Numismatic Evidence

After discussing the historical circumstances responsible for the flow of Byzantine coins to *barbaricum* we should now turn to the other main problem, the function of money in societies living beyond the frontier of Early Byzantium. It is widely accepted that money loses its face value beyond the political borders of the issuing authority. That is not to say that coins cannot perform any economic function whatsoever. It basically means that the state no longer guarantees the value of the currency, the exchange rate, and the enforcement of other regulations in place. This fact alone affects Byzantine money in different ways depending on the intrinsic value. Gold and silver coins were hardly the currency used on a daily basis at the marketplace. In the Byzantine world the main purpose of gold was to create a means for the payment of salaries and the collection of taxes and to serve as medium of exchange in large-scale transactions. As for silver coinage, it served a purely ceremonial function until the introduction of the hexagram, although it was loosely struck on the weight standard of the *siliqua* or the *miliarense*. Clearly, we should not attach any monetary value to gold and silver Byzantine coins found in *barbaricum*. Despite the Roman law prohibiting the export of precious metal, millions of coins were sent to *barbaricum* in the form of political and diplomatic payments, almost never to return back to Byzantium. But this was bullion, not cash. Precious-metal coins gained non-monetary attributes after being converted into pendants, rings, and appliqués, as well as through their ritual deposition in graves; many were simply melted down to provide raw material for the production of jewelry and dress accessories.

The function of copper coinage, however, is much more problematic given its fiduciary nature. This was the currency most frequently circulated in the Byzantine provinces, being the main facilitator of small-scale transactions in urban markets. Although the highly militarized environment of the northern Balkans dominated by hilltop fortresses rather than urban agglomerations was not characterized by a "market economy," copper coins still performed their designated monetary purpose. Did coins retain this function once they crossed the Empire's frontier? Given the high concentration of finds in today's Romania, Moldova, Ukraine, and Georgia most scholars have preferred an economic interpretation of these coins, under the assumption that the Byzantine monetary economy somehow extended beyond the frontier. Indeed, the presence of Byzantine copper coins has been described almost exclusively in terms of an "intense monetary circulation," or at least an "active circulation," especially after the reform of Anastasius which supposedly brought an "economic revival" in *barbaricum*.[1]

Historians commonly ascribe the use of small-value currency beyond the frontier, in modern-day Romania, to the local Daco-Roman population, as an ethnic antithesis to waves of migratory peoples who did not have the benefit of a time-honored tradition of economic contact with the Roman world. Unfortunately, the nationalistic agenda driving the interpretation of the archaeological material discussed in the previous chapters also applies to the numismatic evidence. According to such views, Byzantine coins fueled internal trade, horizontal exchanges between

---

[1] C. Chiriac, *Civilizația bizantină și societatea din regiunile extracarpatice ale României în secolele VI–VIII* (Brăila, 2013), 95 ("real coin circulation"); C. Preda, "The Byzantine coins – an expression of the relations between the Empire and the populations north of the Danube in the 6th–13th centuries," in *Relations*, 221 ("active coin circulation"); L. Bârzu, *La continuité de la création matérielle et spirituelle du peuple roumain sur le territoire de l'ancienne Dacie* (Bucharest, 1980), 80 ("intensified coin circulation"); L. M. Stratulat, "Continuitate și discontinuitate la nordul Dunării de Jos (secolele IV–VIII d. Hr.)," *Carpica* 31 (2002): 71 ("intense coin circulation"); A. Madgearu, *Continuitate și discontinuitate culturală la Dunărea de Jos în secolele VII–VIII* (Bucharest, 1997), 68 ("coin circulation and frequent transactions"); I. Corman, *Contribuții la istoria spațiului pruto-nistrian în epoca evului mediu timpuriu (sec. V–VII d.Chr.)* (Chișinău, 1998), 98–99 ("coin circulation"); Ș. Olteanu, *Societatea carpato-danubiano-pontică în secolele IV–XI. Structuri demo-economice și social-politice* (Bucharest, 1997), 174 ("coin circulation"); A.-M. Velter, *Transilvania în secolele V–XII. Interpretări istorico-politice și economice pe baza descoperirilor monetare din bazinul Carpatic, secolele V–XII* (Bucharest, 2002), 33–35 ("coin circulation and active trade"); N. Stoicescu, *The Continuity of the Romanian People* (Bucharest, 1983), 205 ("coin circulation and commercial relations"); D. G. Teodor, *East Carpathian Area of Romania in the V–XI Centuries AD* (Oxford, 1980), 14 ("uninterrupted coin circulation"); Teodor recently reinforced his position, for which see D. G. Teodor, "Considerații privind unele aspecte ale etnogenezei românești," *AM* 34 (2011): 180. For similar arguments in favor of monetary circulation in Georgia, see N. Iu. Lomouri, "Arkheopolis-Tsikhegodzhi-Nokalakevi," in *Nokalakevi-Arkeopolisi: III. Arkeologiuri gatchrebi 1983–1989*, ed. P. Zakaraia (Tbilisi, 1993), 136–139. For the lands north of the Black Sea, see E. S. Stolyarik, *Essays on Monetary Circulation in the North-Western Black Sea Region in the Late Roman and Early Byzantine Periods: Late 3rd Century–Early 13th Century AD* (Odessa, 1993), 68.

communities in *barbaricum* which complemented the vertical dealings with Byzantium.[2] Following this line of reasoning, interruptions in "coin circulation" were used for dating the arrival of new ethnic groups, usually peoples ignorant of monetary transactions and generally bent on destruction, who disrupted the cultural dealings of the autochthonous population with the Byzantine world.[3] Although the uncompromising thesis of a true coin circulation has been undermined in more recent studies, the larger paradigm has not been challenged.[4] Lip service has been given to alternative functions performed by coins and to the realization that societies of different ethnic background handled Byzantine coins, but such vistas have not been properly pursued.[5] A careful reassessment of the evidence shows that the economy of northern *barbaricum* was not a natural extension of the Byzantine economy and coins did not perform any monetary function whatsoever beyond the political frontier. Much like other non-urban civilizations, communities north of the Danube developed an exchange system based on barter or on the use of less standardized media of exchange, not always visible in the archaeological record. Just like the Byzantine imports discussed in the previous chapters, Byzantine copper coins brought to *barbaricum* abandoned their original economic

---

[2] S. Brezeanu, "The Lower Danube frontier during the 4th–7th centuries. A notion's ambiguity," *Annuario Istituto Romeno di Cultura e Ricerca Umanistica* 5 (2003): 37; Corman, *Contribuții la istoria,* 99; Velter, *Transilvania,* 35; Chiriac, *Civilizația bizantină,* 57–58; Olteanu, *Societatea,* 172.

[3] S. Musteață, *Moneda bizantină în regiunile carpato-nistrene în secolele VI–X* (Chișinău, 2014), 119; Chiriac, *Civilizația bizantină,* 106; D. G. Teodor, *Descoperiri arheologice și numismatice la est de Carpați (contribuții la continuitatea daco-romană și veche românească)* (Bucharest, 1997), 12; E. Oberländer, "Barbaricum apropiat – populațiile din Muntenia și Imperiul Bizantin (secolele VI–X) – mărturia numismaticii," *Ialomița* 4 (2004): 332–358; S. Dolinescu-Ferche, "La culture Ipotești–Ciurel–Cîndești (Ve–VIIe siècle). La situation en Valachie," *Dacia* 28 (1984): 120. For a more nuanced interpretation, see E. S. Teodor, "Ceramica așezărilor din secolul al VI-lea de la Dulceanca," in *Istro-Pontica: Muzeul tulcean la a 50-a aniversare, 1950–2000; omagiu lui Simion Gavrilă la 45 de ani de activitate*, eds. M. Iacob, E. Oberländer-Târnoveanu, and F. Topoleanu (Tulcea, 2000), 330, n. 195, who argued that the Slavs could also be interested in handling Byzantine coins, only to conclude elsewhere that the interruption of the coin flow may be connected with the massive arrival of Slavic groups, for which see E. S. Teodor, "O frontieră incertă a lumii romane – Cîmpia Dunării de Jos în epoca lui Justinian," *Cercetări arheologice* 12 (2003): 334.

[4] See especially E. Oberländer-Târnoveanu, "La monnaie byzantine des VIe-VIIIe siècles au-delà de la frontière du Bas-Danube. Entre politique, économie et diffusion culturelle," *Histoire et Mesure* 17, no. 3 (2002): 177–181; A. Lakatos, "Monede bizantine din perioada avară în Transilvania, vestul și nord-vestul României," *EN* 12 (2002): 239–246.

[5] Oberländer, "La monnaie byzantine," 182. For the function of Byzantine coins as raw material for the production of bronze jewelry and dress accessories, see A. Gandila, "Face value or bullion value? Early Byzantine coins beyond the Lower Danube border," in *Byzantine Coins*, 455–459.

designation and gained social and symbolic attributes. Some were melted down to produce jewelry, others were included in burial assemblages, and many were hoarded and buried as "wealth deposits" or as votive offerings.

In other parts of the northern *barbaricum* historians and archaeologists paid little attention to the social function performed by Byzantine coins. Unfortunately, the numismatic evidence, due to its complex nature and chronological sensitivity is very susceptible to methodological abuse. In the steppe north of the Black Sea and the northern Caucasus, Early Byzantine coin finds were mainly used by Soviet archaeologists to date burial assemblages and to build relative chronologies for Early Medieval artifacts. In a seminal early article, A. K. Ambroz argued that the dating of burials based on coins should not take into consideration the date when the coin was issued, since coins arrived in the region much later and at least a hundred years must be added in order to reach the approximate date of the burial.[6] This was not treated as a mere hypothesis but as a true axiom that needed to be applied to every case. Although it was rooted in the fact that Early Byzantine coins were sometimes found together with later Islamic coins, in reality this solution was needed in order to reconcile the conflicting chronologies of the cultural complexes studied by Ambroz. However, since it was not founded on a careful study of the Byzantine monetary economy, this arbitrary "delay" principle influenced his huge chronological sequence that covered the territory extending from the Ural Mountains to the Middle Danube. Such an interpretation of the numismatic evidence has created a large gap between the chronology of the Black Sea region and the one established by Hungarian archaeologists working on the Avar period, who have criticized Ambroz's principles.[7]

The historiography of the Avar age is itself not free of controversy. As we have seen in the previous chapter, the Middle Danube region was a major recipient of Early Byzantine coins. Starting from the second half of the sixth century the rise of the Avar Khaganate as the hegemonic power in

---

[6] A. K. Ambroz "Problemy rannesrednevekovoi khronologii Vostochnoi Evropy," *SA* no. 2 (1971): 96–123. For this methodological problem, see recently O. V. Komar, "Kuda "zapazdyvaiut" monety? (K voprosu o roli monet v datirovke rannesrednevekovykh pamiatnikov Vostochnoi Evropy VI–VIII vv.)," in *Peterburgskii apokrif. Poslanie ot Marka*, ed. O. V. Sharov (Chişinău, 2011), 555–566.

[7] C. Bálint, "Über die Datierung der osteuropäischen Steppenfunde des frühen Mittelalters. Schwierigkeiten und Möglichkeiten," *Mitteilungen des Archäologischen Instituts der Ungarischen Akademie der Wissenschaften* 14 (1985): 137–147; C. Bálint, "Probleme der archäologischen Forschung zur awarischen Landnahmen," in *Ausgewählte Probleme europäischer Landnahmen des Früh- und Hochmittelalters*, eds. M. Müller-Wille and R. Schneider (Sigmaringen, 1993), 195–273.

barbaricum brought a huge quantity of gold coins sent by Byzantine rulers as annual tribute. Hungarian historians and archaeologists are still trying to determine the fate of this huge accumulation of gold, given that the number of surviving *solidi* is perplexingly small.[8] A major point of debate has been the transition from the Early to the Middle Avar period, which relies heavily on the nature of the numismatic evidence. As early as 1940 Gyula László suggested that the cultural changes visible in the archaeological record were brought about by the arrival ca. 670–680 of a new group led by Kuber after the Bulgars had been forced westward under the pressure of the Khazars.[9] The theory was further developed and refined by István Bóna who sustained the immigrationist thesis by looking at coin hoards from the Carpathian Basin and the overall reduction in coin finds toward the end of the seventh century.[10] Although the theory has been largely refuted since then,[11] the numismatic evidence remains one of the central points in the debate regarding the interpretation of the striking cultural parallels found in Ukraine for the Middle Avar period.[12] Much like the Romanian case, changes in the ethnic structure of Eastern Europe has been the main issue at stake and the numismatic evidence has provided powerful chronological arguments. As a consequence of such debates – not always dispassionate – the social value of Byzantine coins in the Avar-age *barbaricum* has not been fully explored and a systematic assessment of the coins in their archaeological context is only beginning to address wider implications.

---

[8] I. Bóna, "Byzantium and the Avars: the archaeology of the first 70 years of the Avar era," in *From the Baltic to the Black Sea. Studies in Medieval Archaeology*, eds. D. Austin and L. Alcock (London, 1990), 113–118. A corpus of Byzantine coin finds in "Avaria" has been published by P. Somogyi, *Byzantinische Fundmünzen der Awarenzeit* (Innsbruck, 1997). For updates, see P. Somogyi, "Byzantinische Fundmünzen der Awarenzeit. Eine Bestandsaufnahme, 1998–2007," *AAC* 42–43 (2007–2008): 231–298; P. Somogyi, *Byzantinische Fundmünzen der Awarenzeit in ihrem europäischen Umfeld* (Budapest, 2014).

[9] Gy. László, "Die Reiternomaden der Völkerwanderungszeit und das Christentum in Ungarn," *Zeitschrift für Kirchengeschichte* 59 (1940): 126–146.

[10] I. Bóna, "Avar lovassír Iváncsáról," *ArchÉrt* 97 (1970): 243–261.

[11] C. Bálint, "Der Beginn der Mittelawarenzeit und die Einwanderung Kubers," *Antaeus* 29–30 (2008): 29–61, with the historiographical background of the debate.

[12] See recently P. Somogyi, "New remarks on the flow of Byzantine coins in Avaria and Wallachia during the second half of the seventh century," in *The Other Europe in the Middle Ages: Avars, Bulgars, Khazars and Cumans*, ed. F. Curta (Leiden, 2008), 83–149; P. Somogyi, "Neue Überlegungen über den Zustrom byzantinischer Münzen ins Awarenland (Numismatischer Kommentar zu Csanád Bálints Betrachtungen zum Beginn der Mittelawarenzeit)," *Antaeus* 29–30 (2008–2009): 347–393; C. Bálint, "Antwortschreiben an Péter Somogyi," *Antaeus* 29–30 (2008–2009): 395–401.

7.2 New Barbarians: Primitive Cash and Non-Economic Value of Colonial Money

Difficulties in handling the numismatic evidence are compounded by the fact that contemporary accounts tell us little about the use of Byzantine coins outside the frontier. There is virtually no useful information about trade aside from the occasional anecdote. Furthermore, our knowledge regarding the political organization and social structure of societies in *barbaricum* is fragmentary at best and comes exclusively from Byzantine writers who filtered realities from *barbaricum* through their own cultural sieve. Archaeology can certainly shed more light on these issues, especially future research if conducted with such questions in mind. For the time being, however, the functions performed by Byzantine money in "barbarian" hands can be revealed by analogy with more recent traditional societies in contact with capitalist states using a carefully regulated currency. The methodological limitations of such an approach are readily apparent but not impossible to overcome. The economy of early modern Europe and the economy of Early Byzantium were driven by different mechanisms, although they were both monetized. Moreover, the distinctive culture of each "primitive" society studied by anthropologists, whose particular set of values influenced the way foreign currencies were perceived and adopted, invites caution in pressing the analogy beyond the level of generality. At the very least the comparison can be reduced to the lowest common denominator of cultural contact between monetized states and non-monetized rural societies.[13]

With this caveat in mind, some similarities make this a worthwhile exercise. They can be fleshed out by asking questions inspired by world-systems analysis, an approach whose merits have been assessed in the previous chapters. Although Byzantine influence in *barbaricum* cannot be equated with the modern colonial experience, the exposure of village societies to a world system relying on the use of money might have elicited comparable responses regardless of time and space. Territories in *barbaricum* were never annexed or directly administered by Byzantium. No

---

[13] Several collections of essays over the past two decades have provided important insights for this type of comparison. See in particular H. Donnan and T. M. Wilson, eds., *Border Approaches: Anthropological Perspectives on Frontiers* (Lanham, MD, 1994); T. Wendl and M. Rösler, eds., *Frontiers and Borderlands: Anthropological Perspectives* (Frankfurt am Main, 1999); L. Russell, ed., *Colonial Frontiers: Indigenous–European Encounters in Settler Societies* (Manchester, 2001); B. J. Parker and L. Rodseth, eds., *Untaming the Frontier in Anthropology, Archaeology and History* (Tucson, AZ, 2005).

administrative ambitions are documented in the northern Balkans aside from the settlement of various ethnic groups as *foederati* with the purpose of defending the frontier. As a result, the use of money was never officially implemented, nor was taxation, although communities in *barbaricum* were well aware of the functions performed by coins in the Byzantine world. However, just like in many colonial settings, foreign coinage could be perceived as the cultural agent of an expansionist power and a potentially dangerous interference with local customs emphasizing gift-giving and reciprocity.

Unlike some colonial settings, the lands north of the Byzantine frontier on the Danube had been in contact with monetized cultures since the Hellenistic age if not earlier, going back to the Greek colonies established on the Black Sea coast. Tribal confederations rose and fell but a true monetary economy was never established and communities in *barbaricum* never rose above the status of peripheries or "mini-systems" at the edge of ancient empires, despite their tendency to imitate Greek and Roman silver coins.[14] Modern examples from Madagascar, which is perhaps the best documented case, show us that the island had been in contact with the monetized Arab world since the Fatimid period and yet modern coinages in the eighteenth and nineteenth century were still perceived as alien intrusions into the social fabric of the island. Similar to many of the colonial examples discussed below, Early Byzantine coins contributed to the creation of social distinction through their non-monetary use, their face and even intrinsic value being converted into social meaning. A stronger emphasis on such functions was also favored by the changing cultural landscape in Late Antiquity. The contraction of urban culture and Roman political weakness on the Middle and Lower Danube eroded the structures that had allowed Roman coinage to play an economic role in the previous centuries. This is not to say that local economic systems ever reached the point of requiring a high degree of monetization. Historically, the need for money in *barbaricum* was maintained artificially through

---

[14] Romanian numismatists have almost unanimously attributed the practice of imitation to the development of a monetary economy in Dacia and the neighboring regions; see in particular C. Preda, *Monedele geto-dacilor* (Bucharest, 1973); V. Mihailescu-Bîrliba, *La monnaie romaine chez les Daces orientaux* (Bucharest, 1980), 217–221 and 235–250; M. Chițescu, *Numismatic Aspects of the History of the Dacian State. The Roman Republican Coinage in Dacia and Geto-Dacian Coins of Roman Type* (Oxford, 1981), 46–61. For non-monetary uses of imitations, see M. Peter, "Imitations of Roman coins in non-Roman contexts: some remarks," in *Roman Coins Outside the Empire: Ways and Phases, Contexts and Functions*, eds. A. Bursche, R. Ciołek, and R. Wolters (Wetteren, 2008), 389–394.

contact with the Greco-Roman world rather than developing organically through the growing complexity of local culture. As the connection to Rome became weaker, the non-economic function of money became stronger.

Although the role of Byzantine coins in *barbaricum* may not be perfectly analogous to the function of money in "primitive societies," much can be learned from local responses to the introduction of European currency in the early stages of contact predating direct annexation and even during the colonial period. Three topics in particular can furnish valuable insights: alternative "monetary instruments" used by traditional societies, the non-monetary use of foreign currencies, and the morality of exchange mediated by money. They will be the focus of the next pages.

The type of coinage introduced in the ancient Mediterranean world and inherited by modern states did not become current in many parts of the world until the creation of modern colonial empires. However, the fact that traditional societies did not use money with the physical resemblance and the general purpose function of western currencies does not mean they did not employ other instruments of exchange.[15] What makes them different from the European all-purpose money is their dual function as economic tools and symbolic objects used in rituals and ceremonies. Their power was not so much derived from their intrinsic properties, although that was also important, as from their socially embedded value. This duality reflects the dichotomy between economic and non-economic exchange which can be noticed in many cultures, the Melanesian case studied by Malinowski being the classic example.[16]

---

[15] For primitive money, see C. Haselgrove and S. Krmnicek, "The archaeology of money," *ARA* 41 (2012): 235–250; P. Sibilla, "A proposito di moneta. Lineamenti di un percorso di ricerca," in *Antropologia dello scambio e della moneta*, ed. P. Sibilla (Torino, 2006), 9–46. From the older literature, see especially P. Bessaignet, "Monnaie primitive et théorie monétaire," *RESS* 21 (1970): 37–65; G. Tucci, Origine et développement de la monnaie primitive," *RESS* 21 (1970): 17–36; K. Polanyi, "The semantics of money uses," in *Primitive, Archaic, and Modern Economies: Essays of Karl Polanyi*, ed. G. Dalton (Garden City, NY, 1968), 175–203; G. Dalton, "Primitive money," *AA* 67, no. 1 (1965): 44–65; P. Einzig, *Primitive Money in Its Ethnological, Historical, and Economic Aspects*, 2nd ed. (New York, NY, 1966).

[16] B. Malinowski, *Argonauts of the Western Pacific: An Account of Native Enterprise and Adventure in the Archipelagoes of Melanesian New Guinea* (London, 1922). See more recently A. Gell, "Inter-tribal commodity barter and reproductive gift-exchange in Old Melanesia," in *Barter, Exchange and Value: An Anthropological Approach*, eds. C. Humphrey and S. Hugh-Jones (Cambridge, 1992), 142–168. See also the essays in *Money and Modernity*. For the duality, see K. Hart, "Heads or tails? Two sides of the coin," *Man* 21, no. 4 (1986): 637–656; M. Godelier, *Perspectives in Marxist Anthropology* (Cambridge, 1977), 128–129.

In the early modern period cowrie shells were used as the main medium of exchange. The cowrie (*cypraea moneta*) cannot be fully defined as "international currency," despite the fact that it was widely used from Africa to Oceania, because its value and exchange rate were locally determined based on idiosyncratic criteria seldom dictated by economic principles. Nevertheless, the use of such standardized objects as medium of exchange was facilitated by the development of long-distance trade where a mutually accepted instrument was required. Cowries and beads introduced by Europeans played this role for the greater part of the modern period. Moreover, cowries should not be treated as an eminently primitive monetary instrument. The cowrie system knew various lower denominations, forgeries, agreed upon prices, and exchange rates, as well as the dire consequences of inflation which could render large accumulations practically worthless.[17] The "modern" flavor of cowrie-based transactions is best illustrated by the economy of Kapauku Papuans, who had a primitive monetary economy, profit-motivated transactions, and prices regulated by demand and supply.[18]

Other monetary instruments included coins made of clay of different shapes, usually pierced, used by the Sao peoples in Cameroon, Chad, and Nigeria.[19] Most of them were star-shaped and their value depended on the number of corners and whether they were pierced or not. Much like other primitive forms of currency, such clay coins were also used as symbolic offerings.[20] Clay was not the only material employed for this purpose. The Buduma in the region of Lake Chad, the Lamba from Congo, and the Baruya from Papua New Guinea used units of salt as their main form of currency.[21] The Kotoko from Chad used stone in the pre-colonial period, mainly stone axes and smaller pieces of stone as lower denominations.[22] Rolled strips of cotton and a variety of iron objects counted among the

---

[17] C. A. Gregory, *Savage Money: The Anthropology and Politics of Commodity Exchange* (Amsterdam, 1997), 236–242.
[18] L. J. Pospisil, *The Kapauku Papuans of West New Guinea* (New York, NY, 1963), 300–309.
[19] For a comprehensive list of primitive money across the ages, see Einzig, *Primitive Money*, 29–308.
[20] J.-P. Lebeuf, "Monnaies archaïques africaines de terre cuite," *RESS* 21 (1970): 67.
[21] A. Dorsinfang-Smets, "Les moyens d'échange traditionnels dans le bassin congolais," *RESS* 21 (1970): 101; Lebeuf, "Monnaies archaïques," 81; M. Godelier, "'Monnaie de sel' et circulation des merchandises chez les Baruya de Nouvelle Guinée," *RESS* 21 (1970): 134.
[22] Lebeuf, "Monnaies archaïques," 81–83; The circulation of polished stone-axes was an old practice of Neolithic Europe, for which see E. Thirault, "The politics of supply: the Neolithic axe industry in Alpine Europe," *Antiquity* 79 (2005): 34–50.

acceptable monetary instruments in Central Africa.[23] In pre-colonial Madagascar cattle was the main medium of exchange and means of storing wealth.[24] Moving to the Western Hemisphere, various agricultural products and cotton were used in the Andes as monetary instruments in the pre-Columbian period, while in Mesoamerica cocoa beans and large white cotton cloaks (*quachtli*) served this purpose.[25] Even in the early colonial period cocoa beans and Spanish coins circulated side by side with regulated exchange rates between these two accepted monetary instruments. No sign of such instruments can be detected in the sixth-century archaeological record north of the Danube, but if any organic materials served this purpose they would no longer be traceable.

The adoption of metal coinage for either monetary on non-monetary purposes often relied on existing traditions. The use of metal in different forms and shapes as currency was a well-known ancient practice in Africa, documented by the author of *The Periplus of the Erythraean Sea* in the first century AD.[26] Copper bars continued to be used as currency in Niger, a fact recognized by Ibn Battuta who visited the region in 1352.[27] Small wire-like objects (3–4 cm long) called "fils à double tête" were used in political centers of the empires of Ghana and Mali between the eleventh and the fourteenth century and various copper ingots were used in the Copperbelt region of Central Africa.[28] The Mongo from Congo used red copper cylinders or copper jewelry as media of exchange. In addition, the so-called Katanga crosses made of copper (weighing ca. 750 g or more) were valued for the metal and melted down to produce copper jewelry. The smaller versions are often found in burial assemblages dating from the early modern period.[29] Similarly,

---

[23] Lebeuf, "Monnaies archaïques," 72–80; Dorsinfang-Smets, "Les moyens d'échange," 102–103.

[24] J. Dez, "Monnaie et structures traditionelles à Madagascar," *RESS* 21 (1970): 185.

[25] C. Lazo García, *Economia colonial y regimen monetario. Peru: siglos XVI–XIX. Tomo I: Nascimiento e instauración del sistema económico monetario colonial (siglo XVI)* (Lima, 1992), 55–57; J. L. de Rojas, *La moneda indígena y sus usos en la Nueva España en el siglo XVI* (Tlalpan, DF, 1998), 183–187.

[26] *Periplus Maris Erythraei*, 6: καὶ ὠρόχαλκος, ᾧ χρῶνται πρὸς κόσμον καὶ εἰς συγκοπὴν ἀντὶ νομίσματος.

[27] N. Levtzion and J. F. P Hopkins, eds., *Corpus of Early Arabic Sources for West African History*, trans. J. F. P. Hopkins (Princeton, NJ, 2000), 302.

[28] L. Garenne-Marot, "'Fils à double tête' and copper-based ingots: copper money-objects at the time of the Sahelian Empires of ancient Ghana and Mali," in *Money in Africa*, 1–8; P. de Maret, "L'évolution monétaire du Shaba Central entre le 7e et le 18e siècle," *African Economic History* 10 (1981): 125–128.

[29] Dorsinfang-Smets, "Les moyens d'échange," 104; de Maret, "L'évolution monétaire," 128–143.

the Tiv people in Nigeria used three-foot brass rods as money, which they often melted down to cast jewelry.[30]

The main motivation behind the use of foreign currencies was the demand for cash revenue, which forced cultivators to sell a portion of their crops as well as manufactured goods to raise money. Indeed, much like the case of Byzantine villages, in well-established colonial settings money was needed to pay taxes. Besides taxation, in most situations foreign money was the only form of payment one could use to purchase foreign goods needed in the household or acquired to increase the social prestige of the owner.[31] Evidence shows that European coins introduced in Congo in the 1920s were used primarily to procure Western goods.[32] The Azande saw money as a special type of instrument needed to gain access to goods they could not produce themselves but almost nothing was spent on subsistence goods.[33] The Hausa people in Nigeria first encountered Western coins when traders from the Mediterranean coast of North Africa extended their business to the south. Payment had to be made in coin and the local elite had to raise cash in order to buy Western products such as weapons.[34] In Asia, the Lhomi from Nepal used money only for purchasing cooking oil, lamps, and medicine from the bazaar.[35] In most cases, however, coinage was not needed or was even banned from the purchase of food or other locally produced subsistence goods and the general impression is that nothing indispensable was bought with coins. All these developments took place under colonial regimes and there is no evidence that Western money was used in the pre-colonial period. This is an important point to consider when studying the Byzantine case since no provinces were created in *barbaricum*. Byzantine coins could have been acquired with the sole purpose of using them to purchase luxury goods from the frontier region, and only by those communities close enough to the Danube or the Black Sea.

One of the keys to understanding whether communities in *barbaricum* accepted Byzantine coins as a form of payment is to determine the level of

---

[30] P. Bohannan, "The impact of money on an African subsistence economy," *The Journal of Economic History* 19, no. 4 (1959): 498.
[31] C. J. Fuller, "Misconceiving the grain heap: a critique of the concept of the Indian Jajmani system," in *Money and Morality*, 45.
[32] Dorsinfang-Smets, "Les moyens d'échange," 108–110.
[33] C. R. Reining, "The role of money in the Zande economy," *AA* 61, no. 1 (1959): 40.
[34] G. Nicolas, "Circulations des biens et échanges monétaires en pays haoussa (Niger)," *RESS* 21 (1970): 114.
[35] C. Humphrey, "Barter and economic disintegration," *Man* 20, no. 1 (1985): 57.

trust needed for such transactions to take place. The value of the copper *follis* fluctuated a great deal in the sixth century, usually downwards, being constantly depreciated in relation to the gold *solidus*. Ethnographic parallels suggest that non-monetized village communities were reluctant to use money and preferred barter, unless the intrinsic value of foreign money was particularly appealing. People as diverse as the Nepalese, the Nigerians, the Kwaio from Solomon Islands, and the Greek villagers from Ambéli on the island of Euboea distrusted money because of its unstable value and fiduciary nature.[36] Money was an instrument eminently unsecure, something to get rid of before it becomes worthless.

Moreover, no issuing state wants to see its coinage drain outside the frontier, especially when it is not token coinage but essentially commodity money. The Byzantine legislation prohibiting the export of precious-metal coins finds an interesting equivalent in modern concerns with the same issue. The natives of Madagascar got so fond of European silver coins that they accepted only monetary payments in exchange for their goods, although they had no intention of releasing those coins back on the market. Fearing that large quantities of silver would be lost, European powers were desperately trying to discourage this practice complaining that "the silver 5 Franc pieces are diligently sought by the natives from Madagascar in exchange for their products which they would not sell, most often, unless they are paid in piasters which they bury with their dead or convert into ornaments and jewelry."[37] Such practices were sometimes a form of resistance to the ambitions of the colonial state, as in British West Africa where the Africans – perhaps as an act of defiance – continued to melt down European money and use indigenous currencies instead.[38]

---

[36] P. M. Shipton, *Bitter Money: Cultural Economy and Some African Meanings of Forbidden Commodities* (Washington, DC, 1989), 6. Humphrey, "Barter and economic," 63; J. du Boulay, *Portrait of a Greek Mountain Village* (Oxford, 1974), 37; S. Heap, "'A Bottle of gin is dangled before the nose of the natives': gin currency in colonial Southern Nigeria," in *Money in Africa*, 35; D. Akin, "Cash and shell money in Kwaio, Solomon Islands," in *Money and Modernity*, 109–113.

[37] The account dates to 1867; see J. Chauvicourt and S. Chauvicourt, *Numismatique malgache. Fasc. 3. Les premières monnaies introduites à Madagascar* (Antananarivo, 1968), 24–25, "Quant aux pièces de 5 francs en argent elles sont recherchées avec avidité par les naturels de Madagascar en échange de leur produits qu'ils ne cèdent le plus souvent qu'à la condition d'être payés en piastres destinées à être enfouies chez eux ou converties en ornements ou parures."

[38] H. Fuller, "From cowries to coins: money and colonialism in the Gold Coast and British West Africa in the early 20th Century," in *Money in Africa*, 60. African nickel coins, which had a hole in the center, were used by carpenters and smiths as washers for nails and screws; see A. A. Lawal, "The currency revolution in British West Africa: an analysis of some early problems," in *Money in Africa*, 63.

In the initial phase of contact, silver coins were acquired like any other European object and used as ornaments in necklaces or bracelets. The most common silver coins were piasters, reali ("pieces of eight"), and especially Maria Theresa thalers.[39] Again, the economic vs. non-economic duality is present. Pre-colonial Kilwa Islamic coinage is a case in point. The town of Kilwa Kisiwani on the Swahili coast minted its own coinage in the name of various sultans from the eleventh through the fifteenth century. Most of the coins were copper issues destined for local circulation but their function was not exclusively economic. Many were used as commemorative objects and some five percent of the coins were pierced indicating that they were used as pendants.[40] This is strikingly similar to the figure of ca. seven percent calculated for the number of pierced *folles* of Justinian, probably used for the same purpose.[41] On the other hand, monetary dealings with foreigners were done only in precious-metal coinage. No doubt the natives had more confidence in the purity of coined silver and recognized coins as instruments carefully regulated by the issuing authority. Nicolas Mayeur, an eighteenth-century trader and traveler in Madagascar drew attention to the fact that the Merina are willing to accept "any coins provided they are of silver and have the proper weight," adding that "they may accept scrap or crafted silver but prefer it monetized and are even willing to lower their prices if they know that payment will be done in coin."[42] The same sentiment was expressed by M. Blancart, a French trader who regretted the good old days when barter alone could do the job: "in the past everything was done with goods; and right now the natives only

---

[39] A. E. Tschoegl, "Maria Theresa's Thaler: a case of international money," *Eastern Economic Journal* 27, no. 4 (2001): 443–462.

[40] S. Wynne-Jones and J. Fleisher, "Coins in context: local economy, value and practice on the East African Swahili coast," *Cambridge Archaeological Journal* 22, no. 1 (2012): 32.

[41] A. Gandila, "Early Byzantine coin circulation in the eastern provinces: a statistical approach," *AJN* 21 (2009): 177. For the pierced Byzantine coins used as religious amulets see C. Morrisson, "Monnaies et amulettes byzantines à motifs chrétiens: croyance ou magie?" in *Les savoirs magiques et leur transmission de l'Antiquité à la Renaissance*, eds. V. Dasen and J.-M. Spieser (Florence, 2014), 414–449. More generally on pierced coins during Roman, Byzantine, and Early Medieval times at C. Perassi, "Monete romane forate: qualche riflessione su 'un grand theme européen' (J.-P. Callu)," *Aevum* 85, no. 2 (2011): 257–315.

[42] N. Mayeur, "Voyage dans le sud et dans l'intérieur des terres et plus particulièrement au pays d'Hancove," *Bulletin de l'Académie Malgache* 12 (1913): 163: "Toutes espèces monnayées quelconques, pourvu qu'elles soient d'argent et que le poids y soit, leur conviennent. Ils reçoivent aussi l'argent coupé ou travaillé mais ils donnent la préférence à celui qui est monnayé, et même font une diminution assez grande sur le prix des objets quand ils savent qu'ils seront payés de cette manière."

accept piasters."[43] The adoption of European coins as an accepted form of currency in Madagascar led to the practice of cutting the coins in halves and quarters and they would cut as many as 720 small pieces from an original coin in order to be used as lower denominations.[44]

Still, the non-monetary use of European money often took precedence. One of the most important functions of foreign coins in primitive societies on four different continents was that of jewelry or bullion for the production of bracelets, necklaces, and earrings (Figure 38).[45] This practice is clearly reflected in Jacques Dez's observations in Madagascar:

> In this non-monetized country coins were originally integrated in the local system according to their intrinsic value not based on their monetary function. Coins were nothing else but objects to be bartered. They could be assembled to create dress sets or melted down to produce silver jewelry or silver blades to be deposited in royal coffins.[46]

Sometimes foreign coins were used as jewelry with only minor modifications. The Fali from Cameroon used pierced French and English silver coins to adorn leather bands worn around their heads.[47] In Asia, the Lhomi from Nepal melted down silver coins to produce bracelets or belts or used the coins as jewelry, sewing them on women's hats or turning them into finger rings.[48] The same social prestige was sought by villagers from Ambéli on Euboea (Greece) who displayed their wealth by having a gold coin sewn onto the front of shoes to be worn on special occasions.[49] Iconography is also important as testified by the case of the silver five franc piece displaying Hercules and two muses (Trinity allegory) often

---

[43] L. Molet, "Les monnaies à Madagascar," *RESS* 21 (1970): 206: "Autrefois, tout se faisait avec des marchandises; et maintenant les naturels ne veulent plus que des piastres."

[44] S. Kus and V. Raharijaona, "Small change in Madagascar: sacred coins and profane coinage," in *The Archaeology of Politics: The Materiality of Political Practice and Action in the Past*, eds. P. G. Johansen and A. M. Bauer (Newcastle upon Tyne, 2011), 39; Chauvicourt and Chauvicourt, *Numismatique malgache*, 18.

[45] Chauvicourt and Chauvicourt, *Numismatique malgache*, 4.

[46] Dez, "Monnaie et structures," 181: "La monnaie à l'origine, dans ce pays qui ne connaissait pas la monnaie, sera également reçue comme devant être intégrée dans ce système, c'est-à-dire prise dans sa nature matérielle et non comme signe monétaire. Elle ne sera rien d'autre qu'un objet de troc, et les pièces de monnaie se retrouveront réunies en parure, ou fondues pour faire de bijoux d'argent, ou des lames d'argent qui seront déposées dans les cercueils royaux." It was said that king Radama, who died in 1828, was buried in a silver coffin made from 14,000 Spanish silver coins, weighing almost 375 kg and several other examples are known from the nineteenth century, for which see Chauvicourt and Chauvicourt, *Numismatique malgache*, 7.

[47] J.-P. Lebeuf, *Vêtements et parures du Cameroun français* (Paris, 1946), 37–38 and pl. II/D, III/A, and VI/B–C.

[48] Humphrey, "Barter and economic," 63.   [49] du Boulay, *Portrait of a Greek*, 244.

7.2 New Barbarians: Primitive Cash and Colonial Money 257

Figure 38 First-to-third-century mummy portraits with coin-necklaces and coin-pendants

used as pendant on silver necklaces worn by young men from Madagascar.[50] In light of such examples, the tendency to mount Byzantine coins into sets, necklaces, pendants, and finger rings in "barbarian" cultures from the Carpathians to the Caucasus comes as no surprise.

Finally, the morality of monetary exchanges is a concern that goes back to Aristotle and has long fascinated anthropologists who study the use of money in traditional societies. A wealth of literary evidence shows that contempt for monetary transactions – banking, usury, and profit stored in monetary form – was common in the Roman world and some of these taboos carried over into the Middle Ages.[51] Moreover, it is undeniable that money gained a negative symbolism in many societies around the world.[52] The traditional system of exchange in most village societies of the early modern age was some form of barter. In many cases this remained the preferred form of exchange even after the introduction of European money. Whether we are talking about the Lhomi of Nepal, the Merina of Madagascar or the east African farmers in Kenya, barter was dominated by the idea of equal exchange, a morally acceptable and socially fulfilling means of acquiring subsistence goods.[53]

European money was seen as a potential threat to the social structures in place. Money served to depersonalize social relations, to simplify them, and reduce their meaning. The case of Madagascar remains the best documented. The Merina drew a clear distinction between unpaid work performed as community service (*miasa*) and wages received from foreigners (*mikarama*), the latter gaining a negative connotation when they interfered with ancestral laws.[54] For the peoples of the eastern coast, "money is presented as having a power eminently corrosive, it is the main reason for the destruction of kinship, the binding solidarities of the village."[55] As a consequence, those who were employed and received monetary wages from foreigners were excluded from the village community, becoming themselves strangers through their economic position.[56] The same threat to the authority of the elders can be perceived in the function of money in

---

[50] Kus and Raharijaona, "Small change," 47–48.
[51] M. Hénaff, *The Price of Truth: Gift, Money, and Philosophy* (Stanford, CA, 2010).
[52] J. Parry and M. Bloch, "Introduction: money and the morality of exchange," in *Money and Morality*, 21; N. Morley, *Trade in Classical Antiquity* (Cambridge, 2007), 79–89.
[53] Humphrey, "Barter and economic," 64; Dez, "Monnaie et structures," 180.
[54] M. Bloch, "The symbolism of money in Imerina," in *Money and Morality*, 175.
[55] G. Althabe, "Circulation monétaire et communautés villageoises malgaches," *RESS* 21 (1970): 149: "L'argent [...] est présenté alors comme possédant une puissance singulièrement corrosive, il est le grand destructeur des lignages, des solidarités constitutives du village."
[56] Althabe, "Circulation monétaire," 164.

other parts of the world. The Dande communities from Zimbabwe were slightly more liberal with the acceptance of coins so long as it did not challenge ancestral customs.[57] The Kwaio from Solomon Islands are still more conservative and refuse to allow the use of cash in prestige economy, drawing a clear distinction between European and traditional Kwaio practices.[58] This custom has a long history. On New Georgia local clam shell rings used as money (*poata*) were divided into sacred shells associated with deities and ordinary shells used in routine exchange which could be officially traded for British pounds, shillings, and pence.[59]

The means by which money was acquired was also important. In Kenya and Gambia, money obtained through theft, usury or by accident is considered "bitter money," boding ill for its owner.[60] For such reasons, money was often "purified" to gain a neutral or even positive symbolism. In Madagascar money was often obtained as payment for agricultural products – an immoral practice – but was spent on prestige-gaining activities such as building houses or honoring the ancestors by erecting funerary monuments.[61] Another popular form of purification was the royal ceremony in which the king received tokens of deference (*hasina*) in the form of coins.[62] We find similar concerns in Fiji where the traditional ritual of fundraising presupposed the purification of money through the ceremony of "drinking cash."[63]

Coins could have a magical function usually connected to the symbolism of precious metals or to their apotropaic force recognized since ancient times.[64] In Madagascar coins were used in purification rituals by being thrown into water before the ceremony of washing and in other cases to

---

[57] D. Lan, "Resistance to the present by the past: mediums and money in Zimbabwe," in *Money and the Morality*, eds. Parry and Bloch, 203.

[58] Akin, "Cash and shell money," 113–126. The fear that money posed a threat to social structures was not universal. See for instance the case of the Kwanga from Papua New Guinea who did not draw an opposition between money and local media of exchange, K. Brison, "Money and the morality of exchange among the Kwanga, East Sepik Province, Papua New Guinea," in *Money and Modernity*, 155–161.

[59] N. Thomas, *Exchange, Material Culture, and Colonialism in the Pacific* (Cambridge, MA, 1991), 46–47.

[60] Shipton, *Bitter Money*, 28 and 72–73.   [61] Althabe, "Circulation monétaire," 156.

[62] D. Graeber, *Toward an Anthropological Theory of Value: The False Coin of Our Own Dreams* (New York, NY, 2001), 232–237.

[63] C. Toren, "Drinking cash: the purification of money through ceremonial exchange in Fiji," in *Money and Morality*, 151.

[64] H. Maguire, "Magic and money in the Early Middle Ages," *Speculum* 72, no. 4 (1997): 1037–1054.

ensure immunity before appearing in court.[65] In India silver rupee coins could symbolize deities and were kept in clay pots storing the spiritual wealth of the clan.[66] In the Andes foreign coins are still hoarded and buried into the ground, constituting the treasure of the community, dug up and counted every year during a rain-calling ceremony called *Chaopincha*.[67] In Mexico, Central America, and Colombia money was "baptized" to become officially acceptable.[68] Common monetary instruments or specially designed ones were used as part of the traditional bride price in many primitive societies, such as Musanga shell disc money from Congo, but also on the Greek island of Euboea where gold coins were stored in chests to be given away as dowry.[69] Communities from four different continents are thus linked by this constant preoccupation with purifying coins seen as external agents potentially harmful to social harmony.

The ways in which the coinage of expanding colonial powers affected the economic and cultural life of traditional village communities in different parts of the world can guide our analysis of earlier situations where textual evidence is far less abundant. Foreign currency was adapted rather than adopted and seldom replaced the existing norms governing local exchange systems. Although traditional societies may have been in close contact with a monetized world system, not adhering to its practices was a form of cultural resistance, a deliberate effort to preserve ancestral customs. Barter or ad hoc monetary instruments dominated an economic activity deeply embedded in social norms and rituals, which never became the equivalent of the impersonal framework typical of capitalist societies. Since the Early Byzantine economy is often described as a pre-capitalist monetized market economy, we should be even less inclined to accept the survival of the monetary function once Byzantine coins crossed the frontier to become part of cultures governed by different values.[70] Although only certain types of behavior documented in the colonial period are directly traceable in the Byzantine record, it behooves us to approach the issue from a wider perspective and abandon the strictly economistic interpretation.

---

[65] Dez, "Monnaie et structures," 182–183.   [66] Gregory, *Savage Money*, 71–72.

[67] Ethnographic research and footage taken in 1996 by Axel Nielsen, Consejo Nacional de Investigaciones Científicas y Técnicas, Buenos Aires, Argentina, in the province of Nor Lipez, Department Potosí, Bolivia.

[68] Shipton, *Bitter Money*, 75.

[69] Dorsinfang-Smets, "Les moyens d'échange," 107; du Boulay, *Portrait of a Greek*, 244.

[70] See most recently J.-M. Carrié, "Were Late Roman and Byzantine economies market economies? A comparative look at historiography," in *Trade and Markets in Byzantium*, ed. C. Morrisson (Washington, DC, 2012), 13–26.

7.3 The Price of Money on the Northern Frontier of Byzantium

What was, then, the function of sixth- and seventh-century Byzantine coins in *barbaricum*? Gold and silver coins clearly served no monetary purpose. They were stored for their intrinsic value and constituted objects of prestige, much like Roman coins in the previous centuries.[71] As we have seen in the previous chapters, precious-metal coinage was often the preferred medium used by Byzantine emperors to establish political alliances with various tribes. Collections such as found at Chibati and Nokalakevi in Georgia, Malo Pereshchepyne in Ukraine, and Zemiansky Vrbovok in Slovakia are fragmentary reflections of political payments sent directly from Constantinople. The large number of gold coins found in burials and the frequency of *solidi* and *tremisses* pierced or modified to be worn as jewelry indicates that Byzantine coins acted as status markers in societies from *barbaricum*. In addition, the number of gold-plated imitations of Byzantine *solidi* found in the Carpathian Basin, the Pontic steppe, and the Ciscaucasus, probably produced for those who could not afford genuine pieces, confirms the high demand for coins and underscores their non-economic function.[72]

Finds of *solidi* from the core regions of the Avar Khaganate confirm the flow of gold described by written sources. It seems that the Avars kept the gold in monetary form mostly to be included in burial assemblages, much like the natives of Madagascar observed by the Marquis de Mondevergue in 1868: "If they possessed any coins, they would bury them with their dead."[73] Graves from Kölked-Feketekapu, Tiszagyenda Gói tó, Pécs Alsómakár-dűlő, and Szentendre in Hungary produced gold coins of Justin II,

---

[71] A. Bursche, *Later Roman–Barbarian Contacts in Central Europe: Numismatic Evidence* (Berlin, 1996). See also A. Bursche, "Function of Roman coins in *Barbaricum* of Later Antiquity. An anthropological essay," in *Roman Coins Outside the Empire: Ways and Phases, Contexts and Functions*, eds. A. Bursche, R. Ciołek, and R. Wolters (Wetteren, 2008), 395–416; For a monetary interpretation of finds, cf. S. K. Drummond and L. H. Nelson, *The Western Frontiers of Imperial Rome* (Armonk, NY, 1994), 109–110.

[72] I. Bóna, ""Barbarische" Nachahmungen von byzantinischen Goldmünzen im Awarenreich," *RIN* 95 (1993): 529–538; Y. A. Prokopenko, "K voprosu o severo-kavkazskikh podrazhaniiakh vizantiiskim monetnim obrazcam," *Vestnik stavropol'skogo gosudarstvennogo pedagogicheskogo universiteta* 1 (1995): 63–67; S. V. Gusev, *Severo-Vostochnyi Kavkaz v epokhu srednevekov'ia: monety rasskazyvaiut* (Moscow, 1995), 19–24; Somogyi, *Byzantinische Fundmünzen der Awarenzeit*, 243–245, table 4; K. V. Golenko, "Imitacii solida VII v. iz Podneprov'ya," *VV* 11 (1956): 292–294.

[73] Chauvicourt and Chauvicourt, *Numismatique malgache*, 7 ("S'ils ont quelques pièces de monnaie, ils les enterrent avec leurs morts").

Tiberius II, Maurice, and Phocas.[74] Sometimes the coins are uncirculated (Szentendre) and many were used as *oboli*, judging by their position in the grave, regardless of the social status of the deceased. Others were local imitations, including "mules" such as the piece from Tác-Gorsium, a hybrid imitation of *solidi* of Tiberius II and Maurice.[75] An imitation of Maurice was also found in Transylvania at Rupea (Romania) evidencing the extension of this practice to the east.[76] Copper coins were themselves deposited as *oboli* but they were also part of waist purses as indicated by the burial assemblages from Jutas, Kölked-Feketekapu, Egerlövő, and Várpalota in Hungary.[77] They were found together with other small objects, but no other coins, so the existence of coin purses is out of the question. In other cases, the coins were perforated to be worn on a necklace or perhaps attached to a piece of garment, but the fashion of using Byzantine coins as jewelry would become more popular on coins of the Heraclian house.[78] After the failed siege of Constantinople (626) the Avar khagan could not hope to obtain any more gold from Byzantium so the social value of Byzantine coins in the Avar world increased accordingly. The tendency to use seventh-century Byzantine coins as jewelry (rings and pendants), rather than simply melting them down, is documented archaeologically in a wide region from Transylvania to the eastern Merovingian world.[79]

Although the picture might be distorted by the fact that Avar archaeology has been devoted almost exclusively to the study of cemeteries, the abundance of Byzantine coins and their imitations in graves cannot be ignored. Although many were used as *oboli*, almost 20 percent of the gold coins were de-monetized, perhaps reflecting a double role as jewelry and *obolus*, as well as the act of appropriation through physical modification.[80] Many such coins seem to be associated with female graves, although more data is needed before advancing any hypothesis. In many cases the perforated gold coins are placed in the area of the left or right shoulder, a clear

---

[74] Somogyi, *Byzantinische Fundmünzen*, 56, no. 39; 57, no. 41/2; 87–88, no. 77; and 88–89, no. 78; Somogyi, "Byzantinische Fundmünzen," 279–280, no. 10 and 284–285, no. 15.
[75] Somogyi, *Byzantinische Fundmünzen*, 89–90, no. 80.   [76] Velter, *Transilvania*, 298, no. 144.
[77] Somogyi, *Byzantinische Fundmünzen*, 38–39, no. 21; 48–49, no. 33; 57, no. 41/1; and 93, no. 84.
[78] Nyíregyháza-Kertgazdaság (a lightweight *solidus* perforated twice) and Tác-Gorsium (fourrée *solidus*): Somogyi, *Byzantinische Fundmünzen*, 67–68, no. 52 and 89–90, no. 80.
[79] Somogyi, *Byzantinische Fundmünzen*, 142; J. Militký, "Finds of the Early Byzantine coins of the 6th and 7th century in the territory of the Czech Republic," in *Byzantine Coins*, 364; J. Drauschke, "Byzantinische Münzen des ausgehenden 5. bis beginnenden 8. Jahrhunderts in den östlichen Regionen des Merowingerreiches," in *Byzantine Coins*, 283 and 292.
[80] Somogyi, *Byzantinische Fundmünzen der Awarenzeit*, 141–151.

sign that Avar women liked to attach Byzantine coins to their clothes.[81] When they appear in male graves, they are associated with military equipment and/or horse gear.[82] In such warrior burials Byzantine coins were included to highlight the elevated social status of the deceased. Interestingly, none of the copper coins found in Avar graves were pierced suggesting that only gold coins served this function in *Avaria*.[83] The same is true for burial assemblages from the Caucasus where genuine Byzantine *solidi* mounted to work as pendants are surpassed in number by imitations and bracteates made of thin gold-plated foil, which clearly had a ritual function and not a monetary one.

Nevertheless, many gold coins were melted down to produce spectacular jewelry. Fewer than 200 gold coins have been found in the Carpathian Basin dominated by the Avars, a paltry residue of the huge quantity of *solidi* sent by Byzantine emperors to *Avaria* as tribute. This is clear indication of the fact that most coins served as raw material for the Avar jewelry now on display in many Central European museums. The use of coins to produce jewelry in *barbaricum* has already been tested by means of correlation between the weight of coins and that of small pieces of jewelry, usually earrings with pendants and bracelets.[84] However, such calculations are not required to demonstrate that coins were used for this purpose. Goldsmiths cut coins as needed to produce their jewelry and this is testified by the eighth-century workshop found at Beth She'an in Palestine where pieces of gold jewelry were found together with cut gold coins.[85] The use of *solidi* for such purposes is also confirmed by contemporary accounts. When discussing the external politics of rival Persia, Theophylact Simocatta did not miss the chance to emphasize the Persians' weakness for being compelled to send 40,000 gold *solidi* every year to the Turks to keep them quiet. Lavished by such gifts "this particular nation had turned to great extravagance; for they hammered out gold couches, tables, goblets,

---

[81] P. Somogyi, "Byzantinische Fundmünzen als Quelle zur Archäologie der Awaren," figs. 2–4, forthcoming.

[82] A similar practice was documented in Early Medieval mounted warrior graves from Serpovoe, Tambov region, Russia where coins were affixed on leather straps; see V. V. Kropotkin, *Klady vizantiiskikh monet na territorii SSSR* (Moscow, 1962), 29, no. 125.

[83] This was not the case in the Byzantine world where pierced copper coins are found in sixth-century graves; e.g. P. Delougaz, "Coins," in *A Byzantine church at Khirbat Al-Karak*, eds. P. Delougaz and R. C. Haines (Chicago, IL, 1960), 50–52 and pl. 46/12–17.

[84] Bóna, "Byzantium and the Avars," 117; J. Werner, "Die frühgeschichtlichen Grabfunde vom Spielberg bei Erlbach, Ldkr. Nördlingen, und von Fürst, Ldkr. Laufen a.d. Salzach," *BV* 25 (1960): 171–172.

[85] I owe this information to Gabriela Bijovsky, Israel Antiquities Authority, Jerusalem.

thrones, pedestals, horse-trappings, suits of armor, and everything which has been devised by the inebriation of wealth."[86] The account may have been exaggerated for propagandistic purposes, but the practice itself was real.

Official payments from Constantinople were not the only means of transferring gold coins to *barbaricum*. Additional channels include plunder, ransom for prisoners, and enslavement of captives taken from the Byzantine provinces; they are well documented in written sources and underscore the non-economic dimension of cultural interaction. Roman POWs and especially VIPs fallen into captivity were ransomed for gold coins without exception when a monetary ransom was involved. Since we have to rely on anecdotal evidence, the actual amounts often appear arbitrary. In the fifth century the Huns required nine gold pieces for each Roman POW.[87] By 600, the Avars had much more modest demands when they requested one *solidus* for each prisoner. The khagan was ready to bargain when Emperor Maurice refused the initial offer and lowered the sum to a half-*solidus*, but according to Theophanes the Byzantine ruler would not even agree to pay four *keratia* (one *solidus* = 24 *keratia*) so the khagan slew the prisoners angered at the Emperor's "Markianism."[88] By comparison, an unspecified number of prisoners had been ransomed from the Goths in 517 against 1,000 pounds of coined gold (*mille librarum auri denarios*), the equivalent of 72,000 *solidi*.[89] Important prisoners were worth much more. The "Bulgars" who invaded Scythia and Moesia sometime at the beginning of Justinian's reign managed to capture Constantiolus, the commander of the Roman army. According to Theophanes, the emperor paid 1,000 gold coins to ransom his careless general, while Malalas, writing closer to the time of the event but not necessarily better informed, advanced the sum of 10,000 *solidi*.[90]

---

[86] Theophylact Simocatta, *Historia*, 3.6.10–11 (trans. Whitby): πολυχρύσου τοίνυν τῆς τῶν Τούρκων ἀρχῆς ὑπὸ τῶν Περσῶν γεγονυίας, ἐς μεγάλην τοῦτο δὴ τὸ ἔθνος ἐτέτραπτο πολυτέλειαν κλίνας τε γὰρ ἐσφυρηλατοῦντο χρυσᾶς καὶ τραπέζας καὶ κύλικας καὶ θρόνους καὶ βήματα ἱππικούς τε κόσμους καὶ πανοπλίας, καὶ ὅσα τῇ μέθῃ τοῦ πλούτου ἐπινενόηται.

[87] Priscus, *History*, 1 (Blockley).

[88] Theophanes, *Chronographia*, 280, AM 6092 [599/600]. Not just the khagan was annoyed by the Emperor's unwillingness to strike a deal, but also the Christian-minded population of Constantinople who chanted slogans mocking the emperor for his avarice; see M. Graebner, "'Μαυρίκιε Μαρκιανιστά.' A note," *Byzantina* 11 (1982): 181–188.

[89] Marcellinus, *Chronicon*, a. 517.

[90] Theophanes, *Chronographia*, 218, AM 6031 [538/9]; Malalas, *Chronographia*, 18.21, who dates the event a decade earlier.

Many ransoms of less conspicuous captives remained unrecorded and brought additional gold to *barbaricum*.[91] That much can be inferred from the large number of Romans enslaved by barbarians during their frequent inroads south of the Danube, which prompted Justinian's appeal to local churches, urging them to sell property in order to redeem the captives.[92] These episodes became almost a *topos* in the writings of Procopius who always mentioned the combination of booty and prisoners taken by Cutrigurs, Antes, Slavs, and Gepids who invaded the Balkans during the reign of Justinian. When provided, numbers seem inflated – the 120,000 prisoners taken by the Cutrigurs comes to mind – but the problem itself was very real and forced population movements could further erode the social, economic, and defensive structures of the Balkans.[93] In the embassy sent by the Utigurs to Justinian, thousands of Roman prisoners taken by the Cutrigurs were invoked in support of their request to be granted the subsidies once due to the Cutrigurs. Apparently, the monetary payments received thus far had been put to good use as the Utigurs jealously sneered at their Cutrigur rivals who were "wearing gold and had no lack of fine clothes that are embroidered and overlaid with gold."[94] Justinian's savvy diplomatic maneuvers bore fruit when many Roman captives, tens of thousands taken by the Cutrigurs during their incursions, managed to take advantage of the war with the Utigurs and returned home unharmed.[95]

---

[91] On captivity in Late Antiquity, see N. Lenski, "Captivity and Romano-Barbarian interchange," in *Romans, Barbarians, and the Transformation of the Roman World. Cultural Interaction and the Creation of Identity in Late Antiquity*, eds. R. Mathisen and D. Shanzer (Farnham, 2011), 185–198. On the topic of ransomed prisoners we can still rely on E. Levy, "Captivus redemptus," *Classical Philology* 38, no. 3 (1943): 159–176.

[92] *Corpus Iuris Civilis*, Novella 120, Cap. 9: ταῖς δὲ ἁγιωτάταις ἐκκλησίαις Ὀδησσοῦ καὶ Τόμεως τῶν πόλεων ἐπιτρέπομεν ἐκποιεῖν πράγματα ἀκίνητα ὑπὲρ τῆς τῶν αἰχμαλώτων ἀναρρύσεως. Novella LXV from 538 further alludes to fund raising organized by the Moesian Church to ransom Romans taken into captivity: *ita ut in venditionis instrumento ipsa verba testatoris exprimantur, ubi ei placuit venditionem fieri et redemptionem ex his captivorum vel alimonias pauperum celebrari*.

[93] Procopius, *Bella*, 6.4.6. Elsewhere Procopius mentions large numbers of prisoners, without providing figures, taken by the Antes in the early 540s before they became allies of the Empire; Procopius, *Bella*, 7.14.11.

[94] Procopius, *Bella*, 8.19.17 (trans Dewing, rev. Kaldellis): καὶ χρυσοφοροῦσιν οἱ πλανῆται καὶ ἱματίων οὐκ ἀμοιροῦσι λεπτῶν τε καὶ πεποικιλμένων καὶ καταληλειμμένων χρυσῷ. For Justinian's *Realpolitik* in the region north of the Black Sea, see D. Syrbe, "Reiternomaden des Schwarzmeerraums (Kutriguren und Utiguren) und byzantinische Diplomatie im 6. Jahrhundert," *Acta Orientalia* 65, no. 3 (2012): 291–316. A hoard of 50 lightweight *solidi* of Justinian, dated 542–565, found at Beloyariv'ka near Saur Mogil'skiy in the Donets'k region (Ukraine) may reflect political payments sent to the Cutrigurs and Justinian's political game of manipulating the Cutrigur–Utigur feud; see Kropotkin, *Klady vizantiiskikh*, 36, no. 253.

[95] Procopius, *Bella*, 8.19.2.

Although the scale of the event may have been dramatized once more, this was a recurring episode. There can be no doubt that the Slavic invasions around 550 led to additional displacements of population north of the Danube. The Slavs took booty (χρήματα) and enslaved "the young and the old alike" and later sacked Toperos on the Black Sea killing 15,000 men and enslaving tens of thousands of women and children.[96] In the end they crossed the Danube back to their homeland with "countless thousands of prisoners."[97]

We should not treat these accounts with undue suspicion, especially since this had been an endemic problem in the Balkans since the fifth century.[98] In addition, Procopius is not the only author to mention the multitude of Romans taken into captivity by barbarians. Slavic attacks intensified in the last quarter of the sixth century and provided contemporary writers further opportunity to lament the miserable fate of the population from the Balkan provinces. According to Menander, after a retaliation staged by Tiberius II in 579 in cooperation with the Avars, tens of thousands of Roman captives north of the Danube were set free by the khagan.[99] Unfortunately, the Byzantine maneuvers north of the Danube backfired. John of Ephesus informs us that the Slavs ravaged the Balkans for four years (581–584), took more captives and got rich with the gold and silver plundered from the Romans.[100] As far as the prisoners are concerned, such accounts are at odds with what we otherwise know about the Slavs' attitude toward Roman captives from the anonymous author of the *Strategikon* who tells us that prisoners were free to return home for a small monetary ransom (μισθός), unless they decided to stay and become full members of the community.[101] Some of these prisoners who remained in

---

[96] Procopius, *Bella*, 7.29.1: κτείνοντες καὶ ἀνδραποδίζοντες τοὺς ἐν ποσὶν ἡβηδὸν ἅπαντας καὶ τὰ χρήματα ληϊζόμενοι; and *Bella*, 7.38.18.

[97] Procopius, *Bella*, 7.38.23: καὶ ἀπ' αὐτοῦ μυριάδας αἰχμαλώτων ἐπαγόμενοι ἀριθμοῦ κρείσσους ἐπ' οἴκου ἀπεκομίσθησαν ἅπαντες.

[98] On captivity in the fifth century, with a special emphasis on the Balkans, see N. Lenski, "Captivity among the barbarians and its impact on the fate of the Roman Empire," in *The Cambridge Companion to the Age of Attila*, ed. M. Maas (Cambridge, 2014), 230–246.

[99] Menander, *Historia*, fr. 25.1 (Blockley). This is not the only instance when large numbers of Roman prisoners in the lands north of the Danube were released from their captivity. Procopius tells us about a similar episode from the mid 540s when the Herules defeated the Slavs who had taken many prisoners after a recent expedition in the Balkans, for which see *Bella*, 7.13.24–25.

[100] John of Ephesus, *Historia Ecclesiastica*, 6.25 (trans. Brooks): *et divites facti sunt et aurum et argentum lucrati sunt et armenta equorum et arma multa*.

[101] *Strategikon*, 11.4.12–16. For a different interpretation, see F. Curta, "Invasion or inflation? Sixth-to-seventh century Byzantine coin hoards in Eastern and Southeastern Europe," *Annali*

Sklavinia of their own accord might be the "refugees" against whom the author of the *Strategikon* warned for they "have given in to the times, forget their own people, and prefer to gain the good will of the enemy."[102]

Coinage seems to have circulated along with people inevitably leaving a mark on cultures beyond the frontier. Would such former prisoners provide additional impetus to cultural and economic exchanges between the lands south and north of the Danube? While it is not clear what their contribution may have been to the dissemination of coinage in the frontier region, they are more likely to have acted as cultural brokers in the general sense. Our sources are unfortunately silent on this matter, although we might extrapolate from the fifth-century story of the Greek merchant taken captive by the Huns. Priscus of Panium introduces him as a Greek-speaking Roman who had been taken prisoner but regained his freedom after he distinguished himself in the Hunnic army (against the Romans). Bitterly disillusioned with Roman leadership, as a free man he chose to take up "Scythian" customs, acquired a "barbarian" wife, and remained in the service of the Huns adopting a hybrid identity.[103] Such practices remained current under the Avars two centuries later with even more dramatic consequences. In the 680s we learn about a group of descendants of the Roman prisoners taken by the Avars who later participated as warriors in Avar campaigns. They wanted to return to their homeland south of the Danube, but they received a cold reception being perceived as half-Romans ("Sermesianoi") because they had long mixed with barbarians.[104] This type

---

dell'Istituto Italiano di Numismatica 43 (1996): 107, "to return to their own homes with a small recompense," following the German translation of G. T. Dennis (Philadelphia, 1984), 120. However, paying ransom rather than receiving recompense for being released from captivity is a more plausible interpretation.

[102] *Strategikon*, 11.4.133–135 (trans. Dennis): τοὺς δὲ λεγομένους ρεφούγους ἐπιστελλομένους καὶ στράτας δεικνύειν καὶ μηνύειν τινὰ δεῖ ἀσφαλῶς φυλάττειν κἂν γὰρ Ῥωμαῖοί εἰσι τῷ χρόνῳ ποιωθέντες καὶ τῶν ἰδίων ἐπιλαθόμενοι τὴν πρὸς τοὺς ἐχθροὺς εὔνοιαν ἐν προτιμήσει ποιοῦνται, οὓς εὐγνωμονοῦντας μὲν εὐεργετεῖν, κακουργοῦντας δὲ τιμωρεῖσθαι προσήκει. For alternative interpretations of this passage, see V. V. Muntean, "Creștinism primar la Dunărea inferioară. Noi revizuiri," in *Slujitor al bisericii și al neamului. Părintele Prof. Univ. Dr. Mircea Păcurariu, membru corespondent al Academiei Române, la împlinirea vârstei de 70 de ani* (Cluj-Napoca, 2002), 209; A. Madgearu, "About Maurikios, Strategikon, XI.4.31," *RESEE* 35, nos. 1–2 (1997): 119–121; C. Daicoviciu, "Romeii lui Maurikios," *Apulum* 9 (1971): 731–733.

[103] Priscus, *History*, 2.407–510 (Blockley).

[104] *Miracula Sancti Demetrii*, 284–287. For the episode, see also S. Brezeanu, "'Romains' et 'barbares' dans les Balkans au VIIe siècle à la lumière des 'Miracles de Saint Démetrius'. Comment on peut devenir l'autre'," *RESEE* 24, no. 3 (1986): 130–131; M. Pillon, "L'exode des Sermésiens et les grandes migrations des Romains de Pannonie dans les Balkans durant le Haut Moyen Âge," *EB* 38, no. 3 (2002): 103–141.

of cultural hybridization was no longer welcomed in the climate of uncertainty in which the Balkans had descended after the collapse of the frontier.

Ransom paid for POWs and enslaved Romans taken to *barbaricum* may indeed account for some of the gold found beyond the frontier. A lot of wealth was concentrated north of the Danube if we believe sixth-century writers. This impression comes out most forcefully from the motivation invoked by Menander for Baian's eagerness to accept Tiberius II's seductive proposition to attack the Slavs located in eastern Wallachia. The khagan of the Avars was extremely upset that the Slavs had dared to refuse his suzerainty and was anxious to put them in their place while hoping that "he would find the land full of gold, since the Roman Empire had long been plundered by the Slavs whose own land had never been raided by any other people at all."[105] While the scale of the frequent plunder expeditions into the Balkans is up for debate, at least two episodes suggest that Slavs did handle Byzantine gold coins. Procopius informs us that the Gepids who controlled the crossing of the Danube taxed one *stater* (*solidus*) per head to ferry the Slavs across the river with the booty and prisoners taken from the Balkans.[106] In addition, the "false Chilbudius" from the well-known anecdote recorded by the Byzantine historian was bought with gold (χρυσίον) by the Antes from the Slavs.[107]

Surprisingly, this litany of tragic events left few archaeological traces in the Slavic world although one would expect a significant catalogue of coin hoards. Finds of silver and gold objects are in fact extremely rare north of the Danube, while gold coins themselves are not very frequent. There is certainly nothing to match the rich burial assemblages of the Avars. Where is the wealth taken by the Slavs from Thracia and Illyricum? Was this a deliberate mystification orchestrated by Byzantine writers? One may speculate that the Avars did a thorough job and plundered *Sklavinia* taking all its riches, but this is not entirely convincing. Despite the fact that the Slavs entered the political orbit of the Avars and probably paid tribute, they were also known to make inroads south of the Danube on their own. There are several possible explanations for this situation and they are not mutually exclusive. First, it may well be that the Slavic social structure did not rely so heavily on the possession of gold which they gave away more easily than the Avars. The *Strategikon* does not describe them as being

---

[105] Menander, *Historia*, fr. 21 (Blockley): ἅμα καὶ πολυχρήματον τὴν χώραν εὑρήσειν οἰόμενος, ἅτε ἐκ πολλοῦ τῆς Ῥωμαίων ὑπὸ Σκλαβηνῶν <πεπορθημένης>, τῆς δὲ κατ' αὐτοὺς γῆς πρὸς ἑτέρου τινὸς τῶν πάντων ἐθνῶν οὐδαμῶς.
[106] Procopius, *Bella*, 8.25.5.   [107] Procopius, *Bella*, 7.14.19.

excessively gold-thirsty, although Byzantine writers tried to use this stereotype as often as they could when they described "barbarians." Even if Slavs did value gold, the chronic political instability north of the Danube did not favor the steady accumulation of wealth. Second, their inroads into the Balkans may have been successful in acquiring prisoners and other tangible treasures and not so much coinage, especially since the Danubian provinces were not particularly wealthy and coined gold (as well as copper) tended to be buried for safekeeping in times of insecurity.[108]

Finally, although the Slavs frequently plundered the Balkan provinces, the successful campaigns led by the Byzantine army north of the Danube in the last decade of the sixth century led to an inversion of roles. Now the Roman commander was the one proud to send to Constantinople booty and prisoners.[109] In the western Balkans the campaign against the Avars occasioned a confrontation of the Gepids, in fact the slaughter of some 30,000 Gepids caught unawares as they were celebrating a feast. According to Theophylact, at the end of the campaign 3,000 Avars, 8,000 Slavs, and 6,200 other barbarians were taken prisoner, among them Gepids if we believe Theophanes, who gives different figures.[110] On the eve of the mutiny which led to the deposition of Maurice in 602, the soldiers vociferated against the idea of spending the winter in the lands north of the Danube, because they were anxious to bring home the booty taken from the Slavs.[111] It is hard to determine whether such events ruined the Slavs to the point of justifying an archaeological record lacking any luster. For the time being, it seems more prudent to treat these possible explanations in a complementary fashion.

"Barbarians" preferred high value *solidi* but copper coins were more readily available. Some may have been among the personal possessions of captives taken from the Balkans, low-born Romans who rarely had the privilege of touching gold. The fact that many copper coins are stray finds along major river valleys suggests plenty of movement. Displaced Romans dropping low-value coins from their pockets are a good alternative to the multitude of traders envisaged in previous scholarship, for which we lack any information in the sources. We are on even more solid ground if we

---

[108] Most sixth-century hoards from the Balkans appear to be emergency deposits; see *Trésors*; F. Curta and A. Gandila, "Hoards and hoarding patterns in the Early Byzantine Balkans," *DOP* 65–66 (2012): 45–111.
[109] Theophylact Simocatta, *Historia*, 6.8.7.
[110] Theophylact Simocatta, *Historia*, 8.3.15; Theophanes, *Chronographia*, 282, AM 6093 [600/1]: 3000 Avars, 800 Slavs, 200 Gepids, and 2,000 other barbarians.
[111] Theophylact Simocatta, *Historia*, 8.6.2.

seek the explanation in Justinian's politics of recruitment. We have already seen that Herules, Gepids, and Cutrigurs were enlisted in Justinian's armies operating on various fronts. The Antes became allies of the Empire after Justinian offered them the fortress of Turris in 545 and acted as federates defending the frontier on the Lower Danube and the Delta.[112] The non-Roman pottery found in frontier fortresses from Scythia may belong to Antes serving in Roman garrisons. Plenty of literary and archaeological evidence exists for a firm placement of the Herules in the frontier region of northern Illyricum.[113] Slavs and other foreigners also served in the Byzantine army as far as Italy and some distinguished themselves in the Balkans, like Chilbudius, whose campaigns north of the Danube in the late 520s and the early 530s were extremely successful, as well as Tatimer who served under Maurice.[114]

Warlords of different ethnic background like Mundus (Gepid), Ildiges (Lombard), and Sinnion (Cutrigur) often changed their political allegiance, which points both to the fluid nature of power relations in the frontier region as well as to military talent being the main asset of *barbaricum*.[115] Such cases, including the "false Chilbudius" episode, are typical examples of reinvention of one's self which post-colonial anthropology has ascribed to frontier landscapes.[116] Not only warlords could reinvent themselves. Frontier garrisons on the Lower Danube were ethnically mixed as suggested by the archaeological evidence discussed in the previous chapters.[117] Such groups were neither barbarian nor Roman. Their identity as "Romans" was defined by their legal position and actual function in the Byzantine defense system and of course by the regular payment received

---

[112] Procopius, *Bella*, 7.14.32. See G. Kardaras, "The Byzantine–Antic treaty (545/46 AD) and the defense of the Scythia Minor," *Byzantinoslavica* 58 (2010): 74–85. For the location of Turris, see A. Madgearu, "The placement of the fortress Turris," *BS* 33, no. 2 (1992): 203–208.

[113] V. Ivanišević and M. Kazanski, "Geruly Iustiniana v Severnom Illirikume i ikh arheologicheskie sledy," *Stratum plus* (2010), no. 5: 141–157; A. Sarantis, "The Justinianic Herules: from allied barbarians to Roman provincials," in *Neglected Barbarians*, 361–402.

[114] H. Ditten, "Slawen im byzantinischen Heer von Justinian I. bis Justinian II," in *Studien zum 7. Jahrhundert in Byzanz. Probleme der Herausbildung des Feudalismus*, eds. H. Köpstein and F. Winkelmann (Berlin, 1976), 59–72; F. Curta, *The Making of the Slavs: History and Archaeology of the Lower Danube Region, c. 500–700* (Cambridge, 2001), 83–84.

[115] On barbarian warlords switching allegiance, see W. Pohl, "Justinian and the barbarian kingdoms," in *The Cambridge Companion to the Age of Justinian*, ed. M. Maas (Cambridge, 2005), 448–476.

[116] M. Naum, "Re-emerging frontiers: postcolonial theory and historical archaeology of the borderlands," *Journal of Archaeological Method and Theory* 17, no. 2 (2011): 105–107.

[117] For the Danubian fortresses, see D. Bondoc, *The Roman Rule to the North of the Lower Danube during the Late Roman and Early Byzantine Period* (Cluj-Napoca, 2009), 180–192.

for their services.[118] Regardless of their status as "second-class citizens" in the frontier region, there can be little doubt that many of the bronze coins handled in the hilltop sites placed along the Lower Danube belonged to "barbarians" settled on the frontier who also contributed to the distribution of such coins in their homeland. They were the chief cultural brokers of the Danubian borderlands.

What was the function of Byzantine copper coins in *barbaricum*? The theory that they primarily reflect trade between the Empire and communities beyond the frontier or even transactions between communities in *barbaricum* is untenable. To be sure, there is no reason to maintain that trade mediated by coinage was non-existent. Despite the fact that written sources have nothing to say on this topic, the *Strategikon* in particular gives us precious clues as to what may have interested Roman military officials or even traders who hoped to make a profit by supplying the army with provisions. The main concern was to ensure access to reliable sources of supply while campaigning in the Danube plain. The author of the *Strategikon* warns against the destruction of agricultural fields and argues for the protection of the peasants who can supply the army with food.[119] Although this advice probably referred to the Danubian provinces, the priorities remained the same when campaigning in *barbaricum*. The author emphasized the care which should be given to the food provisions secured from raids of plunder in enemy territory.[120] Moreover, it was strongly advised to gather all the available food and bring it back to the Empire on pack animals and boats along the rivers flowing into the Danube.[121]

Food shortage had been an endemic problem of the Balkans which Justinian's administrative reform and the creation of the *quaestura exercitus* did not really solve. On the other hand, the Romans were not alone in seeking the agricultural products of the Danubian plain. The Avars were equally interested in ensuring adequate supplies for the army. According to Michael the Syrian the khagan was ready to make the people from "two Roman towns and other fortresses" an offer they could not refuse: "sow and harvest, we shall claim only half of your due," a clear

---

[118] On Roman identity, see G. Greatrex, "Roman identity in the sixth century," in *Ethnicity and Culture in Late Antiquity*, eds. S. Mitchell and G. Greatrex (London, 2000), 267–292; D. A. Parnell, "Barbarians and brothers-in-arms: Byzantines on barbarian soldiers in the sixth century," *BZ* 108, no. 2 (2015): 809–826. On legal identity, see R. Mathisen, "*Peregrini, Barbari*, and *Cives Romani*: concepts of citizenship and the legal identity of barbarians in the Later Roman Empire," *The American Historical Review* 111, no. 4 (2006): 1011–1040.
[119] *Strategikon*, 1.9.9.   [120] *Strategikon*, 9.3.14.   [121] *Strategikon*, 11.4.136–140.

reference to the regular tax paid to the Byzantine treasury.[122] We are not sure if frontier communities were ready to sell their allegiance to the highest bidder, but the Avars were clearly interested in receiving tribute in kind, as suggested by the conditions imposed on the Lombards in return for their help against the Gepids in the late 560s: the Avars would receive one tenth of all the livestock that the Lombards possessed.[123] In addition, the Avars wanted to extend their control over the lands of the Gepids, Transylvania with its salt resources being especially attractive to pastoralists.[124] The region had strategic resources to offer and competition clearly stiffened in the last decades of the sixth century, but there is no reason to believe that monetary mediation was ever needed.

Alternative media of exchange may have existed but none was preserved and it is possible that peoples in *barbaricum* used perishable materials for this purpose, if they used any monetary instruments at all. Nevertheless, it has been suggested that Byzantine merchants paid with copper coin for the agricultural products acquired from *barbaricum*, while "barbarians" used the same coins to pay for manufactured products from the Empire.[125] This view is widely shared but suffers from preconceived ideas about the nature of exchange and the role of money. Ethnographic parallels have taught us that "primitives" were only inclined to accept coin if it was essentially commodity money, which the Byzantine *follis*, with its fluctuating weight and exchange rate to the *solidus* was certainly not. There is every reason to believe that barter alone would have sufficed to facilitate exchange north of the Danube. Anthropological studies indicate that barter remained the most important form of exchange in traditional societies, even during the colonial period, and the nature of the sixth-century society north of the Danube as reflected in the archaeological record suggests that a market economy did not exist.[126] Although "barbarians" did not develop their own

---

[122] Michael the Syrian, *Chronicon*, 10.21 (ed. Chabot, 361). For the Avar subsistence economy, see W. Pohl, "Herrschaft und Subsistenz. Zum Wandel der byzantinischen Randkulturen an der Donau vom 6.-8. Jahrhundert," in *Awarenforschungen*, ed. F. Daim, vol. I (Vienna, 1992), 13–24.

[123] Menander, *Historia*, fr. 12.2 (Blockley).

[124] K. Horedt, "The Gepidae, the Avars, and the Romanic population in Transylvania," in *Relations*, 111–22; D. Ciobanu, "The role of salt deposits in the political-military history of the Carpatho-Danubian space in the I–XIII centuries," *Studia antiqua et archaeologica* 9 (2003): 436–437.

[125] D. G. Teodor, *Romanitatea carpato-dunăreană și Bizanțul în veacurile V-XI* (Iași, 1981), 28.

[126] Market systems themselves can exist even without the use of money; on this question, see recently, B. L. Stark and C. P. Garraty, "Detecting marketplace exchange in archaeology: a methodological review," in *Archaeological Approaches to Market Exchange in Ancient Societies*, ed. B. L. Stark and C. P. Garraty (Boulder, CO, 2010), 35.

coinage, imitations after Byzantine bronze coins from 512–538 have been found in Danubian Illyricum and downstream on the frontier line, but none are known in *barbaricum*.[127] They probably reflect attempts by the Gepid rulers in Sirmium to usurp the emperor's prerogative of issuing coinage and perhaps provide currency for the needs of the city and the surrounding regions in Pannonia.

Copper coins were not a good investment for communities in *barbaricum* unless they were located very close to the Danube and frequent contact with the Byzantine fortresses permitted them to spend those coins fast. The only conceivable monetary transactions probably took place in Oltenia where the presence of a few Byzantine bridge-head fortresses on the left bank made the dangerous crossing of the Danube unnecessary. Nonetheless, bronze coins have been found over a much wider area, sometimes very far from the Danube. Many were probably brought home by the soldiers who served in the Roman army or in the garrisons defending the Danube frontier. In light of more recent parallels, their function is not hard to guess. "Big men" or simply village chiefs, some of whom may have served in the Roman army or led plunder expeditions in the Empire, could only retain their prestige if the way in which they manipulated wealth served the needs of the community.[128] In societies where prestige depended largely on access to Roman goods, coins were yet another type of import, to be worn as jewelry, to be given away as gifts, or to be used in ceremonies and rituals. To be sure, Byzantine merchants may have used coins to pay for various products bought from the region close to the Danube, but similar to the Merina from Madagascar, communities in *barbaricum* treated coins like any other Byzantine commodity. Coins were kept and melted down never to return to Byzantium. Much like the French authorities who complained that the silver five franc pieces "disappeared" in Madagascar, the Byzantine government probably discouraged the private export of

---

[127] I. Iurukova, "Imitations barbares de monnaies de bronze byzantines du VIe siècle," *Byzantinoslavica* 30 (1969): 83–87; D. Gaj-Popović, "The appearance of the barbarized folises (folles) in the 6th century in the Balkan Peninsula," *Balcanoslavica* 2 (1973): 95–100; D. Vladimirova-Aladzhova, "Oshte za barbarskite imitatsii v monetnoto obrashtenie prez VI vek," *Numizmatika i Sfragistika* 5, no. 1 (1998): 70–75.

[128] Curta, *The Making of the Slavs*, 325–332.

coin, especially when inflation struck and the supply of metal needed to issue fresh coins became limited.[129]

Finally, what is the evidence for the use of bronze coins as raw material for the production of jewelry? We have already seen that gold clearly served this purpose, not only in *barbaricum*, but also in the Empire, where coins could be mounted or melted down (Figure 39).[130] Pierced coins, gold or copper, are also known from the Early Byzantine provinces proving that the distinction between money and ornament is not as clear-cut as some may think (Figure 40).[131] Unsurprisingly, such coins are also found in *barbaricum* and their number is probably higher for copper coins, which are most often published without illustration and with insufficient details regarding alterations (e.g. piercing). We have already seen that metalwork was a widespread activity north of the Danube, evidenced by the large number of tools (crucibles and metallurgical ladles) and stone molds used for the production of copper jewelry.[132] There are reasons to believe that coins were a constant and reliable source of copper. Unfortunately, very few coins have been found in a clear archaeological context. The old finds from the sixth-century settlements excavated in Bucharest have not been properly published and their association with other objects is unknown.[133] In other cases coins were found with Early Medieval pottery, but no stratigraphical information is available; such finds include the *folles* from the Early Medieval settlements at Alcedar-Odaia and Lopatna in Moldova where they were found together with Luka Raikovetskaia ceramics, the *folles* of Justin I, Justinian, and Justin II from Horga, Sărățeni, and Fălciu (Moldavia), respectively, found with wheelmade and handmade pottery, and the early seventh-century coins of Phocas and Heraclius from

---

[129] Such a crisis becomes evident in the last decade of the sixth century and the beginning of the seventh when fresh bronze coins were overstruck on older coins due to the shortage of metal, for which see, A. Gandila, "Heavy money, weightier problems: the Justinianic reform of 538 and its economic consequences," *RN* 168 (2012): 370–371.

[130] See especially A. E. Jones, "'Lord, Protect the Wearer':" Late Antique Numismatic Jewelry and the Image of the Emperor as Talismanic Device," PhD Dissertation, Yale University, 2011. See also, A. Oddy, "La monnaie d'or dans la bijouterie à travers les ages," *Aurum* 15 (1983): 10–16; J.-A. Bruhn, *Coin and costume in Late Antiquity* (Washington, DC, 1993).

[131] Morrisson, "Monnaies et amulettes," 409–430.

[132] For metallurgical activity in *barbaricum*, see above Chapter 2, Figure 9–Figure 10.

[133] D. V. Rosetti, "Siedlungen der Kaiserzeit und der Völkerwanderungszeit bei Bukarest," *Germania* 18 (1934): 210; S. Morintz and D. V. Rosetti, "Din cele mai vechi timpuri și pînă la formarea Bucureștilor," in *Bucureștii de odinioară în lumina săpăturilor arheologice* (Bucharest, 1959), 33–34; M. Constantiniu, "Săpăturile de la Străulești-Măicănești. Așezarea feudală II," *CAB* 2 (1965): 189, fig. 93/1–3.

Figure 39 Coins as jewelry: necklace with a mounted *solidus* from Dzhiginka, Russia (1); coin-set from Malo Pereshchepyne, Ukraine (2); early modern coin-necklace from Madagascar (3)

Figure 40 Early Byzantine gold (1–6, 8), silver (10), and bronze (7, 9) coins modified to be displayed as jewelry

Grumezoaia and Comănești (Moldavia), associated with Early Medieval ceramic remains.[134]

We are best informed about the two early *folles* of Justinian found at Botoșana in Moldavia, very far from the Danube. The sunken-featured building no. 20 produced a *follis* dated 527–537 in association with a crucible and a ladle used to pour the metal. The coin was not cut or damaged but this was not absolutely necessary.[135] Recent research at Nicopolis in Moesia II has revealed unusually large accumulations of Late Roman copper coins together with scrap metal collected for recycling and although none of the coins, which are smaller than the Early Byzantine pieces, were folded, cut or damaged, the association with metalwork is quite evident.[136] Similarly, no damage can be traced on coins from the hoard found at Horgești in Moldavia. However, they were unlikely to have served any monetary function; the coins were hidden in a copper pitcher (ca. 1.3 kg) together with a copper chain (ca. 250 g) and small scrap pieces of copper.[137]

---

[134] Alcedar-Odaia: I. A. Rafalovich, *Slaviane VI–IX vekov v Moldavii* (Kishinew, 1972), 40, fig. 9/2; V. V. A. Rikman and I. A. Rafalovich, "K voprosu o sootnoshenii cherniakhovskoi i ranneslavianskoi kul'tur v dnestrovsko-dunaiskom mezhdurech'e," *KSIA* 105 (1965): 49, fig. 3/4. Lopatna: Kropotkin, *Klady vizantiiskikh*, 38, no. 293, fig. 17/26. Horga: V. M. Butnariu, "Răspîndirea monedelor bizantine din secolele VI–VII în teritoriile carpato-dunărene," *BSNR* 131–133 (1983–1985): 220, nos. 72–73; Teodor, *Descoperiri arheologice*, 101, no. 363 (including a "Slavic" bow fibula). Sărățeni: Butnariu, "Răspîndirea monedelor," 222, no. 136; Teodor, *Descoperiri arheologice*, 144, no. 619. Comănești: Butnariu, "Răspîndirea monedelor," 218, nos. 35–36; D. G. Teodor, *Teritoriul est-carpatic în veacurile V–XI e.n.: contribuții arheologice și istorice la problema formării poporului român* (Iași, 1978), 23, fig. 16/6–7; Grumezoaia: G. Coman, "Contribuții la cunoașterea fondului etnic al civilizației secolelor V–XIII în jumătatea sudică a Moldovei," *Carpica* 11 (1979): 206, fig. 11/1–2. Fălciu: Butnariu, "Răspîndirea monedelor," 219, no. 49; Teodor, *Descoperiri arheologice*, 88, no. 288.

[135] Cut or damaged Byzantine bronze coins have been found at Osijek (Croatia) and Pavlivka (Ukraine) but no archaeological context is available. A hexagram of Heraclius cut in half was found in a grave from Linz. See H. Göricke-Lukić, "Justinijanov novac iz Slavonije i Baranje," in *Radovi XIII. Međunarodnog kongresa za starokršćansku arheologija. Split-Poreč (25.9–1.10.1994)*, vol. II, eds. N. Cambi and E. Marin (Vatican, 1998), 1152, no. 28 and 1159, fig. 28 (Osijek); P. O. Karyshkovski, "Nakhodki pozdnerimskikh i vizantiiskikh monet v Odesskoi oblasti," *Materialy po arkheologii Severnogo Prichernomor'ia* 7 (1971): 81, no. 10 (Pavlivka); W. Hahn, "Die Fundmünzen des 5.–9. Jahrhunderts in Österreich und den unmittelbar angrenzenden Gebieten," in *Die Geburt Mitteleuropas. Geschichte Österreichs vor seiner Entstehung, 378–907*, ed. H. Wolfram (Vienna, 1987), 459 (Linz).

[136] A. G. Poulter, "Interpreting finds in context: Nicopolis and Dichin revisited," in *Objects in Context, Objects in Use: Material Spatiality in Late Antiquity*, eds. L. Lavan, E. Swift, and T. Putzeys (Boston, MA, 2007), 694–698.

[137] V. Căpitanu, "Tezaurul de monede bizantine descoperit la Horgești," *Carpica* 4 (1971): 253–269; G. Buzdugan, "Notă suplimentară despre tezaurul bizantin de la Horgești (jud. Bacău)," *Carpica* 6 (1974): 47–63. For the objects, see S. Musteață, "Unele concretizări privind vasul de metal din tezaurul monetar de la Horgești, jud. Bacău, Romania," in *Arheologia între*

It is quite obvious in such cases that we are dealing with accumulations of metal rather than collections of coins. There is evidence that bronze pieces were diligently collected for their scrap value. Older coins, no longer in circulation, which had arrived north of the Danube centuries earlier were probably found accidentally in the sixth century and gathered to be recycled. Such may be the case of the 12 Roman imperial bronze coins from Marcus Aurelius to Philip I found in the sixth-century settlement from Căţelu Nou near Bucharest, the bronze coin of Nerva found together with scrap pieces of bronze in the settlement from Ipoteşti (Olt, Romania), or the bronze coin of Trajan found in a sixth-to-seventh-century context at Târgşoru Vechi (Prahova, Romania).[138] Unfortunately, the mixed composition of copper alloys of various Byzantine mints and denominations makes them unsuited for analyses of metal composition and comparison with copper-alloy artifacts which would provide definitive evidence.[139] Still, this practice must have been common in the sixth-century *barbaricum*, since a reliable source of copper was needed for producing jewelry and coins could have easily fulfilled this function. An exceptional

ştiinţă, politică şi economia de piaţă, eds. S. Musteaţă, A. Popa, and J.-P. Abraham (Chişinău, 2010), 99–127.

[138] P. Roman and S. Dolinescu-Ferche, "Cercetările de la Ipoteşti (jud. Olt) (observaţii asupra culturii materiale autohtone din sec. al VI-lea în Muntenia)," *SCIVA* 29, no. 1 (1978): 73–93; B. Ciupercă and A. Măgureanu, "Locuinţe din a doua jumătate a mileniului I p. Chr. descoperite la Târgşoru Vechi," in *Arheologia mileniului I p. Chr. Cercetări actuale privind istoria şi arheologia migraţiilor*, ed. L. M. Voicu (Bucharest, 2010), 155–156. Roman coins appear in sixth-century burial assemblages in Hungary and Transylvania. See M. Nagy,
"A hódmezővásárhely-kishomoki gepida temető (elemzés)," *MFMÉ* 10 (2004): 129–139; C. Găzdac and C. Cosma, "Monede romane şi statut social într-o necropolă de secolele VI-VII. 'Groapa lui Hărăstăşan', Noşlac, jud. Alba, România," *Analele Banatului* 21 (2013): 107–116. Ancient silver coins were also retrieved in the sixth century and are sometimes found in residences; occasionally they were pierced and functioned as pendants; see the finds at Kavetchina: L. V. Vakulenko and O. M. Prikhodniuk, *Slavianskie poseleniia I tys. n.e. u s. Sokol na Srednem Dnestre* (Kiev, 1984), 81 (denarius of Hadrian). Bucharest–Dămăroaia: C.-M. Vintilă, E.-F. Gavrilă, and T.-A. Ignat, "Două locuinţe din sec. VI–VII descoperite în situl Bucureşti-Dămăroaia," *Buletinul Muzeului Judeţean Teleorman* 6 (2014), 106–107 (Getic silver imitation). Moreşti: K. Horedt, *Moreşti. Grabungen in einer vor- und frühgeschichtlichen Siedlung in Siebenbürgen* (Bucharest, 1979), 70 (denarius of Elagabalus).

[139] For coins, see T. Padfield, "Analysis of Byzantine copper coins by X-Ray methods (with a numismatic commentary by P. Grierson)," in *Methods of Chemical and Metallurgical Investigation of Ancient Coinage*, eds. T. Hall and D. M. Metcalf (London, 1972), 219–236. For objects, see H. K. Cooper, "Analysis of Late Roman-Byzantine copper alloy artifacts from Northern Jordan," MA thesis, University of Arkansas, 2000. Still, Krzysztof Dąbrowski has analyzed a few dozen Roman fibulae found in *barbaricum* and concluded that they were produced by melting down early Roman coins; see K. Dąbrowski, "Nouvelles données concernant l'orfévrerie sur le territoire de la voévodie d'Olsztyn (Pologne)," *Archaeologia Polona* 19 (1980): 238–239.

confirmation of this practice comes from the spectacular hoard found at Kuzebaevo (Udmurtia, Russia), including more than one thousand tools and objects, most of which are directly related to metallurgical production: crucibles, ladles, molds, and a large quantity of scrap copper. Several Central Asian copper coins from the sixth-to-seventh centuries were part of the hoard and they were clearly used as raw material for the production of jewelry and dress accessories, whose models were also part of the hoard.[140]

Let me pull the strands of my argument together. Whether used as souvenirs, apotropaic amulets, jewelry, objects of prestige, or simply raw material for the production of copper-alloy items, Early Byzantine coins rarely returned to the Empire. If any transactions required the mediation of coins they were undertaken in Byzantine fortresses on the Lower Danube where peasants could come to sell their surplus. If Byzantine merchants venturing into the dangerous world of "barbarians" paid with coin for the products they acquired it was a unidirectional monetary transaction. The communities living in the shadow of the Empire bought coins like any Byzantine commodity because they needed the metal or simply because they were looking to use them as jewelry to adorn their clothes or to hang on necklaces. In small isolated communities such exotica could gain powerful attributes. Through the same channels of cooperation and conflict, along with Roman prisoners, the main agents for the vehiculation of Byzantine money in *barbaricum* were barbarian soldiers in the empire's service who brought some coins back home. They were not driven by a civilizing mission of starting a local monetary economy but by a desire to display their new identity forged in the cultural crucible of the Danubian borderlands.

---

[140] T. I. Ostanina et al., *Kuzebaevskii klad iuvelira VII v. kak istoricheskii istochnik* (Izhevsk, 2011), fig. 7–23–27 (for the coins). Some 400 km to the east a hoard of Heraclian hexagrams was found at Bartym, for which see R. D. Goldina, I. Iu. Pastushenko, and E. M. Chernykh, "The Nevolino culture in the context of the 7th-century East-West trade: the finds from Bartym," in *Constructing the Seventh Century*, ed. C. Zuckerman (Paris, 2013), 865–930; 876–881, figs. 8–13.

Conclusions

Two interpretations have shaped our understanding of the role played by the Danube frontier in Late Antiquity. One relied faithfully on the testimony of contemporary writers who epitomized the river as the ideal boundary between civilized Romans and savage "barbarians," while the other clung on to the legacy of the former transdanubian province of Dacia to claim that the Empire never completely abandoned its political ambitions north of the river during Late Antiquity. Both are correct, albeit not always for the reasons invoked by their proponents. The external policy of an empire is rarely straightforward and unequivocal and Early Byzantium makes no exception. On one hand, Roman emperors were interested in securing the Balkans by closely guarding the river, on the other communication and contact with *barbaricum* became integral to the frontier strategy which included interaction, exchange, and the recruitment of "barbarians" in the Roman army. No "Grand Strategy" was applied on the Danube frontier but a larger repertoire of solutions depending on the balance of power and the Empire's agenda at one time or another.

Undoubtedly, the Danube met the necessary preconditions to become a defensible frontier and consolidate its venerable reputation as the most strategically advantageous line of political separation in the ancient Balkans. In the sixth century this fact was recognized not only by the Empire but also by its bellicose neighbors – Gepids, Avars, Slavs, Antes, and Cutrigurs – who pressed against the Danube like a string of unstable molecules at the edge of a dense nucleus. Roman emperors of the old days who engineered the frontier system took the necessary precautions and complemented the natural virtues of the river with a strong fleet and a chain of fortifications running along its southern bank, but the functioning of this elaborate machine ultimately depended on the Empire's capacity to maintain internal stability. Managing the cascade of crises between the fifth and the seventh century often entailed the serious neglect of one frontier in favor of another. The Balkan region rarely ranked high in the Empire's list of priorities, although it was never completely overlooked. Through a combination of ideological pressure, imperial will, and military necessity, in the sixth century the center of gravity often shifted from Italy to

Anatolia bypassing the Balkans where efficient defense remained the only ambition. In other words, it was not the systemic inadequacy of the Danube as a frontier that led to its fateful breakdown but the way in which it was consciously managed by Early Byzantine emperors who had limited resources at their disposal.

When speaking about the Danube frontier we must distinguish between two different layers. The upper is high politics, which included the defense of Constantinople and the prosperity of Thracia and Illyricum, as well as political dealings with "barbarian" groups living north of the Danube. The lower layer is the individual experience of people living on the frontier and whose actions, which might be broadly labeled as private initiative or individual agency, gave shape to cultural change in the frontier region and led to the cultural realignment of entire groups. The former layer is shrouded in the rhetoric of contemporary writers while the latter can only be illuminated by turning to the archaeological evidence. The interaction between the two spheres falls within the realm of core–periphery relations to which world-systems analysis still has a lot to offer.

Coins are the most chronologically accurate testament of such efforts and can help us add more depth to the conceptual analysis drawing on the world-systems paradigm discussed in the previous chapters. From ca. 490 to ca. 615 the Danube frontier acted as a semiperiphery with the dual function of producing culture through interaction with the periphery and transmitting policy from the center, mainly the Byzantine concern with the safety of the northern frontier. During this time the periphery (*barbaricum*) gradually transitioned through two different stages. From ca. 490 to ca. 570 it developed the outlook of a "negotiated periphery" or a "middle ground" with the Romans in the driving seat but the speed and direction being the result of negotiation and hybridization. After the Avars established their hegemony in *barbaricum* the region morphed into a "contested periphery" resulting in growing militarization, frequent conflict and instability, a phase which lasted from ca. 570 to ca. 615. Throughout these two phases, cultural interaction with the Byzantine world was defined by a yin-yang-like combination of cooperation and conflict, an entwined process sustaining the circulation of Byzantine goods and fashions in *barbaricum*, contributing to the creation of identities in relation to Byzantium, and stimulating competition. For this reason I chose the term "bipolar periphery" to describe this duality fueled by similar motivations but enacted through conflicting channels. When the Byzantine frontier on the Danube finally collapsed ca. 615, the region's function as a semiperiphery vanished and the Byzantine core itself contracted under the pressure of Avars, Slavs, and Bulgars. As a result, some areas of the Balkans descended to the status of peripheral regions bordering the new Bulgar state, dangerously close to Constantinople where "Maurice's ditch" raised in the 580s foreshadowed the medieval contraction of the Byzantine state.

The political history of the Danube region is well known but the cultural impact of the Byzantine frontier policy leaves a lot of room for ambiguity. Often the archaeological record seems to be at variance with the written sources where the polarizing "us vs. them" mentality reigns supreme. The difference between the "Romans" who defend the frontier behind the thick walls of fortresses placed on the Danube and the "Barbarians" bent on destroying the civilized world is purely situational. Events from the long sixth century have taught us that today's "Barbarians" are often the "Romans" of tomorrow who may well begin by plundering the provinces of the Balkans, only to end up defending them later as *foederati, symmachoi,* or through more ad hoc arrangements. The northern Balkans in Late Antiquity was clearly a multiethnic environment and barbarian soldiers in the empire's service acted as cultural brokers. Traffic and communication between the two sides of the river occurred naturally and the archaeological evidence shows that it was encouraged so long it was done peacefully and without upsetting the upper layer, that of high politics. Ideally, constant interaction would attract "barbarian" communities into the Empire's cultural orbit and help restore peace and prosperity in the Balkans after more than a century of alarming decline.

Early Byzantine culture did not invent barbarians but it encouraged them to reinvent themselves in the Danubian borderlands. The Byzantine artifacts most frequently found in *barbaricum* are precisely those related to the militarized environment of the northern Balkans: fragments of LR1 and LR2 amphorae, the containers in which soldiers received their allowances of oil and wine, a variety of jewelry and dress accessories for both sexes fashionable in the frontier fortresses, as well as Byzantine coins. We can speculate that the actual list of Byzantine goods was much more diverse and included perishable items that seldom leave any trace in the archaeological record. Even with an incomplete dossier at our disposal we can still discern certain patterns. Cultural influences were not unidirectional and were not spread uniformly in the transdanubian world. The stylistic evolution and geographical distribution of the so-called "Slavic" bow fibulae best illustrates cultural influences coming from outside the Empire. In fact, there are very few artifacts produced in the northern Balkans which can be described as reflecting just one cultural identity. Fashions developing on the sixth-century Danube frontier reflect the multiethnic background of their carriers, blending several cultural traditions relying on the Roman technology of producing jewelry and combining imagery derived from the cultures of the steppe and from Germanic styles. The long standing academic obsession with identifying Slavs, Gepids, or "proto-Romanians" in the lands north of the Danube based on the degree of contact with the Roman world is a futile quest that finds little confirmation in the archaeological record. In reality, cultural spheres were constantly intersecting and overlapping, a process that modern ideologies, including nationalism and communism, had a hard time acknowledging.

Analyzing the distribution of Byzantine artifacts found in *barbaricum* is helpful in coming to grips with the widely different social and cultural complexities they encompass. Communities living outside the Empire emulated the Roman way of life by seeking access to the objects and goods most often encountered in the frontier region. Expressing ethnic and social identity in *barbaricum* was a process whose mechanics depended not only on the cultural pull of Byzantium but also on cultural contact and relations of power between groups within *barbaricum*. Distribution maps clearly reveal specific preferences, although most Byzantine goods reflect the *annona militaris* and soldiers' expenditure in the frontier region. Regardless of particular tastes, "barbarians" of all kinds were attracted by the Empire's culture and wealth. Although archaeology has been used to demonstrate the cultural predominance of a Romanized population north of the Danube – the descendants of the Roman colonists in Dacia who supposedly were the primary recipients of Roman goods – there is very little evidence that sixth-century Byzantium showed any preference. Out of political pragmatism, Byzantine emperors divided the world of *barbaricum* into friends and foes and showed plenty of flexibility for the reevaluation of such roles which were by no means immutable. Well-established sedentary communities in the Danube valley and the Carpathian region – numerically superior but dominated politically – were joined by incoming Germanic and Slavic population groups into the process of appropriation and modification of Byzantine cultural traits for the construction of identities and social distinction.

The diffusion of Byzantine artifacts suggests that local communities were not passive recipients. Finds of amphorae concentrate in Oltenia and Moldavia pointing to important regions for the recruitment of soldiers and the development of a local elite culture which required access to Roman wine and oil. Oil lamps including bronze liturgical lamps are found almost exclusively on the territory of Trajanic Dacia, while pectoral crosses are encountered predominantly south and east of the Carpathians.

Metallurgical activity and the production of bronze jewelry and dress accessories of Byzantine inspiration was most intense in the Subcarpathian hills of Wallachia and Moldavia, which are also important regions for the distribution of Byzantine military buckles and brooches. All these convey an image of communities living in the shadow of the Empire but adopting only certain cultural practices. The cultural process at work can be described more in terms of borrowing than assimilation into the dominant culture. The unsystematic adoption of Christianity, one of the most important components of Roman identity in the sixth-century Balkans, reveals the limits of Byzantine influence in the lands beyond the frontier. Furthermore, as the political grip of the imperial power weakened, the selectivity of cultural traits adopted in *barbaricum* increased and allowed for a mélange of Byzantine and Avar influences to prevail in the late sixth and seventh centuries.

The steady flow of precisely dated coins to the transdanubian world suggests an uninterrupted traffic of people and goods across the frontier. Numismatic evidence has been seldom used to understand the complex nature of Early Byzantine frontiers although it is uniquely positioned to complement – and sometime challenge – conclusions drawn from other types of sources. Most often than not, Byzantine coins played their designated role in the scenario emphasizing separation, in which coin finds were seen as the result of plunder, or in the one illustrating contact, with coins being the instrument of a local monetary economy. The latter has been particularly contentious. The monetary economy of Early Byzantium could display very different traits depending on the type of settlement, which could be a large coastal town, a landlocked administrative center, a frontier fortress, or a small village. Outside the confines of large urban markets monetary transactions were just one of the ways in which exchange took place. Hilltop military sites from the Balkans were not engaged in a full-blown market economy; local monetary circulation was closely dependent on the payment of soldiers' salaries and transactions which often involved the state as the most important agent. Frontier fortresses could not export a monetized economy in the lands north of the Danube simply because they did not develop one themselves.

Barbarians needed gold and silver but there is very little evidence to suggest that they also needed a currency. What exactly communities outside the Empire had to offer in exchange for Byzantine coins remains a matter for conjecture. Trade was just one, certainly not the dominant, manner in which Byzantine coins arrived in *barbaricum.* In Transcaucasia, the Carpathian Basin, and the Lower Danube region gold and ceremonial silver issues reflect political and diplomatic payments made by Byzantine emperors as *tributum pacis* or as incentives meant to gain stable allies in volatile regions. Many of those coins, redistributed to the local elite in a top-down fashion, found their way into burials often after having been converted into ornaments. Byzantine gold and silver coins were not used as instruments of economic exchange; they were displayed as jewelry and became important pillars in the architecture of social status. The Avars in particular chose to melt down Byzantine gold coins in order to produce spectacular jewelry which would serve a similarly important social function. Those coins that were not melted ended up in warrior burials as objects of prestige displayed by members of the Avar aristocracy who had access to money coming from Constantinople. Coined gold became the quintessential symbol of the khagan's ability to force the Byzantine emperor into submissiveness.

The analysis of Byzantine coins from *barbaricum* in their historical and archaeological context rejects once more the existence of a uniform policy in the frontier region. In fact we are dealing with many frontiers and many types of responses and this realization appears in a clearer light when we place the Lower Danube in the wider peripheral context of the northern world. The diffusion of Early Byzantine coins from Central Europe to the Caspian Sea shows that adaptation rather than rigid planning characterizes imperial action at the periphery. At least three major patterns of distribution can be distinguished: Transcaucasia, dominated by regular and ceremonial silver coinage, the Lower Danube region where copper coin finds are overwhelming, and the Carpathian Basin where gold issues predominate.

The explanation lies in the particular nature of each of these frontier regions, the strategic priorities of the Empire, and the strength of its enemies in *barbaricum*. Lazica and Iberia guarded the strategic passes in the Caucasus Mountains through which poured not only spices and exotica from the East but also nomadic raiders from the endless Asian steppe. The danger was deemed serious enough to require the joint action of the two great empires, the Byzantine and the Persian, in one of the rare instances of collaboration. Failure to control movement in the Caucasus exposed the Byzantine heartland and the Black Sea coast. Procopius was perhaps exaggerating when he suggested that the loss of Lazica could lead to a major invasion by sea toward Constantinople, but the danger itself was very real. Sixth-to-seventh-century Byzantine emperors took every precaution to secure this region. Gifts of silver and gold coins were sent to Lazi kings and to smaller Caucasian tribes in order to gain their loyalty and huge quantities of silver hexagrams were spent by emperors of the Heraclian dynasty to keep Transcaucasia in the Byzantine orbit.

Very little of this policy applies to the Lower Danube. Unlike Transcaucasia where the frontier was eminently unstable and depended primarily on diplomacy, on the Danube the frontier was more entrenched and relied on the heavily fortified southern bank of the river. Transcaucasia had many tribes but no coherent defense system, while the Lower Danube had many fortifications but few Romans to defend it and an impoverished hinterland to supply it. At least this is the message conveyed by authors such as Agathias who lamented the state of the garrisons as early as 559 when Zabergan's Cutrigurs cut their way through the Balkans to reach the Great Wall. The high density of hilltop sites in the Danube valley indeed required many defenders, most of whom were recruited from *barbaricum*. Historians and archaeologists have looked for natural resources or strategic roads to explain Byzantium's interest in the region when in reality people and their military skill, rather than objects or goods were the greatest asset of the lands north of the river. They were the owners of the Byzantine bronze coins found in abundance in the transdanubian *barbaricum*, which they had acquired while serving the Empire in the frontier region or in more distant campaigns.

The energy and resources invested in Transcaucasia ensured that the Anatolian provinces would not be invaded and depopulated by "barbarians." In the Balkans, however, such events were commonplace in the sixth century. The Danube was frequently crossed back and forth usually by small bands of raiders but sometimes by larger invading parties. Booty and thousands of enslaved Romans were taken north of the Danube, although contemporary observers often exaggerated numbers for dramatic effect. This continuous movement of people further explains the large quantity of bronze coins available in the northern Balkans and by extension in *barbaricum*. Because of the nature of this traffic, such coins did not have any monetary function outside the Empire except for isolated transactions in the region close to the Danube. Much like the gold *solidi*, copper coins were used as raw material for the production of dress accessories as testified by single finds, hoards, and numerous stone molds designed to cast small pieces of jewelry. Others were kept as souvenirs or amulets pierced to be worn as pendants and became an index of social distinction.

Copper coins did not play a significant social function in the Carpathian Basin, where the legacy of the Huns had engendered a strong preference for gold. The Lower Danube region remains alone in its emphasis on bronze coinage. For all intents and purposes the Middle Danube, the

Drava, and the Sava rivers flowing from the Alps were lost to the Empire and no coherent system of fortification can be found there to help distribute Byzantine copper coins in the Carpathian Basin. Such coins are rare and were mostly brought from Italy, rather than the Balkans, where prospects of enrichment through warfare during the age of Justinian attracted ambitious men from *barbaricum*. The archaeological and numismatic evidence shows that they did not return home empty-handed. The region became once again a frontier of the Roman Empire after Justinian's reconquest of Dalmatia and northern Italy and its strategic significance increased accordingly. Large quantities of gold in the form of *solidi* were sent to the Gepids, the Lombards, and the Avars to name only the most powerful confederations. These allies and adversaries at the same time were of a different caliber than the Slavs, the Antes, and the Cutrigurs in the Danube and the northern Black Sea regions. Justinian's *divide et impera* strategy backfired in the last quarter of the sixth century when his successors were forced to dispatch increasing amounts of gold *solidi* as tribute to the Avars. From this perspective, the flow of Byzantine money to the Carpathian Basin resembles more closely the situation in Transcaucasia where political payment was a common tool used by Byzantine emperors. On the other hand, military operations in *Avaria* cannot be compared with the massive campaigning unfolded in the Eastern theater which absorbed huge quantities of silver hexagrams destined for the war effort. Annual tribute rather than extraordinary military expenditure brought coin to the Carpathian Basin. Clearly, Byzantine emperors did not have the necessary human and material resources to sustain an aggressive policy on every frontier and they were rarely in the position of devising a uniform strategy for all its peripheral regions.

To conclude, warfare and service in the Roman army define Roman frontiers in Late Antiquity. By necessity, emperors were forced to prioritize and the failure of certain frontiers reflects neglect more than barbarian pressure. Adaptation and, indeed, improvisation and quick reaction time were crucial survival skills in marginal regions. No longer able to play the role of an aggressive and expansionist empire, Byzantium pulled out the cultural card drawing on centuries of study in acculturation and appeasement. Without defenders, Justinian's system of fortification in the Balkans was nothing more than an artificial and expensive showroom. The Danubian frontier of exclusion needed a strong cultural component of attraction in order to remain efficient. Coins are an excellent testimony of such concerns and together with other categories of artifacts can open a window to the world of *barbaricum* where individual agency and culturally constructed responses were often shaped in relation to Byzantium. Both written accounts and the available archaeological evidence point to a complex society developing in the frontier region, drawing its cultural energy from multiple sources and blending Roman and "barbarian" influences. Identities were constantly renegotiated and reinvented on the periphery in the ever-changing world of conflict and cooperation between Romans and Barbarians, whose very definitions came to be blurred as the Empire grew weaker.

Bibliography

Primary Sources

Agathias. *Cycle*. Edited and translated by W. R. Paton. *The Greek Anthology*. Vol. I. New York, NY: G. P. Putnam & Sons, 1920.

Historiae. Edited by R. Keydell. Berlin: De Gruyter, 1967. Translated by J. D. Frendo. Berlin: De Gruyter, 1975.

Ammianus Marcellinus. *Res Gestae*. Edited and translated by John C. Rolfe. Vol. III. Cambridge, MA: Harvard University Press, 1939.

Annaeus Florus. *Epitome of Roman History*. Edited by T. E. Page, E. Capps, and W. H. D. Rouse. Translated by E. S. Forster. London: William Heinemann Ltd., 1929.

Annales Regni Francorum. Edited by G. H. Pertz and F. Kurz. Hannover: Hahn, 1895.

Aristotle. *De Mirabilibus Auscultationibus*. Edited by G. Vanotti. Padova: Edizioni Studio Tesi, 1997.

Aurelius Victor. *De Caesaribus*. Edited by F. Pichlmayr. Leipzig: Teubner, 1911.

Auxentius of Durostorum. *Epistula de Fide Vita et Obitu Wulfilae*. Edited by F. Kaufmann. Strasbourg: Karl J. Trübner, 1899.

Cassius Dio. *Historia Romana*. Edited by L. Dindorf. Vols. III–IV. Leipzig: Teubner, 1874.

Chalcocondyl. *Historiarum Libri Decem*. Edited by I. Bekker. Corpus Scriptorium Historiae Byzantinae 32. Bonn: Weber, 1843.

Codex Diplomaticus Hungariae Ecclesiasticus ac Civilis. Edited by G. Fejér. Vol. IV, part 1. Buda: Typis Typogr. Regiae Universitas Ungaricae, 1829.

Corippus, *In Laudem Iustini Augusti Minoris*. Edited and translated by A. Cameron. London: Athlone Press, 1976.

Corpus Iuris Civilis. Edited by P. Krueger, R. Schoell, and W. Kroll. Vols. II–III. 5th ed. Berlin: Weidmann, 1928–1929.

De Rebus Bellicis. Edited and translated by E. A. Thompson. New York, NY: Arno Press, 1979.

Einhard. *Vita Karoli Magni*. Edited by O. Holder-Egger. *MGH: SS.* Hannover: Impensis bibliopolii Hahniani, 1911.

Epiphanius. *Audians*. In *Epiphanius III: Panarion Haer. 65–80; De Fide*. Edited by K. Holl and J. Dummer. Berlin: Akademie Verlag, 1985.

Eusebius. *Vita Constantini*. Edited by F. Winkelmann. Berlin: Akademie Verlag, 1975.
Evagrius. *Historia Ecclesiastica*. Edited by J.-P. Migne. Patrologia Graeca 86/2. Paris, 1865.
Fredegar. *Chronicae*. Edited by B. Krusch. *MGH: SRM* 2: 1–193. Hannover: Impensis bibliopolii Hahniani, 1888.
Geographus Ravennas. *Cosmographia*. Edited by I. Schnetz. *Itineraria Romana II*. Leipzig: Teubner, 1940.
Georgios Pisides. *Bellum Avaricum*. Edited and translated by A. Pertusi. Studia patristica et Byzantina 7. Ettal: Buch-Kunstverlag, 1959.
Herodotus. *Historiae*. Edited by A. D. Godley. Vol. II. Loeb Classical Library 118. New York, NY, G.P. Putnam's Sons, 1921.
Ioannes Lydus. *On Powers or the Magistracies of the Roman State*. Introduction, critical text, translation, commentary, and indices by A. C. Bandy. Philadelphia, PA: American Philosophical Society, 1983.
Jerome. *Epistulae*. Edited by J.-P. Migne. Patrologia Latina 22. Paris: Migne, 1864.
Letters and Select Works. In *A Select Library of the Nicene and Post-Nicene Fathers of the Christian Church. Second Series*. Vol. VI. Edited by Philip Schaff. Translated by W. H. Fremantle. Peabody: Hendrickson Publishers, 1994.
John of Antioch. *Historia Chronike*. Edited by C. Müller. *FHG* 4. Paris: A. Firmin Didot, 1851.
John of Biclar. *Chronica*. Edited by T. Mommsen. Chronica Minora 2. Berlin: Weidmann, 1894.
John of Ephesus. *Johannis Ephesini Historiae Ecclesiasticae Pars Tertia*. Edited by E. W. Brooks. Louvain: Ex Officina Orientali et Scientifica, 1936.
John of Nikiu. *Chronicle*. Edited and translated by H. Zotenberg. Paris: Imprimerie Nationale, 1883.
Jordanes. *Getica*. Edited by T. Mommsen. *MGH: AA* 5.1. Berlin: Weidmann, 1882.
Kedrenos. *Synopsis Historion (Compendium Historiarum)*. Edited by I. Bekker. Corpus Scriptorum Historia Byzantinae 14/2. Bonn: Weber, 1939.
Leo the Deacon. *Historia*. Edited by C. B. Hase. Bonn: Weber, 1828.
Libanius. *Libanii Opera*. Edited by R. Foerster. Vol. IV. Leipzig: B. G. Teubner, 1908.
Oratio LIX. Translated by M. H. Dodgeon, revised by M. Vermes and S. Lieu. In *From Constantine to Julian: Pagan and Byzantine Views: A Source History*, edited by S. N. C. Lieu and D. Montserrat, 159–209. New York, NY: Routledge, 1996.
Malalas. *Chronographia*. Edited by I. Thurn. Berlin: de Gruyter, 2000. Translated by E. Jeffreys, M. Jeffreys, and R. Scott. Melbourne: Australian Association for Byzantine Studies, 1986.
Marcellinus Comes. *Chronicon*. Edited by J.-P. Migne. Patrologia Latina 51. Paris, 1861.

Mauropos. *Iohannis Euchaitorum Metropolitae Quae Supersunt*. Edited by P. de Lagarde. Amsterdam: Adolf M. Hakkert, 1979 [1882].

Menander Protector. *Historia*. Edited and translated by R. C. Blockley. Liverpool: Francis Cairns, 1985.

Michael the Syrian. *Chronicon*. Edited by J. B. Chabot. Vol. II. Paris: Ernest Leroux, 1901.

Miracula Sancti Demetrii. Edited and translated by P. Lemerle. Paris: Éditions du Centre National de la Recherche Scientifique, 1979–1981.

Nikephoros. *Breviarum Historicum*. Edited and translated by C. Mango. Washington, DC: Dumbarton Oaks, 1990.

Nikephoros. *On Strategy*. Edited and translated by G. T. Dennis. *Three Byzantine Military Treatises*. Washington DC: Dumbarton Oaks, 1985.

Orosius. *Historiarum adversus Paganos Libri VII*. Edited by C. Zangemeister. Leipzig: Teubner, 1889. Translated by A. T. Fear. Liverpool: Liverpool University Press, 2010.

Panegyrici Latini. Edited by R. A. B. Mynors. Translated by C. E. V. Nixon and B. S. Rodgers. Berkeley, CA: University of California Press, 1994.

Periplus Maris Erythraei. Edited and translated by L. Casson. Princeton, NJ: Princeton University Press, 1989.

Philostorgius. *Historia Ecclesiastica*. Edited by J. Bidez. Die griechischen christlichen Schriftsteller der ersten drei Jahrhunderte 21. Leipzig: J. C. Hinrichs'sche Buchhandlung, 1913.

Priscus of Panium. *History*. Edited and translated by R. C. Blockley. Liverpool: Francis Cairns, 1981.

Procopius. *Opera Omnia*. Edited by J. Haury and G. Wirth. Leipzig: Teubner, 1962–1964. Translated by H. B. Dewing. Cambridge, MA: Harvard University Press/New York, NY: G. P. Putnam's Sons, 1914–1940. Revised translation by A. Kaldellis. *The Wars of Justinian*. Indianapolis, IN/Cambridge: Hackett, 2014.

Historia Arcana. Edited and translated by A. Kaldellis.*The Secret History with Related Texts*. Indianapolis, IN/Cambridge: Hackett, 2010.

Psellos. *Chronographia*. Edited by E. Renauld. Paris: Belles Lettres, 1928.

Pseudo-Zachariah. *The Chronicle of Pseudo-Zachariah Rhetor: Church and War in Late Antiquity*. Edited by G. Greatrex. Translated by R. R. Phenix and C. B. Horn. Liverpool: Liverpool University Press, 2011.

Seneca. *Naturales Quaestiones*. Edited by H. M. Hine. Leipzig: Teubner, 1996. Translated by H. M. Hine. Chicago, IL: University of Chicago Press, 2010.

Socrates. *Historia Ecclesiastica*. Edited by R. Hussey and W. Bright. Oxford: Clarendon Press, 1893.

Sozomen. *Historia Ecclesiastica*. Edited by J. Bidez and G. C. Hansen. Die griechischen christlichen Schriftsteller der ersten Jahrhunderte 4. Berlin: Akademie Verlag, 1995.

Staurakios. *Logos eis ta Thaumasia tou Agiou Dimitriou*. Edited by I. Iviritou, *Makedonika* 1 (1940): 324–376.

Strategikon. Edited by G. T. Dennis. Vienna: Verlag der Österreichischen Akademie der Wissenschaften, 1981. Translated by G. T. Dennis. Philadelphia, PA: University of Pennsylvania Press, 1984.

Suetonius. *Opera*. Edited by M. Ihm. Vol. I. Leipzig: Teubner, 1907.

Tacitus. *Annales*. Edited by J. Jackson. Loeb Classical Library. Vol. II. Cambridge, MA: Harvard University Press, 1962.

Germania. Edited by M. Hutton. Loeb Classical Library. Cambridge, MA: Harvard University Press, 1946.

Themistius. *Orationes*. Edited by L. Dindorf. Leipzig: C. Cnobloch, 1832.

Theophanes. *Chronographia*. Edited by C. de Boor. Leipzig: Teubner, 1883. Translated by C. Mango and R. Scott. Oxford: Clarendon Press, 1997.

Theophylact Simocatta. *Historia*. Edited by C. de Boor and P. Wirth. Stuttgart: Teubner, 1972. Translated by Mary Whitby and Michael Whitby. Oxford: Oxford University Press, 1986.

Zosimus. *Historia Nova*. Edited by L. Mendelssohn. Leipzig: Teubner, 1887. Translated by J. J. Buchanan and H. T. Davis. San Antonio, TX: Trinity University Press, 1967.

Secondary Sources

Abdy, R. and G. Williams. "A catalogue of hoards and single finds from the British Isles c. 410–675." In *Coinage and History in the North Sea World, c. AD 500–1250. Essays in Honour of Marion Archibald*, edited by B. Cook and G. Williams, 11–73. Leiden: Brill, 2006.

Abramishvili, T. "Nokalakevskii klad" [Nokalakevi hoard]. *VV* 23 (1963): 158–165.

"Ochamchireshi aghmochenili sp'ilendzis bizant'iuri monet'ebi" [Byzantine copper coins found in Ochamchire]. *Akad. S. Janashias sachelobis sakartvelos sachelmts'ipo muzeumis moambe* 24-B (1963): 56–74.

Sakartvelos sakhelmts'ipo muzeumis bizant'iuri monet'ebi [Byzantine Coins in the National Museum of Georgia]. Tbilisi: Mecniereba, 1965.

"Bizant'iuri okros monet'ebi (Chibatis gandzi)" [Byzantine gold coins (Chibati hoard)]. *Akad. S. Janashias sachelobis sakartvelos sachelmts'ipo muzeumis moambe* 25-B (1968): 159–176.

"Klad monet iz Magraneti" [Coin hoard from Magraneti]. In *Numizmaticheskii sbornik posviashchaetsia pamiati D. G. Kapanadze*, edited by V. A. Lekvinadze, 73–82. Tbilisi: Mecniereba, 1977.

"Nokalakevisa da nojikhevis monet'ebi" [Coins from Nokalakevi]. In *Nokalakevi-Arkeopolisi. II. Arkeologiuri gatkhrebi 1978–1982*, edited by P. Zakaraia, 274–286. Tbilisi: Mecniereba, 1987.

Sakartvelos sakhelmts'ipo muzeumis bizant'iuri monet'ebi (1966–1984) [Byzantine Coins in the National Museum of Georgia (1966–1984)]. Tbilisi: Mecniereba, 1989.

"Nokalakevis arkeologiuri ekspeditsiis mier bolo ts'legshi gamovlenili numizmat'ik'uri masla" [Numismatic material recently found by the Nokalakevi archaeological expedition]. In *Nokalakevi-Arkeopolisi: III. Arkeologiuri gatchrebi 1983–1989*, edited by P. Zakaraia, 270–272. Tbilisi: Mecniereba, 1993.

Afanas'ev, G. "Na karavannoi trope" [On the caravan trail]. *Stavropol'e literaturno-khudozhestvennyi al'manakh* (1973), no. 3: 73–74.

Ahrweiler, H. "La frontière et les frontières de Byzance en Orient." In *Actes du XIVe congrès international des études byzantines: Bucarest, 6–12 septembre 1971*, edited by M. Berza and E. Stănescu, Vol. I, 209–230. Bucharest: Editura Academiei RSR, 1974.

Aibabin, A. I. "Khronologiia mogil'nikov Kryma pozdnerimskogo i rannesrednevekovogo vremeni" [Chronology of Crimean burials in the Late Roman and Early Medieval period]. *MAIET* 1 (1990): 5–68.

Akhmedov, I. "Rannevizantiiskie nakhodki na R. Oke v central'noi Rossii (predvaritel'nye soobshchenie)" [Early Byzantine finds on River Oka in central Russia (preliminary report)]. In *Od Bachórza do Światowida ze Zbrucza. Tworzenie się słowiańskiej Europy w ujęciu źródłoznawczym. Księga jubileuszowa Profesora Michała Parczewskiego*, edited by B. Chudzińska, M. Wojenka, and M. Wołoszyn, 171–177. Cracow/Rzeszów: Wydawnictwo Uniwersytetu Rzeszowskiego, 2016.

"Vizantiiskie i slavianskie nakhodki v riazano-okskikh drevnostiakh" [Byzantine and Slavic artifacts in Riazan'-Oka assemblages]. In *Drevnosti Pooch'ia. Sbornik nauchnkykh rabot k 60-letiiu V. V. Sudakova*, edited by A. O. Nikitin, 64–87. Ryazan: Riazanskoe istoriko-kul'turnoe obshchestvo, 2016.

Akin, D. "Cash and shell money in Kwaio, Solomon Islands." In *Money and Modernity*, 103–130.

Alconini, A. "The dynamics of military and cultural frontiers on the southeastern edge of the Inka Empire." In *Untaming the Frontier in Anthropology, Archaeology and History*, edited by B. J. Parker and L. Rodseth, 115–146. Tucson, AZ: University of Arizona Press, 2005.

Aldea, I. A. "Două monede bizantine descoperite la Sebeş" [Two Byzantine coins found at Sebeş]. *Apulum* 6 (1967): 625–628.

Alemany, A. "Sixth-century Alania: between Byzantium, Sasanian Iran and the Turkic world." In *Ērān ud Anērān. Studies Presented to Boris Il'ich Marshak on the Occasion of His 70th Birthday*, edited by M. Compareti, P. Raffetta, and G. Scarcia, 43–50. Venice: Libreria Editrice Cafoscarina, 2006.

Alföldi, A. "The moral barrier on Rhine and Danube." In *The Congress of Roman Frontier Studies, 1949*, edited by E. Birley, 1–16. Durham: Durham University Press, 1952.

Alföldi, M. R. *Die constantinische Goldprägung: Untersuchungen zu ihrer Bedeutung für Kaiserpolitik und Hofkunst*. Mainz: Verlag des Römisch-Germanischen Zentralmuseums Mainz, 1963.

Allen, M. "Contested Peripheries: Philistia in the Neo-Assyrian World-System." PhD Dissertation, University of California, Los Angeles, CA, 1996.

Althabe, G. "Circulation monétaire et communautés villageoises malgaches." *RESS* 21 (1970): 149–174.

Ambroz, A. K. "Problemy rannesrednevekovoi khronologii Vostochnoi Evropy" [Problems regarding the Early Medieval chronology of Eastern Europe]. *SA* 2 (1971): 96–123.

Anamali, S. and H. Spahiu. "Varrëza arbërore e Krujes" [An Albanian cemetery in Kruje]. *Iliria* 9–10 (1979–1980): 47–103.

Andreev, S. I. and N. V. Filimonova. "Ranneslavianskie kul'tury v Tambovskoi obl." [Early Slavic culture in Tambov Oblast]. In *Verkhnee Podon'e: arkheologiia, istoriia. Vypusk 3 k 65-letiiu so dnia rozhdeniia B.A. Folomeeva (1942–2001) i 25-letiiu so dnia nachala arkheologo geograficheskikh rabot na Kulikovom pole (1982–2007)*, edited by O. V. Burova, A. N. Naumov, and N. K. Fomin, 18–24. Tula: Gosudarstvennyi muzei-zapovednik "Kulikovo pole," 2009.

Angelov, D. "La formation de la nationalité bulgare." *EB* 4 (1969): 14–37.

Angelova, S. "Po vuprosa za rannoslavianskata kultura na iug i na sever ot Dunav prez VI-VII v" [On the question of early Slavic culture south and north of the Danube in the 6th–7th c.]. *Arkheologiia* 12, no. 4 (1980): 1–12.

Angelova, S. and R. Koleva. "Archäologische Zeugnisse frühslawischer Besiedlung in Bulgarien." In *Post-Roman Towns. Trade and Settlement in Europe and Byzantium. Vol. II: Byzantium, Pliska, and the Balkans*, edited by J. Henning, 281–307. Berlin/New York, NY: Walter de Gruyter, 2007.

Anghelinu, M. "Failed revolution: Marxism and the Romanian prehistoric archaeology between 1945 and 1989." *ArchBulg* 11, no. 1 (2007): 1–36.

Antonova, V. "Arkheologicheski prouchvaniia na Shumenskata krepost (Prevaritelno suobshtenie za trakiiskoto, rimskoto i rannovizantiiskoto selishte)" [Archaeological excavations of the Shumen fortress (preliminary report on the Thracian, Roman and Early Byzantine settlement)]. *Izvestiia na Narodniia Muzei Shumen* 6 (1973): 127–158.

Apakidze, A. M., ed. *Didi Pit'iunt'i. Arkeologiuri gatkhrebi Bich'vint'ashi* [Great Pitiunt. Archaeological finds at Pitsunda]. Vol. II. Tbilisi: Mecniereba, 1977.

Arce, J. "Frontiers of the Late Roman Empire: perceptions and realities." In *The Transformation of Frontiers. From Late Antiquity to the Carolingians*, edited by W. Pohl, I. Wood, and H. Reimitz, 5–13. Transformation of the Roman World 10. Leiden/New York, NY: Brill, 2001.

Arrignon, J. P. and J. F. Duneau. "La frontière chez deux auteurs byzantins: Procope de Césarée et Constantin VII Porphyrogénète." *Geographica Byzantina* (1981): 17–30.

Asdracha, C. "Inscriptions chrétiennes et protobyzantines de la Thrace orientale et de l'île d'Imbros (IIIe–VIIe siècles): Présentation et commentaire historique." *ArchDelt* 53 (1998): 455–521.

Atanasov, G. "Martyrium et ἁγιασμον dans le castel bas-byzantin près du village de Golech, région de Silistra (communication préliminaire)." In *Von der Scythia zur Dobrudža*, edited by Kh. Kholiolchev, R. Pillinger, and R. Hahrreiter, 127–139. Vienna: Verlag "Freunde des Hauses Wittgenstein," 1997.

Aulikh, V. V. *Zimnyvs'ke gorodishche: slov'ians'ka pam'iatka VI–VII n.e. v zakhydnyi Voliny* [The Zimno stronghold: a Slavic monument of the sixth and seventh century]. Kiev: Naukova dumka, 1972.

Ausenda, G., P. Delogu, and C. Wickham, eds. *The Langobards Before the Frankish Conquest: An Ethnographic Perspective*. Rochester, NY: Boydell Press, 2009.

Avenarius, A. *Die byzantinische Kultur und die Slawen: zum Problem der Rezeption und Transformation (6. bis 12. Jahrhundert)*. Vienna: R. Oldenbourg, 2000.

Babić, S. "Still innocent after all these years? Sketches for a social history of archaeology in Serbia." In *Archäologien Europas. Geschichte, Methoden und Theorien*, edited by P. F. Biehl, A. Gramsch, and A. Marciniak, 309–321. Münster: Waxmann, 2002.

Bálint, C. "Über die Datierung der osteuropäischen Steppenfunde des frühen Mittelalters. Schwierigkeiten und Möglichkeiten." *Mitteilungen des Archäologischen Instituts der Ungarischen Akademie der Wissenschaften* 14 (1985): 137–147.

 "Kontakte zwischen Iran, Byzanz und der Steppe. Das Grab von Üç Tepe (Sowj. Azerbajdžan) und der beschlagverzierte Gürtel im 6. und 7. Jahrhundert." In *Awarenforschungen*, edited by F. Daim, 309–496. Vienna: Institut für Ur- und Frühgeschichte der Universität Wien, 1992.

 "Probleme der archäologischen Forschung zur awarischen Landnahme." In *Ausgewählte Probleme europäischer Landnahmen des Früh- und Hochmittelalters*, edited by M. Müller-Wille and R. Scheider, 195–273. Sigmaringen: Thorbecke, 1993.

 "Der Beginn der Mittelawarenzeit und die Einwanderung Kubers." *Antaeus* 29–30 (2008): 29–61.

 "Antwortschreiben an Péter Somogyi." *Antaeus* 29–30 (2008–2009): 395–401.

Băluță, C. L. "Lămpile antice din colecția Severeanu" [Ancient lamps in the Severeanu Collection]. *Apulum* 31 (1994): 199–225.

Banfi, E. "Cristianizzazione nei Balcani e formazione della lega linguistica balcanica." In *Christianity Among the Slavs: The Heritage of Saints Cyril and Methodius. Acts of the International Congress Held on the Eleventh Centenary of the Death of St. Methodius, Rome, October 8–11, 1985*, edited by G. Farrugia, R. F. Taft, and G. K. Piovesana, 145–163. Rome: Pont. Institutum Studiorum Orientalium, 1988.

Bangert, S. "Menas ampullae: a case study of long-distance contacts." In *Incipient Globalization? Long-Distance Contacts in the Sixth Century*, edited by A. Harris, 27–33. Oxford: Archaeopress, 2007.

Bărbulescu, M. "Paleocreștinismul în România. Probleme metodologice și aspecte istoriografice românești și străine" [Early Christianity in Romania.

Methodological questions and Romanian and foreign historiographical issues]. In *Slujitor al bisericii și al neamului. Părintele Prof. Univ. Dr. Mircea Păcurariu, membru corespondent al Academiei Române, la împlinirea vârstei de 70 de ani*, 171–178. Cluj-Napoca: Editura Renașterea, 2002.

Barnea, A. "Einige Bemerkungen zur Chronologie des Limes an der unteren Donau in spätrömischer Zeit." *Dacia* 34 (1990): 283–290.

——— "Voies de communication au bas-Danube aux IVe–VIe s. ap. J. C." *EBPB* 3 (1997): 29–43.

Barnea, I. "Contributions to Dobrudja History under Anastasius I." *Dacia* 4 (1960): 363–374.

——— "Perioada Dominatului (sec. IV–VII)" [The Dominate (4th–7th c.)]. In *Din istoria Dobrogei*, edited by R. Vulpe and I. Barnea, Vol. II. Bucharest: Editura Academiei, 1968.

——— *Les monuments paléochrétiens de Roumanie*. Vatican: Pontificio Istituto di Archeologia Christiana, 1977.

——— *Christian Art in Romania. Vol. I: 3rd–6th Centuries*. Bucharest: Publishing House of the Bible and Mission Institute of the Romanian Orthodox Church, 1979.

——— "Le christianisme sur le territoire de la Republique Socialiste de Roumanie aux IIIe–XIe siècles." *EB* 1 (1985): 92–106.

——— "Sur les rapports avec Byzance du territoire situé au Nord du Bas Danube durant la période Anastase Ier–Justinien Ier (491–565)." *EBPB* 2 (1991): 47–57.

——— "Le Danube, voie de communication byzantine." In *He epikoinonia sto Byzantio. Praktika tou B' diethnous symposiou, 4–6 oktobriou 1990*, edited by N. Moschonas, 577–595. Athens: Kentro Byzantinon Ereunon, 1993.

——— "Menasampullen auf dem Gebiet Rumäniens." In *Akten XII*, 509–514.

——— ed. *Tropaeum Traiani. I. Cetatea*. Bucharest: Editura Academiei, 1979.

Barnea, I. and A. Barnea. "Săpăturile de salvare de la Noviodunum" [Rescue excavations at Noviodunum]. *Peuce* 9 (1984): 97–105.

Barnea, I., O. Iliescu, and C. Nicolescu. *Cultura bizantină în România* [Byzantine culture in Romania]. Bucharest: Editura Meridiane, 1971.

Barnes, T. D. "The victories of Constantine." *ZPE* 20 (1976): 149–55.

Bartel, B. "Colonialism and cultural responses: problems related to Roman provincial analysis." *World Archaeology* 12, no. 1 (1980): 11–26.

Bartosiewicz, L. and A. M. Choyke. "Animal remains from the 1970–1972 excavations of Iatrus (Krivina), Bulgaria." *AAASH* 43 (1991): 181–209.

Bârzu, L. *La continuité de la création matérielle et spirituelle du peuple roumain sur le territoire de l'ancienne Dacie*. Bucharest: Editura Academiei RSR, 1980.

——— *Ein gepidisches Denkmal aus Siebenbürgen: das Gräberfeld Nr. 3 von Bratei*. Cluj-Napoca: Accent, 2010.

Bârzu, L. and S. Brezeanu. *Originea și continuitatea românilor. Arheologie și tradiție istorică* [The origin and continuity of the Romanian people. Archaeology and historical tradition]. Bucharest: Editura Enciclopedică, 1991.

Bausovac, M. "Late Roman amphorae from Rifnik near Celje (Slovenia)." In *LRCW3. Late Roman Coarse Wares, Cooking Wares and Amphorae in the Mediterranean. Archaeology and Archaeometry. Comparison Between Western and Eastern Mediterranean*, edited by S. Menchelli, 695–701. Oxford: Archaeopress, 2010.

Bavant, B. "Un moule d'orfèvre protobyzantin au British Museum." In *Mélanges Jean-Pierre Sodini*, edited by F. Baratte, V. Déroche, C. Jolivet-Lévy, and B. Pitarakis, 627–644. Travaux et Mémoires 15. Paris: Collège de France-CNRS, 2005.

Beda, C. "Descoperiri monetare antice şi bizantine, jud. Teleorman" [Ancient and Byzantine coin finds from Teleorman County]. *CN* 3 (1980): 127–147.

Bejan, A. "Un atelier metalurgic de la Drobeta-Turnu Severin" [A metallurgical workshop at Drobeta-Turnu Severin]. *AMN* 13 (1976): 257–268.

Beliaev, O. S. and I. O. Molodchikova. "Pokhovannia kochyvnikov na r. Orel" [A nomadic burial on the Orel River]. *Arkheolohiia* 28 (1978): 84–92.

Bendall, S. "Some comments on the anonymous silver coinage of the fourth to sixth centuries AD." *RN* 158 (2002): 139–159.

Berdan, F. F. "Borders in the Eastern Aztec Empire." In *The Postclassic Mesoamerican World*, edited by M. E. Smith and F. F. Berdan, 73–77. Salt Lake City, UT: University of Utah Press, 2003.

Berndt, G. M. "Shifting frontiers in the Caucasus Mountains: the Suani." In *Shifting Cultural Frontiers in Late Antiquity*, edited by D. Brakke, D. Deliyannis, and E. Watts, 255–270. Burlington, VT: Ashgate, 2012.

Bessaignet, P. "Monnaie primitive et théorie monétaire." *RESS* 21 (1970): 37–65.

Bezuglov, S. I. "O monete iz Bol'shoi Orlovki (k ocenke datiruiushchikh vozmozhnostei)" [On the coin from Bol'shaia Orlovka (dating possibilities)]. In *Srednevekovye drevnosti Dona*, edited by I. K. Guguev, 114–118. Moscow/Jerusalem: Mosty kul'tury/Gesharim, 2007.

Bezuglov, S. I. and S. A. Naumenko. "Novye nakhodki vizantiiskikh i iranskikh importov v stepiakh Podon'ia" [New finds of Byzantine and Iranian imports from the Don steppe]. *Donskaia arkheologiia* 1 (1999): 35–42.

Bhabha, H. *The Location of Culture*. London: Routledge, 1994.

"Culture's in-between." In *Questions of Cultural Identity*, edited by S. Hall and P. du Gay, 52–60. London: Sage, 1996.

Biernacka-Lubańska, M. *The Roman and Early Byzantine Fortifications of Lower Moesia and Northern Thrace*. Wrocław: Zaklad Narodowy im. Ossolinskich, 1982.

Bitenc, P. and T. Knific, eds. *Od Rimljanov do Slovanov Predmeti* [From Romans to Slavs]. Ljubljana: Narodni Muzej Slovenije, 2001.

Bjelajac, L. "La céramique et les lampes." In *Caričin Grad II: Le quartier sud-ouest de la ville haute*, edited by B. Bavant, V. Kondić, and J. M. Spieser, 161–190. Rome: École Française de Rome, 1990.

Blackburn, J. *The White Men: The First Response of Aboriginal Peoples to the White Men*. London: Orbis, 1979.

Blesl, C. "Gräber des 6. Jahrhunderts zwischen der Traisen und dem Wienerwald in Niederösterreich." In *Kulturwandel in Mitteleuropa: Langobarden, Awaren, Slawen: Akten der Internationalen Tagung in Bonn vom 25. bis 28. Februar 2008*, edited by J. Bemmann and M. Schmauder, 319–330. Bonn: R. Habelt, 2008.

Bloch, M. "The symbolism of money in Imerina." In *Money and Morality*, 165–190.

Blockley, R. C. "Roman–barbarian marriages in the Late Empire." *Florilegium* 4 (1982): 63–79.

Bodianskii, A. V. "Arkheologicheskie nakhodki v Dneprovskom nadporozh'e" [Archaeological finds in the region of the Dnieper Cataracts]. *SA* (1960), no. 1: 274–277.

Bogdan Cătăniciu, I. and A. Barnea. "Ceramica şi descoperiri mărunte" [Pottery and small finds]. In *Tropaeum Traiani. I. Cetatea*, edited by I. Barnea, 177–226. Bucharest: Editura Academiei, 1979.

Bohannan, P. "The impact of money on an African subsistence economy." *Journal of Economic History* 19, no. 4 (1959): 491–503.

Boia, L. *History and Myth in Romanian Consciousness*. Budapest: Central European University Press, 2001.

Bolta, L. *Rifnik pri Šenturju. Poznoantična naselbina in grobišče* [Rifnik near Šentur. The Late Antique settlement and cemetery]. Ljubljana: Narodni muzei, 1981.

Bóna, I. "Avar lovassír Iváncsáról" [Grave of an Avar horseman at Iváncsa]. *ArchÉrt* 97 (1970): 243–261.

"Gepiden in Siebenbürgen, Gepiden an der Theiss." *AAASH* 23, nos. 1–2 (1979): 9–50.

"Studien zum frühawarischen Reitergrab von Szegvár." *AAASH* 32 (1980): 31–95.

"Byzantium and the Avars: the archaeology of the first 70 years of the Avar era." In *From the Baltic to the Black Sea. Studies in Medieval Archaeology*, edited by D. Austin and L. Alcock, 113–118. London: Unwin Hyman, 1990.

"'Barbarische' Nachahmungen von byzantinischen Goldmünzen im Awarenreich." *RIN* 95 (1993): 529–538.

"Die Awarenfeldzüge und der Untergang der byzantinischen Provinzen an der Unteren Donau." In *Kontakte zwischen Iran, Byzanz und der Steppe im 6.-7. Jahrhundert*, edited by C. Bálint, 163–183. Budapest: Archäologisches Institut der UAW, 2000.

"Review of P. Somogyi, Byzantinische Fundmünzen der Awarenzeit." *AAASH* 54, nos. 1–2 (2003): 294–296.

Bóna, I. and M. Nagy. *Gepidische Gräberfelder am Theissgebiet I*. Budapest: Magyar Nemzeti Múzeum, 2002.

Bonev, C. "Les Antes et Byzance." *EB* 19 (1983), 3: 109–120.

Boozer, A. L. "Frontiers and borderlands in imperial perspectives: exploring Rome's Egyptian frontier." *AJA* 117, no. 2 (2013): 275–292.

Boshkova, B. "Coins from the excavations of the antique town Ratiaria." *Ratiarensia* 2 (1984): 105–116.

Böttger, B. "Die Gefäßkeramik aus dem Kastell Iatrus." In B. Döhle, B. Böttger, G. Gomolka-Fuchs, E. Hajnalová, and K. Wachtel, *Iatrus Krivina. Spätantike Befestigung und frühmittelalterliche Siedlung an der unteren Donau. Band II: Ergebnisse der Ausgrabungen 1966-1973*, 33–148. Berlin: Akademie Verlag, 1982.

du Boulay, J. *Portrait of a Greek Mountain Village*. Oxford: Clarendon Press, 1974.

Bounegru, O. and M. Zahariade. *Les forces navales du Bas Danube et de la Mer Noire aux Ier VIe siècles*. Oxford: Oxbow Books, 1996.

Braudel, F. *Méditerranée et le monde méditerranéen à l'époque de Philippe II*. 2nd edn. Paris: A. Colin, 1966.

Braund, D. "Coping with the Caucasus: Roman responses to local conditions in Colchis." In *The Eastern Frontier of the Roman Empire. Proceedings of a Colloquium Held at Ankara in September 1988*, edited by D. French and C. Lightfoot, 31–43. BAR International Series 553. Oxford: BAR, 1989.

"Procopius on the Economy of Lazica." *Classical Quarterly* 41, no. 1 (1991): 221–225.

Georgia in Antiquity: A History of Colchis and Transcaucasian Iberia, 550 BC– AD 562. Oxford: Oxford University Press, 1994.

"River frontiers in the environmental psychology of the Roman world." In *The Roman Army in the East*, edited by D. Kennedy, 43–47. Journal of Roman Archaeology Supplementary Series no. 18. Ann Arbor, MI: JRA, 1996.

Brezeanu, S. "'Romains' et 'barbares' dans les Balkans au VIIe siècle à la lumière des 'Miracles de Saint Démétrius'. Comment on peut devenir 'l'autre'." *RESEE* 24, no. 3 (1986): 127–131.

"The Lower Danube frontier during the 4th–7th centuries. A notion's ambiguity." *Annuario Istituto Romeno di Cultura e Ricerca Umanistica* 5 (2003): 19–46.

Brison, K. "Money and the morality of exchange among the Kwanga, East Sepik Province, Papua New Guinea." In *Money and Modernity*, 151-163.

Bruhn, J.-A. *Coin and Costume in Late Antiquity*. Washington, DC: Dumbarton Oaks Research Library and Collection, 1993.

Budaj, M. "Byzantská minca z Gajar" [A Byzantine coin from Gajary]. *Zborník Slovenského národného Múzea – Archeológia* 19 (2009): 219–224.

Budaj, M. and P. Proháska. "Ein Solidus des oströmischen Kaisers Anastasius I. aus Čataj." *Zborník Slovenského národného Múzea – Archeológia* 24 (2014): 145–149.

Bugarski, I. and V. Ivanišević. "Pogranich'e rimskoi imperii i varvarov: sistema oborony imperii ot Kutsiia do Lederaty" [The Roman frontier and the barbarians: the defense system from Cutia to Lederata]. In *Lesnaja i lesostepnaia zony vostochnoi Evropy v epohi rimskikh vliianii i velikogo pereseleniia narodov*, 482–511. Tula: Gosudarstvennyi muzei-zapovednik "Kulikovo pole," 2012.

von Bülow, G., B. Böttger, and S. Conrad, eds. *Iatrus-Krivina. Spätantike Befestigung und frühmittelalterliche Siedlung an der unteren Donau. Band VI: Ergebnisse der Ausgrabungen 1992–2000*. Mainz am Rhein: Verlag Phillip von Zabern, 2007.

Buora, M. "La ceramica di importazione (sigillata africana e anfore) come indicatore archeologico per il periodo bizantino nell'alto Adriatico." *Quaderni friulani di archaeologia* 15 (2005): 163–167.

Burns, T. S. *Barbarians Within the Gates of Rome: A Study of Roman Military Policy and the Barbarians, ca. 375–425 AD*. Bloomington, IN: Indiana University Press, 1994.

Bursche, A. *Later Roman–Barbarian Contacts in Central Europe: Numismatic Evidence*. Berlin: Mann, 1996.

"Function of Roman coins in *barbaricum* of Later Antiquity. An anthropological essay." In *Roman Coins Outside the Empire: Ways and Phases, Contexts and Functions*, edited by A. Bursche, R. Ciołek, and R. Wolters, 395–416. Wetteren: Moneta, 2008.

Butnariu, V. M. "Răspîndirea monedelor bizantine din secolele VI–VII în teritoriile carpato-dunărene" [The diffusion of Byzantine coins from the 6th–7th century in the Carpatho-Danubian region]. *BSNR* 131–133 (1983–1985): 199–235.

"Monedele romane postaureliene în teritoriile carpato-dunăreano-pontice (anii 275–491): I. Perioada 275–324" [Post-Aurelian Roman coins in the lands between the Carpathians, the Danube, and the Black Sea (275–491): Phase I: 275–324]. *AM* 11 (1987): 113–140.

"Monedele romane postaureliene în teritoriile carpato-dunăreano-pontice (anii 275–491): II. Perioada 323–383." *AM* 12 (1988): 131–196.

"Monedele romane postaureliene în teritoriile carpato-dunăreano-pontice (anii 275–491): III. Perioada 383–491." *AM* 14 (1991): 67–107.

Campbell, B. *Rivers and the Power of Ancient Rome*. Chapel Hill, NC: University of North Carolina Press, 2012.

Cândea, I. "Descoperiri monetare pe teritoriul județului Brăila, sec. XIV–XIX" [Coin finds from Brăila County, 14th–19th c.]. *Istros* 1 (1980): 375–399.

Cantea, G. "Cercetările arheologice pe dealul Mihai Vodă și împrejurimi" [Archaeological excavations on Mihai Vodă hill and its surroundings]. In *Bucureștii de odinioară în lumina săpăturilor arheologice*, edited by I. Ionașcu, 93–143. Bucharest: Editura Științifică, 1959.

Carile, A. "Il Caucaso e l'Imperio bizantino (secoli VI–XI)." In *Il Caucaso: cerniera fra culture dal Mediterraneo alla Persia (secoli IV–XI)*. Vol. I, 9–80. Spoleto: Centro italiano di studi sull'alto Medioevo, 1996.

Carrié, J.-M. "1993: ouverture des frontières romaines?" In *Frontières terrestres, frontières célestes dans l'antiquité*, edited by A. Rousselle, 31–53. Paris: Diffusion De Boccard, 1995.

"Were Late Roman and Byzantine economies market economies? A comparative look at historiography." In *Trade and Markets in Byzantium*, edited by C. Morrisson, 13–26. Washington, DC: Dumbarton Oaks Research Library and Collection, 2012.

Cârstea, S. D. "Creștinismul românesc din primele secole. Puncte de vedere" [Early Romanian Christianity. Some viewpoints]. *Revista Teologica* 2 (2008): 122–134.

Casey, J. *A Catalogue of the Greek, Roman and Byzantine Coins in Sinop Museum (Turkey) and Related Historical and Numismatic Studies*. London: Royal Numismatic Society, 2010.

Catrinoiu, I. "Rolul Bizanțului în viața religioasă din Muntenia în secolele IV–VI în lumina izvoarelor literare și arheologice" [The role of Byzantium in the religious life in Wallachia during the 4th–6th c. in light of literary and archaeological sources]. *BOR* 110, no. 7 (1983): 589–599.

Chase-Dunn, C. and T. D. Hall. "Conceptualizing core/periphery hierarchies for comparative study." In *Core/Periphery Relations in Precapitalist Worlds*, edited by C. Chase-Dunn and T. D. Hall, 5–44. Boulder, CO: Westview Press, 1991.

Rise and Demise: Comparing World-Systems. Boulder, CO: Westview Press, 1997.

Chauvicourt, J. and S. Chauvicourt. *Numismatique malgache. Fasc. 3. Les premières monnaies introduites à Madagascar*. Antananarivo: Trano Printy Loterana, 1968.

Cherry, D. *Frontier and Society in Roman North Africa*. Oxford: Clarendon Press, 1998.

Chiriac, C. "Expediția avară din 578–579 și evidența numismatică" [The Avar expedition of 578–579: the numismatic evidence]. *AM* 16 (1993): 191–203.

"Unele observații asupra informațiilor literar-istorice bizantine privitoare la regiunea Dunării de Jos în secolele V–X" [Some observations regarding the Byzantine literary sources concerning the Lower Danube region in the 5th–10th c.]. *AM* 20 (1997): 107–126.

Civilizația bizantină și societatea din regiunile extracarpatice ale României în secolele VI–VIII [Byzantine civilization and the society south and east of the Romanian Carpathians in the 6th–8th c.]. Brăila: Istros, 2013.

Chirica V. and M. Tanasachi. *Repertoriul arheologic al județului Iași* [The archaeological gazetteer of Iași County]. Vol. II. Iași: Institutul de Istorie și Arheologie, 1985.

Chirilă, E. and A. Socolan. *Tezaure și descoperiri monetare din colecția Muzeului județean Maramureș* [Coins and coin hoards in the collection of the Maramureș County Museum]. Baia Mare: Muzeul Județean Maramureș, 1971.

Chițescu, M. *Numismatic Aspects of the History of the Dacian State. The Roman Republican Coinage in Dacia and Geto-Dacian Coins of Roman Type*. BAR International Series 112. Oxford: BAR, 1981.

Christie, N. *The Lombards: The Ancient Longobards*. Cambridge, MA: Blackwell, 1995.

"From the Danube to the Po: the defence of Pannonia and Italy in the fourth and fifth centuries AD." In *Transition*, 547–578.

Christou, K. *Byzanz und die Langobarden: von der Ansiedlung in Pannonien bis zur endgültigen Anerkennung (500–680)*. Athens: Historical Publications St. D. Basilopoulos, 1991.

Chrysos, E. "Die Nordgrenze des byzantinischen Reiches im 6. bis 8. Jahrhundert." In *Die Völker Südosteuropas im 6. bis 8. Jarhrhundert*, edited by B. Hänsel, 27–40. Munich: Selbstverlag der Südosteuropa-Gesellschaft, 1987.

Chrzanovski, L. and D. Zhuravlev. *Lamps from Chersonesus in the State Historical Museum – Moscow*. Rome: L'Erma di Bretschneider, 1998.

Ciobanu, D. "The role of salt deposits in the political-military history of the Carpatho-Danubian space in the I–XIII centuries." *Studia Antiqua et Archaeologica* 9 (2003): 429–446.

Ciołek, R. "Skarb złotych monet z Mrzezina (Gm. Puck) a zespół z Brzezina Gdańskiego" [The hoard of gold coins of Mrzezino and the complex of Brzeźno Gdańskie]. *Wiadomości Numizmatyczne* 42 (1998): 59–67.

"Znaleziska monet rzymskich z terenów Pomorza przechowywanie w zbiorach Muzeum Kulturalno-Historycznego w Stralsundzie" [Finds of Roman coins from the Pomeranian area kept in the collection of the Museum of Culture and History in Stralsund]. *Wiadomości Numizmatyczne* 43 (1999): 169–186.

"Der Zufluss von Solidi in die südlichen Ostseegebiete." In *Byzantine Coins*, 217–230.

Cîrciumaru, M. and E. Ionescu. "Semințe de cereale și leguminoase din așezarea de la Histria (secolul al VI-lea e.n.)" [Grain and vegetable seeds at Histria (6th c. AD)]. *SCIVA* 36, no. 4 (1977): 267–270.

Ciupercă, B. and A. Măgureanu. "Unele observații asupra problemei tiparelor din secolele V–VII descoperite în spațiul extra-carpatic" [Some observations on the question of 6th-to-7th-century molds found in Wallachia and Moldavia]. *Buletinul Muzeului Județean Teleorman* 1 (2009): 149–157.

"Locuințe din a doua jumătate a mileniului I p. Chr. descoperite la Târgșoru Vechi" [Residences from the second half of the first millennium AD found at Târgșoru Vechi]. In *Arheologia mileniului I p. Chr. Cercetări actuale privind istoria și arheologia migrațiilor*, edited by L. M. Voicu, 152–174. Bucharest: Oscar Print, 2010.

Cojocaru, V. "Descoperiri de monede antice și medievale la Dunărea de Jos basarabeană" [Ancient and medieval coin finds from the Lower Danube region in Bessarabia]. In *Simpozion de Numismatică. Organizat în memoria martirilor căzuți la Valea Albă, la împlinirea a 525 de ani (1476–2001),*

Chișinău, 13–15 mai 2001. Comunicări, studii și note, edited by E. Nicolae, 113–124. Bucharest: Editura Enciclopedică, 2002.

Coman, G. "Cercetări arheologice cu privire la secolele V–XI în sudul Moldovei (stepa colinară Horincea-Elan-Prut)" [Archaeological research in southern Moldavia, 5th–11th c. (Horincea-Elan-Prut steppe)]. *AM* 6 (1969): 277–315.

"Contribuții la cunoașterea fondului etnic al civilizației secolelor V–XIII în jumătatea sudică a Moldovei" [Contributions to the ethnic study of 5th-to-13th-century culture in the southern half of Moldavia]. *Carpica* 11 (1979): 181–216.

"Noi cercetări arheologice cu privire la secolele V–XI în partea de sud a Moldovei" [New archaeological research in southern Moldavia, 5th–11th century]. *Acta Moldaviae Meridionalis* 1 (1979): 71–100.

Comșa, M. "Contribution à la question de la pénétration des Slaves au sud du Danube durant les VIe–VIIe siècles d'après quelques données archéologiques de Dobroudja." In *I Międzynarodowy Kongres Archeologii Slowiańskiej. Warszawa 14–18 IX-1965*. Vol. III, 322–330. Wrocław: Ossolineum, 1970.

"Die Slawen im karpatischen-donauländischen Raum im 6.–7. Jahrhundert." *ZfA* 7 (1973): 197–223.

"Unele considerații cu privire la originea și apartenența etnică a complexelor cu fibule digitate de tip Gîmbaș (jud. Alba)-Coșoveni (jud. Dolj)" [Some observations regarding the origin and ethnic character of assemblages with bow fibulae, type Gîmbaș (Alba County)-Coșoveni (Dolj County)]. *Apulum* 11 (1973): 259–272.

"Unele date cu privire la Banatul de sud în sec. IV–VII" [Some observations regarding South Banat during the 4th–7th c.]. In *In Memoriam Constantini Daicoviciu*, edited by H. Daicoviciu, 85–97. Cluj: Dacia, 1974.

"Socio-economic organization of the Daco-Romanic and Slav population on the Lower Danube during the 6th–8th centuries." In *Relations*, 171–200.

"Les formations politiques (cnezats de vallée) du VIe siècle sur le territoire de la Roumanie." *Prace i materiały. Muzeum Archeologicznego i Etnograficznego w Lodzi. Seria Archeologiczne* 25 (1978): 109–117.

"La Province de la Scythie Mineure (Dobroudja) et les Slaves pendant les VI–VII ss." In *Istoriia i kul'tura drevnik i srednevekovykh slavian*, edited by V. V. Sedov, 301–313. Moscow: Editorial URSS, 1999.

Condurachi, E., I. Barnea, and P. Diaconu. "Nouvelles recherches sur le Limes byzantin du Bas-Danube aux Xe–XIe siècles." In *Proceedings of the XIIIth International Congress of Byzantine Studies. Oxford, 5–10 September 1966*, edited by J. M. Hussey, D. Obolensky, and S. Runciman, 179–193. London: Oxford University Press, 1967.

Condurachi, E., D. M. Pippidi, D. Teodor, S. Dimitriu, V. Zirra, M. Coja, V. Eftimie, P. Alexandrescu, E. Popescu, D. Berciu, and C. Preda. "Șantierul arheologic Histria" [Archaeological excavations at Histria]. *MCA* 4 (1957): 9–101.

Constantinescu, E.-M. *Memoria pământului dintre Carpați și Dunăre* [The memory of the land between the Carpathian Mountains and the Danube]. Buzău: Muzeul Județean Buzău, 1999.

Constantiniu, M. "Șantierul arheologic Băneasa-Străulești" [Archaeological excavations at Bucharest–Băneasa-Străulești)]. *CAB* 2 (1965): 75–98.

— "Săpăturile de la Străulești-Măicănești. Așezarea feudală II" [Excavations at Bucharest–Străulești-Măicănești. The medieval settlement no. II]. *CAB* 2 (1965): 174–189.

— "Elemente romano-bizantine în cultura materială a populației autohtone din partea centrală a Munteniei în secolele VI–VII e.n." [Roman-Byzantine influence in the material culture of the native population from central Wallachia in the 6th–7th c. AD]. *SCIV* 17, no. 4 (1966): 665–678.

Cooper, H. K. "Analysis of Late Roman-Byzantine copper-alloy artifacts from Northern Jordan." MA thesis. University of Arkansas, 2000.

Corman, I. *Contribuții la istoria spațiului pruto-nistrian în epoca evului mediu timpuriu (sec. V–VII d.Chr.)* [Contributions to the history of Moldova in the Early Middle Ages (5th–7th c. AD)]. Chișinău: Cartdidact, 1998.

Čorović-Ljubinković, M. "Les Slaves du centre balkanique du VIe au XIe siècle." *Balcanoslavica* 1 (1972): 43–54.

Cosentino, S. "Constans II and the Byzantine Navy." *BZ* 100, no. 2 (2007): 577–603.

Covacef, Z. and E. Corbu. "Considerații asupra unei categorii de opaițe descoperite în sectorul V al cetății Capidava" [Some observations regarding a category of lamps found at Capidava, Sector V]. *Pontica* 24 (1991): 282–297.

Crawford J. Stephens. *The Byzantine Shops at Sardis*. Cambridge, MA: Harvard University Press, 1990.

Croke, B. "Mundo the Gepid: from freebooter to Roman general." *Chiron* 12 (1982): 125–135.

Croke, B. and J. Crow. "Procopius and Dara." *JRS* 73 (1983): 143–159.

Crow, J. "Amida and Tropaeum Traiani: a comparison of Late Antique fortress cities on the Lower Danube and Mesopotamia." In *Transition*, 435–455.

Csallány, D. *Archäologische Denkmäler der Gepiden im Mitteldonaubecken*. Budapest: Verlag der ungarischen Akademie der Wissenschaften, 1961.

Cseh, J., E. Istvánovits, E. Lovász, K. Mesterházy, M. Nagy, I. M. Nepper, and E. Simonyi. *Gepidische Gräberfelder im Theissgebiet II*. Budapest: Magyar Nemzeti Múzeum 2005.

Csiky, G. and P. Magyar-Hárshegyi. "Wine for the Avar elite? Amphorae from Avar period burials in the Carpathian Basin." In *The Danubian Lands between the Black, Aegean and Adriatic Seas (7th Century BC–10th Century AD): Proceedings of the Fifth International Congress on Black Sea Antiquities (Belgrade – 17–21 September 2013)*, edited by G. R. Tsetskhladze, A. Avram, and J. Hargrave, 175–182. Oxford: Archaeopress, 2015.

Curta, F. "The changing image of the Early Slavs in the Rumanian historiography and archaeological literature. A critical survey." *SF* 53 (1994): 235–276.

"Invasion or inflation? Sixth-to-seventh century Byzantine coin hoards in Eastern and Southeastern Europe." *Annali dell'Istituto Italiano di Numismatica* 43 (1996): 65–224.

"Limes and cross: the religious dimension of the sixth-century Danube frontier of the Early Byzantine Empire." *Starinar* 51 (2001): 45–67.

"Peasants as 'makeshift soldiers for the occasion': sixth-century settlement patterns in the Balkans." In *Urban Centers and Rural Contexts in Late Antiquity*, edited by T. S. Burns and J. W. Eadie, 199–217. Lansing, MI: Michigan State University Press, 2001.

The Making of the Slavs: History and Archaeology of the Lower Danube Region, c. 500–700. Cambridge: Cambridge University Press, 2001.

"The Prague type: a critical approach to pottery classification." *ArchBulg* 5 (2001): 73–106.

"Before Cyril and Methodius: Christianity and barbarians beyond the sixth- and seventh-century Danube frontier." In *East Central and Eastern Europe in the Early Middle Ages*, edited by F. Curta, 181–219. Ann Arbor, MI: University of Michigan Press, 2005.

"Byzantium in Dark-Age Greece (the numismatic evidence in its Balkan context)." *BMGS* 29, no. 2 (2005): 113–146.

"Frontier ethnogenesis in Late Antiquity: the Danube, the Tervingi, and the Slavs." In *Borders, Barriers, and Ethnogenesis. Frontiers in Late Antiquity and the Middle Ages*, edited by F. Curta, 173–204. Turnhout: Brepols, 2005.

"The Early Slavs in Bohemia and Moravia: a response to my critics." *Archeologické rozhledy* 61 (2009): 725–754.

"New remarks on Christianity beyond the sixth- and early seventh-century frontier of the Empire." In *Keszthely-Fenékpuszta im Kontext spätantiker Kontinuitätsforschung zwischen Noricum und Moesia*, edited by O. Heinrich-Tamáska, 303–321. Budapest/Leipzig: Marie Leidorf, 2011.

"Werner's Class I C: *erratum corrigendum cum commentariis*." *EN* 21 (2011): 63–110.

"Slavic" bow fibulae: twenty years of research." *Bericht der Römisch-Germanischen Kommission* 93 (2012): 235–342.

"Horsemen in forts or peasants in villages? Remarks on the archaeology of warfare in the 6th to 7th c. Balkans." In *War and Warfare in Late Antiquity*, edited by A. Sarantis and N. Christie, 809–852. Leiden/Boston, MA: Brill, 2013.

"Amphorae and seals: the "Sub-Byzantine" Avars and the quaestura exercitus." In *Festschrift for Csanád Bálint*, edited by Á. Bollók, 1–28. Budapest: Magyar Nemzéti Múzeum, 2016.

"Shedding light on a murky matter: remarks on 6th to early 7th century clay lamps in the Balkans." *AB* 20, no. 3 (2016): 51–116.

Curta, F. and A. Gandila. "Too much typology, too little history: a critical approach to the classification and interpretation of cast fibulae with bent stem." *ArchBulg* 15, no. 3 (2011): 51–81.

Curta, F. and A. Gandila. "Hoards and hoarding patterns in the Early Byzantine Balkans." *DOP* 65–66 (2012): 45–111.

Curta, F. and A. Gandila. "Sixth-century fibulae with bent stem." *Peuce* 11 (2013): 101–176.

ed. *Borders, Barriers, and Ethnogenesis. Frontiers in Late Antiquity and the Middle Ages*. Turnhout: Brepols, 2005.

Curzon, George N., Lord of Kedleston. *Frontiers. The Romanes Lecture 1907*. 2nd edn. Oxford: Clarendon Press, 1908.

Cusick, J. C. "Historiography of acculturation: an evaluation of concepts and their application in archaeology." In *Studies in Culture Contact: Interaction, Culture Change, and Archaeology*, edited by J. C. Cusick, 126–145. Carbondale, IL: Southern Illinois University, 1998.

Dąbrowski, K. "Nouvelles données concernant l'orfévrerie sur le territoire de la voévodie d'Olsztyn (Pologne)." *Archaeologia Polona* 19 (1980): 235–241.

Dagron, G. "Byzance et la frontière. Idéologie et réalité." In *Frontiers in the Middle Ages: Proceedings of the Third European Congress of Medieval Studies (Jyväskylä, 10–14 June 2003)*, edited by O. Merisalo, 303–318. Louvain-la-Neuve: Fédération internationale des instituts d'études médiévales, 2006.

Dagron, G. and C. Morrisson. "Le Kentènarion dans les sources Byzantines." *RN* 17 (1975): 145–162.

Daicoviciu, C. "Romeii lui Maurikios" [The Romans of Maurice]. *Apulum* 9 (1971): 731–733.

Dalton, G. "Primitive money." *AA* 67, no. 1 (1965): 44–65.

Damian, O. *Bizanțul la Dunărea de Jos (secolele VII–X)* [Byzantium on the Lower Danube (7th–10th c.)]. Brăila: Istros, 2015.

Dancheva-Vasileva, A. "Serdika i slavianskite nashestviia vuv Vizantiiskata imperiia VI–VII v." [Serdica and the 6th–7th century Slavic invasions in the Byzantine Empire]. In *Eurika. In honorem Ludmilae Donchevae-Petkovae*. edited by V. Grigorov, M. Daskalov, and E. Komatarova-Balinova, 79–92. Sofia: Natsionalen Arkheologicheski Institut s Muzei, 2009.

Dănilă, N. "Tipare de turnat cruci din secolele IV–VI descoperite pe teritoriul României" [Molds for crosses from the 4th to 6th century found in Romania]. *BOR* 101 (1983): 557–561.

"Izvoare literare, epigrafice, arheologice și numismatice privind prezența bizantină în Banat în secolele IV–VI" [Literary, epigraphic, archaeological, and numismatic sources regarding the Byzantine presence in Banat in the 4th–6th century]. *Mitropolia Banatului* 34, nos. 3–4 (1984): 150–161.

"Viața creștină în secolele IV–VI în lumina documentelor romano-bizantine" [Christian life in the 4th–6th century in light of Roman-Byzantine sources]. *Mitropolia Olteniei* 36, nos. 5–6 (1984): 325–341.

Daskalov, M. "Kalupi za metalni nakiti i kolanni ukrasi (VI–VII v.) ot Iuzhna Bulgariia" [Molds for metal ornaments and belt decorations from southern Bulgaria (6th–7th c.]. *Arkheologiia* 45, nos. 1–2 (2004): 91–95.

Kolani i kolanni ukrasi ot VI–VII vek (ot dneshna Bulgariia i susednite zemi) [Sixth-to-seventh-century belt sets and ornaments (on the basis of artifacts from present-day Bulgaria and the neighboring countries)]. Sofia: Craft House, 2012.

Daskalov, M. and D. I. Dimitrov. "Za proizvodstvoto na nakiti prez VI–VII v. v bulgarskite zemi" [The production of jewelry in Bulgaria during the 6th–7th c.]. *Arkheologiia* 42, nos. 3–4 (2001): 69–74.

Daskalov, M. and K. Trendafilova. "Kolanut v iuzhnodunavskite vizantiiski provintsii prez VI–VII v." [Sixth-to-seventh-century belt sets from the Byzantine provinces south of the Danube]. In *The Bulgarian Lands in the Middle Ages 7th–18th Centuries. International Conference, a Tribute to the 70th Anniversary of Prof. Alexander Kuzev, Varna, Septembre 12th–14th, 2002*, edited by V. Iotov, 7–18. Varna: Regionalen Istoricheski Muzei, 2005.

De'Spagnolis, M. C. and E. De Carolis. *Le Lucerne di bronzo*. Vatican: Musei della Biblioteca Apostolica Vaticana, 1986.

Dejan, M. *Elemente răsăritene în ținuturile extracarpatice (secolele VI–X)* [Eastern elements in the extra-Carpathian territories (6th–10th c.)]. Suceava: Editura Karl A. Romstorfer, 2015.

Delougaz, P. "Coins." In *A Byzantine church at Khirbat Al-Karak*, edited by P. Delougaz and R. C. Haines, 50–52. Chicago, IL: University of Chicago Press, 1960.

Demo, Ž. *Ostrogothic Coinage from Collections in Croatia, Slovenia and Bosnia and Herzegovina*. Ljubljana: Narodni Muzej, 1994.

Dez, J. "Monnaie et structures traditionelles à Madagascar." *RESS* 21 (1970): 175–202.

Diaconescu, A. "Lămpi romane târzii şi paleobizantine din fosta provincie Dacia" [Late Roman and Early Byzantine lamps from the former province of Dacia]. *EN* 5 (1995): 255–299.

Diaconescu, A. and C. Opreanu. "Cîteva puncte de vedere în legătură cu evoluţia societăţii autohtone în epoca daco-romană tîrzie şi în perioada migraţiilor" [Some viewpoints regarding the development of native culture in the late Daco-Roman period and the age of migrations]. *Anuarul Institutului de Istorie şi Arheologie din Cluj* 29 (1989): 571–595.

Diaconu, P. "Fibula digitată descoperită la Dervent (reg. Dobrogea)" [A bow fibula found at Dervent (Dobrudja)]. *SCIV* 13, no. 2 (1962): 447–449.

"Cui aparţine cultura Ciurel?" [To whom does the Ciurel culture belong?]. *Istros* 10 (2000): 491–493.

Dignas, B. and E. Winter. *Rome and Persia in Late Antiquity: Neighbours and Rivals*. Cambridge: Cambridge University Press, 2007.

Dijkstra, J. H. F. and G. Fisher, eds. *Inside and Out: Interactions between Rome and the Peoples on the Arabian and Egyptian Frontiers in Late Antiquity*. Leuven: Peeters, 2014.

Dimian, I. "Cîteva descoperiri monetare bizantine pe teritoriul RPR." [A few Byzantine coin finds from Romania]. *SCN* 1 (1957): 189–216.

Dimitrijević, D. "O etničkim problemima Vojvodine u vreme doseljenja Slovena" [On the ethnic problems of Vojvodina at the time of the Slavic settlement]. In *Simpozijum "Predslavenski etnički elementi na Balkanu u etnogenezi južnih Slovena," održan 24–26. oktobra 1968 u Mostaru*, edited by A. Benac, 85–94. Sarajevo: Akademija nauka i umjetnosti Bosne i Hercegovine, 1969.

Dimitrijević, D. and M. Girić. "Pesak près de Bočar, nécropole gépide." In *Époque préhistorique et protohistorique en Yougoslavie - Recherches et résultats*, edited by G. Novak, A. Benac, M. Garašanin, and N. Tasić, 190–193. Belgrade: Société archéologique de Yougoslavie, 1971.

Dimitrov, D. P., M. Chichikova, B. Sultov, and A. Dimitrova. "Arkheologicheskie raskopki v vostochnom sektore Nove v 1962 godu" [Archaeological excavations in the eastern sector at Novae (1962)]. *IAI* 27 (1964): 218–235.

"Arkheologicheskie raskopki v vostochnom sektore Nove v 1963 godu." *IAI* 28 (1965): 43–62.

Dimitrov, K. "Poznorzymskie i wczesnobizantyjskie monety z odcinka iv w Novae z lat 294–612" [Late Roman and Early Byzantine coins from 294–612 found in Sector IV at Novae]. *Novensia* 11 (1998): 99–112.

Dinchev, V. "Household substructure of the Early Byzantine settlements on the present Bulgarian territory." *ArchBulg* 1 (1997): 47–63.

"The fortresses of Thrace and Dacia in the Early Byzantine period." In *Transition*, 479–546.

Ditten, H. "Slawen im byzantinischen Heer von Justinian I. bis Justinian II." In *Studien zum 7. Jahrhundert in Byzanz. Probleme der Herausbildung des Feudalismus*, edited by H. Köpstein and F. Winkelmann, 59–72. Berlin: Akademie Verlag, 1976.

Dolinescu-Ferche, S. "Un complex din secolul al VI-lea la Sfințești" [A sixth-century archaeological assemblage found at Sfințești]. *SCIV* 18, no. 1 (1967): 127–134.

"Așezarea din sec. VI e.n. de la Olteni-județul Teleorman" [A sixth-century settlement at Olteni, Teleorman County]. *MCA* 10 (1973): 203–208.

Așezările din secolele III și VI în sud-vestul Munteniei. Cercetările de la Dulceanca [Third- and sixth-century settlements in soutwestern Wallachia: archaeological research at Dulceanca]. Bucharest: Editura Academiei RSR, 1974.

"Ciurel, habitat des VIe–VIIe siècles des notre ère." *Dacia* 23 (1979): 179–230.

"La culture Ipotești–Ciurel–Cîndești (Ve–VIIe siècles). La situation en Valachie." *Dacia NS* 28 (1984): 117–147.

"Cercetările arheologice din com. Vedea (jud. Teleorman)" [Archaeological excavations at Vedea (Teleorman County)]. *MCA* 16 (1986): 202–207.

Dolinescu-Ferche, S. and M. Constantiniu. "Un établissement du VIe siècle à Bucarest (Découvertes de la rue Soldat Ghivan)." *Dacia* 25 (1981): 289–329.

Donnan, H. and T. M. Wilson, eds. *Border Approaches: Anthropological Perspectives on Frontiers*. Lanham, MD: University Press of America, 1994.

Dorsinfang-Smets, A. "Les moyens d'échange traditionnels dans le bassin congolais." *RESS* 21 (1970): 93–110.

Drake, H. A. *Constantine and the Bishops: The Politics of Intolerance*. Baltimore, MD: Johns Hopkins University Press, 2002.

Drauschke, J. "Byzantinische Münzen des ausgehenden 5. bis beginnenden 8. Jahrhunderts in den östlichen Regionen des Merowingerreiches." In *Byzantine Coins*, 279–324.

Droberjar, E. "À propos des contacts entre l'empire d'Orient et les germans de l'Elbe au VIe siècle." In *Pontic-Danubian Realm*, 297–316.

Dumanov, B. "The Late Antique workshops of jewelry south of the Lower Danube. Direct and indirect evidence of local production." In *The Lower Danube Roman Limes (1st–6th c. AD)*, edited by L. Vagalinski, N. Sharankov, and S. Torbatov, 405–428. Sofia: National Archaeological Institute and Museum, 2012.

Dumistrăcel, S. and D. Hreapcă. "Histoire des dialects dans la Romania: Romania du Sud-Est." In *Romanische Sprachgeschichte/ Histoire linguistique de la Romania: Ein internationales Handbuch zur Geschichte der romanischen Sprachen/ Manuel international d'histoire linguistique de la Romania*, edited by G. Ernst, M.-D. Gleßgen, C. Schmitt, and W. Schweickard, 2459–2476. Berlin: Walter de Gruyter, 2008.

Dumitroaia, G. "Materiale şi cercetări arheologice din nord-estul judeţului Neamţ" [Archaeological research in the northeastern region of Neamţ County]. *Memoria Antiquitatis* 18 (1992): 63–143.

Drummond, S. K. and L. H. Nelson. *The Western Frontiers of Imperial Rome*. Armonk, NY: M. E. Sharpe, 1994.

du Nay, A. *The Origin of the Rumanians: The Early History of the Rumanian Language*. Toronto/Buffalo: Mathias Corvinus Publishing, 1996.

Dyczek, P. "Lamps of the 3rd–6th century AD from the civil architecture in Sector IV at Novae." In *Lychnological Acts 2*, 73–78.

Dyson, S. L. "The role of comparative frontier studies in understanding the Roman frontier." In *Actes du IXe Congrès international d'études sur les frontières romaines, Mamaia 6–13 sept. 1972*, edited by D. M. Pippidi, 277–283. Bucharest: Editura Academiei RSR, 1974.

Dzhalagania, I. *Inozemnaia moneta v denezhnom obrashchenii Gruzii V–XIII vv.* [Foreign coins in the monetary circulation of Georgia, 5th–13th c.]. Tbilisi: Mecniereba, 1979.

Monety klady Gruzii: klad sasanidskikh i vizantiiskikh monet iz Tsiteli Tskaro (pervaia chast') [Coin hoards in Georgia: a hoard of Sasanian and Byzantine coins from Tsitelitskaro (part one)]. Tbilisi: Mecniereba, 1980.

Eadie, J. W. "Peripheral vision in Roman history: strengths and weaknesses of the comparative approach." In *Ancient and Modern: Essays in Honor of Gerald*

F. Else, edited by J. H. D'Arms and J. W. Eadie, 215–234. Ann Arbor, MI: Center for Coordination of Ancient and Modern Studies, 1977.

Eggers, J. H. *Der römische Import im freien Germanien.* Hamburg: Hamburgisches Museum für Völkerkunde und Vorgeschichte, 1951.

Einzig, P. *Primitive Money in Its Ethnological, Historical, and Economic Aspects.* 2nd edn. New York, NY: Pergamon Press, 1966.

Ellis, L. "Elusive Places: A chorological approach to identity and territory in Scythia Minor." In *Romans, Barbarians, and the Transformation of the Roman World. Cultural Interaction and the Creation of Identity in Late Antiquity*, edited by R. W. Mathisen and D. Shanzer, 241–251. Farnham: Ashgate, 2011.

Elton, H. *Frontiers of the Roman Empire.* Bloomington, IN: Indiana University Press, 1996.

Engelhardt, I. *Mission und Politik in Byzanz: ein Beitrag zur Strukturanalyse byzantinischer Mission zur Zeit Justins und Justinians.* Munich: Institut für Byzantinistik und Neugriechische Philologie der Universität, 1974.

Ennabli, A. *Lampes chrétiennes de Tunisie (Musées du Bardo et de Carthage).* Paris: Centre National de la Recherche Scientifique, 1976.

Erdrich, M. *Rom und die Barbaren. Das Verhältnis zwischen dem Imperium Romanum und den germanischen Stämmen vor seiner Nordwestgrenze von der späten römischen Republik bis zum Gallischen Sonderreich.* Römisch-Germanische Forschungen 58. Mainz am Rhein: Verlag Philipp von Zabern, 2001.

Falkner, R. K. "The pottery." In A. G. Poulter, *Nicopolis ad Istrum: A Roman to Early Byzantine City. The Pottery and Glass*, 55–296. London: Leicester University Press, 1999.

Febvre, L. "La Frontière: le mot et la notion." *Revue de Synthèse Historique* 45 (1928): 31–44.

Feissel, D. "L'architecte Viktôrinos et les fortifications de Justinien dans les provinces balkaniques." *Bulletin de la Société Nationale des Antiquaires de France* (1988): 136–146.

Feuer, B. A. *Boundaries, Borders and Frontiers in Archaeology: A Study of Spatial Relationships.* Jefferson, NC: McFarland & Co, 2016.

Fiala, A. "K objavu miliarense Constansa II. z pokladu zo Zemianskeho Vrbovku" [Miliarensia of Constans II from the Zemiansky Vrbovok hoard]. *Numismatický sborník* 17 (1986): 15–20.

"Byzantské mince na Slovensku (6.–12. storočie)" [Byzantine coins in Slovakia (6th–12th c.)]. *Slovenská Numizmatika* 10 (1989): 57–64.

Fiedler, U. *Studien zu Gräberfeldern des 6. bis 9. Jahrhunderts an der unteren Donau.* Bonn: Habelt, 1992.

"Biertan. Ein Zeugnis heidnischer Opfersitten im nachrömischen Siebenbürgen." *Dacia* 40–42 (1996–1998): 389–397.

"Die slawischen Bügelfibeln von Joachim Werners Gruppe I. Bemerkungen zum Forschungsstand unter besonderer Berücksichtigung des Typs I C." In *Între stepă și imperiu. Studii în onoarea lui Radu Harhoiu*, edited by A. Măgureanu and E. Gáll, 225–252. Bucharest: Renaissance, 2010.

Fiema, Z. T. "Late-Antique Petra and its hinterland: recent research and new interpretations." In *The Roman and Byzantine Near East. Vol. III: Late-Antique Petra, Nile Festival Buildings at Sepphoris, Deir Qual'a Monastery, Khirbet Qana Village and Pilgrim Site, 'Ain-'Arrub Hiding Complex, and Other Studies*, edited by J. H. Humphrey, 191–252. JRA Supplementary Series 49. Portsmouth, RI: JRA, 2002.

Filipescu, B. "Cercetări în stațiunea arheologică Malu Roșu, com. Fierbinți-tîrg, jud. Ialomița" [Archaeological research at Malu Roșu (Fierbinți-tîrg, Ialomița County)]. *Cercetări arheologice* 7 (1984): 129–135.

Flerova, V. E. "Podkurgannye pogrebreniia vostochnoevropeiskikh stepei i puti slozheniia kul'tury Khazarii" [Barrow inhumations in the Eastern European steppe lands and the path to the rise of Khazaria]. In *Stepi Evropy v epokhu srednevekov'ia. Khazarskoe vremia*, edited by A. V. Evgelevskii, 163–190. Donetsk: Institut Arkheologii NAN Ukrainy/Donetskii Nacional'nyi Universitet, 2001.

Fleșer, G. and A. Popa. "Monede bizantine în colecția muzeului din Sebeș" [Byzantine coins in the Sebeș museum]. *Apulum* 12 (1974): 296–298.

Forni, G. "Limes. Nozioni e nomenclature." In *Il confine nel mondo clasico*, edited by M. Sordi, 272–294. Contributi dell'Istituto di storia antica 13. Milan: Pubblicazioni della Università Cattolica del Sacro Cuore, 1987.

Fowden, G. *Empire to Commonwealth: Consequences of Monotheism in Late Antiquity*. Princeton, NJ: Princeton University Press, 1994.

Frend, W. H. C. "Persecutions: genesis and legacy." In *The Cambridge History of Christianity. Vol. I: Origins to Constantine*, edited by M. M. Mitchell and F. M. Young, 503–523. Cambridge: Cambridge University Press, 2006.

Frezouls, E. "Les fluctuations de la frontière de l'Empire Romain." In *La géographie administrative et politique d'Alexandre à Mahomet: actes du Colloque de Strasbourg, 14–16 juin 1979*, 177–225. Leiden: Brill, 1981.

Frolova, N. A. and E. Ia. Nikolaeva. "Il'ichevskii klad monet 1975 g." [The Il'ich coin hoard (1975)]. *VV* 39 (1978): 173–179.

Fulford, M. G. "Roman and barbarian: the economy of Roman frontier systems." In *Barbarians and Romans in North-West Europe: From the Later Republic to Late Antiquity*, edited by J. C. Barrett, A. P. Fitzpatrick, and L. Macinnes, 81–95. BAR International Series 471. Oxford: BAR, 1989.

Fuller, C. J. "Misconceiving the grain heap: a critique of the concept of the Indian Jajmani system." In *Money and Morality*, 33–63.

Fuller, H. "From cowries to coins: money and colonialism in the Gold Coast and British West Africa in the early 20th century." In *Money in Africa*, 54–61.

Furasiev, A. "Byzance et la Crimée du sud-ouest au VIe siècle: relations culturelles et particularités du costume feminine." In *Pontic-Danubian Realm*, 363–380.

Gaj-Popović, D. "The appearance of the barbarized follises (folles) in the 6th century in the Balkan Peninsula." *Balcanoslavica* 2 (1973): 95–100.

Galaty, M. L. "World-systems analysis and anthropology: a new détente?" *Reviews in Anthropology* 40 (2011): 3–26.

Galestin, M. C. "Roman artefacts beyond the northern frontier: interpreting the evidence from the Netherlands." *European Journal of Archaeology* 13, no. 1 (2010): 64–88.

Galinier, M. "La Colonne trajane: images et imaginaire de la frontière." In *Frontières terrestres, frontières célestes dans l'antiquité*, edited by A. Rousselle, 273–288. Paris: Diffusion De Boccard, 1995.

Galkina, E. G. "K voprosu o roli Velikoi Bulgarii v etnopoliticheskoi istorii Vostochnoi Evropy" [On the role of Great Bulgaria in the ethnopolitical history of Eastern Europe]. *Studia Slavica et Balcanica Petropolitana* 9 (2011), no. 1: 5–32.

Gandila, A. "Early Byzantine Capidava: the numismatic evidence." *CN* 12–13 (2006–2007): 97–122.

"Some aspects of monetary circulation in the Byzantine province of Scythia during the 6th and 7th century." In *Numismatic, Sphragistic and Epigraphic Contributions to the History of the Black Sea Coast*, edited by I. Lazarenko. Vol. I, 301–330. Varna: Zograf, 2008.

"Face value or bullion value? Early Byzantine coins beyond the Lower Danube border." In *Byzantine Coins*, 449–472.

"Early Byzantine coin circulation in the Eastern provinces: a statistical approach." *AJN* 21 (2009): 151–226.

"Un tezaur de monede bizantine timpurii descoperit la Capidava" [An Early Byzantine coin hoard from Capidava]. *CN* 15 (2009): 87–105.

"Heavy money, weightier problems: the Justinianic reform of 538 and its economic consequences." *RN* 168 (2012): 363–402.

"A few rare Byzantine coins found in Dobrudja and the extent of Byzantine control in the seventh-century Balkans." *CN* 17 (2016): 53–64.

"Going east: western money in the Early Byzantine Balkans, Asia Minor and the Circumpontic region (6th–7th c.)." *RIN* 117 (2016): 129–88.

Garam, É. "A közép avarkor sírobolussal keltezhető leletköre" [The Middle Avar horizon dated with Charon's obol]. *ArchÉrt* 105 (1978): 206–216.

Funde byzantinischer Herkunft in der Awarenzeit vom Ende des 6. bis zum Ende des 7. Jahrhunderts. Budapest: Magyar Nemzeti Múzeum, 2001.

Gardner, A. "Fluid frontiers: cultural interaction on the edge of empire." *Stanford Journal of Archaeology* 5 (2007): 43–60.

Garenne-Marot, L. "'Fils à double tête' and copper-based ingots: copper money-objects at the time of the Sahelian empires of ancient Ghana and Mali." In *Money in Africa*, 1–8.

Gavritukhin, I. O. "Fibuly vizantiiskogo kruga v Vostochnoi Evrope (litye dunaisko-illiriiskie)" [Byzantine brooches in Eastern Europe (Danubian-Illyrian cast brooches)]. *MAIET* 9 (2002): 229–50.

"Fibula iz Luki-Kavechinskoi v kontekste slaviano-vizantiiskih sviazei" [The fibula from Luka-Kavechinskaya in the context of Slavic-Byzantine relations]. In *Słowianie i ich sąsiedzi we wczesnym średniowieczu*, edited by M. Dulinicz, 197–206. Lublin/Warsaw: Uniwersytetu Marii Curie-Skłodowskiej, 2003.

Gavritukhin, I. O. and M. Kazanski. "Bosporus, the Tetraxite Goths, and the Northern Caucasus region during the second half of the fifth and the sixth centuries." In *Neglected Barbarians*, 83–136.

Găzdac, C., L. Călian, and Á. Alföldy-Găzdac. *The Ancient and Byzantine Gold Coinages in the National History Museum of Transylvania*. Cluj-Napoca: Mega, 2007.

Găzdac, C. and C. Cosma. "Monede romane și statut social într-o necropolă de secolele VI–VII. 'Groapa lui Hărăstășan', Noșlac, jud. Alba, România" [Roman coins and social status in a sixth-seventh-century cemetery: "Groapa lui Hărăstășan," Noșlac, Alba County, Romania]. *Analele Banatului* 21 (2013): 107–116.

Găzdac, C., F. Humer, and E. Pollhammer. *In the Shadow of the Heathens' Gate: The Black Book of the Gold Coins from Carnuntum*. Cluj-Napoca: Mega Publishing House, 2014.

Gell, A. "Inter-tribal commodity barter and reproductive gift-exchange in Old Melanesia." In *Barter, Exchange and Value: An Anthropological Approach*, edited by C. Humphrey and S. Hugh-Jones, 142–168. Cambridge: Cambridge University Press, 1992.

Gening, V. F. "Pamiatniki u s. Kushnarenkovo na r. Beloi (VI–VII vv. n.e.)" [Archaeological sites near Kushnarenkovo on the Belyi River (6th–7th c.)]. In *Issledovaniia po arkheologii Iuzhnogo Urala*, edited by R. G. Kuzeev, N. A. Mazhitov, and A. Kh. Pshenichniuk, 90–136. Ufa: Institut istorii, iazyka i literatury AN SSSR Bashkirskii filial, 1976.

Gherghe, P. and L. Amon. "Noi date în legătură cu podul lui Constantin cel Mare de la Sucidava" [New information regarding Constantine's bridge at Sucidava]. *Pontica* 40 (2007): 359–369.

Gill, M. A. V. and N. T. Şen. "Roman and Early Byzantine terracotta lamps. With a discussion and two appendices by C. S. Lightfoot." In *Amorium Reports II. Research Papers and Technical Reports*, edited by C. S. Lightfoot, 25–63. BAR International Series 1170. Oxford: Archaeopress, 2003.

Gkoutzioukostas, A. and X. M. Moniaros. *He peripheriake dioiketike anadiorganose tes byzantines autokratorias apo ton Ioustiniano A' (527–565): he periptose tes quaestura Iustiniana exercitus*. Thessaloniki: Banias, 2009.

Glad, D. "The Empire's influence on the barbarian elites from the Pontic region to the Rhine (5th–7th Centuries)." In *Pontic-Danubian Realm*, 349–362.

Glumac, M. "Glinene svetiljke iz kasnoantichke zbirke Narodnog Muzeja u Beogradu" [Late Antique terracotta lamps from the collection of the National Museum in Belgrade]. *Zbornik Narodnog Muzeja* 17, no. 1 (2001): 213–227.

Godelier, M. "'Monnaie de sel' et circulation des merchandises chez les Baruya de Nouvelle Guinée." *RESS* 21 (1970): 121–147.

Perspectives in Marxist Anthropology. Cambridge: Cambridge University Press, 1977.

Godłowski, K. "Das Aufhören der germanischen Kulturen an der mittleren Donau und das Problem des Vordringens der Slawen." In *Die Völker an der mittleren und unteren Donau im fünften und sechsten Jahrhundert*, edited by H. Wolfram and F. Daim, 225–232. Vienna: Verlag der Österreichischen Akademie der Wissenschaften, 1980.

Gogu, M. "Monedele bizantine aflate în colecția numismatică a Muzeului Național al Bucovinei din Suceava" [Byzantine coins in the National Museum of Bucovina in Suceava]. *Suceava* 26–28 (1999–2001): 283–310.

Gökalp, Demirel Z. *Malatya Arkeoloji Müzesi bizans sikkeleri kataloğu*. Istanbul: Arkeoloji ve Sanat Yayınları, 2014.

Goldina, R.D., Iu. Pastushenko, and E. M. Chernykh. "The Nevolino culture in the context of the 7th-century East–West trade: the finds from Bartym." In *Constructing the Seventh Century*, edited by C. Zuckerman, 865–930. Paris: Association des Amis du Centre d'histoire et civilisation de Byzance, 2013.

Goldina, R. D. and N. V. Vodolago. *Mogil'niki nevolinskoi kul'tury v Priural'e* [Burials belonging to the Nevolino culture in Priural'e]. Irkutsk: Izdatel'stvo Irkutskogo universiteta, 1990.

Golenko, K. V. "Imitacii solida VII v. iz Podneprov'ya" [Imitations of seventh-century solidi from the Dnieper region]. *VV* 11 (1956): 292–294.

"Klad vizantiiskikh monet VII v., naidennyi bliz Anapy" [A seventh-century hoard of Byzantine coins found near Anapa]. *VV* 26 (1965): 162–165.

Gomolka-Fuchs, G. "Die Kleinfunde vom 4. bis 6. Jh. aus Iatrus." In B. Döhle, B. Böttger, G. Gomolka-Fuchs, E. Hajnalová, and K. Wachtel, *Iatrus-Krivina II. Ergebnisse der Ausgrabungen 1966–1973*, 149–206. Berlin: Akademie Verlag, 1982.

Gomolka-Fuchs, G., ed. *Die Sîntana de Mureş-Cernjachov-Kultur: Akten des internationalen Kolloquiums in Caputh vom 20. bis 24. Oktober 1995*. Bonn: Habelt, 1999.

Göricke-Lukić, H. "Justinijanov novac iz Slavonije i Baranje" [Justinianic coins from Slavonia and Baranja]. In *Radovi XIII. Međunarodnog kongresa za starokrščansku arheologija. Split-Poreč (25.9–1.10.1994)*, edited by N. Cambi and E. Marin, Vol. II, 1144–1159. Vatican/Split: Pontificio Istituto di Archeologia Cristiana/Arheološki Muzej, 1998.

Gosden, C. *Archaeology and Colonialism: Cultural Contact from 5000 BC to the Present*. Cambridge: Cambridge University Press, 2004.

Gračanin, H. "Gepidi, Heruli, Langobardi i južna Panonija" [Gepids, Herules, Lombards and south Pannonia]. *Scrinia slavonica* 7 (2007): 7–64.

Graeber, D. *Toward an Anthropological Theory of Value: The False Coin of Our Own Dreams*. New York, NY: Palgrave, 2001.

Graebner, M. "'Μαυρίκιε Μαρκιανιστά.' A note." *Byzantina* 11 (1982): 181–188.

Graham, M. W. *News and Frontier Consciousness in the Late Roman Empire*. Ann Arbor, MI: University of Michigan Press, 2006.

Gray, E. W. "The Roman Eastern limes from Constantine to Justinian." *Proceedings of the African Classical Association* 12 (1973): 24–40.

Greatrex, G. "Roman identity in the sixth century." In *Ethnicity and Culture in Late Antiquity*, edited by S. Mitchell and G. Greatrex, 267–292. London: Duckworth and the Classical Press of Wales, 2000.

"Byzantium and the East in the sixth century." In *The Cambridge Companion to the Age of Justinian*, edited by M. Maas, 477–509. Cambridge: Cambridge University Press, 2005.

Greatrex, G. and S. N. C. Lieu *The Roman Eastern Frontier and the Persian Wars. Part II, AD 363-630. A Narrative Sourcebook*. London/New York, NY: Routledge, 2002.

Green, S. W and S. M. Perlman. "Frontiers, boundaries, and open social systems." In *The Archaeology of Frontiers and Boundaries*, edited by S. W. Green and S. M. Perlman, 3–13. New York, NY: Academic Press, 1985.

Greenwood, T. W. "A corpus of Early Medieval Armenian inscriptions." *DOP* 58 (2004): 27–91.

"Armenian neighbours: 600–1045." In *The Cambridge History of the Byzantine Empire c. 500-1492*, edited by J. Shepard, 333–364. Cambridge: Cambridge University Press, 2008.

Gregory, C. A. *Savage Money: The Anthropology and Politics of Commodity Exchange*. Amsterdam: Harwood Academic, 1997.

Gubitza, K. "A kishegyesi régibb középkori temető" [The old medieval cemetery in Kishegy]. *ArchÉrt* 31 (1907): 346–363.

Gudea, N. and I. Ghiurco. "Un opaiț de bronz bizantin de la Porolissum" [A Byzantine bronze lamp from Porolissum]. *Acta Musei Porolissensis* 10 (1986): 209–214.

Din istoria creștinismului la români. Mărturii arheologice [History of Christianity in Romania: archaeological evidence]. Oradea: Editura Episcopiei Ortodoxe Române a Oradiei, 1988.

Gusev, S. V. *Severo-Vostochnyi Kavkaz v epokhu srednevekov'ia: monety rasskazyvaiut* [Northeast Caucasus in the middle ages: numismatic evidence]. Moscow: Institut etnologii i antropologii RAN, 1995.

Haas, C. "Mountain Constantines: the Christianization of Aksum and Iberia." *Journal of Late Antiquity* 1, no. 1 (2008): 101–126.

Hahn, W. "Emission und Lustrum in der byzantinischen Münzprägung des 6. Jahrhunderts." *Anzeiger* 108 (1971): 215–221.

"Die Fundmünzen des 5.–9. Jahrhunderts in Österreich und den unmittelbar angrenzenden Gebieten." In *Die Geburt Mitteleuropas. Geschichte Österreichs vor seiner Entstehung, 378-907*, edited by H. Wolfram, 453–464. Vienna: Kremayr & Scheriau, 1987.

Hajnal, Z. "Mécsesek a Kölked-Feketekapui avar telepről" [Clay lamps from the Avar-age settlement in Kölked-Feketekapu]. *ArchÉrt* 128 (2003): 177–209.

"Késő antik jellegű kerámia a Kölked-Feketekapui avar kori telepről 2005" [Late Antique pottery from the Avar-age settlement at Kölked-Feketekapu (2005)]. *CAH* (2005): 477–480.

Hall, T. D. "Frontiers, ethnogenesis, and world-systems: rethinking the theories." In *A World-Systems Reader: New Perspectives on Gender, Urbanism, Cultures, Indigenous Peoples, and Ecology*, edited by T. D. Hall, 237–270. Lanham, MD: Rowman and Littlefield, 2000.

"Puzzles in the comparative study of frontiers: problems, some solutions, and methodological implications." *Journal of World-Systems Research* 15, no. 1 (2009): 25–47.

Hall, T. D., P. N. Kardulias and C. Chase-Dunn. "World-systems analysis and archaeology: continuing the dialogue." *Journal of Archaeological Research* 19 (2011): 233–279.

Hammarberg, I., B. Malmer, and T. Zachrisson. *Byzantine Coins Found in Sweden*. London: Spink & Son, 1989.

Hâncu, I. "Semnificația unor vestigii de cult la Hansca-Ialoveni" [The significance of some archaeological religious finds at Hansca-Ialoveni]. *Analele Științifice ale Universității de Stat din Moldova – seria științe socio-umane* (1998): 29–31.

Hansen, U. L. *Römischer Import im Norden: Warenaustausch zwischen dem Römischen Reich und dem freien Germanien während der Kaiserzeit unter besonderer Berücksichtigung Nordeuropas*. Copenhagen: Det Kongelige nordiske Oldskriftselskab, 1987.

Hanson, W. S., ed. *The Army and Frontiers of Rome. Papers Offered to David J. Breeze on the Occasion of his Sixty-Fifth Birthday and his Retirement from Historic Scotland*. JRA Supplementary Series 74. Portsmouth, RI: JRA, 2009.

Hardt, M. "The nomad's greed for gold: from the fall of the Burgundians to the Avar treasure." In *The Construction of Communities in the Early Middle Ages: Texts, Resources and Artefacts*, edited by R. Corradini, M. Diesenberger, and H. Reimitz, 95–107. Transformation of the Roman World 12. Leiden: Brill, 2003.

Harhoiu, R. *Die frühe Völkerwanderungszeit in Rumänien*. Bucharest: Editura Enciclopedică, 1997.

"Quellenlage und Forschungsstand der Frühgeschichte Siebenbürgens im 6.–7. Jahrhundert." *Dacia* 43–45 (2001): 97–158.

"Allgemeine Betrachtungen zum Bestattungssittenbild Siebenbürgens im 4. und bis zur Mitte des 9. Jahrhunderts." *Dacia* 48–49 (2004–2005): 283–334.

"Where did all the Gepids go? A sixth- to seventh-century cemetery in Bratei (Romania)." In *Neglected Barbarians*, 209–244.

Härke H. and A. Belinsky. "Nouvelles fouilles de 1994–1996 dans la necropole de Klin-Yar." In *Les sites archéologiques en Crimée et au Caucase durant l'antiquité tardive et le haut Moyen-Âge*, edited by M. Kazanski and V. Soupault, 193–210. Leiden/Boston, MA: Brill, 2000.

Hart, K. "Heads or tails? Two sides of the coin." *Man* 21, no. 4 (1986): 637–656.

Harțuche, N. and O. Bounegru. "Opaițe grecești și romane din colecțiile Muzeului Brăila" [Greek and Roman lamps from Brăila Museum]. *Pontica* 15 (1982): 221–234.

Haselgrove, C. and S. Krmnicek. "The archaeology of money." *ARA* 41 (2012): 235–250.

Heap, S. "'A bottle of gin is dangled before the nose of the natives': gin currency in colonial Southern Nigeria." In *Money in Africa*, 30–37.

Heather, P. and J. Matthews. *The Goths in the Fourth Century*. Liverpool: Liverpool University Press, 1991.

Hedeager, L. "A quantitative analysis of Roman imports in Europe north of the limes (0–400 AD), and the question of Roman–Germanic exchange." In *New Directions in Scandinavian Archaeology*, edited by K. Kristiansen and C. Paludan-Müller, 191–216. Copenhagen: Aarhus University Press, 1979.

Heinrich-Tamáska, O. "Megjegyzések a fenékpusztai II. számú kora keresztény bazilika keltezéséhez" [Remarks on the dating of the second early Christian church in Fenékpuszta]. *MFMÉ* 12 (2011): 225–234.

Hénaff, M. *The Price of Truth: Gift, Money, and Philosophy*. Stanford, CA: Stanford University Press, 2010.

Hendy, M. F. *Studies in the Byzantine Monetary Economy c. 300–1450*. Cambridge: Cambridge University Press, 1985.

Herrmann, J. "Die archäologischen Forschungen des Zentralinstituts für Alte Geschichte und Archäologie 1973 und im ersten Halbjahr 1974." *Ausgrabungen und Funde* 19, no. 6 (1974): 295–308.

Himmler, F. *Untersuchungen zur schiffsgestützten Grenzsicherung auf der spätantiken Donau (3.–6. Jh. n. Chr.)*. BAR International Series 2197. Oxford: Archaeopress, 2011.

Hodgson, N. "Relationships between Roman river frontiers and artificial frontiers." In *Roman Frontier Studies 1995. Proceedings of the XVIth International Congress of Roman Frontier Studies*, edited by W. Groenman-Van Waateringe, 61–66. Oxford: Oxbow, 1997.

Horedt, K. "Eine lateinische Inschrift des 4. Jahrhunderts aus Siebenbürgen." *Anuarul Institutului de Studii Clasice* 4 (1941–1943): 10–16.

"Avarii în Transilvania" [The Avars in Transylvania]. *SCIV* 7, nos. 3–4 (1956): 393–406.

Contribuții la istoria Transilvaniei în secolele IV–XIII [Contributions to the history of Transylvania, 4th–13th c.]. Bucharest: Editura Academiei RPR, 1958.

"The Gepidae, the Avars, and the Romanic population in Transylvania." In *Relations*, 111–122.

"Kleine Beiträge." *Dacia* 23 (1979): 341–346.

Moreşti: Grabungen in einer vor- und frühgeschichtlichen Siedlung in Siebenbürgen. Bucharest: Kriterion, 1979.

Hornstein, F. "ΙΣΤΡΟΣ ΑΜΑΞΕΥΟΜΕΝΟΣ. Zur Geschichte eines literarischen Topos." *Gymnasium* 64 (1957): 154–161.

Horsnaes, H. "Late Roman and Byzantine coins found in Denmark." In *Byzantine Coins*, 231–270.

Howard-Johnston, J. "Heraclius' Persian campaigns and the revival of the Eastern Roman Empire, 622–630." *War in History* 6, no. 1 (1999): 1–44.

——— "Armenian historians of Heraclius: an examination of the aims, sources and working-methods of Sebeos and Movses Daskhurantsi." In *The Reign of Heraclius (610–641): Crisis and Confrontation*, edited by G. J. Reinink and B. H. Stolte, 41–62. Leuven: Peeters, 2002.

——— *Witnesses to a World Crisis: Historians and Histories of the Middle East in the Seventh Century.* Oxford: Oxford University Press, 2010.

Humphrey, C. "Barter and economic disintegration." *Man* 20, no. 1 (1985): 48–72.

Hunka, J. "Finds of Byzantine coins from the 5th–10th century from the northern part of the Carpathian Basin." In *Byzantine Coins*, 395–402.

Iconomu, C. "Descoperiri de tipare de opaiţe la Tomis" [Lamp molds found at Tomis]. *Pontica* 9 (1976): 135–145.

Ierusalimskaia, A. *Die Gräber der Moščevaja Balka: frühmittelalterliche Funde an der nordkaukasischen Seidenstrasse.* Munich: Editio Maris, 1996.

Ilić, O. "Early Christian imports and local imitations of imported goods in the territory of the Central Balkans." In *The Roman Empire and Beyond: Archaeological and Historical Research on the Romans and Native Cultures in Central Europe*, edited by E. C. De Sena and H. Dobrzanska, 35–50. Oxford: Archaeopress, 2011.

Illyés, E. *Ethnic Continuity in the Carpatho-Danubian Area.* Boulder, CO: East European Monographs, 1988.

Iluk, J. "The export of gold from the Roman Empire to barbarian countries from the 4th to the 6th centuries." *Münstersche Beiträge zur antiken Handelsgeschichte* 4, no. 1 (1985): 79–102.

——— "Bałtycki epizod wczesnobizantyskich dziejów. Znaleziska solidów na Pomorzu Nadwiślańskim z V–VI wieku" [A Baltic episode of Early Byzantine history: Fifth-to sixth-century solidi found in the Lower Vistula region of Pomerania]. In *Gdańsk średniowieczny w świetle najnowszych badań archeologicznych i historycznych*, edited by H. Paner, 51–63. Gdańsk: Muzeum Archeologiczne, 1998.

Inaishvili, N. and N. Vashakidze. "Typology and chronology of Greek, Roman and Early Byzantine amphorae from Petra-Tsikhisdziri." In *PATABS I: Production and Trade of Amphorae in the Black Sea: actes de la table ronde internationale de Batoumi et Trabzon, 27–29 avril 2006*, edited by D. Kassab Tezgör and N. Inaishvili, 151–152. Paris: Institut français d'études anatoliennes–Georges Dumezil, 2010.

Ionescu, I. *Începuturile creștinismului românesc daco-roman (sec. II–VI, VII)* [The beginnings of Romanian Daco-Roman Christianity]. Bucharest: Editura Universității din București, 1998.

Ireland, S. and S. Ateşoğulları. "The ancient coins in Amasra Museum." In *Studies in Ancient Coinage from Turkey*, edited by R. Ashton, 115–137. London: Royal Numismatic Society, 1996.

Greek, Roman and Byzantine Coins in the Museum at Amasya. London: Royal Numismatic Society, 2000.

Irimia, M. "Cuptoarele romano-bizantine de ars ceramica de la Oltina" [Roman-Byzantine pottery kilns at Oltina]. *Pontice* 1 (1968): 379–408.

Isaac, B. "The meaning of the term *limes* and *limitanei*." JRS 78 (1988): 125–147.

The Limits of Empire. The Roman Army in the East. Oxford: Clarendon Press, 1990.

Isvoranu, T. and G. Poenaru Bordea. "Monede bizantine de la Tomis şi împrejurimi în colecția Institutului de Arheologie 'Vasile Pârvan' [Byzantine coins from Tomis and its surroundings in the collection of the Archaeological Institute "Vasile Pârvan"]. In *Simpozion de numismatică dedicat împlinirii a 125 de ani de la proclamarea independenței României, Chişinău, 24–26 septembrie 2002. Comunicări, studii şi note*, edited by E. Nicolae, 137–161. Bucharest: Editura Enciclopedică, 2003.

Iurukova, I. "Imitations barbares de monnaies de bronze byzantines du VIe siècle." *Byzantinoslavica* 30 (1969): 83–87.

Ivanišević, V. "Vizantijski novac sa Beogradske tvrđave" [Byzantine coins from the Belgrade fortress]. *Numizmatičar* 10 (1987): 88–107.

"Vizantijski novac (491–1092) iz zairke Narodnog Myzeja y Pojarevci" [Byzantine coins (491–1092) in the National Museum in Pojarevac]. *Numizmatičar* 11 (1988): 87–99.

"La monnaie paléobyzantine dans l'Illyricum du nord." In *Mélanges Cécile Morrisson*, 441–454. Travaux et Mémoires 16. Paris: Centre d'Histoire et Civilisation de Byzance, 2010.

Ivanišević, V. and I. Bugarski. "Western Banat during the Great Migration period." In *The Turbulent Epoch: New Materials from the Late Roman Period and the Migration Period*, edited by B. Niezabitowska-Wiśniewska, P. Łuczkiewicz, and S. Sadowski, 39–61. Lublin: Instytut Archeologii UMCS, 2008.

Ivanišević, V. and M. Kazanski. "Geruly Iustiniana v Severnom Illirikume i ikh arheologicheskie sledy" [Justinian's Herules in Northern Illyricum and their archaeological footprint]. *Stratum plus* (2010), no. 5: 141–157.

Ivanišević, V. and S. Stamenković. "'Glass' workshop from Caričin Grad (Iustiniana Prima)." In *Glass Along the Silk Road from 200 BC to AD 1000. International Conference Within the Scope of the "Sino-German Project on Cultural Heritage Preservation" of the RGZM and the Shaanxi Provincial Institute of Archaeology, December 11th–12th 2008*, edited by B. Zorn, 39–52. Mainz: Verlag des Römisch-Germanischen Zentralmuseums, 2010.

Ivanišević, V., M. Kazanski, and A. Mastykova. *Les nécropoles de Viminacium à l'époque des grandes migrations*. Paris: Centre d'Histoire et Civilisation de Byzance, 2006.

Ivanov, I. "Bolgi, Bersili, Esegeli – osnovni prabulgarski rodove na Kavkaz, Volga, Dunav i v Makedoniia" [Bolgi, Bersili, Esegeli – main proto-Bulgar groups of the Caucasus, Volga, Danube, and Macedonia]. In *Bulgariia v svetovnoto kulturno nasledstvo. Materialy ot tretata natsionalna konferentsiia po istoriia, arkheologiia i kulturen turizum. Putuvane kum Bulgariia - Shumen, 17–19.05.2012 g.*, edited by I. Iordanov, 179-193. Shumen: Universitetsko izadatelstvo "Episkop Konstantin Preslavski," 2014.

Ivanov, R., ed. *Roman and Early Byzantine Settlements in Bulgaria*. Vol. II. Sofia: Ivray, 2002.

Ivanov, S. A. "Oborona Vizantii i geografiia 'varvarskikh' vtorzhenii cherez Dunai v pervoi polovine VI v." [The defense of Byzantium and the geography of the "barbarian" invasions across the Danube in the first half of the sixth century]. *VV* 44 (1983): 27-47.

Ivanyi, D. *Die Pannonischen Lampen: eine typologisch-chronlogische Übersicht*. Budapest: Numismatic and Archaeological Institute, 1935.

Jagodziński, M. F. *Archeologiczne ślady osadnictwa między Wisłą a Pasłęką we wczesnym średniowieczu. Katalog stanowisk* [Archaeological remains of settlements between the Vistula and the Pasłęka in the Early Middle Ages: a gazetteer]. Warsaw: Instytut Archeologii i Etnologii Polskiej Akademii Nauk, 1997.

Janković, Đ. "Pozdneantičnie fibuli VI–VII vekov i slaviane" [Late antique fibulae of the 6th–7th century and the Slavs]. In *Rapports du IIIe Congres International d'archéologie slave. Bratislava 7–14 Septembre 1975*. Vol. I, 171-181. Bratislava: VEDA, 1980.

Podunavski deo oblasti Akvisa u VI i pochetkom VII veka [The Danubian area of Aquis in the sixth and the begining of the seventh century]. Belgrade: Arheološki Institut, 1981.

Jeremić, G. "Glass artefacts from Roman and Late Roman fortification at Saldum on the Middle Danube. Social and economic background." In *Annales du 18e Congrès de l'Association internationale pour l'histoire du verre. Thessaloniki, 2009*, edited by D. Ignatiadou and A. Antonaras, 284-291. Thessaloniki: Association Internationale pour l'Histoire du Verre, 2012.

Jones, A. E. "'Lord, protect the wearer:' Late Antique numismatic jewelry and the image of the Emperor as talismanic device." PhD Dissertation, Yale University, 2011.

Jovanović, A. "The problem of the location of Lederata." In *Roman Limes on the Middle and Lower Danube*, edited by P. Petrović, 69-72. Belgrade: Archaeological Institute, 1996.

Kadar, Z. "Die Menasampulle von Szombathely." In *Akten XII*, 886-888.

Kaegi, W. E. *Muslim Expansion and Byzantine Collapse in North Africa*. Cambridge: Cambridge University Press, 2010.

Kagan, K. "Redefining Roman Grand Strategy." *Journal of Military History* 70, no. 2 (2006): 336–362.

Kaiser, T. "Archaeology and ideology in Southeast Europe." In *Nationalism, Politics, and the Practice of Archaeology*, edited by P. L. Kohl and C. Fawcett, 99–119. Cambridge: Cambridge University Press, 1995.

Kalchev, K. "Antichni i kusnoantichni lampi ot Stara Zagora" [Ancient and Late Antique lamps from Stara Zagora]. *IMIB* 5 (1982): 7–22.

Kaldellis, A. "Classicism, barbarism, and warfare: Prokopios and the conservative reaction to Later Roman military policy." *American Journal of Ancient History* 3–4 (2004–2005): 189–218.

Kamera, M. I. and K. V. Golenko. "Leninakanskii klad sasanidskikh i vizantiiskikh monet (1956 g.)" [Hoard of Sasanian and Byzantine coins from Leninakan]. *VV* 19 (1961): 172–193.

Karagianni, F. "Networks of Medieval city-ports on the Black Sea (7th–15th century). The archaeological evidence." In *Harbours and Maritime Networks as Complex Adaptive Systems*, edited by J. Preiser-Kapeller and F. Daim, 83–104. Mainz: Verlag des Römisch-Germanischen Zentralmuseums, 2015.

Karagiorgou, O. "LR2: a container for the military *annona* on the Danubian border?" In *Economy and Exchange in the East Mediterranean during Late Antiquity. Proceedings of a Conference at Somerville College. Oxford – 29th May 1999*, edited by S. Kingsley and M. Decker, 129–166. Oxford: Oxbow Books, 2001.

Kardaras, G. "Ho 'dromos tou Dounabe' kata ten Hystere Archaioteta (4os–7os ai.)." In *He methorios tou Dounabe kai o kosmos ten sten epoche tes metanasteuses ton laon (4os-7os ai.)*, edited by S. Patoura-Spanou, 267–284. Athens: Ethniko Hidryma Ereunon/ Instituto Vyzantinon Ereunon, 2008.

"The Byzantine–Antic treaty (545/46 AD) and the defense of the Scythia Minor." *Byzantinoslavica* 58 (2010): 74–85.

To Byzantio kai oi Abaroi, 6.–9. ai. Politikes, diplomatikes kai politismikes scheseis. Athens: Ethniko Hidryma Ereunon/Instituto Vyzantinon Ereunon, 2010.

Kardulias, P. N. "Preface." In *World-Systems Theory in Practice: Leadership, Production, and Exchange*, edited by P. N. Kardulias, xvii–xxi. Lanham, MD: Rowman and Littlefield, 1999.

"Negotiation and incorporation on the margins of world-systems: examples from Cyprus and North America." *Journal of World-Systems Research* 13, no. 1 (2007): 55–82.

Karyshkovski, P. O. "Nakhodki pozdnerimskikh i vizantiiskikh monet v Odesskoi oblasti" [Finds of Late Roman and Byzantine coins in the Odessa region]. *Materialy po arkheologii Severnogo Prichernomor'ia* 7 (1971): 78–86.

Katsougiannopoulou, C. "Studien zu ost- und südosteuropäischen Bügelfibeln." PhD Dissertation, University of Bonn, 1999.

Kazanski, M. "Contribution à l'histoire de la défense de la frontière pontique au Bas-Empire." *Travaux et Mémoires* 11 (1991): 487–526.

Kazanski, M. and V. A. Mastykova. "Centry vlasti i togoviye pouti Zapadnoi Alanii V–VI vv." [Centers of power and trade routes in fifth-to-sixth-century Western Alania]. In *Severnyi Kavkaz: istoriko-arkheologicheskie ocherki i zametki*, edited by M. P. Abramova and V. I. Markovin, 138–161. Moscow: Rossiiskaia akademiia nauk, 2001.

Les peuples du Caucase du Nord. Le début de l'histoire (Ier–VIIe siècle apr. J.-C.). Paris: Editions Errance, 2003.

Kharalambieva, A. "Dva tipa kusnoantichni fibuli vuv Varnenskiia muzei" [Two types of Late Antique fibulae in the Varna Museum]. *INMV* 25 (1989): 25–40.

"Fibuli ot I–VII v. v Dobrichkiia muzei" [Fibulae from the 1st–7th c. in the Dobrich Museum]. *Dobrudzha* 9 (1992): 127–140.

"Bügelfibeln aus dem 7. Jh. südlich der unteren Donau." In *Actes du XIIe Congrès international des sciences préhistoriques et protohistoriques, Bratislava, 1–7 septembre 1991*, edited by J. Pavuj, 25–32. Bratislava: Institut Archéologique de l'Académie Slovaque des Sciences, 1993.

"Fibulite ot I–VII v. v muzeia na Dulgopol" [Fibulae from the 1st–7th c. in the Dulgopol Museum]. *INMV* 32–33 (1996–1997): 89–129.

"Production of dress ornaments in the fortresses and small settlements in North Bulgaria during the period from the 5th till the 7th century AD." In *The Roman and Late Roman City. The International Conference (Veliko Turnovo 26–30 July 2000)*, edited by L. Ruseva-Slokoska, R. T. Ivanov, and V. Dinchev, 393–397. Sofia: Akademichno izdatelstvo "Prof. Marin Drinov," 2002.

"Gepids in the Balkans: a survey of the archaeological evidence." In *Neglected Barbarians*, 245–262.

Kharalambieva, A. and G. Atanasov. "Novopostupili fibuli ot III–VII v. v Shumenskiia muzei" [Newly acquired fibulae from the 3rd–7th c. in the Shumen Museum]. *INMV* 28 (1992): 57–73.

Khrisimov, N. "Der frühmittelalterliche Gürtel von Üç Tepe (Azerbajdžan) und die dazugehörige Ausrüstung. Ein Rekonstruktionsversuch." *ArchBulg* 8, no. 1 (2004): 79–96.

"Ranneslavianskie pamiatniki v severo-vostochnoi chasti Balkanskogo poluostrova" [Early Slavic monuments in the northeastern region of the Balkan Peninsula]. *Stratum plus* (2015), no. 5: 309–344.

Kim, H. J. *The Huns*. New York, NY: Routledge, 2016.

Kiss, A. "Heruler in Nordserbien." In *Interaktionen der mitteleuropäischen Slawen und anderer Ethnika im 6.–10. Jahrhundert. Symposium Nové Vozokany 3.–7. Oktober 1983*, edited by P. Šalkovský, 133–137. Nitra: Archäologisches Institut der slowakischen Akademie der Wissenschaften, 1984.

"Die Goldfunde des Karpatenbeckens vom 5.–10. Jahrhundert (Angaben zu den Vergleichsmöglichkeiten der schriftlichen und archäologischen Quellen)." *AAASH* 38 (1986): 105–145.

"Die "barbarischen" Könige des 4.–7. Jahrhunderts im Karpatenbecken, als Verbündete des römischen bzw. byzantinischen Reiches." *CAH* (1991): 115–128.

"Germanen im awarenzeitlichen Karpatenbecken." In *Awarenforschungen*, edited by F. Daim. Vol. I, 35–134. Vienna: Institut für Ur- und Frühgeschichte der Universität Wien, 1992.

Das awarenzeitlich-gepidische Gräberfeld von Kölked-Feketekapu A. Innsbruck: Universitätsverlag Wagner, 1996.

"Régészeti és numizmatikai adatok a Duna-Tisza-köz 5. század második felének és a 6. század első felének településtörténetéhez" [Archeological and numismatic data on the history of settlements in the Danube-Tisza region in the second half of the 5th century and the first half of the 6th century]. *MFMÉ* 4 (1998): 189–194.

Das awarenzeitliche Gräberfeld in Kölked-Feketekapu B. Budapest: Magyar Nemzeti Múzeum/Magyar Tudományos Akadémia Régészeti Intézete, 2001.

"A gepidák avar kori továbbélésének vizsgálatáról" [A reassessment of the survival of the Gepids under Avar rule]. In *Középkortörténeti tanulmányok 6. A VI. Medievisztikai PhD-konferencia (Szeged, 2009. június 4–5. előadásai)*, edited by P. G. Tóth and P. Szabó, 119–134. Szeged: Szegedi Középkorász Műhely, 2010.

Klein, K. L. "Reclaiming the "F" word, or being and becoming postwestern." *Pacific Historical Review* 65, no. 2 (1996): 179–215.

Kóčka-Krenz, H. "The beginning of metal casting in Polish territories in the Early Middle Ages (the 6th–13th centuries)." In *Trudy V Mezhdunarodnogo Kongressa arkheologov-slavistov. Kiev 18–25 sentiabria 1985 g.*, edited by P. P. Tolochko, 83–89. Kiev: Naukova Dumka, 1988.

Koicheva, K. and A. Kharalambieva. "Fibuli ot Istoricheskiia muzei v Gabrovo (III–VII vek)" [Fibulae from the History Museum in Gabrovo (3rd–7th c.)]. *Godishnik na muzeite ot Severna Bulgariia* 19 (1993): 57–72.

Komar, O. V. "'Kubrat' i 'Velyka Bulgariia': problemy dzhereloznavchogo analizu" [Kubrat and Great Bulgaria: analyzing the facts]. *Skhodoznavstvo* (2001), nos. 13–14: 133–155.

"Kuda 'zapazdyvaiut' monety? (K voprosu o roli monet v datirovke rannesrednevekovykh pamiatnikov Vostochnoi Evropy VI–VIII vv.)" [Where are the "late" coins? (on the role of coins in the dating of Early Medieval complexes in sixth–eighth century Eastern Europe)]. In *Peterburgskii apokrif. Poslanie ot Marka*, ed. O. V. Sharov, 555–566. Chişinău: Universitet "Vyshskaia antropologicheskaia shkola," 2011.

"Zachepilovskii ('Novosanzharskii') kompleks rubezha VII–VIII vv" [The Zachepilovka ("Novosanzhary") assemblage of the late seventh and early eighth century]. In *Stepi Evropy v epokhu srednevekov'ia. Khazarskoe vremia. Sbornik nauchnykh trudov*, edited by A. V. Evgelevskii, 243–296. Donetsk: Doneckii Nacional'nyi universitet, 2012.

Komar, O. V. and V. M. Khardaev. "Kolekciia Zachepylivs'kogo ('Novosanzhars'-kogo') kompleksu 1928 r.: vtrachene i zberezhene" [The collection in the Zachepylivka ("Novosanzharsky") complex of 1928: lost and preserved]. In *Starozhytnosti livoberezhnogo Podniprov'ia 2011. Zbirnyk naukovykh prats'*, edited by G. Iu. Ivakin, I. F. Koval'ova, and I. Kulatova, 101–115. Kiev/Poltava: Tsentr pam'iatkoznavstva NAN Ukraini i UTOPIK, 2011.

Kopytoff, I. "The Roman frontier and the uses of comparison." In *Frontières d'empire. Nature et signification des frontières romaines: Actes de la table ronde internationale de Nemours, 21-22-23 mai 1992*, edited by P. Brun, S. van der Leeuw, and C. R. Whittaker, 143–148. Nemours: Édition de l'Association pour la Promotion de la Recherche Archéologique en Ile-de-France, 1993.

Korzukhina, G. F. "Klady i sluchainye nakhodki veshchei kruga 'drevnostei antov' v srednem Podneprov'e. Katalog pamiatnikov" [Treasures and stray finds from the culture of the Antes on the Middle Dnieper: a gazetteer]. *MAIET* 5 (1996): 352–435; 586–705.

Kos, P. "The monetary circulation in the Southeastern Alpine region ca 300 BC–AD 1000." *Situla* 24 (1984–1985): 1–254.

―― *Die Fundmünzen der römischen Zeit in Slowenien*. Vols. I–III. Berlin: Mann, 1988.

Kosianenko, M. "Pogrebenie u slobody Bol'shaia Orlovka - rannii pamiatnik saltovo-maiackoi kul'tury" [The Bol'shaia Orlovka burial - an early Saltovo assemblage]. In *Problemy khronologii arkheologicheskikh pamiatnikov stepnoi zony Severnogo Kavkaza*, edited by V. Ia. Kiiashko, 113–117. Rostov-na-Donu: Izdatel'stvo Rostovskogo universiteta, 1983.

Košnar, L. "Raně středověký depot stříbrných předmětů z Poštorné, okr. Břeclav" [Early Medieval hoard of silver objects from Poštná, Břeclav County]. *Praehistorica* 21 (1994): 69–103.

Kostova, K. and D. Dobreva. "Roman, Late Roman and Early Byzantine lamps from National Archaeological Reserve 'Deultum-Debelt'." In *Lychnological Acts 2*, 161–169.

Kramer, J. "Bemerkungen zu den christlichen Erbwörtern des Rumänischen und zur Frage der Urheimat der Balkanromanen." *Zeitschrift für Balkanologie* 34 (1998): 15–22.

―― "Sprachwissenschaft und Politik. Die Theorie der Kontinuität des Rumänischen und der balkanische Ethno-Nationalismus im 20. Jh." *Balkan-Archiv* 24–25 (1999–2000): 105–163.

Križanac, M. "Glass from Early Byzantine Gradina on Mount Jelica (Serbia)." In *Late Antique/Early Byzantine Glass in the Eastern Mediterranean*, edited by E. Laflı, 265–284. Izmir: Hürriyet Matbaası, 2009.

Kropotkin, V. V. *Klady vizantiiskikh monet na territorii SSSR* [Finds of Byzantine coins on the territory of the USSR]. Moscow: Izd-vo Akademii nauk SSSR, 1962.

"Novye nakhodki vizantiiskikh monet na territorii SSSR" [New finds of Byzantine coins on the territory of the USSR]. *VV* 26 (1965): 166–189.

Les trouvailles de monnaies byzantines en URSS. Edited by G. Depeyrot. Wetteren: Moneta, 2006.

Kruglov, E. V. "Obrashchenie vizantiiskikh monet VI–VIII vv. v vostochnoevropeiskikh stepiakh" [The circulation of Byzantine coins from the sixth and seventh centuries in the Eastern European steppe]. In *Vizantiia: obshchestvo i cerkov'*, edited by S. N. Malakhov and N. D. Barabanov, 168–177. Armavir: Armavirskii gosudarstvennyi pedagogicheskii universitet, 2005.

Kühn, H. "Das Problem der masurgermanischen Fibeln in Ostpreussen." In *Documenta Archaeologica Wolfgang La Baume dedicata 8.II.1955*, edited by O. Kleeman, 79–108. Bonn: L. Rohrscheid, 1956.

Kulikowski, M. *Rome's Gothic Wars: From the Third Century to Alaric*. Cambridge: Cambridge University Press, 2007.

Kurnatowska, Z. "Słowianie Południowi" [The Southern Slavs]. In *Wedrowka i etnogeneza w starozytnosci i sredniowieczu*, edited by M. Salamon and J. Strzelczyk, 203–218. Cracow: Towarzystwo Wydawnicze Historia Iagellonica, 2004.

Kurtz, E. "Eshchte dva neizdann'ikh proizvedeniia Konstantina Manassi" [Two more unpublished works of Constantine Manasses]. *VV* 12 (1906): 69–98.

Kus, S. and V. Raharijaona. "Small change in Madagascar: sacred coins and profane coinage." In *The Archaeology of Politics: The Materiality of Political Practice and Action in the Past*, edited by P. G. Johansen and A. M. Bauer, 29–55. Newcastle upon Tyne: Cambridge Scholars Publishing, 2011.

Kutchen, L. F. "The neo-Turnerian frontier." *Early American Literature* 40, no. 1 (2005): 163–171.

Kuzmanov, G. "Ceramica del primo periodo bizantino a Ratiaria." *Ratiarensia* 3–4 (1987): 111–118.

"Ranovizantiiska bitova keramika ot Gradishteto (severozapaden sector)" [The Early Byzantine kitchen wares from Gradishte (the northwestern sector)]. In V. Dinchev et al., *Bulgaro-britanski razkopki na gradishteto pri s. Dichin. Velikoturnovska oblast. 1996–2003: rezultati ot prouchvaniiata na bulgarskiia ekip*, 153–206. Razkopki i prouchvaniia, no. 39. Sofia: Bulgarska Akademiia na Naukite, 2009.

Lakatos, A. "Monede bizantine din perioada avară în Transilvania, vestul și nord-vestul României" [Byzantine coins from Avar-age Transylvania and the western and northwestern region of Romania]. *EN* 12 (2002): 237–256.

Lambert, C. and P. P. Demeglio. "Ampolle devozionali ed itinerari di pellegrinaggio tra IV e VII secolo." *Antiquité Tardive* 2 (1994): 205–231.

Lan, D. "Resistance to the present by the past: mediums and money in Zimbabwe." In *Money and Morality*, 191–208.

Langu, S., C. Onel, and C. Giurcanu. "Note asupra unor monede dintr-o colecție bârlădeană" [Notes on some coins from a collection in Bârlad]. *Elanul* 93, (November, 2009): 3–5.

László, Gy. "Die Reiternomaden der Völkerwanderungszeit und das Christentum in Ungarn." *Zeitschrift für Kirchengeschichte* 59 (1940): 126–146.

Lászlovszky J. and Cs. Siklódi. "Archaeological theory in Hungary since 1960: theories without theoretical archaeology." In *Archaeological Theory in Europe: The Last Three Decades*, edited by I. Hodder, 272–298. London/New York, NY: Routledge, 1991.

Lattimore, O. *Inner Asian Frontiers of China*. 2nd edn. Boston, MA: Beacon Press, 1962.

Lawal, A. A. "The currency revolution in British West Africa: an analysis of some early problems." In *Money in Africa*, 62–67.

Lazăr, V. "Repertoriul arheologic al județului Mureș" [The archaeological gazetteer of Mureș County]. Târgu Mureș: Casa de Editură "Mureș," 1995.

Lazaridis, P. "Nea Anchialos." *ArchDelt* 20 (1965): 326–334.

Lazo García, C. *Economia colonial y regimen monetario. Peru: siglos XVI–XIX. Tomo I: Nascimiento e instauración del sistema económico monetario colonial (siglo XVI)*. Lima: Banco Central de Reserva del Perú, 1992.

Leahu, V. "Raport asupra săpăturilor arheologice efectuate în 1960 la Cățelu Nou" [Report on excavations conducted at Cățelu Nou in 1960]. *Cercetări arheologice în București* 1 (1963): 34–43.

Lebeuf, J.-P. *Vêtements et parures du Cameroun français*. Paris: Éditions Arc-en-Ciel, 1946.

"Monnaies archaïques africaines de terre cuite." *RESS* 21 (1970): 67–91.

Lenski, N. "The Gothic civil war and the date of the Gothic conversion." *Greek, Roman and Byzantine Studies* 36 (1995): 51–87.

Failure of Empire: Valens and the Roman State in the Fourth Century AD. Los Angeles, CA: University of California Press, 2002.

"Captivity and Romano-Barbarian interchange." In *Romans, Barbarians, and the Transformation of the Roman World. Cultural Interaction and the Creation of Identity in Late Antiquity*, edited by R. Mathisen and D. Shanzer, 185–198. Farnham: Ashgate, 2011.

"Captivity among the Barbarians and its impact on the fate of the Roman Empire." In *The Cambridge Companion to the Age of Attila*, edited by M. Maas, 230–246. Cambridge: Cambridge University Press, 2014.

Levtzion, N. and J. F. P Hopkins, eds. *Corpus of Early Arabic Sources for West African History*. Translated by J. F. P. Hopkins. Princeton, NJ: Markus Wiener Publishers, 2000.

Levy, E. "Captivus redemptus." *Classical Philology* 38, no. 3 (1943): 159–176.

Liebeschuetz, J. H. W. G. "The refugees and evacuees in the age of migrations." In *The Construction of Communities in the Early Middle Ages*, edited by R. Corradini, M. Diesenberger, and H. Reimitz, 65–79. Transformation of the Roman World 12. Leiden: Brill, 2003.

"The Lower Danube under pressure: from Valens to Heraclius." In *Transition*, 101–134.

Lightfoot, K. G. and A. Martinez. "Frontiers and boundaries in archaeological perspective." *Annual Review of Anthropology* 24 (1995): 471–492.

Linscheid, P. "Untersuchungen zur Verbreitung von Menasampullen nördlich der Alpen." In *Akten XII*, 982–986.

Liubenova, V. "Selishteto ot rimskata i rannovizantiiskata epokha" [The Roman and Early Byzantine settlement]. In *Pernik I. Poselishten zhivot na khulma Krakra ot V khil. pr. n. e. do VI v. na n. e.*, edited by T. Ivanov, 107–203. Sofia: Izdatelstvo na Bulgarskata Akademiia na Naukite, 1981.

Lorthkhiphanidze, O. D. *Vani archeologiceskie raskopki* [Archaeological excavations at Vani]. Vol. IV. Tbilisi: Mecniereba, 1979.

Loskotová, Z. "Lombard burial grounds and graves of social elites north of the Middle Danube in the light of recent research." In *Macht des Goldes, Gold der Macht. Herrschafts- und Jenseitsrepräsentation zwischen Antike und Frühmittelalter im mittleren Donauraum. Akten des 23. internationalen Symposiums der Grundprobleme der frühgeschichtlichen Entwicklung im mittleren Donauraum, Tengelic, 16.–19.11.2011*, edited by M. Hardt and O. Heinrich-Tamáska, 321–338. Weinstadt: Bernhard Albert Greiner, 2013.

Lüdtke, H. *Der Ursprung der romanischen Sprachen. Eine Geschichte der sprachlichen Kommunikation*. Kiel: Westensee, 2005.

Lungu, I. *Școala Ardeleană. Mișcare culturală națională iluministă* [The Transylvanian School: a national cultural movement in the Age of Enlightenment]. Bucharest: Editura Viitorul Românesc, 1995.

Luttwak, E. N. *The Grand Strategy of the Roman Empire. From the First Century AD to the Third*. Baltimore, MD: Johns Hopkins University Press, 1976.

The Grand Strategy of the Byzantine Empire. Cambridge, MA: Harvard University Press, 2009.

Macarie, V. "Un vas bizantin de cult descoperit la Iași" [A Byzantine liturgical vessel found at Iași]. *SCIVA* 32, no. 2 (1981): 299–302.

Machajewski, H. "Skandynawskie elementy kulturowe na Pomorzu Zachodnim z okresu wędrówek ludów (2. połowa IV w.–początek VI w.)" [Scandinavian cultural elements in West Pomerania from the migration age (second half of the 4th century–beginning of 6th century)]. *Przegląd Archeologiczny* 40 (1992): 71–96.

Mackensen, M. "Amphoren und spatheia von Golemanovo Kale." In *Die Spätantiken Befestigungen von Sadovec (Bulgarien). Ergebnisse der deutsch-bulgarisch-österreichischen Ausgrabungen 1934–1937*, edited by S. Uenze, K. Dietz, J. Jurukova, G. Kuzmanov, M. Mackensen, H. Todorova, P. Valev, V. P. Vasilev, V. Velkov, and J. Werner, 239–254. Munich: C. H. Beck'sche Verlagsbuchhandlung, 1992.

Madgearu, A. "The placement of the fortress Turris." *BS* 33, no. 2 (1992): 203–208.

"Despre cataramele de tip Pápa și unele probleme ale secolului al VII-lea." *SCIVA* 44, no. 2 (1993): 171–183.

"Romanizare și creștinare la nordul Dunării în secolele IV–VII" [Romanization and Christianization north of the Danube in the 4th–7th c.]. *Anuarul Institutului de Istorie "A. D. Xenopol"* 31 (1994): 479–502.

"The province of Scythia and the Avaro-Slavic invasions (576–626). *BS* 37, no. 1 (1996): 35–61.

"About Maurikios, Strategikon, XI.4.31." *RESEE* 35, nos. 1–2 (1997): 119–121.

Continuitate și discontinuitate culturală la Dunărea de Jos în secolele VII–VIII [Cultural continuity and discontinuity on the 7th–8th c. Lower Danube]. Bucharest: Editura Universității București, 1997.

"The Sucidava type of buckles and the relations between the Late Roman Empire and the barbarians in the 6th century." *AM* 21 (1998): 217–222.

"Dunărea în epoca bizantină (secolele X–XII): o frontieră permeabilă" [The Byzantine Danube (10th–12th c.): a permeable frontier]. *Revista Istorică* 10, nos. 1–2 (1999): 41–55.

Rolul creștinismului în formarea poporului român [The role of Christianity in the genesis of the Romanian people]. Bucharest: All, 2001.

"A buckle of Pápa type found in the Early Byzantine fortress Halmyris (Murighiol, Tulcea County)." *Peuce* 15 (2003): 169–176.

"The 6th century Lower Danubian bridgeheads: location and mission." *EN* 13 (2003): 295–314.

"The spreading of the Christianity in the rural areas of post-Roman Dacia (4th–7th centuries)." *Archaeus* 8 (2004): 41–59.

"Semnificația purtării crucilor pectorale descoperite la nord de Dunăre în secolele VI–VII" [The significance of pectoral crosses found north of the Danube (6th–7th c.)]. *AM* 30 (2007): 129–136.

"The significance of the Early Christian artefacts in post-Roman Dacia." In *Christianisierung Europas. Entstehung, Entwicklung und Konsolidierung im archäologischen Befund. Internationale Tagung im Dezember 2010 in Bergisch-Gladbach*, edited by O. Heinrich-Tamáska, N. Krohn, and S. Ristow, 299–317. Regensburg: Schnell & Steiner, 2012.

"Military operations commanded by Constantine the Great north of the Danube." In *Cruce și misiune. Sfinții Împărați Constantin și Elena - promotori ai libertății religioase și apărători ai Bisericii*, edited by E. Popescu and V. Ioniță. Vol. II, 581–594. Bucharest: Basilica, 2013.

"Militari 'sciți' și 'daci' în Egipt, Italia și Palestina în secolele VI–VII" ["Scythian" and "Dacian" soldiers in Egypt, Italy, and Palestine (6th–7th c.)]. *SCIVA* 65, nos. 1–2 (2014): 49–58.

Maguire, H. "Magic and money in the Early Middle Ages." *Speculum* 72, no. 4 (1997): 1037–1054.

Măgureanu, A. "Fibulele turnate romano-bizantine" [The Roman-Byzantine cast fibulae]. *MCA* 4 (2008): 99–155.

"About power in the sixth–seventh century in the Extra-Carpathian area." In *Potestas et Communitas. Interdiciplinary Studies of the Constitution and*

Demonstration of Power Relations in the Middle Ages East of the Elbe, edited by A. Paroń, S. Rossignol, B. Szmoniewski, and G. Vercamer, 73–86. Warsaw: Instytut Archeologii i Etnologii Polskiej Akademii Nauk/ Deutsches Historisches Institut Warschau, 2010.

Măgureanu, A. and B. Ciupercă. "The 6th–8th centuries metallurgical activity from Budureasca Valley. The molds." *AMN* 41–42, no. 1 (2004–2005): 291–318.

Măgureanu, A. and B. S. Szmoniewski. "Domestic dwellings in Moldavia and Wallachia in the initial phase of the Early Middle Ages." *AAA* 38 (2003): 111–136.

Makarova, T. I. "Bospor-Korchev po arkheologicheskim dannym" [Bospor-Korchev: the archaeological evidence]. In *Vizantiiskaia Tavrika. Sbornik nauchnykh trudov (v XVIII kongressu vizantinistov)*, edited by P. P. Tolochko, 121–141. Kiev: Naukova Dumka, 1991.

Makkai, L. "The emergence of the Estates (1172–1526)." In *History of Transylvania*, edited by B. Köpeczi, 178–243. Budapest: Akadémiai Kiadó, 1994.

Malenko, V. "Ranosrednovekovnata materijalna kultura vo Okhrid i Okhridsko" [The Early Medieval material culture at Ohrid]. In *Okhrid i Okhridsko niz istorijata*, edited by M. Apostolski, 269–315. Skopje: Sobranie na opshtina Okhrid, 1985.

Malinowski, B. *Argonauts of the Western Pacific: An Account of Native Enterprise and Adventure in the Archipelagoes of Melanesian New Guinea*. London: Routledge, 1922.

Mann, C. J. "The frontiers of the Principate." In *Aufstieg und Niedergang der römischen Welt. II. Principat. 1. Politische Geschichte (Allgemeines)*, edited by H. Temporini, 508–533. Berlin: Walter de Gruyter & Co., 1974.

Mănucu-Adameşteanu, G. and E. Popuşoi. "Monede bizantine descoperite la est de Carpaţi" [Byzantine coins found east of the Carpathians]. *AM* 23–24 (2000–2001): 349–360.

Mărculeţ, V. "Un problème de géopolitique de la politique danubienne du Constantin le Grand (324–337): la reconquête et la domination de la Dacie méridionale." *Pontica* 41 (2008): 299–312.

de Maret, P. "L'évolution monétaire du Shaba Central entre le 7e et le 18e siècle." *African Economic History* 10 (1981): 117–149.

Martin-Hisard, B. "La domination Byzantine sur le littoral oriental du Pont Euxin (milieu du VIIe–VIIIe siècles)." *Byzantinobulgaria* 7 (1981): 141–156.

Martínez, O. *Border People. Life and Society in the US–Mexico Borderlands*. Tucson, AZ: University of Arizona Press, 1994.

Matei, C. "Cercetări arheologice în zona instalaţiei portuare antice de la Capidava (II)" [Archaeological research in the ancient port at Capidava]. *Cultură şi Civilizaţie la Dunărea de Jos* 5–7 (1988–1989): 121–141.

Mathisen, R. W. "*Peregrini, barbari*, and *cives romani*: concepts of citizenship and the legal identity of barbarians in the Later Roman Empire." *The American Historical Review* 111, no. 4 (2006): 1011–1040.

"*Provinciales, gentiles*, and marriages between Romans and Barbarians in the Late Roman Empire." *JRS* 99 (2009): 140–55.

Mathisen, R. W. and D. Shanzer, eds. *Romans, Barbarians, and the Transformation of the Roman World. Cultural Interaction and the Creation of Identity in Late Antiquity*. Farnham: Ashgate, 2011.

Matthies Green, U. and K. E. Costion. "Modeling ranges of cross-cultural interaction in ancient borderlands." In *Frontiers of Colonialism*, edited by C. D. Beaule, 480–539. Gainesville, FL: University Press of Florida, 2017.

Mattingly, D. J. and J. Salmon, eds. *Economies Beyond Agriculture in the Classical World*. London/New York, NY: Routledge, 2001.

Mayeur, N. "Voyage dans le sud et dans l'intérieur des terres et plus particulièrement au pays d'Hancove." *Bulletin de l'Académie Malgache* 12 (1913): 139–176.

Merisalo, O., ed. *Frontiers in the Middle Ages: Proceedings of the Third European Congress of Medieval Studies (Jyväskylä, 10–14 June 2003)*. Louvain-la- Neuve: Fédération internationale des instituts d'études médiévales, 2006.

Metcalf, D. M. *The Origins of the Anastasian Currency Reform*. Chicago, IL: Argonaut, 1969.

"The joint reign gold of Justin I and Justinian I." In *Studies in Early Byzantine Gold Coinage*, edited by W. Hahn and W. E. Metcalf, 19–27. New York, NY: American Numismatic Society, 1988.

"Viking-age numismatics 1: Late Roman and Byzantine gold in the northern lands." *NC* 155 (1995): 413–441.

Miclea, I. and R. Florescu. *Daco-romanii*. Vol. II. Bucharest: Meridiane, 1980.

Mihăilescu-Bîrliba, V. *La monnaie romaine chez les Daces orientaux*. Bucharest: Editura Academiei RSR, 1980.

Mihăilescu-Bîrliba, V. and V. Butnariu. "Descoperiri monetare din Moldova. I" [Coin finds in Moldavia (part I)]. *AM* 12 (1988): 311–320.

Mihăilescu-Bîrliba, V. and C. Mihai. "Descoperiri monetare la Târgu Frumos, jud. Iași" [Coin finds at Târgu Frumos, Iași County]. *AM* 19 (1996): 253–259.

Mihaylov, S. "Seventh-to-eighth century Byzantine bronze coins from northeastern Bulgaria." *Cultură și Civilizație la Dunărea de Jos* 26 (2008): 77–85.

"Vidovete nominali v monetnoto obrashtenie na bizantiiskite provintsii Scitiia i Vtora Miziia (498–681 g.)" [Types of coin denominations in circulation in the Byzantine provinces of Scythia and Moesia II (498–681)]. In *Numismatic, Sphragistic and Epigraphic Contributions to the History of the Black Sea Coast*, edited by I. Lazarenko. Vol. I, 278–300. Varna: Zograf, 2008.

"Etapi v parichata tsirkulatsiia prez rannovizantiiskata epocha (498–681) v provintsiia Vtora Miziia" [Stages in coin circulation in the province of Moesia II in the Early Byzantine age (498–681)]. *Numizmatika, sfragistika i epigrafika* 6 (2010): 109–122.

Mikhailov, S. "Rannosrednovekovni fibuli v Bulgariia" [Early Medieval fibulae from Bulgaria]. *IAI* 24 (1961): 37–60.

"Die Bügelfibeln in Bulgarien und ihre historische Interpretation." In *Archäologie als Geschichtswissenschaft. Studien und Untersuchungen*, edited by J. Herrmann, 317–327. Berlin: Akademie Verlag, 1977.

Milavec, T. "Late antique settlements in Slovenia after the year 600." In *Pontic-Danubian Realm*, 71–88.

Militký, J. "Finds of the Early Byzantine coins of the 6th and 7th century in the territory of the Czech Republic." In *Byzantine Coins*, 357–394.

"Finds of Greek, Roman and Early Byzantine coins in the territory of the Czech Republic. I. Bohemia." Wetteren: Moneta, 2010.

Miller, D. H. "Frontier societies and the transition between Late Antiquity and the Early Middle Ages." In *Shifting Frontiers*, 158–174.

Mirnik, I. and A. Šemrov. "Byzantine coins in the Zagreb Archaeological Museum numismatic collection. Anastasius I (AD 497–518)–Anastasius II (AD 713–715)." *Vjesnik Arheološkog Muzeja u Zagrebu* 30–31 (1997–1998): 129–258.

Mitrea, B. "Découvertes récentes de monnaies anciennes sur le territoire de la République Populaire Roumaine." *Dacia* 4 (1960): 587–591.

"Descoperiri recente și mai vechi de monede antice și bizantine în Republica Populară Română" [Old and recent finds of ancient and Byzantine coins in Romania]. *SCIV* 13, no. 1 (1962): 215–224.

"Découvertes récentes et plus anciennes de monnaies antiques et byzantines sur le territoire de la République Populaire Roumaine." *Dacia* 7 (1963): 589–599.

"Descoperiri recente și mai vechi de monede antice și bizantine în Republica Populară Română." *SCIV* 14, no. 2 (1963): 466–474.

"Découvertes récentes et plus anciennes de monnaies antiques et byzantines sur le territoire de la République Populaire Roumaine." *Dacia* 10 (1966): 403–414.

"Descoperiri recente și mai vechi de monede antice și bizantine în Republica Socialistă România." *SCIV* 18, no. 1 (1967): 188–202.

"Descoperiri recente și mai vechi de monede antice și bizantine în Republica Socialistă România XV." *SCIV* 23, no. 1 (1972): 133–147.

"Date noi cu privire la secolul VII. Tezaurul de hexagrame bizantine de la Priseaca (jud. Olt)" [New evidence from the seventh century: the hoard of Byzantine hexagrams from Priseaca (Olt County)]. *SCN* 6 (1975): 113–125.

"Découvertes monétaires en Roumanie, 1976 (XX)." *Dacia* 21 (1977): 375–381.

"Découvertes monétaires en Roumanie: 1981, 1982 et 1983 (XXV, XXVI et XXVII)." *Dacia* 28 (1984): 183–190.

Mitrea, I. "Cîteva fibule romano-bizantine descoperite în Moldova" [A few Roman-Byzantine fibulae found in Moldavia]. *SCIV* 24, no. 4 (1973): 663–664.

Comunități sătești la est de Carpați în epoca migrațiilor. Așezarea de la Davideni din secolele V–VII [Village communities east of the Carpathian Mountains: the settlement from Davideni in the 5th–7th c.]. Piatra Neamț: Muzeul de Istorie, 2001.

"Considerații privind etnicitatea si spiritualitatea la est de Carpați în secolul al VI-lea pe baza surselor arheologice" [Some remarks about sixth-century ethnicity and religion in the lands east of the Carpathian Mountains in light of the archaeological evidence]. In *Adevărul omenește posibil pentru rânduirea binelui*, edited by L. Cornea, M. D. Drecin, and B. B. Ștefănescu, 299–306. Oradea: Editura Muzeului Țării Crișurilor, 2001.

"Romanitate și creștinism în secolele V-VI în lumea satelor din spațiul carpato-nistrean" [Romanization and Christianity in village communities in the lands between the Carpathian Mountains and the Dniester]. *Zargidava* 1 (2002): 17–44.

"Observații privind sfârșitul culturii Sântana de Mureș și începuturile culturii Costișa-Botoșana-Hansca, în stadiul actual al cercetărilor arheologice" [Some observations regarding the end of the Sântana de Mureș culture and the beginning of the Costișa-Botoșana-Hansca culture in light of the archaeological evidence]. *Carpica* 34 (2005): 131–42.

Mitrea, I. and A. Artimon. "Descoperiri prefeudale la Curtea Domnească Bacău" [Early Medieval finds at Curtea Domnească Bacău]. *Carpica* 4 (1971): 225–252.

Mitrea, I. and C. Eminovici. "Ștefan cel Mare, jud. Bacău." In *Cronica Cercetărilor Arheologice în România 1983–1992. A XXXI-a sesiune națională de rapoarte arheologice*, 105–106. Bucharest: CIMEC, 1997.

Mitrea, I., C. Eminovici, and V. Momanu. "Așezarea din secolele V–VII de la Ștefan cel Mare, jud. Bacău" [The 5th–6th century settlement at Ștefan cel Mare, Bacău County]. *Carpica* 18–19 (1986-1987): 215–250.

Mitrofanov, A. G. "Bancerovskoe gorodishche" [Ancient Bancerovoe]. In *Belorusskie drevnosti. Doklady k konferencii po arkheologii Belorussii (ianvar'-fevral' 1968)*, edited by V. D. Bud'ko, I. G. Zverugo, V. F. Isaenko, and K. P. Shuta, 243–261. Minsk: Institut istorii Akademii Nauk BSSR, 1967.

Mitu, S. *National Identity of Romanians in Transylvania*. Budapest: Central European University Press, 2001.

Modrijan, Z. "Keramika." In *Poznoantična utrjena naselbina Tonovcov grad pri Kobaridu. Najdbe*, edited by Z. Modrijan and T. Milavec, 121–219; 514–554. Ljubljana: Institut za arheologijo ZRC SAZU, 2011.

Moga, V. "Observații asupra unor piese paleocreștine inedite" [Notes on a few unpublished early Christian artifacts]. *Apulum* 37, no. 1 (2000): 429–435.

Moisil, C. "Monete și tezaure monetare găsite în România și în Ținuturile românești învecinate (vechiul teritoriu geto-dac)" [Coins and coin hoards found in Romania and the neighboring regions (ancient Geto-Dacian realm)]. *BSNR* 20, July–December (1913): 62–64.

"Creșterea colecțiilor cabinetului numismatic" [New additions to the collection of the numismatic department]. *Creșterea Colecțiilor* 49–53 (1944): 1–125.

Moisil, D. "The Danube *limes* and the *barbaricum* (294–498 AD): a study in coin circulation." *Histoire et Mesure* 17, nos. 3–4 (2002): 79–120.

Molet, L. "Les monnaies à Madagascar." *RESS* 21 (1970): 203–234.

Montinaro, F. "Byzantium and the Slavs in the reign of Justinian: comparing the two recensions of Procopius' Buildings." In *Pontic-Danubian Realm*, 89–114.

Morintz, S. and D. V. Rosetti. "Din cele mai vechi timpuri și pînă la formarea Bucureștilor" [Bucharest since ancient times]. In *Bucureștii de odinioară în lumina săpăturilor arheologice*, ed. I. Ionașcu, 11–47. Bucharest: Editura Științifică, 1959.

Morley, N. *Trade in Classical Antiquity*. Cambridge: Cambridge University Press, 2007.

Morrisson, C. "Byzantine money: its production and circulation." In *Economic History of Byzantium*, edited by A. Laiou, 909–966. Washington, DC: Dumbarton Oaks, 2002.

"Monnaies et amulettes byzantines à motifs chrétiens: croyance ou magie?" In *Les savoirs magiques et leur transmission de l'Antiquité à la Renaissance*, edited by V. Dasen and J.-M. Spieser, 409–30. Florence: Sismel, 2014.

"Byzantine coins in Early Medieval Britain: a Byzantinist's assessment." In *Early Medieval Monetary History: Studies in Memory of Mark Blackburn*, edited by M. Allen, R. Naismith, and E. Screen, 207–242. New York, NY: Routledge, 2016.

Mousheghian, Kh. *Denezhnoe obrashchenie Dvina po numizmaticheskim dannym* [Monetary circulation at Dvin in light of the numismatic evidence]. Yerevan: Izdatel'stvo Akademii Nauk Armianskoi SSR, 1962.

Denezhnoe obrashchenie v Armenii (V v. do n.e.–XIV v.n.e.) [Monetary circulation in Armenia (5th c. BC–14th c. AD)]. Yerevan: Izdatel'stvo Akademii Nauk Armianskoi SSR, 1983.

The Numismatics of Armenian History. Yerevan: Anahit, 1997.

Mousheghian, Kh., A. Mousheghian, and C. Bresc. *History and Coin Finds in Armenia: Coins from Ani, Capital of Armenia, 4th c. BC–19th c. AD*. Wetteren: Moneta, 2000.

Mousheghian, Kh., A. Mousheghian, C. Bresc, G. Depeyrot, and F. Gurnet. *History and Coin Finds in Armenia: Coins from Duin, Capital of Armenia, 6–7th c.: Inventory of Byzantine and Sasanian Coins in Armenia, 6–7th c*. Wetteren: Moneta, 2000.

Müller, R. "Sági Károly temetőfeltárása a Keszthely-fenékpusztai erőd déli fala előtt" [Károlyi Sági's excavation of the cemetery by the southern wall at Keszthely-Fenékpuszta]. *Zalai Múzeum* 9 (1999): 153–179.

Die Gräberfelder vor der Südmauer der Befestigung von Keszthely-Fenékpuszta. Budapest/Leipzig: Magyar Tudományos Akadémia Régészeti Intézet/Geisteswissenschaftliches Zentrum Geschichte und Kultur, 2010.

Muntean, V. V. "Creștinism primar la Dunărea inferioară. Noi revizuiri" [Early Christianity on the Lower Danube: new remarks]. In *Slujitor al bisericii și al neamului. Părintele Prof. Univ. Dr. Mircea Păcurariu, membru corespondent al Academiei Române, la împlinirea vârstei de 70 de ani*, 203–210. Cluj-Napoca: Editura Renașterea, 2002.

Murygin, A. M. "Poselenie Usugorsk III na srednei Mezeni" [Settlement Usugorsk III on the middle Mezen']. *Materialy po arkheologii Evropeiskogo Severo-Vostoka* 8 (1980): 71–91.

Mușețeanu, C. "Ceramica romană de la Durostorum" [The Roman pottery from Durostorum]. Ph.D. dissertation, University of Bucharest, 1992.

Mussurov, A. I., and L. V. Nosova. "Nakhodki vizantiiskikh monet V–VI vv. na Nizhnem Dnestre" [Finds of Byzantine coins (6th–7th c.) on the Lower Dniester]. *Stratum plus* (2001–2002), no. 6: 304–306.

Musteață, S. "Unele concretizări privind vasul de metal din tezaurul monetar de la Horgești, jud. Bacău, Romania" [Some observations regarding the copper pitcher from the coin hoard found at Horgești, Bacău County, Romania]. In *Arheologia între știință, politică și economia de piață*, edited by S. Musteață, A. Popa, and J.-P. Abraham, 99–127. Chișinău: Pontos, 2010.

Moneda bizantină în regiunile carpato-nistrene în secolele VI–X [Byzantine coins in the lands between the Carpathian Mountains and the Dniester (6th–10th c.)]. Chișinău: Arc, 2014.

Nagy, M. *Awarenzeitliche Gräberfelder im Stadtgebiet von Budapest.* Budapest: Magyar Nemzeti Múzeum/MTA Régészeti Intézete, 1998.

"A hódmezővásárhely-kishomoki gepida temető (elemzés)" [The Gepid cemetery at Hódmezővásárhely-Kishomok: an analysis]. *MFMÉ* 10 (2004): 129–139.

Nagy, S. "Nekropola kod Aradca iz ranog sredn'eg veka" [The Early Medieval cemetery at Aradac]. *Rad Vojvodanskich Muzeja* 8 (1959): 45–102.

Naum, M. "Re-emerging frontiers: postcolonial theory and historical archaeology of the borderlands." *Journal of Archaeological Method and Theory* 17, no. 2 (2011): 101–131.

Naumenko, A. and S. I. Bezuglov. "Új bizánci és iráni importleletek a Don-vidék sztyeppéiről" [New Byzantine and Iranian imports from the Don steppe]. *MFMÉ* 2 (1996): 247–257.

Nestor, I. "L'établissement des Slaves en Roumanie à la lumière de quelques découvertes archéologiques récentes." *Dacia* 5 (1961): 429–448.

Nestor, I. and C. S. Nicolaescu-Plopșor. "Der völkerwanderungszeitliche Schatz Negrescu." *Germania* 22, no. 1 (1938): 33–41.

Nicasie, M. J. *Twilight of Empire. The Roman Army from the Reign of Diocletian until the Battle of Adrianople.* Amsterdam: J. C. Gieben, 1998.

Nicolas, G. "Circulations des biens et échanges monétaires en pays haoussa (Niger)." *RESS* 21 (1970): 111–120.

Niculescu, A. "Le daco-roumain – *Romania antiqua, Romania nova* et la continuité mobile. Une synthèse." In *Actes du XVIIIe Congrès international de linguistique et philologie romanes: Université de Trèves (Trier) 1986*, edited by D. Kremer, 86–104. Tübingen: Niemeyer, 1992.

Niculescu, G. A. "Archaeology, nationalism, and the 'History of the Romanians'." *Dacia* 48–49 (2004–2005): 99–124.

Nikolov, V. "Die bulgarische Archäologie im letzten Jahrzehnt des 20. Jahrhunderts." In *Archäologien Europas. Geschichte, Methoden und Theorien*, edited by P. F. Biehl, A. Gramsch, and A. Marciniak, 303–307. Münster: Waxmann, 2002.

Nouzille, J., *La Transylvanie: terre de contacts et de conflits*. Strasbourg: Revue d'Europe centrale, 1994.

Novaković, P. "The present makes the past: the use of archaeology and changing national identities in Former Yugoslavia." In *Auf der Suche nach Identitäten: Volk, Stamm, Kultur, Ethnos. Internationale Tagung der Universität Leipzig vom 8.-9. Dezember 2000*, edited by S. Rieckhoff and U. Sommer, 181–192. BAR International Series 1705. Oxford: Archaeopress, 2007.

Nudel'man, A. A. *Topografiia kladov i nakhodok edinichnykh monet* [Gazetteer of hoards and single coin finds]. Arkheologicheskaia karta Moldavskoi SSR 8. Kishinew: Shtiinca, 1976.

Oanță-Marghitu, R. "Argamum între Imperiul Roman Târziu și "barbari." Obiectele mărunte ca ipostaze ale comunicării" [Argamum between the Late Roman Empire and the 'barbarians': small items as evidence of contact]. In *Orgamé/Argamum. Supplementa I. À la recherche d'une colonie. Actes du Colloque International à l'occasion du 40ème anniversaire des fouilles à Orgamé/Argamum, Bucarest-Tulcea-Jurilovca, 3–5 octobre 2005*, edited by M. Mănucu-Adameșteanu, 345–373. Bucharest: AGIR, 2006.

Oberländer-Târnoveanu, E. "Monnaies byzantines des VIIe–Xe siècles découvertes à Silistra dans la collection de l'Académicien Péricle Papahagi conservées au Cabinet des Medailles du Musée National d'Histoire de Roumanie." *CN* 7 (1996): 97–127.

"Societate, economie și politică – populațiile de pe teritoriul Moldovei și lumea sud-est europeană în secolele IV–XIV în lumina descoperirilor monetare" [Society, economy, and politics: communities in Moldavia and the southeastern European world in light of the numismatic evidence (4th–14th c.)]. *Suceava* 26–28 (1999–2001): 311–355.

"From the Late Antiquity to the Early Middle Ages – the Byzantine coins in the territories of the Iron Gates of the Danube from the second half of the 6th century to the first half of the 8th century." *EBPB* 4 (2001): 29–69.

"La monnaie byzantine des VIe–VIIIe siècles au-delà de la frontière du Bas-Danube. Entre politique, économie et diffusion culturelle." *Histoire et Mesure* 17, no. 3 (2002): 155–196.

"La răscruce de vremuri: tranziția de la antichitate la evul mediu timpuriu în zona Porților de Fier ale Dunării – un punct de vedere numismatic" [Facing an age of change: the transition from Late Antiquity to the Early Middle Ages in the Danube's Iron Gates region in light of the numismatic evidence]. *CN* 8 (2002): 121–172.

"Barbaricum apropiat – populațiile din Muntenia și Imperiul Bizantin (secolele VI–X) – mărturia numismaticii" [Neighboring Barbaricum: the population of

Wallachia and the Byzantine Empire in light of numismatic sources (6th-10th c.)]. *Ialomița* 4 (2004): 323–368.

"Tranziția de la antichitate la evul mediu timpuriu la marginea imperiului (II). De la prima dispariție a circulației monetare la renașterea ei în zona Porților de Fier ale Dunării (circa 375–565)" [The transition from antiquity to the Early Middle Ages at the edge of empire (part II): from the breakdown of coin circulation to its revival in the Danube's Iron Gates region (ca. 375–565)]. *Muzeul Național* 16 (2004): 39–83.

Oberländer-Târnoveanu, E. and E.-M. Constantinescu. "Monede romane târzii și bizantine din colecția Muzeului Județean Buzău" [Late Roman and Byzantine coins from the collection of the Buzău County Museum]. *Mousaios* 4 (1994): 311–341.

Oberländer-Târnoveanu, E. and G. Mănucu-Adameșteanu. "O monedă de la începutul secolului al VIII-lea descoperită în București, pe amplasamentul 'Teatrul Național'" [A coin from the beginning of the eighth century found on the site of the old National Theatre in Bucharest]. In *Teatrul Național din București (1846–1947): cercetări arheologice*, edited by G. Mănucu-Adameșteanu, 357–375. Bucharest: Muzeul Municipiului București, 2005.

Oberländer-Târnoveanu, E. and E. Popușoi. "Monede bizantine din colecția muzeului 'Vasile Pârvan' din Bîrlad" [Byzantine coins in the "Vasile Pârvan" Museum, Bîrlad]. *Carpica* 13, no. 2 (1992): 223–245.

Obolensky, D. "Byzantine frontier zones and cultural exchanges." In *Actes du XIVe congrès international des études byzantines: Bucarest, 6–12 septembre 1971*, edited by M. Berza and E. Stănescu. Vol. I, 303–313. Bucharest: Editura Academiei RSR, 1974.

Oddy, A. "La monnaie d'or dans la bijouterie à travers les ages." *Aurum* 15 (1983): 10–16.

Oltean, I. *Dacia: Landscape, Colonisation, and Romanisation*. London: Routledge, 2007.

Olteanu, Ș. *Societatea carpato-danubiano-pontică în secolele IV–XI. Structuri demo-economice și social-politice* [Local communities in the lands between the Carpathian Mountains, the Danube, and the Black Sea: demographic, economic, social, and political structures]. Bucharest: Editura Didactică și Pedagogică, 1997.

Olteanu, Ș., M. Rusu, and R. Popa. "Modul de viață a comunităților umane: așezări, locuințe, necropole, credințe" [Aspects of life: settlements, residences, cemeteries, and beliefs]. In *Istoria românilor 3*, 70–93.

Opaiț, A. "O săpătură de salvare în orașul antic Ibida" [Rescue excavations at ancient Ibida]. *SCIVA* 41, no. 4 (1990): 19–54.

Opreanu, C. "Creștinismul și neamurile germanice în secolele IV–V în Transilvania" [Christianity and the Germanic peoples in fourth-to-fifth-century Transylvania)]. *EN* 5 (1995): 227–254.

Dacia romană și Barbaricum [Roman Dacia and Barbaricum]. Timișoara: Mirton, 1998.

"The north-Danube regions from the Roman province of Dacia to the emergence of the Romanian language (2nd–8th centuries)." In *History of Romania: Compendium*, edited by I. A. Pop, I. Bolovan, and S. Andrea, 59–132. Cluj-Napoca: Romanian Cultural Institute, 2006.

"The barbarians and Roman Dacia. War, trade and cultural interaction." In *The Roman Empire and Beyond*, edited by E. C. De Sena and H. Dobrzanska, 125–136. BAR International Series 2236. Oxford: Archaeopress, 2011.

Opriș, I. C. *Ceramica romană târzie și paleobizantină de la Capidava în contextul descoperirilor de la Dunărea de Jos (sec. IV–VI p. Chr.)* [The Late Roman and Early Byzantine pottery at Capidava in Lower Danubian context (4th–6th c.)]. Bucharest: Editura Enciclopedică, 2003.

Ostanina, T. I., O. M. Kanunnikova, V. P. Stepanov, and A. B. Nikitin. *Kuzebaevskii klad iuvelira VII v. kak istoricheskii istochnik* [An artisan's treasure at Kuzebaevo as a historical source]. Izhevsk: Izdatel'stvo "Udmurtiia," 2011.

Oța, L. "Hunii în Dobrogea" [The Huns in Dobrudja]. *Istros* 10 (2000): 363–387.

Özyurt Özcan, H. "Erzurum Arkeoloji Müzesi'ndeki bizans sikkeleri." *Araştırma Sonuçları Toplantısı* 24, no. 1 (2007): 1–16.

Păcurariu, M. *Geschichte der Rumänischen Orthodoxen Kirche*. Erlangen: Lehrstuhl für Geschichte und Theologie des Christlichen Ostens, 1994.

Padfield, T. "Analysis of Byzantine copper coins by X-ray methods (with a numismatic commentary by P. Grierson)." In *Methods of Chemical and Metallurgical Investigation of Ancient Coinage*, edited by T. Hall and D. M. Metcalf, 219–236. London: Royal Numismatic Society, 1972.

Pallas, D. "Données nouvelles sur quelques boucles et fibules considérées comme avares et slaves et sur Corinthe entre le VIe et le IXe s." *Byzantino-bulgarica* 7 (1981): 295–318.

Pamlényi, E. ed. *A History of Hungary*. London: n.p., 1975.

Papasima, T. "Monede bizantine inedite din colecția Muzeului Județean Călărași" [Unpublished Byzantine coins from the Călărași County Museum]. *Pontica* 28–29 (1995–1996): 279–285.

Papuc, G. "Opaițe de import la Tomis" [Import lamps at Tomis]. *Pontica* 9 (1976): 201–205.

"O fibulă digitată de la Tropaeum Traiani și cîteva considerații asupra fibulelor de acest tip" [A bow fibula from Tropaeum Traiani and a few observations regarding this type of fibulae]. *Pontica* 20 (1987): 207–215.

Părău, V. "La diffusione delle lucerne nordafricane dei sec. IV–VI D. C. nelle ex-provincie central e sud danubiane. La lucerna del tipo Atlante VIII–X con chrismon." In *Lychnological Acts 2*, 197–206.

Parker, B. J. "Understanding of borderland processes." *AAnt* 71, no. 1 (2006): 77–100.

Parker, P. *The Empire Stops Here. A Journey along the Frontiers of the Roman World*. London: Jonathan Cape, 2009.

Parker, S. T. "The defense of Palestine and Transjordan from Diocletian to Heraclius." In *The Archaeology of Jordan and Beyond: Essays in Honor of James A. Sauer*, edited by L. E. Stager, J. A. Greene, and M. D. Coogan, 367–388. Winona Lake, IN: Eisenbrauns, 2000.

Parlasca, K. *Repertorio d'arte dell'Egitto Greco-Romano*. Edited by A. Adriani. Series B/Vols. I–II. Palermo: Fondazione "Ignazio Mormino" del Banco di Sicilia, 1969–1977.

Parnell, D. A. "Barbarians and brothers-in-arms: Byzantines on barbarian soldiers in the sixth century." *BZ* 108, no. 2 (2015): 809–826.

Parry, J. and M. Bloch. "Introduction: money and the morality of exchange." In *Money and Morality*, 1–32.

Pârvan, V. "Cetatea Ulmetum. III" [The Ulmetum fortress (part III)]. *Academia Română Memoriile Secției Istorice* 37 (1914–1915): 265–304.

Patoura, S. "Une nouvelle considération sur la politique de Justinien envers les peuples du Danube." *Byzantinoslavica* 58 (1997): 78–86.

"Ho Dounabes stis istoriographikes peges kata ten periodo tes metanasteuseos ton laon; mythoi kai pragmaikoteta." *Historikogeōgraphika* 9 (2002): 399–412.

"Emporio kai synallages ste dounabike methorio: he Autokratoria kai hoi 'barbaroi'." In *He methorios tou Dounabe kai o kosmos tes sten epoche tes metanasteuses ton laon (4os-7os ai.)*, edited by S. Patoura-Spanou, 195–221. Athens: National Hellenic Research Foundation/ Institute for Byzantine Research, 2008.

Pauker, M. "Monete antice și grecești, romane și bizantine găsite la Piua Pietrei" [Ancient Greek, Roman, and Byzantine coins found at Piua Pietrei]. *Cronica numismatică și arheologică* 135–136, July–December (1945): 51–54.

Paunov, E. "Konstantinoviiat most na Dunava pri Escus – Sukidava izobrazen na bronzov medal'on" [Constantine's Danube bridge at Oescus-Sucidava depicted on a bronze medallion]. *Reverse* 1, no. 1 (2016): 28–33.

Pavel, V. "Monede de aur romane imperiale și bizantine în colecția Muzeului din Alba Iulia" [Roman and Byzantine gold coins in the Alba Iulia Museum]. *Apulum* 15 (1977): 663–670.

Peacock, D. P. S. and D. F. Williams. *Amphorae and the Roman Economy. An Introductory Guide*. New York, NY: Longman, 1986.

Perassi, C. "Monete romane forate: qualche riflessione su 'un grand theme européen' (J.-P. Callu)." *Aevum* 85, no. 2 (2011): 257–315.

Petac, V. "Descoperiri inedite de monede antice și bizantine" [Unpublished finds of ancient and Byzantine coins]. *BSNR* 86–87 (1992–1993): 319–322.

Petković, S. "Late Roman Romuliana and Mediaeval Gamzigrad from the end of 4th to 11th centuries AD." In *Keszthely-Fenékpuszta im Kontext spätantiker Kontinuitätsforschung zwischen Noricum und Moesia*, edited by O. Heinrich-Tamáska, 267–284. Leipzig: Marie Leidorf, 2011.

Petre, A. "Predvaritel'nye svedeniia v sviazi s khronologiei mogil'nika v Piatra Frecăței" [Preliminary information regarding the chronology of the cemetery at Piatra Frecăței]. *Dacia* 6 (1962): 215–234.

"Contribuția atelierelor romano-bizantine la geneza unor tipuri de fibule 'digitate' din veacurile VI–VII e.n." [The contribution of Roman-Byzantine workshops to the development of certain sixth–seventh century 'bow' fibulae]. *SCIV* 17, no. 2 (1966): 255–275.

"Contribuția culturii romano-bizantine din secolele VI–VII la geneza culturii feudale timpurii din spațiul balcano-ponto-danubian" [The contribution of Roman-Byzantine culture to the development of Early Medieval culture in the lands between the Balkan Mountains, the Danube, and the Black Sea (6th–7th c.)]. In *2050 de ani de la făurirea de către Burebista a primului stat independent și centralizat al geto-dacilor*, 193–214. Bucharest: Universitatea București, 1980.

La romanité en Scythie Mineure (IIe–VIIe siècles de notre ère). Recherches archéologiques. Bucharest: Institut des Études Sud-Est-Européennes, 1987.

Petre-Govora, G. I. "Continuitatea daco-romană în nordul Olteniei în sec. IV–VII e.n. în lumina noilor descoperiri arheologice și numismatice" [Daco-Roman continuity in northern Oltenia (4th–7th c.) in light of recent archaeological and numismatic evidence]. *Drobeta* 2 (1976): 112–116.

Petrescu, F. *Repertoriul monumentelor arheologice de tip Sântana de Mureș-Cerneahov de pe teritoriul României* [Gazetteer of Sântana de Mureș-Chernyakhov archeological finds in Romania]. Bucharest: Ars Docendi, 2002.

Petridis, P. *La céramique protobyzantine de Delphes: une production et son contexte*. Athens: École française d'Athènes, 2010.

Petsas, P. "Archaiotetes kai mnemeia Kentrikes Makedonias." *ArchDelt* 24 (1969): 302–311.

Pichler, F. *Repertorium der steirischen Münzkunde. II. Die Münzen der römischen und byzantinischen Kaiser in der Steiermark*. Graz: Leuschner & Lubensky, 1867.

Piganiol, A. *L'empire chrétien (325–395)*. Paris: Presses universitaires de France, 1947.

Pillon, M. "L'exode des Sermésiens et les grandes migrations des Romains de Pannonie dans les Balkans durant le Haut Moyen Âge." *EB* 38 (2002), no. 3: 103–141.

"Armée et defense de l'Illyricum byzantin de Justinien à Héraclius (527–641). De la reorganization justinienne à l'émergence des 'armées de cité'." *Erytheia* 26 (2005): 7–85.

Pioro, I. S. *Krymskaia Gotiia (Ocherki etnicheskoi istorii naseleniia Kryma v pozdnerimskii period i rannee srednevekov'e)* [Crimean Gothia: essays on the ethnic history of the Crimean population in the Late Roman period and the Early Middle Ages]. Kiev: Lybid', 1990.

Pippidi, D. M., G. Bordenache, and V. Eftimie. "Șantierul arheologic Histria" [Archaeological excavations at Histria]. *MCA* 7 (1961): 229–264.

Poenaru Bordea, G. and P. I. Dicu. "Monede romane tîrzii și bizantine (secolele IV–XI) descoperite pe teritoriul județului Argeș." [Late Roman and Byzantine coins (4th–11th c.) found in Argeș County]. *SCN* 9 (1989): 75–88.

Poenaru Bordea, G. and B. Mitrea. "Découvertes monétaires en Roumanie–1992 (XXXVI)." *Dacia* 37 (1993): 307–320.

Poenaru Bordea, G. and R. Ocheșeanu. "Probleme istorice dobrogene (secolele VI–VII) în lumina monedelor bizantine din colecția Muzeului de Istorie Națională și Arheologie din Constanța." [Questions concerning the history of Dobrudja (6th–7th c.) in light of the Byzantine coins from the National History and Archaeology Museum Constanța]. *SCIVA* 31, no. 3 (1980): 377–396.

Poenaru Bordea, G., E. Nicolae, and A. Popescu. "Contributions numismatiques à l'histoire de Noviodunum aux VIe–VIIe siècles." *SCN* 11 (1995): 135–161.

Pohl, W. "Die Gepiden und die Gentes an der mittleren Donau nach dem Zerfall des Attilareiches." In *Die Völker an der mittleren und unteren Donau im fünften und sechsten Jahrhundert*, edited by H. Wolfram and F. Daim, 239–305. Vienna: Verlag der Österreichischen Akademie der Wissenschaften, 1980.

Die Awaren: Ein Steppenvolk in Mitteleuropa, 567–822 n. Chr. Munich: C. H. Beck, 1988.

"Herrschaft und Subsistenz. Zum Wandel der byzantinischen Randkulturen an der Donau vom 6.–8. Jahrhundert." In *Awarenforschungen*, edited by F. Daim, 13–24. Vienna: Institut für Ur- und Frühgeschichte der Universität Wien, 1992.

"The Empire and the Lombards: treaties and negotiations in the sixth century." In *Kingdoms of the Empire: The Integraton of Barbarians in Late Antiquity*, edited by W. Pohl, 75–134.Transformation of the Roman World 1. Leiden/New York, NY: Brill, 1997.

"Conclusion: the transformation of frontiers." In *The Transformation of Frontiers. From Late Antiquity to the Carolingians*, edited by W. Pohl, I. Wood, and H. Reimitz, 247–260. Transformation of the Roman World 10. Leiden/New York, NY: Brill, 2001.

Polanyi, K. "The semantics of money uses." In *Primitive, Archaic, and Modern Economies: Essays of Karl Polanyi*, edited by G. Dalton, 175–203. Garden City, NY: Doubleday, 1968.

Popa, A. "Academia Română și descoperirile arheologice de pe valea superioară a Mureșului" [The Romanian Academy and the archaeological finds on the upper Mureș]. *Marisia* 6 (1976): 11–24.

Popescu, E. *Inscripțiile grecești și latine din secolele IV–XIII descoperite în România* [The Greek and Latin inscriptions from the 4th–13th c. found in Romania]. Bucharest: Editura Academiei RSR, 1976.

Christianitas daco-romana. Florilegium studiorum. Bucharest: Editura Academiei, 1994.

"Le village en Scythie Mineure (Dobroudja) à l'époque protobyzantine." In *Les villages dans l'Empire byzantin (IVe–XVe siècle)*, edited by J. Lefort, C. Morrisson, and J.-P. Sodini, 363–380. Paris: Lethielleux, 2005.

Popilian, G. "Stăpânirea romano-bizantină la Dunărea de Jos" [The Roman-Byzantine rule on the Lower Danube]. In *Istoria românilor 2*, 607–616.

Popilian, G. and M. Nica. *Gropșani. Monografie arheologică*. Bucharest: Institutul Român de Tracologie, 1998.

"Așezarea prefeudală de la Craiova (Fântâna Obedeanu)" [An Early Medieval settlement at Craiova (Fântâna Obedeanu)]. *Drobeta* 15 (2005): 148–165.

Popinceanu, I. *Religion, Glaube und Aberglaube in der rumänischen Sprache*. Nuremberg: Verlag Hans Carl, 1964.

Popović, M. "Svetinja, novi podaci o ranovizantijskom Viminacijumu" [Svetinja: new data on the Early Byzantine Viminacium]. *Starinar* 38 (1987): 1–37.

Popović, V. "La descente des Koutrigours, des Slaves et des Avars vers la Mer Égée: le témoignage de l'archéologie." *Comptes rendus de l'Académie des Inscriptions et Belles-Lettres* 6 (1978): 596–648.

"Byzantins, Slaves et autochtones dans les provinces de Prévalitane et Nouvelle Epire." In *Villes et peuplement dans l'Illyricum protobyzantin. Actes du colloque organisé par l'École Française de Rome, Rome 12–14 mai 1982*. Rome: École Française de Rome, 1984.

"Trois inscriptions protobyzantines de Bregovina." *Starinar* 40–41 (1989–1990): 279–290.

Popovici, R. "Două piese vestimentare din secolele VI–VII descoperite la Borniș-Neamț" [Two dress accessories from the 6th–7th c. found at Borniș-Neamț]. *AM* 12 (1988): 249–251.

Pospisil, L. J. *The Kapauku Papuans of West New Guinea*. New York, NY: Holt, Rinehart and Winston, 1963.

Postică, G. *Civilizația medievală timpurie din spațiul pruto-nistrean (secolele V–XIII)* [Early Medieval civilization in the lands between the rivers Prut and Dniester (5th–13th c.)]. Bucharest: Editura Academiei Române, 2007.

Poulou-Papadimitriou, N. "Lampes paléochrétiennes de Samos." *Bulletin de correspondance hellénique* 110, no. 1 (1986): 583–610.

Poulter, A. G. *Nicopolis ad Istrum: A Roman to Early Byzantine City. The Pottery and Glass*. London: Leicester University Press, 1999.

"Cataclysm on the Lower Danube: the destruction of a complex Roman landscape." In *Landscape of Change: Rural Evolutions in Late Antiquity and the Early Middle Ages*, edited by N. Christie, 223–253. Aldershot: Ashgate, 2004.

"Interpreting finds in context: Nicopolis and Dichin revisited." In *Objects in Context, Objects in Use: Material Spatiality in Late Antiquity*, edited by L. Lavan, E. Swift, and T. Putzeys, 685–705. Leiden/Boston, MA: Brill, 2007.

"The Lower Danubian frontier in Late Antiquity: evolution and dramatic change in the frontier zone, c. 296–600." In *Zwischen Region und Reich: das Gebiet der oberen Donau im Imperium Romanum*, edited by P. Herz, P. Schmid, and O. Stoll, 11–42. Berlin: Frank & Timme, 2010.

Preda, C. "Tipar pentru bijuterii din secolul al VI-lea e.n. descoperit la Olteni (r. Videle, reg. București) [A sixth-century mold for jewelry found at Olteni (Videle County)]. *SCIV* 18, no. 3 (1967): 513–520.

——— "Circulația monedelor bizantine în regiunea carpato-dunăreană" [Byzantine coin circulation in the lands between the Carpathian Mountains and the Danube]. *SCIV* 23, no. 3 (1972): 375–415.

——— *Monedele geto-dacilor*. Bucharest: Editura Academiei RSR, 1973.

——— "Circulația monedelor postaureliene în Dacia" [Coin circulation in Dacia after Aurelian]. *SCIVA* 26, no. 4 (1975): 441–486.

——— "The Byzantine coins – an expression of the relations between the Empire and the populations north of the Danube in the 6th–13th centuries." In *Relations*, 219–233.

——— "O monedă bizantină de argint inedită" [An unpublished Byzantine silver coin]. *BSNR* 86–87 (1992–1993): 123–124.

——— "Descoperiri inedite de monede antice și bizantine" [Unpublished finds of ancient and Byzantine coins]. *BSNR* 80–85 (1986–1991): 289–296.

Preda, C. and H. Nubar. *Histria III. Descoperirile monetare de la Histria 1914–1970* [Histria III: Coin finds (1914–1970)]. Bucharest: Editura Academiei, 1973.

Prendi, F. "Një varrëze e kulturës arbërore në Lezhë" [An early medieval Albanian cemetery in Lezhë]. *Iliria* 9–10 (1979–1980): 123–170.

Press, L., L. Dąbrowski, L. Kajzer, A. Nadolski, T. Sarnowski, W. Szubert, and Z. Tabasz. "Novae - sektor zachodni. 1971. Sprawozdanie tymczasowe z wykopalisk ekspedycji archeologicznej Uniwersytetu Warszawskiego" [Novae - western sector: preliminary report of the archaeological excavations conducted by the University of Warsaw in 1971]. *Archeologia* 24 (1973): 101–146.

Prigent, V. "Le rôle des provinces d'Occident dans l'approvisionnement de Constantinople (618–771). Témoignages numismatique et sigillographique." *Mélanges de l'École Française de Rome, Moyen Âge* 118, no. 2 (2006): 269–299.

Priimak, V. V. "Kulturnye transformatsii i vzaimovliianiia v Dneprovskom regione na iskhode rimskogo vremei i v rannem Srednevekov'e" [Cultural transformations and mixed influences in the Dnieper region at the end of Roman times and in the Early Middle Ages]. In *Doklady nauchnoi konferentsii, posviashchennoi 60-letiiu so dnia rozhdeniia E. A. Goriunova (Sankt Peterburg, 14–17 noiabria 2000 g.)*, edited by V. M. Goriunova and O. A. Shcheglova, 282–287. St. Petersburg: Petersburgskoe vostokovedenie, 2004.

Pringle, D. *The Defence of Byzantine Africa from Justinian to the Arab Conquest. An account of the Military History and Archaeology of the African Provinces in the Sixth and Seventh Centuries*. BAR International Series 99. Oxford: BAR, 1981.

Profantová, N. "Die frühslavische Besiedlung Böhmens und archäologische Spuren der Kontakte zum früh- und mittelawarischen sowie merowingischen Kulturkreis." In *Kulturwandel in Mitteleuropa. Langobarden, Awaren, Slawen. Akten der Internationalen Tagung in Bonn vom 25. Bis 28. Februar 2008,* edited by J. Bemmann and M. Schmauder, 619–644. Bonn: Rudolf Habelt, 2008.

"Awarische Funde in der Tschechischen Republik – Forschungsstand und neue Erkenntnisse." *AAC* 45 (2010): 203–270.

Prohászka, P. "Altneue byzantinische Münzen der Awarenzeit (Ergänzungen zum Buch von Péter Somogyi: Byzantinische Fundmünzen der Awarenzeit. Innsbruck, 1997)." *AAASH* 55 (2004): 101–113.

"Beiträge zum spätrömischen und byzantinischen Goldmünzverkehr zwischen dem 4. und 8. Jahrhundert in Siebenbürgen." *CN* 12–13 (2006–2007): 89–96.

Prokopenko, Y. A. "K voprosu o Severo-Kavkazskikh podrazhaniiakh bizantiiskim monetn'im obraztsam" [On the issue of North Caucasian imitations of Byzantine coinage]. *Vestnik stavropol'skogo gosudarstvennogo pedagogichescogo universiteta* 1 (1995): 63–67.

"Byzantine coins of the 5th–9th century and their imitations in the Central and Eastern Ciscaucasus." In *Byzantine Coins*, 417–448.

Protase, D. *Problema continuității în Dacia în lumina arheologiei și numismaticii* [The question of continuity in Dacia in light of archaeological and numismatic sources]. Bucharest: Editura Academiei RSR, 1966.

Autohtonii în Dacia II: Dacia postromană până la slavi [The native population of Dacia (part II): Post-Roman Dacia to the Slavic migration]. Cluj-Napoca: Risoprint, 2000.

"Populația autohtonă în Dacia postromană (anul 275–secolul al VI-lea)" [The autochthonous population in post-Roman Dacia (from 275 to the 6th century]. In *Istoria românilor. Vol. II: Daco-romani, romanici, alogeni*, edited by D. Protase and A. Suceveanu, 555–606. Bucharest: Editura Enciclopedică, 2001.

Pröttel, P. M. *Mediterrane Feinkeramikimporte des 2. bis 7. Jahrhunderts n. Chr. im oberen Adriaraum und in Slowenien*. Espelkamp: Marie Leidorf, 1996.

Prykhodniuk, O. M. *Arkheolohychny pam'iatki seredn'ogo Pridnyprov'ia VI–X st. n. e.* [Sixth-to-ninth century archaeological assemblages of the Middle Dnieper region]. Kiev: Naukova Dumka, 1980.

"Tekhnologiia vyrobnytsva ta vytoki iuvelirnogo styliu metalevykh ptykras Pastyrs'kogo gorodyshcha." [Production techniques and sources of the jewelry style of metal adornments from the Pastyr settlement]. *Arkheologia* 2 (1994): 61–77.

Pen'kovskaia kul'tura [Penkovka culture]. *Kul'turno-khronologicheskii aspekt issledovaniia*. Voronezh: Voronezhskii universitet, 1998.

Pyiatnisky, Y. "New evidence for Byzantine activity in the Caucasus during the reign of the Emperor Anastasius I." *AJN* 18 (2006): 113–122.

Quast, D. "Die Langobarden in Mähren und im nördlichen Niederösterreich - ein Diskussionsbeitrag." In *Archaeology of Identity – Archäologie der Identität*, edited by W. Pohl and M. Mehofer, 93–110. Vienna: Verlag der Österreichischen Akademie der Wissenschaften, 2009.

Radić, V. and V. Ivanišević. *Byzantine Coins from the National Museum in Belgrade*. Belgrade: Narodni Muzej, 2006.

Radomerský, P. "Byzantské mince z pokladu v Zemianském Vrbovku" [The hoard of Byzantine coins from Zemiansky Vrbovok]. *Památky Archeologické* 44 (1953): 109–122.

Rădulescu, A. "Casa cnezială de la Udeşti" [The princely residence from Udeşti]. *Magazin Istoric* 11 (1977): 49.

Rafalovich, I. A. *Slaviane VI–IX vekov v Moldavii* [The Slavs in Moldova (6th–9th c.)]. Kishinew: Shtiinca, 1972.

"Issledovaniia ranneslavianskikh poselenii v Moldavii" [Studies of early Slavic settlements in Moldavia]. In *Arkheologicheskie issledovaniia v Moldavii v 1970–1971 gg.*, edited by G. F. Chebotarenko, 134–154. Kishinew: Shtiinca, 1973.

Dancheni. Mogil'nik cherniakhovskoi kul'tury [Dănceni: a Chernyakhovian cemetery]. Kishinew: Shtiinca, 1986.

Rafalovich, I. A. and V. L. Lapushnian. "Raboty Reutskoi arkheologicheskoi ekspedicii" [The activity of the Răut expedition]. In *Arkheologicheskie issledovaniia v Moldavii (1972 g)*, 110–147. Kishinew: Shtiinca, 1973.

Raica, I. and I. A. Aldea. "Două monede bizantine descoperite la Sebeş" [Two Byzantine coins found at Sebeş]. *Apulum* 6 (1967): 625–628.

Rankov, B. "Do rivers make good frontiers?" In *Limes XIX. Proceedings of the XIXth International Congress of Roman Frontier Studies Held in Pécs, Hungary, September 2003*, edited by Z. Visy, 175–181. Pécs: University of Pécs, 2005.

Rashev, R. *Prabulgarite prez V–VII vek* [The Bulgars between the 5th and the 7th c.]. Veliko Turnovo: Faber, 2000.

Rassamakin, J. "Die Archäologie der Ukraine: vom 'entwickelten' Sozialismus zur 'Selbstständigkeit'." In *Archäologien Europas. Geschichte, Methoden und Theorien*, edited by P. F. Biehl, A. Gramsch, and A. Marciniak, 271–282. Tübinger archäologische Taschenbücher 3. Münster: Waxmann, 2002.

Rautman, M. "Handmade pottery and social change: the view from Late Roman Cyprus." *Journal of Mediterranean Archaeology* 11, no. 1 (1998): 81–104.

Redfield, R., R. Linton, and M. J. Herskovits. "Memorandum for the study of acculturation." *AA* 38 (1936): 149–152.

Reining, C. R. "The role of money in the Zande economy." *AA* 61, no. 1 (1959): 39–43.

Repnikov, N. I. "Nekotorye mogil'niki oblasti Krymskikh gotov" [A few cemeteries of the Crimean Gothic region]. *Zapiski Odesskogo obshchestva istorii i drevnostei* 27 (1907): 101–148.

Rice, P. M. "Context of contact and change: peripheries, frontiers, and boundaries." In *Studies in Culture Contact: Interaction, Culture Change, and Archaeology*, edited by C. Cusick, 44–66. Carbondale, IL: Southern Illinois University, 1998.

Rikman, A. and I. A. Rafalovich. "K voprosu o sootnoshenii cherniakhovskoi i ranneslavianskoi kul'tur v dnestrovsko-dunaiskom mezhdurech'e" [On the question of the connection between Chernyakhovian and early Slavic culture in the Dniester-Danube interfluve]. *KSIA* 105 (1965): 42–58.

Riley, J. A. "The coarse pottery from Berenice." In *Excavations at Sidi Khrebish. Benghazi (Berenice)*, edited by J. A. Lloyd, Vol. V/2, 91–467. Tripoli: Department of Antiquities, 1979.

Rodseth L. and B. J. Parker. "Introduction: theoretical considerations in the study of frontiers." In *Untaming the Frontier in Anthropology, Archaeology and History*, edited by B. J. Parker and L. Rodseth, 3–21. Tucson, AZ: University of Arizona Press, 2005.

de Rojas, J. L. *La moneda indígena y sus usos en la Nueva España en el siglo XVI*. Tlalpan, DF: Centro de Investigaciones y Estudios Superiores en Antropología Social, 1998.

Roman, P. and S. Dolinescu-Ferche. "Cercetările de la Ipotești (jud. Olt) (observații asupra culturii materiale autohtone din sec. al VI-lea în Muntenia)" [Archaeological research at Ipotești (Olt County): observations regarding the native material culture in sixth-century Wallachia]. *SCIVA* 29, no. 2 (1978): 73–93.

Rosetti, D. V. "Siedlungen der Kaiserzeit und der Völkerwanderungszeit bei Bukarest." *Germania* 18 (1934): 206–214.

Ross, J. B. "Two neglected Paladins of Charlemagne: Erich of Friuli and Gerold of Bavaria." *Speculum* 20 (1945): 212–235.

Rossi, L. *Trajan's Column and the Dacian Wars*. Ithaca, NY: Cornell University Press, 1971.

Rousselle, A., ed. *Frontières terrestres, frontières célestes dans l'antiquité*. Paris: Diffusion de Boccard, 1995.

Rtveladze, E. V. and A. P. Runich. "Nakhodki indikacii vizantiiskikh monet vblizi Kislovodska" [Finds of Byzantine coins and imitations near Kislovodsk]. *VV* 32 (1971): 219–222.

"Novye nahodki vizantiiskikh monet i indikacii v okrestnostiakh Kislovodska" [New finds of Byzantine coins and imitations in the environs of Kislovodsk]. *VV* 37 (1976): 151–155.

Rubin, Z. "The conversion of the Visigoths to Christianity." *Museum Helveticum* 38 (1981): 34–54.

Rubright, J. C. "Lamps from Sirmium in the Museum of Sremska Mitrovica." In *Sirmium III. Archaeological Investigations in Syrmian Pannonia*, edited by V. Popović and E. L. Ochsenschlager, 45–84. Belgrade: Archaeological Institute, 1973.

Russell, L., ed. *Colonial Frontiers: Indigenous–European Encounters in Settler Societies*. Manchester: Manchester University Press, 2001.

Rusu, M. "Paleocreștinismul nord-dunărean și etnogeneza românilor" [Early Christianity north of the Danube and the Romanian ethnogenesis]. *Anuarul Institutului de Istorie și Arheologie* 26 (1983–1984): 35–84.

"Paleocreștinismul din Dacia romană" [Early Christianity in Roman Dacia]. *EN* 1 (1991): 81–112.

Rutkivs'ka, L. M. "Arkheologicheskie pamiatniki IV–VI vv. v raione Kremenchugskogo moria (Ukraina)" [Archaeological monuments from the 4th–6th c. in the area of the Kremenchuk Reservoir (Ukraine)]. *Slovenská Archeológia* 27 (1979): 316–361.

Rybakov, B. A. "Drevnie rusi. K voprosu ob obrazovanii iadra drevnerusskoi narodnosti v svete trudov I. V. Stalina" [The ancient Rus'. On the issue of the formation of the Old Russian cradle according to the works of I. V. Stalin]. *SA* 17 (1953): 23–104.

Sala, M. *De la latină la română* [From Latin to Romanian]. Bucharest: Univers Enciclopedic, 1998.

Salamon, A. and I. Erdély. *Das völkerwanderungszeitliche Gräberfeld von Környe*. Budapest: Akadémia Kiadó, 1971.

Saramandu, N. *Originea dialectelor românești* [The origin of Romanian dialects]. Bucharest: Editura Academiei Române, 2005.

"À propos de l'origine du roumain." *RESEE* 47 (2009): 315–321.

Sarantis, A. "War and diplomacy in Pannonia and the northwest Balkans during the reign of Justinian. The Gepid threat and imperial responses." *DOP* 63 (2009): 15–40.

"The Justinianic Herules: from allied barbarians to Roman provincials." In *Neglected Barbarians*, 361–402.

Justinian's Balkan Wars: Campaigning, Diplomacy and Development in Illyricum, Thrace and the Northern World AD 527–65. Prenton: Francis Cairns, 2016.

Sarris, P. "Bubonic plague in Byzantium: the evidence of non-literary sources." In *Plague and the End of Antiquity: The Pandemic of 541–750*, edited by L. K. Little, 119–132. Cambridge: Cambridge University Press, 2008.

Scărlătoiu, E. *Istroromânii și istroromâna: relații lingvistice cu slavii de sud: cuvinte de origine veche slavă* [Istro-Romanians and Istro-Romanian: linguistic contacts with the Southern Slavs: old Slavic words]. Bucharest: Editura Staff, 1998.

Schmiedehelm, M. and S. Laul. "Asustusest ja etnilistest oludest Kagu-Eestis I aastatuhande" [The settlement and ethnic profile of the southeastern region of Estonia during the first millennium]. In *Studia archaeologica in memoriam Harri Moora*, edited by M. Schmiedehelm, L. Jaanits, and J. Selirand, 154–163. Tallinn: Kirjastus "Valgus," 1970.

Schneider, J. "Was there a precapitalist world-system?" *Peasant Studies* 6, no. 1 (1977): 20–29.

Scholl, T. "The chronology of Jerash lamps: Umayyad period." *Archeologia* 42 (1991): 65–84.

Schramm, G. *Ein Damm bricht. Die römische Donaugrenze und die Invasionen des 5.-7. Jahrhunderts im Lichte von Namen und Wörtern*. Munich: R. Oldenbourg, 1997.

Schulze-Dörrlamm, M. *Byzantinische Gürtelschnallen und Gürtelbeschläge im Römisch-Germanischen Zentralmuseum. Teil I: Die Schnallen ohne Beschläg, mit Laschenbeschläg und mit festem Beschläg des 5. bis 7. Jahrhunderts*. Mainz: Verlag des Römisch-Germanischen Zentralmuseums, 2002.

Scorpan, C. "Imitații getice după opaițe greco-romane" [Getic imitations of Greco-Roman lamps]. *Pontice* 2 (1969): 253–268.

"Ceramica romano-bizantină de la Sacidava" [Roman-Byzantine pottery from Sacidava]. *Pontica* 8 (1975): 263–313.

"Descoperiri arheologice diverse la Sacidava" [Various archaeological finds at Sacidava]. *Pontica* 11 (1978): 155–180.

Seibt, W. "Westgeorgien (Egrisi, Lazica) in frühchristlicher Zeit." In *Die Schwarzmeerküste in der Spätantike und im frühen Mittelalter*, edited by R. Pillinger, A. Pülz, and H. Vetters, 137–144. Vienna: Verlag der Österreichischen Akademie der Wissenschaften, 1992.

Semenov, Λ. "Petropavlovskii mogil'nik VI–VII vv. V iuzhnoi Udmurtii" [The sixth-to-seventh century Petropavlovo cemetery in southern Udmurtia]. *Voprosy arkheologii Urala* 7 (1967): 164–171.

"K vyiavleniiu central'noaziatskikh elementov v kul'ture rannesrednevekovykh kochevnikov Vostochnoi Evropy" [On the identification of Central Asian elements in the culture of the Early Medieval nomads of Eastern Europe]. *ASGE* 29 (1988): 97–111.

"Vizantiiskie monety Kelegeiskogo kompleksa" [Byzantine coins from the Kelegeia complex]. *ASGE* 31 (1991): 121–130.

Sgîbea, M. "Fibule din sec. III și VI e.n. descoperite în săpăturile arheologice de la Militari" [Fibulae from the third and the sixth century found during archaeological excavations at Bucharest–Militari]. *CAB* 1 (1963): 373–384.

Shablavina, E. A. "O rannesrednevekovoi produkcii Bosporskikh iuvelirov (na primere orlinogolovykh priazhek)" [On the Early Medieval activity of Bosporan jewelers (primarily on the basis of eagle-headed buckles)]. *Arkheologicheskie vesti* 13 (2006): 230–251.

Shablavina, E. A. and B. S. Szmoniewski. "The forming model of the Kertch type finger-shaped fibula." *Sprawozdania Archeologiczne* 58 (2006): 519–526.

Shamba, S. M. *Monetnoe obrashchenie na territorii Abkhazii: (V v. do n.e.–XIII v. n.e.)* [Coin circulation on the territory of Abkhazia (5th–13th c)]. Tbilisi: Mecniereba, 1987.

Shipton, P. M. *Bitter Money: Cultural Economy and Some African Meanings of Forbidden Commodities*. Washington, DC: American Anthropological Association, 1989.

Shortman, E. M. and P. A. Urban. "Culture contact structure and process." In *Studies in Culture Contact: Interaction, Culture Change, and Archaeology*, edited by C. Cusick, 102–125. Carbondale, IL: Southern Illinois University, 1998.

Shovkoplias, A. M. "Ranneslavianskaia keramika s gory Kiselevki v Kieve" [Early-Slavic ceramics from the Kiselevka mountain in Kiev]. In *Slaviane nakanune obrazovaniia Kievskoi Rusi*, edited by B. A. Rybakov, 138–144. Moscow: Izd-vo Akademii Nauk SSSR, 1963.

Shukriu, E. "Frühchristliche Lampen aus der antiken Provinz Dardania." *Mitteilungen zur Christlichen Archäologie* 9 (2003): 19–23.

Sibilla, P. "A proposito di moneta. Lincamenti di un percorso di ricerca." In *Antropologia dello scambio e della moneta*, edited by P. Sibilla, 9–46. Torino: Libreria Stampaori, 2006.

Simion, G. "Necropola feudal-timpurie de la Nalbant (jud. Tulcea)" [The Early Medieval cemetery from Nalbant (Tulcea County)]. *Peuce* 2 (1971): 221–248.

"Un nouveau groupe de fibule digitales découvertes dans la région du Dobroudja." *Studia antiqua et medievalia. Miscellanea in honorem annos LXXV peragentis Professoris Dan Gh. Teodor oblata*, edited by D. Aparaschivei, 411–420. Bucharest: Editura Academiei Române, 2009.

Simoni, K. "Zagreb i okolica u ranom srednjem vijeku" [Zagreb and its surroundings in the Early Middle Ages]. In *Arheološka istraživanja u Zagrebu i njegovoj okolici*, edited by Ž. Rapanić, 155–168. Zagreb: Hrvatsko Arheološko društvo, 1981.

Skvorcov, K. N. "Avarskaia replika vizantiiskogo solida na Sambiiskom poluostrove" [An Avar imitation of Byzantine solidus found in the Sambia Peninsula]. *Materialy po arkheologii i istorii antichnogo i srednevekovogo Kryma* 6 (2014): 547–558.

Smedley, J. "Seventh-century Byzantine coins in Southern Russia and the problem of light weight solidi." In *Studies in Byzantine Gold Coinage*, edited by W. Hahn and W. E. Metcalf, 111–130. New York, NY: American Numismatic Society, 1988.

Smilenko, A. T. "Nakhodka 1928 g. u g. Novye Senzhary (Po materialam obsledovaniia A. K. Takhtaia)" [The 1928 find in Novye Senzhary (on the basis of the materials of A. K. Takhtai's research)]. In *Slaviane i Rus'*, edited by E. I. Krupnov, 158–166. Moscow: Nauka, 1968.

Sodini, J.-P. "The transformation of cities in Late Antiquity within the provinces of Macedonia and Epirus." In *Transition*, 311–336.

Sokolova, I. V. "Monety Pereshchepinskogo klada" [Coins from the Pereshchepyne hoard]. In *Sokrovishcha Khana Kubrata*, edited by O. Fedoseenko, 17–41. St. Petersburg: AO Slaviia, 1997.

Sommer, C. S. "Why there? The positioning of forts along the riverine frontiers of the Roman Empire." In *The Army and Frontiers of Rome. Papers Offered to David J. Breeze on the Occasion of his Sixty-Fifth Birthday and his Retirement from Historic Scotland*, edited by W. S. Hanson, 103–114. JRA Supplementary Series 74. Portsmouth, RI: JRA, 2009.

Somogyi, P. "Bemerkungen zu den silbernen Münzimitationen vom Typ Kiskörös." In *A Népvándorláskor fiatal kutatoinak IV. összejövetele. Visegrád, 1993, szeptember 20–22*, edited by I. Borsody, 79–89. Visegrád: Mátyás Király Múzeum, 1995.

Byzantinische Fundmünzen der Awarenzeit. Innsbruck: Universitätsverlag Wagner, 1997.

"Ismeretlen levéltári adatok a Firtos hegyén 1831-ben talált bizánci aranyakról" [Unpublished archival data on the Byzantine gold found at Firtos in 1831]. In *Hadak útján. A népvándorlás kor fiatal kutatóinak konferenciája*, edited by L. Bende, G. Lőrinczy, and C. Szalontai, 197–204. Szeged: Csongrad Megye Múzeumi Igazgatósága, 2000.

"Byzantinische Fundmünzen der Awarenzeit. Eine Bestandsaufnahme, 1998-2007." *AAC* 42–43 (2007–2008): 231–298.

"New remarks on the flow of Byzantine coins in Avaria and Wallachia during the second half of the seventh century." In *The Other Europe in the Middle Ages: Avars, Bulgars, Khazars and Cumans*, edited by F. Curta, 83–149. Leiden/Boston, MA: Brill, 2008.

"Neue Überlegungen über den Zustrom byzantinischer Münzen ins Awarenland (Numismatischer Kommentar zu Csanád Bálints Betrachtungen zum Beginn der Mittelawarenzeit)." *Antaeus* 29–30 (2008–2009): 347–393.

"Der Fund von Kleinschelken (Siebenbürgen, 1856) im Lichte neuentdeckter Archivdaten." In *Byzantine Coins*, 417–448.

"Byzantinische Fundmünzen der Awarenzeit. Ergebnisse und Möglichkeiten." Ph.D. Dissertation, Eötvös Loránd University, Budapest, 2011.

Byzantinische Fundmünzen der Awarenzeit in ihrem europäischen Umfeld. Budapest: Institut für Archäologische Wissenschaften, 2014.

Speck, P. *Zufälliges zum Bellum Avaricum des Georgios Pisides*. Munich: Institut für Byzantinistik, neugriechische Philologie und byzantinische Kunstgeschichte der Universität, 1980.

Špehar, P. "The Danubian *limes* between Lederata and Aquae during the Migration Period." In *Pontic-Danubian Realm*, 35–56.

Stanc, S. *Relațiile omului cu lumea animală. Arheozoologia secolelor IV–X pentru zonele extracarpatice de est și de sud ale României* [Human relations with the animal world: the zooarchaeology of eastern and southern Romania between the 4th and the 10th century]. Iași: Editura Universității Al. I. Cuza, 2006.

Stanciu, I. "Gepizi, avari și slavi timpurii (sec. V–VII p. Chr.) în spațiul vestic și nord-vestic al României" [Gepids, Avars, and Early Slavs in the western and northwestern regions of Romania (5th–7th c.)]. *EN* 12 (2002): 203–236.

Stare, V. *Kranj. Nekropola iz časa preseljevanja ljudstev* [A cemetery from the Migration Period]. Ljubljana: Narodni muzej, 1980.

Stark, B. L. and C. P. Garraty. "Detecting marketplace exchange in archaeology: a methodological review." In *Archaeological Approaches to Market Exchange in Ancient Societies*, edited by B. L. Stark and C. P. Garraty, 33–58. Boulder, CO: University Press of Colorado, 2010.

Stefanov, S. "Kusnorimski fibuli ot Nove" [Late Roman fibulae from Novae]. In *Izsledvaniia v pamet na Karel Shkorpil*, edited by K. Miiatev and V. Mikov, 341–350. Sofia: Izsledvaniia na Bulgarskata Akademiia na Naukite, 1961.

Stein, E. *Studien zur Geschichte des byzantinischen Reiches, vornehmlich unter den Kaisern Justinus II u. Tiberius Constantinus*. Stuttgart: J. B. Metzler, 1919.

Stein, G. J. "From passive periphery to active agents: emerging perspectives in the archaeology of interregional interaction." *AAnth* 104, no. 3 (2002): 903–916.

Steinacher, R. "The Herules: fragments of a history." In *Neglected Barbarians*, 319–360.

Stepanov, T. "Danube and Caucasus – the Bulgar(ian)s' real and imagined frontiers." In *Donaulimes*, 299–310.

Stephenson, P. *Byzantium's Balkan Frontier: A Political Study of the Northern Balkans, 900–1204*. Revised edn. Cambridge: Cambridge University Press, 2006.

Stoikov, V. "Kusnoantichni lampi ot Karasura (Predvaritelno suobshtenie)" [Late Antique lamps from Karasura (preliminary report)]. In *Paleobalkanistika i starobulgaristika. Vtori esenni mezhdunarodni cheteniia Profesor "Ivan Gulubov." Veliko Turnovo. 14–17 noemvri 1996*, edited by I. Kharalambiev, K. Popkonstantinov, and S. Iordanov, 503–513. Veliko Turnovo: Universitetsko izdatelstvo "Sv. sv. Kiril i Metodii," 2001.

Stolyarik, E. S. "Klad vizantiiskikh bronzovykh VI v. iz Starye Beliary, Odesskoi oblasti" [A hoard of sixth-century Byzantine bronze coins from Stary Biliary, Odessa region]. In *Severnoe Prichernomor'e: materialy po arkheologii: sbornik nauchnykh trudov*, edited by G. A. Dzis-Raiko, 136–138. Kiev: Nauk dumka, 1984.

"Novye nakhodki pozdnerimskich i vizantiiskikh monet v Pruto-Dunaiskom mezhdurech'e" [New finds of Late Roman and Byzantine coins in the Prut-Danube interfluve]. In *Dnestro-Dunaiskoe mezhdurech'e v I–nachale II tys. n. è.*, edited by A. T. Smilenko, A. V. Gudkova, and A. A. Kozlovskii. Kiev: Nauk dumka, 1987.

Essays on Monetary Circulation in the Northwestern Black Sea Region in the Late Roman and Early Byzantine Periods: Late 3rd Century–Early 13th Century AD. Odessa: Polis Press, 1993.

Stratulat, L. M. "Continuitate şi discontinuitate la nordul Dunării de Jos (secolele IV–VIII d. Hr.)" [Continuity and discontinuity north of the Lower Danube between the fourth and the eighth century]. *Carpica* 31 (2002): 59–78.

Stupperich, R. "Bemerkungen zum römischen Import im sogenannten Freien Germanien." In *Aspekte römisch-germanischer Beziehungen in der frühen Kaiserzeit: Vortragsreihe zur Sonderausstellung "Kalkriese-Römer im Osnabrücker Land," 1993 in Osnabrück*, edited by G. Franzius, 45–98. Espelkamp: Marie Leidorf, 1995.

Suceveanu, A. and A. Barnea. *La Dobroudja romaine*. Bucharest: Editura Enciclopedică, 1991.

Suciu, V. "Noi descoperiri monetare în judeţul Alba" [New coin finds from Alba County]. *Apulum* 38 (2001): 251–260.

Swan, V. G. "Dichin (Bulgaria): interpreting the ceramic evidence in its wider context." In *Transition*, 260–265.

Syrbe, D. "Reiternomaden des Schwarzmeerraums (Kutriguren und Utiguren) und byzantinische Diplomatie im 6. Jahrhundert." *Acta Orientalia* 65, no. 3 (2012): 291–316.

Székely, Z. "Așezări din secolele VII–VIII în bazinul superior al Tîrnavei Mari" [Seventh- and eighth-century settlements from the upper Tîrnava Mare]. *SCIVA* 39, no. 2 (1988): 169–198.

"Așezări din secolele VI–XI p. Ch. în bazinul Oltului superior" [Settlements from the upper Olt region between the sixth and the eleventh century]. *SCIVA* 43, no. 2 (1992): 245–306.

Szmoniewski, B. S. "Production of Early Medieval ornaments made of non-ferrous metals: dies from archaeological finds in North-East Romania." *AAC* 37 (2002): 111–135.

"The Antes: eastern 'brothers' of the Sclavenes?" In *Neglected Barbarians*, 53–82.

Takács, M. and I. V. Tătar. "O monedă bizantină inedită din zona Aiudului" [An unpublished Byzantine coin from the Aiud area]. *Apulum* 37 (2000): 443–447.

Tănase, D. and M. Mare. "Piese de port și de podoabă din secolele III–VII în colecția Pongrácz. Catalog" [Jewelry and dress accessories from the third to the seventh century in the Pongrácz collection. Catalogue]. *Analele Banatului* 9 (2001): 181–206.

"Piese de aur din epoca migrațiilor în colecția Muzeului Banatului din Timișoara" [Gold from the Migration Age in the Banat Museum in Timișoara]. In *Între stepă și Imperiu. Studii în onoarea lui Radu Harhoiu*, edited by A. Măgureanu and E. Gáll, 141–147. Bucharest: Renaissance, 2010.

Tancheva-Vasilieva, N. "Antichni glineni lampi ot Muzeia v Iambol" [Ancient terracotta lamps from the Yambol Museum]. *IMIB* 5 (1982): 23–31.

Tavlinceva, Iu. "K voprosu o metallicheskom bisere v riazno-okskikh mogil'nikakh (po materialam Shoshinskogo mogil'nika)" [On the question of the metallic beads of the Riazan'-Oka cemeteries]. In *Nauchnoe nasledie A. P. Smirnova i sovremennye problemy arkheologii Volgo-Kam'ia. Materialy nauchnoi konferencii*, edited by I. V. Belocerkovskaia, 109–115. Moscow: Gosudarstvennyi istoricheskii muzei, 2000.

Teall, J. L. "The barbarians in Justinian's armies." *Speculum* 40, n. 2 (1965): 294–322.

Țeicu, D. "Căldarea de lut paleocreștină de la Periam" [A clay liturgical vessel from Periam]. *Thraco-Dacica* 11 (1990): 153–156.

Tenchova, A. "Beobachtung der Münzzirkulation am Mittellauf des Maritzaflusses im 6.-7. Jahrhundert." Paper given at 22nd International Congress of Byzantine Studies, Sofia, 22–27 August 2011.

Tentiuc, I. "Siturile din secolele V–VII de la Molești-Ialoveni (Republica Moldova)" [The fifth- and sixth-century settlements from Molești-Ialoveni (Moldova)]. *AM* 21 (1998): 201–212.

Teodor, D. G. "Elemente și influențe bizantine în Moldova în sec. VI–XI" [The Byzantine cultural influence in Moldavia between the sixth and the eleventh century]. *SCIV* 21, no. 1 (1970): 97–128.

"La pénétration des Slaves dans les régions du sud-est de l'Europe d'après les données archéologiques des régions orientales de la Roumanie." *Balcanoslavica* 1 (1972): 29–42.

"Teritoriul est-carpatic în veacurile V–XI e.n.: contribuții arheologice și istorice la problema formării poporului român" [The East-Carpathian area between the fifth and the eleventh century: archaeological and historical contributions to the question of the Romanian ethnogenesis]. Iași: Junimea, 1978.

The East-Carpathian Area of Romania in the V–XI Centuries AD. BAR International Series 81. Oxford: BAR, 1980.

Romanitatea carpato-dunăreană și Bizanțul în veacurile V–XI [Byzantium and the Romanic culture north of the Lower Danube, 5th–11th c.]. Iași: Junimea. 1981.

Civilizația romanică la est de Carpați în secolele V–VII (așezarea de la Botoșana-Suceava) [Romanic culture east of the Carpathians between the fifth and the seventh century (the settlement from Botoșana-Suceava)]. Bucharest: Editura Academiei, 1984.

"Considerații privind fibulele romano-bizantine din secolele V–VII în spațiul carpato-danubiano-pontic" [Some remarks regarding the fifth-to-seventh-century Roman-Byzantine fibulae found in Romania]. *AM* 12 (1988): 197–223.

Creștinismul la est de Carpați de la origini și pînă în secolul al XVI-lea [Christianity in Moldavia from the beginnings to the sixteenth century]. Iași: Junimea, 1991.

"Éléments et influences byzantins dans la civilisation des VIe–VIIe siècles après J. Chr. au nord du Bas-Danube." *EBPB* 2 (1991): 59–72.

"Piese vestimentare bizantine din secolele VI–VIII în spațiul carpato-dunăreano-pontic" [Byzantine dress accessories from the 6th–8th c. found in Romania]. *AM* 14 (1991): 117–138.

"Fibule digitate din secolele VI–VII în spațiul carpato-dunăreano-pontic" [Sixth-seventh-century bow fibulae found in Romania]. *AM* 15 (1992): 119–152.

"Slavii la nordul Dunării de Jos în secolele VI–VII d.H." [The Slavs north of the Lower Danube in the 6th–7th c]. *AM* 17 (1994): 223–251.

"Creștinism și păgânism la est de Carpați în a doua jumătate a mileniului I d. Hr." [Christian and pagan beliefs in Moldavia during the second half of the first millennium]. *Pontica* 28–29 (1994–1995): 215–226.

Meșteșugurile la nordul Dunării de Jos în secolele IV–XI [Crafts north of the Lower Danube between the fourth and the eleventh century]. Iași: Helios, 1996.

Descoperiri arheologice și numismatice la est de Carpați (contribuții la continuitatea daco-romană și veche românească). [Archaeological and numismatic finds in Moldavia: Daco-Roman and old Romanian continuity]. Bucharest: Muzeul Național de Istorie a României, 1997.

"Christian Roman Byzantine imports north of the Lower Danube." *Interacademica* 2–3 (2001): 118–130.

"Populația autohtonă din regiunile extracarpatice în secolele V–VII" [The native population in Moldavia and Wallachia (6th–7th c.)]. In *Istoria românilor 2*, 639–662.

Spațiul carpato-dunăreano-pontic în mileniul marilor migrații [The area between the Carpathians, the Danube and the Black Sea in the millennium of the Great Migrations]. Buzău: Alpha, 2003.

"Considerații privind continuitatea autohtonă în spațiul carpato-dunărean în mileniul I d. Hr." [Some remarks concerning the continuity of the native population in Romania in the first millennium AD]. *Carpica* 34 (2005): 143–150.

"Tipare din secolele V–XI d. Hr. în regiunile carpato-nistrene" [Molds from the fifth to the eleventh century from the area between the Carpathians and the Dniester]. *AM* 28 (2005): 159–174.

"Ateliers byzantins des VIe–VIIIe siècles au nord du Bas-Danube." *EBPB* 5 (2006): 198–201.

"Considerații privind unele aspecte ale etnogenezei românești" [Some remarks regarding the Romanian ethnogenesis]. *AM* 34 (2011): 177–185.

Teodor, D. G. and C. Chiriac. "Noi fibule digitate din Dobrogea" [Bow fibulae recently found in Dobrudja]. *Peuce* 3–4 (2005–2006): 241–250.

Teodor, E. S. "Ceramica așezărilor din secolul al VI-lea de la Dulceanca" [Pottery from the sixth-century settlement at Dulceanca]. In *Istro-Pontica: Muzeul tulcean la a 50-a aniversare, 1950–2000; omagiu lui Simion Gavrilă la 45 de ani de activitate*, edited by M. Iacob, E. Oberländer-Târnoveanu, and F. Topoleanu, 295–342. Tulcea: Consiliul Județean, 2000.

"Ceramica de uz comun din Muntenia de la sfârșitul veacului al V-lea până la mijlocul veacului al VII-lea" [The ceramics from Wallachia, from the end of the fifth to the middle of the seventh century]. PhD Dissertation, A. I. Cuza University, Iași, 2001.

"Epoca romană târzie și cronologia atacurilor transdanubiene. Analiza componentelor etnice și geografice (partea a doua, de la 565 la 626)" [The chronology of transdanubian attacks in Late Antiquity: an ethnic and geographical analysis (part two, from 565 to 626)]. *Muzeul Național* 15 (2003): 3–36.

"O frontieră incertă a lumii romane – Cîmpia Dunării de Jos în epoca lui Justinian" [The Lower Danubian plane under Justinian: an uncertain frontier]. *Cercetări arheologice* 12 (2003): 325–360.

"Handmade pottery from the Late Roman fortress at Capidava." In *Between the Steppe and the Empire. Archaeological Studies in Honour of Radu Harhoiu at 65th Anniversary*, edited by A. Măgureanu and E. Gáll, 211–223. Bucharest: Renaissance, 2010.

Teodor, E. S. and I. Stanciu. "About crosses on wet clay as cultural markers." *EN* 19 (2009): 129–155.

Teodorescu, V. "O nouă cultură arheologică recent precizată în țara noastră, cultura Ipotești-Cîndești (sec. V–VII)" [A new archaeological culture in Romania: Ipotești-Cîndești, 5th–7th c.]. In *Sesiunea de comunicări științifice a muzeelor de istorie, dec. 1964*, Vol. II, 104–130. Bucharest: n.p., 1971.

"Centre meșteșugărești din sec. V/VI–VII în București" [Artisan workshops in Bucharest, 5th–7th c.]. *București* 9 (1972): 73–99.

"Les anciens Roumains." *Roumanie. Pages d'histoire* 5 (1980): 56–91.

Teodorescu, V., D. Lichiardopol, M. Peneș, and V. Sandu. "Așezarea daco-romană din secolele IV–V de la Cireșanu, jud. Prahova" [The Daco-Roman settlement from Cireșanu, Prahova County (4th–5th c.)]. *MCA* 17 (1993), Vol. II: 389–416.

Terjal, J. "Cultural or ethnic changes? Continuity and discontinuity on the Middle Danube ca AD 500." In *Pontic-Danubian Realm*, 115–188.

Tettamanti, S. *Das awarenzeitliche Gräberfeld in Vác-Kavicsbánya*. Budapest: Magyar Nemzeti Múzeum, 2000.

Thirault, E. "The politics of supply: the Neolithic axe industry in Alpine Europe." *Antiquity* 79 (2005): 34–50.

Thomas, E. B. "Die Romanität Pannoniens im 5. und 6. Jahrhundert." In *Germanen, Hunnen und Awaren: Schätze der Völkerwanderungszeit: Germanisches Nationalmuseum, Nürnberg, 12. Dezember 1987 bis 21. Februar 1988: Museum für Vor- und Frühgeschichte der Stadt Frankfurt am Main, 13. März bis 15. Mai 1988*, edited by W. Menghin, T. Springer, and E. Wamers, 284–294. Nuremberg: Verlag Germanisches Nationalmuseum, 1987.

Thomas, N. *Exchange, Material Culture, and Colonialism in the Pacific*. Cambridge, MA: Harvard University Press, 1991.

Thomson, R. W. "Mission, conversion, and Christianization: the Armenian example." *Harvard Ukrainian Studies* 12–13 (1988–1989): 28–45.

"Eastern neighbours: Armenia (400–600)." In *The Cambridge History of the Byzantine Empire c. 500–1492*, edited by J. Shepard, 156–172. Cambridge: Cambridge University Press, 2008.

trans., *Rewriting Caucasian History. The Medieval Armenian Adaptation of the Georgian Chronicles*. Oxford: Clarendon Press, 1996.

Timotin, A. "Paleocreștinismul carpato-danubian" [Early Christianity in Romania]. *Archaeus* 2, no. 2 (1998): 43–172.

Toncheva, G. "Keramichna rabotilnica krai s. Kranevo" [A ceramic workshop near the village of Kranevo]. *Izvestiia Bulgarskoto Arkheologichesko Druzhestvo* 9 (1952): 81–104.

Topoleanu, F. *Ceramica romană și romano-bizantină de la Halmyris* [The Roman and Early Byzantine pottery from Halmyris]. Tulcea: Institutul de Cercetări Eco-Muzeale, 2000.

"Ceramica." In A. Suceveanu, M. Zahariade, F. Topoleanu, and G. Poenaru Bordea, *Halmyris I. Monografie arheologică*. Cluj-Napoca: Nereamia Napocae, 2003.

Lămpile antice din colecțiile Muzeului Județean de Istorie și Arheologie Prahova – Ploiești [Ancient lamps from the collection of the Prahova County History and Archaeology Museum in Ploiești]. Ploiești: Oscar Print, 2012.

"Vase de tip ploscă descoperite recent în Dobrogea (sec. VI p. Chr.)" [Sixth-century flasks recently found in Dobrudja]. In *Moesica et Christiana. Studies in Honour of Professor Alexandru Barnea*, edited by A. Panaite, R. Cîrjan, and C. Căpiță, 455–461. Brăila: Istros, 2016.

Topoleanu, F. and E. S. Teodor. "Handmade pottery from Halmyris and its cultural context." *Peuce* 7 (2009): 347–360.

Torbatov, S. "Quaestura exercitus: Moesia Secunda and Scythia under Justinian." *ArchBulg* 1 (1997): 78–87.

Monetnata tsirculatsiia v gradishteto krai Odurtsi [Coin circulation in the fortress near Odurtsi]. Turnovo: Faber, 2002.

Ukrepitelnata sistema na provintsiia Skitiia (kraia na III–VII v.) [The fortification system of the province of Scythia (from the end of the third to the seventh century)]. Turnovo: Faber, 2002.

Toren, C. "Drinking cash: the purification of money through ceremonial exchange in Fiji." In *Money and Morality*, 142–164.

Toropu, O. *Romanitatea tîrzie și străromânii în Dacia traiană sud-carpatică (secolele III–XI)* [Late Romanic culture and proto-Romanians in Trajanic Dacia south of the Carpathian Mountains (3rd–11th c.)]. Craiova: Scrisul Românesc, 1976.

Toropu, O., V. Ciucă, and C. Voicu. "Noi descoperiri arheologice în Oltenia" [Recent archaeological finds in Oltenia]. *Drobeta* 2 (1976): 98–102.

Tóth, E. "The Roman province of Dacia." In *History of Transylvania*, edited by B. Köpeczi, 28–61. Budapest: Akadémiai Kiadó, 1994.

"Die awarische Schatzkammer und die Franken." In *Thesaurus Avarorum. Régészeti tánulmanyok Garam Éva tiszteletére*, edited by T. Vida, 773–782. Budapest: Magyar Nemzeti Múzeum, 2012.

Toumanoff, C. "Caucasia and Byzantium." *Traditio* 27 (1971): 111–158.

Trousset, P. "La frontière romaine et ses contradictions." In *La frontière: séminaire de recherche*, edited by Y. Roman, 25–33. Travaux de la Maison de l'Orient no. 21. Paris: Diffusion de Boccard, 1993.

"La notion de 'ripa' et les frontières de l'empire." In *Le fleuve et ses métamorphoses. Actes du Colloque international tenu à l'Université Lyon 3 – Jean Moulin les 13, 14 et 15 mai 1992*, edited by F. Piquet, 141–152. Paris: Didier Érudition, 1994.

Tschoegl, A. E. "Maria Theresa's Thaler: a case of international money." *Eastern Economic Journal* 27, no. 4 (2001): 443–462.

Tsetskhladze, G. R. *Pichvnari and Its Environs, 6th c BC–4th c AD*. Annales littéraires de l'Université de Franche-Comté no. 659. Paris: Presses Universitaires Franc-Comtoises, 1999.

Tsotselia, M. *History and Coin Finds in Georgia: Sasanian and Byzantine Coins from Tsitelitskaro (AD 641)*. Wetteren: Moneta, 2002.

History and Coin Finds in Georgia: Sasanian Coin Finds and Hoards. Wetteren: Moneta, 2003.

Coin Finds in Georgia: (6th Century BC–15th Century AD). Wetteren: Moneta, 2010.

Tsukhishvili, I. "Bich'vint'is bizant'iuri monet'ebi" [Byzantine coins from Pitsunda]. In *Didi Pit'iunt'i. Arkeologiuri gatkhrebi Bich'vint'ashi*, Vol. II, edited by A. Apakidze, 305–334. Tbilisi: Mecniereba, 1977.

Tsukhishvili, I. and G. Depeyrot. *History and Coin Finds in Georgia: Late Roman and Byzantine Hoards (4th–13th c.)*. Wetteren: Moneta, 2003.

Tucci, G. "Origine et développement de la monnaie primitive." *RESS* 21 (1970): 17–36.

Tudor, D. "Sucidava III. Quatrième (1942), cinquième (1943) et sixième (1945) campagnes de fouilles et de recherches archéologiques dans la forteresse de Celei, département de Romanați." *Dacia* 11–12 (1945–1947): 166–208.

"Sucidava IV. Campania a șaptea (1946) și a opta (1947) de săpături și cercetări arheologice în cetățuia dela Celei, reg. Craiova, raionul Corabia" [Report on the seventh (1946) and eighth (1947) archaeological campaign at Celei, Craiova region, Corabia County]. *Materiale arheologice privind istoria veche a RPR*, Vol. I, 693–742. Bucharest: Editura Academiei RPR, 1953.

"Comunicări epigrafice II" [Epigraphic notes II]. *SCIV* 16, no. 1 (1965): 177–188.

Les ponts romains du Bas-Danube. Bucharest: Editura Academiei RSR, 1974.

Oltenia romană [Roman Oltenia]. Bucharest: Editura Academiei RSR, 1978.

Tufescu, V. "Teritoriul și populația României" [Land and people in Romania]. In *Istoria românilor 1*.

Turčan, V. "K historickému pozadiu uloženia depotu v Zemianskom Vrbovku" [The historical context of the hoard from Zemiansky Vrbovok]. In *Byzantská kultúra a Slovensko. Zborník štúdií*, edited by V. Turčan, 41–47. Bratislava: Slovenské Národné Múzeum/Archeologické Múzeum, 2007.

Turcu, M. and C. Marinescu. "Considerații privind 'Foișorul Mavrocordaților'" [Remarks about 'Foișorul Mavrocordaților', Bucharest]. *București. Materiale de istorie și muzeografie* 6 (1968): 119–129.

Turner, F. J. *The Frontier in American History*. New York, NY: Holt, Rinehart and Winston, 1893. Reprint, New York, NY: Holt, Rinehart and Winston, 1962.

Uenze, S. "Die Schnallen mit Riemenschlaufe aus dem 6. und 7. Jahrh." *Bayerische Vorgeschichtsblätter* 31, nos. 1–2 (1966): 142–181.

"Gegossene Fibeln mit Scheinumwicklung des Bügels in den östlichen Balkanprovinzen." In *Studien zur vor- und frühgeschichtlichen Archäologie: Festschrift für Joachim Werner zum 65. Geburtstag*, edited by G. Kossack and G. Ulbert, 483–494. Munich: C. H. Beck, 1974.

Die Spätantiken Befestigungen von Sadovec (Bulgarien). Ergebnisse der deutsch-bulgarisch-österreichischen Ausgrabungen 1934–1937. Munich: C. H. Beck, 1992.

Vachkova, V. "Danube Bulgaria and Khazaria as parts of the Byzantine *oikoumene*." In *The Other Europe in the Middle Ages: Avars, Bulgars, Khazars, and Cumans*, edited by F. Curta, 339–362. Leiden/Boston, MA: Brill, 2008.

Vagalinski, L. "Zur Frage der ethnischen Herkunft der späten Strahlenfibeln (Finger- oder Bügelfibeln) aus dem Donau-Karpaten-Becken (M. 6.-7. Jh.)." *ZfA* 28 (1994): 261–305.

Vakulenko, L. V. and O. M. Prykhodniuk. *Slavianskie poseleniia I tys. n.e. u s. Sokol na Srednem Dnestre* [Slavic settlements from the first millennium at Sokol on the Middle Dniester]. Kiev: Naukova Dumka, 1984.

Van Esbroeck, M. "Lazique, Mingrélie, Svanéthie et Aphkhazie du IVe au IXe siècle." In *Il Caucaso: cerniera fra culture dal Mediterraneo alla Persia (secoli IV–XI)*, Vol. I, 195–218. Spoleto: Centro italiano di studi sull'alto Medioevo, 1996.

Vang Petersen, P. "Excavations at sites of treasure trove finds at Gudme." In *The Archaeology of Gudme and Lundeborg. Papers presented at a Conference at Svendborg, October 1991*, edited by P. O. Nielsen, K. Randsborg, and H. Thrane, 30–40. Copenhagen: Akademisk Forlag, 1994.

Varsik, V. "Byzantinische Gürtelschnallen im mittleren und unteren Donauraum im 6. und 7. Jahrhundert." *Slovesnká Archeológia* 40, no. 1 (1992): 77–106.

Vasić, M. "Le limes protobyzantin dans la province de Mésie Première." *Starinar* 45–46 (1994–1995): 41–53.

Vasić, M. and V. Kondić. "Le limes romain et paléobyzantin des Portes de Fer." In *Studien zu den Militärgrenzen Roms III. 13. internationaler Limeskongreß Aalen 1983. Vorträge*, 542–560. Stuttgart: Konrad Theiss Verlag, 1986.

Velkov, V. *Cities in Thrace and Dacia in Late Antiquity*. Amsterdam: Adolf M. Hakkert, 1977.

"Napis na tsar Anastasiie (491–518) ot Ratiariia" [An inscription of Emperor Anastasius (491–518) from Ratiaria]. *Arkheologiia* (1984), nos. 1–2: 92–94.

"L'état ethnique de Dobrudža au cours du IVe–VIe s." In *Dobrudža. Études ethno-culturelles: recueil d'articles*, edited by D. S. Angelov and D. Ovcharov, 13–21. Sofia: Editions de l'Académie bulgare des sciences, 1987.

Velter, A.-M. "Unele considerații privind circulația monetară din secolele V–XII în bazinul carpatic (cu privire specială asupra teritoriului Romîniei)" [Some observations regarding coin circulation in the Carpathian Basin from the fifth to the twelfth century (with particular emphasis on present-day Romania)]. *SCIV* 39, no. 3 (1988): 251–274.

Transilvania în secolele V–XII. Interpretări istorico-politice și economice pe baza descoperirilor monetare din bazinul Carpatic, secolele V–XII [Transilvania from the fifth to the twelfth century: a political and economic history on the basis of coin finds from the Carpathian Basin]. Bucharest: Paideia, 2002.

Versluys, M. J. "Understanding objects in motion. An archaeological dialogue on Romanization." *Archaeological Dialogues* 21, no. 1 (2014): 1–20.

Viargei, V. S. "Poseleniia prazhskoi kul'tury Belorusskogo Poles'ia" [Prague culture settlements in Polesia, Belarus]. in *Problemy slavianskoi arkheologii*, edited by V. V. Sedov, 28–38. Moscow: Institut Arkheologii RAN, 1997.

Vida, T. *Die Awarenzeitliche Keramik I. (6.–7. Jh.)*. Berlin/Budapest: Balassi Kiadó, 1999.

———. "The Byzantine vessels of the Avars." In *The Gold of the Avars. The Nagyszentmiklós Treasure. Magyar Nemzeti Múzeum, Budapest, 24 March-30 June, 2002*, edited by T. Kovács and É. Garam, 113–119. Budapest: Helikon Kiadó, 2002.

Vidrih Perko, V. "Seaborne trade routes in the North-East Adriatic and their connections to the hinterland in the Late Antiquity." In *L'Adriatico dalla tarda antichità all'età carolingia*, edited by G. Broglio and P. Delogu, 49–77. Rome: All'Insegna del Giglio, 2005.

Vikić-Belančić, B. *Antičke Svjetiljke u Arheološkom Muzeju u Zagrebu* [Ancient lamps from the Archaeological Museum in Zagreb]. Zagreb: Arheološki Muzej, 1976.

Vîlceanu, D. and A. Barnea. "Ceramica lucrată cu mîna din aşezarea romano-bizantină de la Piatra Frecăţei (sec. VI e.n.)" [Hand-made pottery from the Early Byzantine settlement at Piatra Frecăţei (6th c.)]. *SCIVA* 26, no. 2 (1975): 209–218.

Vîlcu, A. *Les monnaies d'or de la Bibliothèque de l'Académie roumaine. II. Monnaies Byzantines*. Wetteren: Moneta, 2009.

Vîlcu, A. and E. Nicolae. "Monede bizantine descoperite la Sucidava" [Byzantine coins found at Sucidava]. In *Arheologia mileniului I p. Chr. Cercetări actuale privind istoria şi arheologia migraţiilor*, edited by B. Ciupercă, 285–321. Bucharest: Oscar Print, 2010.

Vîlcu, A., T. Isvoranu, and E. Nicolae. *Les monnaies d'or de l'Institut d'Archéologie de Bucarest*. Wetteren: Moneta, 2006.

Vinski, Z. "Arheološki spomenici velike seobe naroda u Srijemu" [The archaeological monuments of the Great Migration period in the region of Srem]. *Situla* 2 (1957): 1–77.

Vintilă, C.-M., E.-F. Gavrilă, and T.-A. Ignat. "Două locuinţe din sec. VI-VII descoperite în situl Bucureşti-Dămăroaia" [Two sixth- to seventh-century dwellings from Bucharest 'Dămăroaia']. *Buletinul Muzeului Judeţean Teleorman* 6 (2014): 105–126.

Visy, Z. "Similarities and differences in the Late Roman defense system on the European and Eastern frontiers." In *Limes XVIII: Proceedings of the XVIIIth International Congress of Roman Frontier Studies, Amman, Jordan (September 2000)*, edited by P. Freeman, J. Bennett, Z. T. Fiema, and B. Hoffmann, 71–75. Oxford: Archaeopress, 2002.

Vitelli, K. D. "The lamps." In G. E. Bass and F. H. van Doorninck Jr., *Yassı Ada. Vol. I. A Seventh-Century Byzantine Shipwreck*, 189–201. College Station: Texas A&M University Press, 1982.

Vladimirova-Aladzhova, D. "Oshte za barbarskite imitatsii v monetnoto obrashtenie prez VI vek" [More about the barbarous imitations in circulation during the sixth century]. *Numizmatika i Sfragistika* 5, no. 1 (1998): 70–75.

Voronov, Iu. N. "The Eastern Pontus within the sphere of Byzantine political and cultural activities, the sixth–eighth centuries." In *XVIIIth International Congress of Byzantine Studies. Selected Papers: Main and Communications, Moscow 1991. Vol. II: History, Archaeology, Religion, Theology*, edited by I. Shevchenko and G. G. Litavrin, 167–172. Shepherdstown, WV: Byzantine Studies Press, Inc, 1996.

Tsibilium: la nécropole apsile de Tsibilium (VIIe av. J.-C.–VIIIe ap. J.C). (Abkhazie, Caucase). Oxford: John and Erica Hedges Ltd., 2007.

Voronov, Iu. N. and O. Kh. Bgazhba. *Materialy po arkheologii Tsebel'dy (itogi issledovanii Tsibiliuma v 1978–1982 gg.)* [Archaeological materials from Tsebelda (1978–1982 campaigns)]. Tbilisi: Mecniereba, 1985.

Voronov, Iu. N. and V. A. Iushin. "Pogrebenic VII v. n. e. v s. Tsebel'da v Abkhazii" [A seventh-century burial from Tsebelda, Abkhazia]. *KSIA* 128 (1971): 100–105.

Vulov, V. "Ranni zaselvaniia na slaviani v pridunavskite oblasti na Balkanskiia poluostrov" [Early Slavic settlements in the Danubian region of the Balkans]. In *Bulgariia 1300. Institutsii i durzhavna traditsiia. Dokladi na tretiia kongres na Bulgarskoto Istorichesko Druzhestvo, 3–5 oktombri 1981*, edited by E. Buzhashki, Vol. II, 169–177. Sofia: Bulgarsko Istorichesko Druzhestvo, 1982.

Vynokur, I. S. *Slov'ians'kyi iuveliry Podnistrov'ia. Za materialamy doslidzhen' Bernashivs'kogo kompleksu seredyny I tys. n. e.* [The Slavic jewelry of the Dniester Valley, according to the materials of excavations in the Bernashivka complex of the middle of the first millenium AD]. Kam'ianets' Podil's'kyy: Oium, 1997.

Wallerstein, I. "A world-system perspective on the social sciences." *The British Journal of Sociology* 27, no. 3 (1976): 345–346.

Wamser, L. and R. Gebhard, eds. *Gold: Magie, Mythos, Macht. Gold der alten und neuen Welt*. Stuttgart: Arnoldsche, 2001.

Webster, J. "Creolizing the Roman provinces." *AJA* 105, no. 2 (2001): 209–225.

Wells, C. M. *The German Policy of Augustus. An Examination of the Archaeological Evidence*. Oxford: Clarendon Press, 1972.

Wells, P. S. "Tradition, identity, and change beyond the Roman frontier." In *Resources, Power and Interregional Interaction*, edited by E. M. Shortman and P. A. Urban, 175–187. New York, NY: Plenum Press, 1992.

"Production within and beyond imperial boundaries: goods, exchange, and power in Roman Europe." In *World-Systems Theory in Practice: Leadership, Production, and Exchange*, edited by P. N. Kardulias, 85–101. Boulder, CO: Rowman and Littlefield, 1999.

Wendel, M., S. Angelova, G. Gomolka-Fuchs, J. Herrmann, and E. Schönert-Geiß. *Iatrus-Krivina. Spätantike Befestigung und frühmittelalterliche Siedlung an der unteren Donau. Band III: Die mittelalterlichen Siedlungen.* Berlin: Akademie Verlag, 1986.

Wendl T. and M. Rösler. "Frontiers and borderlands. The rise and relevance of an anthropological research genre." In *Frontiers and Borderlands: Anthropological Perspectives,* edited by T. Wendl and M. Rösler, 1–27. Frankfurt am Main: Peter Lang, 1999.

Werner, J. "Slawische Bügelfibeln des 7. Jahrhunderts." In *Reinecke Festschrift zum 75. Geburtstag von Paul Reinecke am 25. September 1947,* edited by G. Behrens and E. Schneider, 150–172. Mainz: E. Schneider, 1950.

"Byzantinische Gürtelschnallen des 6. und 7. Jahrhunderts aus der Sammlung Diergardt." *Kölner Jahrbuch für Vor- und Frühgeschichte* 1 (1955): 36–48.

"Die frühgeschichtlichen Grabfunde vom Spielberg bei Erlbach, Ldkr. Nördlingen, und von Fürst, Ldkr. Laufen a.d. Salzach." *BV* 25 (1960): 164–179.

"Neues zur Frage der slawischen Bügelfibeln aus süd-osteuropäischen Ländern." *Germania* 38 (1960): 114–120.

Der Grabfund von Malaja Pereščepina und Kuvrat, Kagan der Bulgaren. Munich: C.H. Beck'sche Verlagsbuchhandlung, 1984.

Wheeler, M. *Rome beyond the Imperial Frontier.* London: Bell, 1954.

Whitby, M. "Justinian's bridge over the Sangarius and the date of Procopius' *de Aedificiis.*" *Journal of Hellenic Studies* 105 (1985): 129–148.

"Procopius' description of Dara ("Buildings" II 1–3)." In *The Defence of the Roman and Byzantine East. Proceedings of a Colloquium Held at the University of Sheffield in April 1986,* edited by P. Freeman and D. L. Kennedy, Vol. II, 737–783. BAR International Series 297. Oxford: BAR, 1986.

The Emperor Maurice and His Historian: Theophylact Simocatta on Persian and Balkan Warfare. Oxford: Clarendon Press, 1988.

"Recruitment in Roman armies." In *The Byzantine and Early Islamic Near East III: State, Resources and Armies,* edited by A. Cameron, 61–125. Princeton, NJ: The Darwin Press, 1995.

White, R. *The Middle Ground: Indians, Empires and Republics in the Great Lakes Region, 1650–1815.* Cambridge: Cambridge University Press, 1991.

Whittaker, C. R. *Les frontières de l'Empire romain.* Paris: Belles Lettres, 1989.

Frontiers of the Roman Empire. A Social and Economic Study. Baltimore, MD: Johns Hopkins University Press, 1994.

"Frontiers." In *The Cambridge Ancient History. Volume XI: The High Empire, AD 70–192,* edited by A. K. Bowman, P. Garnsey, and D. Rathbone, 293–319. Cambridge: Cambridge University Press, 2000.

Rome and Its Frontiers: The Dynamics of Empire. New York, NY: Routledge, 2004.

Whittow, M. *The Making of Byzantium, 600–1025.* Los Angeles, CA: University of California Press, 1996.

Wilkes, J. J. "The Roman Danube: an archaeological survey." *JRS* 95 (2005): 124–225.

Williams, D. *The Reach of Rome. A History of the Roman Imperial Frontier 1st–5th Centuries AD*. New York, NY: St. Martin's Press, 1996.

Williams, H. and P. Taylor. "A Byzantine lamp hoard from Anamur (Cilicia)." *Anatolian Studies* 25 (1975): 77–84.

Wilmott, T. "Towers and spies on Chinese and Roman frontiers." In *The Army and Frontiers of Rome. Papers Offered to David J. Breeze on the Occasion of his Sixty-Fifth Birthday and his Retirement from Historic Scotland*, edited by W. S. Hanson, 127–133. JRA Supplementary Series 74. Portsmouth, RI: JRA, 2009.

Winkler, I. "Despre activitatea numismatică a lui Michael Pap Szatmári (1747–1812)" [Notes regarding the numismatic contributions of Michael Pap Szatmári (1747–1812)]. *SCN* 3 (1960): 433–447.

Winter, H. "Die byzantinischen Fundmünzen aus dem österreichischen Bereich der Avaria." In *Die Awaren am Rand der byzantinischen Welt: Studien zu Diplomatie, Handel und Technologietransfer im Frühmittelalter*, edited by F. Daim, 45–66. Innsbruck: Universitätsverlag Wagner, 2000.

"Die byzantinischen und karolingischen Fundmünzen aus dem österreichischen Bereich der Avaria – eine Neubearbeitung." In *Byzantine Coins*, 325–356.

Wolfram, H. *The Roman Empire and Its Germanic Peoples*. Los Angeles, CA: California University Press, 1997.

Wołoszyn, M. "Die byzantinischen Fundstücke in Polen. Ausgewählte Probleme." In *Byzantium and East Central Europe*, edited by G. Prinzing and M. Salamon, 49–59. Cracow: "Historia Iagellonica"/ Jagiellonian University, 2001.

"Byzantine coins from the 6th and 7th c. from Poland and their East-Central European context." In *Roman Coins Outside the Empire: Ways and Phases, Contexts and Functions*, edited by A. Bursche, R. Ciołek, and R. Wolters, 195–224. Wetteren: Moneta, 2008.

"Byzantinische Münzen aus dem 6.–7. Jh. in Polen." In *Byzantine Coins*, 473–530.

Wozniak, F. "Byzantine diplomacy and the Lombardic–Gepid wars." *BS* 20 (1979): 139–158.

Wynne-Jones, S. and J. Fleisher. "Coins in context: local economy, value and practice on the East African Swahili coast." *Cambridge Archaeological Journal* 22, no. 1 (2012): 19–36.

Xanthopoulou, M. *Les lampes en bronze à l'époque paléochrétienne*. Turnhout: Brepols, 2010.

Zábojník, J. "Das Awarische Kaganat und die Slawen an seiner nördlichen Peripherie (Probleme der archäologischen Abgrenzung)." *Slovenská Archeológia* 47, no. 1 (1999): 153–173.

"Antike Münzen im Gebiet der Slowakei aus der Zeit des Awarischen Khaganats." In *Byzantine Coins*, 403–416.

Zaharia, E. "La station n. 2 de Bratei, dép. de Sibiu (VIe–VIIIe siècles)." *Dacia* 38–39 (1994–1995): 297–356.

Zakaraia, P., ed. *Nokalakevi-Arkeopolisi. Arkeologiuri gatkh'rebi*. Vols. I–III. Tbilisi: Mecniereba, 1981–1993.

Zamtaradze, M. "Nokalakevshi aghmochenili amforebi" [Amphora finds at Nokalakevi]. In *Nokalakevi-Arkeopolisi: III. Arkeologiuri gatchrebi 1983–1989*, edited by P. Zakaraia, 158–175. Tbilisi: Mecniereba, 1993.

Zanini, E. "Confini e frontiera: il limes danubiano nel VI secolo." In *MILION. Studi et ricerche d'arte bizantina*, edited by. C. Barsanti, A. G. Guidobaldi, and A. Iacobini, 257–271. Rome: Biblioteca di Storia Patria, 1988.

Zaseckaia, I. P. "Datirovka i proiskhoidenie palchatikh fibul bosporskogo nekropolia rannesrednevekovogo perioda" [The chronology and origin of bow fibulae from the Early Medieval cemetery of Bosporus]. *MAIET* 6 (1997): 394–478.

Zirra, V. and G. Cazimir. "Unele rezultate ale săpăturilor arheologice de pe Cîmpul lui Boja din cartierul Militari" [Some results from the archaeological excavations conducted at Cîmpul lui Boja, Bucharest–Militari]. *CAB* 1 (1963): 56–71.

Zrinyi, A. "Repertoriul localităților din jud. Mureș cu descoperiri arheologice din secolele IV–XIII e.n." [Gazetteer of settlements and archaeological finds from Mureș County (4th–13th c.)]. *Marisia* 6 (1976): 125–151.

Zsoldos, A. "Hongria als segles XII i XIII." In *Princeses de terres llunyanes. Catalunya i Hongria a l'edat mitjana*, edited by F. Makk, M. Miquel, R. Sarobe, and C. Tóth, 145–163. Barcelona/Budapest: Generalitat de Catalunya, Departament de Cultura i Mitjans de Comunicació/Okatási és kulturális minisztérium, 2009.

Zuckerman, C. "The Early Byzantine strongholds in Eastern Pontus." *Travaux et Mémoires* 11 (1991): 527–540.

Zugravu, N. "Cu privire la jurisdicția asupra creștinilor nord-dunăreni în secolele II-VIII" [Notes concerning the jurisdiction over the Christian community north of the Danube between the second and the eighth century]. *Pontica* 28–29 (1995–1996): 164–181.

Geneza creștinismului popular al românilor [The genesis of Romanian Folk Christianity]. Bucharest: Institutul Român de Tracologie, 1997.

Erezii și schisme la Dunărea de Mijloc și de Jos în mileniul I [Heresies and schisms on the Lower and Middle Danube in the first millennium]. Iași: Presa Bună, 1999.

Index

12-nummia, *225–226*, *233*, *235*
Abasgi, *192*, *198*, *200*, *204–205*, *217*
Abasgia, *201*, *203–204*
Abkhazia, *96*, *199*, *201*, *204*, *210*
Accres, *86*
acculturation, *136*, *287*
Adamclisi, *55–56*, *73*, *79*, *93*, *182*
Adjovski gradec, *48*
Adriatic Sea, *53*, *63*, *148*, *157*, *222*
Aegean Sea, *53*, *63–64*, *162*, *182*
Agathias, *18*, *22*, *176*, *194*, *201*, *286*
Aila, *191*
Ak'ura, *213*
Akhali Atoni, *201*
Akhaltsikhe, *207*
Akhtopol, *189*
Alamans, *26*
Alans, *192*, *202–203*, *207*
Alba-Iulia, *55–56*, *61*, *64*, *107*
Albania, *18*, *90*, *194*, *196*, *206–208*, *211*
Alboin, king, *230*
Alcedar-Odaia, *274*
Alexandretta, *235*
Alexandria, *189*, *201*, *225–226*, *233*, *235*
Alföldi, Andreas, *11*, *20*
Almăjel, *171*
Alps, *122*, *217*, *232*, *287*
Amasra, *201*
Amasya, *196*
Ambéli, *254*, *256*
Ambroz, A. K., *246*
Amorium, *57*
amphorae, *6*, *40–41*, *46*, *48–50*, *69*, *80*, *139*, *142*, *170–171*, *201*, *205*, *283*
  LR1, LR2, *48*, *51*, *142*, *282*
  Pontic, *51*
  spatheia, *48*, *64*
Anastasius, *8*, *96*, *137*, *152*, *157*, *160*, *162–163*, *168*, *170*, *192*, *199*, *202*, *207*, *221–223*, *228*, *244*
Anatolia. *See* Asia Minor
Anchialus, *181*
Andes Mountains, *252*, *260*

Anemurium, *55*, *58*
Ani, *199*, *204*, *206*, *209*
Annaeus Florus, *22*
annona, *46*, *48*, *69*, *139*, *142*, *150*, *162*, *283*
Antes, *4*, *86*, *92*, *128*, *141*, *144*, *156*, *173*, *190*, *265*, *268*, *270*, *280*, *287*
Antioch, *159*, *172*, *177*, *180–181*, *185*, *200–201*, *207*
Apalina, *225*
Apsili, *192*, *198*, *200*, *205*
Apsilia, *201*, *204–205*
Apulum. *See* Alba-Iulia
Aquis, *56*, *59*, *80*, *96*, *115*, *184*
Arabia, *132*, *152*, *203*, *232*
Arabs, *1*, *187*, *214–215*
Arad, *236*
Araxes river, *208*, *215*
Archaeopolis, *157*, *198*, *200*, *207*, *209*, *212–213*
Archar, *53*
Ardagast, *170*, *182*
Argamum, *74*
Argeș river, *170*
aristocracy. *See* elites
Aristotle, *258*
Armenia, *7*, *194*, *198–200*, *202*, *204*, *206*, *209–211*, *213–215*, *217*
  Prima, *196*
  Secunda, *196*
Arnoldstein, *231*
Artaxata, *19*
Asia Minor, *53*, *56–59*, *96*, *99*, *183*, *193*, *207*, *211*
Asparuch, *188*
Assyria, *15*
At'ots'i, *215*
Athanaric, *26*, *107*
Athens, *53*, *64*
Attila, *24*, *26*, *112*, *114*, *137*, *147*, *161*, *190*, *217*, *220*
Augustus, *228*
Aurelian, *33*, *138*, *160*
Austria, *223*, *226–227*, *233*, *236*, *238*

Auxentius, *106*
Avaria, *9*, *49*, *53*, *67*, *74–75*, *98*, *122*, *124–125*, *230–231*, *233*, *235–236*, *240*, *263*, *287*
Avars, *4*, *7*, *19*, *26–27*, *30*, *49*, *76*, *79*, *93*, *98–99*, *126*, *134*, *140*, *147–148*, *176*, *179–183*, *186*, *190*, *193*, *205*, *209–211*, *217*, *220*, *229–232*, *236*, *239*, *261*, *263–264*, *266–269*, *271–272*, *280–281*, *285*, *287*
Axiopolis, *179*, *185*
Azande, *253*
Azov Sea, *216*

Bacău, *86*, *175*, *180*
Bački Monoštor, *236*
Bahram, general, *208*
Baian, *27*, *268*
Băiceni, *173*
Balaton, lake, *79*
Balatonfüzfő-Szalmássy, *122*
Balotaszállás, *222*
Balta Verde, *99*
Baltic Sea, *75*, *157*, *178*, *193*, *221*
Banat, *126*, *162*, *176–178*, *184*, *224*
Banatski Karlovac, *225*
Bancerovoe, *75*
Bârlad, *167*, *182*, *188*
Bârlălești, *85*
Bartel, Brad, *136*
barter, *272*
Bartym, *279*
Baruya, *251*
Batumi, *199*
Bavaria, *226–227*
Beclean, *226*
Bejan, Adrian, *82*
Béla IV, *20*
Belarus, *75*, *84*, *189*
Belgrade, *6*, *96*, *223–224*
Belisarius, *115*, *226*
Beloyariv'ka, *172*, *265*
Berezeni, *189*
Bernashivka, *73–75*, *88*
Beroe, *38*, *55*, *59*
Beth She'an, *263*
Bhabha, Homi, *136*
Biertan, *108–109*
Bjelovar, *227*
Black Sea, *64*, *98*, *154*, *172*, *187*, *196*, *200–201*, *203*, *209*, *253*
  coast, *48*, *55*, *63*, *96*, *99*, *162*, *181–182*, *189*, *191*, *193*, *196*, *199*, *202*, *206*, *211–212*, *215*, *249*, *266*, *285*
  east of, *15*, *205*
  north of, *51*, *74*, *138*, *148*, *152*, *169*, *171*, *185–186*, *244*, *246*, *261*, *265*, *287*
  west of, *49*, *63*, *65*, *175*, *189*
Blancart, M., *255*
Boa, *202*
Bočar, *225*
Bohemia, *157*, *222*, *228*, *235*, *238*
Bohouňovice, *232*
Bohuslavice, *234*, *238*
Bol'shaia Orlovka, *216*
Boljetin, *179*
Bóna, István, *247*
Bonosus, *127*
Borniș, *84*, *97*
Borolea, *171*
Borșeni, *85*
Bosman, *182*
Bosnia, *223*
Bosporus, *202*
Botoșana, *36*, *49*, *73–74*, *124*, *170*, *277*
bracteates, *215*, *221*, *263*
Bratei, *52*, *67*, *93*
British West Africa, *254*
Brody, *96*
brooches, *6*, *41*, *49–50*, *58*, *97*, *124*, *142*, *150*, *278*, *284*
  bow, *87–88*, *90–93*, *118*, *180*, *277*, *282*
  cast, with bent stem, *76–77*, *81–82*, *84–86*, *144*
  Cividale, *85*
  East Germanic, *88*
  with bent stem, *76–77*, *79–81*, *85*, *88*, *92*, *125*, *142*, *180*
  Zaseckaia, *77*
Brown, Peter, *8*
Bucharest, *37*, *79*, *126*, *147*, *170*, *178*, *189*, *274*
  Băneasa, *50*
  Cățelu Nou, *37*, *50*, *278*
  Ciurel, *37*
  Foişorul Mavrocordaților, *50*
  Măgurele, *169*
  Mihai Vodă, *50*
  Militari, *79–80*
  Soldat Ghivan, *49–50*, *52*, *67*, *75*
  Străulești, *74–75*
  Străulești-Lunca, *37*, *124*
  Străulești-Măicănești, *37*, *50*
  Tei, *88*
buckles, *6*, *41*, *49–50*, *58*, *74*, *94*, *97*, *99*, *124*, *142*, *150*, *180*, *284*
  Beroe, *94*, *96*
  Corinth, *90*

Pápa, *97–98*
Salona-Histria, *97–98*
Sucidava, *84*, *94*, *96*, *98*, *118*, *125*, *144*
Syracuse, *97–99*
Bucovina, *36*
Budapest, *156*, *236*
Buduma, *251*
Budureasca, *73–75*, *147*
Bujanovac, *53*
Bukhlichskii Khutor, *84*
Bulgaria, *4*, *44*, *64*, *80*, *82*, *90*, *96*, *168*, *189*
Bulgars, *22*, *155*, *173*, *186–190*, *237*, *247*, *282*
   first state, *44*
Bumbeşti, *55*
Butrint, *93*
Buzău, *147*, *180–181*, *185*
Byllis, *18*

Calafat, *175*
Caliphate, *214–215*
Callatis, *59*
Callinicum, *19*
Cameroon, *251*, *256*
Cândeşti, *67*
Capidava, *5*, *40*, *53*, *55–57*, *59*, *61*, *179*, *184*
Căprioara, *90*
Capris. See Koper
Caričin Grad, *58*, *61*, *63*, *67*, *73–74*, *82*, *92–93*
Carinthia, *231*
Cârja, *171*
Carnuntum, *227*, *232–233*, *235*
Carolingian. See Charlemagne
Carpathian
   barrow culture, *36*
   Basin, *7*, *148*, *154–155*, *157*, *159*, *161*, *169*, *217*, *220*, *224*, *226*, *229–230*, *232*, *234*, *240*, *247*, *261*, *263*, *284–287*
   Mountains, *7*, *21*, *42*, *49–50*, *75*, *85–86*, *99*, *102*, *118*, *120*, *125*, *138*, *148*, *160*, *167*, *170–171*, *173*, *258*, *283*
Carpi, *36–37*
Carthage, *188–189*, *201*, *211*, *228*, *232–233*, *235*, *238*
Caspian Sea, *178*, *206*, *285*
Catania, *235*, *239*
Caucasus Mountains, *7*, *15*, *96*, *191–193*, *200*, *205*, *208*, *210*, *217*, *237*, *240*, *258*, *263*, *285*
   Dariel, *202*, *208*
   Gates, *192–193*, *211*
   Klukhor, *200*

Marukha, *200*
north of, *203*, *207*, *210*, *212*, *215–216*, *246*, *261*
Celje, *231*, *238*
centenarium, *203*, *205*
Červený Hrádek, *228*
Cetea, *226*
Ch'andrebi, *213*
Ch'iatura, *210*
Ch'iora, *213*
Ch'khalt'a, *201*
Ch'orvila, *215*
Chad, *251*
Chad, lake, *251*
Chaopincha, *260*
Charlemagne, *230*
Chełm, *228*
Chernyakhov culture, *34*, *36*, *76*, *88*, *137*, *161*
Cherry, David, *152*
Chersonesus, *56*, *64*, *175*, *201*
Chibati, *212*, *240*, *261*
Chilbudius, *28*, *114–115*, *138*, *172*, *175*, *268*, *270*
China, *11*
Chkhorotsqu, *205*
Chmi, *210*
Chornivka, *84*
Chosroes I, *203*
Chosroes II, *20*, *208–210*, *213–214*
Chotusice, *222*
Christianity
   artifacts, *107*, *116*, *118*, *128*
      crosses, *73*, *97*, *116*, *120*, *127*, *144*, *148*, *150*
         Maltese, *74*, *122*, *125*
      flasks, *116*, *120*, *126*, *177*
         Menas, *122*, *128*
      lamps, *108*, *116–117*, *120*, *124–125*
   bishoprics, *119–120*
   burials, *102*
   canons, *103*, *119*
   cemeteries, *117–118*
   churches, *108*, *117*, *120*, *201*, *265*
   Folk, *102*
   identity, *17*, *84*, *124*, *142*, *151*
   in *barbaricum*, *101*, *103–106*, *109*, *112*, *115–117*, *120*, *126*, *128–130*, *144*, *284*
   in Transcaucasia, *198*, *201*
   lamps, *283*
   missions, *119*
   practices, *52*, *63*, *107*, *117*, *126*, *144*
   symbolism, *84*, *118*, *120*, *125–126*, *153*

Christianity (cont.)
   transdanubian, *3, 41*
   Trinity, *256*
   vocabulary, *110*
Chufut Kale, *93*
Cilicia, *55, 215*
Ciołek, Renata, *222*
Cioroiu Nou, *175*
Cividale, *236*
Coada Izvorului, *180*
Colchis. *See* Lazica
Cologne, *25*
Colombia, *260*
Comănești, *185, 277*
Congo, *251–253, 260*
Constans II, *186, 188, 214–216, 235, 237–240*
Constanța, *55–57, 63–64, 189*
Constantine IV, *187–189, 214–215, 237, 240*
Constantine the Great, *25, 27–28, 34, 103–105, 107, 112–113*
Constantinople, *26, 32, 55–58, 96, 112, 119, 122, 131, 138, 147, 190, 193, 208, 213, 216, 224, 227, 229, 261, 264, 269, 281–282, 285*
   mint, *159, 172, 175, 177, 232*
   siege of, *49, 186–187, 220, 236–237, 262*
Constantiolus, *264*
Constantius Chlorus, *113*
Constantius II, *106–107*
continuity thesis, *3, 5, 43, 110, 118*
Corinth, *64*
Coșoveni, *188*
Coșovenii de Jos, *88, 90*
Cotești, *185*
Cotiso, king, *22*
cowrie, *251*
Craiova, *126–127, 169*
Crete, *53*
Crimea, *51, 56, 63, 74, 77, 88, 91, 93, 98–99, 170, 172*
Cristuru Secuiesc, *74*
Crnomelj, *48*
Croatia, *63, 223, 226–227, 277*
Cucorăni, *126, 177*
Cudalbi, *171*
Cunimund, king, *230–231*
Curcani, *188*
curopalates, *208*
Curzon, Lord of Kedleston, *21*
Cutrigurs, *22, 30, 138, 172–173, 190, 205, 265, 270, 280, 286–287*
Cyprus, *38, 40*

Cyzicus, *185*
Czech Republic, *75, 157, 222–223, 226–229, 232, 234–235, 238*

Dacia, *122*
   diocese, *80, 114*
   kingdom, *23, 33, 249*
   Mediterranea, *58, 63, 80, 93*
   Ripensis, *55, 63, 80, 82, 98, 184*
   transdanubian, *21, 23, 25–26, 37, 42–44, 53, 61, 63, 67, 75, 101, 103–105, 107, 109–110, 112–113, 117–118, 120, 124, 128, 137–138, 142, 147–148, 150, 160, 280, 283*
Dacians, *22*
Dacicus Maximus, *105*
Daco-Roman, *43, 87, 101–102, 108, 110, 118, 162, 244*
Dafne, *25, 30, 105, 113*
Dagistheus, *206*
Dalmatia, *63–64, 122, 128, 148, 221, 231, 287*
Dănceni, *93, 118*
Dande, *259*
Dănești, *97, 118*
Danube, *269*
   as cultural interface, *6, 150, 152*
   as frontier, *2, 6, 8, 11, 16, 18–22, 24–27, 30, 32–33, 36, 41, 48, 52, 76, 80, 91–92, 97–98, 105, 111, 117, 120, 128–129, 131, 133–134, 136, 138–139, 141–142, 144, 148, 151–152, 154, 167, 171–173, 176, 181–183, 185, 187, 189–190, 193–194, 206, 216, 249, 253, 270, 273, 280–282, 287*
   Delta, *6, 188–189, 270*
   fortifications, *18, 38, 81, 96, 114, 119, 140, 142, 171, 180, 183, 217, 223, 279, 282*
   god *Danubius*, *26*
   Iron Gates of, *80, 82, 86, 93, 115, 127, 142, 167, 173, 175, 181, 223*
   Lower, *5, 7, 14, 20–21, 26, 28, 36, 38, 48, 53, 55–58, 61, 63, 65, 69, 84, 87, 90, 94, 98–99, 104, 106, 112, 115, 118, 129, 137, 144, 147, 154–155, 159, 161, 169–170, 180, 183, 187, 190, 193, 196, 203–204, 217, 220–221, 227, 235, 249, 271, 284–286*
   Middle, *48, 64, 67, 80, 85, 94, 98–99, 124, 147–148, 178, 182, 217, 221, 227, 229, 231, 237, 246, 249, 286*

north of, *27–28*, *31*, *36*, *41*, *43*, *49*, *51–52*, *57–58*, *64*, *69*, *71*, *74*, *76*, *81*, *85*, *87*, *92–93*, *97–100*, *102–107*, *109*, *111–112*, *114–116*, *118–119*, *122*, *124–125*, *127–128*, *130–132*, *135*, *139–140*, *142*, *144*, *148*, *151–153*, *161–162*, *175–177*, *179–184*, *194*, *226*, *231*, *252*, *266–268*, *270*, *272*, *274*, *278*, *281*, *283–284*, *286*
provinces, *73*, *84*, *111*, *124*, *127*, *134*, *140*, *150*, *156*, *162*, *168*, *173*, *179–180*, *182–183*, *269*, *271*
road along, *30*
south of, *4*, *22*, *81*, *86*, *88*, *90*, *110*, *124*, *128*, *159*, *265*, *267–268*
Upper, *219*, *223*
Dara, *19*
Dardania, *53*
Darius the Great, *22*
Davideni, *73–74*, *79–80*, *84–85*, *122*, *125*
decanummium (¼ *follis*), *77*, *160*, *169*, *175*, *182*, *185*, *226*, *228*, *231–233*, *235*
Dedoplitskaro, *213*
Dej, *53*
Delphi, *63*
Denmark, *239*
Dervent, *91*
Deultum, *65*
Dez, Jacques, *256*
Diaconescu, Alexandru, *65*
Didi Chqoni, *212*
Dierna. See Orşova
Dinogetia, *38*, *61*, *91*, *96*, *142*
Dionysopolis, *63*
Dmanisi, *202*, *207*
Dnieper river, *51*, *79–80*, *85*, *171*, *173*
Dniester river, *81*, *184*
Dobrudja, *44*, *61*, *65*, *90*, *120*, *189*
Domneşti, *170*
Don river, *216*
donativum, *177*
Donets'k, *265*
Dorobanţi, *168*, *223*
Dorotheus, *199*
drachm, Sasanian, *7*, *204*, *208–209*, *212–214*
Drăgăşani, *187–188*
Dranda, *210*
Drava river, *217*, *223*, *237*, *287*
Drobeta, *30*, *57*, *64*, *82*, *97–98*, *167–169*, *175*, *177*, *179*, *181*, *184*, *193*
Dubovac, *90*
Dulceanca, *36*, *50*, *126*, *140*

Dunafalva, *240*
Dunăreni, *55*
Dunaújváros, *67*
Durostorum, *55*, *96*, *184*, *189*
Dusheti, *204*
Dvin, *206*, *209*, *211*, *214*
Dzhaga, *215*
Dzhiginka, *202*, *208*

earrings, *76*
Echmiazdin, *215*
Edessa, *91*
Egerlövő, *262*
Egypt, *11*, *31*, *53*, *63*, *122*, *183*, *211*
Einhard, *230*
Eisenstadt, *227*
Elbe river, *222*, *237*
elites, *6*, *50*, *76*, *116*, *128*, *150*, *213*, *225*, *228*, *230*, *234*, *239*, *285*
England, *156*
Ephesus, *53*
Epirus, *93*
Erzurum, *196*
Eski Kermen, *93*
Estonia, *74*
Euboea, *260*. See Ambéli
Euphrates, *18*, *26*, *193*, *200*
Eusebius of Caesarea, *106*
Evagrius, *232*

Fălciu, *274*
Fali, *256*
Feldioara-Războieni, *58*
Fclnac, *88*
Fenékpuszta, *117*
Feteşti, *181*
fibulae. See brooches
Fiji, *259*
Firtuşu, *234*
foederati, *221*, *249*, *282*
follis, *96*, *160*, *167–168*, *170*, *175*, *177*, *180*, *185*, *189*, *201*, *207*, *226*, *231*, *235*, *238*, *254–255*, *272*, *274*, *277*
Franks, *226*
Fritigern, *107*

Gaatha, *112*
Gabrovo, *81*
Găeşti, *171*
Galaţi, *188*
Gambia, *259*
Gaza, *53*
General Kantardzhievo, *79–80*

Georgia, *157, 194, 196, 200, 204, 206, 208, 210, 212, 214, 216, 240, 244, 261*
Georgios Pisides, *27*
Gepidia, 9, 224
Gepids, *4, 19, 30, 93, 99, 114–115, 128, 138, 147, 162, 168, 176, 190, 221–222, 224–226, 230, 265, 268–270, 272, 280, 283, 287*
Germanic, *38, 128, 132, 161, 217, 222, 229, 235, 283*
Ghana, *252*
Ghassanids, *132*
Gheorghe Doja, *225*
Gherla, *65, 168, 223*
Gibbon, Edward, *11*
Giurgița, *179*
Goddas, *112*
Gogoșu, *181*
Goicea, *181*
Golesh, *79*
Gorna Sekirna, *74*
Goryachi Klyuch, *202*
Gothia, 105–107, 119
Goths, *19, 24, 26, 105–106, 109, 112, 114, 137*
  Crimean, *99*
  Ostrogoths, *162, 167, 220–223, 226, 264*
  Tetraxite, *202, 205*
Grand Strategy, *6, 12–13, 15, 280*
Gratian, *98*
Greece, *53, 58, 61, 63–64, 91*
Grepes, king, *119*
Grod, king, *119, 202*
Grodzisko Dolne, *238*
Gropeni, *179, 184*
Gropșani, *37*
Grtchi, *214*
Grumezoaia, *277*
Guaram, *208*
Gubazes, king, *203–205*
Gudme, *239*
Gurjaani, *216*
Gutinaș, *50*
Gvank'iti, *216*
Gveso, *200*
Gyenesdiás, *237*
Gyula, *225*
Gyumri, *215*

Hadrian, *23*
Haemimontus, *168*
Hajdúdorog-Városkert, *235*
Hajdúnánás-Fürjhalom-járás, *236–237*

half-follis, 175–177, 182, 184, 206–207, 228, 231–232, 235
Halmyris, *38, 53, 55–57, 59, 61*
Hansca, *50, 75, 85*
hasina, 259
Hausa, *253*
Heraclius, *8, 20, 27, 157, 180, 184, 186, 211–214, 229, 233–238, 274, 277*
Hercules, *256*
Herodotus, *22*
Herules, *114, 128, 138, 141, 148, 168, 176, 190, 222–224, 226, 266, 270*
hexagrammon, 157, 187, 189, 196, 211–214, 236, 238, 240, 243, 277, 279, 286–287
Histria, *56, 58, 77, 96, 98, 140*
Holy Land. *See* Syria-Palestine
Horga, *274*
Horgești, *109, 182, 239, 277*
Hormizd, *208*
Hradec Králové, *228*
Hradyz'ke, *80*
Hrozová, *157, 238*
Hrozová river, *238*
Hungary, *4, 20, 44, 79–80, 124, 222, 227, 231, 233, 236–237, 240, 261–262, 278*
Huns, *24, 26, 29, 34, 107, 112, 137, 147, 161–162, 190, 264, 267, 286*
  Sabir, *202–203, 207*

Iași, *126*
Iatrus, *56, 59, 127, 140*
Iberia, *7, 192, 194, 196, 202, 204, 206–209, 213, 215–217, 285*
Ibida, *84*
Ibn Battuta, *252*
Iğdır, *214*
Igren', *79*
Ildiges, *270*
Illyricum, *18, 38, 53, 61, 74, 81, 98, 107, 109, 112, 114, 126, 148, 167, 173, 180, 182, 184, 223–224, 232, 268, 270, 273, 281*
Ilych, *205*
imitations, *135, 171*
  amphorae, *49, 52*
  brooches, *81, 84*
  buckles, *94, 97*
  coins, *168, 178, 201, 207, 212, 221, 227–228, 231, 249, 261–263, 273, 278*
    Kiskőrös, *240*
  lamps, *61, 63–65, 150*
inflation, *180, 242, 251*

Inka, *16*
Innocent IV, pope, *20*
Ipotești, *49, 278*
Isaac, Benjamin, *1*
Istanbul. See Constantinople
Italy, *48, 63, 115, 122, 148, 175, 188, 190, 201, 220–222, 224, 226–227, 229, 231, 235, 238–239, 270, 280, 287*
Iuzhnoe, *184*
Izvoru Dulce, *74*

Jerome, *24*
Jerusalem, *183*
jewelry, *41, 45, 49–50, 71, 73, 75–76, 97, 100, 124, 150, 171, 186, 221, 225, 230, 238–240, 243, 252, 254, 263, 274, 278–279, 282, 284, 286*
  bracelets, *91, 256*
  coins, *3, 210, 235, 261–262, 273, 285*
  earrings, *74, 85, 256*
    Deszk, *74*
    silver, *85, 90*
    star-shaped, *240*
  finger rings
    coins, *230, 262*
  necklaces, *203, 256*
    coins, *262*
  pendants, *73*
    coins, *171, 230, 262–263, 286*
    precious stones, *202*
    star-shaped, *85, 90*
Jireček Line, *111*
Jiu river, *171*
John Chrisostomos, *198*
John Dacnas, general, *205*
John of Biclar, *206*
John of Ephesus, *266*
John of Nikiu, *186*
Jordanes, *224*
Julian, *18, 196*
Jupiter, *128*
Justin I, *157, 169–171, 199, 202, 210, 222–223, 225, 228, 274*
Justin II, *19, 26, 77, 157, 159, 176–179, 182, 204, 206–208, 230–232, 239, 261, 274*
Justinian, *2, 8, 18, 27, 29–30, 32, 34, 40, 61, 64, 77, 81, 96, 103, 112–113, 115, 119–120, 128–129, 134–135, 138–139, 141, 144, 148, 150, 157, 159, 169–177, 179, 182, 185, 191, 196, 198–205, 207, 217, 221–223, 225–229, 231, 238, 255, 264–265, 270–271, 274, 287*

Justinian II, *189, 215–216*
Justiniana Prima. See Caričin Grad
Jutas, *262*

K'rts'anisi, *202*
Kabardino-Balkaria, *208*
Kalaja, *53*
Kamenovo, *90*
Kamunta, *207, 210*
Kapauku Papuans, *251*
Kapitan Dimitrovo, *86*
Karachayevo-Cherkesiya, *215*
Karasura, *59, 65*
Karlino, *221*
Karnobat, *99*
Karsibór, *221*
Katanga, *252*
Kavetchina, *81*
Kelegeia, *186*
Kenya, *258–259*
keration, *264*
Kerch, *56, 74*
Keszthely, *80*
Keszthely-Fenékpuszta, *127*
Kharalambieva, Anna, *82*
Khazars, *215–216, 247*
Kherson, *170*
Kiev, *51, 169*
Kilwa, *255*
Kirovohrad, *186*
Kiselivka, *169*
Kiskundorozsma, *237*
Kislovodsk, *208, 212*
Kiss, Attila, *236*
Kiszombor, *222*
Kiszombor-Tanyahalom-dűlő, *235*
Klimovka, *51*
Klosterneuburg, *227*
Kluk, *235*
Kobuleti, *205*
Kodyn, *36*
Kolín, *223, 238*
Kölked-Feketekapu, *48, 67, 74, 85, 98–99, 231, 261–262*
Koper, *48, 63*
Koprivets, *182*
Korbovo, *80*
Korchak, *38, 92, 126*
Környe, *97*
Kosh, *215*
Kotoko, *251*
Kötschach-Laas, *227*
Kozloduy, *63*

Kramolin, *80*
Kranevo, *55*
Kranj, *48*, *227*
Krasnodar, *201–202*, *205*, *212*
Križna gora, *48*
Kruje, *90*
Kšely, *234*, *238*
Kuber, *247*
Kubrat, *186*, *237*
Kunbábony, *49*
Kupusina, *236*
Kushnarenkovo, *49*
Kutaisi, *200*, *207*, *209*
Kuzebaevo, *279*
Kuzhendeevsky, *75*
Kwaio, *254*, *259*
Kwanga, *259*

L'viv, *81*
Lamba, *251*
lamps, *6*, *41*, *75*, *142*, *150*, *253*, *283*
    Anatolian, *59*
    bronze, *52–53*, *63*, *108*, *122*, *148*
    Danubian, *53*, *55–58*, *61*, *125*
    hand-made, *50*, *67*, *171*
    North African, *61*, *63–64*, *125*, *127*, *148*
    Palestinian, *65*, *177*
László, Gyula, *247*
Latin (language), *3*, *8*, *106*, *110–111*, *115*, *142*
Lattimore, Owen, *11*
Lăureni, *225*
Lazica, *191–192*, *194*, *198–200*, *202–207*, *209–210*, *212*, *215*, *217*, *285*
Lederata, *29*, *115*
Leo I, *26*, *137*
Leontius, *216*
Lezhë, *88*, *90*
Lhomi, *253*, *256*, *258*
Libanius, *22*
limes, *12*, *28*, *41*, *90*, *152*, *184–185*, *223*
Linz, *236*, *277*
Lipova, *53*
Litterata, *113*
Liuliakovo, *88*, *90*
Ljubljana, *223*
Łódź, *232*
Lombards, *4*, *128*, *138*, *222–223*, *226–227*, *229–230*, *272*, *287*
Loosi, *74*
Lopatna, *274*
Lovosice, *226*
Luchistoe, *74*, *93*
Luciu, *53*, *120*

Luka Raikovetskaia, *274*
lustrum, *159*
Luttwak, Edward, *12*, *20*
Lužice, *222*, *227*
Lydia, *56*
Lyon, *25*

Macedonia, *61*, *77*, *93*
Madagascar, *249*, *252*, *254–256*, *258–259*, *261*, *273*
Magraneti, *157*, *214*
Măgureanu, Andrei, *49*
Magyars, *4*, *44*
Mainz, *25*
Maistrov, *186*
Malalas, *264*
Malatya, *196*
Małechowo, *221*
Mali, *252*
Malinowski, Bronisław, *250*
Malo Pereshchepyne, *186*, *261*
Mănăstioara, *178*
Maratice, *227*
Marcian, *167*
Marcus Aurelius, *278*
Maria Saal, *233*, *235*
Maria Theresa. *See* thaler
Mars, *128*
Martin, general, *205*
Martínez, Oscar, *136*
marzban, *206*
Masis, *214*
Maurice, *20*, *27–28*, *30*, *144*, *180–182*, *207–210*, *212–213*, *233–234*, *236*, *262*, *264*, *269–270*, *282*
Maximianus, *18*
Mayeur, Nicolas, *255*
Media Atropatene, *192*
Mediterranean, *128*, *160*, *200–201*, *228*, *232–233*, *235*, *238*, *250*, *253*
Melanesia, *250*
Melitene, *207*
Menander Protector, *30*, *179*, *194*, *266*, *268*
Mercury, *128*
Merina, *255*, *258*, *273*
Mermeroes, *204–205*
Mesoamerica, *252*
Mesopotamia, *19*
metallurgical activity, *69*, *71*, *147*, *170*, *274*, *279*, *284*
Metcalf, D. M., *221*
Mexico, *260*
miasa, *258*

Michael the Syrian, *271*
mikarama, *258*
miliarense, *7*, *159*, *176*, *196*, *200–202*, *205*, *222*, *227*, *240–241*, *243*
Misimia, *205*
Misimiani, *198*, *200*, *205*
Miskolc, *236*
Mitterndorf, *227*
Moesia, *22–23*, *113*, *144*, *264*
  Prima, *82*, *98*, *169*, *184*
  Secunda, *44*, *55*, *79*, *82*, *84*, *86*, *92*, *97–98*, *172*, *188*, *277*
  Upper, *136*
Moigrad, *53*, *107*, *122*
Mokranjske Stene, *56*, *96*
Mokraya Balka, *208*, *210*
Mokronog, *223*
Moldavia, *36–37*, *46*, *80*, *84*, *86*, *97–99*, *109*, *118*, *120*, *122*, *124*, *126*, *142*, *144*, *147*, *161*, *170–171*, *173*, *175*, *177–178*, *182*, *184*, *188–189*, *239*, *274*, *277*, *283–284*
Moldova, *118*, *167*, *170*, *181*, *244*, *274*
Moldoveni, *80*, *118*
molds, *45*, *49–50*, *55*, *59*, *61*, *69*, *71*, *73–75*, *82*, *88*, *100*, *120*, *124–125*, *127*, *144*, *148*, *274*, *279*, *286*
Mondevergue, Marquis de, *261*
Mongo, *252*
Mongols, *20*
Moravia, *232*, *238*
Moreşti, *225*
Mostová, *238*
Movileni, *185*
Movses Dashkurantsi, *211–212*
Mrzezino, *221*
Mtkvari river, *207*, *215*
Mtskheta, *202*, *209*, *213*
Muawiya, *214–215*
Mundus, *202*, *223*, *270*
Mureş river, *222*, *225*
Murighiol, *55*
Musanga, *260*

Naissus, *24*
Nalbant, *67*
Narses, *226*
nationalism, *3*, *10*, *42–44*, *101*, *110*, *244*, *283*
Nea Anchialos, *61*, *77*, *96*
Near East. See Syria-Palestine
Nedao, battle, *221*
Nekresi, *209*

Nepal, *253*, *256*, *258*
Nerva, *278*
Neulengbach, *238*
New Georgia, *259*
Nicomedia, *159*, *177*, *207*, *232*
Nicopolis, *277*
Niger, *252*
Nigeria, *251–252*
Nikephoros, *186*
Nisibis, *19*
Nokalakevi. See Archaeopolis
Noricum, *224*
Normandy, *96*
North Africa, *1*, *12*, *14*, *48*, *61*, *64*, *115*, *152*, *188*, *201*, *221*, *229*, *235*, *238–239*, *253*
North Ossetia-Alania, *207*, *210*
Nost'e, *202*
Novaci, *188*
Novae, *56–57*, *61*, *86*, *96*, *184*
Novi Banovci, *127*
Noviodunum, *55*, *184*
Novosils'ke, *181*
Nubia, *119*

Oarda de Jos, *226*
Obârşeni, *188*
obolus, *230*, *237*, *262*
Oceania, *251*
Ochamchire, *210*
Odessos, *96*
Odishi, *213*
Oescus, *25*, *74*, *96*, *105*
Ok'ami, *216*
Oka river, *79*
Olari, *171*
Olt river, *37*, *67*, *171*, *188*
Olteni, *50*, *74*, *124*
Oltenia, *55*, *126*, *142*, *147*, *160*, *171*, *176–178*, *184–185*, *188*, *240*, *273*, *283*
Olteniţa, *184*
Oltina, *55*
Orlea, *181*
Orosius, *23*
Orşova, *30*, *56*, *97*, *113*, *122*, *169*, *184*
Osijek, *226*, *277*
Ostrogoths. See Goths
Ostrovu Banului, *179*
Ostrovu Mare, *181*
Ostrówek, *235*
Ottomans, *21*, *26*

Palestine, *31*. See Syria-Palestine
Palmyra, *96*

Pannonia, *56*, *79*, *107*, *109*, *112*, *148*, *176*, *221*, *224*, *227*, *230–231*, *273*
Papua New Guinea, *251*, *259*
Parker, Bradley, *15–16*
Parutyne, *175*
patricius, *186*
Pavlivka, *182*, *277*
Pechanka, *207*
Pechenaya, *186*
Pecica, *226*
Pécs, *227*
Pécs-Alsómakár-dűlő, *261*
Penkovka, *38*, *92*
pentanummium (⅛ *follis*), *160*, *169–170*, *175*, *180*, *199*, *226*
Periam, *126*
Pernik, *59*, *80*, *84*, *96*
Persia, *7*, *18–20*, *32*, *132*, *152*, *157*, *181*, *191*, *194*, *198*, *205–206*, *208–211*, *213*, *221*, *232*, *263*
Persians, *25*, *183*, *186*, *191–192*, *202–204*, *208*, *211*, *263*
Pet Mogilii, *79*
Petra, *31*, *198*, *203–204*
Petropavlovo, *96*
Petrus, general, *28*, *181–182*
Phasis, *206*. See Poti
Phasis river, *192*
Philip I, *278*
Phocas, *180*, *183–184*, *210*, *212–213*, *231*, *233–235*, *262*, *274*
piaster, *256*
Piatra Frecăței, *85*, *91*, *94*
Pinsk, *189*
Pisides, Georgios, *26*
Pityus, *157*, *193*, *196*, *198*, *201*, *203–204*, *207*, *209*, *211*, *216*
Piua Petrii, *188*
Ploiești, *65*
poata, *259*
Poděbrady, *238*
Podgornenskii, *216*
Poian, *80*
Pojejena, *169*
Poland, *221–222*, *226–227*, *232*, *234–236*, *238*
Pomerania, *221–222*
Pompey, *192*
Pontic. See Black Sea
Pontus Polemoniacus, *198*
Porolissum. See Moigrad
Portus Altus. See Batumi
Poštorná, *238*
Potaissa. See Turda

Poti. See Phasis
Prague, *228*
Předlánce, *223*
Priscus of Panium, *24*, *26*, *267*
Priscus, general, *181–182*
Priseaca, *188*, *240*
prisoners, *34*, *103*, *106*, *125*, *128*, *135*, *138*, *151*, *234*, *264*, *266*, *269*, *279*
Procopius, *18–19*, *24*, *28–30*, *71*, *105*, *113–114*, *125*, *131*, *172*, *175*, *191–192*, *194*, *199*, *203–204*, *221*, *265–266*, *268*, *285*
Provadiia, *182*
Prundu, *181*
Pruneni, *93*
Prut river, *170*, *184*
Przemyśl, *226*
Ptuj, *231*, *235*, *238*
Pulchra Theodora, *113*
Pulst, *227*

quachtli, *252*
quaestura exercitus, *51*, *150*, *271*

Rabka-Zdrój, *227*
Răcari, *65*, *169*
Radama, king, *256*
Rakita, *182*
Rashkiv, *36*, *122*
Ratiaria, *167*, *184*
Ravenna, *189*, *226*, *228*, *231*, *233*, *236*
Realpolitik, *3*, *152*
Recidiva, *29*, *113*, *115*
Reisberg, *223*
Reșca, *53*, *61*, *178*, *188*
Reselec, *182*
Rhine, *11*, *18*, *21*, *25–26*
Rhodopolis, *198*
Rifnik, *226–227*, *231*
Rivne, *186*
Romania, *3*, *43*, *101*, *110*, *124*, *167–168*, *170–171*, *179–180*, *185*, *187–189*, *225*, *233*, *244*, *262*, *278*
Romanization, *5*, *9*, *44*, *101*, *103*, *107*, *110*, *115*, *137*, *241*, *283*
Romanovskaya, *216*
Rome, *175*, *189*, *207*, *226*, *228*, *231*, *235*, *239*
Romula. See Reșca
Romuliana, *56*
Ruginoasa, *122*
Rupea, *262*
Russia, *49*, *65*, *74–75*, *77*, *79*, *87*, *96*, *187*, *216*, *279*

Rustavi, *202*, *215*
Rusticus, *205*
Ryazan Finns, *87*

Săbăoani, *118*
Sacidava, *55*, *59*, *67*, *98*
Sadovets, *53*, *58–59*, *73–74*, *77*, *182*
Šaľa, *238*
Salcia, *184*
Salona, *175*, *231*
Salovo, *216*
Samo, *237–238*
Samos, *57*
Sangarius, *27*
Sângeorgiu de Câmpie, *225*
Sânmiclăuș, *74*, *124*
Sânnicolaul Mare, *236*
Sânpetru German, *235*
Sântana de Mureș. *See* Chernyakhov culture
Sao, *251*
Sarapana, *192*
Sărata-Monteoru, *37*, *85*, *93*, *98*, *118*, *147*, *171*
Sărățeni, *171*, *274*
Sardis, *56*
Sarmatians, *22*, *36*, *38*
Sarmizegetusa, *64*, *107*
Saskhari, *208*
Sava river, *217*, *287*
Scanda, *192*
Scandinavia, *221*
Scurta, *189*
Scymni, *198*
Scythia, *38*, *40*, *44*, *55–56*, *58–59*, *63–64*, *67*, *73*, *77*, *79*, *84–86*, *91–94*, *96–98*, *112*, *120*, *122*, *140*, *144*, *167*, *170*, *172*, *177*, *179–182*, *184–185*, *188*, *264*, *270*
Sebastopolis, *193*, *196*, *198*, *200*, *203–204*, *215*
Secuieni, *118*
Șeica Mică, *225*
Seliște, *73*, *93*
Sempeter, *231*
Seneca, *24*
Sennaya, *212*
Serbia, *64*, *90*, *96*, *115*, *168*, *178*, *225*, *233*, *240*
Sermesianoi, *267*
Serpovoe, *216*
Sfințești, *36*
Shapur III, *206*
Shemokmedi, *215*
Shilda, *213*
Shilovo, *87*
Shumen, *58*, *82*

Sibiu, *122*
Sicily, *235*, *239*
siliqua, *159*, *209–210*, *213*, *226*, *243*
Silk Road, *193*
Singidunum. *See* Belgrade
Sinnion, *270*
Sinop, *201*
Siret river, *170*, *185*
Sirmium, *19*, *30*, *93*, *114–115*, *168*, *180*, *224*, *230–231*, *273*
Sisak, *63*, *226–227*, *235*
Siscia, *63*. *See* Sisak
Sittas, *199*
Skalistoe, *93*
Sklavinia, *9*, *267–268*
Slatinska Reka, *179*
Slava Rusă, *91*, *182*
Slavs, *27*, *30*, *36–37*, *44*, *86–87*, *92–93*, *99*, *114*, *118–119*, *125*, *139–140*, *144*, *147*, *156*, *173–174*, *176*, *178–180*, *182–183*, *185*, *189–190*, *211*, *237*, *245*, *265–266*, *268–270*, *280*, *282–283*, *287*
Slobozia Mare, *167*
Slovakia, *187*, *222–223*, *232–233*, *235*, *237–240*, *261*
Slovenia, *48*, *223*, *226–227*, *231*, *238*
Smbat Bagratuni, *215*
Sochi, *201*
Socrates, *106*
solidus, *3*, *7*, *157*, *169*, *171–172*, *178*, *180–181*, *183*, *185–186*, *188*, *200–203*, *205*, *207–210*, *212–215*, *221–222*, *225*, *229–231*, *233–235*, *237–238*, *241*, *247*, *254*, *261–264*, *268–269*, *272*, *286–287*
  light weight, *181*, *186*, *208*, *210*, *224*, *231*, *234*, *241*
Solomon Islands, *254*, *259*
Șomcuta Mare, *226*
Somogyi, Péter, *234*, *237*
Somova, *91*
Soterichus, *205*
Sozomen, *106*
Spain, *48*, *206*
Șpălnaca, *231*
St Paul im Lavanttal, *227*
Staasdorf, *223*
Stara Zagora, *65*
Stari Dubovac, *115*
Stari Kostolac, *77*, *79–80*
Starodzhereliyevskaya, *212*
Stary Biliary, *173*

stater. *See* solidus
Stejanovci, *240*
Stepanavan, *215*
Stephen I, king, *213*
Stillfried, *226*
Stobi, *61*
Strategikon, *86*, *116*, *129*, *139*, *144*, *156*, *183*, *266*, *268*, *271*
Studeno, *223*
Štúrovo, *223*, *235*
Suani, *192*, *198*, *200*, *205*, *208*, *217*
Suceava, *86*
Suceava-Șipot, *126*
Sucidava, *25*, *30*, *46*, *57*, *59*, *61*, *74*, *80*, *94*, *97*, *105*, *113*, *142*, *169*, *174*, *177*, *179*, *181*, *184*, *193*
Sukhumi, *216*
Sulejów, *232*
Supruty, *75*
Suuk Su, *77*, *80*, *93*
Sv. Erazmo, *93*
Sv. Kirik, *99*
Svetil'ne, *51*
Sviatoslav, *26*
Swahili coast, *255*
symmachoi. *See* foederati
Syracuse, *189*
Syria. *See* Syria-Palestine
Syria-Palestine, *65*, *211*
Szadzko, *236*, *238*
Székkutas, *124*
Szendrő, *235*
Szentendre, *231*, *261*
Szolnok, *80*
Szombathely, *122*
Szőreg, *222*

Tác-Gorsium, *262*
Taman, *202*
Tápiógyörgye, *53*
Târgșoru Vechi, *52*, *278*
Tatimer, *270*
Tbilisi, *209*, *211*, *213*
Tecuci, *175*
Tekija, *179*
Terechovo, *77*
Tetrarchy, *18*, *25*
thaler, *255*
Themistius, *114*
Theodora, *113*
Theodoric the Great, *220*, *224*
Theodoropolis, *113*
Theodosius I, *196*

Theodosius II, *61*, *198*
Theophanes Confessor, *128*, *264*, *269*
Theophylact Simocatta, *30*, *181*, *263*, *269*
Thessalonica, *159*, *176–179*, *181*, *206*, *209*, *232*
Thracia, *18*, *173*, *181*, *224*
  diocese, *61*, *65*, *74*, *139*, *182*, *185*, *268*, *281*
  province, *168*
Thuringians, *222*
Tiberius II, *179*, *206–208*, *232*, *262*, *266*, *268*
Tiberius II Constantine, *30*
Tiberius III, *189*, *216*
Tigris, *15*
Tisza, *222*, *224*
Tisza river, *49*, *148*, *162*, *217*, *222*, *224*
Tiszagyenda-Gói-tó, *261*
Tiszakeszi, *232*
Tiszavasvári, *49*
Tiszavasvári-Kashalom-dűlő, *235*
Tiv, *253*
Tolenji, *204*
Tolisa, *227*
Tomis, *55*
Toperos, *266*
Trąbki Małe, *221*
trade, *16*, *34*, *41*, *48*, *51*, *69*, *138–139*, *161*, *163*, *199*, *201*, *213*, *244*, *248*, *251*, *271*, *284*
  barter, *254–255*, *258*, *260*
Trajan, *21–23*, *25–28*, *105*, *113*, *135*, *278*
Trajan Decius, *232*
Transcaucasia, *7*, *14*, *119*, *132*, *152*, *155*, *157*, *159*, *190–191*, *193–194*, *196*, *198–200*, *203–206*, *209–211*, *214–217*, *225*, *227*, *232*, *235–236*, *239*, *241*, *284–287*
Transmarisca, *25*
Transylvania, *4–5*, *44*, *52*, *58*, *81*, *99*, *109*, *111*, *147*, *160*, *162*, *168*, *221*, *223–225*, *231*, *234*, *236*, *262*, *272*, *278*
Trapezus, *191*, *196*
Trbinc, *223*
tremissis, *157*, *168*, *171*, *181*, *222–223*, *226–227*, *261*
Ts'ints'karo, *213*
Tsarevets, *92*
Tsebelda, *205*
Tsibilium, *96*, *201*, *204*
Tulcea, *91*
Tunisia, *63*, *239*
Turda, *61*, *107*
Turkey, *196*, *199*

Turks, *207–208, 211–212, 263*
Turner, Frederick, *11*
Turnov, *228*
Turris, *270*
Týn Nad Vltavou, *227*
Tzani, *198, 201, 204*
Tzath, king, *119, 198*
Tzikishdziri. See Petra
Tzimiskes, *26*

Udești, *185*
Uenze, Syna, *77, 82*
Ukraine, *75, 81, 84, 87–88, 170, 173, 175, 178, 182, 186, 244, 247, 261, 265, 277*
Ulfilas, *106, 119*
Ulmeni, *170, 175*
Ulmetum, *56*
Unirea, *182*
Ural Mountains, *96, 246*
Urbnisi, *200, 204, 212*
Usugorsk, *75*
Utigurs, *128, 138, 141, 172, 205, 207, 265*

Vác-Kavicsbánya, *75*
Vădaș, *225*
Vădastrița, *171*
Vadu Săpat, *75*
Vadul lui Isac, *170*
Valea Teilor, *188*
Valea Voievozilor, *122*
Valens, *24, 26, 107, 196*
Valentinian I, *26, 98*
Van Lake, *209*
Vanadzor, *204*
Vandals, *1*
Vardan, *206*
Vardenut, *207*
Várpalota, *262*
Vârtop, *188*
Vășcăuți, *181*
Vasylivka, *181*
Veliko Gradište, *179*
Veliko Orašje, *179*
Veliko Turnovo, *55*
Venchan, *80, 84*
Verbovyi Log, *216*
Vețel, *226*
Vienna, *56, 226, 233*
Viktorinos, *18*
Viminacium, *115, 168, 184*
Viničani, *93*
Vinkovci, *227*

Vitalianus, *167*
Vojvodina, *233*
Volga river, *51, 73, 75*
Volos'ke, *80*
Vosketap, *207*
Vranje, *48*
Vrh Pri Pahi, *227*

Wallachia, *30, 36, 48, 52, 67, 97–99, 118, 120, 122, 124, 126, 144, 161, 171–172, 178–182, 184, 188, 268, 284*
Wallerstein, Immanuel, *133–134, 137*
Werner, Joachim, *87, 94*
White, Richard, *135, 151*
Whittaker, C. R., *13–14*
Wiener Neustadt, *238*
world-systems analysis, *131, 133, 137, 148, 248, 281*
  coevolving interaction, *137*
  core, *2, 133–134, 141, 187, 281*
  hierarchical interaction, *137*
  hybridization, *2, 136, 268, 281*
  interdependent borderland, *136*
  interstitial agency, *136*
  middle ground, *135, 151, 281*
  mini-systems, *249*
  periphery, *2, 133–134, 141, 187, 190, 249, 281, 288*
    bipolar, *6, 135, 152, 281*
    contested, *281*
    negotiated, *6, 133, 281*
  semiperiphery, *2, 134, 141, 148, 187, 190, 281*
  Third Space, *136*

Yassı Ada, *53, 58–59*
Yemen, *119*
Yosypivka, *186*

Zabergan, *22, 286*
Zachepylivka, *186*
Zaldapa, *182*
Zašovice, *227*
Žďár nad Sázavou, *228*
Zdravkovec, *79*
Zemiansky Vrbovok, *239–240, 261*
Zenobius, *108*
Zernes. See Orșova
Zeugitania, *238*
Zhebot'a, *213*
Zimbabwe, *259*
Zimne, *73, 75*

Zimnicea, *181*
Žinkovy, *228*
Żółków, *234*, *238*
Zolotonosha, *173*
Zoroastrianism, *203*, *206*

Zosimus, *24*
Zugdidi, *200*, *215*
Zulud, *182*
Zvonets'ke, *79*, *85*
Żywiec, *227*